THE OXFORD INTERNATIONA

THE OXFORD INTERNATIONAL LAW LIBRARY

This series features works on substantial topics in international law which provide authoritative statements of the chosen areas. Taken together they map out the whole of international law in a set of scholarly reference works and treatises intended to be of use to scholars, practitioners, and students.

# THE WORLD TRADE ORGANIZATION

## *Law, Practice, and Policy*

Mitsuo Matsushita
Thomas J. Schoenbaum
and
Petros C. Mavroidis

OXFORD
UNIVERSITY PRESS

Great Claredon Street, Oxford OX2 6DP

Oxford University Press is a department of the University of Oxford.
It furthers the University's objective of excellence in research, scholarship,
and education by publishing worldwide in

Oxford New York

Auckland Bangkok Buenos Aires Cape Town Chennai
Dar es Salaam Delhi Hong Kong Istanbul Karachi Kolkata
Kuala Lumpur Madrid Melbourne Mexico City Mumbai Nairobi
São Paulo Shanghai Taipei Tokyo Toronto

Oxford is a registered trade mark of Oxford University Press
in the UK and in certain other countries

Published in the United States
by Oxford University Press Inc., New York



First published 2003

Published new in paperback 2004



British Library Cataloguing in Publication Data
Data available

Library of Congress Cataloging in Publication Data
Data available

ISBN 0-19-876472-3 (hbk)

ISBN 0-19-927425-8 (pbk)

1 3 5 7 9 10 8 6 4 2

Typeset by Kolam Information Services Pvt. Ltd, Pondicherry, India
Printed in Great Britain
on acid-free paper by
Biddles Ltd., King's Lynn

# PREFACE

This book combines the thinking and scholarship of three academicians, one from Japan, one from North America, and the third from Europe. All three have worked in the field for many years and have extensive experience in developing countries. We have pitched the levels of analysis to appeal not only to specialists in law, political science and economics, but also to intelligent laypersons interested in the phenomenon of "globalism". We believe that this book will contribute to a better understanding of the important and far-reaching work of one of the most controversial institutions of our time, the World Trade Organization.

The authors would like to acknowledge Sylvia A. Rhodes, Esq. of Bryan Cave, LLP, Washington D.C. for the special part she played in the creation of this book. For over a year, Sylvia was able to join us as co-author. The book was strengthened immeasurably by her input. She bears no responsibility, of course, for any errors or omissions.

Mitsuo Matsushita
Thomas J. Schoenbaum
Petros C. Mavroidis
October, 2002

# CONTENTS — SUMMARY

# CONTENTS

# TABLE OF WTO AND GATT AGREEMENTS, TREATIES, AND OTHER INTERNATIONAL INSTRUMENTS

# TABLES OF NATIONAL LAWS AND REGULATIONS

**Germany**



**Ghana**



**Japan**

**Nigeria**



**Switzerland**



**US**

# TABLES OF WTO AND GATT DECISIONS

NOTE: In this book, the authors have cited WTO and GATT cases sometimes in the long citation form, but mostly in short citation form. These tables include all relevant information on WTO and GATT cases, the full texts of which are available on the WTO website.

**WTO Decisions**

**Gatt Decisions**

# TABLES OF COURT AND ADMINISTRATIVE DECISIONS

## European Commission



## European Court of Justice and Court of First Instance

**France**



**Germany**

## International Court of Justice



## Japan

**NAFTA Dispute Panel**



**UK**



**US**

## US International trade Commission (USITC)

# OVERVIEW

The aim of this book is to provide in one accessible volume a snapshot of the law and practice of the World Trade Organization (WTO) at the dawn of the twenty-first century, eight years after its founding. It is safe to say that the WTO has become one of the most interesting and important intergovernmental organizations of our time. Not only does the WTO provide a forum for continued trade negotiations and the focus of the global trading system, it also oversees and administers a complex matrix of international treaty law, and it operates the busiest and perhaps most important international dispute settlement system on the world scene.

Despite its prominence, the WTO is poorly understood. There is a need for an explanation of the basics of the WTO that explains both how it functions as an organization and the scope of its authority and power. The book is aimed primarily at persons — lawyers, economists, political scientists, and members of the public — who are not specialists in international economic law but wish to understand the WTO. Second, we have taken care to provide enough detail and to integrate the law contained in the WTO Agreements with the burgeoning jurisprudence of WTO dispute settlement panels and the Appellate Body to make the book appeal to students of the subject, when used in conjunction with the primary sources. We believe we have provided a synthesis and insight into these primary sources. Third, we believe the book will be useful even to the specialist who may want a quick and handy reference work.

As indicated by the title, our perspective is primarily legal but, in the WTO, law is intimately associated with economics[1] and political economy.[2]

The WTO today is embroiled in controversy. It is "public enemy number one" on the anti-globalist agenda. The charges are serious:

1. The WTO serves the interests of transnational corporations to the detriment of developing nations and the poor.
2. The WTO is anti-democratic and violates national sovereignty.

---

[1] For the economics perspective, see Jagdish Bhagwati, FREE TRADE TODAY (2002) and Douglas A. Irwin, FREE TRADE UNDER FIRE (2002).

[2] For the political economy perspective, see Bernard M. Hoekman and Michael M. Kostecki, THE POLITICAL ECONOMY OF THE WTO (2d ed. 2001).

3. The WTO elevates property interests over human rights and health. It particularly "enshrines" intellectual property rights.
4. The WTO is hostile to protection of the environment, workers' rights, agriculture, food safety, and social welfare generally because it strikes down protection of such interests as trade barriers.

In summary, to some, the WTO and globalization are forces for oppression, exploitation, and injustice.

The authors largely disagree with this judgment, although we believe that there is room for improvement in many aspects of the WTO's work. Our primary purpose, however, is to present a picture of the WTO on its own terms, what it is, its functions, the rules it administers and the scope of its involvement. Governments, companies, and individuals all over the world are affected by the WTO's work, but that influence is largely indirect. Unlike its sister agencies, the International Monetary Fund and the World Bank, the WTO has no power of independent executive action; it restricts itself to the administration of WTO agreements formulated by its 146 Members.

We believe that the law of the WTO can best be analysed in five separate categories. First, there is the institutional law, comprising Chapters 1 to 5: the WTO as an international organization; the dispute settlement system, the sources of law and remedies, and the ways the international law of the WTO is transformed into the municipal law of member states.

Second, we take up the principal substantive WTO obligations in Chapters 6 to 11: tariffs, quotas, and barriers to trade; most-favoured nation and national treatment; safeguards; export controls; and services. These obligations establish the regime of free trade on a worldwide basis but temper free trade with safeguards.

Third, we take up the issue of unfair trade in Chapters 12 and 13, considering subsidies and dumping.

Fourth, we cover two difficult issues in Chapters 14 and 15, namely, regional trading arrangements and developing countries. In both contexts, the WTO tolerates principled discrimination for the purpose of achieving certain goals. Although concerns overlap, there are considerations unique to each of these subjects. For regional trading groups, the problem is to assure their openness. Developing countries need special and differential treatment to attain economic development.

Finally, with the coming of globalism, it is clear that the rules of international trade inevitably become linked with additional matters normally considered domestic issues or far removed from trade. This comes about for two reasons: First, with greater integration and interdependence, trade becomes intertwined with other issues such as intellectual property, competition policy and investment. Second, trade is looked upon by some as a threat to certain values, such as the protection of the environment, health and workers' rights. These matters are treated in Chapters 16 to 20.

Chapter 21 is our perspective on future challenges facing the WTO. In our view, three categories of challenges are prominent. First, the WTO must rethink carefully its internal structures and decision-making processes. We believe there is an imbalance between the highly legalistic and efficient dispute settlement process, on the one hand, and the very cumbersome and inefficient political decision-making process, on the other.[3] Second, the WTO must do a better job of responding to the societal issues raised by the broader civil society. Third, the WTO must do more to allow developing countries to participate in and benefit from trade. We believe the future success of the WTO hinges on these issues. Of course, the WTO still faces a host of work stemming from its so-called built-in agenda and the negotiating agenda adopted at the Doha Ministerial Conference in 2001. We summarize these questions as well.

The story of the WTO is remarkable. Although a world trade organization was envisaged at the Bretton Woods, New Hampshire economic conference in 1944, it took fifty-one years before political conditions permitted its creation. The WTO's predecessor, the General Agreement on Tariffs and Trade (GATT), was operated from 1947 to 1994 almost informally by states as a forum to conduct multilateral trade negotiations and, increasingly, to deal with contentious trade disputes. The GATT attracted more and more members, and with each success in lowering post-World War II trade barriers, got involved in broader market access problems, such as technical barriers to trade and investment policy. By the 1980s, it became clear that international trade has implications for a wide variety of societal concerns, such as protection of the environment, health, human rights, workers' rights, and world poverty. The fall of the Soviet Union and the end of the Cold War opened the way for the GATT to give way to the WTO, which is in the process of becoming a membership organization of virtually all the states (and various customs unions) of the

[3] On this point, we agree with and have benefited from the views expressed by Claude E. Barfield, Free Trade, Sovereignty, Democracy, the Future of the WTO (2001).

world. The attraction of the WTO (no state is compelled to join) is basically threefold: (1) trade is conducted according to rules formulated and agreed upon by members, (2) there is a system for resolving disagreements between members, and (3) there is opportunity to help formulate future rules and trade policies. Another attraction is that each member, formally at least, has equal voting power, so no state or group of states can dominate. But the disadvantage here is that this control pattern frequently leads to deadlock. As a result, the WTO is slow to change even bad or outdated policies and practices.

The tensions between GATT/WTO rules and societal concerns came as a surprise. The WTO regards its mission as trade liberalization. It is only slowly coming to grips with broader societal concerns, and the WTO's role must be sorted out with other specialized intergovernmental agencies that have primary responsibility for these societal issues.

# 1

# THE WORLD TRADE ORGANIZATION



## 1. Bretton Woods and the failure of the International Trade Organization

The idea of founding an international organization to develop and coordinate international trade was put forward in 1944 at a conference on economic matters held in Bretton Woods, New Hampshire, but the details were left for later. After the founding of the United Nations in 1945, multilateral trade negotiations were conducted within the framework of the UN Economic and Social Council, which in 1946 adopted a resolution in favour of forming an International Trade Organization (ITO).

Negotiations over the ITO and the post-war international trading system were held in several stages: at Lake Success, New York in 1947; in Geneva in 1947; and in Havana in 1948. The Geneva meetings, which were pivotal, had three objectives: (1) draft an ITO charter, (2) prepare schedules of tariff reductions and (3) prepare a multilateral treaty containing general principles of trade, namely, the General Agreement on Tariffs and Trade (GATT). By the end of 1947, work had been completed on the tariff reductions and the GATT. The final work to complete a charter for the ITO was put off until 1948.

The governments of the countries engaged in the negotiations were left with a problem: how to bring the tariff cuts and the GATT into force right away without waiting on the final round of negotiations to form the ITO. The solution was to adopt a Protocol of Provisional Application to apply the GATT "provisionally on and after January 1, 1948."[1] In this way, the GATT and its tariff schedules could immediately enter into force, later the GATT could be revised to be consistent with the charter, and the GATT and the charter could finally be adopted.

The countries participating in the Havana Conference of 1948 completed work on the ITO charter, but the ITO charter never entered into force. Because the support of the United States was critical, other countries that were ready to adopt the ITO charter waited to see its fate in the United States. President Truman submitted the ITO charter to Congress, but the Republicans won control of Congress in the 1948 election. In 1950, the Truman administration announced that it would no longer seek congressional approval for the ITO. The ITO was dead.

## 2. The GATT becomes an international organization

The failure to adopt the ITO meant the absence of the "third pillar"[2] on which the Bretton Woods economic structure was to be built. The GATT, which was not intended to be an international organization, gradually filled this void. The contracting parties of the GATT — the GATT could have no

[1] Protocol of Provisional Application to the General Agreement on Tariffs and Trade, 30 October 1947, 55 U.N.T.S. 308.

[2] The two "pillars" that came into existence as agreed at the Bretton Woods Conference were the International Monetary Fund and the World Bank.

members — held meetings every year, and new contracting parties were gradually added. The Interim Commission for the ITO became the GATT Secretariat. The GATT evolved into an international organization based in Geneva, taking as its "charter" the GATT, practice under the GATT and additional understandings and agreements.

Nevertheless, the GATT always suffered from what Professor Jackson has termed "birth defects", inherent weaknesses that handicapped its operation.[3] These birth defects included:

1. The lack of a charter granting the GATT legal personality and establishing its procedures and organizational structure;
2. The fact that the GATT had only "provisional" application;
3. The fact that the Protocol of Provisional Application contained provisions enabling GATT contracting parties to maintain legislation that was in force on accession to the GATT and was inconsistent with the GATT (so-called grandfather rights);[4] and
4. Ambiguity and confusion about the GATT's authority, decision-making ability and legal status.

## 3. A summary of GATT obligations

The GATT lowers tariffs by limiting tariff charges to those agreed in the Schedules of Concessions (Article II) and giving the benefit of these concessions to all GATT contracting parties (Article I). The tariff schedules are annexed to the GATT.[5] The GATT is a code of general rules regulating the conduct of the parties. Most of these rules are designed to assure that the tariff concessions work as intended and are not undermined. The GATT contains the following additional provisions:

1. A requirement of national treatment of imports with respect to taxes and regulations (Article III);

[3] John H. Jackson, *Designing and Implementing Effective Dispute Settlement Procedures: WTO Dispute Settlement, Appraisal and Prospects*, in THE WTO AS AN INTERNATIONAL ORGANIZATION 161, 163 (Anne O. Krueger ed., 1998).

[4] John H. Jackson, THE JURISPRUDENCE OF GATT AND THE WTO: INSIGHTS ON TREATY LAW AND ECONOMIC RELATIONS 84 (2000) (discussing grandfather rights).

[5] GATT Art. XXXIV.

2. A prohibition on quotas, import or export licenses and other measures, with some exceptions (Article XI), and a special provision relating to quotas on cinematograph films (Article IV);
3. Guarantees of freedom of transit (Article V);
4. Rules relating to subsidies and antidumping and countervailing duties (Articles VI and XVI);
5. Rules on valuation for customs purposes (Article VII);
6. Rules on fees and formalities connected with importation and exportation (Article VIII);
7. Rules on marks of origin (Article IX);
8. Rules on transparency and publication of national trade regulations (Article X);
9. Rules on currency exchange regulation (Article XV);
10. Rules on state-trading enterprises (Article XVII); and
11. Rules on government assistance to economic development (Article XVIII).

In addition, the GATT contains provisions that allow some exceptions to the basic GATT rules:

1. Exceptions for quotas for balance-of-payments purposes (Articles XII, XIII, XIV, XV and XVII, Section B);
2. Exceptions for developing countries (Article XVIII and Part IV);
3. An exception for emergency action where serious injury is caused or threatened to a domestic industry (Article XIX) (the so-called escape clause);
4. An exception for health, safety, the protection of natural resources and other matters (Article XX);
5. An exception for national security (Article XXI);
6. An exception for customs unions and free trade areas (Article XXIV);
7. An exception for waivers by the contracting parties (Article XXV); and
8. An exception allowing a GATT contracting party to "opt out" of a GATT relationship on a one-time basis only, when a new contracting party joins the GATT (Article XXXV).[6]

[6] Under the WTO Agreement, the "opt-out" procedure is continued in modified form. The WTO agreements in Annexes 1 and 2 of the WTO Agreement do not apply between a Member and any other Member if either, at the time of becoming a Member, does not consent. However, as between the *original* WTO Members, this opt-out procedure may be exercised only where GATT Article XXXV had been previously invoked and was still effective on 1 January 1995. *See* WTO Agreement Art. XIII:1 and :2.

Two GATT provisions are central to the settlement of disputes: Article XXII, which provides for consultation, and Article XXIII, which allows a GATT contracting party to make a complaint and permits the GATT Contracting Parties[7] to investigate and make recommendations for resolving the dispute. These provisions were the basis on which the GATT system of dispute resolution was developed and are the foundation for WTO dispute settlement procedures.

Finally, the GATT contains a number of provisions relating to procedure:

1. Procedures for modifying the Schedules of Concessions (Article XXVIII) and conducting tariff negotiations (Article XXVIII *bis*);
2. Procedures for withholding or withdrawing concessions if a state withdraws or fails to become a contracting party (Article XXVII);
3. Procedures defining which countries may be the contracting parties and for accession to the GATT (Articles XXXII and XXXIII);
4. Procedures for amending the GATT (Article XXX);
5. Procedures for withdrawing from the GATT on six months' notice (Article XXXI); and
6. Procedures for acceptance, entry into force and registration of the GATT (Article XXVI).

The GATT also contains an Annex with notes and supplementary interpretations of various Articles. The GATT was modified and superseded in part by the GATT 1994, one of the WTO agreements. The "original" GATT, as amended, is now known as the GATT 1947.

## 4. The GATT tariff negotiating rounds

Despite its birth defects, the GATT served as the basis for eight "rounds" of multilateral trade negotiations. These rounds were held periodically to reduce tariffs and other barriers to international trade and were increasingly complex and ambitious. All were successful.

The principal accomplishment of the GATT was its success in reducing tariffs and other trade barriers on a worldwide basis.

[7] The GATT uses the terms "contracting party" and "contracting parties" as well as the term "CONTRACTING PARTIES." The latter is used when the contracting parties are "acting jointly." GATT Art. XXV:1. This work uses the term "Contracting Parties" in place of "CONTRACTING PARTIES."

The various negotiating rounds were named after the place in which the negotiations began or the person associated with initiating the round. The names and dates of the rounds are as follows:

- Geneva 1947
- Annecy 1949
- Torquay 1950
- Geneva 1956
- Dillon 1960–61
- Kennedy 1962–67
- Tokyo 1973–79
- Uruguay 1986–94

The objectives of the early GATT negotiating rounds were primarily to reduce tariffs. Non-tariff barriers later emerged as a vital concern as well. The objectives of the Tokyo and Uruguay Rounds were primarily to reduce non-tariff barriers. The Uruguay Round culminated in the creation of an immense new body of international law relating to trade: the basic texts of the WTO agreements exceeded 400 pages, and the Final Act signed in Marrakesh, Morocco on 15 April 1994 was over 26,000 pages.

The Final Act of the Uruguay Round transformed the GATT into a new, fully fledged international organization called the World Trade Organization (WTO).

## 5. The creation of the WTO

The idea of creating a World Trade Organization emerged slowly from various needs and suggestions. Even at the beginning of the Uruguay Round, negotiators and observers realized that significant new agreements would require better institutional mechanisms and a better system for resolving disputes. One of the 15 negotiations undertaken at the beginning of the Round was on the "functioning of the GATT system", dubbed with the acronym "FOGS". Negotiators were particularly concerned with how new agreements would come into force and whether they would be binding on all GATT contracting parties. Many countries wanted to avoid the problems of the Tokyo Round, which had resulted in significant new "side agreements" that were binding only on those GATT contracting parties that accepted them (GATT à la carte).

Thus, Uruguay Round negotiators were receptive to the suggestion, first made by Professor Jackson, to use the Uruguay Round as an occasion to found a new "World Trade Organization".[8] Jackson argued that it was time to cure the "birth defects" of the GATT by creating an organization that would be a United Nations specialized agency with an organizational structure and a dispute settlement mechanism. The creation of such an organization could solve the problems of "GATT à la carte". It would be necessary to accept all the Uruguay Round agreements to be a Member of the new World Trade Organization.

The idea of a new world trade organization was taken up in the FOGS negotiation. When the Draft Final Act of the Uruguay Round was issued in 1991, it contained a proposal for a new "Multilateral Trade Organization". Working groups and negotiators did further work, and the name was changed to the World Trade Organization. The Draft Final Act included agreements on transitional arrangements and the termination of the GATT 1947 and the Tokyo Round agreements on subjects covered by new WTO agreements. Finally, the negotiators decided that the WTO would come into being on 1 January 1995.[9] The package of agreements that brought the WTO into being was opened for signature at Marrakesh on 15 April 1994. The package consisted of multilateral trade agreements annexed to a single document, namely, the Marrakesh Agreement Establishing the World Trade Organization (WTO Agreement).[10] Through this ingenious device, all agreements annexed to the WTO Agreement become binding on all Members as a single body of law. [11]

Annex 1 of the WTO Agreement is divided into three parts. Annex 1A consists of the GATT 1994 and the following agreements:

- Agreement on Agriculture
- Agreement on the Application of Sanitary and Phytosanitary Measures
- Agreement on Textiles and Clothing

[8] John H. Jackson, RESTRUCTURING THE GATT SYSTEM 38–41 (1990).

[9] For details of the complex negotiations, see Amelia Porges, *The Marrakesh Agreement Establishing the World Trade Organization*, in THE WORLD TRADE ORGANIZATION 63 (T. P. Stewart ed., 1996).

[10] The WTO is established formally by Article I of the WTO Agreement. No reservations may be made to the WTO Agreement; reservations to the multilateral trade agreements are allowed only if their terms permit them. WTO Agreement Art. XVI:5. The WTO Agreement is registered in accordance with Article 102 of the United Nations Charter. *Id.* Art. XVI:6.

[11] *Id.* Art. II:2.

- Agreement on Technical Barriers to Trade
- Agreement on Trade Related Investment Measures
- Agreement on Implementation of Article VI of the General Agreement on Tariffs and Trade 1994 (Antidumping Agreement)
- Agreement on Implementation of Article VII of the General Agreement on Tariffs and Trade 1994 (Customs Valuation Agreement)
- Agreement on Preshipment Inspection
- Agreement on Rules of Origin
- Agreement on Import Licensing Procedures
- Agreement on Subsidies and Countervailing Measures
- Agreement on Safeguards

Annex 1A includes a General Interpretive Note that provides that, if there is a "conflict" between provisions of the GATT 1994 and another Annex 1A Agreement, the provision of the latter controls.[12]

Annex 1B consists of the General Agreement on Trade in Services (GATS) and its annexes. Annex 1C consists of the Agreement on Trade-Related Aspects of Intellectual Property Rights (TRIPs Agreement).

Annex 2 consists of the Understanding on Rules and Procedures Governing Settlement of Disputes (Dispute Settlement Understanding or DSU), which establishes the procedures for resolving trade disputes among WTO Members.

Annex 3 consists of the Trade Policy Review Mechanism, which establishes a periodic review of each WTO Member's compliance with WTO agreements and commitments.

Annex 4 consists of the Plurilateral Trade Agreements:

- Agreement on Trade in Civil Aircraft
- Agreement on Government Procurement
- International Dairy Agreement
- International Bovine Meat Agreement

The plurilateral agreements are binding only on the parties that have accepted them.[13] The International Dairy Agreement and the

[12] General Interpretive Note to Annex 1A, Multilateral Agreements on Trade in Goods, of the WTO Agreement, reprinted in WTO, The Legal Texts: The Results of the Uruguay Round of Multilateral Trade Negotiations 16 (1999).

[13] WTO Agreement Art. II:3.

International Bovine Meat Agreement, however, were terminated in 1997.[14]

The WTO Agreement formally replaced the GATT 1947 with the GATT 1994, which is a new and legally distinct agreement. The GATT 1994 consists of the GATT 1947, excluding the Protocol of Provisional Application, as amended by all legal instruments that entered into force under the GATT before 1 January 1995, the date of the entry into force of the WTO Agreement.[15] Such legal instruments include various protocols, decisions on waivers, other decisions and understandings and the Marrakesh Protocol to the GATT 1994. Thus, the WTO Agreement incorporates the GATT as it existed in 1994 rather than the original GATT.

## 6. The WTO: functions and structure

The WTO exists to "facilitate the implementation, administration, and operation as well as to further the objectives" of the WTO agreements.[16] Beyond this general purpose, the WTO has four specific tasks: (1) to provide a forum for negotiations among Members both as to current matters and any future agreements; (2) to administer the system of dispute settlement; (3) to administer the Trade Policy Review Mechanism; and (4) to cooperate as needed with the IMF and the World Bank, the two other Bretton Woods institutions.[17]

The WTO is formally endowed with existence, legal personality and legal capacity as an international organization. It must be accorded privileges and immunities that are in accordance with its functions.[18]

The WTO has two governing bodies: the Ministerial Conference and the General Council. The Ministerial Conference is the supreme authority. It is composed of representatives of all WTO Members and meets at least once every two years. The General Council is the chief decision-making and

[14] WTO, *Deletion of the International Dairy Agreement from Annex 4 of the WTO Agreement, Decision of 10 December 1997*, WT/L/251, 17 December 1997; WTO, *Deletion of the International Bovine Meat Agreement from Annex 4 of the WTO Agreement, Decision of 10 December 1997*, WT/L/252, 16 December 1997.

[15] GATT Art. II:4 and Annex 1A.

[16] *Id.* Art. III:1.

[17] *Id.* Art. III.

[18] *Id.* Arts. I, VIII.

policy body between meetings of the Ministerial Conference.[19] The General Council also discharges the responsibilities of two important subsidiary bodies, namely, the Dispute Settlement Body and the Trade Policy Review Body.[20] The General Council is composed of all WTO Members and meets "as appropriate".

Specialized Councils and Committees that report to the General Council do much of the day-to-day work of the WTO. The WTO Agreement establishes these Councils: a Council for Trade in Goods; a Council for Trade in Services; and a Council for Trade-Related Aspects of Intellectual Property Rights (TRIPS).[21] These Councils have the power to establish committees (or subsidiary bodies) as required.[22] The Ministerial Conference has also established committees: a Committee on Trade and Development; a Committee on Balance of Payments; a Committee on Budget, Finance and Administration;[23] and, by special action on 14 April 1994, a Committee on Trade and Environment. Additional councils and committees oversee the Plurilateral Trade Agreements. These also report to the WTO General Council.[24]

The WTO has a Secretariat located in Geneva and presided over by a Director-General, who is appointed by the Ministerial Conference.[25] The Ministerial Conference sets the powers and term of office of the Director-General, and the Director-General has the power to appoint the staff and direct the duties of the WTO Secretariat.[26] Neither the Director-General nor the Members of the Secretariat may seek or accept instructions from any national government, and both must act as international officials.[27]

The General Council has control over the WTO budget, which is prepared by the Director-General and the Committee on Budget, Finance and Administration.[28] The General Council has authority to arrange for cooperating

---

[19] GATT Art. IV:1 and :2.

[20] *Id.* Art. IV:3.

[21] *Id.* Art. IV:5.

[22] *Id.* Art. IV:6.

[23] *Id.* Art. IV:7.

[24] *Id.* Art. IV:8.

[25] WTO Agreement Art. VI:1.

[26] *Id.* Art. VI:1, :2 and :3.

[27] *Id.* Art. VI:4. The Secretariat staff members "to the extent practicable" are to be appointed from the pre-existing GATT Secretariat. *Id.* Art. XVI:2.

[28] *Id.* Art. VII. Each WTO Member contributes to the budget according to its share of world trade in goods.

with other inter-governmental organizations and non-governmental organizations.[29]

To deal with the plethora of matters that may arise concerning trade, the WTO commonly establishes *ad hoc* Working Parties and committees consisting of representatives of WTO Members who participate on a voluntary, though official, basis.

## 6.1 Membership, accession, and withdrawal

The original WTO Membership consisted of all GATT contracting parties as of the entry into force of the WTO Agreement on 1 January 1995 and the European Community.[30] Countries may join the WTO only after negotiating terms of accession.[31] The Ministerial Conference must approve the terms of accession by a two-thirds majority of the WTO Members.[32] In practice, accession is accomplished through obtaining a consensus of all WTO Members.

Accession to the WTO is a difficult and time-consuming process. In the case of China, for example, a prerequisite to the negotiation of a "Protocol of Accession" to the WTO was the requirement of negotiating bilateral market access packages with interested WTO Members. Thus, China entered into a series of bilateral trade agreements, notably with the United States[33] and the European Community.[34] Only after these bilateral negotiations were completed did substantive discussions on the text and annexes of a Protocol of Accession begin. The entire accession process, which extended over 14 years, was finally completed when China became a WTO Member by decision of the Fourth Ministerial Conference of the WTO in November 2001.

---

[29] *Id.* Art. V.

[30] *Id.* Art. XI:1. A Member also must have negotiated appropriate Schedules of Concessions. *Id.* The WTO Agreement had to be accepted formally by each original Member. *Id.* Art. XIV.

Although the European Community is a WTO Member, the number of votes of the European Community and its Member States may not exceed the number of votes of the Member States of the European Community. *Id.* Art. IX.

[31] *Id.* Art. XII.

[32] *Id.* Art. XII:1 and :2.

[33] *See Summary of U.S.–China Bilateral WTO Agreement, February 2, 2000* (visited 4/8/02) http://www.uschina.org/public/wto/ustr/generalfacts.html.

[34] *Highlights of the EU–China Agreement on WTO* (visited 4/8/02) http://www.europa.eu.int/comm/trade/bilateral/china/high.htm.

Any Member may withdraw from the WTO Agreement after giving notice to the Director-General six months before the date on which it intends to withdraw.[35]

## 6.2 Decision-making

The WTO's decision-making processes are quite unusual. The procedures and customary practices under the old GATT are generally retained.[36] There are several types of decisions.

### *6.2.1 General decision-making*

There are two primary modes of decision-making: decision by consensus and voting. For general decision-making, WTO bodies continue to follow the practice of the GATT 1947 of deciding by consensus. The WTO provides that "[t]he body concerned shall be deemed to have decided by consensus if no Member, present at the meeting when the decision is taken, formally objects to the proposed decision".[37] Thus, consensus differs from unanimity. In consensus decision-making, the minority will normally go along with the majority unless it has a serious objection. The majority will, in turn, not ramrod decisions through by vote but will deal with the objections of the minority. The consensus decision-making process takes a great deal of time.

Voting occurs in the WTO only when a decision cannot be taken by consensus. In the Ministerial Conference and the General Council, decisions are taken by "a majority of the votes cast" unless otherwise specified in the relevant WTO agreement.[38] Each Member has one vote.[39] Thus, the decision-making process of the WTO is quite different from the IMF and the World Bank, where weighted voting favours the larger, more important states.

### *6.2.2 Interpretations*

The WTO has a rather strict rule concerning interpretations of the WTO agreements because WTO Members realized the complexity of the huge mass of verbiage and did not want official "glosses" to be adopted by subsidiary bodies. Thus, the WTO Agreement provides that only the Ministerial Conference and the General Council have the power to adopt interpretations of the WTO agreements by a three-fourths majority of the

[35] WTO Agreement Art. XII:1. [36] *Id.* Art. XVI:1. [37] *Id.* Art. IX:1.
[38] *Id.* Art. IX:1. [39] *Id.* Art. IX:1.

Members. The interpretation authority may not, however, be used to undermine the amendment provisions of the WTO Agreement.[40]

### 6.2.3 *Waivers*

Safeguards have been built into the WTO waiver process in the light of difficult experiences with the waiver provision (Article XXV) of the GATT 1947.[41] Only the Ministerial Conference by three-fourths of the Members can make a decision on a waiver of any obligation under the WTO agreements. A decision to grant a waiver of any obligation subject to staged implementation or a transitional period may be taken only by consensus.[42]

Waivers are subject to annual review, after which they may be extended, modified or terminated.[43]

At the Fourth WTO Ministerial Conference in Doha, Qatar, in November 2001, waivers were accepted to settle the *Bananas* case between the United States and certain Latin American banana producers on the one hand, and the European Community on the other.[44] One waiver allows the EC to continue discriminating in favour of imports of banana producers from Africa, the Caribbean and the Pacific;[45] a second waiver grants the EC the right to give tariff preferences to developing countries, including Latin American countries, on a variety of other products.[46] The EC, in return for the waiver, has promised to replace its discriminatory tariff-quota regime for bananas with a tariff system by 1 January 2006.[47]

### 6.2.4 *Amendments*

Amending the WTO agreements is very difficult. To ensure against surprise proposals, an amendment must be formally tabled for at least 90 days before

[40] *Id.* Art. IX:2.

[41] Pre-WTO waivers granted under the GATT 1947 terminated as of the date of entry into force of the WTO Agreement. Understanding in Respect of Waivers of Obligations under the General Agreement on Tariffs and Trade 1994, para. 2, reprinted in WTO, THE LEGAL TEXTS: THE RESULTS OF THE URUGUAY ROUND OF MULTILATERAL TRADE NEGOTIATIONS 29 (1999).

[42] *Id.* Art. IX:3.

[43] *Id.* Art. IX:4.

[44] *See* Ministerial Conference — Fourth Session — Doha, 9–14 November 2001 — European Communities — The ACP-EC Partnership Agreement, Decision of 14 November 2001, WT/MIN(01)/15, 14 November 2001.

[45] *Id.* para. 1.

[46] *Id.* Annex para. 1.

[47] *See EU Waivers Approved as Latin Americans Drop Banana Demands,* INSIDE U.S. TRADE, 15 November 2001, at 10.

being submitted for acceptance.[48] The Ministerial Conference has exclusive competence to vote on amendments. Certain provisions of the agreements may be amended only by unanimous vote.[49] Other provisions can be amended by two-thirds vote, but such an amendment is binding only on those Members accepting it.[50] The Ministerial Conference, by three-fourths vote, can decide that all Members must accept an amendment, and recalcitrant Members either must withdraw from the WTO or remain a Member with the consent of the Ministerial Conference.[51]

### 6.3 The WTO as an international organization[52]

The WTO Agreement created the WTO as a new international organization with a legal personality, legal capacity, and sufficient privileges and immunities.[53] It also endowed the WTO with decision-making processes, an institutional structure, and distinctive functions. If it maintains the support of its Members and gains public understanding and support, the WTO will continue to play a key global economic role in the twenty-first century.

## 7. Suggestions for improving the WTO

In creating the WTO, the international community has overcome the "birth defects" surrounding the GATT and its functions. Two primary difficulties remain. First, decision-making is too cumbersome. Second, the WTO needs to be more "externally" transparent.

First, the primary modes of decision-making, namely, consensus and voting, are too cumbersome for an organization that has 145 Members (as at the time of writing). These modes may lead to deadlock or back-room deals and other low-visibility decisions. Both are to be avoided if possible.

[48] WTO Agreement Art. X:1.

[49] *Id.* Art. X:2. For example, the following provisions of the WTO agreements may only be amended by unanimous vote: the amendment provision of the WTO Agreement (Article X), Arts I and II of the GATT, Art. II:1 of GATS, Art. 4 of TRIPS and Art. IX of the WTO Agreement. *Id.*

[50] *Id.* Art. X:3 and :4.

[51] *Id.* Art. X:5.

[52] See generally The WTO as an International Organization, above note 3.

[53] *Id.* Arts. I, II.

Deadlock obviously impairs the function of the WTO, while low-visibility decisions cause resentment among WTO Members and by the public.

A more efficient yet fair method of decision-making is needed. One solution would be to create an "Executive Body" of the General Council that would have general decision-making power. The Members of the Executive Body should be chosen according to objective criteria based on such factors as (1) GDP; (2) share of world trade; and (3) population. Other criteria could assure representation by developing countries and a geographic balance. The Executive Body should have both permanent Members and a rotating group of Members that would serve fixed terms. Thus, every WTO Member would have a seat on the Executive Body at regular intervals. A weighted voting system could be devised to replace consensus decision-making. Some variant of this proposal is needed to improve the WTO's decision-making process.[54]

A second need is to improve the WTO's external transparency. Greater public disclosure of the WTO's business would promote public understanding of the benefits of trade and the complex issues that must be decided. Transparency also would lead to more input by the global public.

Canada,[55] for example, has proposed several need transparency reforms:

- Enhanced transparency of trade policy reviews, including broadcast over the Internet of Canada's interim trade policy review, scheduled to be conducted in December 2000, as such a "Webcasting" exercise would provide the public with a greater understanding and appreciation of the WTO peer review process;
- Increased public access to WTO documentation, including adoption of a liberal "de-restriction" policy for documents such as WTO secretariat working papers, formal contributions from WTO Members, draft meeting agendas, minutes of meetings and notes of discussions, and improved access to trade policy review documentation;
- Expanded use of the WTO's Internet site to disseminate information on the organization and its work, including provision of "hot links" to the Internet sites of trade-related, nongovernmental organizations;

[54] *See Symposium: Democratizing International Trade Decision-Making*, 27 CORNELL INT'L L.J. 699 (1994).

[55] Posted at www.dfait-maeci.gc.ca/tna-nac/wto-e.asp#canada. For a similar proposal made by the United States, see INSIDE U.S. TRADE, 7 April 2000, at 20. For more far-reaching reforms, *see* Steve Charnovitz, *Opening the WTO to Nongovernmental Interests*, 24 FORDHAM INT'L L.J. 173 (2000).

- Improved dialogue with the public through (1) allocation of a portion of the WTO secretariat's budget to outreach initiatives such as symposia, workshops and improvements to the WTO Internet site; and (2) use of the WTO's outreach budget for more frequent and more structured meetings with journalists and non-governmental organizations;
- Consideration (1) of convening annual meetings for WTO bodies and committees to which nongovernmental observers would be invited or to which they could make written submissions; and (2) of conducting a series of dialogues among WTO Members, academics, the media, and non-governmental organizations;
- In the longer term, creation of a mechanism for parliamentary input into international trade policy debates, including the possibility of regular informal meetings of WTO Member parliamentarians; and
- Creation of *ad hoc* advisory boards made up of experts in specialized areas to provide nonbinding advice to the WTO Membership on issues such as trade and sustainable development and electronic commerce, similar to those created by the Asia-Pacific Economic Cooperation (APEC) forum, the World Intellectual Property Organization (WIPO), and the Organisation for Economic Co-operation and Development (OECD).

A variant of these proposals is needed to improve the WTO's public image and to open the decision-making process related to trade.

# 2

# DISPUTE SETTLEMENT

## 1. Introduction

One of the strengths of the WTO is the dispute settlement system, which came into operation on 1 January 1995. This system has rapidly become arguably the most important international tribunal. The WTO dispute settlement institutions function very much like a court of international trade: there is compulsory jurisdiction, disputes are settled largely by applying rules of law, decisions are binding on the parties and sanctions may be imposed if decisions are not observed.

From its inception, the WTO dispute settlement mechanism has been very busy; more than 80 cases were filed in the first two years, and more than 270 cases had been filed at the time of this writing. This activity implies confidence in the system and places political pressure on all states to comply, because many, including the most important trading nations, are both complainants and respondents in the various trade disputes considered.[1]

[1] For an excellent detailed treatment of the subject, see Ernst-Ulrich Petersmann, The GATT-WTO Dispute Settlement Mechanism, International Law, International Organizations and Dispute Settlement (1997). For a practical handbook, see N. David Palmeter and Petros C. Mavroidis, Dispute Settlement in the World Trade Organization (1999). For suggestions and evaluations, see *Symposium on The First Three Years of the WTO Dispute Settlement System*, 32 Int'l Law 609 (1998).

## 2. Dispute settlement in the GATT

The WTO dispute settlement system is the result of over 40 years of experience and the evolution of dispute settlement under the GATT 1947. The WTO system can be appreciated only against the background of the GATT regime.

The GATT avoids mention of the term "dispute". The drafters of the GATT did, however, foresee that problems would arise due to future actions or non-actions of one or more GATT contracting parties concerning the matters covered in the GATT. The principal mechanism for dealing with these problems is diplomatic consultation. There are 19 provisions for consultation in the GATT 1947.[2] One of these, Article XXII, is a general provision calling for "sympathetic consideration" and consultation "with respect to any matter affecting the operation of this Agreement".[3]

Article XXIII of the GATT creates a specific mechanism to correct "nullification or impairment" of the GATT. Nullification or impairment can occur for any one of three reasons: (1) failure of a party to carry out its obligations under the GATT; (2) the application of a measure by a party regardless of whether the measure conflicts with the GATT or (3) the existence of any other "situation" that is troublesome.[4] Thus, dispute settlement addresses more than just breaches of the GATT.

Article XXIII specifies a series of steps for dealing with a possible nullification or impairment. Each step is an escalation to be taken if previous attempts to settle the matter are ineffective:

1. The party concerned addresses "written representations or proposals" to the other contracting party or parties, which must give these representations or proposals "sympathetic consideration".[5]
2. The matter may be referred to the Contracting Parties, which "shall promptly investigate" and make appropriate recommendations to the parties concerned.[6] Alternatively, this may take the form of a "ruling on the matter". In the course of the investigation, the Contracting Parties may consult with contracting parties, "any appropriate inter-governmental organization" or the UN Economic and Social Council.[7]

---

[2] John H. Jackson, WORLD TRADE AND THE LAW OF GATT (1969), § 8.2, at 164.
[3] GATT Art. XXII:1.
[4] GATT Art. XXIII:1(a)–(c).
[5] *Id.* Art. XXIII:1.
[6] *Id.* Art. XXIII:2.
[7] *Id.*

3. The Contracting Parties may authorize a contracting party or parties to suspend the application of concessions or obligations under the GATT as a countermeasure if "the circumstances are serious enough".[8] The party against which this action is directed may then withdraw from the GATT on 60 days' notice.[9]

Article XXIII and dispute settlement under the GATT 1947 were shaped by state practice. At first, diplomatic negotiations were the sole means of dealing with controversies. Then, "working parties" began to be established to investigate and formulate recommendations. Working parties were typically composed of representatives of various countries who received instructions from their governments. In 1955, the GATT Contracting Parties began referring disputes to "panels", *ad hoc* groups of experts who acted as neutrals, not government representatives. Panel decisions had no official or binding effect but were referred to the GATT Council,[10] which could make the "appropriate recommendations".[11]

The GATT panel decision process of dispute resolution was successful. Because it was frequently utilized, it became necessary to formalize the panel procedures. This led to a series of agreements and understandings on dispute settlement[12] to supplement the skeleton approach of Article XXIII. Over the years, panels began to take a more rule-oriented, judicial approach to settling disputes. Parties invoked Article XXIII to vindicate their legal rights under the GATT. The panels' recommendations rested on legal, rather than merely diplomatic, grounds. To a remarkable degree, the decisions of the GATT panels adopted by the GATT Council were imple-

[8] GATT Art. XXIII:2.

[9] *Id.*

[10] The GATT Council, which was set up by resolution of the Contracting Parties in 1960, "consisted of representatives of all GATT contracting parties who wished to assume the responsibility of such membership", and met almost monthly. John H. Jackson, THE WORLD TRADING SYSTEM 63 (2d ed. 1997).

[11] For detailed treatment of this history, see especially Ernst-Ulrich Petersmann, *The Dispute Settlement System of the World Trade Organization and the Evolution of the GATT Since 1948*, 31 COMMON MKT. L. REV. 1157 (1994); Robert E. Hudec, ENFORCING INTERNATIONAL TRADE LAW: THE EVOLUTION OF THE MODERN GATT LEGAL SYSTEM 9 (1993).

[12] These are as follows: (1) The 1966 Decision on Procedures under Article XXIII, 5 April 1966, GATT B.I.S.D. (14th Supp.) at 18 (1966) (applying to disputes between a developing country contracting party and a developed country contracting party); (2) Understanding Regarding Notification, Consultation, Dispute Settlement and Surveillance, 28 November 1979, GATT B.I.S.D. (26th Supp.) at 210 (1979); (3) The 1982 Decision on Dispute Settlement Procedures, 29 November 1982, GATT B.I.S.D. (29th Supp.) at 9, 13–16 (1983); (4) The

mented and observed by states. This was not due to the threat of suspension of concessions,[13] but rather was an accomplishment of the dynamics of the process. A losing party could not ignore a decision based on legal principles. To do so would threaten the entire legal order on which the GATT system was based and which the losing party would need (and might be on the winning side of) in other cases.

Despite the success of the GATT panel dispute resolution process, serious shortcomings inhibited its effectiveness. Such shortcomings included delays in the formation of panels and the panel process, blocking of the adoption of panel reports in the GATT Council and delays in the implementation of Council recommendations. The Tokyo Round of multilateral trade negotiations added dispute resolution procedures to the various Codes approved in 1979. The result was dispute resolution procedures that were confusing in number and were largely uncoordinated.[14]

These difficulties were addressed in the new system of dispute settlement adopted by the WTO.

## 3. WTO dispute settlement

In the negotiations leading to the establishment of the WTO dispute settlement mechanism, the debate focused on whether a negotiation

1984 Decision on Dispute Settlement Procedures, 30 November 1984, GATT B.I.S.D. (31st Supp.) at 9 10 (1984); and (5) The 1989 Decision on Improvements to the GATT Dispute Settlement Rules and Procedures, 12 April 1989, GATT B.I.S.D. (36th Supp.) at 61 (1989).

[13] The suspension of concessions was authorized in only one case under the GATT. This case involved import restrictions on dairy products maintained by the United States. After a GATT Working Party found that these restrictions were inconsistent with the GATT, the Contracting Parties authorized The Netherlands to suspend concessions so that the importation of wheat flour would be limited to 60,000 metric tons in 1953. Netherlands Measures of Suspension of Obligations to the United States, 8 November 1952, GATT B.I.S.D. (1st Supp.) at 33 (1952). Both The Netherlands and the United States abstained from voting on this authorization. The Netherlands never acted to implement this suspension, presumably because it would have been ineffective. *See* Robert E. Hudec, *Retaliation Against Unreasonable Foreign Trade Practices*, 59 Minn. L. Rev. 461, 505–07 (1975).

[14] *See* Amelia Porges, *The New Dispute Settlement: From the GATT to the WTO*, 8 Leiden J. Int'l L. 115 (1995); Norio Komuro, *The WTO Dispute Settlement Mechanism: Coverage and Procedures of the WTO Understanding*, 29 J. World Trade, No. 4, at 5, 17–37 (1995); John P. Gaffney, *Due Process in the World Trade Organization: The Need for Procedural Justice in the Dispute Settlement System*, 14 Am. U. Int'l L. Rev. 1173 (1999).

approach would be superior to a more legalistic, rule-oriented approach.[15] Fears were expressed that reforms to give primacy to legal rules would impair the WTO's credibility because powerful states would inevitably ignore the rules when they go against their national interests.[16]

For better or worse, the judicialized, rule-oriented approach to dispute resolution has prevailed at the WTO.

## 3.1 General considerations

The WTO dispute settlement system is built on the pre-existing GATT regime. The document establishing the new system is the Uruguay Round Understanding on Rules and Procedures Governing the Settlement of Disputes (Dispute Settlement Understanding or DSU). Article 3.1 of the DSU affirms the application of Articles XXII and XXIII of GATT 1947. In addition, the WTO Agreement provides that "[e]xcept as otherwise provided under this Agreement or the Multilateral Trade Agreements, the WTO shall be guided by the decisions, procedures and customary practices followed by the Contracting Parties to GATT 1947. . . ."[17]

## 3.2 Institutions

Three institutions administer the WTO dispute settlement system. The first institution is the Dispute Settlement Body (DSB), which establishes panels, adopts panel and Appellate Body Reports, supervises the implementation of recommendations and rulings, and authorizes sanctions for failure to comply with dispute settlement decisions.[18] The General Council of the WTO serves as the DSB, but the DSB has its own chairman and follows separate procedures from those of the General Council.[19]

The DSU creates an Appellate Body to review panel rulings.[20] The Appellate Body is a standing institution composed of seven persons appointed by the DSB for four-year terms.[21] The members of the Appellate

[15] Jackson, above note 10, at 85–88.

[16] Hudec, above note 11, at 362–66; Edwin Vermulst and Bart Driessen, *An Overview of the WTO Dispute Settlement System and Its Relationship with the Uruguay Round Agreements: Nice on Paper but Too Much Stress for the System?*, 29 J. World Trade, No. 2, at 131, 146 (1995).

[17] WTO Agreement Art. XVI:1.

[18] DSU Art. 2.1.

[19] WTO Agreement Art. IV:3.

[20] DSU Art. 17.

[21] *Id.* Art. 17.1 and 17.2.

Body must be persons with demonstrated expertise in law and international trade who are not affiliated with any government. The Appellate Body membership must be "broadly representative of membership in the WTO".[22] The Appellate Body members hear cases in divisions of three, but each member is required to "stay abreast" of the dispute settlement activities of the WTO.[23]

The WTO system continues the panel system of the GATT 1947. Panels are composed of three (exceptionally five) persons, "well qualified governmental and/or non-governmental individuals", selected from a roster of persons suggested by WTO Members.[24] Panel members serve in their individual capacities and not as representatives of WTO Members.[25]

## 3.3 Scope of application

The competence of the WTO Dispute Settlement Body is set out in Article 1 of the DSU. Any dispute arising out of any of the multilateral WTO agreements may be resolved according to the rules and procedures of the DSU.[26] These agreements, which are referred to collectively as the "covered agreements", are listed in Appendix I of the DSU.[27] Some WTO agreements contain special or additional rules and procedures, and the DSU incorporates these rules and procedures as well.[28] In the event of conflict, the special or additional rules and procedures prevail.[29]

In its interpretation of the covered agreements, panels and the Appellate Body are guided by "customary rules of interpretation of public international law",[30] a reference to the Vienna Convention on the Law of Treaties.[31] Interpretations of the WTO agreements by panels and the Appellate Body are not, however, definitive. Only the Ministerial Conference and the General Council have the authority to adopt definitive interpretations.[32]

[22] *Id.* Art. 17.3.

[23] *Id.* Art. 17.1.

[24] *Id.* Art. 8.4, 8.5 and 8.6

[25] *Id.* Art. 8.9.

[26] *Id.* Art. 1.1.

[27] *Id.*

[28] *Id.* Art. 1.2.

[29] *Id.*

[30] *Id.* Art. 3.2.

[31] Vienna Convention on the Law of Treaties, available at http://www.un.org/law/ilc/texts/treatfra.htm.

[32] WTO Agreement Art. IX:2.

An interesting and unresolved issue is whether WTO panels and the Appellate Body have jurisdiction to decide questions of public or private international law (or even Member State law) when such issues arise in connection with a controversy under a covered agreement. An example is the dispute brought by the European Community before the WTO concerning the U.S. Helms-Burton law's provision imposing economic sanctions on persons and companies that own certain property in Cuba.[33] This dispute concerned provisions of a "covered agreement", GATT (Article XXI), as well as questions of public international law regarding extraterritorial jurisdiction and the doctrine of non-intervention. At the EC's request, this dispute was suspended when the United States waived application of key provisions of the disputed law.

To avoid a piecemeal decision that does not resolve the dispute, it is advisable that the WTO institutions have competence to consider all aspects of a dispute, including those involving legal issues not strictly arising under a covered agreement. Article 11 of the DSU arguably provides this authority by granting to panels the authority to "make such other findings as will assist the DSB in making the recommendations or in giving the rulings provided for in the covered agreements". In addition, the Vienna Convention, Article 31.2(c), provides for the application of "any relevant rules of international law applicable in the relations between the parties", in connection with the interpretation of a treaty. Because the DSU incorporates this interpretive principle,[34] panels and the Appellate Body should be able to apply such rules where relevant.[35] Alternatively, a legal question involving public international law could be the subject of a request by the WTO for an Advisory Opinion from the International Court of Justice (ICJ).[36] The Advisory Opinion procedure, however, would appear to be impractical and time consuming because the DSB and the General Council would have

[33] United States — The Cuban Liberty and Democratic Solidarity Act, WT/DS38 (suspended at the request of the EC, the complaining Member).

[34] DSU Art. 3.2.

[35] Therefore, the WTO/GATT is not a self-contained legal regime. *See* P. J. Kuyper, *The Law of GATT as a Special Field of International Law: Ignorance, Further Refinement or Self-Contained System of International Law*, 25 NETH. Y.B. INT'L L. 227, 229–32 (1994). For an argument that WTO panels have broad authority to decide all relevant questions of public international law, *see* Joost Pauwelyn, *The Role of Public International Law in the WTO: How Far Can We Go?*, 95 AM. J. INT'L L. 535, 554–59 (2001).

[36] Statute of the International Court of Justice, 26 June 1945, Arts. 65–68, 59 Stat. 1055, T.S. No. 993 (1945), available at http://www.icj-cij.org/icjwww/ibasicdocuments/ibasictext/ibasicstatute.htm.

to agree to make the request and the matter would have to be argued and decided separately by the ICJ.

## 3.4 The legal effect of panel and Appellate Body reports

WTO panel and Appellate Body reports are binding on the parties to the dispute once the Dispute Settlement Body adopts them.[37] They are not binding interpretations of the WTO agreements, however, and have no legal effect on other WTO Members. They also are not precedents that are legally binding in subsequent cases. Nevertheless, such reports constitute evidence of treaty practice, and subsequent dispute settlement panels and the Appellate Body are free to cite them and rely on their reasoning. To the extent their reasoning is persuasive, even unadopted reports may be cited and relied on by subsequent panels.[38] In fact, panels and the Appellate Body closely examine precedents when dealing with a dispute and try not to deviate from the interpretations established by the precedents.

## 3.5 Dispute resolution procedures

### *3.5.1 Objectives*

As under the GATT, the WTO dispute settlement system is based on the central idea that the rights and obligations of the Members under the WTO agreements are to be preserved and safeguarded.[39] To that end, the prompt settlement of "situations" in which a Member considers its rights to be impaired is "essential to the effective functioning of the WTO".[40] Thus, the objective of WTO dispute settlement is to secure the withdrawal of any measure that is found to be inconsistent with any agreement or to foster a mutually acceptable solution that is consistent with the WTO agreements.[41] All settlements and solutions must be consistent with the covered agreements.[42]

[37] Professor Jackson argues convincingly against the contrary view that reports are not legally binding but only require that the losing party pay "compensation". *See* John H. Jackson, *Designing and Implementing Effective Dispute Settlement Procedures: WTO Dispute Settlement, Appraisal and Prospects, in* The WTO as an International Organization 161, 169–70 (Anne O. Krueger ed., 1998).

[38] This has been authoritatively stated. *See* Appellate Body Report, *Japan — Taxes on Alcoholic Beverages*, at Part E, para. 8.

[39] DSU Art. 3.2.

[40] *Id.* Art. 3.3.

[41] *Id.* Art. 3.7.

[42] *Id.* Art. 3.5 and 3.6.

### 3.5.2 *Initiation: request for consultations*

The DSU cautions WTO Members to be judicious about invoking the dispute settlement procedures. They should consider whether the action "would be fruitful" and would "secure a positive resolution to a dispute".[43] The first step is to make a request for consultations with the other Member or Members. Only after this consultation do the parties have a right to invoke the panel process.

Upon a request for consultations, the Member concerned must reply within 10 days and must enter into good faith consultations within 30 days after receiving the request.[44]

### 3.5.3 *Standing to bring claims*

A WTO panel and the Appellate Body, in *EC — Bananas*, addressed the matter of standing to pursue a claim. In that case, the European Communities questioned the "legal interest" of the United States to bring a dispute involving bananas because U.S. banana production was minimal and the United States did not export bananas. The Appellate Body concluded that a WTO Member has broad discretion in deciding to bring a case under the DSU:

> The wording of Article XXIII:1 of the GATT 1994 and of Article 3.7 of the DSU suggests, furthermore, that a Member is expected to be largely self-regulating in deciding whether any such action would be "fruitful". We are satisfied that the United States is a producer of bananas, and a potential export interest by the United States cannot be excluded. The internal market of the United States for bananas could be affected by the EC banana regime, by the effects of that regime on world supplies and world prices of bananas.
>
> We agree with the panel report that "neither Article 3.3 nor 3.7 of the DSU nor any other provision of the DSU contains any explicit requirement that a Member must have a 'legal interest' as a prerequisite for requesting a panel". We do not accept that the need for a legal interest is implied in the DSU or in any other provision of the *WTO Agreement*.[45]

This is, in effect, the recognition of an "*actio popularis*" because all WTO Members would seem to have an interest in any material breach of the covered agreements. The liberal approach to standing is quite new and controversial; there was no tradition of such complaints under the GATT.

---

[43] DSU Art. 3.7.

[44] *Id.* Art. 4.3.

[45] *See* Appellate Body Report, *European Communities—Bananas*, para. 132.

In addition, any WTO Member that is not a party to the original dispute may intervene in one of two ways. First, such a Member "having a substantial interest in a matter before a panel" has an opportunity to be heard both orally and in writing.[46] Second, such a "third party" to a dispute may freely bring an original complaint under the normal dispute settlement procedures.[47] Whenever "feasible," a single panel will handle both (or all) complaints related to the original matter.[48]

### *3.5.4 Good offices, conciliation, and mediation*

The DSU provides that the parties to a dispute may agree "voluntarily" to employ good offices, conciliation, or mediation as a settlement technique.[49] Such procedures may begin or be terminated at any time.[50] An agreement to use these procedures, however, does not preclude the establishment of a dispute settlement panel. The complaining party must allow a period of 60 days after the date of the request for consultations before requesting the establishment of a panel. If the parties agree, procedures for good offices, conciliation, or mediation may proceed even after a panel has been established.[51]

Normally, the WTO Director-General, acting in an ex-officio capacity, will offer good offices, conciliation, or mediation.[52] These three procedures are similar in that a neutral third party is involved to aid the process of dispute settlement. A good officer is more of a channel of communication than an active participant in the dispute settlement process. A conciliator independently investigates the dispute and makes a written proposal for its resolution. A mediator is an active participant in the dispute settlement process, bringing the parties together in an informal setting and making suggestions for resolution and closure of the dispute. In practice, the three procedures tend to blend. These procedures are useful not only in resolving issues of law and fact but also in dealing with non-justiciable issues that an adjudicative process cannot settle.

---

[46] DSU Art. 10.2. [47] *Id.* Art. 10.4. [48] *Id.* Art. 9.1.
[49] *Id.* Art. 5. [50] *Id.* [51] *Id.* Art. 5.
[52] *Id.* Art. 5.6.

### 3.5.5 *Arbitration*

WTO Members can agree to use binding arbitration as an alternative means of dispute settlement.[53] In such a case, the parties to the dispute can define the issues and the procedures to be followed. Any arbitration award is then enforceable through the WTO. DSB and WTO sanctions may be imposed for non-compliance.

## 3.6 The panel process

If consultations fail to settle the dispute within 60 days (20 days "in cases of urgency"), the complaining party may request the establishment of a panel.[54] A panel *must* be established at the next DSB meeting unless it is decided by consensus not to establish a panel.[55] Panels are composed of three (exceptionally five) qualified governmental or non-governmental individuals chosen from lists maintained by the Secretariat. The parties to a dispute have 20 days to agree on the panellists; if they fail to agree, panellists are appointed by the Director-General. Citizens of the states that are parties to the dispute (including citizens of the same customs union or common market) cannot serve as panellists.[56] The parties to the dispute also have 20 days from the establishment of the panel to agree on the "terms of reference" of the panel; otherwise, standard terms of reference will be used.[57]

Frequently, more than one Member requests the establishment of a panel, and the interests of more than two parties are involved in a dispute. In such cases, a single panel can consider the disputes of multiple complainants,[58] and third parties that have an interest in a dispute have the right to be heard by the panel.[59]

A panel's function is to assist the DSB in resolving the dispute.[60] The panel operates on a timetable that, generally, shall not exceed six months (three months in cases of urgency).[61] The panel process involves the

---

[53] DSU Art. 25.

[54] *Id.* Art. 4.7 and 4.8.

[55] *Id.* Art. 6.1. The "negative consensus" process of decision making is a key innovation of the DSU.

[56] *Id.* Art. 8.3.

[57] *Id.* Art. 7.1.

[58] *Id.* Art. 9.1.

[59] *Id.* Art. 10.2.

[60] *Id.* Art. 11. The Working Procedures for panels are set out in Appendix 3 of the DSU.

[61] *Id.* Art. 12.8.

following: (1) written submissions of parties and third parties; and (2) meetings (oral hearings) with parties and third parties.[62]

The panel may seek information and technical advice from any appropriate source.[63] In addition, the panel may request an advisory report in writing from an Expert Review Group.[64] The panel then submits a draft report to the parties to the dispute. After comments by the parties, the panel prepares an interim report consisting of findings of fact, and conclusions of law. The interim report is circulated to the parties, which can request a meeting with the panel to discuss the issues. At the conclusion of this interim review process, the panel prepares a final report and transmits it to the DSB.[65]

The DSB may consider the report 20 days after it has been circulated to Members.[66] Objections to the report must be made at least 10 days before the DSB is to meet.[67] Within 60 days after the submission of the report, the DSB must adopt it unless there is a consensus against adoption.[68] If a party has notified its decision to appeal, the DSB may not consider the report until after the completion of the appeal.[69]

## 3.7 The appeal process

Any party to a dispute (but not third parties) may appeal a panel report to a seven-member standing Appellate Body established for this purpose.[70] The Appellate Body sits in divisions of three members.[71] Appellate Body members are appointed for four-year terms and cannot be affiliated with any government.[72] The Appellate Body has the power to uphold, modify or reverse the legal interpretations adopted by the panel.[73] Generally, the

---

62 *Id.* Art. 12.

63 *Id.* Art. 13.1.

64 *Id.* Art. 13.2. The rules and procedures governing Expert Review Groups (ERGs) are set out in Appendix 4 of the DSU. Their function is to make available technical and scientific expertise to panel members. ERGs work under the authority of the panels, which decide their terms of reference and their working procedures. *Id.* Appendix 4, para. 1. Their final reports are advisory only. *Id.* Appendix 4, para. 6.

65 *Id.* Art. 15. The deliberations of the panels are confidential. *Id.* Art. 14.

66 *Id.* Art. 16.1.

67 *Id.* Art. 16.2.

68 *Id.* Art. 16.4.

69 *Id.*

70 *Id.* Under Article 17.9 of the DSU the Appellate Body has authority to draft its Working Procedures.

71 *Id.* Art. 17.1.

72 *Id.* Art. 17.2 and 17.3.

73 *Id.* Art. 17.13.

appellate process must be completed within 60 days but shall in no case exceed 90 days.[74] Within 30 days following the circulation of an Appellate Body report, the report must be adopted by the DSB and "unconditionally accepted by the parties to the dispute" unless the DSB decides by consensus not to adopt the report.[75]

## 3.8 Implementation

The losing party must inform the DSB of its intentions "in respect of implementation of the recommendations and rulings of the DSB" within 30 days of the date of the adoption of a panel or Appellate Body report.[76]

### *3.8.1 Reasonable period for implementation*

Losing parties have an obligation to comply with the recommendations and rulings of the DSB within "a reasonable period of time".[77] What is a reasonable period is determined under Article 21.3 of the DSU by any one of the following three methods:

1. A period set by the DSB after a proposal by the Member concerned,
2. A period agreed by the parties to the dispute, or
3. A period determined through binding arbitration within 90 days after adoption of the relevant report. In this case, the suggested period should not exceed 15 months from the date of the adoption of the report but may be shorter or longer depending on the circumstances.[78]

### *3.8.2 Compliance and the "sequencing" problem*

A problem with the implementation of WTO dispute settlement recommendations and rulings is the lack of guidance over what exactly a losing party must do to comply. The tendency has been for the losing party to take minimal steps and declare itself in full compliance. The winning party often disagrees.[79] One solution is to refer the matter to a compliance panel under

[74] DSU Art. 17.5.

[75] *Id.* Art. 17.4.

[76] *Id.* Art. 21.3.

[77] *Id.*

[78] *Id.*

[79] *E.g., U.S., Korea Clash Over Implementation of WTO Panel Dumping Ruling,* Inside U.S. Trade, 16 April 1999.

Article 21.5 of the DSU. In the *EC — Bananas* case,[80] the matter of compliance was referred to a WTO panel that ruled that the revised EC banana regulations violated the GATT and the GATS. The panel also ruled that no presumption of consistency or inconsistency attaches to regulations revised by a losing party.[81] But the winning party may not want to wait for the decision of a compliance panel. In the *Bananas* case, at the United States' request, a WTO arbitral panel established under DSU Article 22.6 set the amount of compensation authorized due to continued nullification or impairment of trade benefits.[82]

The confusion between the provisions of Articles 21 and 22 of the DSU is termed the "sequencing" problem.[83] This problem arises because of a lack of coherence between the two Articles. First, Article 21.5 provides for an expedited compliance procedure:

> Where there is disagreement as to the existence or consistency with a covered agreement of measures taken to comply with the recommendation and rulings such dispute shall be decided through recourse to these dispute settlement procedures, including wherever possible resort to the original panel. The panel shall circulate its report within 90 days after the date of referral of the matter to it. When the panel considers that it cannot provide its report within this time frame, it shall inform the DSB in writing of the reasons for the delay together with an estimate of the period within which it will submit its report.

Article 22.2, however, provides that if the losing party fails to bring its offending measure into compliance within 20 days of the expiry of the reasonable period allotted under Article 21.3, the winning party may request authorization from the DSB to retaliate by suspending trade concessions. The convening of a compliance panel under Article 21.5 is not mentioned. Instead, Article 22.6 states that the DSB must grant

[80] Article 21.5 Panel Report, *European Communities — Bananas, Recourse to Article 21.5 by Ecuador*, WT/DS27/RW/ECU, 12 April 1999. No presumption of consistency with WTO agreements attaches to revised measures under Article 21.5. Article 21.5 Panel Report, *European Communities — Bananas — Recourse to Article 21.5 by the European Communities*, WT/D27/RW/EEC, 12 April 1999.

[81] Article 21.5 Panel Report, *European Communities — Bananas, Recourse to Article 21.5 by Ecuador*, above note 80, para. 6.152.

[82] Arbitration Report, *European Communities — Bananas — Recourse to Arbitration by the European Communities under Article 22.6 of the DSU, Decision by the Arbitrators*, WT/DS27/ARB, 9 April 1999, para. 8.1.

[83] For greater detail, see Cherise M. Valles and Brendan P. McGivern, *The Right to Retaliate under the WTO Agreement: The "Sequencing" Problem*, 34 J. World Trade, No. 2, at 63 (2000).

authorization to suspend trade concessions within 30 days of the expiry of the reasonable period or refer the matter to arbitration, which shall be final.

Thus, as in the *Banana* case, there appears to be, through an oversight in the drafting of the DSU, the possibility of an Article 21.5 compliance panel and an Article 22.6 arbitration both proceeding on parallel and possibly conflicting courses. The confusion is compounded by the fact that there is no appeal from the arbitration but there can be an appeal from the compliance panel.

This state of affairs cannot be dealt with adequately by interpretation; there must be a clarifying amendment of the DSU. This amendment should follow what appears to be the logical sequence intended: Article 22 should be amended so that retaliation may be invoked only after the conclusion of the Article 21.5 compliance determination process. Such an amendment has been proposed.[84] In current practice at the WTO, arbitration under Article 22 is suspended until the Article 21.5 compliance proceeding has run its course.

## 3.9 Compensation for failure to comply and retaliation

Two sanctions are specified if the recommendations and rulings of the DSB are not implemented within a reasonable period: compensation and retaliation (or suspension of concessions). Both sanctions are temporary. Neither is intended to be a substitute for implementing a recommendation or ruling to conform to the WTO agreements.[85]

The first option for sanctions is compensation. Compensation consists of additional trade concessions by the losing party, usually in related economic areas to the dispute, that are acceptable to the winning party as a substitute for maintaining the trade barriers in dispute. Compensation is voluntary and the subject of agreement between the parties to the dispute. If no satisfactory compensation is agreed within 20 days of the expiration of the reasonable period, any party having invoked the dispute settlement procedures may request authorization from the DSB to retaliate.[86]

[84] *Agreement on Dispute Settlement Changes Unlikely Before DOHA*, Inside U.S. Trade, 3 August 2001, at 1, 20.

[85] DSU Art. 22. It is unclear whether the sanction procedure under Article 22 can go forward before the Article 21.5 and 21.6 procedures are complete. In *EC — Bananas*, the United States argued that Article 22 may be invoked before the completion of Article 21 proceedings. In fact, the WTO arbitrators released both findings at once. This seems to be a precedent that Article 21 and 22 proceedings can go forward simultaneously.

[86] DSU Art. 22.2.

The second option is retaliation (suspension of concessions). The level of retaliation authorized by the DSB must be equivalent to the nullification or impairment. There are three types of retaliation: (1) parallel retaliation by suspending concessions with respect to the same economic sector in which the nullification or impairment has been found; (2) cross-sector retaliation, which is the suspension of concessions relating to different sectors in the same agreement; and (3) cross-agreement retaliation, which is the suspension of concessions specified in a different agreement.[87] The preferred option is parallel retaliation; cross-sector and cross-agreement retaliation will be authorized only if parallel retaliation is impractical.[88]

Disputes over retaliation can be referred to arbitration if the losing party objects to the level of retaliation or appropriate procedures are challenged where the complaining party has requested cross-retaliation. The original panel or an arbitrator appointed by the Director-General carries out the arbitration.[89] The arbitration must be completed within 60 days.[90]

The DSB must both authorize and monitor the retaliation taken.[91] Unilateral retaliation is prohibited.[92] Retaliation is deemed temporary and will be terminated once the inconsistent measure has been removed, the losing party has provided a solution to the nullification or impairment of benefits, or the parties have reached a satisfactory solution.[93]

The United States has proposed that retaliation lists be rotated periodically to increase the pressure for compliance. The EC and other Members oppose this so-called carousel procedure.

## 3.10 Special dispute resolution procedures

The DSU is primarily concerned with the settlement of disputes that involve an infringement of an obligation assumed under one or more of the WTO agreements. Such an infringement is considered a *prima facie* nullification or impairment of a trade benefit accruing to other WTO Members. Following GATT practice, however, the DSU provides for dispute settlement concerning complaints that there is a nullification or impairment of benefits without an infringement of a WTO obligation. The DSU contains provisions for resolving two such complaints described in

[87] *Id.* Art. 22.3. [88] *Id.* Art. 22.3(e). [89] *Id.* Art. 22.6.
[90] *Id.* [91] *Id.* Art. 22.8. [92] *Id.* Art. 23.2.
[93] *Id.* Art. 22.8.

GATT Article XXIII: (1) non-violation complaints; and (2) situation complaints.

### *3.10.1. Non-violation complaints*

In accordance with GATT Article XXIII:1(b), Article 26.1 of the DSU authorizes a complaint against "a measure" by a Member even if such measure does not conflict with any WTO agreement, if the complaining Member considers that any benefit under a covered agreement is being nullified or impaired or the attainment of any objective of a covered agreement is being impeded as a result of the application of the measure.

This procedure is available where not specifically excluded by the relevant covered agreement to secure the removal of trade barriers that impede market access even if there is no violation of the agreement. The burden of proof is on the complainant, which must present a "detailed justification" of the complaint. This involves (1) defining the "benefit" being nullified or impaired or the objective being impeded; (2) defining the "measure" responsible; and (3) showing a causal relationship between the measure and the nullification or impairment or impeding of objectives.[94]

These three points are all rather vague. The meagre case law on non-violation complaints suggests that "benefit" refers to assurance of better market access;[95] that nullification or impairment depends on a showing of adverse effect and frustration of reasonable expectations;[96] that "measure" may be a specific action[97] or omission;[98] and that the causal factor refers to a propensity to have an adverse effect, not any specific proof of a change in the volume of trade.[99]

[94] DSU Art. 26. *See also* Armin von Bogdandy, *The Non-Violation Procedure of Article XXIII:2: Its Operational Rationale*, 26 J. World Trade, No. 4, at 95, 101–08 (1992).

[95] *See* European Communities — Payments and Subsidies Paid to Processors and Producers of Oilseeds-Related Animal Feed Proteins, 25 January 1990, GATT B.I.S.D. (37th Supp.) at 86, para. 148 (1991) [hereinafter *Oilseeds* case]. Often the benefit is a tariff concession. The Australian Subsidy on Ammonium Sulfate, 3 April 1950, GATT B.I.S.D. II at 188, para. 10 (1952); Treatment of Germany Imports of Sardines, 31 October 1952, GATT B.I.S.D. (1st Supp.) at 53, paras 16–17 (1953) [hereinafter *Germany Sardines* case].

[96] *Oilseeds* case, above note 95, para. 150. *See also* Adrian T. L. Chua, *Reasonable Expectations and Non-Violation Complaints in GATT/WTO Jurisprudence*, 32 J. World Trade, at 27 1998.

[97] *Id.* para. 154.

[98] *Germany Sardines* case, above note 95, para. 16.

[99] This causal requirement stems from the necessity of showing the nullification or impairment is "as a result of" the measure. *See Oilseeds* case, above note 95, para. 150. However, is not necessary to show the specific volume of trade caused by the measure. *Id.* paras 150–52.

Where the elements of a non-violation complaint are proved, however, there is no obligation to withdraw the measure in question. The panel or the Appellate Body must recommend that the Member concerned make a "mutually satisfactory adjustment".[100]

The non-violation complaint procedure may appear to lack teeth. Article 26.1(c), however, provides for non-binding arbitration "upon the request of either party". Arbitrators may determine the level of benefits impaired or suggest ways of resolving the dispute. Compensation may be part of a "mutually satisfactory adjustment as final settlement of the dispute". This procedure, although technically non-binding, places pressure on the parties to reach an agreement to resolve the dispute.

### *3.10.2 Situation complaints*

In accordance with GATT Article XXIII:1(c), Article 26.2 of the DSU authorizes a complaint by a Member that considers that any benefit under a covered agreement is being nullified or impaired or the attainment of any objective of the agreement is being impeded by the existence of "any situation" other than those covered by the violation and non-violation complaint procedures. The chief utility of the situation complaint procedure is that causes of the frustration of market access expectations can be addressed other than measures. Presumably, the term "situation" allows more nebulous conditions or states of affairs to be addressed. No panels, however, have been called on to address "situations" in the 50-year history of the GATT/WTO.

The utility of the situation complaint procedure is very limited. Not only are the elements of such a complaint nebulous but also the only effect is that the findings of the panel will be circulated to Members. The panel report may be appealed to the Appellate Body. The adoption of the panel report as well as surveillance and implementation of recommendations and rulings is subject to pre-WTO rules that allow blocking and delay of panel rulings.

## 3.11 Adverse inference

Article 13.1 of the DSU provides that each panel has the right to seek information and technical advice from "any individual and body" the panel deems appropriate. This broad investigative power is essential if the panel is to fulfil its mandate under DSU Article 11 to make an "objective assessment of the matter before it, including an objective assessment of the facts of the case".

[100] DSU Art. 26.1(b).

In *Canada — Aircraft*, the Appellate Body ruled that panels have authority to draw an adverse inference from the refusal of a party to supply necessary information without good reason.[101] This case involved an alleged subsidy by Canada to its aircraft industry that Brazil regarded as contrary to the SCM (Subsidies and Countervailing Measures) Agreement. The panel asked Canada for certain information related to the alleged subsidy. In response, Canada asked for a special procedure to protect proprietary information. The panel complied, but Canada still refused to supply the information.

The panel did not draw an adverse inference, and Brazil appealed this ruling to the Appellate Body. The Appellate Body upheld the panel's discretion but stated that, under the circumstances of the case, the panel could have drawn an adverse inference and could have found a violation of DSU Article 13, which concerns the panel's right to seek information.

*Canada — Aircraft*, therefore, established the principle that an adverse inference may be drawn from non-cooperation of a party if the lack of cooperation is without any reasonable ground. After *Canada — Aircraft*, the Appellate Body confirmed that panels and the Appellate Body may draw an adverse inference from non-cooperation on the part of a party to a dispute under certain circumstances.[102]

## 3.12 *Amicus curiae*

Whether or not panels and the Appellate Body may accept and consider *amicus curiae* briefs from persons other than the parties to a dispute (the disputing parties and the third parties) has been a controversial issue. The recent rulings of the Appellate Body, however, show that the power of panels and the Appellate Body to accept and consider *amicus curiae* briefs is an established principle. In the *Shrimp/Turtle* case, the panel declined to accept an *amicus curiae* brief, but the Appellate Body reversed and stated that Article 13.1 of the DSU confers power on panels to "seek" information from any

[101] *Canada — Measures Affecting the Export of Civilian Aircraft*, Report of the Appellate Body (AB-1999), 2 August 1999, WT/DS70/AB/R, para. 203

[102] *United States — Definitive Safeguard Measures on Imports of Wheat Gluten from the European Communities*, Report of the Appellate Body (AB-2000–2–10), 22 December 2000, WT/DS166/AB/R, para. 172

individual or body, and the power to "seek" information should be interpreted to include the power to accept and consider *amicus curiae* briefs.[103]

Subsequently, the Appellate Body ruled that two methods exist for the submission and consideration of *amicus curiae* briefs.[104] First, since it is up to each participant in a dispute settlement proceeding to determine what to include in its submissions, an *amicus curiae* brief may be submitted either to a panel or to the Appellate Body with the consent of a participating WTO member.[105] Second, private organizations and individuals may submit *amicus curiae* briefs directly to a panel under DSU Article 13.1 and to the Appellate Body under DSU Article 17.9.[106] In the *EC — Asbestos* case, the Appellate Body established a special procedure for accepting *amicus curiae* briefs.[107] A person submitting an *amicus curiae* brief must also submit a short summary of the brief limited to 20 pages and should not repeat the arguments of the parties. Whether to accept or consider an *amicus curiae* brief is up to the discretion of the panels and the Appellate Body.

At the meetings of the WTO General Council, certain WTO members, especially developing countries, have criticized the decision of the Appellate Body to consider *amicus curiae* submissions on the ground that the WTO is a contract among the members who have accepted it, and it is inappropriate to permit outside parties to influence adjudicative interpretations and decisions.[108]

Nevertheless, in the *EC — Sardines*[109] case, the Appellate Body accepted a portion of an *amicus curiae* brief submitted by the Government of Morocco, while rejecting as unhelpful an *amicus* brief submitted by a private party.

[103] *United States — Import Prohibition of Certain Shrimp and Shrimp Products*, Report of the Appellate Body (AB-1998-4), 12 October 1998, WT/DS58/R, para. 104

[104] *European Communities — Trade Description of Sardines*, Report of the Appellate Body (AB 2002–3), 26 September 2002, WT/DS231/AB/R, para. 156–157.

[105] *Id.* para. 156

[106] *Id.* para. 157. In *United States — Imposition of Countervailing Duties on Certain Hot-rolled Carbon Steel Products Originating in the United Kingdom*, Report of the Appellate Body (AB 2000–1) 5 October 2000, WT/DS138/AB/R, para. 36–42, the Appellate Body first invoked DSU Article 17.9 for this purpose, reasoning that if panels are authorized to accept *amicus* briefs, the Appellate Body, which has authority to adopt its own working procedures, could do the same.

[107] *European Communities — Measures Affecting Asbestos and Asbestos-Containing Products*, Report of the Appellate Body (AB – 2000–11), 12 March 2001, WT/DS135, AB/R, paras 51–52

[108] General Council Meeting on 22 November 2000, WT/GC/38 (12 Dec. 2000).

[109] *EC — Sardines*, Report of the Appellate Body, paras. 153–170.

## 3.13 Burden of proof

Burden of proof concerns the issue of which of the disputing parties is responsible for proving the illegality or legality of the conduct under question. In *United States — Shirts and Blouses*,[110] India argued that it was incumbent on the United States (the respondent) to prove that its imposition of import restrictions on shirts and blouses imported from India was not contrary to the safeguard provisions in the WTO Agreement on Textile and Clothing (ATC). India argued that the United States had the burden of proving that its conduct was not contrary to the requirements of safeguard measures as provided for in the ATC since the United States was invoking the safeguard provision in the ATC, which is an exception to the general principle, and the party which invokes an exception to the general principle is responsible for proving that it is justified.

The Appellate Body held that the safeguard measure should not be regarded as an exception to the general principle and that it is incumbent on the party challenging the conduct of another party to adduce *prima facie* evidence of facts and law to show that the conduct of the challenged party is in violation of the provision in question. When such a proof is established, the burden of proof is shifted to the party under challenge to adduce a rebuttal that the allegation of the challenging party is not based on an appropriate ground.

In *EC — Hormones*,[111] the issue was the allocation of the burden of proof under Articles 3.1 and 3.3 of the SPS (Sanitary and Phytosanitary Measures) Agreement. Article 3.1 stipulates that Members shall base their SPS measures on international standards, guidelines or recommendations where they exist, and Article 3.3 provides that Members may introduce or maintain SPS measures which result in a higher level of SPS protection than would be achieved by measures based on international standards. The Panel assigned to the respondent (EC) the burden of proof to show that the measure would be justified under Article 3.3. The Appellate Body reversed the Panel's ruling and held that the burden of proof is on the complaining party to establish a prima facie case of inconsistency with a provision of the SPS Agreement.

110 *United States — Measures Affecting Imports of Woven Wool Shirts and Blouses from India*, Report of the Appellate Body (AB 1997–1), 25 April 1997, WT/DS33/AB/R.

111 *EC — Hormones*, Report of the Appellate Body, 13 February 1998, WT/DS26/AB/R; WT/DS/48/R, para. 104.

In *EC — Sardines*[112] the issue was who bears the burden of proof under the TBT (Technical Barriers to Trade) Agreement when a Member departs from the obligation to follow international standards under Article 2.4 of the TBT Agreement for the reason that the relevant international standards are not effective. Although the Panel held that the party which invokes the portion of Article 2.4 of the TBT Agreement which permits a departure from international standards had the burden of proof, the Appellate Body reversed and held that the complaining party (Peru) had the burden of proving that the relevant international standards were not relied upon, and such international standards were effective and appropriate to fulfil the legitimate objectives pursued by the respondent (EC).

A review of the precedents on this issue seems to reveal that the rule of the burden of proof established by *United States — Shirts and Blouses* has been followed by the Appellate Body, and that it has been firmly established that a party which makes an affirmative claim, whether it is the complaining party or the defending party, bears the burden of proof.

## 3.14 Judicial economy

Judicial economy is a recognized principle of the judicial and administrative process whereby an adjudicating body is authorized to deal only with issues necessary to dispose of the dispute in question while skipping other issues raised by the parties. In the WTO, while panels are free to employ judicial economy, Article 17.12 of the DSU states that the Appellate Body shall address each of the issues raised during the appellate proceeding. Therefore, contrary to the practice of panels, the Appellate Body is not free to exercise judicial economy. The reason for this difference comes from the role assigned to the Appellate Body. The Appellate Body is charged with the responsibility not only of resolving disputes but also of establishing interpretations of WTO agreements. Therefore, the Appellate Body must address each legal issue raised in an appellate proceeding regardless of whether it is necessary to resolve the dispute.

In the *United States — Line Pipe Safeguard*[113] case, which involved a safeguard measure by the United States, Korea raised a claim regarding the

[112] *EC — Trade Description of Sardines*, Report of the Appellate Body, 26 September 2002, WT/DS231/AB/R, para. 260–282.

[113] *United States — Definitive Safeguard Measures on Imports of Circular Welded Carbon Quality Line Pipe from Korea*, Report of the Appellate Body (AB-2002–1) 15 February 2002, WT/DS202/13/AB/R.

non-application of a safeguard measure to members of a free trade agreement under Article XXIV of GATT 1994. The Appellate Body, however, did not deal with this issue on the ground that the dispute had been resolved by its holding on "parallelism." In light of the text of DSU Article 17.12, which states that the Appellate Body shall deal with each legal issue raised in an appellate proceeding, the dismissal by the Appellate Body of the issue raised by Korea regarding the applicability of Article XXIV of the GATT 1994 is problematic.

## 3.15 Standard of review

Article 11 of the DSU states that a panel should make an objective assessment of the matter before it, including an objective assessment of the facts of the case and the applicability and conformity with the relevant covered agreements. This requires that a panel treat pieces of evidence produced before it with objectivity and not distort or ignore them and that a panel analyse the matter before it without bias and reach a reasonable conclusion. In short, this means that a panel must observe due process of law.[114] To facilitate this, Article 13 of the DSU accords panels a wide scope of investigative power including the power to seek information from any individual or body, and Members are obligated to cooperate and provide information requested by a panel. Although Articles 11 and 13 of the DSU do not refer to the Appellate Body, it is obvious that the Appellate Body is under the obligation to observe due process of law as well.

Article 17.6(i) of the Antidumping Agreement provides for a special standard of review for antidumping proceedings. This Article requires that if the establishment of facts by a national antidumping authority was proper and the evaluation was unbiased and objective, even though the panel might have reached a different conclusion, the panel shall not overturn the evaluation. Article 17.6(ii) of the Antidumping Agreement requires that where the panel finds that a relevant provision of the Agreement admits of more than one permissible interpretation, the panel shall find the national antidumping authority's measure to be in conformity with the Agreement if it rests upon one of those permissible interpretations.

When one compares the wording of Article 17.6 of the Antidumping Agreement and Article 11 of the DSU, one might have the impression that

[114] This was the explicit determination of the Appellate Body in *Chile — Price Band System and Safeguard Measures Relating to Certain Agricultural Products*, Report of the Appellate Body (AB 2002–2), 23 September 2002, WT/DS207/AB/R.

Article 17.6 declares a deference principle according to which WTO bodies are obligated to respect determinations of national antidumping authorities as an exception to Article 11 of the DSU. However, in *U.S. — Hot-rolled Steel*,[115] the Appellate Body stated that Article 17.6 of the Antidumping Agreement is supplementary to Article 11 of the DSU with regard to antidumping matters and should not be interpreted as superseding Article 11 of the DSU. This interpretation seems reasonable since Article 3.2 of the DSU requires panels and the Appellate Body to interpret provisions of WTO agreements, including Article 11 of the DSU, according to the established rules of public international law for interpreting treaties (which are incorporated in the Vienna Convention), and Article 17.6 of the Antidumping Agreement contains the requirement that the rules of interpretation established in public international law should be observed. Therefore, both Article 11 of the DSU and Article 17.6 of the Antidumping Agreement incorporate the same rules of interpretation as expressed in Article 31 (1) and (2) of the Vienna Convention.

There are two principles with regard to standards of review: the deference principle and the *de novo* principle. Under the deference principle, WTO bodies defer to findings of the national authority and do not, in principle, engage in new findings of fact or law unless the findings of the national authority are clearly unreasonable. Under the *de novo* principle, WTO bodies take a more active role and use evidence that was not before the national authority. Neither of these principles has been applied in their extreme forms. Panels and the Appellate Body have taken a middle-of-the-road approach and applied a test which is a mixture of these two principles depending on the particulars of the case concerned. In *EC — Hormones*,[116] the Appellate Body stated that the proper standard of review is neither the deference principle nor the *de novo* principle, but the proper test is "the objective assessment" as provided for in Article 11 of the DSU.

In *Guatemala Cement*,[117] the Appellate Body enunciated the deference principle by stating: "... in our review of the investigative authorities' evaluation of the facts, we will first need to examine evidence considered by the investigating authority. That is, we are not to examine any new

[115] *United States — Anti-Dumping Measures on certain Hot-Rolled Products from Japan*, Report of the Appellate Body, 23 August 2001, WT/DS184/AB/R.

[116] Report of the Appellate Body, para. 116.

[117] *Guatemala – Anti-Dumping Investigation Regarding Portland Cement from Mexico*, Report of the Appellate Body, 25 November 1998, WT/DS60/AB/R.

evidence that was not part of the record of the investigation". This expresses the deference principle with regard to fact findings and, according to this rule, panels should not look for facts that were not before the investigating authority.

However, the recent trend of Appellate Body rulings seem to shift toward "judicial activism". In *Thailand — Anti-Dumping Duties on Angles, Shapes and Sections of Iron or Non-Alloy Steel H-Beams from Poland,*[118] the issue was an interpretation of Article 3.1 of the Antidumping Agreement. The Appellate Body stated that panels are given broad authority to investigate whether the antidumping authority of a Member did a proper job in fact-finding, and suggested that panels can examine not only evidence before the antidumping authority but also other evidence. This seems to be a departure from the principle established by *Guatemala Cement.*

An interesting aspect of this ruling by the Appellate Body is that it allowed the Panel to base its findings on evidence not shown to the parties.[119] This finding may invite criticism that parties are not accorded a sufficient opportunity to be heard.

This trend was exhibited again in *U.S. — Lamb*[120] in which the issue was the scope of review by the Panel of fact-findings by the U.S. International Trade Commission. The Panel took the view that its task was limited to a review of the determination made by the U.S. International Trade Commission and to examining whether the published report provides an adequate explanation of how the facts as a whole support the determination of threat of injury by the U.S. International Trade Commission. However, the Appellate Body stated that a panel need not confine itself to the arguments of the investigating authority, and must be open to the possibility that the explanation given by the competent authorities is not reasoned or adequate.

However, in *U.S. — Transitional Safeguard Measure on Combed Cotton Yarn from Pakistan,*[121] the Appellate Body stated that panels must not conduct a *de novo* review of the evidence and should not substitute their judgment for that of the competent authority.

---

[118] *Thailand – Anti-Dumping Duties,* para. 113–120.

[119] *Thailand – Anti-Dumping Duties on Angles, Shapes and Sections of Iron or Non-Alloy Steel H-Beams from Poland,* Report of the Appellate Body, 5 April 2001, WT/DS122/AB/R.

[120] *United States – Safeguard Measures on Imports of Fresh, Chilled or Frozen Lamb Meat from New Zealand and Australia,* Report of the Panel and Report of the Appellate Body, 16 May 2001, WT/DS177; WT/DS178.

[121] Report of the Appellate Body, 5 November 2001, WT/DS192/AB/R.

On the whole, however, it seems that a departure from the rule established by *Guatemala — Cement* is clear. The question is whether this trend will continue in future. If the investigate powers of panels are extended beyond a certain limit, there may be criticism that WTO bodies act beyond their authority.

## 3.16 Critique of the DSU

The WTO dispute settlement system is a valiant attempt to subject controversies over international trade to the rule of international law. This ambitious goal will be advanced if this system continues to be respected, especially by larger states, so that rule-oriented settlements prevail over power-oriented dispute settlement. The WTO system has unabashedly adopted the judicial model of dispute settlement.

This effort deserves high praise, but, even if it is successful, there have been some criticisms raised against the dispute settlement process at the WTO. Some argue that the Appellate Body has overstepped the boundary assigned to it and, in fact, "made law" instead of interpreting law.[122] We refrain from making any judgment as to whether the Appellate Body did overstep the boundary or not. However, the Appellate Body has the final word in a dispute settlement since the report of the Appellate Body in a dispute is adopted automatically by negative consensus voting at the DSB, and the winning party always favours its adoption. Even if the Appellate Body makes a mistake, there is no mechanism to correct it. In a domestic jurisdiction, if the Supreme Court makes a mistake, the legislature can enact a law to correct it. However, in the WTO process, the political branch (the General Council and the Ministerial Conference) does not commonly exercise this power.

This means that there are no effective "checks and balances" operating within the WTO. One way to correcting this omission is to modify Article IX:2 of the WTO Agreement to allow the adoption of an interpretation of a WTO agreement by two-thirds or a simple majority of the Members. However, this would mean that the General Council or the Ministerial Conference could overturn a "judicial or quasi-judicial" decision of a panel or the Appellate Body for political reasons. This would be contrary to the idea of establishing a judicialized dispute settlement process.

[122] Claude E. Barfield, FREE TRADE, SOVEREIGNTY, DEMOCRACY, THE FUTURE OF THE WTO 44 (2001).

Another solution may be to create a peer review group in the WTO that would examine reports of the Appellate Body, criticize them if there is any problem of interpretation and periodically publish the results. This group would have no power to overturn the rulings of the Appellate Body, but the Appellate Body could study the reports of this group and gain insight from them. This peer review group would consist of legal experts with established reputations in international law or WTO law, such as academics, judges, and practicing lawyers.

WTO Members would be excluded because the purpose of this "peer review" is not to determine whether rulings of the Appellate Body are politically palatable, but to judge whether they are legally sound and balanced. WTO Members already have the opportunity to express their views when the DSB adopts a report of the Appellate Body.[123]

There is also a need for alternative dispute resolution methods and more diplomatic and negotiation-based dispute settlement. GATT 1947's numerous provisions for diplomatic consultation as well as the DSU's authorization of conciliation, mediation, good offices, arbitration, and expert review are largely overshadowed by the quasi-judicial procedures and the strict timetables of the panels and the Appellate Body. While the WTO system is a vast improvement, there is need to increase the role of the alternative dispute settlement systems that may be more suited to certain types of disputes than the rule-based system.

There is also a need to open the dispute settlement process to allow greater transparency and participation by non-governmental organizations.[124] In addition, there is a need to expand the resources of developing countries to allow them to participate more effectively in the system.

## 4. Trade retaliation under national laws

Several WTO Members, most notably the European Union, Japan, and the United States, have adopted national laws that permit retaliation in response to foreign measures that nullify or impair their rights under international trade law. Although private parties have no right to invoke WTO dispute

[123] DSU Art. 16.2.

[124] *But see* Jeffrey L. Dunoff, *The Misguided Debate Over NGO Participation at the WTO*, 1 J. Int'l Econ. L. 433, 453–56 (1998).

settlement,[125] national trade retaliation laws provide a means whereby a private party can have its complaint espoused by a WTO Member.

## 4.1 The European Union

As a part of its implementation of the Uruguay Round agreements in 1994, the European Community adopted the so-called Trade Barriers Instrument (TBI),[126] which is designed to safeguard the Community's rights under international trade law. This regulation is the successor to the New Commercial Policy Instrument adopted by the EC in 1984, which allowed the EC to retaliate in response to any "illicit commercial practice" by third countries.[127]

The purpose of the TBI is to "ensure the exercise of the Community's rights under international trade rules, in particular those established under the auspices of the World Trade Organization".[128] Three "tracks" are established to vindicate these rights.

First, any natural or legal person or any association (without legal personality) acting on behalf of a Community industry that considers that it has suffered injury as a result of obstacles to trade affecting the Community market may file a complaint with the Commission.[129] "Obstacles to trade" are defined as "any trade practice adopted or maintained by a third country in respect of which international trade rules establish a right of action. Such a right of action exists when international trade rules either prohibit a practice outright or give another party affected by the practice a right to seek elimination of the effect of the practice...."[130] Thus, the first track is intended to cover both violation and non-violation complaints under WTO rules. If the Commission determines that action is necessary to remove the injury or adverse trade effects in question, appropriate retaliatory

[125] There are proposals to allow private parties to proceed directly in the WTO. *See, e.g.*, Thomas J. Schoenbaum, *WTO Dispute Settlement: Praise and Suggestions for Reform*, 47 INT'L & COMP. L.Q. 647, 653–58 (1998).

[126] Council Regulation 3286/94 of 22 December 1994 Laying Down Community Procedures in the Field of the Common Commercial Policy in Order to Ensure the Exercise of the Community's Rights Under International Trade Rules, in Particular Those Established Under the Auspices of the World Trade Organization, 1994 O.J. (L 349) 71 [hereinafter TBI Agreement].

[127] Council Regulation 2641/84 of 17 September 1984 on the Strengthening of the Common Commercial Policy with Regard in Particular to Protection Against Illicit Commercial Practices, 1984 O.J. (L 252) 1 (no longer in force).

[128] TBI Agreement, above note 126, Art. 1.

[129] *Id.* Art. 3.1.

[130] *Id.* Art. 2.1.

commercial policy measures may be adopted. Retaliatory action, however, must be in accordance with the recommendations of an appropriate international dispute settlement body.

The second track the TBI permits is that EU Member states may request the Commission to initiate an investigation into whether obstacles to trade are affecting either the Community market or third-country markets.[131]

The third track allows any community enterprise suffering adverse trade effects to request that the Commission investigate obstacles to trade in third-country markets.[132]

All three tracks require the Commission to seek and abide by international dispute settlement procedures.[133]

## 4.2 Japan

Japanese Customs and Tariffs Law and a Cabinet Order which implements the Law provide for the Japanese government to retaliate against foreign discriminatory treatment of Japanese goods, shipping, or airlines.[134] Retaliation, which has never been authorized, is limited to imposing customs duties, and authorization by the WTO is required.[135]

## 4.3 The United States

The United States has championed the need for retaliation under national trade laws to open foreign markets and to combat foreign trade barriers. The U.S. government has invoked section 301 of the Trade Act of 1974[136] and variants known as Super 301,[137] Special 301,[138] and other laws[139] frequently

[131] *Id.* Art. 6.

[132] *Id.* Art. 4.

[133] *Id.* Art. 12.

[134] Kanzei Teiritsu Hō [Customs and tariff law], Law No. 54 of 1910, as amended.

[135] *Id.* Arts. 6 and 7.

[136] 19 U.S.C.A. § 2411. For the history of this law, see Thomas O. Bayard and Kimberly Ann Elliott, Reciprocity and Retaliation in U.S. Trade Policy (1994).

[137] 19 U.S.C.A. § 2420. Super 301 requires the United States Trade Representative to identify trade priorities, including priority countries and priority practices to be investigated under section 301.

[138] 19 U.S.C.A. § 2242(a). This section allows retaliation against countries that do not protect U.S. intellectual property rights.

[139] *See* Telecommunications Trade Act of 1988, 19 U.S.C.A. § 3111, which authorizes retaliation against countries that do not open their telecommunications markets; the Buy America Act of 1988, 41 U.S.C.A. § 10a–10d, which authorizes retaliation against countries

since the mid-1980s. For example, in 1993, the year before the Uruguay Round accords, the U.S. Trade Representative conducted 91 investigations under Section 301 and Special 301, and imposed sanctions in 11 cases.[140]

Section 301 and its progeny[141] authorize the United States to take unilateral action to retaliate against perceived unfair trade practices either allowed or undertaken by other nations. Section 301 grew out of Congressional concern over foreign barriers to U.S. exports that could not be addressed easily in trade negotiations under the GATT; it has been strengthened progressively over the years.[142] Many other nations have adopted their own versions of Section 301, even as they sharply criticized its use by the United States.[143]

Section 301 authorizes both mandatory and discretionary action by the U.S. Trade Representative. Mandatory action is required if a foreign act or practice:

- Denies U.S. rights under any trade agreements;[144]
- Violates, is inconsistent with, or denies benefits under a trade agreement with the United States;[145] or
- Is "unjustifiable and burdens or restricts United States Commerce".[146]

---

not in compliance with the WTO Government Procurement Code; and the Primary Dealers Act of 1988, 22 U.S.C.A. § 5342, which authorizes retaliation against countries that discriminate against U.S. financial institutions.

[140] *See* Komuro, above note 14, at 74.

[141] The discussion will focus on the basic Section 301, 19 U.S.C.A. § 2411, as a paradigm for all of the Section 301 variants. Super 301 differs little from basic 301 except that, in its original 1988 form, countries — not only practices — could be designated as "unfair," and an annual determination is required; 19 U.S.C. § 2420. Those features also are present in Special 301, 19 U.S.C.A. § 2242(a). There is little indication that these additional features have had much impact, and they actually may be counterproductive. For a capsule summary, see Bayard and Elliott, above note 136, at 25–32.

[142] For a history of the evolution of Section 301, see Bayard and Elliott, above note 136, at 326–27.

[143] For example, after the conclusion of the Uruguay Round, the European Union adopted a strengthened version of Section 301 that allows retaliation against "illicit commercial practices" by foreign trading partners. *See* Council Regulation 3286/94, above note 126.

[144] 19 U.S.C.A. § 2411(a)(1)(A).

[145] 19 U.S.C.A. § 2411(a)(1)(B)(i).

[146] 19 U.S.C.A. § 2411(a)(1)(B)(ii). "Mandatory" Section 301 is somewhat less than mandatory because it gives the USTR several escape routes. Retaliation can be avoided in "extraordinary cases," where retaliation would cause serious harm to national security, and where retaliation would have a disproportionately adverse impact on the U.S. economy. *Id.* § 2411(a)(2)(B)(iv), (v). Mandatory, therefore, does not mean compulsory.

This wording makes clear that *mandatory* Section 301 is concerned with enforcing the rights of the United States under international law. The first two categories concern legal violations, denial of rights and denials of benefits under trade agreements. This is considered a *per se* enforcement matter, since no showing is required that U.S. commerce is restricted or burdened. The third category concerns unjustifiable acts, policies, and practices; and the word "unjustifiable" is defined as illegal, i.e., "in violation of, or inconsistent with the international legal rights of the United States",[147] which further is defined to mean: without limitation, denial of "national or most-favored-nation treatment or the right of establishment or protection of intellectual property rights".[148] This sub-paragraph also requires a burden or restriction on U.S. commerce. But the effect of this is to broaden the operation of mandatory Section 301, because "commerce" is defined to include services (including transfers of information) and investment as well as goods.[149]

*Discretionary* Section 301, in contrast, is designed to reach any foreign act, practice, or policy that is "unreasonable or discriminatory and burdens or restricts United States Commerce".[150] This subsection goes beyond merely enforcing international law obligations; it permits U.S. unilateral determination and enforcement of appropriate standards of behaviour in international business transactions.

This becomes evident when one considers how "unreasonable" is defined, as denying fair and equitable opportunities for the establishment of:

- Adequate and effective protection of intellectual property rights (even where a country is in compliance with the WTO Agreement on Trade-Related Aspects of Intellectual Property);
- Non-discriminatory market access for companies that rely on intellectual property protection;
- Market opportunities, including the "toleration . . . of systematic anticompetitive activities" by enterprises in a foreign country;

[147] 19 U.S.C.A. § 2411(d)(4)(A).

[148] 19 U.S.C.A. § 2411(d)(4)(B).

[149] 19 U.S.C.A. § 2411(d)(4)(A), (B). Commerce may be burdened by foreign shipbuilding subsidies as well.

[150] 19 U.S.C.A. § 2411(b).

- Export targeting; and
- Workers' rights.[151]

The term "discriminatory," the other half of discretionary Section 301, is defined in terms of denying national or MFN treatment,[152] but such conduct is actionable even if no international law obligation is involved. Once again, commerce is defined broadly[153] so that discretionary Section 301 can reach business dealings involving services and investment as well as goods.

Proceedings under both variants of Section 301 may be initiated by the filing of a petition by an "interested person"[154] or by the U.S. Trade Representative.[155] If the U.S. Trade Representative accepts a petition, there is an investigation and a request for consultations with the foreign country concerned.[156] The matter then proceeds according to a strict timetable designed to produce a final determination within 18 months after the investigation is initiated, in most cases.[157]

The relief granted will generally be a solution negotiated with the foreign country involved. This will take the form of a binding agreement to end the objectionable act, policy or practice, or to provide the United States with compensatory trade benefits.[158] If there is no negotiated settlement, the USTR is authorized to take unilateral retaliatory action. This can involve a wide variety of sanctions, such as import duties or restrictions, suspension of trade benefits, and termination of duty free export treatment.[159] The USTR does not have to limit retaliation to the subject matter of the unfair trade practice; he can cross-retaliate: levy sanctions against completely different goods or subject matter.[160]

---

[151] 19 U.S.C.A. § 2411(d)(3)(B).

[152] 19 U.S.C.A. § 2411(d)(5).

[153] 19 U.S.C.A. § 2411(d).

[154] 19 U.S.C.A. § 2412(a). An "interested person" encompasses a wide variety of private business, organizations and individuals, including unions, workers, domestic firms and consumers.

[155] 19 U.S.C.A. § 2412(b).

[156] 19 U.S.C.A. § 2413(a)(1).

[157] 19 U.S.C.A. § 2414(a)(2)(A)(ii).

[158] 19 U.S.C.A. § 2411(c)(1)(D).

[159] 19 U.S.C.A. § 2411(c).

[160] 19 U.S.C.A. § 2411(c)(B).

## 4.4 Critique of trade retaliation under national laws

The question arises whether these national laws allowing retaliation as a response to foreign trade barriers conform to the Members' legal obligations. The WTO Agreement specifically requires Members to ensure the conformity of their laws and regulations to their obligations under all of the WTO agreements.[161] The DSU, Article 23, contains a broad prohibition against unilateral retaliatory measures; Members must have recourse to the WTO dispute settlement procedures and must not suspend trade obligations or concessions without DSB authorization.

Thus, national laws permitting retaliation conform to WTO rules only if they are exercised in accordance with the DSU. Conformity with the DSU is required under the laws of Japan and the European Union, and even U.S. law can be consistent: one of the "escapes" from "mandatory" action under Section 301 is a negative DSB ruling, so the U.S. Trade Representative can terminate a Section 301 proceeding on this ground.

U.S. law, however, differs from the other two in that it leaves open the possibility of unilateralism. Such trade unilateralism generally is now a violation of international law and would be subject to appropriate WTO sanctions.

The United States may raise the argument that a unilateral measure may be justified as a countermeasure under international law and that although the unilateral measure is a violation of international law, it is intended as a proportionate response to an action or inaction by another state that is itself a violation of international law. Such a "self-help" measure is an accepted measure of redress under international law.[162] The difficulty of this position, however, is that in most cases the WTO dispute settlement procedure would be available to correct violations of international law so there is no need for such countermeasures under the WTO system.[163]

---

161 WTO Agreement Art. XVI:4.

162 *See The Naulilaa* case *(Germany and Portugal)* 2 Rep. Int. Awards 1011 (1928); Case Concerning the Air Services Agreement, 27 March 1946 (United States-France), Arbitral Award, 9 December 1978, 54 INT'L L. REP. 304 (1979); 18 R.I.A.A. 416 (1979) [hereinafter *Air Services* case].

163 However, under the *Air Services* case, a countermeasure may be undertaken even where arbitral recourse is available. *See Air Services* case, above note 162, at 305.

Unilateralism under U.S. Section 301 was the subject of a WTO panel decision: *United States — Sections 301–310 of the Trade Act of 1974.*[164] In that case, the panel, although finding that Sections 301–310 are a *prima facie* violation of the DSU Article 23 prohibition against unilateralism, accepted as legally binding the assurances of the U.S. administration that it has a duty to exercise the discretion given under the statutory language in a way consistent with WTO obligations.[165] This confirms that trade unilateralism is broadly precluded under WTO rules.

[164] Panel Report, *United States — Sections 301–310 of the Trade Act of 1974*, WT/DS152/R, 22 December 1999.

[165] *Id.* paras 7.116–7.122.

# 3

# SOURCES OF LAW[1]



## 1. Introduction

Modern discussions of the sources of international law usually begin with a reference to Article 38(1) of the Statute of the International Court of Justice (ICJ),[2] which provides:

> The Court, whose function is to decide in accordance with international law such disputes as are submitted to it, shall apply:

[1] This chapter is based on N. David Palmeter and Petros C. Mavroidis, *The WTO Legal System: Sources of Law*, 92 AM. J. INT'L L. 398 (1998).

[2] Statute of the International Court of Justice, 26 June 1945, 59 Stat. 1055, T.S. No. 993 (1945), available at http://www.icj-cij.org/icjwww/ibasicdocuments/ibasictext/ibasicstatute.htm.

(a) international conventions, whether general or particular, establishing rules expressly recognized by the contesting states;
(b) international custom as evidence of a general practice accepted as law;
(c) the general principles of law recognized by civilized nations;
(d) subject to the provisions of Article 59, judicial decisions and the teachings of the most highly qualified publicists of the various nations, as subsidiary means for the determination of rules of law.[3]

The WTO Agreement is a "particular" international convention within the meaning of Article 38(1)(a), as are the agreements and legal instruments annexed thereto. The agreements annexed to the WTO Agreement are known as the WTO agreements or the covered agreements. The Dispute Settlement Understanding (DSU) governs resolution of disputes concerning the substantive rights and obligations of WTO Members under the covered agreements. In the words of Article 38(1)(a), the rules of the DSU "are expressly recognized by the contesting states" that are parties to WTO dispute settlement procedures.

The fundamental source of law in the WTO is, therefore, the texts of the relevant covered agreements themselves. All legal analysis begins there. In the words of the WTO Appellate Body, which was established by Article 17 of the DSU, "The proper interpretation of the Article is, first of all, a textual interpretation".[4]

The Agreements, however, do not exhaust the sources of potentially relevant law. On the contrary, all of the subparagraphs of Article 38(1) are potential sources of law in WTO dispute settlement. More specifically, prior practice under the WTO's predecessor, the General Agreement on Tariffs and Trade (GATT), including reports of GATT dispute settlement panels; WTO practice, particularly reports of dispute settlement panels and the WTO Appellate Body; custom; the teachings of highly qualified publicists; general principles of law; and other international instruments — all contribute to the rapidly growing and increasingly important body of law known as "WTO law".

While there is no explicit equivalent to Article 38(1) in the Dispute Settlement Understanding or any other of the covered agreements, its terms

[3] ICJ Statute Art. 38(1). *See, e.g.*, Ian Brownlie, PRINCIPLES OF PUBLIC INTERNATIONAL LAW 15 (5th ed. 1998); Barry E. Carter and Phillip R. Trimble, INTERNATIONAL LAW 18 (2d ed. 1994); Rosalyn Higgins, PROBLEMS AND PROCESS: INTERNATIONAL LAW AND HOW WE USE IT 17–18 (1994); Malcolm N. Shaw, INTERNATIONAL LAW 59 (1991). Article 59 of the Statute, referred to in Article 38(1)(d), provides simply: "The decision of the Court has no binding force except between the parties and in respect of that particular case".

[4] Appellate Body Report, *Japan — Alcoholic Beverages*, at Part G, para. 1.

are effectively brought into WTO dispute settlement by Articles 3.2 and 7 of the DSU. Article 3.2 specifies that the purpose of dispute settlement is to clarify the provisions of the WTO Agreements "in accordance with customary rules of interpretation of public international law". Article 7 specifies that the terms of reference for panels shall be "to examine, in the light of the relevant provisions in [... the covered agreement(s) cited by the parties to the dispute], the matter referred to the DSB" and to "address the relevant provisions in any covered agreement or agreements cited by the parties to the dispute".[5]

The "DSB" is the Dispute Settlement Body, established by the DSU, with "the authority to establish panels, adopt panel and Appellate Body reports, maintain surveillance of implementation of rulings and recommendations, and authorize suspension of concessions and other obligations under the covered agreements".[6]

## 2. Sources of law

### 2.1 Covered agreements

The term "covered agreements" in Article 7 of the Dispute Settlement Understanding means all of the agreements annexed to the WTO Agreement. In addition, the DSU applies to disputes between the parties to the two plurilateral agreements that are also part of the WTO.[7] These texts, as noted, are the starting point for dispute settlement proceedings, because Article 6.2 of the DSU requires that a request for the establishment of a panel identify the legal basis for the request. The legal basis for a request would be the specific provisions of a particular agreement or agreements. Implicit in this requirement is a due process consideration of fair notice, which has led the Appellate Body to observe, "It is incumbent upon a panel to examine the request for the establishment of the panel very carefully to

[5] DSU Art. 7.1 and 7.2.

[6] *Id.* Art. 2.1.

[7] These are the Agreement on Civil Aircraft and the Agreement on Government Procurement. Two other plurilateral agreements, the International Dairy Agreement and the International Bovine Meat Agreement, were terminated at the end of 1997. WTO, *Deletion of the International Dairy Agreement from Annex 4 of the WTO Agreement, Decision of 10 December 1997*, WT/L/251, 17 December 1997; WTO, *Deletion of the International Bovine Meat Agreement from Annex 4 of the WTO Agreement, Decision of 10 December 1997*, WT/L/252, 16 December 1997.

ensure its compliance with both the letter and the spirit of Article 6.2 of the DSU".[8]

The texts of several covered agreements explicitly refer to other international agreements, which, in this sense, may be considered to be "covered agreements". These are considered below in the section "Other international instruments".

## 2.2 Reports of prior panels and the Appellate Body

Other than the texts of the WTO Agreements themselves, no source of law is as important in WTO dispute settlement as the reported decisions of prior dispute settlement panels. These include the reports of GATT panels as well as WTO panels, and now, of course, reports of the Appellate Body.

"Judicial decisions" are among the "subsidiary" sources of international law specified in Article 38(1)(d) of the ICJ Statute. Read together with Article 59 of the Statute, which confines the binding force of a decision of the Court to the parties, Article 38(d)(1) has produced a system of precedent that the Court essentially refers to and considers its prior decisions, but is not legally required to follow. As Judge Mohamed Shahabuddeen has observed, however, "though having the power to depart from them, [the Court] will not lightly exercise that power".[9] The law of the WTO effectively duplicates this system.

### *2.2.1 Adopted and unadopted panel reports*

The WTO Agreement specifies that the WTO shall be guided by the decisions, procedures, and customary practices followed by the Contracting Parties to GATT 1947 and the bodies established in the framework of GATT 1947.[10] Implementing this requirement in the context of trade in goods, one of the most important of the WTO Agreements, GATT 1994, specifies that the Agreement includes "decisions of the CONTRACTING PARTIES to GATT 1947".[11]

The question whether adopted GATT panel reports represent "decisions" of the Contracting Parties to GATT 1947 arose in *Japan — Alcoholic Beverages*.[12] Without referring explicitly to Article 38(1)(d) of the World

[8] Appellate Body Report, *EC — Bananas*, para. 142.

[9] Mohamed Shahabuddeen, PRECEDENT IN THE WORLD COURT 2–3 (1996).

[10] WTO Agreement Art. XIV:1 (except as otherwise provided under the Agreement or the multilateral WTO agreements).

[11] *Id.*

[12] Appellate Body Report, *Japan — Alcoholic Beverages*, at Part E, para. 1–8.

Court Statute, the panel effectively treated adopted reports as if they had the status of judicial decisions. Specifically, it determined that adopted reports are an integral part of GATT 1994 since they are "other decisions of the CONTRACTING PARTIES to GATT 1947" within the meaning of Article 1(b)(iv) of GATT 1994.[13] The Appellate Body disagreed, but in the end, it is difficult to detect any practical difference resulting from the disagreement, which may have been largely semantic.[14]

The Appellate Body in *Japan — Alcoholic Beverages* held that a "decision" to adopt a panel report is not a "decision" within the meaning of Article 1(b)(iv). It did not say what adopted reports are if they are not "decisions," other than to say that they are "an important part of the GATT acquis".[15] This is somewhat confusing, both because the legal source of this "acquis" is not specified and because, in its discussion of the issue, the Appellate Body itself refers to "a decision" and "decisions" to adopt panel reports.[16]

The Appellate Body apparently was concerned that the panel's conclusion could be interpreted as holding that adopted reports "constitute a definitive interpretation of the relevant provisions of GATT 1947".[17] A "definitive interpretation" would presumably be controlling and thus, on this theory, could amount to importation of rigid *stare decisis* into the WTO, if not amendment *sub rosa* of its very texts. If this were the concern, it seems misplaced. The panel treated adopted reports as "subsidiary" sources of WTO law, comparable in status to judicial decisions in the World Court. It did not say that adopted reports were controlling. Rather, it said that they "have to be taken into account by subsequent panels dealing with the same or a similar issue".[18] It specified, however, that "it does not necessarily have to follow their reasoning or results".[19] Thus, in the panel's view, an adopted report does not "constitute a definitive interpretation" of an agreement; it is simply a "decision" that has to be considered — but not necessarily followed — by the panel. The panel effectively agreed with Judge Shahabuddeen's invocation of Shabtai Rosenne: "Precedents may be followed or discarded, but not disregarded".[20]

[13] *Id.* at Part E, para. 1.

[14] This discussion is based on section E of the Appellate Body's report, Appellate Body Report, *Japan — Alcoholic Beverages.*

[15] *See id.* at Part E, para. 6.

[16] *Id.*

[17] *Id.* at Part E, para. 4.

[18] *See* Panel Report, *Japan — Alcoholic Beverages*, para. 6.10.

[19] *Id.*

[20] Shabtai Rosenne, The Law and Practice of the International Court 56 (2d rev. ed. 1985), quoted in Shahabuddeen, above note 9, at 131.

In its description of adopted reports, the Appellate Body came very close to saying the same thing: "[Adopted reports] are often considered by subsequent panels. They create legitimate expectations among WTO Members, and, therefore, should be taken into account where they are relevant to any dispute. However, they are not binding, except with respect to resolving the particular dispute between the parties to that dispute".[21]

This statement reads very much like Article 38(1)(d) of the ICJ Statute and its reference to "subsidiary" sources of international law. Indeed, in a footnote to this passage, the Appellate Body went on to draw a parallel to the practice of the World Court:

> It is worth noting that the Statute of the International Court of Justice has an explicit provision, Article 59, to the same effect. This has not inhibited the development by that Court (and its predecessor) of a body of case law in which considerable reliance on the value of previous decisions is readily discernible.[22]

All of this discussion took place in the context of GATT reports. However, the same reasoning, *mutatis mutandis*, would apply to adopted WTO reports themselves, not only those concerned with GATT 1994, but also those concerned with the General Agreement on Trade in Services, the Agreement on Trade-Related Aspects of Intellectual Property Rights, and the plurilateral trade agreements. In the end, the result seems to be that adopted reports are not binding precedent and do not control subsequent panels; neither may they "add to or diminish the rights and obligations provided in the covered agreements".[23] Nevertheless, panels "should" consider them. Adopted reports have strong persuasive power and may be viewed as a form of nonbinding precedent, whose role is comparable to that played by jurisprudence in the contemporary civil law of many countries, such as France, and that played by decisions of courts at the same level in the United States. As a practical matter, parties will continue to cite prior reports to panels, and panels will continue to take them into account by adopting their reasoning — in effect, following precedent — unless panels conclude, for good and articulated reasons, that they should do otherwise.

The role of unadopted panel reports is somewhat less, but they remain relevant. The Appellate Body agreed with the panel in *Japan — Alcoholic Beverages* that unadopted reports "have no legal status in either the GATT or the WTO system since they have not been endorsed through decisions by the

---

[21] *See* Appellate Body Report, *Japan — Alcoholic Beverages*, at Part E, para. 6.

[22] *Id.* note 30.

[23] DSU Art. 3.2.

CONTRACTING PARTIES to GATT or WTO Members".[24] The Appellate Body also agreed that "a panel could nevertheless find useful guidance in the reasoning of an unadopted panel report that it considered to be relevant".[25]

The persuasive power of the prior reports rests not only on the reasoning they contain, important as this is, but also on the mere fact that once a dispute has been decided a certain way, subsequent panels are likely to agree even if they believe they might have decided the case otherwise had they been viewing the question in the first instance. Continuity and consistency are valuable attributes in any legal system: application of the same rules to the same factual issues, regardless of the parties involved — treating like cases alike — is an important source of legitimacy for any adjudicator. It is particularly important for international adjudicators, who, unlike their municipal counterparts, lack a monopoly of enforcement power and have only the power to persuade the addressees of their decisions that those decisions are correct.[26] Thus, if a panel decides not to treat like cases alike by not following a prior report, the panel most certainly "should" — to use the words of the Appellate Body — address that report, which "created legitimate expectations among WTO Members". To do otherwise would call into serious question the very legitimacy of the process.

Tribunals choose to follow previous cases not only for reasons of fairness and legitimacy, but also for reasons of efficiency. Today's tribunal benefits from the work done yesterday on the same legal question; the wheel does not have to be reinvented. Finally, following precedent tends to make the law clearer and more certain, which is also of benefit to the legal system and those that take part in it.

Nevertheless, the panel in *Japan — Alcoholic Beverages* itself declined to follow the reasoning in two prior panels, one unadopted, the other adopted. As to the unadopted report, the panel said that it "was not persuaded by the reasoning", and, as to the adopted report, that it had "decided not to follow the interpretation of the term 'like product' as it appears in GATT Article III:2, first sentence, advanced by the 1992 Malt Beverages report in so far as it incorporates the aim-and-effect test", which it had previously discussed at length and dismissed.[27]

[24] Appellate Body Report, *Japan — Alcoholic Beverages*, at Part E, para. 8 (quoting Panel Report, *Japan — Alcoholic Beverages*, para. 6.10).

[25] *Id.*

[26] *See* Thomas M. Franck, FAIRNESS IN INTERNATIONAL LAW AND INSTITUTIONS 26–46 (1995).

[27] *See* Panel Report, *Japan — Alcoholic Beverages*, para. 6.18.

Each of these panels stated why it had decided not to follow the previously adopted reports. This need to justify departures from prior cases is key for an international adjudicating body in its quest for legitimacy. Sir Gerald Fitzmaurice expressed a similar view with respect to the functioning of the World Court:

> It would seem that, although the Court is not obliged to decide . . . on the basis of previous decisions *as such*, what it can do is to take them fully into account in arriving at subsequent decisions, and that . . . it is mandatory for it to apply judicial decisions in the sense of employing them as part of the process whereby it arrives at its legal conclusions in the case.[28]

No doubt in part because prior panel reports are not legally binding, and perhaps in part because of GATT's diplomatic heritage, parties and panels use peculiar language in referring to earlier decisions. They "note" prior reports[29]; they "recall" them.[30] They "concur" with the reasoning of the prior panel.[31] In one of the early WTO panel reports, the panel quoted another report at length and said, "We see great force in this argument".[32] Whatever word or words they use, however, panels are likely to "follow" the reports of previous panels unless those reports can be distinguished from the cases before them or the panels can be convinced that the previous panels were in error.[33]

Nevertheless, panels can sometimes seem to be trains passing in the night, as indicated by two reports arising out of the Agreement on Textiles and Clothing that were faced at the outset with the question of the appropriate standard of review. The first panel, *United States — Underwear*, found "great

[28] *See* Gerald Fitzmaurice, 2 The Law and Procedure of the International Court of Justice 584 (1986).

[29] *See* Panel Report, *Japan — Alcoholic Beverages*, para. 6.11; Panel Report, *United States — Reformulated Gasoline*, para. 6.11.

[30] Panel Report, *United States — Reformulated Gasoline*, paras 6.10, 6.40; Panel Report, *Japan — Alcoholic Beverages*, para. 6.19.

[31] Panel Report, *United States — Reformulated Gasoline*, para. 6.14.

[32] Panel Report, *United States — Underwear*, para. 7.12 (referring to *New Zealand — Imports of Electrical Transformers from Finland*, 18 July 1985, GATT B.I.S.D. (32d Supp.) at 55 (1986)).

[33] This wording suggests that the drafters of these reports were aware of comparable wording in reports of the Permanent Court of International Justice. *See* Shahabuddeen, above note 9, at 18. The phraseology continues in the World Court, as evidenced by Gabcikovo-Nagymaros Project (Hung. v. Slovk.), 1997 ICJ Rep. 7, 92 (25 September): "The Court recalls that it has recently had occasion to stress . . ." (para. 53); "The Court recalls that, in the Fisheries Jurisdiction case . . ." (para. 104); "The Court will recall in this context that, as it said in the North Sea Continental Shelf cases . . ." (para. 141); but more authoritatively, "The Permanent Court of

force" in the argument of a 1985 panel.[34] Two months later, the second panel, *United States — Shirts and Blouses*, dismissed the 1985 report along with other reports cited by the parties:

> We do not consider that the reports cited by the parties are relevant to the present dispute.... [They] were adopted many years ago...and they interpreted different agreements in different contexts. ...The ATC has instituted a new regime for textile products and the DSU has instituted new rules for panels.[35]

The panel in *United States — Shirts and Blouses* not only saw the prior reports very differently; it did not even refer to the panel report in *United States — Underwear* and its consideration of the same question. Given the sizable records in both cases, the fact that the nearly contemporaneous proceedings overlapped to a considerable degree and the time constraints on panels, this result is not surprising. It is more than likely that the panel in *United States — Shirts and Blouses* was not even aware of the report on *United States — Underwear* at the time it prepared its own report.

Finally, the question of the degree to which facts found by a previous panel may be relevant to a later panel has not arisen often. Nevertheless, one of the early WTO panels had occasion to consider the purely factual conclusion of an earlier GATT panel. After quoting the previous panel's factual finding, the WTO panel said, "Following its independent consideration of the factors mentioned in the 1987 Panel Report, the Panel agreed with this statement".[36] It went on to observe that the responding Member had "offered no further convincing evidence that the conclusion reached by the 1987 Panel Report was wrong", thus clearly stating the otherwise always implicit burden on the party challenging a prior report, as to law or fact, to demonstrate its error.[37]

In one of the early instances, a panel referred to an Appellate Body report in language reminiscent of that used by panels in "recalling" and referring affirmatively to other panel reports: "The Panel recalled in this respect the conclusions of the Appellate Body in its report on *United States — Standards for Reformulated and Conventional Gasoline* where it stated that

International Justice stated in its Judgment of 13 September 1928 in the case concerning the Factory at Chorzow..." (para. 149) (emphasis added).

[34] Panel Report, *United States — Underwear*, paras 7.11–7.12.

[35] Panel Report, *United States — Shirts and Blouses*, para. 7.15.

[36] Panel Report, *Japan — Alcoholic Beverages*, para. 6.23.

[37] *Id.*

'an interpreter is not free to adopt a reading that would result in reducing whole clauses or paragraphs of a treaty to redundancy or inutility' ".[38] The panel in *United States — Shirts and Blouses*, on the other hand, adopted a slightly more deferential tone with respect to reports of the Appellate Body, suggestive of the way that panels are likely to view those reports in practice: "We note that the Appellate Body has made clear. . . . The Appellate Body also concluded that. . . ."[39]

The panel's stating that with regard to one point the Appellate Body "made clear," and that with regard to another point it "concluded", is at least suggestive of a tendency to treat Appellate Body reports as controlling the decisions of panels in subsequent cases. Thus, it seems more likely that, rather than explicitly declining to follow a decision of the Appellate Body, a panel would attempt to distinguish the case before it.

The Appellate Body is likely to be even more prone than panels to follow its own prior decisions. This is because the Appellate Body is effectively a standing judicial body, while panels are not. Panels are chosen *ad hoc* from a roster of individuals whose names have been put forward by WTO Members.[40] They are generally present or former members of nonparty Geneva delegations to the WTO, or academics — law professors and economists.[41] Those sitting on a particular panel have probably never served together before, and are likely never to serve together again, although a number of persons have served on several panels.

The Appellate Body, by contrast, operates on a "collegial" basis. While only three of the seven members sit on any one "division" to hear a particular appeal, and that division retains full authority to decide the case,[42] views on the issues are shared with the other Appellate Body members before a decision is reached.[43] Consequently, members of the Appellate Body, in confronting prior decisions, are far more likely to be confronting their own decisions, or those of their close colleagues, than are WTO panellists. This relationship seems likely to lead to a stronger attachment to the reasoning and results of

---

[38] Panel Report, *Japan — Alcoholic Beverages*, para. 6.22.

[39] *See* Panel Report, *United States — Shirts and Blouses*, para. 7.15.

[40] DSU Art. 8.4.

[41] Panels are normally composed of three individuals, with one serving as chair. The parties may agree, however, to a five-member panel provided they do so within 10 days of the establishment of the panel by the DSB. *Id.* Art. 8.5.

[42] *See* DSU Art. 17.1.

[43] Appellate Body, Working Procedures for Appellate Review, Rule 4, WT/AB/WP/3, 28 February 1997.

those decisions. "Once standing judicial bodies have come into existence", Judge Shahabuddeen has observed, "they provide an additional mechanism for the further development of the law".[44]

An early example appears in the Appellate Body's second opinion, *Japan — Alcoholic Beverages*, where it made two references to its first opinion, *United States — Reformulated Gasoline*, dealing with treaty interpretation:

> 1. "In *United States — Standards for Reformulated and Conventional Gasoline*, we stressed the need to achieve such clarification by reference to the fundamental rule of treaty interpretation set out in Article 31(1) of the Vienna Convention"[45]; and
> 2. "In *United States — Standards for Reformulated and Conventional Gasoline*, we noted that. . . ."[46]

While the words "we stressed" and "we noted" are not the same, in a legal context, as "we held", there is an authoritative tone to them that suggests more than mere persuasion. The tone suggests that, in the view of the Appellate Body, those issues are closed.

The extent to which the Appellate Body should depart from its prior decisions presents it with something of a dilemma. On the one hand, stability in the law — and treating like cases alike — is served by declining to depart from prior decisions, even those which, in retrospect, may seem ill-advised, leaving it to the Members to change the text of an agreement should they believe the Appellate Body to be wrong. On the other hand, the virtual certainty that reports of the Appellate Body will be adopted, and the fact that negotiations leading to changes in text are so infrequent and so difficult, mean that there is no practical way members can easily change the texts of a covered agreement — and thereby change the law — if they disagree with the Appellate Body. Therefore, the likelihood that its rulings will be the final word on the subject should arguably lead the Appellate Body to a greater willingness to re-examine them, for finality does not equate with infallibility. The Appellate Body, in substance if not in form, is a court of last resort, and "courts of last resort have come to accept that they are not obliged to follow their previous decisions; within careful bounds, they may depart".[47]

---

[44] Shahabuddeen, above note 9, at 45.

[45] *See* Appellate Body Report, *Japan — Alcoholic Beverages*, at Part D, para. 1.

[46] *Id.* at Part D, para. 8.

[47] Shahabuddeen, above note 9, at 238–39. The words of former U.S. Supreme Court Associate Justice Robert H. Jackson are relevant:

## 2.3 Custom

Customary international law plays a specific role in WTO dispute settlement by virtue of Article 3.2 of the Dispute Settlement Understanding, which specifies that the purpose of dispute settlement is to clarify the provisions of the WTO Agreements "in accordance with customary rules of interpretation of public international law". In practice, Article 3.2 has led panels and the Appellate Body to Articles 31 and 32 of the Vienna Convention on the Law of Treaties, which have been held to codify customary international law on the subject.[48] These customary rules of interpretation are, so far, the only portions of customary international law to have found their way meaningfully into WTO dispute settlement.

The issue of custom did arise in one important WTO proceeding. This was the question whether the precautionary principle is part of customary international law.[49] In *EC — Hormones*, the panel stated that "even if" the precautionary principle were considered customary international law, it would not override explicit provisions of the WTO Agreements.[50] This conclusion was affirmed by the Appellate Body, which noted that the status of the precautionary principle in international law is the subject of debate.[51] The Appellate Body also stated that, while the precautionary principle might have crystallized into a general principle of customary international environmental law, it is less than clear whether it has been widely accepted as a principle of general or customary international law.[52] The opinion does not reveal what the consequences would be if, in the view of the Appellate

> Whenever decisions of one court are reviewed by another, a percentage of them are reversed. That reflects a difference in outlook normally found between personnel comprising different courts. However, reversal by a higher court is not proof that justice is thereby better done. . . . We are not final because we are infallible, but we are infallible only because we are final.

*Brown v. Allen*, 344 U.S. 443, 540 (1953) (Jackson, J., concurring).

[48] *See, e.g.*, Appellate Body Report, *United States — Reformulated Gasoline*, at Part IV, para. 4.

[49] The "precautionary principle" holds generally that, "where there are threats of serious or irreversible damage, lack of full scientific certainty shall not be used as a reason for postponing cost-effective measures to prevent environmental degradation". United Nations Conference on Environment and Development: Rio Declaration on Environment and Development, 14 June 1992, Principle 15, 31 I.L.M. 874, 879 (1992). *See also* Franck, above note 26, at 370–71; Philippe Sands, 1 Principles of International Environmental Law 208–13 (1995).

[50] Panel Report, *EC — Hormones, Complaint by the United States*, para. 8.157; Panel Report, *EC — Hormones, Complaint by Canada*, para. 8.160.

[51] Appellate Body Report, *EC — Hormones*, para. 123.

[52] *Id.*

Body, the principle had been accepted as part of customary international environmental law but not of international law generally.

But the WTO, like GATT before it, is grounded in agreement, not in custom, and questions of custom are therefore likely to be rare. Even GATT's first and most basic provision, the most-favoured-nation clause (MFN), was not a codification of customary international law; nor did it establish a custom. To the contrary, GATT's MFN obligation extended only to other contracting parties, and contracting parties frequently denied MFN to nonparties, as the United States did, for example, with China. This remains true for the WTO agreements.

Article XVI:1 of the WTO Agreement, as stated earlier, specifies that "the WTO shall be guided by the decisions, procedures and customary practices followed by the CONTRACTING PARTIES to GATT 1947". It is doubtful that the "customary practices" referred to would be recognized as customary international law. Although the customary practices of GATT might meet some of the requirements of custom, it is doubtful that they were accepted by the parties to GATT or are viewed by WTO Members "as law".[53]

## 2.4 Teachings of the most highly qualified publicists

Sporadic references can be found in panel reports to the teachings and writings of highly qualified publicists in GATT law, but these references are rare.[54] In large part, this reluctance may stem from GATT's diplomatic heritage. What is now essentially a judicial system of dispute settlement began as a diplomatic system of "conciliation". Not only were diplomats less likely than lawyers to be aware of or to be influenced by the writings of legal scholars, GATT diplomats for many years were decidedly averse to the notion of turning "conciliation" into a legal proceeding.[55] The views of legal publicists, however qualified, impressed few "old GATT hands".[56]

[53] This is the *opinio juris* requirement, set out in Article 38(1)(b) of the Statute of the International Court of Justice.

[54] *See, e.g.*, United States — Measures Affecting Alcoholic and Malt Beverages, 19 June 1992, GATT B.I.S.D. (39th Supp.) at 206, 285 (1993) (citing the works of Professors John H. Jackson and Robert E. Hudec).

[55] The history is recounted in two volumes by Robert E. Hudec, THE GATT LEGAL SYSTEM AND WORLD TRADE DIPLOMACY (2d ed. 1990), and ENFORCING INTERNATIONAL TRADE LAW: THE EVOLUTION OF THE MODERN GATT LEGAL SYSTEM (1993).

[56] This skeptical attitude to law is apparent from the very title of a work by GATT's second Director General. Olivier Long, LAW AND ITS LIMITATIONS IN THE GATT MULTILATERAL SYSTEM (1985).

If legal scholars are more likely than diplomats to cite the writings of other legal scholars, one of the reasons for the relative absence of scholarship thus far is the relative absence of scholars among the panellists. While some academics have served as panellists, particularly in recent years, for most of GATT's history the practice was not widespread. Indeed, some WTO Members appear to think it undesirable if a potential panellist has expressed any views remotely related to the issue about to be adjudicated — a "paper trail" test that would exclude many scholars. While there are some notable exceptions, and some of these notable exceptions have actually served as panellists, the fact remains that the names of some highly qualified publicists are not even on the roster of panellists (and it is member governments, after all, that establish the roster).

The authors of WTO reports, on the other hand, particularly members of the Appellate Body, seem to be far more willing than their GATT predecessors to refer to the teachings of highly qualified publicists in justifying their positions.[57] This development no doubt reflects recognition of the increasing importance of law to the trading system, made clear by the very establishment of the Appellate Body. The Appellate Body, confined to considering issues of law and legal interpretations of panel reports,[58] of necessity brings a legal perspective to the process; and panels, advised by lawyers (as was not the case for the first few decades of GATT), increasingly deal with complex issues of law, such as standing, adequacy of notice and admissibility of evidence.

## 2.5 General principles of law

On occasion, GATT panels have invoked general principles of law in support of their reasoning, as have WTO panels and the Appellate Body. The principle that an exception to a general rule should be interpreted narrowly has been utilized several times.[59] This principle, however, has been rejected by the Appellate Body, which effectively, and reasonably, has concluded that one portion of the text of an agreement is not superior or

[57] *See, e.g.*, Panel Report, *Argentina — Measures Affecting Imports of Footwear, Textiles, Apparel and Other Items*, notes 176 (John H. Jackson), 184 (Keith Highet) and 185 (Mojtaba Kazazi); Appellate Body Report, *India — Patent Protection for Pharmaceutical and Agricultural Chemical Products*, notes 26 (F. Roessler, E.-U. Petersmann), 28 (E.-U. Petersmann) and 52 (I. Brownlie); Appellate Body Report, *EC — Hormones*, note 92 (P. Sands, J. Cameron, J. Abouchar, P. Birnie, A. Boyle, L. Gundling, A. deMestral and D. Bodansky).

[58] DSU Art. 17.6.

[59] Panel Report, *United States — Underwear*, para. 7.21 (citing several additional cases). *See also Canada — Import Restrictions on Ice Cream and Yoghurt*, 5 December 1989, GATT B.I.S.D.

inferior to another, unless the text itself so indicates.[60] In *United States — Measures Affecting Imports of Softwood Lumber from Canada*, the panel effectively invoked the equitable principle of estoppel in a proceeding involving subsidies and countervailing measures.[61] The interpretive principle that readings that would result in reducing whole clauses or paragraphs of a text to "redundancy or inutility" must be avoided has been recognized several times by the Appellate Body.[62]

Articles 22.4 and 22.6 of the Dispute Settlement Understanding, confining the level of suspension of concessions to the level of the nullification and impairment, are, of course, more than principle. They are the law of the Agreement itself. It is worth noting, however, that these provisions conform to the principle of proportionality recognized by the World Court.[63]

## 2.6 Other international instruments

Other international instruments, or agreements, may become sources of WTO law either because they are referred to specifically in the covered agreements or because the parties to a WTO dispute are also parties to another agreement.

### *2.6.1 Agreements referred to in the WTO agreements*

The texts of several covered agreements explicitly refer to other international agreements, which may therefore serve as direct sources of law in WTO

(36th Supp.) at 68, para. 59 (1990). "The Panel recalled that . . . exceptions were to be interpreted narrowly" (citing *Japan — Restrictions on Imports of Certain Agricultural Products*, 22 March 1988, GATT B.I.S.D. (35th Supp.) at 163 (1989) and *European Economic Community — Restrictions on Imports of Apples — Complaint by the United States*, 22 June 1989, GATT B.I.S.D. (36th Supp.) at 135 (1990)).

[60] Appellate Body Report, *EC — Hormones*, para. 104:

> Merely characterizing a treaty provision as an "exception" does not by itself justify a "stricter" or "narrower" interpretation of that provision than would be warranted by examination of the ordinary meaning of the actual treaty words, viewed in context and in the light of the treaty's object and purpose, or, in other words, by applying the normal rules of treaty interpretation.

[61] *United States — Measures Affecting Imports of Softwood Lumber from Canada*, 27–28 October 1993, GATT B.I.S.D. (40th Supp.) at 358, paras 308–325 (1994).

[62] Appellate Body Report, *United States — Reformulated Gasoline*, at Part IV, para. 4; Panel Report, *Japan — Alcoholic Beverages*, para. 6.22; Appellate Body Report, *Japan — Alcoholic Beverages*, at Part D, para. 1; Appellate Body Report, *United States — Underwear*, at Part IV, 1., para. 9 [p. 16].

[63] "An important consideration is that the effects of a countermeasure must be commensurate with the injury suffered"; this is "the proportionality which is required by international law". Gabcikovo-Nagymaros Project, 1997 ICJ Rep. 92, para. 85.

dispute settlement proceedings. These include the major international intellectual property conventions, the Paris Convention (1967), the Berne Convention (1971), the Rome Convention, and the Treaty on Intellectual Property in Respect of Integrated Circuits, as provided for by the Agreement on Trade-Related Aspects of Intellectual Property Rights (TRIPS Agreement).[64] The Agreement on Subsidies and Countervailing Measures (SCM Agreement) provides, somewhat indirectly, that the grant by governments of export credits in conformity with the provisions of the Arrangement on Guidelines for Officially Supported Export Credits of the Organisation for Economic Co-operation and Development shall not be considered an export subsidy.[65]

As noted above, the reference in Article 3.2 of the DSU to the "customary rules of interpretation of public international law" has been held by the Appellate Body to refer to Articles 31 and 32 of the Vienna Convention, whose provisions become a source of law insofar as they reflect customary international law.[66] Other provisions of the Vienna Convention may also provide law in WTO proceedings. For example, a recent panel considered Article 28 on nonretroactivity of treaties before concluding that it did not apply to the facts of the case.[67] Parties have also cited other Articles of the Convention to panels, including Articles 18 (Obligation not to defeat the object and purpose of a treaty prior to its entry into force), Article 26 (*Pacta sunt servanda*: "Every treaty in force is binding upon the parties to it and must be performed by them in good faith") and Article 30 (Application of

---

[64] TRIPS Agreement Art. 1.3.

[65] SCM Agreement Annex I(k):

> If a Member is a party to an international undertaking on official export credits to which at least twelve original Members to this Agreement are parties as of 1 January 1979 (or a successor undertaking which has been adopted by those original Members), or if in practice a Member applies the interest rates provisions of the relevant undertaking, an export credit practice which is in conformity with those provisions shall not be considered an export subsidy prohibited by this Agreement.

The "international undertaking" described is the "OECD Arrangement," OECD Doc. OCDE/GD(92)95 (1992).

[66] Appellate Body Report, *United States — Reformulated Gasoline*, at Part IV, para. 4. The Vienna Convention opens the way to the potential relevancy of other international agreements that otherwise may have no direct connection with the WTO Agreements. See the section "Customs", above.

[67] Panel Report, *EC — Hormones, Complaint by the United States*, paras 8.24, 8.21; Panel Report, *EC — Hormones, Complaint by Canada*, paras 8.27, 8.28.

successive treaties relating to the same subject matter), although the panels have not yet found it necessary to address them.[68]

An as yet unresolved question is whether the rights and obligations brought into the WTO by these other agreements are only those that were in effect at the time the WTO Agreements became effective, or whether the WTO rights and obligations change as these agreements change. Footnote 2 to the TRIPS Agreement states that references to the intellectual property conventions are to specific versions of those conventions.[69] Presumably, therefore, any rights and obligations negotiated later by the parties to the intellectual property conventions would not affect WTO rights and obligations and thus would not be sources of WTO law. However, a panel established under the North American Free Trade Agreement, in considering a provision of NAFTA preserving the rights of the parties under GATT and agreements negotiated under GATT, concluded that the reference at issue was not simply to GATT as it existed when the NAFTA provision came into effect, but to the GATT regime as it had evolved, eventually, into the WTO.[70] The NAFTA panel also noted that a reference in that Agreement to customary international law was "a reference to an evolving system".[71]

### *2.6.2 Agreements between the parties*

The WTO Agreement, and its annexed covered agreements, are among the many international regulatory agreements entered into by governments, particularly in the post-World War II era, to address economic, environmental, and social problems.[72] Many WTO Members are parties to most of these agreements. Moreover, it seems likely that the number of regulatory agreements is likely to grow, particularly in the environmental field. This

[68] *See, e.g.*, Panel Report, *Brazil — Measures Affecting Desiccated Coconut*, WT/DS22/R, 17 October 1996, paras 23–36, 37–39; Panel Report, *United States — Underwear*, paras 5.224, 7.63.

[69] For example, the text of footnote 2 to the TRIPS Agreement specifies in part: "In this Agreement, 'Paris Convention' refers to the Paris Convention for the Protection of Industrial Property: 'Paris Convention (1967)' refers to the Stockholm Act of this Convention of 14 July 1967".

[70] Arbitral Panel Established Pursuant to Article 2008 of the North American Free Trade Agreement, Final Report, *In re: Tariffs Applied by Canada to Certain U.S.-Origin Agricultural Products*, 2 December 1996, para. 208.

[71] *Id.* para. 134.

[72] The apt phrase "international regulatory agreements" is taken from the subtitle of Abram Chayes and Antonia Handler Chayes, The New Sovereignty: Compliance with International Regulatory Agreements (1995).

raises the question of the extent to which these agreements affect the rights and obligations of WTO Members vis-à-vis other WTO Members.

The issue began to appear in the early 1990s. One instance involved not a multilateral treaty, but a bilateral agreement between Canada and the European Community. In connection with negotiations in the early 1960s concerning Canada's exports of wheat to the Community under the Common Agricultural Policy, the parties entered into an agreement that would have extended the time limits within which Canada could challenge the Community's treatment of its wheat exports under Article XXVIII of GATT. Before an arbitrator agreed to by the parties to resolve a dispute as to whether Canada's Article XXVIII complaint had been made too late, the Community challenged Canada's right to bring a claim based on a bilateral agreement under the multilateral procedures of GATT. The arbitrator disagreed:

> In principle, a claim based on a bilateral agreement cannot be brought under the multilateral dispute settlement procedures of the GATT. An exception is warranted in this case given the close connection of this particular bilateral agreement with the GATT, the fact that the Agreement is consistent with the objectives of the GATT, and that both parties joined in requesting recourse to the GATT Arbitration procedures.[73]

A similar issue arose in a WTO panel's consideration of a recent dispute between Brazil and the Community involving exports of poultry products from Brazil to Europe.[74] Brazil argued that a bilateral agreement between it and the Community (the Oilseeds Agreement) applied to the resolution of the dispute. Although the United States, as third party, argued that the Oilseeds Agreement was not within the terms of reference, the Community did not explicitly object to its consideration by the panel.[75] Noting that the Oilseeds Agreement had been negotiated within the framework of GATT Article XXVIII, and citing the Canada/EC Wheat arbitration, the panel decided to consider the Oilseeds Agreement "to the extent relevant to the determination of the EC's obligations under the WTO agreements vis-à-vis Brazil".[76]

---

[73] Canada/European Communities Article XXVIII Rights, Award by the Arbitrator, GATT B.I.S.D. (37th Supp.) at 80, 84 (1991).

[74] Panel Report, *EC — Measures Affecting the Importation of Certain Poultry Products*, WT/DS69/R (12 March 1998).

[75] *Id.* para. 197.

[76] *Id.* para. 202. The panel also referred to the Banana panel's consideration of the Lomé Convention. *See* Appellate Body Report, *EC — Bananas*.

The first major dispute involving a multilateral agreement, *Tuna Dolphin II*,[77] illustrates the tendency of GATT panels to disregard public international law in interpreting the GATT. In that case, the United States argued that the Convention on International Trade in Endangered Species of Wild Fauna and Flora (CITES)[78] and various other bilateral and plurilateral agreements were relevant to the dispute between GATT parties that were parties to those agreements.[79] After noting, in a tone suggestive of less than wholehearted approval, that "the parties based many of their arguments . . . on environmental and trade treaties", the panel said that "it was first of all necessary to determine the extent to which these treaties were relevant to the interpretation of the text of the General Agreement".[80] The panel concluded that they were not relevant, stating that "the agreements cited by the parties to the dispute were bilateral or plurilateral agreements that were not concluded among the contracting parties to the General Agreement, and that they did not apply to the interpretation of the General Agreement or the application of its provisions".[81]

The panel's conclusion that another international treaty would be relevant to the interpretation of a GATT obligation only to the extent that the treaty was accepted by all GATT parties does not appear to be consistent with Article 31(3)(c) of the Vienna Convention. Article 31(3)(c) specifies that "any relevant rules of international law applicable in the relations between the parties" shall be taken into account in resolving disputes between them.[82] An interpretation of this language to mean only any subsequent agreement among all of the parties to the GATT — and not simply to an agreement among the parties to the dispute — does not seem supportable by the text of Article 31(3)(c). The word "parties", as used in that provision, would seem to refer to the parties to the particular dispute, not to the parties to the multilateral agreement. In any event, the panel's textual emphasis on the word "parties" would itself seem to diminish the relevance of the reasoning of the *Tuna* report in the WTO, inasmuch as the

[77] *United States — Restrictions on Imports of Tuna*, DS29/R, 16 June 1994, reprinted in 33 I.L.M. 839, para. 5.19 (1994) (unadopted) [hereinafter *Tuna Dolphin II*].

[78] Convention on International Trade in Endangered Species of Wild Fauna and Flora, 3 March 1973, 993 U.N.T.S. 243, amended 22 June 1979 and 30 April 1983, available at http://www.cites.org/eng/disc/text.shtml [hereinafter CITES].

[79] *Tuna Dolphin II*, above note 77, paras 3.14, 3.21–3.34.

[80] *Id.* para. 5.18.

[81] *Id.* para. 5.19.

[82] Vienna Convention on the Law of Treaties Art. 31(3)(c).

participants in the WTO are "Members", not "parties" as they were in GATT.

The *Tuna Dolphin II* panel also rejected the argument that practice under the other agreements could be considered "subsequent practice in the application of the treaty which establishes the agreement of the parties regarding its interpretation", as provided for in Article 31(3)(b) of the Vienna Convention. According to the panel, any such practice would constitute practice under those other agreements, not under GATT.[83] This interpretation, too, seems excessively narrow, and not justified by the text of the Convention.

In a widely watched report involving restrictions imposed by the United States on imports of shrimp from countries not meeting U.S. standards for protecting sea turtles in the shrimp-fishing process, all parties to the dispute were also parties to CITES.[84] As in *Tuna*, the *Shrimp/Turtle* panel found CITES not relevant to the dispute, but on more limited grounds that seem more persuasive than the verbal distinctions concerning "parties" drawn in *Tuna*. The United States restricted imports of shrimp, the panel noted, and shrimp are not an endangered species covered by CITES. Turtles are the endangered species, but the United States took no challenged trade action with regard to turtles. Moreover, the United States had itself informed the panel that CITES neither authorized nor prohibited the measures at issue.[85]

The issue of the impact of other international agreements between parties is likely to arise when one WTO Member imposes trade sanctions on the exports of another pursuant to an international agreement, to which both are parties and which calls for sanctions. If the action would otherwise be inconsistent with its WTO obligations, the party taking the action might refer to its obligations under the other agreement in support of an argument that the inconsistency is excused by one or more of the exceptions set forth in GATT Article XX, on the theory that the other agreement constitutes a modification of the WTO legal situation of the participating parties.[86]

---

[83] *Tuna Dolphin II*, above note 77, para. 5.19.

[84] Panel Report, *Shrimp/Turtle*, para. 7.57; Appellate Body Report, *Shrimp/Turtle*, paras 169–171.

[85] *Id.*

[86] *See* Aaditya Mattoo and Petros C. Mavroidis, *Trade, Environment and the WTO: The Dispute Settlement — Practice Relating to Article XX of GATT*, in INTERNATIONAL TRADE LAW AND THE GATT/WTO DISPUTE SETTLEMENT SYSTEM 325, 335 (Ernst-Ulrich Petersmann ed., 1997).

The *Tuna Dolphin II* panel raised another point that is highly germane to the issue of the relevance of other agreements between the parties, although it did so in only a limited way. The panel examined whether the cited treaties could be considered to be subsequent agreements between the parties concerning the interpretation of GATT within the meaning of Article 31 of the Vienna Convention on the Law of Treaties; it concluded, not surprisingly, that they could not be so considered.[87] However, the panel did not look to the question whether GATT and the cited treaties could be considered successive treaties relating to the same subject matter within the meaning of Article 30, rather than Article 31, of the Convention.

Article 30 is likely to be the more relevant provision of the Convention, particularly with regard to international environmental agreements. Article 30(3) specifies that when the disputants are parties to both agreements, the later in time prevails. Article 30(4)(b) also specifies that, as between a state party to both treaties and a state party to only one of the treaties, the treaty to which both are parties governs. This would mean that, in the event that a WTO Member is a party to an environmental agreement and another Member is not a party to that agreement, the environmental agreement would not affect WTO rights and obligations. This result is consistent with the principle *pacta tertiis nec nocent nec prasunt*: a treaty binds only the contracting parties, and neither rights nor duties arise under a treaty for a state not a party.

To the extent that other agreements are relevant to the rights and obligations of WTO Members under the covered agreements, the question arises as to who interprets the pertinent provisions of those agreements. As to agreements specifically brought into the WTO, it now seems settled that WTO panels and the Appellate Body interpret their terms for WTO purposes.

In the *EC — Bananas* case, both the panel and the Appellate Body considered the scope of a waiver of specified obligations granted by the GATT Council and extended by the WTO General Council to the European Community with respect to the Lomé Convention, which required the Community to extend preferential treatment to goods originating in certain African, Caribbean, and Pacific countries (ACP).[88] The substantive question was: what does the Lomé Convention require? The European

[87] *Tuna Dolphin II*, above note 77, para. 5.19.

[88] Panel Report, *EC — Bananas. See also* Appellate Body Report, *EC — Bananas*, paras 27–29.

Community and the ACP argued that the panel was not competent to answer that question. Rather, they contended, the panel should defer to the interpretation advanced by the Community and the ACP, which, as parties, were competent to answer it.[89]

The panel disagreed. It noted that the EC and ACP had originally been granted a waiver by the GATT Contracting Parties to permit the preferential treatment, and that the waiver had been adopted by the WTO. Clearly, the waiver itself was a WTO agreement, within the competence of a WTO panel. "Since the waiver applies to action 'necessary . . . to provide preferential treatment . . . as required by the relevant provisions of the Fourth Lomé Convention' ", the panel said, "we must also determine what preferential treatment is required by the Lomé Convention".[90] The Appellate Body affirmed, observing, "To determine what is 'required' by the Lomé Convention, we must look first to the text of that Convention and identify provisions of it that are relevant to trade in bananas".[91]

Because the waiver had effectively incorporated the Lomé Convention into a WTO agreement, the panel's authority to interpret the waiver, and therefore the Lomé Convention itself, parallels the authority that is likely to be claimed for the agreements explicitly referred to in the covered agreements, such as the intellectual property conventions. The report does not deal with the situation in which the international agreement at issue is not, at least implicitly, a WTO agreement.

## 3. Conflicts of norms

In WTO dispute settlement conflicts of norms may arise in two contexts. First, because, as we have seen, WTO law is not a self-contained system, conflicts may arise between the covered agreements and non-WTO customary or conventional law. This has never directly occurred so far, although, as we have seen, the issue was raised in the *EC — Hormones* case where the precautionary principle was argued by the EC.[92] If such a conflict should arise in the future, WTO adjudicating bodies will have to use recognized public international law interpretative tools to break the conflict. These

[89] Panel Report, *EC — Bananas*, paras 7.95, 7.97.

[90] Panel Report, *EC — Bananas*, para. 7.97.

[91] Appellate Body Report, *EC — Bananas*, paras 167, 169.

[92] Above section 2.3.

include, *inter alia*, the principles that relevant laws or agreements should be construed to be compatible if at all possible, and that, if they are incompatible, the later treaty prevails. No WTO agreement gives guidance on how to resolve these kinds of conflicts.

A second category of conflicts of norms comes up with respect to the covered agreements themselves. Because of their broad scope, there may be overlapping and conflicting obligations. Here there is some guidance. The Agreement Establishing the WTO prevails over any of the other WTO agreements.[93] A conflict between GATT 1994 and another Annex I WTO agreement is resolved in favour of the provision of the other agreement.[94] This is an application of the principle that a specialized agreement prevails over a general one. By the same token, the Agreement on Agriculture prevails over the GATT and other Annex IA agreements.[95]

These rules leave many conflicts questions open that can only be addressed by WTO adjudicating bodies on a case-by-case basis. It has been decided that WTO agreements overlap: in *EC — Bananas*, the panel held that the GATT Articles I and III as well as provisions of the Agreement on Trade Related Investment Measures and the Agreement on Import Licencing Procedures would simultaneously apply.[96] In *Canada — Periodicals* the Appellate Body ruled that even though Canada had not committed to market access for purposes of the General Agreement on Services (GATS) with respect to advertising services, a tax on such services was not exempt from the GATT national treatment clause (Article III).[97] Similarly, in *EC — Bananas*[98] the Appellate Body concluded that the GATS and GATT can overlap.

Thus, future conflicts of norms appear inevitable.

## 4. Conclusions

The WTO is the product of an international agreement, and that agreement and the agreements annexed to it constitute the basic source of WTO law.

[93] WTO Agreement Art. XVI:3.

[94] *Id.* Annex IA General Interpretive Note.

[95] Agreement on Agriculture, Art. 21.1. This rule was applied in the *Chile Price Band* case. *Chile — Price Band System and Safeguard Measures Relating to Certain Agricultural Production*, Report of the Appellate Body (AB 2002–2) 23 September 2002, WT/DS207/AB/R at 190.

[96] Panel Report, *EC — Bananas* paras. 7.90–7.97.

[97] Report of the Appellate Body, *Canada — Periodicals*, pp. 17–20.

[98] Report of the Appellate Body, *EC — Bananas*, paras 217–222.

The reports of panels and the Appellate Body, however, add an important gloss to those texts. Most WTO disputes will be resolved primarily, if not solely, with reference to the texts and to prior reports, and in this sense the WTO legal system may be thought of as largely self-contained.

But if the WTO legal system is largely self-contained, it is not entirely self-contained. To the contrary, it is an important part of the larger system of public international law, as reflected not only by the interpretive principles that are brought to bear on its texts, which are explicitly those of public international law, but also by its increasing recourse to the other traditional sources of public international law: custom, the teachings of publicists, general principles of law, and other international instruments, particularly those incorporated by reference into the WTO and its agreements.

Public international law has clearly made an important contribution to WTO law. It is not yet clear that the reverse will be true, that other international tribunals will begin to see the WTO, as reflected in its adopted reports, as a source of law. Given the growing quantity and high overall quality of those reports, however, it seems likely that it is only a matter of time before this recognition begins to take place, particularly with regard to evidentiary and procedural issues that could have wider application.

# 4

# REMEDIES



## 1. The pre-WTO phase

Neither the GATT nor the various Tokyo Round Codes contained any specific provisions dealing with remedies in cases of violations. This omission was not an anomaly. It often happens that drafters of a treaty do not regulate remedies, thereby leaving judges with discretion to impose an appropriate remedy. GATT jurisprudence is, therefore, particularly relevant to a discussion of remedies.

## 1.1 The usual GATT remedy

Withdrawal of inconsistent measures emerged as the usual remedy through the GATT jurisprudence, which was codified in the 1979 "Understanding Regarding Notification, Consultation, Dispute Settlement and Surveillance".[1] The relevant passage reads:

> The aim of the CONTRACTING PARTIES has always been to secure a positive solution to the dispute. A solution mutually acceptable to the parties to a dispute is clearly to be preferred. In the absence of a mutually agreed solution, the first objective of the CONTRACTING PARTIES is *usually* to secure the withdrawal of the measures concerned if these are found to be inconsistent with the General Agreement.[2]

Thus, GATT panels commonly recommended that the losing party withdraw its inconsistent measures or bring them into compliance with its obligations.

The withdrawal of inconsistent measures has a prospective effect. The bringing of inconsistent measures into compliance with GATT obligations could have a retrospective effect, but the GATT contracting parties have understood it to have a prospective effect.[3]

## 1.2 An alternative remedy: reimbursement and restitution

In several antidumping and countervailing duty cases, GATT panels recommended not only withdrawal of inconsistent measures but also reimbursement of duties found to have been imposed in a manner inconsistent with GATT obligations.[4]

These GATT panels introduced restitution into GATT jurisprudence. They concluded that the antidumping or countervailing duty orders at issue were inconsistent with GATT obligations and, therefore, the duties should not have been imposed in the first place. The withdrawal of these orders and the reimbursement of duties were intended to restore the *status quo ante*.

[1] *See* Understanding Regarding Notification, Consultation, Dispute Settlement and Surveillance, 28 November 1979, GATT B.I.S.D. (26th Supp.) at 210 (1980).

[2] *Id.* Annex, para. 4 (emphasis added).

[3] *See* Robert E. Hudec, Enforcing International Trade Law: The Evolution of the Modern GATT Legal System (1993). This remarkable study constitutes the only comprehensive study of GATT history in this respect.

[4] *See, e.g., United States — Measures Affecting Imports of Softwood Lumber from Canada,* 19 February 1993, GATT B.I.S.D. (41st Supp.) paras 413–415 (1993); *United States — Countervailing Duties on Fresh, Chilled and Frozen Pork from Canada,* 11 July 1991, GATT B.I.S.D. (38th Supp.) at 30, para. 5.2 (1991); *New Zealand — Imports of Electrical Transformers from Finland,* 18 June

The alternative remedy recommended in these antidumping and countervailing duty cases is unique. Restitution was not recommended in any other area. Even in the *City of Trondheim* case, where the panel admitted that the usual GATT remedy was less than satisfactory, restitution was denied.[5] In that case, the United States complained that Norway had illegally awarded a contract for construction of a toll collection system in the city of Trondheim to a Norwegian company. The panel found that Norway had not complied with its obligations under the GATT Government Procurement Code. But because the toll collection system was already in place when the panel made its decision, the panel merely asked Norway to accept the illegality of its act and to provide guarantees for non-repetition.[6]

## 2. Remedies under the Dispute Settlement Understanding

One of the remarkable innovations of the Uruguay Round was the Understanding on Rules and Procedures Governing the Settlement of Disputes

1985, GATT B.I.S.D. (32d Supp.) at 55, paras 4.9–4.11 (1985). *But see, e.g., Korea — Anti-Dumping Duties on Imports of Polyacetal Resins from the United States*, 27 April 1993, GATT B.I.S.D. (40th Supp.) at 205, para. 302 (1993) (recommending that the Committee on Anti-Dumping Practices request that Korea "bring its measure [i.e., the imposition of antidumping duties on 14 September 1991 on polyacetal resins from the United States] into conformity with its obligations" under the Tokyo Round Antidumping Code); *United States — Imposition of Anti-Dumping Duties on Imports of Fresh and Chilled Atlantic Salmon from Norway*, 30 November 1992, GATT B.I.S.D. (40th Supp.) at paras 596–97 (1992) (finding that it "could not recommend that the Anti-dumping Committee request the United States to revoke the anti-dumping duty order and reimburse any duties paid or deposited under this order" and recommending that the United States reconsider the affirmative final determination of dumping); Panel on Canadian Countervailing Duties on Grain Corn from the United States, 26 March 1992, GATT B.I.S.D. (39th Supp.) at 411, para. 6.2 (1992) (recommending that the SCM Committee request Canada "to bring its countervailing duty measure into conformity with Canada's obligations" under the Tokyo Round Subsidies Code). For an examination of the case law in this field, see Ernst-Ulrich Petersmann, *International Competition Rules for the GATT/MTO World Trade and Legal System*, 27 J. World Trade, No. 6, at 35 (1993); Norio Komuro and Edwin Vermulst, *Antidumping Disputes in the GATT/WTO: Navigating Dire Straits*, 31 J. World Trade, No. 1, at 5 (1997).

[5] Panel on Norwegian Procurement of Toll Collection Equipment for the City of Trondheim, 13 May 1992, GATT B.I.S.D. (40th Supp.) at 319, para. 4.26 (1995).

[6] For a critique of the panel's recommendation, see Petros C. Mavroidis, *Government Procurement Agreement, The Trondheim Case: The Remedies Issue*, 48 Aussenwirtschaft 77 (1993). *See also* Hudec, above note 3, at 583 (concluding that, "because the reparation paid was minimal, Norwegians had the incentive to continue the same practices notwithstanding their unilateral declaration to the effect that no such practices would ever be repeated again").

(the Dispute Settlement Understanding or DSU). The DSU is an antidote to the procedural deficiencies of Articles XXII and XXIII of the GATT. In addition, the DSU specifies remedies for all three types of complaints known in the WTO system, namely, violation complaints, non-violation complaints, and situation complaints.

## 2.1 Violation complaints

For violations, the DSU provides that the remedy is a recommendation by a panel or Appellate Body that the Member concerned bring its measure into conformity with the Agreement.[7] In addition, a panel or Appellate Body *may* suggest ways the Member could implement the recommendation.[8]

### *2.1.1 Recommendations and suggestions*

By merely recommending to losing parties that they bring their measures into compliance, WTO adjudicating bodies provide losing parties with ample discretion to choose the appropriate means of compliance.[9] In general, WTO adjudicating bodies have not gone beyond the recommendation stage. In a few cases, however, panels have made suggestions.[10] Notably, these cases have involved antidumping or safeguard measures.

The WTO dispute settlement system favours a practice whereby panels stick to recommendations without suggestions. Various reasons help explain this phenomenon. Most persuasively, though, the answer lies in the institutional structure of panels. Panels, in contrast to the Appellate Body, lack a

[7] DSU Art. 19.1.

[8] *Id.*

[9] *See* Bernard M. Hoekman and Petros C. Mavroidis, *Policy Externalities and High-Tech Rivalry: Competition and Multilateral Cooperation Beyond the WTO*, 9 Leiden J. Int'l L. 273, 286–87 (1996).

[10] Panel Report, *United States — Cotton Yarn Safeguard*, para. 8.5 (recommending that the United States "bring the measure at issue into conformity with its obligations under the ATC" and suggesting that "this can best be achieved by prompt removal of the import restriction"); Panel Report, *Guatemala — Cement*, paras 8.4–8.6 (recommending that Guatemala brings its action into conformity with its obligations under the Antidumping Agreement, which it violated by initiating an investigation when there was not sufficient evidence to justify initiation, and, therefore, suggesting that Guatemala revoke the existing antidumping measure); Panel Report, *United States — Underwear*, para. 8.3 (recommending that the United States "bring the measure challenged by Costa Rica into compliance with U.S. obligations under the ATC" and suggesting "that the United States bring the measure . . . into compliance with U.S. obligations under the ATC by immediately withdrawing the restriction imposed by the measure"). *But see* Appellate Body Report, *United States — Cotton Yarn Safeguard*, para. 129 (merely recommending that the United States bring its measure into conformity with its obligations under the ATC).

permanent composition. Continuity in the GATT/WTO case law has largely depended on the GATT/WTO legal office.[11] Traditionally, panellists are divided among "governmentalists" and "non-governmentalists" (in the GATT/WTO parlance), the former being preferred to the latter in the overwhelming majority of the cases. Practical considerations are more prevalent in the minds of governmental panellists, who know and understand political concerns. Practical considerations generally disfavour remedies that might "rock the boat".

The distinction between recommendations and suggestions, consequently, has been implemented in the overwhelming majority of WTO relevant practice in the sense that the latter remains truly optional.

The only WTO panel to have had the opportunity to pronounce on this issue concluded that suggestions are not binding.[12] This case involved the imposition of antidumping duties by Guatemala. The complaining party (Mexico) asked the panel to rule that the losing party (Guatemala) should revoke and reimburse the imposed duties if it found the imposition of antidumping duties to be inconsistent with the relevant WTO rules.[13]

The panel, after suggesting that the duties be revoked, reached the following conclusion:

> Such suggestions on implementation, however, are not part of the recommendation, and are not binding on the affected Member. Thus, in a dispute where a panel concludes that a Member has violated the provisions of the [Antidumping] Agreement, it is constrained by the language of Article 19.1 to recommend that the Member bring its actions, or its measure, as the case may be, into conformity with the provisions of the [Antidumping] Agreement. In addition the panel could, at most, suggest ways in which it believes the Member could appropriately implement that recommendation. In the first instance, however, the modalities of implementation of a panel, or Appellate Body, recommendation are for the Member concerned to determine.[14]

How should we understand the panel's suggestion that Guatemala revoke the duties? According to Mexico's request, there seems to be no doubt: were

Although none of these cases involved a prohibited subsidy, under the SCM Agreement, a panel must recommend that losing parties withdraw prohibited subsidies "without delay". SCM Agreement Art. 4.7.

[11] Similar points have been made by William J. Davey and Robert E. Hudec. *See* William J. Davey, *Dispute Settlement in GATT*, 11 Fordham Int'l L.J. 51 (1987); Hudec, above note 3.

[12] *See* Panel Report, *Guatemala — Cement*, para. 5.172.

[13] *See id.* para. 7.21.

[14] *Id.* para. 9.5.

Guatemala to revoke the duty order, such action should have a retrospective effect. Because the act giving rise to collection of duties was found to be illegal, all its consequences should be wiped out.[15] However, the panel's ruling that Guatemala revoke the antidumping measure on imports of Mexican cement was only a suggestion, not a recommendation.[16]

In summary, suggestions are not binding on their addressee. They are not, however, devoid of legal consequences. Following suggestions is one way for a losing party to be certain it has corrected the violation. Following panels' and the Appellate Body's suggestions is, therefore, a highly recommendable legal strategy.

### *2.1.2 Prospective and retrospective remedies*

Although the insertion of a distinction between recommendations and suggestions in DSU Article 19 seems to represent a victory for prospective remedies, appearances can be deceiving.

When panels do not go further than the "recommendations" stage, they leave ample discretion to losing parties to choose the appropriate way to implement the recommendation. Limits to such discretion are imposed by a WTO scheme concerning challenges to implementation of panels' recommendations. DSU Article 21.5 reads (in the relevant part): "Where there is disagreement as to the existence or consistency with a covered agreement of measures taken to comply with the recommendations and rulings, such dispute shall be decided through recourse to dispute settlement procedures, including wherever possible resort to the original panel".

In practice, parties might disagree as to the prospective or retrospective function of remedies. This could, in turn, lead to the formation of state practice with respect to remedies in particular fields of WTO law.

The issue of whether Article 19 should be construed to disallow retroactive remedies was put squarely before WTO panel members

[15] The term "revocation" suggests a retrospective effect. Moreover, if this were not the case, the panel could have used the term "withdrawal," which has a prospective effect. If this were the case, however, in cases panels suggest revocation, reimbursement will be an option depending solely on domestic procedures. This, in turn, means that, were panels to continue this practice and stop at the "revocation" stage, they would in effect be suggesting a different remedy (depending on whether domestic procedures allow for reimbursement) for identical violations (illegally imposed antidumping duty orders giving rise to collection of duties).

[16] Panel Report, *Guatemala — Cement*, paras 9.1–9.6. Yet the panel's report was puzzling on this issue because, in making the suggestion, the panel stated that revocation (implying reimbursement) was "the only appropriate means of implementing our recommendation" *Id.* para. 9.6.

in the *Australia — Leather*[17] dispute between the United States and Australia. This dispute involved Australian subsidies to exporters of automotive leather. The United States disagreed with the action taken by Australia to comply with the recommendations of the panel, which had found that the Australian schemes constituted prohibited export subsidies and recommended that Australia withdraw them immediately. The United States requested the establishment of an Article 21.5 compliance panel to examine whether the action taken by Australia brought its measure into compliance with the WTO. The original *Australia — Leather* panel, which had established the illegality of Australian measures in the first place, reconvened under Article 21.5 to examine whether the Australian implementing action taken post-adoption of the report was adequate.[18]

Both the complainant (United States) and the defendant (Australia) agreed that Article 4.7 of the SCM Agreement (which calls for immediate withdrawal of illegal subsidies) is limited to purely prospective action. They disagreed as to the point in time from which the perspectivity determination must be made (the date of the adoption of the report as opposed to end of the reasonable period). It came as no surprise that the European Community followed the same line of reasoning and argued that WTO remedies can only be prospective.

The panel disagreed. Based on the Vienna Convention on the Law of Treaties[19] as well as on the "effectiveness" of the remedy, the panel indicated that retroactive remedies can very well exist within the WTO legal system.[20] In this respect, the panel unambiguously rejected the argument by the United States that DSU Article 19 circumscribes the time function of WTO remedies. The relevant passage reads: "However, we do not believe that Article 19.1 of the DSU, even in conjunction with Article 3.7 of the DSU, requires the limitation of the specific remedy provided for in Article 4.7 of the SCM Agreement to purely prospective action".[21]

The panel's statement came as a shock. It is no surprise that a number of important WTO players criticized its findings vehemently when the panel

17 *See* Article 21.5 Panel Report, *Australia — Leather*, Recourse to Article 21.5 of the DSU by the United States.

18 *See id.*

19 Vienna Convention on the Law of Treaties, available at http://www.un.org/law/ilc/texts/treatfra.htm.

20 *See* Article 21.5 Panel Report, *Australia — Leather*, Recourse to Article 21.5 of the DSU by the United States, para. 6.42.

21 *Id.* para. 6.31.

report was submitted to the DSB for adoption.[22] One can only wonder, though, at such reactions. The panel's findings are sound when viewed from a public international law perspective. In addition, the WTO is a public international law contract. Moreover, contrary to what has been argued by some delegates before the DSB, the panel's findings are not at odds with GATT/WTO practice. As mentioned above, several panel reports in the antidumping or countervailing field opted for retroactive remedies. Adopted GATT reports can provide useful guidance to future panels (and even unadopted panel reports can exercise some persuasive power); the *Australia — Leather* panel report can be seen as part of a *continuum* in this respect.

## 2.2 Non-violation and situation complaints

Petersmann has expressed doubts as to the *raison d'être* of situation complaints and, based on state practice, has made the point that such complaints have fallen into desuetude.[23] It is difficult to understand what could come under a situation complaint, taking into account that in the GATT/WTO context injured parties can attack both illegal (violation complaints) and legal acts (non-violation complaints), to the extent that the latter cause damage. There is no reported case of a situation complaint. Once the EC threatened to submit such a case (the so-called Japanese way-of-life case),[24] but the threat never materialized. In the future, situation complaints seem unlikely. Although there is total absence of case law in this field, one cannot imagine how the remedies in such cases could be any different from those in non-violation complaints. Consequently, our analysis will focus only on non-violation complaints, where there is ample practice.

The *Japan — Film* report captures the nature of non-violation complaints. It states that:

> both the GATT contracting parties and WTO Members have approached this remedy with caution and, indeed, have treated it as an exceptional instrument of dispute settlement.... The reason for this caution is straightforward. Members negotiate the

[22] *See, e.g.*, Minutes of Meeting, Held in the Centre William Rappard on 11 February 2000, WT/DSB/M/75, 11 February 2000, at 5 *et seq.* (angry reactions by the delegates of the United States, Australia, Canada and the European Community).

[23] Ernst-Ulrich Petersmann, *Violation Complaints and Non-Violation Complaints in Public International Trade Law*, 34 German Y.B. Int'l L. 175, 227 (1991).

[24] *See* Bernard M. Hoekman and Petros C. Mavroidis, *Competition, Competition Policy and the GATT*, 17 World Economy 121, 137 (1994).

rules that they agree to follow and only exceptionally would expect to be challenged for actions not in contravention of those rules.[25]

According to GATT case law,[26] three conditions have to be met for a non-violation complaint to be successful:

1. A prior consolidated tariff commitment;
2. A subsequent governmental action that results in
3. Negatively affecting the reasonable expectations created by the consolidated tariff commitment.[27]

Typically, a subsidy scheme would be viewed under (2). The *Japan — Film* dispute, however, made it plain that other governmental measures (an arguably government-induced restrictive business practice) could come into play.[28] The WTO case law has added one more condition: according to the *Japan — Film* panel, non-violation complaints must concern a measure that has a continuing effect and not a measure that has ceased to exist.[29] The latter can only be contested in the context of a violation complaint, where it is the violation as such that is put into question and not the resulting nullification and impairment.[30]

The *Japan — Film* panel states that "the ordinary meaning of this provision limits the non-violation remedy to measures that are currently being applied".[31]

This is the distinguishing factor between violation and non-violation complaints: in the first case, the accent is put on the violation as such; there is a presumption of nullification and impairment of benefits accruing to WTO Members any time the agreement(s) is (are) violated. In the second,

[25] *See* Panel Report, *Japan — Film*, para. 10.36.

[26] *See, e.g., EEC — Payments and Subsidies Paid to Processors and Producers of Oilseeds and Related Animal-Feed Proteins*, 25 January 1990, GATT B.I.S.D. (37th Supp.) at 86, para. 147 *et seq.* (1990).

[27] *See* Petersmann, above note 23.

[28] This point was first argued in the literature by Hoekman and Mavroidis, where the argument was advanced that government-induced restrictive business practices could find their way before a GATT adjudicating body in the context of a non-violation complaint. *See* Hoekman and Mavroidis, above note 24.

[29] Apparently using the term "continuing effect" as Joost Pauwelyn, *The Concept of a "Continuing Violation" of an International Obligation: Selected Problems*, 72 Brit. Y.B. Int'l L. 415–450 (1995).

[30] *See United States — Taxes on Petroleum and Certain Imported Substances*, 17 June 1987, GATT B.I.S.D. (34th Supp.) at 136, para. 5.2.2, at 159–60 (1988).

[31] Panel Report, *Japan — Film*, para. 10.57.

the accent is put on the actual nullification and impairment, independently of whether trade damage also results. This means that, contrary to what we have seen in the context of violation complaints, WTO Members bringing a non-violation complaint will have to show existence of damage (in the form of nullification or impairment of the reasonable expectations created).

Non-violation complaints involve an internationally legal act. In such cases, the withdrawal of the act would be disproportionate because of the compatibility of the act with the international obligations of the losing party. This is presumably why the DSU does not provide for such a remedy and merely specifies a solution where the *effects* of the act will be mitigated without the *act itself* being put into question at all. The relevant DSU provision reads as follows:

> where a measure has been found to nullify or impair benefits under, or impede the attainment of objectives, of the relevant covered agreement without violation thereof, there is no obligation to withdraw the measure. However, in such cases, the panel or the Appellate Body shall recommend that the Member concerned make a mutually satisfactory adjustment.[32]

In *Japan — Film*, the panel rejected the claim advanced by the United States and the United States did not appeal the report. Since *Japan — Film*, no other non-violation complaint lodged before a WTO adjudicating body has been successful. Consequently, so far there is no case law making the vague term "mutually satisfactory adjustment" more precise. What will be determinative in future practice in such cases is the obligation to ensure that such adjustments will not violate the MFN-clause. As noted above, panels can make suggestions about how to reach a mutually satisfactory adjustment, but such suggestions are not binding on the parties.[33]

## 2.3 Compensation for failure to comply and retaliation

### *2.3.1 Overview*

If the losing party fails to comply with the recommendations and rulings of the DSB, the complaining party can seek authorization to suspend concessions.[34] Losing parties may fail to comply because they fail to take any

[32] DSU Art. 26.1(b).

[33] Some economists attach importance to the concept of nullification and impairment. *See, e.g.*, Kyle Bagwell and Robert W. Staiger, *An Economic Theory of GATT*, 89 AM. ECON. REV. 215, 241 (1999) (explaining that the incentive to make concessions will be reduced unless concessions are protected through non-violation complaints).

[34] DSU Art. 22.

action to do so or because a compliance panel found that the action taken was inadequate. Under the "negative consensus" rule, a request for authorization to suspend concessions means that multilateral authorization for countermeasures will be granted.[35] As an alternative, the losing party may grant compensation to the complaining party. Compensation is, however, voluntary. Compensation and suspension of concessions are both temporary measures pending implementation of the report.[36]

Neither compensation nor suspension of concessions are preferred to full implementation.[37] A WTO Member should not be presumed to comply with its international obligations if it continues to violate a WTO agreement, while compensating the winning party or allowing the winning party to suspend concessions. In such a case, the losing party continues to violate such agreement and is not absolved from its international obligations. Compensation and suspension of concessions are intended only as the means that induce eventual compliance with the WTO agreements. Compensation and suspension of concessions are WTO parlance for "countermeasures".

### *2.3.2 Measuring countermeasures*

Countermeasures must be equivalent to the level of nullification or impairment.[38] As a result, there is no room for punitive damages in the WTO context. Moreover, there appears to be no room for proportionate damages because the term "equivalent" is stricter than the term "proportionate." Equivalence is judged by reference to the level of nullification and impairment.[39]

In the GATT regime, the term used in the place of "equivalent" was "appropriate".[40] There is only one reported case in which recourse to countermeasures was envisaged in the GATT era. In that case, the Netherlands was authorized to limit imports of wheat flour from the United States to 60,000 tons based on a determination by a Working Party

1. that the measure proposed by the Netherlands Government is appropriate in character, and
2. that, having regard to

[35] *Id.* Art. 22.6.

[36] *Id.* Art. 22.1.

[37] *Id.*

[38] *Id.* Art. 22.4.

[39] As pointed out above, proportionality of countermeasures in the WTO context is to be judged by reference to the effects rather than to the gravity of the act.

[40] GATT Art. XXIII:2.

(i) the value of the trade involved,
(ii) the broader elements in the impairment suffered by the Netherlands, and
(iii) the statement of the Netherlands Government that its principal objective in proposing the measure in question is to contribute to the eventual solution of the matter in accordance with the objectives of the General Agreement . . .[41]

This matter was also discussed during the aftermath of the adoption of the *United States — Superfund* panel report at the GATT Council, following an EC request to adopt countermeasures against the United States since the latter had not implemented the panel report. There, the Legal Adviser to the Director General of the GATT advanced the following point of view:

> [T]here were a few provisions in the General Agreement where retaliation was foreseen. In two of those, Articles XIX and XXVIII, retaliation was defined as the withdrawal of substantially equivalent concessions. In the case of Article XXIII, the wording was wider, referring to measures determined to be appropriate in the circumstances, which meant that there was a wider leeway in calculating the retaliatory measures under Article XXIII than under Articles XIX or XXVIII . . . A working party in the present case would examine whether the retaliatory measures proposed by the Community would be appropriate in the circumstances; that would include the question of how to calculate the damage and the compensation.[42]

Against this background, Article 22.4 of the DSU is arguably a setback in comparison to Article XXIII:2 of the GATT when it comes to measuring the permissible extent of countermeasures because it imposes a strict equivalence between the damage incurred and the level of countermeasures.

### *2.3.3 Measuring countermeasures: WTO practice*

The WTO has authorized countermeasures in four highly publicized cases (1) the *Hormones*[43] dispute between the United States and the European Community; (2) the *Bananas*[44] case between the United States/Ecuador and the European Community; (3) the *Brazil Aircraft Subsidies*[45] case brought

[41] *See* Netherlands Measures of Suspension of Obligations to the United States, 8 November 1952, GATT B.I.S.D. (1st Supp.) at 32 (1952).

[42] See GATT Doc. C/M/220 at 36. The quoted passage is re-produced in 2 Guide to GATT Law and Practice 651 (6th ed. 1995) (the GATT Analytical Index).

[43] *European Communities — Measures Affecting Livestock and Meat (Hormones)*, WT/DS26/ARB, 12 July 1999 [hereinafter *Hormones* arbitration].

[44] *See EC — Bananas*, Recourse to Arbitration by the European Communities under Article 22.6 of the DSU — Decision by the Arbitrators, WT/DS27/ARB/ECU, 24 March 2000 [hereinafter *Bananas* arbitration].

[45] *Brazil — Export Financing Programme for Aircraft, Recourse to Arbitration by Brazil*, WT/DS46/ABR, 21 August 2000 [hereinafter *Brazil Aircraft* arbitration].

by Canada against Brazil; and the *United States — FSC/ETI*[46] case maintained by the European Community against the United States.

In *Hormones* and *Bananas*, the level of countermeasure was based upon the arbitral panel's calculation of the level of nullification and impairment. In *Hormones*, the panel used the date on which the reasonable time for compliance expired and asked the question: What would annual prospective U.S. exports of hormone-treated beef and beef products to the EC be if the EC had withdrawn the ban on 13 May 1999?[47] It concluded that "this question, like any question about future events, can only be a reasonable estimate".[48] Similarly, in the *Bananas* arbitration, the panel measured the level of nullification and impairment by constructing a hypothetical of the annual exports in absence of the violation.[49]

In the *Brazil Aircraft* case, however, the panel rejected the level of nullification and impairment as the basis of the countermeasure level, using the amount of the subsidy instead.[50] The panel found that "requiring that countermeasures . . . be equivalent to the level of nullification and impairment would be contrary to the principle of effectiveness by significantly limiting the efficacy of countermeasures in the case of prohibited subsidies".[51] The panel's decision can be justified because of the fact that the SCM Agreement, Article 4.10, specifically authorizes "appropriate" countermeasures. The panel found that only a countermeasure equivalent to the level of the subsidy was "appropriate".[52]

In the *United States — FSC Arbitration* the arbitrator ruled consistently with the *Brazil Aircraft* case that the countermeasure should be equivalent to the subsidy, which was found to be US $ 4.043 billion per year. The arbitrator similarly found that the "trade effects" or "nullification and impairment" standard of DSU Article 22.4 was not applicable, and the matter was controlled by SCM Article 4.10 and the word "appropriate".[53]

[46] United States — Tax Treatment for "Foreign Sales Corporations", Recourse to Arbitration by the United States under Article 22.6 of the DSU and Article 4.11 of the SCM Agreement — Decision of the Arbitrator, WT/DS108/ARB, 30 August 2002 [hereinafter *United States FSC Arbitration*].

[47] *Hormones* arbitration para. 38.

[48] *Id.* para. 41.

[49] *Bananas* arbitration para. 100.

[50] *Brazil Aircraft* arbitration para. 3.5.4.

[51] *Id.* paras 3.58, 3.54–3.60.

[52] *Id.* para. 3.60.

[53] *United States — FSC Arbitration*, paras. 5.44–5.49.

Thus, WTO practice with respect to measuring countermeasures employs two different standards: DSU Article 22.4 ("nullification and impairment") and SCM Article 4.10 ("appropriate"). There are huge differences between these seemingly innocuous phrases. "Nullification and impairment" essentially measures the countermeasure in terms of the trade effect on the complaining member; "appropriate" measures the subsidy without regard to trade effects. In the *United States — FSC* case the nullification and impairment was calculated to be US $1.1 billion, but the countermeasure imposed was almost four times as great under the "appropriate" standard. It is not evident why there should be two such different measures.

#### 2.3.3.1 The function of countermeasures

The *EC — Bananas* arbitration underscores that the objective of countermeasures is to induce compliance by the recalcitrant WTO Member.[54] Unless such compliance is induced, the enforcement mechanism of the WTO dispute settlement system cannot function properly.[55]

#### 2.3.3.2 The burden of proof

A WTO Member requesting authorization to impose countermeasures will submit a list of concessions it wishes to suspend. The *Hormones* arbitration established the rule that it is up to the party challenging the proposed countermeasures to rebut the arguments and evidence submitted by the Member requesting authorization to impose countermeasures.[56] This principle was followed in *EC — Bananas* arbitration decision.[57]

If there is no challenge, the complainant must still abide by the Article 22.4 DSU standard, that is, guarantee that countermeasures are equivalent to the level of nullification and impairment. In other words, arbitrators will

---

[54] *See Bananas* arbitration para. 76 (finding that the object and purpose of Article 22 is to induce compliance). The arbitrators also noted that:

> [i]f a complaining party seeking the DSB's authorization to suspend certain concessions or certain other obligations were required to select the concessions or other obligations to be suspended in sectors or under agreements where such suspension would be either not available in practice or would not be powerful in effect, the objective of inducing compliance could not be accomplished, and the enforcement mechanism of the WTO dispute settlement system could not function properly.

[55] *See Bananas* arbitration para. 76.

[56] *See Hormones* arbitration paras 9–11.

[57] *See Bananas* arbitration para. 37.

not rubber stamp the request for suspension of concessions. It is their duty, in accordance with Article 22.7 of the DSU, to ensure that the relevant provisions of the DSU (effectively DSU Article 22.3 and 22.4) are observed.

#### 2.3.3.3 The standard of review

Article 22.7 of the DSU requests arbitrators to verify two things:

1. Whether the Member requesting authorization has complied with the rules and procedures laid down in Article 22.3 of the DSU; and
2. Whether the proposed countermeasures are equivalent to the level of nullification and impairment as requested by Article 22.4 of the DSU.

The wording of Article 22.7 of the DSU makes it clear that arbitrators may modify proposed concessions and that addressees of their decisions must accept the arbitrators' award as final.

With respect to Article 22.4 of the DSU, the text of the DSU imposes an unconditional obligation that the countermeasures must be equivalent to the nullification and impairment. The operative legal consequence is that arbitrators have discretion to downsize over-ambitious submissions. The opposite, though, is not true. If the complainant decides to suspend concessions lower than the level of nullification and impairment, the arbitrators cannot increase it to the level of nullification and impairment. This is so for two reasons: first, the Article 22.4 of the DSU threshold operates as a ceiling beyond which actions are illegal but within which actions are perfectly legal. Second, in accordance with customary international law, the judge should disregard points of fact or law not raised by the parties. Both the *Hormones* and the *EC — Bananas* arbitration decisions reflect this point.

Article 22.3 of the DSU gives the possibility to the complainant to suspend concessions in the same sector,[58] in a different sector under the same agreement,[59] or in a different agreement altogether.[60]

If the complainant avails itself of either of the latter two options, certain procedural obligations come into play: (1) it must "state the reasons" for the request; and (2) notify the relevant WTO Councils and sectoral bodies.[61] In addition, if the complainant is seeking to suspend concessions in other sectors under the same Agreement, it must show that suspending concessions in the *same*[62] sector is not "practicable or effective". If the complainant is seeking to suspend concessions under a different Agreement, it must

[58] DSU Art. 22.3a.
[59] *Id.* Art. 22.3b.
[60] *Id.* Art. 22.3c.
[61] *Id.* Art. 22.3(e).
[62] *Id.* Art. 22.3(b).

also show that it is not "practicable or effective" to suspend concessions in other sectors of the same Agreement and that "the circumstances are serious enough".[63]

Moreover, two overriding principles apply: the complainant (and the arbitrators) must "take into account" (1) trade in the sector and the Agreement violated and its importance to the complainant;[64] and (2) the broader economic consequences of both the violation and the requested countermeasure.[65]

In the *Bananas* arbitration, a broad standard of review was applied to requests for countermeasures in different sectors from the original violation:

> the margin of review by the Arbitrators implies the authority to broadly judge whether the complaining party in question has considered the necessary facts objectively and whether, on the basis of these facts, it could plausibly arrive at the conclusion that it was not practicable or effective to seek suspension within the same sector . . . .[66]

What is puzzling here is that the decision by the arbitrators to reject Ecuador's argument was based precisely on a very artificial distinction. Moreover, the attitude of the arbitrators in this respect underscores the point that, by imposing a meaningful judicial review standard with respect to the procedural obligations contained in Article 22.3 of the DSU, arbitrators will effectively put in question the decision by a WTO Member to take countermeasures in a different sector or agreement.

## 2.4 Countermeasures: how effective?

WTO Members will eventually be persuaded to abandon their WTO-inconsistent practices if countermeasures (or the threat thereof) are indeed credible. Game theory suggests that a threat is credible if players know *ex ante* that it will materialize. Unless countries lose more by keeping their illegal practices intact than vice versa, they will hardly have an incentive to comply.

Moreover, although formally there seems to be a situation of perfect symmetry among the various WTO players when it comes to adopting countermeasures (since countermeasures are limited to the value of damage and do not extend beyond it), in fact, the effectiveness of countermeasures depends on the relative economic importance of the party adopting them. Countermeasures effectively mean exclusion from (or difficult access to)

[63] DSU Art. 22.3(c). [64] *Id.* Art. 22.3(d)(1). [65] *Id.* Art. 22.3(d)(ii).
[66] *See Bananas* arbitration, para. 52.

markets. By definition, countries depending on international trade will be hurt more. An additional complicating factor in this context is the attraction of a particular market for exporters. Not all markets have the same value. The EC and the U.S. markets (because of their overall size and the high-income consumers living there) are not easily replaceable.

Export diversification can be crucial as well. Imagine, for example, a situation where country A exports only to country B, but country B exports to country A but also to 50 other markets. A decision by B to take countermeasures against A can be fatal to A especially if the latter counts a lot on export income. The opposite is not necessarily true.

Most importantly, countermeasures are bad policy. It is commonplace in economics that countermeasures amount to "shooting oneself in the foot". Interestingly, the *EC — Bananas* arbitration acknowledges this point.[67] Through countermeasures, a WTO Member imposes an additional cost on the society. Precisely because of the budgetary constraints, adoption of countermeasures is simply not an option for the poorer WTO Members.

As a result, those WTO Members that can afford to either take or withstand countermeasures will be in a better position. When acting as complaining parties, they will use threat and/or imposition of countermeasures in order to induce compliance; when acting as respondents, they will have at least the luxury of weighing the pros and cons between *changing* the domestic policies at stake (in order to avoid imposition of countermeasures) or simply *keeping* the domestic policies at stake intact (and seeing countermeasures imposed against them).

In an interview, Pascal Lamy, the EC Commissioner responsible for international trade issues, perfectly captured this point by stating the following: "As long as you pay the penalties, you can go on as you are".[68] Lamy did not have to address questions of the type how difficult it is for other weaker WTO members to pursue such policies.[69]

[67] *See Bananas* arbitration para. 86.

[68] *See* Press and Communication Service Brussels, No. 3036, 23 May 2000.

[69] Although the mandate of the WTO is not to deal with all inequalities between players that pre-exist the WTO contract and are anyway hidden behind a concept that has probably lost touch with reality altogether by now: sovereign equality, the mandate of the WTO is to ensure that with respect to its quintessential function, that is adjudication of disputes, all necessary steps will be taken to guarantee that inequalities will not adversely affect the rights of the states concerned.

## 3. The case for re-negotiating remedies

WTO retaliation as a sanction or remedy is the weakest part of the dispute settlement system. Consider that the purpose of dispute settlement is to maintain the balance of trade concessions under the Agreements.[70] Retaliation contravenes this purpose in multiple ways (1) by adding a new incursion into the system; and (2) by removing the incentive to comply since the member being sanctioned is, in effect, choosing to live with the retaliation rather than come into compliance. The result is a new balance of trade relations at more protective levels. Thus, countermeasures at present undermine the entire WTO system, which is based upon mutually agreed trade liberalization.

What should be done? Three possibilities for sanctions rather than retaliation may be considered: (1) making compensation mandatory rather than voluntary; (2) levying fines or damages; and (3) suspending a Member's right to participate in the WTO system.[71] All of these possible solutions pose problems, however. Compensation as a practical matter cannot be forced; it must be conceded by the losing state. But compensation will become more attractive if other available sanctions are put into play. Fines should play a greater role; a system of fines that increase over time and are based upon the size of the Member's economy as well as the size of the violation could provide more incentive to agree to compensation. Finally, denying a non-complying Member the right to participate in WTO business could be effective. This could also be graduated over time. Initially, this may take the form of denial of rights on certain committees and working parties; it could lead to greater denials of rights, including the right to participate in DSB or WTO council meetings or to use the dispute settlement process itself.

The WTO should also devise a remedy to deal with the timing problems associated with non-compliance. Under the present system, remedies — as well as compliance — are prospective only.

A few panels in antidumping and subsidies cases have tried to change that by authorizing retroactivity, but this has been unsuccessful. It is also undesirable to change the system through *ad hoc* pronouncements of chance panel members. Nevertheless, the timing question should be faced by the WTO. Under the present system, a Member can enact "hit and run"

[70] DSU Art. 3.3.

[71] *See generally* Joost Pauwelyn, *Enforcement and Countermeasures in the WTO: Rules are Rules — Toward a More Collective Approach*, 94 Am. J. Int'l L. 335, 345–47 (2000).

protective measures, such as a safeguard quota, that will run its course before the time comes for compliance after dispute settlement has run its course. As in the *City of Trondheim* case, a WTO Member can violate an agreement in a way in which it is impossible to provide prospective relief. In any case in which duties are collected — the antidumping and countervailing duty cases come to mind — prospective relief alone will be insufficient.

The best way of dealing with this situation is an agreed system of compensation or fines (or both). Both compensation and fines could be modulated to reflect both the severity and duration of the violation.

# 5

# WTO LAW AND DOMESTIC LAW



## 1. Introduction

Legal theory posits two basic solutions with respect to the relationship between international law and domestic (sometimes called "municipal") law, the national or internal legal orders of states.

The first theory, namely, *monism*, holds that both international law and domestic law form parts of the same legal order.[1] Exponents of monism commonly conclude that international law is (or should be) directly applicable in domestic law and prevails over inconsistent domestic laws.[2]

The second theory, namely, *dualism*, holds that international law and domestic law are separate systems of law.[3] International law and domestic

[1] For a more complete review of this theory, see Ian Brownlie, PRINCIPLES OF PUBLIC INTERNATIONAL LAW 31–33 (5th ed. 1998).

[2] *See, e.g.*, H. Kelsen, PRINCIPLES OF INTERNATIONAL LAW 553–88 (2d ed. 1966).

[3] For treatment that is more complete, see Brownlie, above note 1, at 31–33. A noted exponent of dualism was Dionisio Anzilotti. *See* Dionisio Anzilotti, CORSO DI DIRITTO INTERNAZIONALE (3d ed. 1928).

law stem from different sources[4] and have different subject matters.[5] Neither has the power to alter the rules of the other. Each is supreme within its own sphere so that a domestic court would apply domestic law in the case of a conflict between domestic law and international law.[6]

Neither monism nor dualism, however, corresponds entirely with contemporary state practice, which combines the monist and dualist approaches. Three propositions characterize contemporary practice.

First, state obligations under international law cannot be excused because they conflict with domestic law or because domestic law is somehow deficient.[7]

Second, it follows from the first proposition that states have a duty to bring their domestic law into conformity with their international obligations. Failure to do so is not itself a breach of international law, but may result in a breach if compliance with domestic law precludes compliance with specific international obligations.[8]

Third, the domestic law of the state concerned determines the effect of international law on domestic law.[9] Thus, international law may or may not be given direct effect or be supreme, depending on the constitutional doctrines of the state concerned.

These propositions apply with respect to the relationship between WTO law as international law and the domestic legal orders of WTO Members. The WTO/GATT system is treaty law in the international law sense; there is little scope for customary international law. The WTO Agreement provides that all agreements and legal instruments that constitute the multilateral trade agreements "are binding on all Members".[10] In addition, each WTO Member has a legal obligation to "ensure the conformity of its laws, regulations, and administrative procedures with its [WTO] obligations".[11]

[4] Lawmaking institutions of sovereign states pass domestic laws, whereas international law is made in a different manner, primarily through treaties and customs accepted as law.

[5] Dualists hold that international law applies to relations between sovereign states while domestic law applies to relations (a) between citizens and (b) between citizens and the government of a sovereign state. *See* Brownlie, above note 1, at 33.

[6] *See id.*

[7] This proposition is well established. *See* Vienna Convention on the Law of Treaties, Art. 27, available at http://www.un.org/law/ilc/texts/treatfra.htm.

[8] Oppenheim's International Law 84–85 (Robert Y. Jennings and Arthur Watts eds., 9th ed. 1992).

[9] Some state constitutions specifically incorporate or recognize the primacy of international law. Japan is an example. *See* Section 4.

[10] WTO Agreement Art. II:2.

[11] WTO Agreement Art. XVI:4.

The implementation of this conformity obligation as well as the effect on domestic law are, however, left to each WTO Member to determine. In this work,[12] only three states will be examined, namely, the United States, the European Community, and Japan.

## 2. The United States

### 2.1 Overview of U.S. law

What is a "treaty" under international law may be called a treaty or an executive agreement under U.S. law.[13] A treaty, to be legally binding on the United States, must be negotiated and ratified by the President after receiving the advice and consent of two-thirds of the members of the U.S. Senate.[14] The President alone, in contrast, can conclude an executive agreement.[15] The executive agreement power may be exercised in conjunction with a treaty or may be authorized in a formal way by Congress.[16] The President also has "inherent power" of uncertain scope to enter into executive agreements.[17] The power to conclude executive agreements is not explicit in the U.S. Constitution, but has been approved by the U.S. Supreme Court.[18] The choice of when to use the treaty power or when to use the executive agreement power is unclear under present constitutional doctrine.[19] In practice, the President makes the choice, but this is often the subject of controversy.[20]

The President treated the WTO Agreement as an executive agreement. Congress authorized the negotiation and approval process in advance under

[12] For more complete treatment, see John H. Jackson and Alan O. Sykes, IMPLEMENTING THE URUGUAY ROUND (1997).

[13] RESTATEMENT (THIRD) OF THE FOREIGN RELATIONS LAW OF THE UNITED STATES § 111 (1987) [hereinafter RESTATEMENT]

[14] U.S. CONST. Art. II, § 2.

[15] *United States v. Belmont*, 301 U.S. 324 (1937); *United States v. Pink*, 315 U.S. 203 (1942).

[16] *See* John H. Jackson et al., LEGAL PROBLEMS OF INTERNATIONAL ECONOMIC RELATIONS 91–92 (4th ed. 2002).

[17] *See id.*

[18] *See* cases cited above note 15.

[19] *See* U.S. DEP'T OF STATE, HANDBOOK ON TREATIES AND OTHER INTERNATIONAL AGREEMENTS § 721.3 (1985).

[20] When the WTO Agreement was submitted to Congress as an executive agreement, many argued that it should be submitted as a treaty under U.S. law. *See The World Trade Organization and U.S. Sovereignty: Hearings Before the Senate Comm. on Foreign Relations*, 103d Cong. (1994).

a procedure known as "fast track". Under the fast-track process, Congress approved legislation authorizing the President to enter into trade negotiations and agreed to consider the necessary implementing legislation under a special legislative process.[21] The process was as follows. First, the bill implementing the executive agreement could not be amended once it was introduced. Second, the appropriate legislative committees and Congress had to vote on the bill within a certain period. Third, the bill would be voted "up" or "down" by each house of Congress. The Uruguay Round results were approved, pursuant to this process, through the approval of the Uruguay Round Agreements Act (URAA) in December 1994.[22]

The function of the U.S. "fast track" procedure for international trade agreements is not only to facilitate Congressional review and approval, but also to reassure negotiating partners that any trade agreement they negotiate with the United States will not be subject to Congressional amendments, restarting the negotiation process. Fast-track authority, most recently called "trade promotion authority," is therefore essential for the President to even conclude serious trade negotiations.

## 2.2 The relationship between WTO law and U.S. law

Do the WTO agreements have direct effect in the domestic legal order of the United States? U.S. constitutional practice recognizes a distinction between self-executing and non-self-executing international agreements. Both treaties and executive agreements can be self-executing,[23] in which case, they have direct effect as part of U.S. domestic law because of the constitutional provision that "treaties," together with the Constitution and U.S. laws, shall be "the Supreme Law of the land".[24]

Whether a particular treaty is self-executing is a matter of considering the terms in question. If the terms of a treaty give the treaty direct effect, the

However, the President's power to conclude a trade agreement was upheld in court. *Made in USA Foundation v. United States*, 56 F. Supp. 3d 1226 (N.D. Ala. 1999).

[21] For a full explanation, see John H. Jackson, *The Great 1994 Sovereignty Debate: United States Acceptance and Implementation of the Uruguay Round Results*, 36 Colum. J. Transnat'l L. 157, 168–69 (1997).

[22] *See id.*

[23] *See Foster v. Neilson*, 27 U.S. 253, 314 (1929); *United States v. Pink*, above note 15. *See also* Restatement, above note 13, § 111.

[24] U.S. Const. Art. VI, § 2.

treaty is self-executing. If the terms indicate that further legislation is needed for direct effect, the treaty is non-self-executing.[25] In addition, some provisions of a treaty may be self-executing, while other provisions are non-self-executing. In U.S. law, multilateral trade agreements such as the GATT have never been held to be self-executing, and leading scholars concur that the GATT is a non-self-executing agreement.[26]

In the Uruguay Round Agreements Act, Congress settled the question of direct effect: section 102 of the Act provides that "no provision of any of the Uruguay Round Agreements, nor the application of any such provision to any person or circumstance, that is inconsistent with any law of the United States shall have effect".[27] This provision means that the WTO agreements have no direct effect on U.S. law.

This provision also means that decisions rendered by WTO dispute settlement panels and the Appellate Body have no direct effect on U.S. law. Even before the URAA, this was the case. In *Footwear Distributors and Retailers of America v. United States*,[28] the U.S. Court of International Trade refused to give direct effect to a GATT panel decision: "However cogent the reasoning of the GATT panels . . . , it cannot and therefore does not lead to the precise domestic, judicial relief for which the plaintiff prays".[29] The U.S. Court of International Trade has also concluded that WTO dispute settlement reports have no binding effect on a U.S. court.[30]

Because neither the WTO agreements nor dispute settlement decisions can directly affect existing U.S. law, it follows that laws passed by Congress after the WTO Agreement and the URAA will be given full effect in domestic law and U.S. courts, even if there is a conflict between such laws and a WTO agreement. U.S. courts have noted that an unambiguous U.S.

---

25 *Foster v. Neilson*, above note 23; *see* John H. Jackson, *Status of Treaties in Domestic Legal Systems: A Policy Analysis*, 86 Am. J. Int'l L. 310, 320 (1992).

26 John H. Jackson, *The General Agreement on Tariffs and Trade in United States Domestic Law*, 66 Mich. L. Rev. 249 (1967); Robert E. Hudec, *The Legal Status of GATT in the Domestic Law of the United States, in* The European Community and GATT 187 (M. Hilf et al. eds., 1986); Ronald A. Brand, *The Status of the General Agreement on Tariffs and Trade in United States Domestic Law*, 26 Stan. J. Int'l L. 479 (1990).

27 19 U.S.C.A. § 3512(a)(1) (1999). *See also* S. Rep. No. 103–412, at 13 (1994) (noting that the Uruguay Round Agreements "are not self-executing and thus their legal effect in the United States is governed by implementing legislation").

28 *Footwear Distributors and Retailers of America v. United States*, 852 F. Supp. 1078 (Ct. Int'l Trade 1994).

29 *Id.* at 1096.

30 *See Hyundai Electronics Co. v. United States*, 53 F. Supp. 2d 1334, 1343 (1999).

law prevails over international law in the event of a conflict between the two.[31] They have also noted that, "absent express language to the contrary, a statute should not be interpreted to conflict with international obligations".[32]

With regard to *U.S. state law*, the URAA similarly provides that

> [n]o State law, or the application of such a State law, may be declared invalid as to any person or circumstance on the ground that the provision or application is inconsistent with any of the Uruguay Round Agreements, except in an action brought by the United States for the purpose of declaring such law or application invalid.[33]

Thus, while U.S. constitutional practice holds that even an executive agreement based solely upon the President's foreign affairs power prevails over inconsistent state law, and the WTO agreements are intended to supersede conflicting state law,[34] a U.S. official or court cannot declare state law invalid on that basis except in an action brought by the federal government.

The United States has adopted virtually a purely dualistic approach to the WTO Agreement. Having been signed by the President, the WTO Agreement is an executive agreement and, therefore, constitutes a binding international obligation of the United States. It is not directly effective, however, in the domestic legal order. Its implementation depends solely upon its transformation by the U.S. Congress into domestic law. No person may assert any cause of action or defence directly under any of the WTO agreements before a U.S. tribunal.[35] Thus, in the United States, the legal issues arising under the WTO agreements will be decided under U.S. legislation, both federal and state, regardless of whether the result is consistent with international law. It is the responsibility of Congress and the President to ensure conformity between U.S. and WTO law.

[31] *See, e.g., Hyundai Electronics Co.*, above note 30, at 1343.

[32] *See, e.g., Hyundai Electronics Co.*, above note 30, at 1344 (citing *Murray v. Schooner Charming Betsy*, 6 U.S. (2 Cranch) 64 (1804).

[33] 19 U.S.C.A. § 3512(b)(2) (1999).

[34] GATT Art. XXIV:12 requires contracting parties to take "reasonable measures" to ensure observance by local and regional governments. This provision has generated an ambiguous jurisprudence in the United States. For a thorough summary and analysis, see Hudec, above note 26, at 219–25. However, GATT Art. XXIV:12 would seem to be superseded by Article XVI:4 of the WTO Agreement. Article XVI:4 mandates conformity to the WTO agreements. *See* 19 U.S.C.A. § 3512(c) (1999) (implementing this obligation into U.S. law).

[35] 19 U.S.C.A. § 3512(c) (1999).

# 3. The European Community

All of the Members of the European Union[36] were contracting parties to the GATT and became founding members of the WTO. Because of the common commercial policy established by the treaties establishing the European Community,[37] the EC represented the Member States in the GATT negotiations.[38] In 1995, the EC formally became a member of the WTO. Thus, the provisions of the WTO agreements are legally binding upon both the EC and its Member States. The EU/EC is not a federal state. It is more like a confederation, and the authority to conduct external relations is shared between the central government and its Member States.

## 3.1 External relations and the EU/EC

The EC Treaty includes a procedure for the negotiation and conclusion of treaties by the Community.[39] The Community's powers are limited to those areas where "the Treaty provides for the conclusion of agreements between the Community and one or more states or international organizations".[40] Insofar as the GATT/WTO is concerned, the central provision authorizing the negotiation and conclusion of multilateral trade agreements reads as follows:

---

[36] The European Union is the political entity founded by the Maastricht Treaty. The legal functions of the EU are still exercised by the European Community.

[37] The three "constitutional" treaties of the European Communities are as follows: (1) Treaty Establishing the European Coal and Steel Community, 18 April 1951, 261 U.N.T.S. 140; (2) Treaty Establishing Euratom, 25 March 1957, 298 U.N.T.S. 9; and (3) Treaty Establishing the European Community, 25 March 1957, 298 U.N.T.S. 11 [hereinafter EC TREATY]. The three European Communities treaties were unified by a Merger Treaty, Treaty on European Union and Consolidated Version of the Treaty Establishing the European Community, done at Maastricht, Rome, and Amsterdam, 7 February 1992, 25 March 1957, 2 October 1997, 37 I.L.M. 56 (1998).

The Treaty of Amsterdam significantly amended the EC Treaty, resulting in the renumbering of the Articles. *See* TREATY OF AMSTERDAM AMENDING THE TREATY ON EUROPEAN UNION, THE TREATIES ESTABLISHING THE EUROPEAN COMMUNITIES AND CERTAIN RELATED ACTS, 2 October 1997, O.J. 1 C340/173 (10 Nov. 1997).

[38] *See* Hugo Paemon and Alexandra Bensch, FROM THE GATT TO THE WTO: THE EUROPEAN COMMUNITY IN THE URUGUAY ROUND (1995).

[39] EC TREATY, above note 37, *Art. 228* (now Art. 300).

[40] EC TREATY, above note 37, *Art. 228* (now Art. 300).

> 1. The common commercial policy shall be based on uniform principles, particularly concerning changes in tariff rates, the conclusion of tariff and trade agreements, the achievement of uniformity in measures of liberalization, export policy, and measures to protect trade such as those to be taken in event of dumping or subsidies.
> 2. The Commission shall present proposals to the Council for implementing the common commercial policy.
> 3. Where agreements with one or more States or international organizations need to be negotiated, the Commission shall make recommendations to the Council, which shall authorize the Commission to open the necessary negotiations.
> The Commission shall conduct these negotiations in consultation with a special committee appointed by the Council to assist the Commission in this task and within the framework of such directives as the Council may issue to it.[41]

This provision has been interpreted by the European Court of Justice (ECJ) to give wide powers to the Community to negotiate and conclude agreements with respect to the common commercial policy.[42]

In addition, the ECJ has ruled that

> each time the Community, with a view to implementing a common policy envisaged by the [EEC] Treaty, adopts provisions laying down common rules, whatever form these may take, the Member States no longer have the right, acting individually or even collectively, to undertake obligations with third countries which affect those rules.[43]

The Member States are constrained from acting, even when the Community has not yet acted, as long as the subject matter is assigned to the Community by treaty.[44] If an agreement involves costs that are to be borne directly by the Member States, however, they can participate in the negotiations with the Community.[45] Such agreements may be termed "mixed agreements".

The respective authority of the Member States and the EC to negotiate and conclude the WTO agreements was decided by the ECJ in *Agreement Establishing the World Trade Organization.*[46] In this case, the ECJ rejected the argument that, because the Member States contribute to the WTO budget, the WTO agreements were, therefore, mixed agreements in which the Member States and Community had joint competence. The Court

[41] EC Treaty, above note 37, *Art. 113* (now Art. 133).

[42] Opinion 1/75, Opinion of the Court Given Pursuant to Article 228 of the EEC Treaty [1975] E.C.R. 1355.

[43] Case 22/70, *Commission v. Council* [1971] E.C.R. 263, 274.

[44] Joined Cases 3, 4 & 6/76, *In re Kramer* [1976] E.C.R. 1279.

[45] Opinion 1/78, *International Agreement on Rubber* [1979] E.C.R. 2871.

[46] Opinion 1/94, *Agreement Establishing the World Trade Organization* [1994] E.C.R. I-5267.

distinguished the *International Rubber* case, which held that the EC and its Member States enjoyed joint competence in the negotiation of an agreement requiring financial commitments from the Member States.[47] Joint competence was found in the *International Rubber* case because it involved a financial policy instrument, while the WTO agreements involved contributing to an operating budget.[48]

The ECJ upheld the exclusive competence of the Community with respect to all matters connected with trade in goods because these matters came within the scope of Article 113 of the EEC treaty and analogous Articles in other relevant treaties.[49] With respect to certain matters connected with trade in services[50] and intellectual property rights,[51] however, the ECJ held that there was joint competence because they were outside the scope of Article 113 and came within the purview of the Member States. The ECJ mandated "close cooperation between the Member States and the Community institutions, both in the process of negotiation and conclusion and in the fulfillment of the commitments entered into. That obligation flows from the requirement of unity in the international representation of the Community".[52]

## 3.2 The relationship between WTO law and the laws of the EC and its Member States

The European Court of Justice has held that certain international agreements concluded by the Community may have "direct effect" in that they create rights on which individuals may rely before Member State courts and Community institutions.[53] The direct effect doctrine has not been

[47] *Id.* at I-5395.

[48] *Id.* at I-5395.

[49] *Id.* at I-5399.

[50] Specifically, the Court ruled that Article 113 of the EC Treaty (now Article 133) covered only cross-border supply of services. Other modes of supply — consumption abroad, commercial presence, and the presence of natural persons — were not within Article 113 (now Article 133). The Court rejected the argument that the Community should have exclusive competence because of its power over these areas at the internal level. External competence only where Community legislation has occupied the field and there is no scope for future Member State action. Before the Community acts, Member States retain competence, even over matters delegated by treaty to the Community. *Id.* at I-5404.

[51] *Id.* at I-5419. The Court pointed out that the Community had not yet exercised its powers to enforce intellectual property rights within the EC.

[52] *Id.* at I-5420.

[53] Case 104/81, *Hauptzollamt Mainz v. C.A. Kupferberg & Cie. KG a. A.* [1982] E.C.R. 3641.

extended, however, to the GATT[54] or the WTO agreements.[55] In *Germany v. Council*,[56] the ECJ reiterated this holding, stating that

> the GATT rules are not unconditional[,] and . . . an obligation to recognize them as rules of international law which are directly applicable in the domestic legal systems of the contracting parties cannot be based on the spirit, general scheme or terms of GATT.[57]

Furthermore, the EC Council, in its decision of 22 December 1994 concerning the conclusion of the Uruguay Round Agreements, stated that "by its nature the Agreement establishing the World Trade Organization, including the Annexes thereto, is not susceptible to being directly invoked in Community or Member State courts".[58]

The European Court of Justice considered the direct effect doctrine in the *Portuguese Textiles* case,[59] in which Portugal sought to annul a Council Decision on market access for textile products originating in India and Pakistan. The ECJ rejected Portugal's argument that WTO agreements could serve as a legal ground for invalidating a Council Decision. It expressly approved the EC Council's determination that the WTO agreements cannot be directly invoked in Community or Member State courts.[60] The Court can review the legality of a Community measure against the WTO agreements only if the Community intends to implement a particular WTO obligation (the so-called *Nakajima* doctrine)[61] or if the Community act in question refers to specific provisions of a WTO agreement (the so-called *Fediol* doctrine).[62]

---

[54] In *International Fruit Co.*, the ECJ held that GATT Article XI "is not capable of conferring on citizens of the Community rights which they can invoke before the courts." Joined Cases 21 to 24/72, *International Fruit Co. v. Produktschap voor Groenten en Fruit* [1972] E.C.R. 1219, 1228. *See also* Case 9/73, *Schlüter v. Hauptzollamt Lörrach* [1973] E.C.R. 1135.

[55] Case C-149/96, *Portugal v. Council* [1998 E.C.R. I-7379].

[56] Case 280/93, *Germany v. Council* [1994] E.C.R. I-4973.

[57] *Id.* at I-5073, para. 110.

[58] 94/800/EC: Council Decision (of 22 December 1994) concerning the conclusion on behalf of the European Community, as regards matters within its competence, of the agreements reached in the Uruguay Round multilateral negotiations, 1994 O.J. (L 336) 1, 11th recital in the preamble.

[59] *Portugal v. Council*, above note 55.

[60] *Id.* para. 48.

[61] *See* Case C-69/89, *Nakajima All Precision Co., Ltd. v. Council* [1991] E.C.R. I-2069, para. 31 [hereinafter *Nakajima v. Council*].

[62] *See* Case 70/87, *Féderation de l'industrie de l'huilerie de la CEE (Fediol) v. Commission* [1989] E.C.R. 1781, paras 19–22 [hereinafter *Fediol v. Commission*]. An application of this doctrine is Case C-89/99, *Schieving-Nijstad v. Groeneveld* [2001] E.C.R. I-340 (holding that Article 50.6 of the TRIPS Agreement must be respected by officials of EU/EC Member States).

The ECJ also has avoided giving direct effect to adopted WTO panel and appellate body reports.[63]

Thus, it would appear that the EC, like the United States, takes a purely dualistic approach to the WTO agreements and, while they are binding obligations for the EC,[64] their implementation is entirely through acts of transformation in the domestic legal order of the EC and Member States. The provisions of a WTO agreement may, accordingly, be invoked in EC law only if the Community act expressly refers to or incorporates such provisions.[65]

# 4. Japan

## 4.1 Overview of Japanese law

The Japanese Constitution provides that treaties and established international law should be given due respect.[66] The relevant constitutional provision has been interpreted to signify the supremacy of a treaty or customary international law.[67] Treaties and customary international law should, therefore, prevail over contrary domestic laws.[68] The GATT enjoyed treaty status in the Japanese legal system because it was signed by the Cabinet as a treaty and approved by the Diet. The WTO Agreement enjoys treaty status for the same reason. When a conflict arises between a

[63] *See, e.g.*, Case C-104/97P, *Atlanta AG v. Commission and Council* [1999] E.C.R. I-06983; Case T-254/97, *Fruchthandelsgesellschaft mbH Chemnitz v. Commission* [1999] E.C.R. II–2743.

[64] The EC is now bound as a party to the WTO. Even before this, the GATT was held to be binding on the Community. *See International Fruit Co.*, above note 54.

[65] *Fediol v. Commission*, above note 62; *Nakajima v. Council*, above note 61.

[66] KENPŌ [Japanese Constitution], Art. 98(2).

[67] *See, e.g.*, Yuji Iwasawa, *Constitutional Problems Involved in Implementing the Uruguay Round in Japan*, in IMPLEMENTING THE URUGUAY ROUND 137, 146 (John H. Jackson and Alan O. Sykes eds., 1997).

[68] *Japan v. Sakata*, 13 KEISHŪ [Sup. Ct. Crim. Cases Rep.] 3225 (Sup. Ct., 16 December 1959). In this case, a person was indicted for trespassing on a U.S. Air Force installation in Japan. The indictment was brought under the Criminal Special Measures Law (Law No. 138 of 1952), which provides for the punishment of anyone who trespasses on the property of U.S. bases in Japan, to implement the Status of Forces Agreement and the Security Treaty between the United States and Japan. The defendant's counsel argued that this law, the agreement and the treaty conflicted with Article 9 of the Constitution, which prohibits Japan from exercising military power for solving international conflicts. The court allowed the indictment to stand.

provision in a WTO agreement and a domestic law, the WTO provision should be interpreted as supreme.[69] What is doubtful, however, is whether the WTO agreements have direct effect in the Japanese legal order.[70]

In the *Kyoto Necktie* case,[71] the issue of direct effect of the GATT arose in connection with the 1976 Raw Silk Price Stabilization Law, which established a price-stabilization scheme for domestically produced raw silk.

To effectively operate this price-stabilization programme, it was necessary also to restrict the import of raw silk because the program would be disrupted if raw silk from abroad were allowed to come in freely when the domestic price was low. Thus, the law was amended to designate a government entity, the Silk Business Agency, as the sole importer of raw silk in Japan. This programme was designed to protect domestic raw silk producers, and the price of raw silk in Japan soared to about twice the world price.

But although raw silk imports were restricted, silk fabric imports were not. As a result, European manufacturers purchased raw silk in China and South Korea, the two major producing countries, and produced silk ties for sale in Japan at low prices.

Japanese fabric producers challenged the Raw Silk Price Stabilization Law under Article XVII:1(a) of the GATT, which stipulates that each contracting party agrees that a state-trading agency under its control should operate its transactions on the basis of commercial considerations only in terms of price, quality and availability. Article II:4 of the GATT also stipulates that, whenever a tariff concession under the GATT has been made for a commodity that is an object of state trading, a contracting party shall not sell the commodity in the domestic market at a price above the actual import price plus the applicable tariff.

The Japanese fabric producers argued that the Silk Business Agency was a state-trading agency, and since the agency was not allowed to sell imported raw silk in the domestic market below the stabilization price, the sales policy envisaged in the legislation violated GATT Articles II and XVII.

The Kyoto District Court rejected this argument and gave the following reasons for upholding the validity of the legislation:

> The exclusive importership and the price stabilization system under consideration . . . are designed to protect the business of raw silk producers from the pressure of imports for a while, and this has the same substance as the emergency measure permitted under

69 Iwasawa, above note 70, at 173.

70 *Id.*

71 *Endō v. Japan*, 530 Hanrei Taimuzu 265 (Kyoto Dist. Ct., 29 June 1984).

article XIX of the GATT. Even though it is reasonable to state that, judging from the nature of such an emergency measure, there should be a limit to the duration of it, such a limit should not be regarded as absolute. Since this duration should be decided in relation to the duration of the pressure of imports, article 12-13-2 of the law providing for enforcing the exclusive importer arrangement for a while cannot be regarded as unreasonable.

Regarding the effectiveness of GATT Articles in relation to domestic laws, the Court stated:

A violation of a provision of GATT pressures the country in default to rectify the violation by being confronted with a request from another member country for consultation and possible retaliatory measures. However, it cannot be interpreted to have more effect than this. Therefore, it cannot be held that the legislation in question is contrary to the GATT and null and void.

Thus, the Kyoto District Court denied the direct effect of the GATT in Japanese law and refused to apply the established principle of Japanese constitutional law that treaties may override statutes, even those enacted later in time. The plaintiffs appealed this judgment to both the Osaka High Court[72] and the Supreme Court,[73] but in both instances the appeal was summarily dismissed. The Supreme Court simply approved the reasoning of the lower court.[74]

The validity of the Court's holding on the relationship between the GATT and a domestic regulation is rather dubious. The Court held that the import restriction in question would be held lawful since the same kind of measure would be allowed under Article XIX of the GATT. However, Article XIX requires that a country invoking a safeguard measure find "serious injury" caused by an increase in imports. In this case, however, not only was "serious injury" not found, but there was no procedure in the law to find such an injury.

Moreover, the Court seems to imply that the fact that a domestic law is contrary to a provision of the GATT will not affect the validity of the law in Japan, although it may trigger a request for consultation or even retaliation by another GATT member country. This view seems to ignore the relevant provision of the Constitution, which provides that a treaty and established rules in international law should be accorded due respect, as well as the established legal interpretation in Japan that a treaty overrides a contrary

[72] Judgment of 25 November 1986, Osaka High Court, 634 Hantei 186.

[73] Judgment of 6 February 1990, Supreme Court, 36 Shomu Geppo 2242.

[74] *Id.* at 2245.

domestic law regardless of the order in which the treaty and the domestic law were enacted.[75]

Nevertheless, the decision of the Kyoto District Court in the *Chinese Silk* case is remarkably consistent with similar cases interpreting the GATT in the European Community and the United States.

[75] Kenpō, above note 66, Art. 98, para. 2.

# 6

# TARIFFS, QUOTAS, AND OTHER BARRIERS TO MARKET ACCESS

## 1. Introduction

Trade barriers still exist even in this age of "globalization". The WTO regularly examines and analyses the trade policies and trade barriers of WTO Members through the Trade Policy Review Mechanism.[1] In addition, major trading nations, such as the United States, the European Community, and Japan, regularly publish reports on barriers to market access maintained by their trading partners.[2] Even a cursory review of these reports is enough to reveal the great variety of trade barriers that remain.

Trade and market access barriers may be grouped into four categories.[3] The first, and most obvious, category consists of border measures maintained by governments. Such measures include tariffs, quotas, customs regulations, import licensing, and practices such as testing and certification. The second category consists of internal regulations and practices that have protective effects. Such regulations and practices are imposed by governments and can include regulations relating to products and services as well as their distribution and sale, subsidies, state-trading monopolies, government procurement policies, technical standards requirements, and health and safety measures. The third category consists of private business practices and customs, including restrictive business practices, social and cultural differences affecting business behaviour, and consumer preferences. The

[1] Trade Policy Review Mechanism, reprinted in WTO, THE LEGAL TEXTS: THE RESULTS OF THE URUGUAY ROUND OF MULTILATERAL TRADE NEGOTIATIONS 380 (1999).

[2] *See, e.g.*, U.S. TRADE REPRESENTATIVE, 2002 NATIONAL TRADE ESTIMATE REPORT ON FOREIGN TRADE BARRIERS (2002); EUROPEAN COMM'N, REPORT ON UNITED STATES BARRIERS TO TRADE AND INVESTMENT 2001 (2001); MINISTRY OF ECONOMY, TRADE AND INDUSTRY, JAPAN, 2001 REPORT ON THE WTO CONSISTENCY OF TRADE POLICIES BY MAJOR TRADING PARTNERS (2001).

[3] The following classification is a modified version of that adopted by John H. Jackson et al., LEGAL PROBLEMS OF INTERNATIONAL ECONOMIC RELATIONS 1206–10 (3d ed. 1995).

fourth category consists of barriers that stem from economic and structural characteristics of the importing country, such as government credit and investment policies, industrial policies, and macroeconomic policies that, for example, induce saving and constrain consumption.

WTO rules do not reach all these categories of obstacles to trade. Because of its nature as an international organization, the WTO has tended to concentrate on explicit and obvious governmentally imposed trade obstacles, such as tariffs, quotas and customs regulations and practices. In the later rounds of trade negotiation, however, notably the Tokyo and Uruguay Rounds, the WTO addressed less obvious governmental measures, such as import licensing, subsidies and technical barriers to trade. Nevertheless, many trade barriers remain outside the purview of WTO agreements. Some of these barriers may be remedied through the nullification or impairment complaint procedure that is part of the GATT/WTO regime. Other barriers remain beyond the reach of international remedies.[4]

## 2. Tariffs and customs rules

### 2.1 The nature of a tariff

A tariff is a tax on imported goods. There are three basic types of tariffs: (1) *ad valorem*; (2) specific; and (3) mixed. An *ad valorem* tariff is a tax that is a percentage of the value of an imported item. A specific tariff is a flat tax per imported item. A mixed tariff combines aspects of the *ad valorem* and specific tariffs. There are also tariff-rate quotas, or tariff-quotas, in which the tariff rate varies depending on the number of products already imported into the country. For example, the first one million imports may be subject to a nine-percent tariff, with all additional imports subject to a 40 per cent tariff.

### 2.2 Welfare effects of tariffs

The welfare effects of a tariff are well known. A tariff reduces the quantity of imports and moves the domestic market closer to its equilibrium without trade. Because the tariff raises the domestic price of the imported product, domestic sellers gain and domestic buyers lose. To determine the total welfare effects of a tariff, it is necessary to add (1) the change in consumer

[4] *See, e.g.*, Panel Report, *Japan — Film — Measures Affecting Consumer Photographic Film and Paper*, WT/DS44/R (adopted by the DSB on 22 April 1998).

surplus, which is usually negative; (2) the change in producer surplus, which is usually positive; and (3) the change in government revenue, which is positive. This calculation is usually a negative number, which represents the "deadweight loss" of the tariff.

A central purpose of the GATT is to reduce and bind tariffs. WTO Members bind tariff rates by including them in Schedules of Concession annexed to the GATT. Tariff bindings add security and predictability to the GATT/WTO system and are a central obligation thereof.[5]

Article II of the GATT is designed to protect the tariff bindings. Article II:1(a) of the GATT embodies this objective by obligating WTO Members to accord tariff "treatment no less favourable" than that provided for in their Schedules. Article II:1(b) provides that imported products shall be exempt from "ordinary customs duties" and "all other duties and charges of any kind" *in excess of* those notified in the Schedule submitted by a WTO Member.[6] The date as of which "other duties and charges" are bound under Article II is 15 April 1994.[7] Article II:1(b) has been interpreted to permit parties to "incorporate into their Schedules acts yielding rights under the General Agreement [on Tariffs and Trade] but not acts diminishing obligations under that Agreement".[8] A U.S. reservation in its Schedule of the right to impose quotas on sugar imports was, therefore, held to be an improper reservation because it constituted a violation of GATT Article XI:1.[9]

The Schedules are an integral part of the GATT.[10] A WTO Member may not impose a duty that is higher than that provided for its Schedule without compensating affected Members. A Member may, however, impose a duty that is less than that provided for in its Schedule. Schedules may not be

[5] *See Panel on Newsprint*, 20 November 1984, GATT B.I.S.D. (31st Supp.) at 114, para. 52, at 132 (1985).

[6] GATT Art. II:1(b). *See, e.g.*, Appellate Body Report, *Canada — Dairy*, paras 142–43 (affirming that Canada acted inconsistently with Article II:1(b) by restricting access to the tariff-rate quota for fluid milk to entries valued at less than C$20 when its Schedule placed no limit on the value of each importation); Appellate Body Report, *Argentina — Textiles and Apparel*, paras 55, 87(a) (finding that Argentina acted inconsistently with Article II:1(b) by applying a type of duty different from the type provided for in its Schedule, because the application thereof resulted in "ordinary customs duties" being levied in excess of those provided for in its Schedule).

[7] Understanding on the Interpretation of Article II:1(b) of the General Agreement on Tariffs and Trade 1994, reprinted in WTO, THE LEGAL TEXTS: THE RESULTS OF THE URUGUAY ROUND OF MULTILATERAL TRADE NEGOTIATIONS 19 (1999).

[8] *United States — Restriction on Imports of Sugar*, 22 June 1989, GATT B.I.S.D. (36th Supp.) at 331, para. 5.2 (1990).

[9] *Id.* para. 6.1, at 344.

[10] GATT Art. II:7.

changed unilaterally, either directly or indirectly.[11] Neither tariff reclassifications,[12] nor changes in the way currencies are converted,[13] nor changes in the methods of determining dutiable value[14] will be allowed to impair the value of trade concessions. Neither will currency revaluations be allowed to impair the value of such concessions.[15] In addition, import monopolies may not be operated to undercut tariff bindings.[16]

## 2.3 Tariff modifications

WTO rules include several provisions that allow WTO Members to modify their tariff Schedules. If a particular tariff binding is too onerous or politically difficult to maintain, a new binding or bindings may be negotiated. Opportunities for re-negotiation include the following:

1. Reopening negotiations after three years,[17]
2. Special circumstance negotiations,[18]
3. Re-negotiations by developing countries,[19]
4. Waiver,[20] and
5. A new round of trade negotiations.[21]

Tariffs may also be modified upon the occurrence of any one of the following circumstances or events:

1. Withdrawal of a WTO Member,[22]
2. Compensatory modifications as a result of the formation or entry into a regional economic union,[23]
3. Invocation of the escape clause,[24]

[11] *Panel on Newsprint*, above note 5, paras 50, 52 (finding that the EC acted inconsistently with Article II of the GATT 1947 by unilaterally reducing its duty-free tariff quota for most-favoured-nation suppliers on newsprint from 1.5 million tonnes to 500,000 tonnes).

[12] GATT Art. II:5.

[13] *Id.* Art. II:3.

[14] *Id.*

[15] *Id.* Art. II:6.

[16] *Id.* Art. II:4.

[17] *Id.* Art. XXVIII:1, :2, :3 and :5. A party may reserve the right of re-negotiation within the three-year period, as well, under paragraph 5.

[18] *Id.* Art. XXVIII:4.

[19] *Id.* Art. XVIII:7.

[20] *Id.* Art. XXV; WTO Agreement Art. IX.

[21] GATT Art. XXVIII *bis*.

[22] *Id.* Art. XXVII.

[23] *Id.* Art. XXIV:6.

[24] *Id.* Art. XIX.

4. Balance-of-payments difficulties,[25] and
5. Sanctions.[26]

Of course, nothing prevents a WTO Member from lowering tariffs unilaterally or as a result of bilateral negotiations. The GATT most-favoured-nation obligation (Article I), however, requires WTO Members to extend the benefit of such tariff concessions to all other Members.

## 2.4 Reclassification

International trade is facilitated if trading countries maintain similar systems of tariff classification. To this end, a Customs Cooperation Council (CCC) was established in 1950 by international agreement.[27] The CCC meets from time to time to consider and decide customs classification questions. Most WTO Members have adopted the Harmonized Commodity Description and Coding System of classification developed by the CCC.

Neither the GATT nor any other WTO Agreements mandate the adoption of any particular system of classification.[28] The GATT contains only vague injunctions that reclassifications may not impair the value of tariff concessions.[29] In general, three issues have arisen concerning tariff reclassifications.

First, if two WTO Members agree that a change in classification impairs a tariff concession but proper treatment cannot be accorded because of a decision of a court or other authority, the Members must negotiate a compensatory adjustment.[30]

Second, a reclassification may involve differentiating between "like" products only on the basis of their country of origin. This may constitute a violation of GATT Article I, which prohibits the discriminatory treatment of "like" products.[31]

---

[25] GATT Art. XII.

[26] *Id.* Art. XXIII.

[27] Convention Establishing a Customs Cooperation Council, Brussels, 15 December 1950, 157 U.N.T.S. 129 (entered into force 4 November 1952).

[28] *Spain — Tariff Treatment of Unroasted Coffee*, 11 June 1981, GATT B.I.S.D. (28th Supp.) at 102, para. 4.4 (1982).

[29] GATT Art. II:3 and II:5.

[30] *Id.* Art. II:5.

[31] *See Spain — Tariff Treatment of Unroasted Coffee*, above note 28, paras 4.4–4.10 (concluding that Spain's tariff sub-classification of unroasted coffee discriminated against unroasted coffee from Brazil in violation of GATT Article I:1). *But see Canada/Japan — Tariff on Imports of Spruce, Pine, Fir (SPF) Dimension Lumber*, 19 July 1989, GATT B.I.S.D. (36th Supp.) at 167 (1990) (upholding Japan's classification system for lumber of species of coniferous trees).

Third, difficult controversies may erupt when new products are developed.[32] Professor Jackson has previously concluded that new products must be deemed bound schedule items where the classification description under national law clearly covers them.[33]

Finally, even if there is not discrimination, a reclassification may deprive WTO Members of the value of trade concessions they reasonably expected. This is, in effect, an example of a measure that is not technically a violation but nevertheless nullifies or impairs a trade concession. In such a case, the aggrieved party has a right to appropriate redress.[34]

## 2.5 Valuation

Tariff values can be greatly skewed by differences or anomalies in the way the valuation of goods is calculated for customs purposes. To eliminate disparities among GATT contracting parties, a so-called Customs Valuation Code was negotiated in the Tokyo Round in 1979.[35] The WTO Valuation Agreement is entitled Agreement on Implementation of Article VII of the General Agreement on Tariffs and Trade 1994.

The Valuation Agreement sets forth five alternative measures of valuation. Generally, goods are to be assessed at their transaction value.[36] Transaction value is the price actually paid or payable for the goods, with adjustments for certain specified costs that are incurred but not reflected in the price, such as selling commissions, packing costs, royalties, license fees, and assets.[37]

---

[32] Greek Increase in Bound Duty, Report by the Group of Experts, GATT Doc. L/580 (9 November 1956).

[33] John H. Jackson, World Trade and the Law of the GATT 214 (1969).

[34] See *Treatment by Germany of Imports of Sardines*, 31 October 1952, GATT B.I.S.D. (1st Supp.) at 53, paras 17–18, at 59 (1953) (concluding that Germany's treatment of imports of sardines substantially reduced the value of the concessions obtained by Norway and, therefore, impaired a benefit accruing to Norway under the GATT). *But see* Appellate Body Report, *European Communities — Customs Classification of Certain Computer Equipment*, paras 107, 111(b) (concluding that the EC's reclassification of Local Area Network equipment by treating such equipment as telecommunications equipment instead of "automatic data processing" machines was consistent with GATT Article II:1); Appellate Body Report, *Canada — Dairy*, paras 125–143.

[35] Agreement on Implementation of Article VII of the General Agreement on Tariffs and Trade 1994, GATT B.I.S.D. (26th Supp.) at 116 (1980); Protocol to the Agreement on Implementation of Article VII of the General Agreement on Tariffs and Trade, GATT B.I.S.D. (26th Supp.) at 151 (1980).

[36] Valuation Agreement Art. 1.

[37] *Id.* Art. 1.

If the transaction value cannot be determined or used, generally because the sale is between related parties, other methods of valuation are specified according to the priority in which they must be used:

1. Transaction value of identical goods,[38]
2. Transaction value of similar goods,[39]
3. Deductive value (defined as the price at which the imported goods or identical or similar imported goods are sold in the greatest aggregate quantity to unrelated persons in the country of importation, with deductions for commissions or profit, general expenses, transport or insurance costs, customs duties and other costs incurred as a result of reselling the goods),[40] or
4. Computed value (determined by summing the cost of producing the good in the country of exportation including an amount for general expenses and profit and all other expenses).[41]

In a rare instance where value cannot be determined using any of these methods, the Valuation Agreement provides that the value is "determined using reasonable means consistent with the principles and general provisions of this Agreement".[42]

The Valuation Agreement eliminates previous valuation abuses, such as the use of the "American Selling Price" by the United States before 1979.[43] It does not, however, eliminate all valuation disparities.[44] For example, the United States utilizes an FOB (free on board) method of valuation for customs purposes, while most other WTO Members use a CIF (cost, insurance, freight) method. The use of an FOB valuation method results in lower U.S. tariff charges than those levied by other countries under identical tariff rates.[45]

---

[38] Valuation Agreement Art. 2.

[39] *Id.* Art. 3.

[40] *Id.* Art. 5.

[41] *Id.* Art. 6.

[42] *Id.* Art. 7.1. This prohibits basing valuation on the selling price in the country of importation of domestically produced goods.

[43] *Id.* Art. 7.2(a).

[44] For cases under the pre-WTO valuation rules, compare *Generra Sportswear Co. v. United States,* 905 F.2d 377 (Fed. Cir. 1990) (textile quota charges properly included in transaction value) with Case 7/83, *Ospig Textilgesellschaft KGW. Ahlers v. Hauptzollamt Bremen-Ost* [1984] E.C.R. 609 (quota charges not included in transaction value).

[45] It is argued that the use of CIF by the United States would be unconstitutional because Article I, section 9, of the U.S. Constitution forbids a preference to the ports of one state over

## 2.6 Rules of origin

Rules of origin are laws used by states to determine the country of origin of goods.[46] States can use rules of origin to implement discriminatory trade policies, such as applying higher tariff rates to imports from non-WTO Members, applying lower tariff rates to imports from free trade areas and certain developing countries, and applying antidumping or countervailing duties or safeguard measures. States can also use rules of origin to establish country-of-origin marking requirements for imported products. In addition, states can use rules of origin as barriers to trade.[47] There is, therefore, a need to adopt international rules on rule-of-origin determinations.

International rules address three categories of concern. First, the GATT permits WTO Members to maintain laws relating to marks of origin on imported products to protect consumers from false and misleading information.[48] Marks of origin may not, however, be discriminatory[49] or unreasonably burdensome.[50] Country-of-origin marking requirements that single out foreign goods may be found to violate GATT's national treatment provisions.[51] Marks of origin may not be misleading or allowed to work to the detriment of products with distinctive regional or geographic names.[52]

another and Article I, section 8, requires import duties to be uniform throughout the United States. Whether CIF valuation would violate the uniformity clause has never been decided.

[46] Agreement on Rules of Origin Art. I:1.

[47] *See, e.g.*, Joseph A. LaNasa III, *Rules of Origin and the Uruguay Round's Effectiveness in Harmonizing and Regulating Them*, 90 Am. J. Int'l L. 625, 626 (1996); Frederick P. Cantin and Andreas F. Lowenfeld, *Rules of Origin, The Canada-U.S. FTA and the Honda Case*, 87 Am. J. Int'l L. 375, 390 (1993).

[48] GATT Art. IX.

[49] *Id.* Art. IX:1.

[50] *Id.* Art. IX:4.

[51] *Id.* Art. III:4. *See also, e.g., Hawaii v. Ho*, 41 Hawaii 565, 571 (1957) (invalidating state law requiring sellers of imported eggs to display a placard bearing the words "we sell foreign eggs" as contrary to GATT Article III:4). Origin marking is not, however, normally required for domestic products. Origin marking under Article IX of the GATT is considered an exception to the national treatment obligations of Article III. *See* John H. Jackson, World Trade and the Law of GATT 461 (1969).

[52] GATT Art. IX:6.

Second, the Kyoto Convention provides that rule-of-origin requirements may not be unduly burdensome. This provision has done little to harmonize rules of origin or correct abuses.[53]

Finally, the WTO Agreement on Rules of Origin was entered into in the Uruguay Round to bring about harmonized rules of origin. The harmonized programme was developed by the WTO in cooperation with the Customs Cooperation Council. The resulting rules of origin must be objective and coherent and must apply equally for all purposes.[54] In general, the "last substantial transformation" test must be used to determine origin.[55] The WTO work programme to harmonize rules of origin is proceeding very slowly.[56]

Until the harmonized programme is completed, WTO Members are required to administer their current rules of origin observing the basic GATT principles of non-discrimination and transparency.[57] The rules of origin may not be instruments of trade policy or disruptive to international trade.[58] The rules of origin that apply to imports and exports may not be more burdensome than those that apply to domestic products.[59] The rules must be based on positive standards.[60] The rules may be implemented through criteria based on change of tariff classification, *ad valorem* percentage increase, or manufacturing or processing requirements.[61] The WTO dispute settlement procedures apply to rule-of-origin disputes.[62]

The adoption of rules of origin is left to the discretion of individual states. Rules of origin come into play most frequently when goods contain parts or components from various countries or are made from various imported materials. Rules of origin are devised especially to govern the case where materials imported from a less favourably treated state into a preference state undergo manufacturing operations before importation into the country of

---

53 International Convention on the Simplification and Harmonization of Customs Procedures, done at Kyoto, 18 May 1973, (entered into force 25 September 1974) [hereinafter Kyoto Convention].

54 Agreement on Rules of Origin Art. 1.2.

55 *Id.* Art. 3(b).

56 *See* Wim Keizer, *Negotiations on Harmonized Non-Preferential Rules of Origin — A Useless Task From a Trade Policy Perspective?*, 31 J. World Trade 145 (1997).

57 Agreement on Rules of Origin Art. 2.

58 *Id.* Art. 2(c).

59 *Id.* Art. 2(d).

60 *Id.* Art. 2(f).

61 *Id.* Art. 2(a).

62 *Id.* Arts. 7–8.

consumption. In this instance, variants of three primary origin rules are used to determine whether the preference state is the state of origin:

1. Did a tariff classification shift occur because of manufacturing operations?[63]
2. Did the manufacturing operations produce a "substantial transformation" in the sense of a change of name, character, and use?[64]
3. Did the manufacturing operations meet a stated percentage of value added in terms of labour and materials in the preference state?[65]

All three tests may be combined into a single rule,[66] and different tests may be used for different purposes.[67]

## 2.7 Customs laws and procedures

The GATT contains few rules concerning customs laws and procedures. Article X of the GATT generally requires (1) transparency through "prompt publication" of trade regulations; (2) the "uniform, impartial, and reasonable" administration of laws, regulations and decisions; and (3) the maintenance of judicial, arbitral or administrative tribunals to afford "prompt review and correction" of administrative actions concerning trade regulation. Numerous other GATT notification provisions further enhance transparency.[68]

Particular issues of customs laws and procedures are, for the most part, left to individual states within the framework of the Kyoto Convention (for those states that have accepted the Convention). The Kyoto Convention contains annexes that harmonize procedures for operations such as the clearance of goods for home use,[69] outward processing[70] of goods (whereby goods are improved or assembled abroad), and inward processing[71] (whereby goods are admitted for in-country processing before being exported). The Kyoto Convention generally allows "drawback," which is the rebate of 99 percent of

[63] This is the primary test used in the EU. *See* Ian S. Forrester, *EEC Customs Law: Rules of Origin and Preferential Duty Treatment*, 5 EUR. L. REV. 167 (1980).

[64] *See, e.g., SDI Technologies, Inc. v. United States*, 977 F. Supp. 1235 (Ct. Int'l Trade 1997).

[65] *E.g., Torrington Co. v. United States*, 764 F.2d 1563 (Fed. Cir. 1985).

[66] *See, e.g., Superior Wire v. United States*, 669 F. Supp. 472 (1987), *aff'd*, 867 F.2d 1409 (Fed. Cir. 1989).

[67] *See* RULES OF ORIGIN IN INTERNATIONAL TRADE: A COMPARATIVE STUDY (E. Vermulst et al. eds., 1994).

[68] These are listed in GUIDE TO GATT LAW AND PRACTICE, Vol. I, pp. 301–05.

[69] Kyoto Convention, above note 53, Annex B.1.

[70] *Id.* Annex E.8.

[71] *Id.* Annex E.6.

duties paid on imported merchandise upon the exportation of articles manufactured or produced with the use of that merchandise, provided the articles are exported within three years of import.[72] The Kyoto Convention also provides for the existence of customs warehouses,[73] which must be open to all importers, and free zones (foreign trade zones where goods may be stored or processed before formal customs entry).[74]

## 2.8 Customs fees and formalities

The GATT requires customs fees and charges to be limited to the approximate cost of services rendered.[75] Fees and charges that represent "indirect protection to domestic products or a taxation of imports" are prohibited.[76] This rule was applied in *United States — Customs User Fee*, in which a GATT panel held that the U.S. system of *ad valorem* fees caused fees to be levied in excess of the cost of services rendered.[77] The United States subsequently adopted a new fee structure to comply with GATT rules.[78]

Article VIII of the GATT sets out two additional general norms: (1) the complexity of customs formalities,[79] including the diversity of fees[80] is to be reduced; and (2) no party can impose "substantial" penalties for minor customs breaches.[81]

## 2.9 Preshipment inspection (PSI)

Preshipment inspection of goods in international trade has become increasingly common as developing country governments supplement their port-of-unloading customs inspections by requiring importers to employ private inspectors to verify price, quality, and other characteristics of goods in the country of origin. This is done for several reasons: to prevent over- or under-invoicing of imports, misclassification and under collection of tariffs by corruptible customs officials. As preshipment inspection has increased,

[72] Kyoto Convention Annex E.4.

[73] *Id.* Annex E.3.

[74] *Id.* Annex F.1.

[75] GATT Arts. II:2(c) and VIII:1(a).

[76] *Id.* Art. VIII:1(a).

[77] *United States — Customs User Fee*, 2 February 1988, GATT B.I.S.D. (35th Supp.) at 276–77 (1989).

[78] U.S. Customs and Trade Act of 1990, 19 U.S.C.A. § 58c.

[79] GATT Art. VIII:1(c).

[80] *Id.* Art. VIII:1(b).

[81] *Id.* Art. VIII:3.

complaints by exporters have risen, charging that preshipment inspection (PSI) has become a significant non-tariff barrier.[82]

To minimize hindrances to trade, the WTO Agreement on Preshipment Inspection specifies certain standards for preshipment inspection activities. Most importantly, pre-inspection entities must observe certain guidelines for price verification of goods.[83] Price comparisons may be made only to "the prices of identical or similar goods offered for export from the same country of exportation at or about the same time, under competitive and comparable conditions of sale, in conformity with customary commercial practices and not of any applicable standard discounts".[84]

In addition, WTO Members must assure that:

1. PSI activities are carried out in a non-discriminatory manner;
2. PSI inspections are performed in accordance with standards agreed between sellers and buyers or, in the absence of such standards, relevant international standards;
3. Conflicts of interest are avoided;
4. Confidential information is respected;
5. PSI activities are carried out in a transparent manner; and
6. PSI activities are conducted without unreasonable delay.

Disputes between PSI entities and exporters are to be resolved by mutual consent.[85] If this is impossible, either party may refer the matter for review to the Independent Entity administered by the WTO that will appoint a panel of three experts to decide the matter within eight working days.[86] The decision of the panel is binding upon the parties.[87]

## 3. Quotas

### 3.1 The nature of a quota

Quotas are numerical restrictions on imports or exports. Unlike tariffs, once the mandated quantity limit is reached, further units are barred. Quotas are

[82] *See generally* Kenneth P. Kansa, *A Cure Worse than the Disease*, 39 Va. J. Int'l L. 1152 (1999).

[83] PSI Agreement Art. 2.20.

[84] *Id.* Art. 2.20(b).

[85] *Id.* Art. 4.

[86] *Id.* Art. 4(e).

[87] *Id.* Art. 4(h).

usually expressed in terms of units of products rather than in terms of value. They are usually set on an annual basis. An import quota, by far the most common type, is an effective trade barrier because it limits the supply of usually cheaper imported goods, allowing more sales of domestic goods, thereby raising the overall price to consumers. How much the price exceeds the lower world market price depends on the stringency of the quota as well as market conditions.

## 3.2 Welfare effects of quotas

The welfare effects of quotas are essentially identical to those of tariffs. A quota increases the welfare of domestic producers and causes deadweight losses. A quota, by its nature, is more certain than a tariff in the effects it produces, because the importing country controls the number of imports. There is, however, one major difference between the two types of trade restrictions: a tariff raises revenue for the importing government, while an import quota creates revenue for foreign producers. The reason for this is that introducing a quota has the effect of raising the price of the imported product since, presumptively, consumer demand is unchanged while the number of goods available is less. This excess profit is not collected by the importing country but accrues to the foreign producers of the product.

## 3.3 Prohibition on quotas and other measures that restrain trade

The GATT prohibits quotas, import and export licenses, and any other measures that prohibit or restrict trade other than duties, taxes, and other charges.[88] This prohibition is set forth in Article XI of the GATT.

GATT Article XI:1, by its terms, reaches restrictions placed on the "importation" of products or the "exportation or sale for export" of any product. Thus, it is to be distinguished from GATT Article III (national treatment), which deals with *internal* requirements that apply to products after they have cleared customs.[89] Thus, Article XI applies to measures that affect the actual *importation* of products, while Article III deals with measures *affecting* imported products. There is some confusion, however, between Article XI:1

[88] GATT Art. XI.

[89] *Canada — Administration of the Foreign Investment Review Act*, 7 February 1984, GATT B.I.S.D. (30th Supp.) at 140, para. 5.14 (1984). *See also Lobsters from Canada*, USA-89–1807–01 (U.S.-Canada FTA Ch. 18 decision), 3 Can. Trade & Commodity Tax Cas. (CCH) 8182 (1990).

and Article III, because *Ad* Article III states that a measure "enforced or collected in the case of an imported product at the time or point of importation" can be regarded, if appropriate, as an internal measure. The difference between the two Articles can be crucial, because Article III permits internal measures that are non-discriminatory as between domestic and imported products, while Article XI:1 prohibits quotas, import and export licenses and any other measures that restrain trade other than duties, taxes, and other charges. It is, for example, permissible to enforce a size limitation on imported lobsters equal to that imposed on domestically caught lobsters. Size is an internal regulation even though it is enforced on importation.[90] It is not permissible, however, to ban imported tuna because of the way it is harvested (without regard to dolphin mortality). This ban is an impermissible import measure and not an internal regulation because the *product as such* is unaffected by a requirement relating to the way in which it is harvested or produced.[91] Distinguishing between Article III and Article XI may be difficult in some cases, as these examples show.[92]

Article XI:1 reaches not only quotas[93] but also "other measures" that restrict imports. "Other measures" can refer to virtually any requirement or regulation designed to inhibit imports or exports. Thus, data collection and monitoring requirements,[94] minimum price systems,[95] prohibiting importation of copyrighted works not manufactured domestically,[96] requiring security deposits,[97] and prohibiting imports not produced in a certain way[98] have all been held to run afoul of Article XI:1.

---

[90] *See Lobsters from Canada*, above note 89.

[91] *United States — Restrictions on Imports of Tuna*, GATT B.I.S.D. (39th Supp.) at 155, paras 5.14–5.15, at 195 (1993), reprinted in 30 I.L.M. 1594 (1991) (unadopted).

[92] *See Canada — Import, Distribution and Sale of Certain Alcoholic Drinks by Provincial Marketing Agencies*, 18 February 1992, GATT B.I.S.D. (39th Supp.) at 27 (1993) (holding that package size limits for beer are subject to GATT Article III:4).

[93] *Japan — Restrictions on Imports of Certain Agricultural Products* is a case of traditional quotas that violate Article XI:1. *Japan — Restrictions on Imports of Certain Agricultural Products*, 22 March 1988, GATT B.I.S.D. (35th Supp.) at 163 (1989). Article XI:1 also covers tariff quotas. *See* Appellate Body Report, *European Communities — Bananas*, para. 194.

[94] *Japan — Trade in Semi-Conductors*, 4 May 1988, GATT B.I.S.D. (35th Supp.) at 116, para. 132, at 162 (1989).

[95] *Id.*

[96] United States Manufacturing Clause, 15–16 May 1984, GATT B.I.S.D. (31st Supp.) at 74 (1985).

[97] *EEC — Programme of Minimum Import Prices, Licenses and Surety Deposits for Certain Processed Fruits and Vegetables*, 18 October 1978, GATT B.I.S.D. (25th Supp.) at 68 (1979).

[98] *Id.*

Article XI:1 also reaches quotas and other measures without regard to the way they are enforced or made effective. Thus, it does not matter if the restrictions in question are enforced in the traditional way, namely, through customs regulation, or if they are enforced in other ways, such as through state-trading companies or import monopolies.[99] Article XI:1 reaches measures that are not legally enforceable if they meet two criteria: (1) there are reasonable grounds to believe that sufficient incentives or disincentives existed for the non-mandatory measures to take effect; and (2) the operation of the measures is essentially dependent on government action.[100]

It is not necessary to show the operation of the quotas or other measures has an effect on trade. Article XI:1 has been interpreted to establish conditions of competition; a quota or other measure will be illegal even if there is no actual effect on trade.[101]

## 3.4 Exceptions to the prohibition on quotas and other measures

There are three exceptions to the general prohibition on quotas and other measures described above.

The first exception permits WTO Members to apply "[e]xport prohibitions or restrictions temporarily . . . to prevent or relieve critical shortages of foodstuffs or other products essential to the exporting . . . party".[102] WTO Members may, therefore, prohibit or restrict exports of a product provided the product is "essential" to that country and the prohibition or restriction is applied temporarily with the objective of preventing or relieving critical shortages of that product.[103]

The second exception permits WTO Members to apply "[i]mport or export prohibitions or restrictions necessary to the application of standards or regulations for the classification, grading or marketing of commodities in international trade".[104] WTO Members may, therefore, prohibit or restrict

[99] *E.g., Canada — Import, Distribution and Sale of Alcoholic Drinks by Canadian Provincial Marketing Agencies*, 22 March 1988, GATT B.I.S.D. (35th Supp.) at 37 (1989); *Canada — Import, Distribution and Sale of Certain Alcoholic Drinks by Provincial Marketing Agencies*, above note 92.

[100] *See Japan — Trade in Semi-Conductors*, above note 94.

[101] *European Economic Community — Payments and Subsidies to Processors and Producers of Oilseeds and Related Animal-Feed Proteins*, 25 January 1990, GATT B.I.S.D. (37th Supp.) at 86 (1991).

[102] GATT Art. XI:2(a).

[103] Guide to GATT Law and Practice, Vol. I, p. 326.

[104] GATT Art. XI:2(b).

imports or exports provided the prohibition or restriction is related to the application of standards or regulations for the classification, grading, or marketing of commodities in international trade and does not go beyond what is "necessary" for the application of those standards or regulations.[105]

The third exception permits WTO Members to apply "[i]mport restrictions on any agricultural or fisheries product... necessary to the enforcement of governmental measures" that:

1. Restrict the marketing or production of the "like" domestic product (or a directly substitutable product if there is no substantial production of the like product);
2. Remove a temporary surplus of a like domestic product (or a directly substitutable product if there is no substantial production of the like product) by making the surplus available to certain groups of domestic consumers free of charge or at prices below the current market level; or
3. Restrict production of any animal product that is directly dependent on the imported commodity, if the domestic production of that commodity is relatively negligible.[106]

This exception allows WTO Members to ensure that imports of agricultural or fisheries products do not interfere with domestic governmental programmes designed to support or allocate agricultural or fish production. Unlike the other two exceptions, this exception does not permit the prohibition of imports but only their restriction. WTO Members restricting imports must give public notice of the total quantity restricted.[107] WTO Members restricting imports of products necessary to the enforcement of a domestic marketing or production restriction must ensure that the import restriction does not reduce the proportion of imports relative to the total of domestic production.[108] As at the time of writing, governmental measures have never been justified under any of these exceptions.[109]

---

[105] *Canada — Measures Affecting Exports of Unprocessed Herring and Salmon*, 22 March 1988, GATT B.I.S.D. (35th Supp.) at 98, para. 4.2, at 112 (1989) (restrictions on export not justified by GATT Art. XI:2(b)).

[106] GATT Art. XI:2(c).

[107] *Id.* Art. XI:2, last subparagraph.

[108] *Id.*

[109] *Canada — Import Restrictions on Ice Cream and Yoghurt*, 5 December 1989, GATT B.I.S.D. (36th Supp.) at 68, para. 84 (1990) (concluding that Canada's import restrictions on ice cream and yoghurt were inconsistent with Article XI:1 and could not be justified under Article

In addition to these three exceptions, another exception from the general prohibition on quotas and other measures is contained in GATT Article XII, which allows restrictions to safeguard balance of payments. This matter is considered in Chapter 9.

Additional exceptions are contained in Article XX (General Exceptions) and Article XXI (Security Exceptions) of the GATT. Moreover, the scope of the Escape Clause (Article XIX of the GATT) must be considered to determine whether the escape clause is another exception.[110]

In the past, important exceptions were granted through waivers[111] under GATT Article XXV, but this is unlikely in the future, because waivers are more difficult to obtain under the WTO than under the GATT.[112]

## 3.5 Licensing

A traditional way of administering quotas is import or export licensing. Import licensing is governed by the Agreement on Import Licensing Procedures (Licensing Agreement).[113] The Licensing Agreement is designed to minimize the trade impact of the procedural aspects of licensing where it is permitted under the GATT. Import licensing must be "neutral in application and administered in a fair and equitable manner".[114] Forms and procedures must be simplified, and licensing rules must be transparent. Consideration may be given in allocating licenses to an applicant's past performance, but there must be a reasonable distribution of licenses to new

XI:2(c)(i) because ice cream and yoghurt are not "like" products to Canadian raw milk and the import restriction on ice cream and yoghurt is not necessary to the enforcement of the Canadian programme for raw milk); *Japan — Restrictions on Imports of Certain Agricultural Products*, above note 93, paras 6.2–6.8, at 243–45 (holding that Japan's import restrictions on agricultural products violate GATT Art. XI:1). *See also European Economic Community — Restrictions on Imports of Dessert Apples* — Complaint by Chile, 22 June 1989, GATT B.I.S.D. (36th Supp.) at 93 (1990); *European Economic Community — Restrictions on Imports of Apples* — Complaint by the United States, 22 June 1989, GATT B.I.S.D. (36th Supp.) at 135 (1990).

[110] *See* Chapter 9.

[111] *E.g.*, Waiver Granted to the United States in Connection with Import Restrictions Imposed Under Section 22 of the Agricultural Adjustment Act (of 1933), as Amended, 5 March 1955, GATT B.I.S.D. (3d Supp.) at 32 (1955).

[112] There now are additional restrictions on waivers. *See* Chapter 1.

[113] Agreement on Import Licensing Procedures, reprinted in WTO, The Legal Texts: The Results of the Uruguay Round of Multilateral Trade Negotiations 223 (1999) [hereinafter Licensing Agreement].

[114] Licensing Agreement Art. 1.3; *see also* Appellate Body Report, *EC—Bananas*, paras 197, 203.

importers, particularly those from developing countries. A Committee on Import Licensing administers the Agreement.

## 4. State-trading enterprises

State-trading enterprises pose what is sometimes called an "interface" problem in international trade. This refers to the fact that the GATT/WTO is founded on principles of free trade in free markets. State trading can easily disrupt or take advantage of this by tilting trade flows.[115] For example, a state monopoly can discriminate between different country markets, adopt artificial prices that are substitutes for tariffs, adopt quotas for imports or exports, and assure more favourable treatment for domestic products by adopting whatever regulations it wants for the distribution and sale of imports. In this way state trading can subvert normal trade concessions in the form of tariff reductions.

To deal with these problems, the GATT addresses state-trading enterprises in several provisions, principally in Article XVII. Although state trading is primarily associated with "non-market economy" states (i.e., states with economic systems based on socialism or communism), Article XVII defines state-trading enterprises in broader terms. Article XVII:1(a) defines "state-trading enterprise" to include any enterprise that benefits, whether formally or *de facto*, from "exclusive or special privileges". This definition includes not only state-owned enterprises as such, but also import or export monopolies and marketing boards. Article XVII would therefore appear to reach, in non-market economy states, private companies under state-planning controls as well as state-owned or state-benefited companies in market-economy states.[116]

In 1999 the WTO Goods Council adopted an Illustrative List of Relationships Between Governments and State Trading Enterprises[117] that broadly defines state trading company activities subject to GATT Article XVII. Such enterprises may be governmental or non-governmental entities; granted exclusive or special rights or privileges; and which influence through purchases or sales the level or direction of exports and imports.

[115] This possibility is explicitly recognized in GATT Art. XVII:3.

[116] An important exclusion is enterprises that buy goods for immediate or ultimate consumption in governmental use. GATT Art. XVII:2.

[117] Adopted, October 15, 1999.

All enterprises covered by Article XVII have a duty of transparency. Article XVII:4 and the 1994 Understanding on the Interpretation of Article XVII of the General Agreement on Tariffs and Trade 1994[118] require notification of state-trading enterprises. Notification must include discussion of their need, practices, and operations. The level of notification must "ensure the maximum transparency possible".[119] The notifications and counter-notifications must be reviewed by the WTO Council for Trade in Goods,[120] which has the power to make recommendations on the "adequacy of notifications and the need for further information".[121]

State-trading enterprises are held to three overriding substantive norms: (1) in purchases or sales involving imports or exports, they must "act in a manner consistent with the general principles of non-discriminatory treatment prescribed in [the GATT] for governmental measures affecting imports or exports by private traders"[122]; (2) they must make such purchases or sales "solely in accordance with commercial considerations, including price, quality, availability, marketability, transportation and other conditions of purchase or sale"[123]; and (3) they must "afford the [other] enterprises . . . adequate opportunity, in accordance with customary business practice, to compete for . . . such purchases or sales".[124]

Thus, the effect of the GATT/WTO system is to accept the existence of state-trading enterprises but to compel them to follow, in general, the economic policies of private companies and adhere to the same normative standards as private companies. There is a substantial question as to whether this policy is realistic. At the same time, under the regime of the GATT, this policy was not severely tested or challenged, because the larger non-market economy states were not parties to the agreement and because of the general economic movement toward the privatization of enterprises.

The norms applicable to state-trading enterprises should be examined closely in five areas. First, in the area of tariffs, it is clear that Schedules of Concession are intended to cover products in which state-trading enterprises are involved. The GATT addresses this explicitly by stating that authorized import monopolies (e.g., state-trading enterprises) "must not

[118] Understanding on the Interpretation of Article XVII of the General Agreement on Tariffs and Trade 1994, reprinted in WTO, The Legal Texts: The Results of the Uruguay Round of Multilateral Trade Negotiations 20 (1999).

[119] *Id.* para. 2.

[120] *Id.* para. 5.

[121] *Id.*

[122] GATT Art. XVII:1(a).

[123] *Id.* Art. XVII:1(b).

[124] *Id.*

afford protection on the average in excess of the amount of protection provided in [the] Schedule".[125] In addition, the GATT provides that import monopolies dealing in products that are *not* the subject of Article II concessions must disclose their import mark-up.[126]

Second, state-trading enterprises must adhere to the most-favoured-nation obligation of Article I of the GATT. It would seem that compliance with Article I is strictly required. There is no derogation from this obligation, and this would seem to be the purpose of the broad requirement in Article XVII to adhere strictly to "commercial considerations".[127] Moreover, state-trading enterprises must adhere to the same "general principles" of non-discriminatary treatment norms applicable to private traders.[128]

Third, it is unclear whether Article XVII embodies the national treatment obligation of Article III. One GATT panel report contains dicta that there is "force" in the argument that "only the most-favoured-nation and not the national treatment obligations fall within the scope of the general principles referred to in Article XVII:1(a)".[129] This view, however, seems erroneous given that this Article, by its terms, requires unqualified adherence to non-discrimination norms. Moreover, other GATT panel decisions have applied Article III national treatment principles to state-trading enterprises.[130]

Fourth, state-trading enterprises are subject to the prohibition on "quotas, import or export licenses or other measures" in Article XI:1 of the GATT. In the 1988 panel report, *Japan — Restrictions on Imports of Certain Agricultural Products*,[131] the GATT panel concluded that Article XI:1 applied to import restrictions made effective through an import monopoly because it is comprehensive and because *Ad* Articles XI, XII, XIII, XIV, and XVIII (i.e., the interpretive notes to these Articles) provide

[125] *Id.* Art. II:4.

[126] *Id.* Art. XVII:4(b).

[127] *Id.*

[128] *Id.* Art. XVII:1(a). Some scholars, however, disagree with this view. *See* Jackson et al., above note 3, at 1144 (arguing that the GATT preparatory work favours a "modified or relaxed form of most-favored-nation treatment," relying also on the fact that Article XVII:1(b) is qualified by the phrase "in accordance with customary business practice").

[129] *Canada — Administration of the Foreign Investment Review Act*, 7 February 1984, GATT B.I.S.D. (30th Supp.) at 140, paras 5.15–5.18, at 163–64 (1984).

[130] *E.g., Canada — Import, Distribution and Sale of Certain Alcoholic Drinks by Provincial Marketing Agencies*, above note 92, paras 5.10–5.16, at 77–80; *Canada — Import, Distribution and Sale of Alcoholic Drinks by Canadian Provincial Marketing Agencies*, above note 99, para. 4.26, at 90.

[131] *Japan — Restrictions on Imports of Certain Agricultural Products*, above note 93, paras 5.2.2.1–5.2.2.2, at 229.

that the terms "import restrictions" and "export restrictions" used in these Articles include restrictions made effective through state-trading enterprises.

Finally, there is no special treatment or derogation granted to state-trading enterprises with respect to subsidies or dumping norms,[132] although practical problems of implementation of antidumping norms may occur if market forces do not determine prices.

## 5. Technical barriers to trade

Every state imposes technical regulations. Technical regulations are requirements to which the characteristics of products must conform. Technical regulations can be trade barriers in three ways. First, a regulation can be unrealistic or unreasonable. Second, even if individual regulations are reasonable, their sheer number can constitute a barrier to trade for companies that want to sell products in many different states. Finally, the procedures for verifying compliance with technical regulations can themselves be barriers to trade, because of either the nature of testing and certification or the proliferation of testing procedures in many different states.

To deal with these problems, the WTO administers an Agreement on Technical Barriers to Trade (TBT Agreement), which seeks to strike a balance between allowing states the freedom to set such regulations and requiring some discipline to minimize their trade effects. The TBT Agreement applies to technical regulations. The term "technical regulation" is defined as *mandatory* laws or provisions specifying the characteristics of products, the processes or production methods for creating products or the terminology, symbols, packaging, marking, or labelling requirements for products.[133]

The TBT Agreement requires WTO Members to apply national treatment and MFN standards with respect to technical regulations.[134] It also requires WTO Members to use international standards when such standards are available, except when such standards "would be an ineffective or inappropriate means for the fulfilment of the legitimate objectives pursued".[135]

In addition to these requirements, WTO Members adopting technical regulations:

---

[132] These are contained generally in Article VI of the GATT 1994 and in the subsidies and antidumping agreements. *See generally* Chapters 12 and 13.

[133] TBT Agreement Annex 1, para. 1. For more complete treatment, *see* Chapter 18.

[134] *Id.* Art. 2.1.

[135] *Id.* Art. 2.4.

1. Must assure transparency, promptly publish technical regulations, and make them generally available.[136]
2. Must not adopt technical regulations that create "unnecessary obstacles to international trade" or are "more trade-restrictive than necessary to fulfil a legitimate objective, taking account of the risks non-fulfilment would create".[137] Such legitimate objectives include "national security requirements; the prevention of deceptive practices; [and] protection of human health or safety, animal or plant life or health, or the environment".[138]
3. Must justify the adoption of any technical regulation that has a significant effect on the trade of another Member.[139]

The TBT Agreement also contains a Code of Good Practice for the Preparation, Adoption and Application of Standards.[140] The term "standard" is defined as a *voluntary* guideline for the characteristics of products.[141] This Code of Good Practice requires WTO Members to participate in and comply with standards codes being formulated by international bodies, such as the International Office for Standardization (ISO) in Geneva.[142]

National conformity assessment procedures for compliance with regulations and standards must not be more strict than necessary and must be transparent and promptly conducted.

A WTO Committee on Technical Barriers administers the TBT Agreement. TBT determinations are subject to WTO dispute settlement procedures.

## 6. Sanitary and phytosanitary measures

Health and safety measures can be barriers to trade. Such measures are called sanitary and phytosanitary measures (SPS measures). The WTO Agreement on the Application of Sanitary and Phytosanitary Measures

136 *Id.* Art. 2.9–2.12. 137 *Id.* Art. 2.2. 138 *Id.* Art. 2.2. 139 *Id.* Art. 2.5.

140 *Id.* Annex 3.

141 *Id.* Annex 1, para. 2.

142 *See also* Decision on Proposed Understanding on WTO-ISO Standards Information System, reprinted in WTO, THE LEGAL TEXTS: THE RESULTS OF THE URUGUAY ROUND OF MULTILATERAL TRADE NEGOTIATIONS 395 (1999); Decision on Review of the ISO/IEC Information Centre Publication, reprinted in WTO, THE LEGAL TEXTS: THE RESULTS OF THE URUGUAY ROUND OF MULTILATERAL TRADE NEGOTIATIONS 396 (1999).

(SPS Agreement) applies to SPS measures and is intended to complement the TBT Agreement. The SPS Agreement sets out more detailed international criteria for SPS measures, which are defined as measures designed:

> (a) to protect animal or plant life or health . . . from risks arising from the entry, establishment or spread of pests, diseases, disease-carrying organisms or disease-causing organisms;
> (b) to protect human or animal life or health . . . from risks arising from additives, contaminants, toxins or disease-causing organisms in foods, beverages or feedstuffs;
> (c) to protect human life or health . . . from risks arising from diseases carried by animals, plants or products thereof, or from the entry, establishment or spread of pests; or
> (d) to prevent or limit other damage . . . from the entry, establishment or spread of pests.[143]

SPS measures include all laws, decrees, regulations, requirements, and procedures relating to products, processes, and production methods.[144]

The SPS Agreement calls for SPS measures to be harmonized "on as wide a basis as possible" and based on international standards, guidelines, or recommendations, where they exist.[145] WTO Members may maintain SPS measures based "on a higher level" of protection, however, provided:

1. They are "based on scientific principles and not maintained without sufficient scientific evidence" (except provisionally)[146];
2. They do not discriminate "arbitrarily or unjustifiably" with respect to both the national treatment and MFN obligations[147]; and
3. They are justified (a) by scientific evidence, or (b) by carrying out an assessment of risk to determine the "appropriate level" of protection. A risk assessment must take into account relevant factors, including the objective of minimizing negative trade effects. The resulting SPS measure must not be more trade restrictive than necessary to achieve the appropriate level of SPS protection.[148]

A WTO Committee on Sanitary and Phytosanitary Measures administers the SPS Agreement. SPS determinations are subject to WTO procedures for the resolution of disputes.

[143] SPS Agreement Annex A, paras 1(a)–(d).

[144] *Id.* para. 1.

[145] SPS Agreement Art. 3.1.

[146] *Id.* Arts. 2.3 and 5.7.

[147] *Id.* Art. 2.3.

[148] *Id.* Arts. 3.3 and 5. Three WTO dispute settlement cases have involved these issues. *See* Chapter 18.

# 7. Sectoral market access agreements

In the history of the GATT, certain economic sectors received special treatment due to special problems or political sensitivity. This tradition was carried over to the WTO, which administers several agreements that create special regimes and rules applicable only to certain market sectors. These agreements cover sectors such as agriculture, textiles and clothing, and information technology. E-commerce has more recently emerged as a sector that merits special treatment.

## 7.1 Agriculture

Agriculture is a sensitive topic in virtually every country. In general, agricultural products are easily exported, so the potential for trade is vast. Yet, every country seeks to maximize economic advantages for its own agricultural sector for social, economic, and political reasons. Thus, agricultural trade has been a topic of almost continuous negotiations[149] and was singled out for special treatment even in the GATT 1947.[150]

Under the GATT, the agricultural sector was bedevilled by the twin problems of protectionism and export subsidies. Both were the subjects of important panel decisions under the GATT dispute settlement regime.[151] Agriculture was a major topic of negotiations during the Uruguay Round, and agreement of sorts (sometimes on ambiguous terms) was reached on the major issues and primarily embodied in the WTO Agreement on Subsidies and Countervailing Measures[152] and the WTO Agreement on Agriculture (Agriculture Agreement).

### *7.1.1 Basic obligations*

The Agriculture Agreement initiates "a process of reform of trade in agriculture"[153] intended to culminate in a market-oriented trading regime that is as

[149] *See* GATT AND TRADE LIBERALIZATION IN AGRICULTURE (M. Honma et al. eds., 1993); Robert L. Paarlberg FIXING FARM TRADE (1992).

[150] GATT Art. XI:2. *See* above discussion in this chapter.

[151] Most of these decisions concerned the GATT subsidy regime that preceded the Uruguay Round. *See, e.g., French Assistance to Exports of Wheat and Wheat Flour*, 21 November 1958, GATT B.I.S.D. (7th Supp.) at 46 (1959); *European Economic Community — Subsidies on Exports of Wheat Flour*, SCM/42, 21 March 1983 (1985) (unadopted); *European Economic Community — Subsidies on Exports of Pasta Products*, 19 May 1983 (1985) (unadopted).

[152] *See* Chapter 12 for a discussion of this agreement.

[153] Agriculture Agreement, preamble.

free as possible from restrictions and distortions. This process progressively integrates international trade in agricultural products into the GATT system. The basic obligations under the Agriculture Agreement are as follows:

1. *Market Access:* WTO Members agreed to convert existing quotas, levies and other non-tariff barriers into equivalent customs tariffs.[154] This process of "tariffication" allows agricultural tariff rates to be incorporated into the Schedules of Concessions each Member is required to deposit under GATT Article II. Tariff rates will also be reduced during an agreed implementation period, an average of 36 percent for developed countries and 24 percent for developing countries. Minimum tariff cuts per product were also agreed: 15 percent for developed and 10 percent for developing countries. With few exceptions, agricultural tariffs are now "bound" under GATT Article II.

In order to increase market access for agricultural products, the rule under the Agriculture Agreement is now "tariffs only". Such tariffs can be quite high and provide protection that is roughly equivalent to previous non-tariff market barriers, but tariffs are more transparent and can be more easily negotiated downwards in the future. In order to assure that this tariffication would not block pre-WTO imports, a system of "tariff quotas" is required: lower tariff rates for specific quantities and higher (often much higher) rates for quantities that exceed the quota.

2. *Domestic Support:* Domestic agricultural support programmes that can distort trade are brought under international discipline. During the phase-in period that ended on 31 December 2000, developed states agreed to reduce their "aggregate measurement of support" by 20 percent.[155] Developing countries agreed to reduce theirs by 13.3 percent over a ten-year period ending on 31 December 2004.[156] Least-developed countries do not need to reduce theirs at all.[157] Certain types of domestic support programmes are exempt that do not have the effect of providing price supports to producers, such as extension and advisory services, food

[154] Agriculture Agreement Art. 4. Most WTO Members have chosen to replace quotas with tariff-rate quotas.

[155] *Id.* Art. 1. The Aggregate Measurement of Support (AMS) is defined as the average of total non-exempt agricultural subsidies during the years of 1986 to 1988, inclusive. *Id.* Annex 3; *see also id.* Annex 4.

[156] *Id.* Art. 15.2. The issue of whether South Korea, as a developing country, had exceeded its AMS obligation was raised by the United States in the *Korean Beef* case. However, the Appellate Body concluded that there was no way to tell whether Korea had exceeded its commitment levels. *See* Report of the Appellate Body, *Korea — Beef*, paras 99–104.

[157] *Id.*

security, and domestic food aid, direct payments to producers, participation in social or crop disaster insurance, structural adjustment assistance, environmental protection, and regional assistance programmes.[158]
3. *Export Subsidies:* Export subsidies will be reduced by developed states an average of 36 percent by value (financial outlay) and 21 percent by volume (subsidized quantities) and by developing states an average of 24 percent by value and 14 percent by volume.[159]
4. *Safeguards:* There are special safeguard (SSG) provisions in the Agriculture Agreement that allow WTO Members to take special emergency action to restrict imports in cases of (a) import surges (when imports of a product exceed a certain trigger level) and (2) falling prices (when the price of a product falls below a certain trigger level).[160] There are technical rules in the Agreement that limit the extent and duration of SSG measures.[161] Members using SSG measures cannot also have recourse to ordinary safeguard measures otherwise permitted under GATT Article XIX.[162]

The Agriculture Agreement provides an implementation period of six years (ten years for developing countries) for reducing tariffs and phasing out impermissible domestic support measures and export subsidies.[163]

### *7.1.2 Tariffication*

The tariffication requirement under the market access commitment has proceeded remarkably smoothly. Article 4.2 of the Agreement ensures against lapses by forbidding any "resort to" non-tariff barriers, which are stated to "include quantitative import restrictions, variable import levies, minimum import prices, discretionary import licensing, non-tariff measures

158 *Id.* Art. 6 and Annex 2. The exempt subsidies are commonly referred to as "green box" and "blue box" subsidies. "Green box" subsidies are listed in Annex 2 of the Agriculture Agreement: important examples include research, infrastructure, damage control, domestic food aid and extension, training, and advisory services. "Blue box" subsidies are listed in Article 6: (1) certain developing country subsidies designed to encourage agricultural production; (2) certain "*de minimis*" subsidies; and (3) certain direct payments aimed at limiting agricultural production. Subsidies that are permissible but subject to limits are called "amber" subsidies. There are no "red" or prohibited subsidies under the Agriculture Agreement.

159 *Id.* Art. 1(e).

160 *Id.* Art. 5.1.

161 *Id.* Art. 5.7

162 *Id.* Art. 5.8.

163 *Id.* Art. 9.

maintained through state trading enterprises, voluntary export restraints, and similar border measures other than ordinary customs duties".

This provision was tested in the *Chile — Price Band*[164] case, which involved a flexible tariff system imposed by Chile on imports of certain agricultural goods. Under the Price Band system, Chile fixed an upper and lower threshold price for imports based upon international prices. Tariffs are calculated based upon reference prices: if reference prices fall duties are increased; if reference prices increase, importers are granted a tariff rebate.

Argentina challenged this system under Article 4.2. Chile modified the Price Band system so that tariffs were capped and could not exceed the GATT-bound rate.

The Appellate Body ruled that Article 4.2 of the Agreement on Agriculture imposes an obligation that is separate and distinct from GATT Article II:1(b), which relates to the tariff binding.[165] It further ruled that the Price Band system was inconsistent with Article 4.2 because it operated as a border measure similar to variable import levies setting minimum import prices. Under Article 4.2 only "ordinary customs duties" are permitted.[166]

### *7.1.3 Subsidies*

The Agriculture Agreement contains a "due restraint" or "peace" clause restricting legal action including countervailing duty proceedings that might otherwise be brought under the SCM Agreement. This "peace" clause expires at the end of 2004.[167]

The types of export subsidies subject to the Agreement on Agriculture are listed with great specificity in Article 9.1: (a) direct subsidies, including payments in kind; (b) the sale or disposal for export of agricultural products at a lower than market price; (c) payments on export that are financed by virtue of government action, such as levies on derived products or the products concerned; (d) provisional subsidies to reduce marketing costs; (e) favourable or reduced transport charges; and (f) subsidies on agricultural products contingent on their incorporation in exported products. In addition, Article 10 of the Agreement covers circumvention of export subsidy commitments, stating that "export subsidies not listed in [Article 9.1] shall not be applied in a manner which results in . . . circumventing of export subsidy commit-

[164] Report of the Appellate Body, *Chile — Price Band System and Safeguard Measures Relating to Certain Agricultural Products* (AB 2002–2), 23 September 2002, WT/DS207/AB/R.

[165] *Id.* p. 190. [166] *Id.* p. 262. [167] *Id.* Art. 13.

ments". In *Canada — Dairy*,[168] a WTO panel and the Appellate Body ruled that Canada's Special Milk Classes Scheme was a prohibited export subsidy under Article 9.1. Under this Scheme, the government set the prices for milk used in processed dairy products for export at a much lower level than milk sold in the Canadian domestic market.

In response to this ruling, Canada created a new system to regulate the export and domestic sale of milk. As far as domestic sales were concerned, Canada continued government price supports tied to a production quota. Milk produced over and above the quota could be sold domestically, but only as Class 4(m) milk to be used for animal feed, at a very low regulated price. Producers of non-quota milk could sell their product as Commercial Export Milk (CEM). The price and volume of CEM was unregulated, left to negotiations between milk processors and producers.

New Zealand and the United States challenged Canada's CEM programme as an export subsidy under Articles 9 and 10 of the Agreement on Agriculture.[169] The first challenge, brought as a compliance complaint under Article 21.5 of the DSU, was inconclusive because the Appellate Body[170] ruled that the WTO panel had failed to use the correct "benchmark" in determining that subsidy "payments" were present.[171] The Appellate Body interpreted Article 9.1(c) of the Agreement on Agriculture to mean that the benchmark for determining the presence of a "payment" is the average total cost of production for all producers.[172]

New Zealand and the United States filed a second complaint against the CEM which, because the Appellate Body lacks remand power, was considered in a second Article 21.5 challenge.[173] This time, the panel issued three important interpretations of Articles 9 and 10 of the Agreement on Agriculture.

First, as to the burden of proof under Articles 9 and 10, the panel ruled that Article 10.3 specifies that it is up to the challenged party to bring forward both evidence and proof after the complaining party has established a *prima facie* case.[174]

[168] *Canada — Measures Affecting the Importation of Milk and the Exportation of Dairy Products*, WT/DS103 and WT/DS113 [hereinafter *Canada-Dairy* case]. Reports of the Panel and the Appellate Body, adopted 27 October 1999.

[169] *Canada — Dairy* (Article 21.5 Recourse), Report of the Panel.

[170] *Canada — Dairy* (Article 21.5 Recourse), Appellate Body Report.

[171] *Id.* paras 82, 85, 104.

[172] *Id.* paras 86–87.

[173] *Canada — Dairy* (Second Article 21.5 Recourse), Report of the Panel.

[174] *Id.* paras 5.15–5.19.

Second, with regard to Article 9.1(c) of the Agreement on Agriculture, the key determinations are whether there is present a "payment" (in terms of the benchmark set by the Appellate Body) by virtue of government action.[175] In the *Canada-Dairy* case, the panel ruled that "payment" can include a price paid by a private processor and that the "government action" issue depends on whether the government involvement has a "significant effect" or is merely incidental.[176] Applying this analysis to the facts, the panel ruled that Canada had failed to rebut the *prima facie* case made by the complainants.[177] Because of the three-class scheme for the marketing of milk put into place by the Canadian government, the "rational processor" of milk is put into a "strong position" to transact a CEM price below the domestic quota price (and thus below the average cost of production) since the only alternative for the producer is to sell at the much lower class 4(m) price.[178]

Third, the panel also ruled, in the alternative, that Canada had failed to rebut the *prima facie* case of a violation of Article 10.1 of the Agreement on Agriculture.[179] The elements of an Article 10.1 violation are (1) the presence of an export subsidy not listed in Article 9.1 and (2) whether this is applied in a manner involving the circumvention of a Member's subsidy commitments.[180] To apply these tests, the panel focused on three general elements of what constitutes an export subsidy[181]: (1) the provision of products for use in export production on terms more favorable than for provision of like products in domestic production; (2) through government action, either directly or indirectly; and (3) on terms more favourable than are commercially available on world markets. The panel found that these elements were present in the *Canada-Dairy* case and that Canada had failed to establish the lack of circumvention.[182]

### *7.1.4 The Doha Agenda*

Under the Doha Development Agenda, agricultural trade is a major focus. The point of departure for the negotiations is Article 20 of the Agriculture Agreement. Article 20 sets a long-term objective of "fundamental reform". The Doha Ministerial Declaration stressed that the long-term objective is to establish a "fair and market-oriented trading system" (referring to the preamble of the Agriculture Agreement) through a programme of "fundamental reform".[183] The two aspects of this reform programme are

175 *Canada—Dairy* paras 5.21–5.26. 176 *Id.* para. 5.27. 177 *Id.* para. 5.34–5.65.
178 *Id.* para. 5.116. 179 *Id.* para. 5.174. 180 *Id.* para. 5.140.
181 *Id.* para. 5.157. 182 *Id.* paras 5.158–5.174.
183 Doha Ministerial Declaration, para. 13.

(1) "reductions of, with a view to phasing out, all forms of export subsidies"; and (2) "substantial reductions in trade-distorting domestic support".[184]

These free-market-oriented goals are balanced, however, with several political goals: (1) special and differential treatment for developing countries; and (2) food security and rural development.

## 7.2 Textiles and clothing

Under the GATT, a special regime, the MultiFibre Arrangement (MFA), was effective for trade in textiles and clothing. The MFA allowed states to impose high quotas on imported clothing and textiles.[185] The WTO Agreement on Textiles and Clothing replaced the MFA.[186] This Agreement provides for the gradual reintegration of textiles and clothing into the normal GATT/WTO regime over a ten-year period. Quotas will be abolished, although tariffs may be bound at relatively high levels.[187] By 2005, all textile and apparel trade among WTO Members will be governed by normal GATT rules. The Agreement creates a new body, the Textiles Monitoring Body (TMB), to administer the agreement.

## 7.3 Information technology

The Ministerial Declaration on Trade in Information Technology Products (ITA) emerged from the Singapore Ministerial Conference in December 1996 as an effort to enhance "market access opportunities for information technology products".[188] Parties to the Declaration agree to "eliminate customs duties and other duties and charges of any kind within the meaning of Article II:1(b)" of the GATT with respect to categories of information technology products and specific information technology products contained in the Declaration's Annex.[189] The primary products covered by the agreement

[184] *Id.* For a more complete discussion, see Kevin C. Kennedy, *Reforming Farm Trade in the Next Round of WTO Multilateral Trade Negotiations*, 35 J. World Trade, at 1061 (2001).

[185] *See* GATT Secretariat, Textiles and Clothing in the World Economy (1984).

[186] Agreement on Textiles and Clothing, reprinted in WTO, The Legal Texts: The Results of the Uruguay Round of Multilateral Trade Negotiations 73 (1999).

[187] *See* Robert C. Cassidy, Jr. and Stuart M. Weiser, *Uruguay Round Textiles and Apparel, in* The World Trade Organization 223 (Terence P. Stewart ed., 1996).

[188] Ministerial Declaration on Trade in Information Technology Products, 13 December 1996, para. 1.

[189] *Id.* para. 2.

include computers, telecommunications products, semiconductors, semiconductor manufacturing equipment, software, and scientific instruments.

Parties to the ITA are to incorporate the commitments to eliminate duties on these products into their WTO schedules.[190] The ITA required that customs duties on covered products be reduced in stages and eventually eliminated by *1 January 2000*.[191] The parties must submit documentation of their implementation plans for review and approval by a consensus of the other parties.[192]

The ITA further stipulates that the duty eliminations are not to be implemented unless parties representing 90 percent of world trade in technology products accede to the Agreement.[193] Twenty-eight parties, representing approximately 93 percent of world trade in technology products, had acceded to the ITA by March of 1998.[194]

## 7.4 Electronic commerce

The WTO has established a comprehensive work programme to deal with all trade-related issues arising from electronic commerce.[195] Three categories of electronic commerce have been identified. The first category consists of tangible goods that may be ordered online and delivered by conventional means. There is broad agreement that such goods should be subject to the rules of the GATT. The second category consists of services delivered over the Internet, such as telecommunications, medical, financial, and travel services. There is agreement that such services should be subject to the General Agreement on Trade in Services (GATS). However, a difference of views exists with respect to the third category, namely, e-products, such as music, books, software, and videos, that were formerly delivered only in tangible form but can now be delivered in electronic form. WTO Members must decide whether these should be treated as goods subject to GATT or as services subject to GATS. Unresolved issues also exist as to how the Telecommunications Annex of GATS should relate to the use of Internet access services.[196]

---

[190] Ministerial Declaration on Trade in Information Technology Products, Annex, para. (1).

[191] *Id.* Annex, para. (2)(a)(i).

[192] *Id.* Annex, para. (2).

[193] *Id.* Annex, para. (4).

[194] WTO, Committee of Participants on the Expansion of Trade in Information Technology Products, Status of Implementation, G/IT/1/Rev.6, 10 June 1998.

[195] WTO, Work Programme on Electronic Commerce, Progress Report to the General Council, S/L/74, 27 July 1999.

[196] *See generally* Stewart A. Baker et al., *E-Products and the WTO*, 35 Int'l Law. 5 (2001).

# 7

# THE MOST-FAVOURED-NATION PRINCIPLE



## 1. What is the most-favoured-nation principle?

The most-favoured-nation (MFN) principle, by name, implies especially favourable treatment. It is nothing of the sort. The MFN principle is a principle of *non-discrimination*, quite the opposite of special treatment. It is a legal obligation to accord equal treatment to all nations accorded the benefit.

The MFN principle dates back to the twelfth century.[1] At first, MFN provisions were used in commercial treaties on a limited basis as a link

[1] The Most-Favored-Nation Provision, Executive Branch GATT Studies, No. 9, 133–35 (1973) (Subcomm. on Int'l Trade, Senate Comm. on Finance, 93d Cong. 2d Sess.), quoted in John H. Jackson et al., LEGAL PROBLEMS OF INTERNATIONAL ECONOMIC RELATIONS 419 (4th ed. 2002).

between specified groups of states.[2] After the demise of mercantilism, MFN provisions were broadly applied to concessions granted to all countries.[3] By the eighteenth and nineteenth centuries, MFN provisions were in general use among European and American trading nations.[4]

## 2. Policy basis

The success of MFN treatment and its continued application are due to the perceived economic and political benefits of its use. First, it ensures the removal of distortions that otherwise would hinder the operation of comparative advantage. Second, it engenders free and fair competition. Third, it protects the value of trade concessions against gradual "erosion" through favours granted to some, but not all, states. Fourth, it is a corollary of the principle of sovereign equality of nations, regardless of their size or importance. Fifth, it protects against corruption and the ability to buy special favours. Sixth, it fosters simplicity of administration, because all nations are to be treated alike. Seventh, it prevents retaliatory cycles of discrimination and consequent animosity between nations. Finally, MFN treatment has a "multiplier effect": through its operation, negotiated trade concessions spread throughout the multilateral trading system.

The disadvantage of MFN treatment is that "free riders" may be encouraged to take advantage of the system by claiming the benefits of liberalization forged by other states while keeping their own markets closed. In the past, the possibility of "free riding" has led some states, including the United States in the nineteenth century,[5] to make MFN treatment conditional on other states granting concessions in return. Although conditional MFN treatment has now largely been abandoned, it still reappears from time to time. For example, the United States conditionally applied three of the Tokyo Round agreements.[6] In the WTO system, those WTO members

[2] The Most-Favored-Nation Provision, above note 1.

[3] *Id.*

[4] *Id.* at 419–20. For a non-GATT application of MFN in a Treaty of Friendship and Commerce Between the United States and Finland, see *Mentula v. State Land Board*, 417 P.2d 581, 583 (Or. 1966) (noting that, "[d]espite centuries of use in many forms of treaties[,] there is a dearth of authority on the meaning and purpose of the most favored nation clause").

[5] *See* The Most-Favoured-Nation Provision, above note 1, at 420.

[6] *See* The Trade Agreements Act of 1979 Pub. L. 96–39, Title I, § 101, 19 U.S.C.A. § 1671(A). The Tokyo Round agreements conditionally applied under U.S. law were the Subsidies Code, the Agreement on Government Procurement and the Standards Code.

that have accepted them in effect apply the "Plurilateral Trade Agreements" conditionally.[7]

There are two main reasons that conditional MFN treatment has largely been abandoned. First, it proved unworkable. As U.S. Secretary of State Charles E. Hughes testified in 1924 before the U.S. Senate Committee on Foreign Relations, "the ascertaining of what might constitute equivalent compensation in the application of the conditional most-favored-nation principle was found to be difficult or impracticable. Reciprocal commercial arrangements were but temporary makeshifts; they caused constant negotiating and created uncertainty".[8] Second, conditional MFN treatment was counterproductive. Instead of securing concessions, it merely provided the opportunity to bargain for equality of treatment.[9]

Unconditional MFN treatment is especially useful in a multilateral system. As Secretary Hughes explained, "[e]ach concession which one country made to another became generalized in favor of all countries to which the country making the concession was obligated by treaty to extend most-favored-nation treatment".[10] Unconditional MFN treatment reduces the transaction costs of entering and maintaining a multilateral trading system. It avoids the enormous difficulty involved in negotiating a multitude of interlocking bilateral agreements. It also counteracts the "prisoners' dilemma" — namely, the temptation to cheat the system — because the putative "cheater" knows that the fruits of his bargain would immediately be claimed by all states. Unconditional MFN treatment has been found to be the simplest system to administer and the most effective way of extending trade.

Unconditional MFN treatment is not, however, unconditional in the sense of being accorded without regard to reciprocity. International practice under bilateral and multilateral treaties, as well as in the WTO system, is that unconditional MFN treatment is accorded only to those states that agree to give it in return. Thus, while details of the multilateral trading system are not reciprocal, the system as a whole is maintained and operated under broad principles of reciprocity and conditionality.

[7] WTO Agreement Art. II:3.

[8] Letter from Charles E. Hughes, Secretary of State, U.S. State Department, to Henry Cabot Lodge, Chairman, Committee on Foreign Relations, U.S. Senate (13 March 1924), quoted in *John T. Bill v. United States*, 104 F.2d 67, 71 (C.C.P.A. 1939).

[9] *Id.*

[10] *Id.*

## 3. The MFN principle in customary international law

Despite the antiquity of the MFN principle, there appears to be no duty to extend MFN treatment under customary international law.[11] Under contemporary state practice, MFN rights can be claimed only through treaty provisions, either bilateral or multilateral.[12]

There have been attempts to establish the MFN principle as a broad principle of international law, but these attempts have not been successful. In 1978, the UN International Law Commission (ILC) concluded a set of draft Articles on MFN treatment and recommended their adoption as a UN Convention.[13] Similarly, the Charter of Economic Rights and Duties of States proclaimed by UN General Assembly in 1974 contains a prohibition against economic discrimination against states based upon differences in political, economic, or social systems.[14] These efforts, however, have remained only political initiatives. Thus, in the absence of treaty, states are free to adopt discriminatory economic policies. Of course, simple discrimination must be distinguished from more drastic measures such as economic sanctions, which present additional issues of economic coercion and non-intervention. These are considered in Chapter 10.

## 4. MFN treatment in the WTO

The MFN principle "has long been a cornerstone of the GATT and is one of the pillars of the WTO trading system".[15] WTO rules require MFN

[11] *See* John Jackson, The World Trading System 134 (ed ed. 1997).

[12] *See, e.g., George E. Warren Corp v. United States,* 71 F.2d 434, 439 (C.C.P.A. 1934) (finding no basis for extending MFN treatment in the absence of a treaty).

[13] United Nations International Law Commission, Draft Articles on Most-Favoured-Nation Clauses, 1978 Yearbook of the ILC, Vol. II, pt. 2; 17 I.L.M. 1518 (1978), available at http://www.un.org/law/ilc/texts/mfnfra.htm.

[14] UNCA Resolution 3281 (XXIX), 14 I.L.M. 25 (1975). *See also* Piet-Hein Houben, *Principles of International Law Concerning Friendly Relations and Cooperation Among States,* 61 Am. J. Int'l L. 703 (1967).

[15] Appellate Body Report, *Canada — Automotive Industry,* para. 69.

treatment with respect to trade in goods,[16] trade in services,[17] and the protection of intellectual property rights.[18]

## 4.1 The MFN obligation under the GATT

The MFN obligation under the GATT is unconditional and quite broad.[19] It includes not only tariffs and associated customs measures, but also, through the incorporation of Article III:2 and Article III:4, internal taxes, charges and regulations affecting the sale, distribution, and use of products. Thus, different tariff rates or border formalities as well as different rates of internal taxation and discriminatory regulations for different WTO Members' like products are prohibited.

Central to the GATT/WTO system is Article I:1 of the GATT. Article I:1 requires MFN treatment with respect to:

1. "[C]ustoms duties and charges of any kind imposed on or in connection with importation or exportation or imposed on the international transfer of payments for imports or exports",
2. "[T]he method of levying such duties and charges",
3. "[A]ll rules and formalities in connection with importation or exportation", and
4. "[M]atters referred to in paragraphs 2 and 4 of Article III".[20]

Under Article I:1, the operative principle with respect to these four areas is that "any advantage, favour, privilege or immunity granted by any contracting party to any product originating in or destined for any other

[16] Article I of the GATT is the main MFN provision, but additional MFN-type obligations are found in the following GATT Articles: Article III:7 (internal quantitative regulations), Article IV(b) (cinematographic films), Article V:2, V:5 and V:6 (transit of goods), Article IX:1 (marks of origin), Article XIII:1 (quantitative restrictions), Article XVII:1 (state trading), Article XVIII:20 (government assistance), and Article XX(j) (short-supply product measures). MFN also applies to certain aspects of countervailing and antidumping proceedings. *See United States — Denial of Most-Favoured-Nation Treatment as to Non-Rubber Footwear from Brazil*, 19 June 1992, GATT B.I.S.D. (39th Supp.) at 128, para. 6.8, at 150 (1993) (holding that the rules and formalities applicable to countervailing duties are within the scope of GATT Art. I).

[17] General Agreement on Trade in Services Art. II. See Chapter 11 for a discussion of the MFN obligation under the GATS.

[18] TRIPS Agreement Art. 4. See Chapter 16 for a discussion of the MFN obligation under the TRIPS Agreement.

[19] *See generally* Gary Clyde Hufbauer et al., *The GATT Codes and the Unconditional Most-Favored-Nation Principle*, 12 Law & Pol'y Int'l Bus. 59 (1980).

[20] GATT Art. I:1.

country shall be accorded immediately and unconditionally to the *like product* originating in or destined for the territories of all other contracting parties".[21]

Article I:1 covers not only *de jure* but also *de facto* discrimination. Measures that explicitly distinguish between foreign goods on the basis of their origin would constitute *de jure*, or "in law", discrimination. Measures that on their face are non-discriminatory but, in practice, impose a heavier burden on foreign goods on the basis of their origin would constitute *de facto*, or "in fact", discrimination. As at the time of writing, *de facto* discrimination has been discussed in one WTO case, namely, *Canada — Automobiles*. In that case, a Canadian exemption from import duties for certain motor vehicles, on its face, imposed no formal restriction on the origin of the imported motor vehicle. The panel found, however, "that, in practice, major automotive firms in Canada import only their own make of motor vehicle and those of related companies".[22] The panel found that the import duty exemption constituted *de facto* discrimination and was, therefore, inconsistent with Article I:1. The Appellate Body upheld this finding and concluded that "[t]he advantage of the import duty exemption is accorded to some motor vehicles originating in certain countries without being accorded to like motor vehicles from *all* other Members".[23] The panel, and subsequently the Appellate Body, recognized that there was a specific historical context for the import duty exemption, namely, that the treatment reserved to Canadian manufacturers was part of Canada's effort to honour a Canada-U.S. auto pact.

The MFN obligation cannot be avoided by establishing different import regimes and maintaining equality within each regime. In *EC — Bananas*, the Appellate Body stated that "the essence of the non-discrimination obligations is that like products should be treated equally, irrespective of their origin. As no participant disputes that all bananas are like products, the non-discrimination provisions apply to all imports of bananas irrespective

[21] GATT Art. I:1. *See also, e.g.*, Appellate Body Report, *Canada — Automobiles*, para. 86 (upholding the panel's conclusion that Canada violated GATT Art. I:1 by according the advantage of the import duty exemption to motor vehicles from certain countries and not according such advantage immediately and unconditionally to like products from the territories of all other WTO Members); Panel Report, *Indonesia — Automobiles*, paras 14.145–14.147 (concluding that Indonesia violated GATT Art. I:1 by charging lower tariffs and taxes with respect to parts and components for "national" cars).

[22] Panel Report, *Canada — Automobiles* para. 10.43.

[23] Appellate Body Report, *Canada — Automobiles*, para. 85 (emphasis in original).

of whether and how a Member categorizes or subdivides these imports for administrative or other reasons".[24]

## 4.2 Types of "advantage" covered by the MFN obligation

A key to the application of the MFN rule is the interpretation given to the term "advantage" in GATT Article I:1. First, the term "advantage" applies to cases of explicit discrimination between products on the basis of their country of origin. Thus, different tariff rates, quotas, and taxation rates for like products from different countries would be prohibited because the difference would afford some an "advantage".

Second, an "advantage" can also take the form of a procedural requirement or practice. For example, in *United States — Denial of Most-Favored-Nation Treatment as to Non-Rubber Footwear from Brazil*, the GATT panel held that the "advantage" of automatic back-dating of the effect of revocation of a countervailing duty order was accorded by the United States to certain countries, while other countries were required to request an injury review for such back-dating.[25] It made no difference whether the products covered by the [antidumping or] countervailing duty orders were "like".

Third, the term "advantage" also covers indirect discrimination where the distinction is not expressly on the basis of countries but is drawn on the basis of conditions that obtain within countries. The leading case is the *Belgian Family Allowances* GATT panel report in 1952.[26] In that case, different levies were made with respect to products purchased by public bodies, based upon whether the products originated in countries with family allowance taxation systems similar to Belgium's. The panel held this to be a violation of GATT Article I:1, stating that "the Belgian legislation would have to be amended insofar as it introduced a discrimination between countries having a given system of family allowances and those which had a different system or no system at all, and made the granting of the

[24] Appellate Body Report, *EC — Bananas*, para. 191.

[25] *United States — Denial of Most-Favored-Nation Treatment as to Non-Rubber Footwear from Brazil*, above note 16, para. 6.9, at 150. *See also* Appellate Body Report, *EC — Bananas*, paras 205–07 (discriminatory export certificate requirements and other administrative and procedural requirements). Another application of this rule is *European Economic Community — Imports of Beef from Canada*, 10 March 1981, GATT B.I.S.D. (28th Supp.) at 92, paras 4.2–4.3, at 98 (1982) (duty waiver certificate conditional on certification by one particular government).

[26] *Belgian Family Allowances (Allocations Familiales)*, 7 November 1952, GATT B.I.S.D. (1st Supp.) at 59 (1953).

exemption dependent on certain conditions".[27] Thus, indirect discrimination between different countries' like products is also forbidden.

## 4.3 Like products

The MFN principle prohibits country-based discrimination with respect to "like products". Products that are not "like" may be treated differently. The Appellate Body has given guidance on interpreting the term "like products" in *Japan — Alcoholic Beverages.*[28] Although this case involved Article III of the GATT, the Appellate Body set out several propositions that apply to "like product" determinations with respect to Article I:1.

First, "there can be no one precise and absolute definition of what is 'like.' The concept of 'likeness' is a relative one that evokes the image of an accordion. The accordion of 'likeness' stretches and squeezes in different places as different provisions of the WTO Agreements are applied".[29] Second, the determination of "likeness" is a case-by-case judgement: "The width of the accordion . . . must be determined by the particular provision in which the term 'like' is encountered, as well as by the context and the circumstances that prevail in any given case".[30] Finally, the determination of "likeness" "will always involve an unavoidable element of individual, discretionary judgement".[31]

With these three propositions in mind, we can approach the issue of "likeness" in GATT Article I:1.

A panel will take into consideration the tariff classifications of the products in question in determining whether such products are "like". In *Canada/Japan — Tariff on Imports of Spruce, Pine, Fir (SPF) Dimension Lumber*,[32] Canada challenged Japan's system of classifying "dimension" lumber (i.e., lumber from whatever species of tree cut into specified dimensions) as discriminatory because different tariffs were applied to dimension lumber based upon the species of tree involved. The GATT panel rejected the challenge, ruling that the burden of challenging tariff classifications rests upon the challenger, and Canada had not proved its case. The concept of

[27] *Belgian Family Allowances (Allocations Familiales)*, above note 26, para. 3, at 60.

[28] Appellate Body Report, *Japan — Taxes on Alcoholic Beverages.*

[29] *Id.* at 21.

[30] *Id.*

[31] *Id.* at 21–22.

[32] *Canada/Japan — Tariff on Imports of Spruce, Pine, Fir (SPF) Dimension Lumber*, 19 July 1989, GATT B.I.S.D. (36th Supp.) at 167 (1990).

"dimension" lumber was a Canadian industry standard that had no acceptance internationally as a tariff category and was not, therefore, an appropriate basis for establishing "likeness".[33] If the particular classification adopted is exceptional or unique, it will be suspect.[34] Tariff classifications are not, however, conclusive in determining whether products are "like".

A panel will also take into consideration the similarity of the physical characteristics of the products involved, their end use (how they are regarded by consumers), and whether they are directly competitive or substitutable in the marketplace, based upon objective measurements such as cross elasticity of demand.[35] In *Spain — Tariff Treatment of Unroasted Coffee*, the GATT panel found that all unroasted, non-decaffeinated coffee beans should be considered "like" products for purposes of GATT Article I:1 because unroasted coffee is sold mainly in the form of blends and is universally regarded as a single product.[36] On the other hand, in *EEC — Measures on Animal Feed Proteins*,[37] the GATT panel upheld an EEC regulation that differentiated between various animal feed protein products, noting that they carried different tariff classifications and had varying contents and differing vegetable, animal, and synthetic origins.[38] Finally, in some cases there is no dispute that the products involved are "like".[39]

## 4.4 Conditional "advantage"

Can a WTO Member structure its tariff and other border advantages to benefit, on a non-discriminatory basis, products from other WTO Members that fulfil certain objective conditions? It may be argued that MFN should not prevent a Member from imposing regulatory or substantive requirements that are open to all to fulfil. For example, Member A could enter into a mutual recognition arrangement (MRA) with Member B to recognize each other's safety approvals for washing machines. If such an MRA scheme were also open to Member C to join, could the scheme be

---

[33] *Id.* para. 5.14, at 199.

[34] *Spain — Tariff Treatment of Unroasted Coffee*, 11 June 1981, GATT B.I.S.D. (28th Supp.) at 102 (1982).

[35] *See Spain — Tariff Treatment of Unroasted Coffee*, above note 34; *Treatment of Germany of Imports of Sardines*, 31 October 1952, GATT B.I.S.D. (1st Supp.) at 53 (1953).

[36] *Id.* para. 4.7, at 112.

[37] *EEC — Measures on Animal Feed Proteins*, 14 March 1978, GATT B.I.S.D. (25th Supp.) at 49, para. 4.2, at 63 (1979).

[38] *Id.* para. 4.2, at 63.

[39] Appellate Body Report, *Canada — Automobiles*, para. 78, note 4.

administered as an MFN advantage without complying with the elements of GATT Article XX or the TBT Agreement? Similarly, could a WTO Member condition an MFN advantage on the maintenance by the exporting Member of certain environmental, safety or health standards?

These interesting questions arose in two WTO dispute settlement proceedings, *Canada — Automobiles* and *Indonesia — Automobiles*. The *Canada — Automobiles* case concerned Japan's complaint that Canada's Motor Vehicle Tariff Order (MVTO), which set out the conditions under which duty-free import eligibility for autos was granted, was discriminatory. The WTO panel found that, although the MVTO was facially origin-neutral, there was *de facto* discrimination because Canada had restricted its application to a small number of countries.[40] The panel stated, however, that "whether an advantage [under] Article I:1 is accorded 'unconditionally' cannot be determined independently of whether it involves discrimination between like products of different countries".[41] The Appellate Body affirmed the panel's findings with regard to *de facto* discrimination[42] but did not rule on the latter point, which was not appealed by the parties.[43] The *Canada — Automobiles* panel, in linking "unconditionally" in Article I:1 exclusively to origin discrimination seems to open the way to MFN conditionality that is origin neutral (*de facto* as well as *de jure*). This would seem to permit the examples above and any other MFN conditions as long as they are origin neutral.

In *Indonesia — Automobiles*, however, the panel took a different view. This case concerned a challenge to Indonesia's programme of conditioning certain exemptions from customs duties and taxes on the exporting country's participation in the Indonesia National Car Program. The panel ruled that this advantage was a violation of Article I:1, not because of *de facto* discrimination, but because autos from Korea received more favourable tariff treatment.[44] Regarding the conditionality, the panel ruled that "GATT case law is clear to the effect that any... advantage (here tax and customs benefits) cannot be made conditional on any criteria that is not related to the imported product itself".[45] The *Indonesia — Automobiles*

[40] Panel Report, *Canada — Automobiles*, para. 14.
[41] *Id.* para. 10.22.
[42] Appellate Body Report, *Canada — Automobiles*, paras 79–86.
[43] *Id.* para. 76.
[44] Panel Report, *Indonesia — Automobiles*, para. 14.145.
[45] *Id.* para. 14.143 (citing the *Belgian Family Allowances* case, above note 26).

ruling thus would not permit MFN conditions, unless they were related to the product itself and were fully subject to the discipline of the "like" product determination of Article I:1, as well as the disciplines of other applicable WTO agreements. The *Indonesia — Automobiles* case was not appealed so the Appellate Body did not have a chance to rule on this question.

On the merits of this argument, two GATT cases can be cited in favour of the *Canada — Automobiles* panel's position. In the *Tuna Dolphin I* case,[46] the panel upheld a U.S. law that allowed use of a "dolphin-safe" label for tuna because it was available on an MFN basis. In the 1978 *EC — Surety Deposit* case,[47] the panel upheld an EC exemption from a surety deposit requirement for suppliers that provided a guarantee that the import price was not less than a specified minimum.

Nevertheless, the *Indonesia — Automobiles* panel's ruling seems correct. Freely allowing conditional MFN contradicts the wording of Article I:1 and potentially subverts numerous other provisions of the WTO agreements.

## 4.5 Discrimination between firms

An intriguing question is whether measures that discriminate between importing or exporting firms violate Article I:1 of the GATT. For example, if certain importing firms are exempted from a particular tax provision that burdens other firms, is this forbidden?

On the one hand, it can be argued that Article I:1 does not reach such discrimination because it prohibits only different treatment of like products from WTO Members. On the other hand, the GATT Secretariat has expressed the view that discrimination among products on the basis of the characteristics of the firms that make or market them violates the MFN obligation.[48]

The point has never been definitively decided. Perhaps the proper inquiry is whether such discrimination is a *de facto* or indirect method of discriminating against a WTO Member. If so, the MFN rule would be violated. Such

[46] *United States — Restrictions on Imports of Tuna*, GATT B.I.S.D. (39th Supp.) at 155, reprinted in 30 I.L.M. 1594 (1991) (unadopted).

[47] *EC — Programme of Minimum Import Prices, Licenses and Surety Deposits for Certain Processed Fruits and Vegetables*, 18 October 1978, GATT B.I.S.D. (25th Supp.) at 68 (1979).

[48] GATT Working Party Report, Accession of Hungary, 30 July 1973, GATT B.I.S.D. (20th Supp.) at 34, para. 12, at 36 (1974).

a measure would probably also violate Article III norms relating to national treatment.[49]

## 5. Exceptions to the MFN obligations

The rule that WTO Members must provide MFN treatment to other Members is subject to two major exceptions. It does not prohibit tariff and trade preferences in connection with the formation of customs unions and free trade areas.[50] Nor does it prohibit trade preferences in favour of developing countries.[51] These matters are considered respectively in Chapters 14 and 15.

Additional exceptions from the MFN treatment rule in the GATT allow the imposition of antidumping and countervailing duties (Article VI), quotas based on balance of payments difficulties (Article XIV), discrimination with respect to safeguards (Article XIX) and for national security (Article XXI).

[49] *See* Chapter 8.

[50] GATT Art. XXIV; *see also* GATS Art. V.

[51] An original exemption in the GATT in Article I:2, I:3 and I:4 allowed special treatment for trade with certain current and former colonies or associated states. This preference has been replaced effectively by more general preferences in favour of developing countries. *See* Chapter 15.

# 8

# THE NATIONAL TREATMENT PRINCIPLE

## 1. What is the national treatment principle?

National treatment is one of the fundamental market access principles of the GATT/WTO system. It imposes an obligation of like treatment and non-discrimination between domestic and imported goods. With respect to goods, national treatment means that, once imported products have cleared customs and the applicable tariff or duty has been collected, they must be treated the same as domestic products. Otherwise, discriminatory treatment could defeat the tariff concessions granted under Article II of the GATT. National treatment applies to products even whose tariffs are not bound.[1] National treatment is also a feature of the General Agreement on Trade in Services (GATS)[2] and many other trade agreements.[3]

The national treatment obligation is set forth in Article III of the GATT. The basic rule is that no law, regulation, or taxation pattern may adversely modify the conditions of competition between like imported and domestic products in the domestic market.[4] This broad formulation reaches both measures giving favour to domestic products and those disfavouring like-product imports. The objective of national treatment is "to protect expectations of the contracting parties as to the competitive relationship between their products and those of the other contracting parties[,] . . . to protect current trade [and] to create the predictability needed to plan future trade".[5] As a result, Article III is generally interpreted to reach both actual

[1] *Brazilian International Taxes*, 30 June 1949, GATT B.I.S.D. II at 181, para. 4 (1952) (concluding that a GATT contracting party was bound by Article III (*i.e.*, the national treatment obligation) regardless of whether the contracting party in question "had undertaken tariff commitments in respect of the goods concerned").

[2] General Agreement on Trade in Services (GATS), Art. XVII, reprinted in WTO, The Legal Texts: The Results of the Uruguay Round of Multilateral Trade Negotiations 286 (1999).

[3] *See, e.g.*, Canada-Chile Free Trade Agreement, 6 February 1997, 36 I.L.M. 1067, Art. 1-1-02; North American Free Trade Agreement, 17 December 1992, 32 I.L.M 289, Arts. 300–01. National treatment is often accorded regarding the right of establishment, the right to set up a subsidiary and offices in another country.

[4] *Italian Discrimination Against Imported Agricultural Machinery*, 23 October 1958, GATT B.I.S.D. (7th Supp.) at 60, para. 12 (1959) (invalidating Italian law providing low-interest loans to purchasers of Italian-made tractors).

[5] *United States — Taxes on Petroleum and Certain Imported Substances*, 17 June 1987, GATT B.I.S.D. (34th Supp.) at 136, para. 5.2.2 (1988) [hereinafter *United States — Superfund*].

and potential discrimination. Thus, it is no excuse that a discriminatory measure is not being enforced or applied.[6]

Article III is constructed to be comprehensive in scope. Article III:1 "contains general principles" and "informs" and provides the context for the rest of Article III.[7] In addition, Article III:1 defines the scope of application of Article III to include: (1) internal taxes and charges; (2) laws, regulations and requirements affecting the sale, transportation, distribution or use of products; and (3) internal quantitative regulations requiring the mixture, processing or use of products in specified proportions. Each of these three matters is dealt with more specifically in subsequent paragraphs of Article III.

The purposes of Article III are to (1) assure that national domestic measures do not subvert the Article II tariff bindings and (2) limit national protective measures to border controls.[8] Accordingly, Article III secures "effective equality of opportunity for imported products" to compete with domestic products.[9]

The national treatment obligation is, therefore, a constraint that operates upon virtually any measure favouring domestic products or disfavouring imported products. An example serves to illustrate its scope. In *Korea — Beef*, the Appellate Body considered whether Korea was infringing the national treatment obligation by maintaining a "dual retail system" for marketing beef that confined sales of imported beef to specialized stores.[10] Korean law created two distinct retail distribution systems for beef: one for domestic beef and another for imported beef. A large retailer could sell both domestic and imported beef as long as it maintained separate sale areas. Retailers selling imported beef were required to display a sign reading "Specialized Imported Beef Store".

The Appellate Body, in analysing whether maintenance of the dual retail system violated Article III, concluded that formal separation does not, in

---

[6] *See, e.g., United States — Section 337 of the Tariff Act of 1930*, 7 November 1989, GATT B.I.S.D. (36th Supp.) at 345, para. 5.13 (1990) [hereinafter *United States — Section 337*] (taking the approach that establishing whether the "no less favourable" treatment standard of Article III is met requires an assessment of whether the law, regulation, or requirement in question in itself may lead to the application to imported products of treatment less favourable than that accorded to domestic products); *United States — Superfund*, above note 5, paras 5.2.1–5.2.2.

[7] Appellate Body Report, *Japan — Alcoholic Beverages*, para. 96.

[8] *Italian Discrimination Against Imported Agricultural Machinery*, above note 4, paras 15, 16.

[9] *United States — Section 337*, above note 6, para. 5.11.

[10] Appellate Body Report, *Korean Beef*, para. 75(c).

itself, necessarily violate the national treatment obligation. The key inquiry is whether the maintenance of separate retail distribution systems for domestic and imported products "modifies the conditions of competition in the Korean beef market to the disadvantage of the imported product".[11] This, in turn, depends upon the effect of the dual retail system. The Appellate Body noted that the effect had been the reduction of retail outlets for imported beef, both in absolute terms and in comparison with the number of retail outlets for domestic beef. This "reduction of competitive opportunity" was not consistent with the requirements of Article III:4 of the GATT.[12]

## 2. National treatment: some key issues

### 2.1 "Like" products

Article III of the GATT prohibits discrimination between imported and domestic "like" products. Because discrimination between unlike products is permissible, the determination as to whether products are "like" is central to the administration of Article III.

The "like" product determination is one of the thorniest in GATT/WTO jurisprudence. Panel and Appellate Body reports routinely state that determinations as to whether products are "like" should be made on a case-by-case basis.[13] The term "like product" does not mean, in any case, that products must be identical to be "like". The term "like" includes "similar" products. The Appellate Body, in *Japan — Alcoholic Beverages*, compared "likeness" to an accordion that "stretches and squeezes in different places as different provisions of the *WTO Agreement* are applied".[14]

[11] Appellate Body Report, *Korean Beef*, para. 144.

[12] *Id.* paras 147–48. The Appellate Body did not rule on the question whether the display sign requirement was a separate Article III violation. *Id.* para. 151.

[13] *See, e.g.*, Appellate Body Report, *Japan — Alcoholic Beverages*, Part H.1(a), para. 8.

[14] *Id.* at Part H.1(a), para. 4. The "like product" issue arises in many different provisions of the WTO agreements, for example, in GATT Arts. I:1, III:2, III:4, VI:1, IX:1, XI:2, XIII:1, XVI:4 and XIX:1; the SCM Agreement; the Antidumping Agreement and the Agreement on Safeguards, just to cite the most important instances. Each provision may be interpreted in a different manner. *See* Appellate Body Report, *European Communities — Asbestos*, para. 89. For a comprehensive list of cases, see *id.* note 58.

Three different approaches have been used for determining whether imported and domestic products are "like" for purposes of the national treatment obligations set forth in Article III:2 and III:4.

### 2.1.1 *Article III:2, first sentence*

Under the first approach, which the Appellate Body has applied to Article III:2, first sentence, involving internal taxes and charges, a case-specific assessment and comparison is made of the two or more products as to their physical properties, nature and quality, end uses, consumers' tastes and habits, and any other relevant point of comparison.[15] The Appellate Body has emphasized that, under this test, the term "like" product is construed narrowly.[16] Since the test is in fact specific, panels are free to use their "best judgement"[17] in making this determination. This test, what we might call the "physical characteristics" test, is the traditional GATT-based test, consistently followed "in almost all adopted panel reports".[18]

### 2.1.2 *Article III:2, second sentence*

The second approach to the like products test applies to the second sentence of GATT Article III:2. Article III:2, second sentence, is the subject of an interpretive note (*Ad* Article III), which provides that the term "like product" refers to a "directly competitive or substitutable product" for purposes of applying this sentence. The Appellate Body has construed this note as mandating a "directly competitive or substitutable products" test for the second sentence of Article III:2.[19] This comprehends, normally, a broader ranger of products than the narrower "like" product test of Article III:2, first sentence.[20] How much broader this may be in any given case "is for the panel to determine based on all the relevant facts".[21] As with the first sentence "like" product determination, the "directly competitive or substitutable products" test is a case-by-case judgment.[22] Panels should consider

[15] Appellate Body Report, *Japan — Alcoholic Beverages. See also Japan — Customs Duties, Taxes and Labelling Practices on Imported Wines and Alcoholic Beverages,* 10 November 1987, GATT B.I.S.D. (34th Supp.) at 83, para. 5.7 (1988) [hereinafter GATT *Japan — Alcoholic Beverages 1987*].

[16] Appellate Body Report, *Japan — Alcoholic Beverages* at 20.

[17] *Id.* at 21.

[18] *Id.* at 22.

[19] *Id.* at 23–24

[20] *Id.* at 25

[21] *Id.*

[22] *Id.*

not only matters such as physical characteristics, common end uses and tariff classifications, but also marketplace factors, competition in the relevant markets, elasticity of substitution and cross-price elasticity of demand.[23]

### *2.1.3 Article III:4*

A third approach to the "like" product issue was used by the Appellate Body in interpreting Article III:4 in *European Communities — Asbestos.*[24] This case best illustrates how the "like product" concept is handled under this provision.[25] The issue was whether chrysotile asbestos fibres are like fibres made from other materials, such as polyvinyl alcohol, cellulose, and glass (PCG fibres).[26]

In answering this question, the Appellate Body began its analysis by stating that Article III:1 sets out an overarching "general principle," namely, avoiding protectionism and ensuring equality of competitive conditions between imported and domestic products, that "informs" the rest of Article III.[27] From this principle, "it follows that the word 'like' in Article III:4 is to be interpreted to apply to products that are in such a competitive relationship. Thus, a determination of likeness under Article III:4 fundamentally is a determination about the nature and extent of a competitive relationship between and among products".[28] The Appellate Body thus concluded that the "scope of 'like' in Article III:4 is broader than the scope of 'like' in Article III:2, first sentence", but is not broader than the combined Article III:2.[29] The Appellate Body then set forth a new test for "like products" that is a synthesis of the physical character and marketplace ideas. The Appellate Body emphasized that "all pertinent evidence" should be marshalled under four general criteria: (1) the properties, nature and quality of the products; (2) their end-uses; (3) consumers' tastes and habits; and (4) tariff classifications of the products.[30] From this evidence, panels should determine likeness exercising "an unavoidable element of discretionary judgment".[31] Applying these cri-

[23] Appellate Body Report, *Japan — Alcoholic Beverages* at 26
[24] Appellate Body Report, *European Communities — Asbestos.*
[25] *Id.*
[26] *Id.*
[27] *Id.* paras 96–98.
[28] *Id.* para. 99.
[29] *Id.*
[30] *Id.* para. 101.
[31] *Id.* paras 100–03.

teria and considering the evidence in the *Asbestos* case, the Appellate Body concluded that, particularly in view of the public health risks of asbestos, the party alleging the Article III violation had failed to carry its burden that chrysotile asbestos fibres are like fibres made from other materials for purposes of Article III:4.[32]

Like product determinations under Article III are to be made on a case-by-case basis that "will always involve an unavoidable element of individual, discretionary judgement".[33]

### *2.1.4 The aim and effects test*

In certain cases under the GATT, panels examined the aim and market effects of the measure at issue to determine whether the imported and domestic products were "like". This approach was used in the *Malt Beverages* case, in which Canada challenged certain U.S. state and federal taxes and sales regulations that discriminated against imported alcoholic beverages.[34] The panel concluded that "like" product determinations should be made "not only in light of criteria such as the products' physical characteristics, but also in light of the purpose of Article III, which is to ensure that internal taxes and regulations 'not be applied to imported or domestic products *so as to afford protection* to domestic production'".[35] This approach came to be known as the "aim and effects" test.

The *Malt Beverages* case illustrates the aim and effects approach. One measure challenged in that case was a Mississippi wine tax imposing a lower tax rate on wines made from a certain grape variety. The panel concluded that there was no public policy purpose for the wine tax other than protecting local producers and that the imported and domestic wines were, therefore, "like" products.[36] The wine tax was found to be inconsistent with Article III.[37] Other measures that were challenged were several state restrictions on the sale of beer that discriminated between types of beer on the basis of alcohol content. The panel concluded that low alcohol content beer and high alcohol content beer "need not be considered as like products," because the purpose

[32] *Id.* para. 141.

[33] Appellate Body Report, *Japan — Alcoholic Beverages,* at Part H.1(a), para. 3. *See also* Appellate Body Report, *European Communities — Asbestos,* para. 101.

[34] *United States — Measures Affecting Alcoholic and Malt Beverages,* 19 June 1992, GATT B.I.S.D. (39th Supp.) at 206 (1993) [hereinafter *Malt Beverages*].

[35] *Id.* para. 5.71 (emphasis added).

[36] *Id.* para. 5.26.

[37] *Id.* para. 5.26.

of the restrictions was to encourage consumption of low alcohol content beer and the restrictions did not create adverse conditions of competition for Canadian producers.[38] These restrictions were found to be consistent with Article III.[39]

The aim and effects test was determinative in *United States — Taxes on Automobiles*,[40] in which the panel concluded that a "like" product determination included an examination of whether the measure at issue had a protective *aim* or *effect*. The panel upheld U.S. luxury and gas guzzler taxes on cars, despite their disproportionate application to imported vehicles, because of the absence of any protective aim or effect.[41] This case was highly controversial, and the Contracting Parties never adopted the panel report because the EC opposed the aim and effects test.

The Appellate Body expressly rejected the aim and effects test in *Japan — Alcoholic Beverages*. In that case, the Appellate Body parsed Article III and concluded that a "like" product determination under Article III:2 does not include an examination of whether the measure at issue has a protective aim or effect.[42] The Appellate Body reasoned that there is no textual basis for the "aim and effects" test.

## 2.2 The product-process distinction

GATT jurisprudence with respect to Article III drew a bright-line distinction between (1) a product and (2) the process or production method (PPM) by which the product is made.[43] This distinction has two bases. First, the scope of applicability of the Article III national treatment obligation has been held

[38] *Malt Beverages*, above note 37, para. 5.75.

[39] *Id.* para. 5.76.

[40] *United States — Taxes on Automobiles*, DS31/R, 11 October 1994, reprinted in 33 I.L.M. 1397, at para. 5.10 (1994) (unadopted) [hereinafter *United States — Taxes on Automobiles*].

[41] *Id.* para. 5.15. The issue of protective effect was analysed, not in terms of actual sales data, but on the basis of *potential* effect. *Id.* para. 5.14. The panel noted that there was not evidence that foreign manufacturers lacked inherent capacity to market automobiles below the high tax thresholds. *Id.* The panel also found that U.S. Corporate Average Fuel Efficiency Rules were in violation of Article III:4 because certain averaging formulas discriminated against foreign vehicles. *Id.* para. 5.55.

[42] For an excellent analysis, see Robert E. Hudec, *GATT/WTO Constraints on National Regulation: Requiem for an "Aim and Effects" Test*, 32 INT'L LAW 619, 630 (1998).

[43] *United States — Restrictions on Imports of Tuna*, GATT B.I.S.D. (39th Supp.) at 155, para. 5.11 (1993), reprinted in 30 I.L.M. 1594 (1991) (unadopted) [hereinafter *Tuna Dolphin I*]; *United States — Restrictions on Imports of Tuna*, DS29/R, 16 June 1994, reprinted in 33 I.L.M. 839, paras 5.8–5.9 (1994) (unadopted) [hereinafter *Tuna Dolphin II*]; *Malt Beverages*, above note 34; *United*

limited to measures that apply to or affect the characteristics of the product itself. Thus, in the *Tuna Dolphin I* case,[44] the panel ruled that the import ban on tuna caught with dolphin-killing methods was not within the scope of Article III because "regulations governing the taking of dolphins incidental to the taking of tuna could not possibly affect tuna as a product".[45] Second, as detailed above, the interpretation of "like" product under Article III:4 does not permit differentiation based on the way a product is made, produced or harvested. These product-process distinctions have been criticized by many commentators.[46]

The WTO, however, has developed a carefully crafted way of permitting certain PPMs through meeting the requirements of GATT Article XX. This is discussed in Chapter 17. In addition, PPMs are addressed in the TBT and SPS Agreements.

## 2.3 Technical regulations and sanitary and phytosanitary measures

An exception to the product-process distinction exists for process or production methods that fall within the scope of the TBT Agreement or the SPS Agreement.

The TBT Agreement applies to technical regulations.[47] The term "technical regulation" is defined to include a mandatory regulation regarding product characteristics or their processes or production methods and "packaging, marking and labelling requirements as they apply to a product, process or production method".[48] The TBT Agreement permits national technical regulations provided such regulations do not have the purpose or

*States — Taxes on Automobiles*, above note 40. Two WTO panel decisions discussed the product-process distinction with approval, although in neither case did the Appellate Body expressly rule on it. *See* Panel Report, *United States — Reformulated Gasoline*, paras 6.11–6.13; Panel Report, *Canada — Periodicals*, paras 5.24–5.25.

[44] *See* above note 43.

[45] 30 I.L.M. at 1618.

[46] *E.g.*, Robert Howse and Donald Regan, *The Product/Process Distinction — An Illusory Basis for Disciplining Unilateralism* Trade Policy, 11 E.J.I.L. 249 (2000); Steve Charnovitz, "The Law of Environmental 'PPMs' in the WTO: Debunking the Myth of Illegality", 27 Yale J. Int'l L. 59 (2000).

[47] Agreement on Technical Barriers to Trade, reprinted in WTO, The Legal Texts: The Results of the Uruguay Round of Multilateral Trade Negotiations 121 (1999) [hereinafter TBT Agreement].

[48] *Id.* Annex 1, para. 1. Such technical regulations may be positively or negatively stated. *See* Appellate Body Report, *European Communities — Asbestos*, para. 69.

effect of creating an unnecessary obstacle to international trade and are not more trade restrictive than necessary to fulfil a legitimate objective.[49]

The SPS Agreement applies to sanitary or phytosanitary measures (SPS measures), which are measures to protect animal, human, or plant life or health within the territory of the adopting state.[50] SPS measures include processes and production methods as well as product requirements. The SPS Agreement permits national SPS measures provided such measures are "applied only to the extent necessary to protect human, animal or plant life or health, [are] based on scientific principles, and [are] not maintained without sufficient scientific evidence".[51] National SPS measures may not arbitrarily or unjustifiably discriminate or be applied in a manner that would constitute a disguised restriction on international trade.[52]

With respect to technical regulations or SPS measures, WTO Members that depart from international standards, guidelines, or recommendations are subject not only to GATT Article III but also to the TBT Agreement or the SPS Agreement. WTO Members may, however, justify the regulation of process or production methods and packaging, marking, or labelling requirements under the TBT Agreement or the SPS Agreement.

Thus, process or production methods that relate to the way a product is made, produced, or harvested can be the subject of import regulations by a WTO Member. Trade restrictions would be legitimate, however, only on the product to which the process or production method requirement is applied, not to an associated product.

## 2.4 Application of Article III to state-trading monopolies

Article III applies to state-trading monopolies because there is no exemption for such monopolies in Article III or Article XVII. As illustrated by the 1992 case, *Canada — Import, Distribution and Sale of Certain Alcoholic Drinks by Provincial Marketing Agencies,*[53] a state-trading company violates Article III:4 if it treats imports less favourably than competing domestic products:

[49] TBT Agreement Art. 2.2.

[50] Agreement on the Application of Sanitary and Phytosanitary Measures, reprinted in WTO, THE LEGAL TEXTS: THE RESULTS OF THE URUGUAY ROUND OF MULTILATERAL TRADE NEGOTIATIONS 59 (1999) [hereinafter SPS Agreement].

[51] *Id.* Art. 2.2.

[52] *Id.* Art. 2.3.

[53] *Canada — Import, Distribution and Sale of Certain Alcoholic Drinks by Provincial Marketing Agencies,* 18 February 1992, GATT B.I.S.D. (39th Supp.) at 27, para. 5.15 (1993) [hereinafter *Canada Beer II*].

> [N]othing in the General Agreement [on Tariffs and Trade] . . . prevented Canada from establishing import and sales monopolies that also had the sole right of internal delivery. The only issue before the Panel was whether Canada, having decided to establish a monopoly for the internal delivery of beer, might exempt domestic beer from that monopoly. The Panel noted that Article III:4 did not differentiate between measures affecting the internal transportation of imported products that were imposed by governmental monopolies and those that were imposed in the form of regulations governing private trade. . . . The Panel recognized that a beer import monopoly that also enjoyed a sales monopoly might, in order properly to carry out its functions, also deliver beer, but it did not for that purpose have to prohibit unconditionally the private delivery of imported beer while permitting that of domestic beer.[54]

In the same report, the panel also invoked Article III:2:

> The Panel noted that Canada taxed both imported and domestic beer by assessing mark-ups through the liquor boards and by levying provincial sales taxes and the federal Goods and Services Tax at the retail level . . . .
>
> The Panel noted that, according to Article III:2, first sentence, imported products "shall not be subject, directly or indirectly, . . . to like domestic products." The Panel considered that this provision applied not only to the provincial and federal sales taxes but also to the mark-ups levied by the liquor boards because they also constituted internal governmental charges borne by products.[55]

Thus, charges levied by state-trading companies and their affiliates must not discriminate between imports and domestic products.

## 2.5 Application of Article III national treatment obligations to sub-federal units of WTO Members

Article III also applies to regulatory restrictions and taxes imposed by sub-federal governmental entities such as U.S. states. It is irrelevant that restrictions imposed on imported products also are imposed on products from other governmental entities within a federal union.[56]

Article XXIV:12 of the GATT addresses this issue as follows: "Each contracting party shall take such reasonable measures as may be available to it to ensure observance of the provisions of this Agreement by the regional and local governments and authorities within its territory". In the Uruguay Round, the following understanding was adopted with regard to Article XXIV:12: "Each Member is fully responsible under the GATT 1994 for the observance of all provisions of GATT 1994, and shall take such

54 *Id.* para. 5.15.
55 *Id.* paras 5.23–5.24.
56 *Malt Beverages*, above note 34, para. 5.17.

reasonable measures as may be available to it to ensure such observance by regional and local governments and authorities within its territory".[57] Thus, Article III norms apply to and must be observed by local and regional governmental units of WTO Members.

## 2.6 The relationship between Article III and Article XI of the GATT

Article III of the GATT interacts with Article XI. Article III applies to internal taxation and regulation, while Article XI applies to quotas, import or export licenses or "other measures... instituted or maintained... on the importation... or exportation... or any product".[58] The word "measures" in Article XI was interpreted in the *Japan Semi-Conductor* case to refer to not only laws and regulations but also non-mandatory government involvement.[59] Thus, Article XI is comprehensive in scope; it deals with everything other than fiscal matters.

In the *Canada Foreign Investment Review Act* case, the GATT panel concluded that Article XI regulated only measures affecting the importation (or exportation) of a product.[60] The panel left the regulation of internal requirements affecting imported products to Article III. Nevertheless, an interpretive note, *Ad* Article III, states that taxes or regulations consistent with Article III may be "collected or enforced" at the border. Thus, the distinction between Articles XI and III often presents difficulty. Ordinarily, a measure should first be analysed under Article III. If it fails the tests of Article III, Article XI automatically applies and, unless it falls under one of the narrow exceptions[61] in that Article, it will fail

[57] Understanding on the Interpretation of Article XXIV of the General Agreement on Tariffs and Trade 1994, in WTO, THE LEGAL TEXTS: THE RESULTS OF THE URUGUAY ROUND OF MULTILATERAL TRADE NEGOTIATIONS 26, para. 13 (1999).

[58] GATT Art. XI.

[59] *Japan — Trade in Semi-Conductors*, 4 May 1988, GATT B.I.S.D. (35th Supp.) at 116, paras 106–09 (1989). The GATT panel set out a two-part test for determining whether non-mandatory government requests could be regarded as "measures" within the meaning of Article XI: first, whether there were sufficient incentives for the requests to take effect and second, whether the operation of the measures was dependent on government action. *Id.* para. 109. The panel determined that non-binding "administrative guidance" by the Japanese government was within the scope of Article XI. *Id.* para. 117–18.

[60] *Canada — Administration of the Foreign Investment Review Act*, 7 February 1984, GATT B.I.S.D. (30th Supp.) at 140, para. 5.14 (1984) [hereinafter *Canada — FIRA*].

[61] Article XI:2 of the GATT excepts three types of measures from the prohibition of Article XI:1: (a) export prohibitions or restrictions to relieve critical shortages of foodstuffs and other

the Article XI tests. This was precisely the panel's analysis in the *Tuna Dolphin* cases.[62] The U.S. embargo on tuna caught by dolphin-unsafe methods was analysed under Article III.[63] When Article III was found inapplicable because the U.S. embargo concerned fishing techniques rather than the product itself, the embargo was judged inconsistent with Article XI.[64]

## 3. Taxes

Article III:2 requires national treatment with respect to internal taxes. Article III:2 is closely related to Articles I and II, which allow tariffs and allow them to be "bound" under GATT/WTO rules. Internal taxes, in contrast to tariffs, are not "bound" but have to be applied on a non-discriminatory basis, with regard to both domestic products and products from other WTO Members.[65]

products "essential" to the exporting party, (b) import or export prohibitions or restrictions necessary to the application of standards or regulations for classifying, grading, or marketing commodities, and (c) import restrictions on agricultural or fisheries products that are necessary to the enforcement of certain governmental policy measures. These exceptions are drawn narrowly and would not be relevant to environmental measures. *See Canada — Measures Affecting Exports of Unprocessed Herring and Salmon*, 22 March 1988, GATT B.I.S.D. (35th Supp.) at 98, para. 4.1 (1989) (restrictions on export not justified by GATT Article XI:2(b)). *See also* Chapter 6 § 3.5.

The difficulty of choosing between the applicability of Articles III and XI in a given case is illustrated by *Lobsters from Canada*, a decision of a binational panel established under Chapter 18 of the U.S.-Canada Free Trade Agreement. *Lobsters from Canada*, USA-89-1807-01 (U.S.-Canada FTA ch. 18 decision), 3 Can. Trade & Commodity Tax Cas. (CCH) 8182 (1990). This case involved a U.S. law that prohibited the transport or importation of lobsters smaller than a certain size. Canada sought relief through the panel on the ground that the restriction violated Article XI of the GATT. Canada alleged *de facto* discrimination against imports because, in colder waters, lobsters tend to be smaller. The majority of the panel upheld the U.S. restriction because the identical restrictions were applied to lobsters caught in U.S. waters. A minority, however, concluded that Article XI should be applied, and that Article III was not applicable because the U.S. law had a protectionist purpose and effect.

[62] *See Tuna Dolphin I* and *Tuna Dolphin II*, above note 43, para. 5.9.

[63] *Tuna Dolphin I*, above note 43, paras 5.9–5.15.

[64] *Tuna Dolphin I*, above note 43, para. 5.18–5.19.

[65] In *Indonesia — Automobiles*, the panel found that tax provisions of the National Car Program violated GATT Article III:2, because like products (imported vehicles and national vehicles with the same end-uses, basic properties, nature and quality) were taxed differently. *See* Panel Report, *Indonesia — Automobiles*, paras 14.121–14.122. Article I, which provides for most-favoured-nation treatment, incorporates internal taxes and regulations into this requirement.

## 3.1 Scope

Tariffs and other charges imposed on or in connection with the importation or exportation of products are outside the scope of Article III:2. The GATT provides no guidance on this distinction except for an interpretive note, *Ad* Article III. This interpretive note provides that a tax that applies to both an imported product and a like domestic product is to be regarded as an internal tax, even if it is collected or enforced at the border with respect to imports. Although no panel report has clarified this distinction,[66] it has not proved overly troublesome in practice.

So-called direct taxes (i.e., those not imposed on products but on income or producers) fall outside the scope of Article III:2. Article III:2 applies to taxes only on products (e.g., sales taxes, excise taxes, value-added taxes). The theory behind restricting the discipline of Article III:2 to taxes on products appears to have been the assumption by the drafters of the GATT that indirect taxes were fully shifted to the purchaser in the price of the good, while the seller or producer absorbed direct taxes. While this is questionable from an economic standpoint,[67] the distinction, nevertheless, remains.

A type of charge outside the scope of Article III is customs fees concerning expenses incurred in assessing duties, inspections and validation of documents. These charges are subject to the discipline of Article VII of the GATT. Article VII limits such charges to the approximate cost of services rendered.

Finally, fees and charges imposed by governments on currency exchange transactions (even in connection with the foreign exchange required to import goods) fall outside the scope of Article III:2 but within the scope of Article XV:4 of the GATT. Article XV:4 provides only a general rule that exchange requirements must not "frustrate the intent of the provisions of this Agreement".

## 3.2 Border tax adjustment

As discussed above, "internal" taxes subject to Article III:2 can be imposed at the border with respect to imports. This convenience permits "border tax adjustment" (BTA) with respect to taxes on products or product compon-

[66] *See* Special Import Taxes Instituted by Greece, 3 November 1952, GATT B.I.S.D. (1st Supp.) at 48 (1953) (concluding that it could not determine whether a "contribution" imposed by Greece on certain imported goods was an internal tax or charge within the meaning of Article III and, therefore, seeking "additional information").

[67] *See generally* John H. Jackson, *National Treatment Obligations and Non-Tariff Barriers*, 10 Mich. J. Int'l L. 207, 216–17 (1989).

ents. With respect to imports, therefore, Article II:2(a) of the GATT grants an exception to the rule limiting border charges to the amount of a scheduled tariff binding for "a charge equivalent to an internal tax imposed consistently with the provisions of paragraph 2 of Article III". On the export side, a nation is allowed to rebate the amount of any internal tax imposed on domestic goods. An interpretive note, *Ad* Article XVI:4, provides that such a rebate shall not be considered a subsidy or be the basis for countervailing or antidumping duties.

## 3.3 The non-discrimination principle

The equality-of-treatment requirements of Article III:2 are very precisely and delicately worded. Article III:2 contains two sentences. The first sentence forbids taxes on imports "in excess of those applied, directly or indirectly, to like domestic products". The second sentence specifically refers to Article III:1 and adopts the standard that internal charges must not be applied to imported or domestic products "so as to afford protection to domestic production".

Because Article III:2, first sentence, does *not* specifically refer to Article III:1, a determination as to whether there has been a violation of Article III:2, first sentence, does *not* require consideration of whether the measure affords protection to domestic production.[68] Because Article III:2, second sentence, does, however, specifically refer to Article III:1, a determination as to whether there has been a violation of Article III:2, second sentence, requires consideration of whether the measure affords protection to domestic production.[69]

The first sentence applies to like products in the sense of "similar", with respect to physical characteristics and end-use.[70] This sentence has been interpreted to demand absolute equality of taxation because the phrase "in excess of" admits no flexibility. It is no defence that the unequal taxation has no trade effect. This sentence does not "protect expectations on export volumes; it protects expectations on the competitive relationship between imported and domestic products".[71]

68 *See id.* at Part H.2 para. 4.

69 *See id.* at 24.

70 See the discussion, above, section 2.1.1.

71 *United States — Superfund*, para. 5.1.9. Cases in which domestic products were subject to less tax than like imported products constitute the principal category of cases decided under Article III:2. *E.g.*, *Japan — Alcoholic Beverages 1987*, Panel and Appellate Body Reports, *Canada — Periodicals*; Panel Report, *Indonesia — Automobiles*; Panel and Appellate Body Reports, *Korea — Alcoholic Beverages*; Panel and Appellate Body Reports, *Chile — Taxes on Alcoholic Beverages.*

The second sentence, on the other hand, permits some flexibility because a small differential in taxation still may satisfy the standard of not affording protection to domestic production.[72] Products that are "like", only in the sense that they are competitive or substitutable, may be tested by the standard of Article III:2, second sentence, alone.[73] Thus, some small tax differences may be permissible between certain "like" imported and domestic products under Article III.

The distinction between the two sentences of Article III:2 is illustrated by the *Japan — Alcoholic Beverages* case.[74] In this case, the Appellate Body considered whether Japan's taxation pattern on domestic and imported alcoholic beverages was discriminatory in violation of Article III:2. Examining the problem under Article III:2, first sentence, involves the consideration of two issues: (1) whether like products are involved; and (2) whether the taxes on the imported product are "in excess of" those on the like domestic product. The Appellate Body concluded that Japanese shochu and vodka are "like" and that vodka was subject to taxes "in excess of" those on shochu. "Even the smallest amount of excess was too much", and this was a violation.

The Appellate Body went on to consider whether the taxation pattern on shochu and a broader range of products, imported gin, whisky, brandy, rum, and liqueurs, violated Article III:2, second sentence. Here, three issues must be considered: (1) whether the products are "directly competitive or substitutable"; (2) whether they are not similarly taxed; and (3) whether this "affords protection" to domestic production. The Appellate Body found that all three tests were met and, consequently, more than a *de minimis* difference in taxation on such alcoholic beverages is impermissible.

The original purpose of the interpretive note to Article III:2, second sentence, was to allow internal taxes on certain imported products to be levied for the purposes of protecting the local production of a related product. That interpretive note provides that an internal tax meeting the

[72] See the leading cases interpreting Article III:2, second sentence: *Korea — Alcoholic Beverages*, para. 117; *Japan — Alcoholic Beverages*, Part H.2(b), para. 3; *Japan — Alcoholic Beverages* 1987 at para. 5.11; and *United States — Superfund*, para. 5.1.9

[73] *Japan — Alcoholic Beverages.* Similarly, in the *Korea — Alcoholic Beverages* case, the Appellate Body affirmed that internal taxes should not be applied to afford protection to domestic production and held that the term "directly competitive or substitutable" should be read expansively to include potentially alternative products. Appellate Body Report, *Korea — Alcoholic Beverages.*

[74] Panel and Appellate Body Reports, *Japan — Alcoholic Beverages.*

requirements of the first sentence of Article III:2 would fail to conform to the second sentence "only in cases where competition was involved between, on the one hand, the taxed product and, on the other hand, a directly competitive or substitutable product which was not similarly taxed". For example, non-discriminatory taxation of domestic and imported oleomargarine may be permitted to protect the local production of butter.[75]

## 4. Government regulations

Article III:4 requires national treatment with respect to regulations and other requirements affecting the internal sale, purchase, transportation, distribution, or use of imported products. Article III:5 and Article III:7 prohibit the use of mixing requirements or internal quantitative requirements (such as local content conditions) that favour domestic products.

The tone was set for the application of Article III:4 by a 1958 GATT panel that considered a complaint by the United Kingdom against Italy. An Italian law provided for loans at preferential rates to Italian farmers that purchased Italian-made tractors. In the panel's report, *Italian Discrimination Against Imported Agricultural Machinery*,[76] Article III:4 was interpreted "to provide equal conditions of competition once goods had been cleared through customs".[77] Furthermore, Article III:4 covered "not only the laws and regulations which directly governed the conditions of sale or purchase but also laws or regulations which might adversely modify the conditions of competition between domestic and imported products".[78] The panel rejected the argument that economic development measures were permitted under this provision: "such protection should be given in ways permissible under the General Agreement".[79] Article III:8(b), which permits "subsidies exclusively to domestic producers, including payments... derived from the proceeds of internal taxes", was declared not applicable because the credit subsidies were being extended to purchasers, not producers.[80]

---

75 *See* Kenneth W. Dam, The GATT 118–19 (1970).

76 *Italian Discrimination Against Imported Agricultural Machinery*, above note 4.

77 *Id.* para. 5.

78 *Id.* para. 12.

79 *Id.* para. 16.

80 *Id.* para. 14.

The basic criterion for determining a violation of the national treatment obligation under Article III:4 is the "no less favourable" treatment standard. This is interpreted to require "effective equality of opportunities for imported products"[81] compared to like domestic products. This cannot be satisfied by balancing less-favourable treatment for imports in some instances and more favourable treatment in others.[82] But it does allow more favourable treatment for imports.[83] Moreover, differences in treatment for imports and domestic products are not conclusively inconsistent with Article III:4, but the WTO Member applying differential treatment must show that the "no less favourable" standard is satisfied.[84]

Article III:4 has been applied in many different contexts. The United States challenged the Canadian Foreign Investment Review Act (FIRA) in 1982, arguing that FIRA's domestic content requirements, which required products made or sold to contain a certain percentage of domestic value, infringed Article III:4. The GATT panel agreed, finding that "undertakings to *purchase goods of Canadian origin*... exclude the possibility of purchasing available imported products so that the latter are clearly treated less favourably than domestic products".[85] In another major case, the European Community successfully challenged Section 337 of the U.S. Tariff Act of 1930. Section 337, under which certain unfair methods of competition, including infringement of intellectual property rights, allowed imported products to be barred from sale in the United States, was found to be inconsistent with Article III:4 because challenging products of foreign origin for unfair competition was easier than challenging domestic "like" products.[86] The United States amended Section 337 in 1994 to comply with this decision.[87]

Thus, Article III:4 has been interpreted broadly to reach all cases of actual or potential discrimination between imports and domestic products in national markets. Even origin-marking requirements, which are permitted under Article IX of the GATT, may infringe Article III if they go beyond

[81] *United States — Section 337*, above note 6, para. 5.11.

[82] *Id.* para. 5.14.

[83] *Id.* para. 5.11.

[84] *Id.*

[85] *Canada — FIRA*, above note 60, para. 5.8 (emphasis in original). The ruling that local content [and trade balancing] requirements infringe Article III:4 was affirmed in the WTO *India — Auto Sector* case. *See* Panel Report, *India — Auto Sector*, para. 8.1(a), (c).

[86] *United States — Section 337*, above n. 6 (overruling a prior panel report that had upheld section 337 in the specific case, but stating that this "did not foreclose future examination of the use of section 337").

[87] Uruguay Round Agreements Act § 321(a), 19 U.S.C.A. § 1337 (1999 & Supp. 2001).

the obligation "to indicate the origin of the imported product".[88] Article III:4 applies to substantive, procedural, and enforcement laws and regulations.[89]

The *Japan — Film* case,[90] however, is an example of an unsuccessful attempt to show infringement of Article III:4. In that case, the United States argued that 23 different Japanese government measures had the combined effect of granting less favourable treatment to imported film and nullified and impaired benefits U.S. producers should have obtained from previous tariff negotiating rounds. The WTO panel's decision rested on the ground that the United States had not sufficiently demonstrated the claims of non-violation or denial of national treatment.[91] Thus, a complainant under Article III:4 must carry a relatively high burden of proof to show "less favourable conditions of competition".

## 5. *De facto* discrimination

Certain taxes and regulatory measures are neutral with respect to imports and domestic products but have a discriminatory effect. A famous example was a U.S. law taxing alcoholic beverages, providing a tax of $10.50 on "each proof gallon or wine gallon below proof". (A "wine gallon" is a gallon of beverage, while a "proof gallon" is a gallon that is 100 proof or 50-percent alcohol by volume.) Although non-discriminatory on its face, this tax favoured domestic producers, who would pay the tax on bottles at full proof and later dilute to the proof necessary for retail sale (86 proof). Importers imported the retail proof bottles and thus paid the wine gallon rate of tax. Thus, domestic producers of scotch whiskeys paid an effective tax of $9.03 per gallon, while importers paid $10.50. It was open for importers to import full proof bottles, but they would have to set up bottling operations in the United States and could not advertise as "bottled in Scotland". This tax was challenged unsuccessfully under Ireland-U.S. and British-U.S. FCN treaties,[92] but was never tested under GATT Article III

[88] *See Hawaii v. Ho*, 41 Hawaii 565, 571 (1957) (invalidating state law requiring sellers of imported eggs to display a placard bearing the words "we sell foreign eggs" as contrary to GATT Article III:4).

[89] *United States — Section 337*, above note 6.

[90] Panel Report, *Japan — Film.*

[91] *Id.* paras 6.79–6.81.

[92] *Schieffelin & Co. v. United States*, 424 F.2d 1396 (C.C.P.A. 1970).

because it was protected by the GATT's "grandfather" clause. The United States voluntarily eliminated this discrimination in 1979.[93]

Beginning with the *Japan — Alcoholic Beverages* case[94] in 1987, GATT and WTO panels have unequivocally ruled that *de facto* discrimination violates Article III. Two methods of analysis are used for this purpose. One is the expansion of the "like" products test to include goods that are competitive or substitutable. This erases arbitrary distinctions used to justify different treatment or taxation.[95] A second way of testing *de facto* discrimination is to apply the effective equality of competitive opportunities for imports test, in light of the purpose of Article III, even to taxes, laws, and regulations that appear to be, on their face, netural.[96] Through a protective effect analysis, *de facto* discrimination can be declared illegal.[97]

*De facto* discrimination is present where the application of formally identical legal provisions results, in practice, in less favourable treatment of imports. Two examples may be cited as illustrative. In *Malt Beverages*,[98] a GATT panel examined the fact that the State of Mississippi (U.S.A.) applied a lower excise tax rate to wines in which a certain variety of grape was used, than to other wines. Although the excise tax rate did not on its face discriminate against imports, the panel found that, because the favoured grape grew only in the State of Mississippi and Mediterranean regions, this tax differential was discriminatory.[99] Similarly, in *Canada — Import, Distribution and Sale of Certain Alcoholic Drinks by Provincial Marketing Agencies*, the GATT panel found that, although Canada maintained minimum prices for both domestic and imported beer, in practice, the minimum prices reflected the lowest possible price for domestic beer, and this adversely affected imports that otherwise would be sold at lower prices.[100]

[93] *See* John H. Jackson et al., LEGAL PROBLEMS OF INTERNATIONAL ECONOMIC RELATIONS 532 (3d ed. 1995).

[94] *Japan — Alcoholic Beverages 1987.*

[95] *Id.* paras 5.7–5.10.

[96] *Id.; see Malt Beverages*, above note 34.

[97] *Japan — Alcoholic Beverages 1987*, para. 5/11/. In *Canada Beer II*, the panel applied the two-part test of *Japan — Alcoholic Beverages 1987* to strike down Canada's restrictive distribution and pricing system for imported beer and wine: "The panel noted that minimum prices applied equally to imported and domestic beer did not necessarily accord equal conditions of competition to imported and domestic beer. Whenever they prevented imported beer from being supplied at a price below that of domestic beer, they accorded in fact treatment to imported beer less favorable than that accorded domestic beer". *See Canada Beer II*, above note 53, para. 5.30.

[98] *Malt Beverages*, above note 34.

[99] *Id.* paras 5.23–5.26.

[100] *See Canada Beer II*, above note 53, para. 5.31.

Although these tools of analysis are quite effective in combating *de facto* discrimination, they may not be appropriate in all such cases. *De facto* discrimination can occur in a wide variety of contexts. In the early 1990s, GATT panels reconsidered their approach in the face of national laws that had valid social purposes. As we have seen, two GATT panels used a new test, the aim and effects test, to judge *de facto* discrimination. This was a more flexible approach: The challenger had to show the tax or regulation in question had both a protectionist purpose and effect.

The Appellate Body in the 1996 *Japan — Alcoholic Beverages* case soon repudiated the aim and effects approach. The purpose of a tax, and by implication a regulation, is irrelevant. The only inquiry is protective effect. The rejection of a purpose inquiry was reaffirmed by the Appellate Body in *European Communities — Bananas*: the "so as to afford protection" language of Article III:1 is not incorporated or referred to in Article III:4.[101] Furthermore, Article XVII:3 of the GATS explicitly adopts an objective test for *de facto* discrimination:

> Formally identical or formally different treatment shall be considered to be less favorable if it modifies the conditions of competition in favour of services or service suppliers of the Member compared to like services or service suppliers of any other Member.

Thus, the WTO seems to be locked into a very restrictive approach to *de facto* discrimination. Professor Robert Hudec has criticized this approach:

> The Appellate Body's responses to these various efforts to employ an "aim and effects" approach suggests an unusually strict attachment to the exact words of the relevant GATT or GATS provisions. One might understand such textual literalism in defense of legal criteria believed to be correct and appropriate, but it is disappointing to see the Appellate Body following such a literalist approach when it results in extending the empty formalism of the traditional "like product" analysis. The disappointment becomes even greater when it is recognized that the issues in these cases go to the very core of the WTO's policing function over domestic regulatory policy — in some respects the most important element of its legal character. We know from the experience of the United States Supreme Court and the European Court of Justice, both of whom are called upon to make very similar rulings, that these are extremely sensitive and difficult issues. Developing an accepted and effective jurisprudence in this area requires a high degree of sensitivity to the balance of the interests involved, and a high degree of creativity in fashioning answers that provide a satisfactory balance. It is not encouraging to think that the Appellate Body has launched itself upon this delicate and sensitive task bound hand and foot to the words of an old, and often badly drafted, instrument.[102]

---

[101] Appellate Body Report, *European Communities — Bananas*, paras 215–16.
[102] Hudec, above note 42, at 633.

The need Professor Hudec sees for a more flexible approach to *de facto* discrimination is confirmed by a consideration of the approaches used by the EC/EU and the United States. The EC/EU uses a balancing rule-of-reason test and the concept of proportionality to test *de facto* discrimination. The U.S. Supreme Court similarly tests facially neutral regulations under the interstate commerce clause of the U.S. Constitution using a balancing test weighing the burden on commerce against putative local benefits.

The "aim and effects" test as a balancing mechanism should be reconsidered by WTO adjudicating bodies. This test entered GATT jurisprudence as a method for deciding the "like" product issue. The Appellate Body rightly rejected the use of the test because there is no textual basis in Article III. Rather, the textual basis for the test is in Article III:1, which contains the phrase "so as to afford protection". This is a statement of aim and effect. Furthermore, because the phrase "so as to afford protection" modifies all three items covered by Article III (internal taxes, regulations, and mixing requirements), and because Article III:1 is a general rule that "informs" the subsequent paragraphs of Article III, it would seem justified to utilize the "aim and effects" test to judge *de facto* discrimination under Article III.[103]

## 6. Article XX exceptions

The general exceptions of Article XX of the GATT are important exceptions to national treatment obligations. These exceptions apply only as limited and conditional exceptions from the GATT obligations, including national treatment. Thus, the applicability of Article III must be determined before an exception can be considered.[104]

Article XX consists of introductory clauses (the so-called chapeau) and lettered clauses. The lettered clauses must be examined individually because each clause has its own requirements. For example, the requirements of Article XX(d) are as follows:

[103] *But see EC — Bananas.* In the *EC — Bananas* case, the Appellate Body concluded that the reasoning applied to the interpretation of Article III:2 in *Japan — Alcoholic Beverages* should be applied to the interpretation of Article III:4. Appellate Body Report, *EC — Bananas*, para. 216. The Appellate Body concluded that because Article III:4 does *not* specifically refer to Article III:1, a determination as to whether there has been a violation of Article III:4 does *not* require a separate consideration of whether a measure affords protection to domestic production. *Id.*

[104] *United States — Section 337*, above note 6, para. 5.9.

- The measures at issue must be "necessary to secure compliance" with laws or regulations, and
- The "laws or regulations" with which compliance is being secured must themselves be "not inconsistent" with the GATT.

In addition, in accordance with the chapeau, the measures at issue must not be "applied in a manner which would constitute a means of arbitrary or unjustifiable discrimination between countries where the same conditions prevail, or a disguised restriction on international trade".[105]

Article XX exceptions have been invoked to justify measures found to violate Article III, particularly in the context of environmental controversies. These issues are covered in Chapter 17.

## 7. Government procurement

Purchases by "government agencies of products purchased for governmental purposes" are exempt from national treatment obligations under the GATT.[106] This exemption proved troublesome for various reasons. First, with the increase in the government sector in many economies, a large proportion of economic activity was beyond the purview of GATT rules. Second, there are unresolved interpretive issues, especially with respect to the terms "governmental agencies" and "governmental purposes".[107]

For these reasons, an Agreement on Government Procurement was negotiated in the Tokyo Round. The Uruguay Round led to the creation of a new Agreement on Government Procurement (Government Procurement Agreement) in 1994. The Government Procurement Agreement is a WTO Plurilateral Agreement that is binding only on those WTO Members that have accepted it.[108]

---

[105] GATT Art. XX(d) and the introductory clauses to Article XX (the so-called chapeau). For discussion of Article XX(d), see Appellate Body Report, *Korea — Beef*, paras 152–66. In this case the Appellate Body held that it was not "necessary" to employ a dual retail system for domestic and imported beef products because traditional enforcement methods are adequate to protect consumers against possible deceptive practices and unfair competition.

[106] GATT Art. III:8.

[107] *Id.*

[108] Only 24 members have accepted the Government Procurement Agreement. For the reasons so few WTO Members have joined the Agreement, see Sue Arrowsmith, *Towards a Multilateral Agreement on Transparency in Government Procurement*, 47 Int'l & Comp. L.Q. 793, 799–780 (1988).

The basic rule adopted by the Government Procurement Agreement is as follows:

**Article III. National Treatment and Non-discrimination**

1. With respect to all laws, regulations, procedures and practices regarding government procurement covered by this Agreement, each Party shall provide immediately and unconditionally to the products, services and suppliers of other Parties offering products or services of the Parties, treatment no less favourable than:

(a) that accorded to domestic products, services and suppliers; and
(b) that accorded to products, services and suppliers of any other Party.

2. With respect to all laws, regulations, procedures and practices regarding government procurement covered by this Agreement, each Party shall ensure:

(a) that its entities shall not treat a locally-established supplier less favourably than another locally established supplier on the basis of degree of foreign affiliation or ownership; and
(b) that its entities shall not discriminate against locally-established suppliers on the basis of the country of production of the good or service being supplied, provided that the country of production is a Party to the Agreement in accordance with the provisions of Article IV.

3. The provisions of paragraphs 1 and 2 shall not apply to customs duties and charges of any kind imposed on or in connection with importation, the method of levying such duties and charges, other import regulations and formalities, and measures affecting trade in services other than laws, regulations, procedures and practices regarding government procurement covered by this Agreement.

Other provisions of the Government Procurement Agreement set forth detailed rules on how to implement this general obligation. These provisions cover rules of origin,[109] technical specifications,[110] tendering procedures,[111] qualification of suppliers,[112] invitation to participate,[113] selection procedures,[114] and negotiation.[115] There are special provisions for information and transparency[116] and for developing countries.[117]

[109] Agreement on Government Procurement, reprinted in WTO, THE LEGAL TEXTS: THE RESULTS OF THE URUGUAY ROUND OF MULTILATERAL TRADE NEGOTIATIONS 383, Art. IV (1999) [hereinafter Government Procurement Agreement].

[110] Id. Art. VI.

[111] *Id.* Arts. VII, XI, XII, XIII and XV.

[112] *Id.* Art. VIII.

[113] *Id.* Art. IX.

[114] *Id.* Art. X.

[115] *Id.* Art. XIV.

[116] *Id.* Arts. XVII–XIX.

[117] *Id.* Arts. V and XVI.

The Government Procurement Agreement features a challenge procedure that entitles a foreign bidder to obtain a statement of reasons why his bid was rejected and impartial review by a court or independent review body.[118] The Agreement also establishes a Committee on Government Procurement to facilitate consultation among the parties.[119]

The WTO Dispute Settlement Understanding governs disputes arising under the Agreement.[120] Several disputes have been considered under the GATT or WTO rules,[121] including a U.S. complaint in connection with the procurement of toll collection equipment for the City of Trondheim, Norway.[122]

The scope of application of the Government Procurement Agreement is limited, however, in several important ways. First, the Agreement covers only those governmental entities, services, and thresholds specifically listed in the Annexes.[123] Second, only contracts over certain value thresholds come within the Agreement.[124] Third, there is a broad exception for national security and national defence.[125]

The Government Procurement Agreement has been only moderately successful. The many exclusions and exceptions protect most governmental

---

[118] *Id.* Art. XX.

[119] *Id.* Art. XXI.

[120] *Id.* Art. XXII:1.

[121] *E.g.*, Panel Report, *Korea — Measures Affecting Government Procurement* (finding that procurement agencies and practices at issue were not covered by the GPA commitments of South Korea); *United States — Procurement of a Sonar Mapping System*, GPR.DS1/R, 23 April 1992, reprinted in 1992 WL 792948 (1992) (United States violated Tokyo Round GPA by exclusion of contract for sonar mapping in Antarctica); *Panel on Value-Added Tax and Threshold*, 16 May 1984, GATT B.I.S.D. (31st Supp.) at 247, para. 28 (1985) (concluding that, for the purpose of determining whether a procurement contract would fall above or below the threshold of the Tokyo GPA, the contract value is the full cost to the entity and would, therefore, include any VAT payable, unless the entity was exempted from paying VAT).

[122] *Panel on Norwegian Procurement of Toll Collection Equipment for the City of Trondheim*, 13 May 1992, GATT B.I.S.D. (40th Supp.) at 319 (1995). The panel ruled that the contract in question did not fall within Tokyo Round GPA's research and development/prototype exception. *Id.* para. 5.1. The panel's report highlights the fact that the GPA does not provide a remedy for an aggrieved foreign bidder in the form of damages, enjoining the award of the contract, or re-tendering. The United States later decided that Norway had adequately implemented the decision. *See* Result of Dispute Settlement Proceeding Initiated Against Norway under the GATT Agreement on Government Procurement Pursuant to Title VII of the Omnibus Trade and Competitiveness Act of 1988, 57 Fed. Reg. 45,232 (1992).

[123] Government Procurement Agreement, above note 109, Art. I(1).

[124] *Id.* Art. II(1).

[125] *Id.* Art. XXIII.

contracting around the world. Despite acceptance of the Government Procurement Agreement, the United States, for example, still maintains "buy American" laws on both the state and federal levels. State "buy American" laws are valid unless they go so far as to constitute an unconstitutional burden on commerce.[126]

[126] *E.g., Bethlehem Steel Corp. v. Board of Commissioners*, 80 Cal. Rptr. 800 (1969).

# 9

# SAFEGUARDS

## 1. Introduction

In the broadest terms, safeguards and safeguard measures refer to the right of a WTO Member to impose temporary tariffs, quotas, tariff-rate quotas or other measures to ensure that its economy or domestic industries do not suffer serious harm from imports and trade concessions.

Unlike rights to impose import restrictions to counteract dumping and subsidies, safeguard remedies are not based on any concept of unfair trade or remedy for distortions by exporters. Safeguard remedies allow fairly traded imports to be restricted.[1] Thus, safeguards are a case in which WTO rules allow the introduction of trade distortions and protective measures.

There are several reasons for allowing safeguards to operate in a system that emphasizes free trade values. First, safeguard measures are a concession to political realities and the fact that political economy is more than just

[1] Appellate Body Report, *United States — Line Pipe Safeguard*, para. 80 (noting that safeguard measures "are remedies that are imposed in the form of import restrictions in the absence of any allegation of an unfair trade practice").

economics. Trade may improve welfare as a whole, but it does not guarantee prosperity for all. Those hurt by trade may, from a public choice perspective, be very powerful politically. Economic considerations may mean that adjustment assistance in the form of job-search help, retraining and temporary financial assistance to allow trade-displaced workers to move to more productive economic sectors may be the most efficient way of accommodating increased trade, but adjustment assistance is often hard to sell politically.

Second, safeguard measures are often considered a political safety valve so that national policymakers will not hesitate to pursue a long-term free trade strategy.

Third, safeguards are sometimes considered just compensation for workers and firms that suffer from trade liberalization. This theory holds that domestic businesses and workers that suffer a trade-related injury have a just claim against the government for compensation.

Fourth, a rationale for safeguards is to provide a "breathing space" to firms and policymakers so they can take the action necessary on a macro- or micro-economic level either to restore competitiveness and efficiency to the industry or to undertake an orderly contraction.

Perhaps all of these theories make up the background for safeguard measures.

## 2. The legal and policy framework for safeguards in the GATT/WTO regime

The GATT/WTO regime establishes two general safeguards provisions as well as methods of invoking safeguards in various economic sectors under specialized agreements involving textiles, agriculture,[2] and services.[3]

The principal safeguards provision is Article XIX of the GATT 1994 as supplemented by the Agreement on Safeguards, which was approved at the conclusion of the Uruguay Round.

The GATT 1994 also contains provisions in Articles XII and XVIII, Section B, allowing the adoption of import restrictions for balance-of-payments reasons. These provisions are of diminished importance today because of floating currency exchange rates.

[2] The Agriculture on Agreement (Article 5) permits WTO Members to impose special safeguards — in the form of additional duties — on an agricultural product that the WTO Member has subjected to "tariffication". This matter is discussed in Chapter 6.

[3] General Agreement on Trade in Services, Art. X.

## 3. GATT Article XIX and the Agreement on Safeguards

### 3.1 GATT Article XIX

Article XIX of the GATT is the so-called escape clause because it allows WTO Members[4] to escape from their WTO obligations by imposing safeguard measures if the following three basic requirements are met. First, there must be an increase of imports of the product in question. Second, the increase of imports must be caused by developments that were not foreseen and must result from obligations that the country applying the safeguard measure must respect under the GATT. Finally, the increase of imports must cause or threaten to cause "serious injury" to a domestic industry producing a "like" or "directly competitive" product. These requirements are set forth in GATT Article XIX:1(a), which reads as follows:

> If, as a result of unforeseen developments and of the effect of the obligations incurred by a contracting party under this Agreement, including tariff concessions, any product is being imported into the territory of that contracting party in such increased quantities and under such conditions as to cause or threaten serious injury to domestic producers in that territory of like or directly competitive products, the contracting party shall be free, in respect of such product, and to the extent and for such time as may be necessary to prevent or remedy such injury, to suspend the obligation in whole or in part or to withdraw or modify the concession.

### 3.2 The Safeguards Agreement

The Safeguards Agreement amplifies and supplements Article XIX of the GATT. It was concluded in the Uruguay Round. In the Tokyo Round, the negotiating parties had discussed an agreement to implement Article XIX but failed to reach agreement. The Safeguards Agreement was influenced by the experience of the United States under Section 201 of the Trade Act of 1974 and reflects the substance of that U.S. law.[5]

---

[4] Note 1 to Article 2.1 of the Agreement on Safeguards allows a customs union to apply a safeguard measure as a single unit or on behalf of a Member State.

[5] *See, e.g.*, Thomas V. Vakerics et al., ANTIDUMPING, COUNTERVAILING DUTY AND OTHER TRADE ACTIONS 271–380 (1987 & Supp.) (discussing practice under § 201 of the Trade Act of 1974).

## 3.3 The relationship between GATT Article XIX and the Safeguards Agreement

The Appellate Body tends to construe the requirements of Article XIX and the Safeguards Agreement together. According to the Appellate Body in the *United States — Line Pipe Safeguard* case,[6] there are two basic inquiries in a safeguards case:

1. Is there a right to apply a safeguard measure?
2. If so, has this right been exercised within the limits set out in the Safeguards Agreement?

In the first cases under the WTO safeguards regime, the issue of the relationship between Article XIX of the GATT and the Safeguards Agreement arose in the context of the "unforeseen developments" requirement.[7] This requirement is included in Article XIX:1(a) of the GATT but is not repeated in the Safeguards Agreement.

One issue was whether Article XIX:1(a) conflicts with provisions of the Safeguards Agreement. In the event of a "conflict", the provisions of the Safeguards Agreement prevail.[8] The term "conflict" is not defined but has been interpreted by the Appellate Body to mean a situation "where adherence to the one provision will lead to a violation of the other provision".[9] The Appellate Body held that Article XIX:(a) and the Safeguards Agreement should be read together since the Safeguards Agreement defines a safeguard measure under this Agreement as that of Article XIX:1(a). This holding implies that there is no conflict between Article XIX:1(a) and the Safeguards Agreement.[10]

The Appellate Body has also concluded that safeguard measures imposed after the entry into force of the WTO Agreement must comply with the provisions of *both* the Article XIX of the GATT and Safeguards

[6] Appellate Body Report, *United States — Line Pipe Safeguard*, para. 84.

[7] *See* Panel Report, *United States — Line Pipe Safeguard*, paras 7.293–7.300, 8.1(6); Appellate Body Report, *United States — Lamb Safeguard*, paras 65–76; Panel Report, *United States — Lamb Safeguard*, paras 7.32–7.45; Appellate Body Report, *Korea — Dairy Safeguard*, paras 68–77; Panel Report, *Korea — Dairy Safeguard*, paras 7.33–7.48; Appellate Body Report, *Argentina — Footwear Safeguard*, paras 76–84; Panel Report, *Argentina — Footwear Safeguard*, paras 8.47–8.69.

[8] General Interpretive Note to Annex 1A, Multilateral Agreements on Trade in Goods, of the WTO Agreement, reprinted in WTO, THE LEGAL TEXTS: THE RESULTS OF THE URUGUAY ROUND OF MULTILATERAL TRADE NEGOTIATIONS 16 (1999).

[9] Appellate Body Report, *Guatemala — Cement*, para. 65.

[10] Appellate Body Report, *Argentina — Footwear Safeguard*, para. 89.

Agreement.[11] The Appellate Body reasoned as follows: Legal effect must be given to all provisions of the WTO Agreement, which includes both the GATT 1994 and the Safeguards Agreement.[12] The Safeguards Agreement "establishes rules for the application of safeguard measures which shall be understood to mean those measures provided for in Article XIX of GATT".[13] The Safeguards Agreement prohibits WTO Members from applying safeguard measures unless such measures conform to the provisions of Article XIX of the GATT 1994 applied in accordance with the Safeguards Agreement.[14] There is no indication that the Uruguay Round negotiators intended to subsume the requirements of Article XIX of the GATT 1994 within the Safeguards Agreement and thereby render those requirements no longer applicable. Thus, safeguard measures are reviewed under both the GATT and the Safeguards Agreement.

## 3.4 Investigation

WTO Members may not impose safeguard measures without first conducting an investigation regarding the necessity of such measures. Article 3.1 of the Safeguards Agreement sets out the requirements for the investigation. The national authorities conducting the investigation must give public notice of the investigation to interested parties. Exporters, importers, and other interested parties must be given an opportunity to express their views on the matter, including their views on whether the application of a safeguard measure would be justified by the public interest. The national authorities must publish a report "setting forth their findings and reasoned conclusions reached on all pertinent issues of fact and law".[15]

In addition, WTO Members must "immediately" notify the Committee on Safeguards of its initiation of an investigation.[16] In the *United States — Wheat Gluten Safeguard* case, the Appellate Body held that a delay of even a few weeks violates this requirement.[17]

[11] *See* Appellate Body Report, *Argentina — Footwear Safeguard*, para. 81; Appellate Body Report, *Korea — Dairy Safeguard*, para. 77.

[12] *See* WTO Agreement Art. II:2 (stating that the agreements included in Annexes 1, 2 and 3 are part of the WTO Agreement). The GATT 1994 and the Safeguards Agreement are both contained in Annex 1A of the WTO Agreement.

[13] Safeguards Agreement Art. 1.

[14] *Id.* Art. 11.1(a).

[15] Safeguards Agreement Art. 3.1.

[16] *Id.* Art. 12.1(a).

[17] Appellate Body Report, *United States — Wheat Gluten Safeguard*, paras 108–112.

## 3.5 Provisional application

WTO Members may impose provisional safeguard measures in "critical circumstances where delay would cause damage which it would be difficult to repair", provided they first make a preliminary determination that there is "clear evidence that increased imports have caused or are threatening to cause serious injury".[18] The maximum period of a provisional measure is 200 days, and the period in which a provisional measure is applied is included in the total period of the safeguard measure.[19] Provisional safeguard measures must take the form of tariff increases.[20]

## 3.6 Determination of increased imports

There must be an increase of imports "in such increased quantities" as to cause or threaten serious injury.[21] The increase can be absolute or relative to domestic production.[22] The Appellate Body found, in *Argentina — Footwear Safeguard*, that the phrase "in such increased quantities" requires that the increase must have been "recent enough, sudden enough, sharp enough and significant enough, both quantitatively and qualitatively, to cause or threaten to cause 'serious injury' ".[23]

## 3.7 Unforeseen developments

The increase of imports must be caused by "unforeseen developments". A literal interpretation of this phrase suggests that a safeguard measure may not be applied unless the injury to a domestic industry was caused by developments that were not foreseen at the time of the latest trade negotiation. The Appellate Body found that the national authorities must demonstrate unforeseen developments before applying a safeguard measure.[24] It is

[18] Safeguards Agreement Art. 6.

[19] *Id.*

[20] *Id.*

[21] GATT Art. XIX:1(a); Safeguards Agreement Art. 2.1.

[22] Safeguards Agreement Art. 2.1.

[23] Appellate Body Report, *Argentina — Footwear Safeguard*, para. 131.

[24] Appellate Body Report, *United States — Lamb Safeguard*, para. 72 (holding that unforeseen developments must be demonstrated "*before* the safeguard measure is applied") (emphasis in original); Appellate Body Report, *Argentina — Footwear Safeguard*, para. 81 (holding that unforeseen developments "must be demonstrated as a matter of fact"); Appellate Body Report, *Korea — Dairy Safeguard*, para. 75 (holding that unforeseen developments "must be demonstrated as a matter of fact").

not sufficient for the national authorities merely to describe certain new developments.[25]

The Appellate Body noted that "unforeseen developments" modifies the phrase "being imported into the territory of that contracting party in such increased quantities and under such conditions as to cause or threaten serious injury to domestic producers in that territory...."[26] The Appellate Body interpreted "unforeseen developments" to be part of "circumstances" in which a sharp increase of imports occurs in such a way as to cause a serious injury to a domestic industry.[27] The Appellate Body concluded that it is necessary for investigating authorities to make findings that unforeseen developments exist and that a logical connection exists between the conditions set forth in Article XIX:1(a) and the circumstances such as "unforeseen developments".[28] If the Appellate Body means that "unforeseen developments" is a requirement that must be established by the country invoking the safeguard measures and is a part of the circumstance surrounding a sharp increase of imports, it means that this requirement must be established independently.

Some commentators have previously suggested that the Report of the Working Party in *Hatters' Fur*[29] read "unforeseen developments" out of Article XIX.[30] In *Hatters' Fur*, the United States invoked a safeguard measure on imported fur products, and Czechoslovakia challenged the measure under Article XIX. The *Hatters' Fur* Working Party found that changes in fashion of women's hats amounted to "unforeseen developments" and upheld the position of the United States.

To state that the *Hatters' Fur* report read "unforeseen developments" out of Article XIX of the GATT seems to be inaccurate (or at least overstated). This report did, however, interpret "unforeseen developments" liberally and, therefore, the threshold for invoking a safeguard measure was set at a

---

[25] Appellate Body Report, *United States — Lamb Safeguard*, para. 73.

[26] Appellate Body Report, *Argentina — Footwear Safeguard*, para. 92.

[27] *Id.*

[28] Appellate Body Report, *United States — Lamb Safeguard*, para. 72.

[29] Report of the Intersessional Working Party on the Complaint of Czechoslovakia Concerning the Withdrawal by the United States of a Concession under the Terms of Article XIX, GATT/CP/106, 27 March 1951.

[30] John H. Jackson, World Trade and the Law of GATT 560–61 (1969); Marco C. E. J. Bronckers, *Voluntary Export Restraints and the GATT 1994 Agreement on Safeguards, in* The Uruguay Round Results: A European Lawyers' Perspective 275 (J. H. J. Bourgeois et al. eds., 1996); Michael J. Trebilcock & Robert Howse, The Regulation of International Trade 228 (2d ed. 1999).

low level. Even if "unforeseen developments" is an independent requirement, it should not be difficult to establish this requirement. Indeed, any development (such as a change in currency value, a technological breakthrough or a change in consumers' preferences) that causes an increase of imports is generally unforeseen at the time of trade negotiation. Who can predict what change in currency value would take place or what technological breakthrough would occur two or three years after the conclusion of a trade negotiation?

A safeguard measure under GATT Article XIX and the Safeguards Agreement is an emergency measure to deal with an increase of imports that is not necessarily unfair. To enable Members to invoke safeguard measures easily would undermine the foundation of the liberal trade order enshrined in the WTO system. In this respect, it makes sense to require the existence of "unforeseen developments" before safeguard measures may be invoked because this requirement will act as a safety mechanism to prevent safeguard measures from being used excessively.

## 3.8 Determination of injury

### *3.8.1 Serious injury or threat of serious injury*

Before imposing safeguard measures, WTO Members must make a determination of serious injury or threat thereof to a domestic injury. The standard of "serious injury" has been found to be higher than that of "material injury", which is the standard for antidumping and countervailing measures.[31] The injury to a domestic industry should be greater when imposing a safeguard measure than when imposing an antidumping or countervailing duty, because safeguards are designed to counteract imports that are not unfair, whereas antidumping and countervailing duties are designed to counteract unfair trade practices. The serious injury standard is intended to strike a balance between the need of a domestic industry for relief from an import surge and that of purchasers of imports and consumers in general for lower-cost imports.

In the *United States — Line Pipe Safeguard* case, the Appellate Body rejected the argument that there must be a discrete determination of both serious injury and threat thereof.[32] Either finding will establish the right to apply safeguard measures.[33] Defining "threat of serious injury" separately

[31] Appellate Body Report, *United States — Lamb Safeguard*, para. 124.
[32] *Id.* paras 171–173.
[33] *Id.* para. 171.

from "serious injury" serves the purpose of "setting a lower threshold for establishing the right to apply a safeguard measure".[34]

### 3.8.1.1 Serious injury

The term "serious injury" is defined to mean "a significant overall impairment in the position of a domestic industry".[35] As the Appellate Body stated in *Argentina — Footwear Safeguard*, there must be a "significant overall impairment" of the situation regarding the domestic industry in question.[36] In other words, there must be not only an upward trend in the volume or market share of imports, but also a deterioration of the situation as a whole with respect to the domestic industry seeking relief.

In *Argentina — Footwear Safeguard*, Argentina found serious injury by comparing figures of imports at two points in time. Although the panel stated that the trend of imports must be examined during the entire period of investigation, it held that, if a decrease of imports is more than temporary, it is doubtful whether there has been an increase of imports. The panel ruled that the government invoking a safeguard measure is required to examine whether an increase of imports and the downward trends of factors of injury coincide, and whether there is a cause other than imports that contributes to the serious injury. The panel held that, in any event, an examination of trends is important. The Appellate Body generally upheld the rulings of the panel.

### 3.8.1.2 Threat of serious injury

The term "threat of serious injury" is defined to mean "serious injury that is clearly imminent".[37] A determination of threat of injury must be based on facts and not merely on allegation, conjecture, or remote possibility.[38] In the *United States — Lamb Safeguard* case, the Appellate Body dealt with the issue of how to interpret the term threat of serious injury. According to the Appellate Body, "threat of serious injury" means that there must be "a high degree of likelihood that the anticipated serious injury will materialize in the very near future".[39]

---

[34] Appellate Body Report, *United States — Lamb Safeguard*, para. 169.
[35] Safeguards Agreement Art. 4.1(a).
[36] Appellate Body Report, *Argentina — Footwear Safeguard*, para. 139.
[37] Safeguards Agreement Art. 4.1(b).
[38] *Id.*
[39] Appellate Body Report, *United States — Lamb Safeguard*, para. 136.

Investigating authorities must explain how the facts relating to prices support a determination that the domestic industry is threatened with serious injury. In *United States — Lamb Safeguard*, the Appellate Body found that over the five-year period of investigation, the price of lamb had generally increased, and then decreased and increased again at the end of the period, and, as a result, the price was higher at the end of the period than it had been at the beginning. The Appellate Body also found that these overall trends raised doubts about the adequacy of the U.S. position. The Appellate Body concluded that the U.S. determination that the domestic industry was threatened with such injury was inconsistent with Article 4.2(a) of the Safeguards Agreement because the United States failed to explain how the facts relating to prices supported its determination.

#### 3.8.1.3 Factors to be considered when determining injury or threat thereof

The national authorities charged with making an injury or threat determination must evaluate "all relevant factors" that are objective and quantifiable and that bear upon the situation of the relevant domestic industry.[40] According to Article 4.2(a) of the Safeguards Agreement, relevant factors include the "rate and amount of the increase in imports of the product concerned in absolute and relative terms, the share of the domestic market taken by increased imports, and changes in the level of sales, production, productivity, capacity utilization, profits and losses, and employment".

The Appellate Body ruled that the national authorities must evaluate all of the factors listed in Article 4.2(a) as well as all other relevant factors, not merely the factors raised by the parties.[41] The Appellate Body qualified its statement by saying that national authorities do not have an open-ended and unlimited duty to investigate all available facts.[42] The Appellate Body recognized that national authorities may not have data pertaining to all domestic producers, but stated that the data must be sufficiently representative to give a true picture of the domestic industry.[43]

Not all factors need to show a downward trend, however, because the issue is whether there is a "significant overall impairment" of the domestic

[40] Safeguards Agreement Art. 4.2(a).

[41] Appellate Body Report, *United States — Wheat Gluten Safeguard*, paras 55–56; Appellate Body Report, *Argentina — Footwear Safeguard*, para. 136.

[42] Appellate Body Report, *United States — Wheat Gluten Safeguard*, para. 56.

[43] Appellate Body Report, *United States — Wheat Gluten Safeguard*, para. 57.

industry or threat thereof.[44] Such impairment can occur even if one or more factors show an upward trend, provided the facts as a whole support the determination of serious injury or threat thereof.

#### 3.8.1.4 Domestic industry

Safeguard measures may be applied to imports when the investigating authorities determine that there is a serious injury or threat thereof to a "domestic industry".[45] Domestic industry is defined as "the producers as a whole of the like or directly competitive products operating within the territory of a Member, or those whose collective output of the like or directly competitive products constitutes a major proportion of the total domestic production of those products".[46] In *United States — Lamb Safeguard*, the Appellate Body dealt with one aspect of the issue of what constitutes a domestic industry. In that case, the United States imposed a safeguard measure on imports of lamb meat. The United States claimed that the producers of lamb meat included growers and feeders of live lambs (*i.e.*, upstream producers) because there is a continuous line of production from the one to the other, and there is commonality of economic interests between the producers of the raw product and the producers of the end product. The panel rejected this argument and held that the domestic industry consists of only producers that have output of like or directly competitive products. The Appellate Body upheld this finding.

### *3.8.2 Causation*

The issue of causation plays a central role in any safeguards investigation. Article 4.2(b) of the Safeguards Agreement provides as follows:

> [An injury or threat determination] shall not be made unless [the] investigation demonstrates . . . the existence of the causal link between increased imports . . . and serious injury or threat thereof. When factors other than increased imports are causing injury to the domestic industry at the same time, such injury shall not be attributed to increased imports.

Article 4.2(b) contains two distinct legal requirements: (1) a causal link between increased imports and the serious injury or threat thereof; and

[44] Appellate Body Report, *Argentina — Footwear Safeguard*, para. 139; Panel Report, *United States — Wheat Gluten Safeguard*, para. 1.85.

[45] Safeguards Agreement Art. 2.1.

[46] *Id.* Art. 4.1(c).

(2) the requirement that other causal factors not be attributed to increased imports.[47] The so-called non-attribution requirement cannot be satisfied by mere assertions. The various causal factors must be disentangled, and there must be a reasoned and adequate explanation of how the factors causing injury and those not causing injury are distinguished.[48]

First, the national authorities conducting the investigation must examine whether increased imports are causing or threatening to cause serious injury. According to the Appellate Body, increased imports will be found to cause or threaten to cause serious injury if such imports clearly contribute to bringing about, producing, or inducing the serious injury or threat thereof.[49] The Appellate Body has pointed out that "the need to distinguish between the effects caused by increased imports and the effects caused by other factors does *not* necessarily imply . . . that increased imports *on their own* must be capable of causing serious injury, nor that injury caused by other factors must be *excluded* from the determination of serious injury".[50]

According to the Appellate Body, the national authorities must determine whether the effects of increased imports establish "*a genuine and substantial relationship* of cause and effect" between the increased imports and serious injury or threat thereof.[51] In determining whether there is "a genuine and substantial relationship of cause and effect" between the increased imports and serious injury or threat thereof, the Appellate Body set out the following "logical process" for national authorities to follow:

1. Distinguish the injurious effects caused to the domestic industry by increased imports from the injurious effects caused by other factors.
2. Attribute to increased imports (on the one hand) and to other relevant factors (on the other hand) "injury" caused by all of these different factors, including increased imports.

[47] Appellate Body Report, *United States — Line Pipe Safeguard*, para. 208.

[48] Appellate Body Report, *United States — Line Pipe Safeguard*, para. 209–214; Appellate Body Report, *United States — Lamb Safeguard*, para. 179; Appellate Body Report, *United States — Wheat Gluten Safeguard*, para. 70.

[49] Appellate Body Report, *United States — Lamb Safeguard*, para. 166; Appellate Body Report, *United States — Wheat Gluten Safeguard*, para. 67.

[50] Appellate Body Report, *United States — Wheat Gluten Safeguard*, para. 70 (emphasis in original).

[51] Appellate Body Report, *United States — Lamb Safeguard*, paras 168, 177, 179 (emphasis added) (citing Appellate Body Report, *United States — Wheat Gluten Safeguard*, para. 69).

3. Determine whether a "causal link" exists between increased imports and serious injury or threat thereof and, if so, whether this causal link involves "a genuine and substantial relationship of cause and effect" between the increased imports and serious injury or threat thereof.[52]

Thus, the Appellate Body concluded that national authorities must explicitly establish, through a reasoned and adequate explanation, that injury caused by factors other than increased imports is not attributed to increased imports. The key is separating or distinguishing the effects of the different factors that bring about the injury.[53] In *United States — Line Pipe Safeguard*,[54] the Appellate Body confirmed this interpretation and added that the standard to be applied is similar to that developed in the context of the Antidumping Agreement. In particular, the Appellate Body cited *United States — Hot-Rolled Steel from Japan*[55] and stated that national authorities must separate and distinguish the injurious effects of the increased imports from the injurious effects of the other factors.

## 3.9 Limits on the application of safeguard measures

The Appellate Body has distinguished the right to apply safeguards under Article XIX and the Safeguards Agreement from the limits on their application. There may be a right to apply safeguard, but a Member must also observe the limits on their application. Thus, in imposing increased tariffs, quotas, tariff-rate quotas, or other safeguard measures, the following limits must be observed.

### *3.9.1 Parallelism*

Parallelism refers to the requirement that WTO Members applying a safeguard measure must maintain a proportion or parallel between (1) the investigation and its findings; and (2) the scope of application of the safeguard measure. The so-called parallelism requirement comes from an interpretation by the Appellate Body of Article 2.1 and 2.2 of the Safeguards Agreement.[56] Article 2.1 concerns the legal conditions that must be fulfilled to invoke safeguard:

52 Appellate Body Report, *United States — Wheat Gluten Safeguard*, para. 69. *See also* Appellate Body Report, *United States — Lamb Safeguard*, para. 177.

53 Appellate Body Report, *United States — Wheat Gluten Safeguard*, para. 68.

54 Appellate Body Report, *United States — Line Pipe Safeguard.*

55 Appellate Body Report, *United States — Hot-Rolled Steel from Japan.*

56 Appellate Body Report, *United States — Line Pipe Safeguard*, paras 179–181.

> A Member may apply a safeguard measure to a product only if that Member has determined, pursuant to the provisions set out below, that such product is being imported into its territory in such increased quantities, absolute or relative to domestic production, and under such conditions as to cause or threaten to cause serious injury to the domestic industry that produces like or directly competitive products.[57]

Article 2.2 concerns the right to apply safeguard: "Safeguard measures shall be applied to a product being imported irrespective of its source".[58]

Both Article 2.1 and Article 2.2 use the phrase "product...being imported". There cannot, therefore, be a gap between the products covered in the investigation and the products subject to the safeguard measure. Rather, the products covered in the investigation and the products subject to the safeguard measure must parallel each other.[59] The parallelism requirement is further elaborated in Article 4.2, which concerns the causal link between increased imports and the serious injury or threat thereof to the domestic industry.[60]

The issue of parallelism between the investigation and the application of a safeguard measure arises most importantly in connection with non-application of a safeguard measure to imports from members of an FTA to which the country applying the measure is also a member. If, for example, Country X (a WTO Member and an FTA member) investigates imports from all sources, but does not apply the safeguard measure to imports from the members of the FTA, Country Y (a WTO Member but not an FTA member) may challenge this non-application as a violation of the Safeguards Agreement as well as, perhaps, the most-favoured-nation treatment principle. The issue of parallelism is closely related to the question of whether, under Article XXIV of the GATT 1994, a country that is a member of an FTA can lawfully apply a safeguard measure with respect to imports from another member of the FTA.

The issue of parallelism was taken up in the *Argentina — Footwear Safeguard* case. In this case, the panel held that the safeguard measure must be applied to imports from all countries, including members of the customs union, if imports from all sources, including those from the other customs union members, were taken into account in the safeguard

---

57 Safeguards Agreement Art. 2.1 (footnote omitted).

58 *Id.* Art. 2.2.

59 Appellate Body Report, *United States — Line Pipe Safeguard*, para. 181.

60 *Id.* para. 188.

investigation.[61] On appeal, the Appellate Body held that Articles 2.1 and 4.2 of the Safeguards Agreement require that an investigation evaluating imports from all sources can lead only to the imposition of safeguard measures on imports from all sources. The Appellate Body ruled that Argentina's investigation, which was based on an investigation of imports from all countries, including the MERCOSUR countries, could not, therefore, serve as a basis for excluding imports from other MERCOSUR countries from the application of the safeguard measure.

In *United States — Wheat Gluten Safeguard*, the panel held that the United States violated Articles 2.1 and 4.2 of the Safeguards Agreement by excluding Canada (a party to NAFTA) from the application of safeguard measures after including imports from all sources in its investigation. The United States appealed this finding, and the Appellate Body rejected the U.S. claims on the ground that it was necessary for the United States to have shown that imports from countries other than Canada cause or threaten to cause serious injury to a domestic industry.

The most recent appellate ruling on this issue came in the *United States — Line Pipe Safeguard* case. In this case, the United States excluded imports from Mexico and Canada from the application of safeguard measures even though an investigation had been conducted with regard to serious injury caused by imports from countries including Mexico and Canada. Korea petitioned to the WTO and argued that the United States violated the principle of most-favoured-nation treatment by excluding Mexico and Canada from the application of the safeguard measure. The panel found a violation of provisions of the Safeguards Agreement on the part of the United States. The panel also found that the United States was entitled to rely on GATT Article XXIV as a defence to a charge that it violated the MFN principle.

Both the United States and Korea appealed. The Appellate Body ruled that the United States did not adduce sufficient evidence to show that imports from countries other than the NAFTA countries (Mexico and Canada) had caused a serious injury to the domestic industry. Regarding the cross-appeal by Korea arguing that the panel was wrong to hold that the United States could rely on Article XXIV as a defence to a charge that it infringed the MFN principle, the Appellate Body stated that the issue was disposed of by the holding and it was not, therefore, necessary to consider this question, and that the part of the panel report dealing with whether

[61] Panel Report, *Argentina — Footwear Safeguard*, para. 111 (citing Safeguards Agreement Art. 2.1, footnote 1).

Article XXIV constitutes a defence to a charge of a violation of the MFN principle was moot and had no legal effect.[62]

In the *United States — Line Pipe Safeguard* case, the Appellate Body held that the exclusion of NAFTA countries Canada and Mexico from a safeguard measure was a *prima facie* violation of the parallelism requirement because Korea had demonstrated that the United States "considered imports from all sources in its investigation" and that "exports from Canada and Mexico were excluded from the safeguard measure at issue".[63] Thus, the burden was on the United States to rebut by providing a "*reasoned and adequate explanation* that *establishes explicitly* that imports from non-NAFTA sources satisfied the conditions for the application of a safeguard measure, as set out in Article 2.1 and elaborated in Article 4.2 of the *Agreement on Safeguards*".[64]

### *3.9.2 Extent of safeguards*

Important limits on the application of safeguards are contained in Article 5.1 of the Safeguards Agreement.

The first sentence of Article 5.1 requires that safeguard measures be applied "only to the extent necessary to prevent or remedy serious injury and to facilitate adjustment". The "extent necessary" requirement is a substantive obligation that the safeguard measure be limited to remedying the serious injury findings in Article 4.2. Thus, a Member cannot apply safeguard to remedy the entirety of the serious injury but only that attributable to increased imports.[65]

The second sentence of Article 5.1 further requires that, if a quota is used as a safeguard measure, it "shall not reduce the quantity of imports below the level of... the average of imports in the last three representative years ..., unless clear justification is given that a different level is necessary to prevent or remedy serious injury". This sentence contains a substantive requirement: if a quota is less than the three-year average, it must be

[62] Appellate Body Report, *United States — Line Pipe Safeguard*, para. 199. Although the Appellate Body exercised "judicial economy" and avoided consideration of this issue, it is probably wrong for the Appellate Body to have dismissed this cross-appeal by Korea because Article 17.12 of the Dispute Settlement Understanding states that the Appellate Body shall address each legal issue raised in an appeal. This wording suggests that the Appellate Body may not exercise judicial economy.

[63] Appellate Body Report, *United States — Line Pipe Safeguard*, para. 187.

[64] Appellate Body Report, *United States — Line Pipe Safeguard*, para. 188 (italics in original).

[65] *Id.* paras 252–260.

necessary to prevent or remedy serious injury. There is also an explicit procedural requirement: "clear justification" means that the Member must make a clear demonstration.[66]

### *3.9.3 Selectivity*

When WTO Members apply safeguard measures in the form of a quota, they may allocate the quota among supplying countries based on an agreement with exporting Members.[67] If an agreement is difficult to reach, they may allocate the quota to Members based on the proportion of products imported from those Members during a representative period, *e.g.*, the past three years.[68] WTO Members may deviate from this principle if the increase of imports from a given Member is disproportionately large in relation to the total increase of imports.[69] This deviation from the principle of non-discrimination is called quota modulation. Quota modulation must be justified and equitable to the Members interested in the matter.[70] Quota modulation is not, however, available in the case of only a threat of serious injury.[71] WTO Members engaging in quota modulation must report to and consult with the WTO Committee on Safeguards.[72]

The issue of whether "selective" safeguard measures should be permissible under GATT/WTO rules was a subject of controversy between the European Community and developing countries. Selective safeguard measures are measures applied to imports from one country but not to imports of other countries. The European Community wanted to include selective safeguard measures, but developing country Members objected because they felt they would be the targets of such measures. Japan sided with developing countries in this issue. A compromise between different views on this subject was quota modulation.

### *3.9.4 Developing countries*

WTO Members must exclude developing country Members whose import share is 3 percent or less from the application of safeguard measures, unless

[66] Appellate Body Report, *United States — Line Pipe Safeguard*, para. 233.

[67] Safeguards Agreement Art. 5.2(a).

[68] *Id.*

[69] *Id.* Art. 5.2(b).

[70] *Id.* WTO Members may not engage in quota modulations if there is only a "threat of serious injury." *Id.; see also, e.g.*, Appellate Body Report, *United States — Line Pipe Safeguard*, para. 173.

[71] Safeguards Agreement Art. 5.2(b).

[72] Safeguards Agreement Art. 5.2(b).

the total import share of all such countries exceeds 9 percent.[73] According to the Appellate Body, "all reasonable steps" must be taken to comply with this exclusion.[74]

### 3.9.5 *GATT Article XIII*

Although GATT Article XIII regarding non-discriminatory administration of import quotas is superseded by the Safeguards Agreement provision on selectivity,[75] two obligations in Article XIII:2(a) remain. First, traditional trade patterns must be respected in allocating quotas.[76] Second, the total amount of imports permitted at the lower tariff rate must be fixed (not merely the individual quotas for each country).[77]

### 3.9.6 *Duration and review*

In principle, safeguard measures are temporary and should not be prolonged beyond the necessary period. In light of this principle, the maximum period for a safeguard measure is four years.[78] A safeguard measure may be extended if the national authorities decide that it is necessary to do so.[79] The total period of a safeguard measure may not be more than eight years. If the period in which a safeguard measure is applied extends beyond one year, there must be a regular reduction of the measure.[80] If the safeguard period is more than three years, there must be an interim review and the measure must be withdrawn or there must be an acceleration of the reduction of the measure.[81] No safeguard measure can be taken with regard to a product on which a safeguard measure was applied at least for the period equal to that in which the safeguard measure was taken and, in any event, no safeguard measure can be taken with regard to that product at least for two years.[82]

A developing country Member has the right to extend the period of safeguard for two years[83] beyond the eight years maximum. It can also reapply a safeguard measure after a period equal to half that during which a

---

[73] *Id.* Art. 9.1.

[74] Appellate Body Report, *United States — Line Pipe Safeguard*, paras 132–133.

[75] *See* above section 3.9.3.

[76] Appellate Body Report, *United States — Line Pipe Safeguard*, para. 79.

[77] *Id.*

[78] Safeguards Agreement Art. 7.1.

[79] *Id.* Art. 7.2.

[80] *Id.* Art. 7.4.

[81] *Id.*

[82] Safeguards Agreement Art. 7.5.

[83] *Id.* Art. 9.2.

previous measure has been previously applied, if the period of non-application is at least two years.[84]

## 3.10 Notification and consultation

Before applying or extending a safeguard measure, WTO Members must provide an "adequate opportunity for prior consultations" to Members "having a substantial interest as exporters" with a view to reaching an understanding on maintaining a "substantially equivalent" balance of trade concessions.[85] Providing an adequate opportunity for prior consultations has been held to mean that the Member proposing to apply the safeguard must provide "sufficient information and time to allow for the possibility, through consultations, for a meaningful exchange" of views.[86] The time for advance notice is determined on a case-by-case basis.[87]

In the *United States — Line Pipe Safeguard* case, the United States announced the safeguard measure in a press release. The Appellate Body held this method of notification to be inadequate and a violation of Safeguards Agreement, Article 12.3 as well as Article 8.1.[88]

## 3.11 Compensation

GATT Article XIX:3 grants to Members affected by safeguard measures the right to suspend "substantially equivalent [trade] concessions" against the Member invoking safeguard measures. The idea is that there should be a rebalancing of trade concessions vis-à-vis the Members either voluntarily or involuntarily.

The Safeguards Agreement modifies this right to a considerable degree. WTO Members invoking safeguard measures must offer to compensate other Members to equalize the loss they would suffer from the invocation of the safeguard measures.[89] If an agreement cannot be reached between the invoking Member and exporting Members, the latter can take retaliatory

[84] Safeguards Agreement Art. 9.2.

[85] Safeguards Agreement Arts. 8.1, 12.3. *See* Appellate Body Report, *United States — Line Pipe Safeguard*, para. 119; Appellate Body Report, *United States — Wheat Gluten Safeguard*, para. 135. There is a link, therefore, between Article 12.3 and Article 8.1, and a violation of the consultation requirement is also a violation of Article 8.1.

[86] Appellate Body Report, *United States — Line Pipe Safeguard*, paras 106–113; Appellate Body Report, *United States — Wheat Gluten Safeguard*, para. 136.

[87] Appellate Body Report, *United States — Line Pipe Safeguard*, para. 113.

[88] Appellate Body Report, *United States — Line Pipe Safeguard*, para. 119.

[89] *Id.* Art. 8.1.

measures.[90] The right to retaliate is, however, limited.[91] If safeguard measures are applied in response to an increase of imports in absolute terms and conform to provisions of the Safeguards Agreement, the exporting Members may not invoke retaliatory measures against those measures for a three-year period.[92] This limitation is provided so that Members can invoke safeguard measures without fear that the exporting Members will retaliate.

The three-year mandatory moratorium in the Safeguards Agreement on the right to suspend concessions creates a dilemma for WTO Members adversely affected by a safeguard measure. Article 8.1 of the Safeguards Agreement provides that Members proposing a safeguard "shall endeavour" to maintain substantially equivalent reciprocal trade concessions, but there may be no practical means to enforce this right. If the Member invoking the safeguard measure refuses consultation[93] and compensation, and safeguard is invoked in violation of the GATT and the Safeguards Agreement, affected parties have options that are less than satisfactory. First, an affected party may bring a complaint under GATT Articles XXII and XXIII and the DSU,[94] but it normally takes a year to get decision by the Appellate Body, and the losing party has up to 15 additional months to comply after the adoption of an Appellate Body report.

Second, an affected party can seek an immediate suspension of equivalent concessions pursuant to Safeguards Agreement Article 8.2, but this is not possible for a safeguard measure taken as a result of an *absolute* increase in imports.

Third, an affected party may seek to invoke GATT Article XXVIII, which allows withdrawal of equivalent trade concessions by Members affected by a modification of another Member's schedule of concessions. However, it would appear that Article XXVIII does not apply and would not, in any case, supersede the Safeguards Agreement, which specifically concerns safeguards and retaliation.

This problem reflects the unresolved tension in the Safeguards Agreement itself regarding the purposes and objectives of safeguards. As discussed

---

[90] *Id.* Art. 8.2.

[91] *Id.* Art. 8.3.

[92] *Id.*

[93] The *Line Pipe* case states that Article 8.1 is enforced in the first instance by the obligation to consult in Safeguards Agreement Art. 12.3. Appellate Body Report, *United States — Line Pipe Safeguard*, para. 119.

[94] Safeguards Agreement Art. 14.

above,[95] a safeguard is a "fair trade remedy",[96] but its purpose is unclear. WTO Members must clarify the basic reason and purpose for a safeguard to clarify the right to compensation and retaliation. If, on the one hand, the purpose of safeguard is to provide compensation for trade-injured workers or allow politicians in the safeguarding country to satisfy the public choice agenda, safeguards should be accompanied by a rebalancing of trade concessions between the safeguarding country and affected WTO Members. This would dictate greater availability of compensation and retaliation by affected Members. In this case, Article 8.3, which restricts this right, should be repealed or modified. If, on the other hand, the purpose of safeguard is to give a "breathing space", allow reforms and provide a "safety valve", the three-year moratorium on the right of retaliation seems justified. Where a Member wrongfully invokes a safeguard, however, provision should be made for a different remedy such as a monetary fine or mandatory compensation.

### 3.12 The standard of review for safeguard disputes

When a WTO panel or the Appellate Body determines whether a safeguard measures is consistent with WTO law, the standard of review is important because, without such a standard, there is no criterion for showing deference to the factual or legal findings of national authorities. Unlike the Anti-dumping Agreement, the Agreement on Safeguards is silent regarding the issue of standard of review. Thus, the applicable standard of review is DSU Article 11. As is evident from the cases discussed above, review by WTO adjudicating bodies tends to be far-reaching, and some violation of the norms in the Safeguards Agreement has been found in every case.

## 4. Safeguard measures for balance-of-payment reasons

### 4.1 The GATT

At the time of GATT 1947, the contracting parties conducted international monetary policy through a system of par-value, fixed currency exchange rates, and the GATT is based upon that system. Under par-value exchange

[95] *See* above section 1.

[96] Appellate Body Report, *United States — Line Pipe Safeguard*, para. 80.

rates, changes in par-value, especially devaluation, are disruptive and to be avoided. Thus, when a country, for any number of reasons, experiences high demand for foreign currencies, crisis can result if currency reserves are inadequate. Two options exist to deal with this problem: (1) trade restrictions to reduce imports; and (2) changes in macro-economic policies.

With the passing of the era of par-value exchange rates and under the current system of floating rates, changes in demand for currencies are reflected in the exchange rate changes. These may vary dramatically over time, but usually only marginally in the short term. As a result, at present, trade restrictions for balance-of-payments reasons are no longer used by most WTO Members with the exception of certain developing countries.[97]

The GATT contains extensive provisions allowing WTO Members to adopt trade restrictions for balance-of-payments reasons.[98] The GATT does not exclude, but does not explicitly require a country experiencing balance-of-payments problems to adopt macroeconomic policies lessening demand.[99]

The substantive requirements for balance-of-payments trade restrictions are contained in Article XII and Article XVIII, Section B, which is reserved to developing countries.[100] Both provisions allow a WTO Member to impose trade restrictions to safeguard its financial position and balance of payments, but only to the extent necessary (1) to forestall the imminent threat of or stop a serious decline in its monetary reserves; or (2) in the case of a country with very low reserves, to achieve a reasonable rate of increase of its reserves.[101]

Both Articles leave the determination as to what is a serious decline in reserves, a low level of reserves, or a reasonable rate of increase to the IMF.[102] Thus, the IMF determines the legality of imposing or continuing balance-of-payments trade restrictions.

---

[97] *E.g.*, see "IMF Approves Loans for Brazil and Uruguay", The International Herald Tribune, 21 June 2002, p. 17, col. 1.

[98] GATT Arts. XII, XIII, XIV, XV and XVIII, section B.

[99] *Id.* Art. XII:3(d). GATT Art. XII:3(a) provides, however, that countries should adopt domestic policies that expand, rather than contract, international trade. See also GATT Art. XVIII:11.

[100] There are small differences between Articles XII and XVIII. *See* Jackson, above note 30, at 689.

[101] GATT Arts. XII:2, XVIII:9.

[102] *Id.* Art. XV:2. *See* Debrah E. Siegel, Legal Aspects of the IMF/WTO Relationship: The Fund's Articles of Agreement and the WTO Agreements, 96 AJIL 561 (2002).

Moreover, both GATT Article XII:2(b) and Article XVIII:11 require the country applying trade restrictions to progressively remove them once balance-of-payments conditions improve. In the *Korean Beef* case, the GATT dispute settlement panel relied upon Article XVIII:11 and the determination of the IMF that South Korea had adequate monetary reserves, to recommend that South Korea work out a timetable for the removal of import quotas on beef that had been maintained since 1967.[103]

In the *India — Agricultural, Textile and Industrial Products* case,[104] the Appellate Body further elaborated on the criteria for maintaining balance-of-payments trade restrictions. First, balance-of-payments trade restrictions may be maintained only if there is a "clear probability" of the occurrence of one of the conditions of GATT Article XVIII:9: (1) a threat of a serious decline in monetary reserves; (2) a serious decline in monetary reserves; or (3) inadequate monetary reserves.[105] Second, in the absence of these conditions, balance-of-payments trade restrictions must be removed and may not be maintained merely because of a "distant possibility" that balance-of-payments difficulties may recur.[106]

As for the products with respect to which trade restrictions may be imposed, the GATT leaves the choice fundamentally to the country applying the restrictions.[107] In making the choice, a country (1) must avoid "unnecessary" damage to the commercial or economic interests of trading partners; (2) must not "prevent unreasonably" the restrictions to impair regular channels of trade; and (3) must not prohibit the importation of commercial samples or "prevent compliance with patent, trademark, copyright, or similar procedures".[108]

Both Article XII and Article XVIII authorize the adoption of only one type of trade restriction — namely, quotas. Generally, quotas must be administered on a non-discriminatory basis[109] and must be allocated among supplier countries based on their expected shares of trade through country-specific quotas or import licenses. The non-discrimination rule

[103] *Republic of Korea — Restrictions on Imports of Beef*, 7 November 1989, GATT B.I.S.D. (36th Supp.) at 268 (1990) [hereinafter the *Korean Beef* case].

[104] Appellate Body Report, *India — Agricultural, Textile and Industrial Products.*

[105] *Id.* paras 110–114.

[106] *Id.* para. 115.

[107] Article XII:3(b) provides that restrictions can be given to the importation of "those products which are more essential". Article XVIII:10 similarly allows "priority to the importation of those products which are more essential in the light of its policy of economic development".

[108] GATT Arts. XII:3(b), XVIII:10.

[109] *Id.* Art. XIII.

may be disregarded "temporarily", with the consent of WTO Members, by the trade-restricting country "in respect of a small part of its external trade" where the benefits to the Member "substantially outweigh" any injury to the trade of other Members.[110]

Procedurally, quotas for balance-of-payments purposes can be adopted unilaterally, but the trade-restricting state must "immediately" enter into consultations with other WTO Members.[111] After the initial consultations, the quotas must be reviewed periodically.[112] If trade restrictions are at any time being applied inconsistently with applicable standards, the WTO may release the aggrieved party or parties from appropriate GATT obligations, thus allowing retaliation through the suspension or modification of trade concessions.[113] A developing country against which trade retaliation is adopted has the right to withdraw from the GATT on 60 days' notice.[114]

In practice, the GATT provision for trade restrictions for balance of payments purposes has never operated the way it apparently was intended, and, in fact, its primary rationale was lost after the end of the Bretton Woods system of par-value exchange rates. Under the current system of floating exchange rates, the need for reserves is now limited to central bank intervention in foreign exchange markets. Rather than intervening to defend exchange rates, countries can simply let the exchange rate move to market-driven levels.

Even before the demise of the Bretton Woods system of par-value exchange rates, balance-of-payments trade restrictions were not used according to GATT norms. When the United States adopted balance-of-payments trade restrictions in August 1971, it imposed a 10–percent import surcharge rather than quotas. This action withstood a court challenge under U.S. law,[115] but was never tested under the GATT. In recent years, the balance-of-payments exception has been invoked only by developing countries. For example, in 1983, Brazil invoked the provisions of GATT Article XVIII to justify 361 quotas.[116] Other countries invoking this provision to justify selected quotas were Ghana, India, Korea, Nigeria, Pakistan

[110] *Id.* Art. XIV.

[111] *Id.* Arts. XII:4(a), XVIII:12(a).

[112] *Id.* Arts. XII:4(b), XVIII:12(b), (c)(i).

[113] *Id.* Arts. XII(c), (d), XVIII:12(c)(ii),(d).

[114] *Id.* Art. XVIII:12(e).

[115] *United States v. Yoshida Int'l Inc.*, 526 F.2d 560 (C.C.P.A. 1975).

[116] Reported in Isaiah Frank, *Import Quotas, the Balance of Payments and the GATT*, 10 World Economy 307 (1987).

and Tunisia, to name a few.[117] This experience shows that the balance-of-payments exception has been used under extremely doubtful circumstances to justify highly selective, rather than across-the-board, quotas.[118]

## 4.2 The WTO

A good case could be made for the abolition of any right under the GATT to impose trade restrictions for balance-of-payment reasons because of the demise of the Bretton Woods par-value exchange system. However, at the conclusion of the Uruguay Round, the negotiating parties chose to retain the GATT provisions unchanged as a part of the GATT 1994 but to adopt an Understanding on the Balance-of-Payments Provisions of the General Agreement on Tariffs and Trade 1994[119] as part of the WTO Agreement. This Understanding makes several changes in the balance-of-payments exception.

In the WTO, the Balance of Payments Committee handles legal and policy questions concerning balance of payments in the first instance, but resort can be made to dispute settlement under the DSU as well.

In the WTO Understanding, Members are authorized to give preference to "price-based" measures for balance-of-payments purposes because such measures have the least disruptive effect on trade.[120] Price-based measures include import surcharges, import deposit requirements, and other equivalent trade restrictions.[121] If quotas are used, Members must provide justification as to the reasons price-based measures are inadequate.[122] The Understanding provides specifically that such price-based measures may be in excess of the GATT-bound duties under GATT Article II.[123] The Understanding, therefore, validates the state practice of the 1960s and early 1970s, when the United States, the United Kingdom, and other countries used price-based measures for balance-of-payments problems.

[117] Reported in Isaiah Frank, above note 116, at 313.

[118] *See, e.g.*, the *Korean Beef* case, above note 103. *See also* Richard Eglin, *Surveillance of Balance of Payments Measures in the GATT*, 10 World Economy 1 (1987).

[119] Understanding on the Balance-of-Payments Provisions of the General Agreement on Tariffs and Trade, reprinted in WTO, The Legal Texts: The Results of the Uruguay Round of Multilateral Trade Negotiations 22 (1999).

[120] *Id.* para. 2.

[121] *Id.*

[122] *Id.* para. 3.

[123] *Id.* paras 2 and 3.

The Understanding also makes several other improvements in balance-of-payments trade measures. Restrictive import measures are to be taken only "to the extent necessary to address the balance of payments situation". Generally, they must not target specific products but must be applied to "control the general level of imports"; only "essential products" may be excluded.[124] The Understanding requires that the trade measures should be administered in a "transparent" manner and must be notified to the WTO General Council.[125] Time schedules for the removal of the trade measures must be announced publicly "as soon as possible".[126]

The WTO Understanding is an improvement over the GATT balance-of-payments provisions because it is based on sound economic principles. If trade intervention is to occur, an across-the-board tariff surcharge is superior to quantitative restrictions. There are several reasons why this is so. First, administratively they are easier to apply and to remove; second, their disruptive effect will be less, to the extent they are spread over many goods and economic sectors; third, a broad-based surcharge will tend to avoid unfair discrimination; and fourth, import surcharges add directly to reserves and still allow imports, at least in principle.

Nevertheless, there are grounds to doubt whether the WTO Understanding, in attempting to preserve an archaic GATT exception, has sewn the seeds of future problems. Although the WTO has gone to great lengths to reform the balance-of-payments provisions so that they will be used as they were during the Bretton Woods system, they almost certainly will not be used that way, since the Bretton Woods system is no more. Instead, the WTO Understanding may open the way for across-the-board import surcharges to cure trade deficit problems and currency exchange imbalances, which have replaced balance-of-payments problems in the post-Bretton Woods world.

Despite the fact that the WTO elected to retain the possibility of trade restrictions to cure balance-of-payments problems, there is reason to believe that current policies make this impossible. This is because the GATT Article XV:2 makes the IMF the sole judge of whether a country has experienced a serious decline, a very low level or a reasonable rate of increase in its monetary reserves. Thus the IMF, in effect, has the power to determine the appropriateness of a country's invocation of Article XII or Article XVII,

124 *Id.* para. 4.

125 *Id.* para. 4 and 9.

126 *Id.* para. 1.

Section B, to justify the restriction of trade. But the IMF's usual remedy for a balance-of-payments crisis is not trade restrictions but fiscal and monetary discipline imposed on a country in return for a loan package.

## 5. Safeguard measures in textile and clothing trade

Before the WTO Agreement entered into force, the Multifibre Arrangement (MFA) authorized country-specific safeguard measures for textile and clothing imports. The MFA operated on the basis of bilateral trade agreements between trading countries. The WTO Agreement on Textiles and Clothing (ATC) replaces the MFA. Under the ATC, safeguard measures are permitted only on a Member-by-Member basis.[127] The ATC permits such safeguard measures because textile industries generally consist of small businesses and employ a large number of people, many of who are unskilled and cannot easily be shifted to other sectors. The ATC is, however, scheduled to terminate after ten years (*i.e.*, at the end of 2004).[128] After this transition period, textile and clothing trade will be integrated into the GATT 1994. Safeguard measures on textile and clothing imports will then be regulated by Article XIX of GATT 1994.

The ATC permits WTO Members to impose safeguard measures if they demonstrate that a particular product is being imported into their territory in such increased quantities as to cause or threaten "serious damage" to the domestic industry producing "like" or "directly competitive" products.[129] The Member seeking to invoke a safeguard measure must consult with exporting Members and notify the Textile Monitoring Board (TMB), a WTO body, with a view to reaching agreement.[130]

If an agreement is reached, an import measure is taken in accordance with the terms of the agreement. If no agreement is reached, the Member can invoke a safeguard measure under the ATC.[131]

The TMB is composed of Members appointed by the Council for Trade in Goods but who serve on an *ad personam* basis. When the TMB issues a recommendation, Members shall "endeavor" to accept it.[132] If a Member is

[127] Understanding on the Balance-of-Payments Provisions of the General Agreement on Tariffs and Trade, above note 126, Art. 6.4.

[128] *Id.* Art. 9.

[129] *Id.* Art. 6.2.

[130] *Id.* Art. 6.7 and 6.9.

[131] *Id.* Art. 6.11.

[132] Panel Report, *United States — Shirts and Blouses.*

unable to comply with the recommendations of the TMB, it must notify it to that effect, and the TMB can issue further recommendations. After further recommendations, either Member can bring the matter before the Dispute Settlement Body and invoke Article XXIII of the GATT and provisions of the DSU. The burden of proof in this instance rests upon the claimant.[133] Thus, Members are under no legal obligation to observe recommendations of the TMB. A Member must, however, exhaust the process of recommendations of the TMB before resorting to the dispute settlement process under Article XXIII of the GATT 1994 or under the DSU.

In *United States — Underwear*, Costa Rica challenged a U.S. import quota on underwear from Costa Rica and argued that the imposition of import quota was based on improper findings of serious damage caused to the domestic industry. The panel agreed that the United States had not demonstrated that serious damage or threat thereof was caused by textile imports,[134] and the Appellate Body added a finding that the U.S. safeguard was illegal because it was imposed with retroactive effect.[135]

## 6. Prohibition on voluntary export restraints

### 6.1 Prohibition in the Safeguards Agreement

Voluntary export restraints (VERs), sometimes called voluntary restraint agreements (VRAs), are agreements between an exporting country and an importing country whereby the exporting country restrains its export of a product to the importing country at a request of the latter. These agreements were used often in the 1960s, 1970s and 1980s between the United States and Japan and the European Community and Japan. Prime examples are the VER in steel, which began in late 1960s and lasted until early 1990s; the VER in automobiles, which began in 1981 and lasted until early 1990s; and the Semiconductor Agreement, which began in 1986 and lasted until early 1990s. Each of them was entered into between the United States and Japan.[136]

[133] Panel Report, *United States — Shirts and Blouses.*

[134] Panel Report, *United States — Underwear.*

[135] Appellate Body Report, *United States — Underwear.*

[136] For brief comments on VERs between the United States and Japan, see Industrial Structure Council, Japan: Report on Unfair Trade Policies by Major Trading Partners (1993), at 66–67, 59–60, 66–69, A5–A6 and A10–A11.

Generally, when there was a surge of imports from one country to another and domestic industries in the latter complained about the import pressures, the former requested the latter to restrain export voluntarily in accordance with its domestic laws and regulations and the latter complied with the request. This was a quick and easy way to resolve trade issues. This way of resolving trade conflicts was called "bilateralism" because issues were dealt with and settled between the two countries.

VERs were, however, criticized as undermining the multilateral trading system, lacking transparency and tending to distort the flow of trade and prolong restrictions.

In the Uruguay Round, the framers of the Safeguards Agreement decided to abolish VERs altogether, and a *quid pro quo* of abolishing VERs was the strengthening of the safeguard system by introducing quota modulation and the restriction of retaliation to import quota under the Safeguards Agreement.

The Safeguards Agreement prohibits Members from engaging in VERs by stating: "a Member shall not seek, take or maintain any voluntary export restraints, orderly marketing arrangements or any other similar measures on the export or the import side".[137] It further continues: "These include actions taken by a single Member as well as actions under agreements, arrangements and understandings entered into by two or more Members". It should be noted that a Member is prohibited not only from taking or maintaining VERs but also from "seeking" them.

In the past, often an importing country conveyed an informal message to an exporting country without any formal trade negotiation that there would be trade issues either by way of imposing import quotas, invocation of antidumping laws, or otherwise, unless import pressure was reduced by whatever means available to the exporting country. The exporting country would agree to this informal request and put into effect a VER restraining export of the products in question to the importing country. Ostensibly, this could be viewed as a unilateral action of the exporting country. It is clear that such a view is contrary to the reality. In fact, the exporting country is pressured into taking this measure by the request of the importing country. One of the prime examples of this is the United States-Japan Automobile Arrangement, which is discussed below.

The framers of the WTO agreements considered this issue and decided to prohibit VERs whether they were formal or informal agreements or whether

[137] Safeguards Agreement Art. 11(b).

they were carried out at the initiative of the exporting country or at the request of importing country.

Although VERs cannot be lawfully maintained under the Safeguards Agreement, protectionist pressures have not died down. What remains to be seen is whether the Safeguards Agreement and Article XIX of the GATT 1994 are effective enough to keep protectionism in bay.

## 6.2 Tension between voluntary export restraints and competition policy

As discussed above, the Safeguards Agreement prohibits VERs,[138] and there are no VERs officially operating today. Protectionists may have shifted their emphasis from VERs to such remedies as antidumping. Also, as seen in indictments returned by the U.S. Justice Department against international cartels, there are underground international cartels that divide world markets and affect international trade in much the same way as VERs. Such private international cartels are more vulnerable than VERs because they do not enjoy the blessings of the governments. At the same time, they are more difficult to detect because they are not authorized by governments and are entered into and enforced in secret.

Past cases of VERs reveal tension between trade policy and competition policy. They also reveal intricate relationships between government policies and private interests. Considering that competition policy in international trade may be an important future agenda in WTO, it may be useful to discuss the past issues of trade and competition and to review some of the important cases of VERs. From among many such cases, two will be discussed.

### *6.2.1 The automobile VER case*

In 1980, the Ford Motor Company, a U.S. automobiles manufacturer, and the United Autoworkers of America (UAW), the labour union, asked the U.S. International Trade Commission (USITC) to investigate whether the U.S. automobile industry was being harmed by imports, pursuant to section 201 of the Trade Act of 1974. For a variety of reasons, the USITC determined that, although the U.S. automobile industry was seriously injured, the injury was not caused by imports of foreign-made cars. The USITC therefore denied the request for the application of section 201.[139]

[138] Safeguard Agreement Art. 11.

[139] *Motor Vehicles and Certain Chassis and Bodies Therefor*, Investigation No. TA-201–44, USITC Publication 1110 (1980).

There were, however, two million workers unemployed in the U.S. automobile industry, and for political reasons it was necessary for the U.S. government to deal with the imports. Because imports of Japanese cars had increased rapidly, the focus of the import issue was Japanese cars. The United States sent a trade mission to Japan and "explained" the troubled situation of the automobile industry and the possibility that the U.S. Congress would restrict imports. The U.S. government did not officially "request" the Japanese government to take measures to restrain export. The Japanese government "voluntarily" decided to set a limit to exports of Japanese-made cars to the United States.

In the view of the Japanese government, the only practical way to implement export restraint of automobiles was for Japanese industry to come up with an export restraint programme. However, if this were to involve an agreement among the Japanese exporters of automobiles, it would be a violation of Section 1 of the Sherman Act.

In the face of this situation, the Japanese government established an intricate device for export restraint. The government issued an individual "directive" to each exporter indicating the maximum number of cars that it could export to the United States. There was no discussion or agreement among the exporters. The government then stated that, should the number of cars exported by an exporter exceed the maximum number as indicated by the directive, it would immediately invoke an order under the Export Control Decree and prohibit the exportation of cars by that exporter.

The purpose of this arrangement was to construct an export scheme in which each exporter would receive the governmental directive individually, without discussion with other exporters, on the number of cars to be exported, and thereby avoid an export cartel agreement, and ensure the effectiveness of the directive by issuing a statement that there would be an invocation of government compulsion if the number of cars exported exceeded the governmental directive. This was to achieve the purpose of reducing the number of cars which would be exported from Japan to the United States and, at the same time, ensure that there would be no export cartel agreement among the exporters which would violate U.S. antitrust laws.

It is ironic, however, that the Japanese government had to resort to a mandatory measure to restrict exports and to deprive private enterprises of the incentive to export solely for the purpose of putting this export scheme outside the reach of U.S. antitrust laws.

The Japanese government requested the view of the U.S. Attorney General as to whether this export scheme would raise any antitrust issues in the United States. The Attorney General replied that "I believe" that this scheme would not raise any antitrust issue.[140]

A feature of this VER is that an export restraint was based on an informal understanding rather than a formal agreement. The U.S. government would have argued that there was no mutual understanding because the role of the U.S. government was merely to "explain" the situation rather than to enter into an understanding with the Japanese government. In this view, it was a unilateral action on the part of the Japanese government to restrain export of cars from Japan to the United States. Realistically, however, the "explanation" was a "request" on the part of the United States to Japan to engage in VER.

Although the U.S. automobile industry was not a part of this trade negotiation, the U.S. government negotiated with the Japanese government on behalf of the U.S. industry, and the economic effect of this deal was no different from that of a cartel between the industries of both countries if they had been engaged in an agreement among themselves to divide the U.S. and Japanese markets.

This case also reveals a potential conflict between trade remedies under trade laws and competition laws. To satisfy the U.S. negotiators, it was necessary for the Japanese government to enforce effectively a measure to restrain export of cars to the United States while, at the same time, it was necessary to do it without violating U.S. antitrust laws. For the sake of trade remedy, an agreement among Japanese exporters of cars under the leadership of the government would have been the easiest and least costly way to carry out VER. This, however, would have invited a challenge under U.S. antitrust laws.

In fact, before the trade negotiation between the United States and Japan, the U.S. Trade Representative consulted with the U.S. Attorney General about potential legal issues that would be involved in the negotiation on issues of imports of automobiles into the United States. The Attorney

[140] Letter from William French Smith, U.S. Attorney General, to Yoshio Okawara, Japanese Ambassador to the United States (7 March 1981), reprinted in U.S. Import Weekly (BNA), 13 May 1981, at M-1 to M-2. On the Auto VER between the United States and Japan, see generally Donald E. deKieffer, *Antitrust and the Japanese Auto Quotas*, 8 Brook. J. Int'l L. 59 (1982); Mitsuo Matsushita and Robert Repeta, *Restricting the Supply of Japanese Automobiles: Sovereign Compulsion or Sovereign Collusion?*, 14 Case W. Res. J. Int'l L. 47 (1982); Michael W. Lochmann, *The Japanese Voluntary Restraint on Automobile Export: An Abandonment of the Free Trade Principles of the GATT and the Free Market Principles of United States Antitrust Laws*, 27 Harvard Int'l L.J. 99 (1986).

General advised that if the U.S. government negotiated with a foreign government informally and an export cartel in the foreign country restraining export to the United States was entered into, such an export cartel would violate U.S. antitrust laws. The U.S. Attorney General further advised that the U.S. negotiators should request the foreign government to invoke a compulsory export restraint and that, if this was achieved, U.S. trade officials would not be held liable under U.S. antitrust laws if a suit under U.S. antitrust laws occurred in respect to the export restraint.[141]

Another striking feature of this trade negotiation and understanding is that, although antitrust implications of the negotiation was discussed and considered, not much attention was paid to GATT implications of them by both governments. This was especially true with the Japanese government. The Japanese government issued a directive whereby Japanese car exporters were restrained from exporting cars above a certain level. This would have been held as contrary to Article XI of the GATT. When the U.S. government and the Japanese government signed a bilateral agreement whereby the Japanese government would restrict the export of semiconductor chips from Japan, the European Communities brought a petition to the GATT arguing that the restraint of export was contrary to GATT Article XI.[142] The issues of the Semiconductor Agreement are discussed in Chapter 20, section 5. In connection with the Auto Pact, however, no such claim was brought, and this agreement lasted until the conclusion of the Uruguay Round brought the WTO into existence.

### *6.2.2 The steel VER case*

A similar problem occurred in the steel voluntary export restraint. In the late 1960s, the U.S. government was faced with an increase of steel imports (especially from Japan). After the Kennedy Round concluded in 1967, the U.S. steel industry requested that imports of steel be restrained. The U.S. government considered various options, including the invocation of the so-called escape clause under the Trade Expansion Act of 1962 that authorized the government to restrain imports after the examination of the matter by the Tariff Commission (now the International Trade Commission). The U.S. government concluded that the best way to deal with the situation was that

[141] Letter from William French Smith, U.S. Attorney General, to William E. Brock, U.S. Trade Representative (18 February 1981), reprinted in U.S. Import Weekly (BNA), 13 May 1981.

[142] *Japan — Trade in Semi-Conductors,* 4 May 1988, GATT B.I.S.D. (35th Supp.) at 116 (1989).

the Japanese exporters restrain voluntarily exports of steel to the United States rather than the U.S. government invoking the escape clause.

The U.S. government initiated negotiations with the Japanese steel industry and requested implicitly to restrain exports of steel to the United States. As a result, Japanese steel exporters engaged in an export cartel to restrain exports to the United States.

A lawsuit was brought in the United States against the U.S. government and Japanese and U.S. steel makers by the Consumers' Union. The reasons for this suit were twofold. The first was a claim that there was a conspiracy among the U.S. government, the Japanese steel makers, and the U.S. steel makers to divide the U.S. and Japanese markets that violated Section 1 of the Sherman Act. The second was a claim that the United States exceeded its authority by asking Japanese exporters to restrain steel exports to the United States by restricting steel imports without an injury determination by the Tariff Commission.

The Consumers' Union withdrew the complaint regarding a violation of the Sherman Act and continued with the suit regarding the government authority to negotiate with foreign entities. The District Court held that the request on the part of the U.S. government to Japanese steel exporters was within the diplomatic power of the President. With regard to the antitrust aspect, the court stated that it could not hand down a decision because the complainant dropped the complaint on this account, but there would have been a serious issue of antitrust violation if the suit had not been dropped.[143] Upon the appeals of both the defendants and plaintiff, the U.S. Court of Appeals held that, with regard to the antitrust aspect, it had ceased to be an issue since the time that this count was dropped, and the court would not make any decision on this issue.[144]

### 6.2.3 *Analysis of the conflict between trade policy and competition policy*

The auto and steel cases are but two of many instances in which VERs were used to settle trade disputes. Both cases, however, illustrate actual and potential conflicts between competition policy and trade policy as well as the philosophies behind these policies. In the auto VER case and steel VER case, there was a possibility of direct conflict between competition laws and trade measures. The case in point is the Consumers' Union case in which the issue of such conflict was raised but withdrawn.

143 *Consumers Union of U.S., Inc. v. Rogers*, 352 F. Supp. 1319, 1323–24 (D.C. 1973).

144 *Consumers Union of U.S., Inc. v. Kissinger*, 506 F.2d 136 (D.C. Cir. 1974).

In the auto case, the Japanese government asked the U.S. Attorney General his view regarding the legality under U.S. antitrust laws of the export control scheme, and he responded by saying that "he believes" that the export control scheme would be lawful in the United States, and the U.S. courts would rule the same way. This conclusion was not, however, tested in U.S. courts, and the legality of this export control scheme under U.S. law remains unclear today.

One could argue that each of the exporters in Japan collected information regarding the export terms (the quantity and price of the products to be exported) of other competitors through the government.[145] One could also argue that the "directive" of the Japanese government could not qualify as an act of state or as government compulsion until the government actually invoked the Export Control Order and put the export of automobiles under legal compulsion.[146]

Such issues reflect tensions and possible conflicts between competition policy and trade remedies. Now that the Safeguards Agreement prohibits the use of voluntary export restraints, there is less justification for the use of restrictive business practices to settle trade disputes.

Under the Safeguards Agreement, both the auto VER and the steel VER would be illegal. Both governments would be held accountable for violating the WTO Agreement, *i.e.*, the Japanese government would be violating the WTO Agreement by employing a VER, and the U.S. government would be held accountable for "seeking" a VER from the Japanese government.

[145] *See Interstate Circuit, Inc. v. United States*, 306 U.S. 208 (1939).

[146] For the view of the U.S. Justice Department, see U.S. Department of Justice, Antitrust Division, Antitrust Enforcement Guidelines for International Operations (10 April 1995), pp. 12–16. For a comprehensive comment on these Guidelines, see Joseph P. Griffin, United States International Antitrust Enforcement, A Practical Guide to the Agency's 1995 Guidelines (Bureau of National Affairs, Inc., 1996).

# 10

# EXPORT CONTROLS AND NATIONAL SECURITY



## 1. Introduction

Exports of goods, services, technology and even capital are, to some degree, regulated by states. Such regulation furthers not only economic objectives but also political and national security objectives. Export controls may, for example, be used to: (1) conserve domestic commodities that are in short supply; (2) conserve natural resources; (3) combat domestic price rises or maintain domestic price controls; (4) maintain world prices of a commodity by withholding supplies; (5) to develop domestic processing industries; (6) enforce "voluntary" export restraints at the behest of an importing country; (7) limit the military or economic capability of another country; and (8) sanction a country or induce it to change its policies.

The United States is the leading proponent of export *sanctions* to accomplish *foreign policy* and national *security* objectives and to punish other states. Although economic sanctions have a poor track record,[1] the United States

[1] Between 1914 and 1990, various countries imposed economic sanctions in 116 cases. They failed to achieve their stated objective in 66 percent of those cases and were only partially successful in most of the rest. Gary Clyde Hufbauer et al., ECONOMIC SANCTIONS RECONSIDERED: HISTORICAL AND CURRENT POLICY (1990).

maintains them against many countries: two-thirds of the world's population is subject to U.S. sanctions, and more than half of the 115 sanction schemes implemented by the United States since World War I have been instituted since 1994.[2]

GATT norms apply to export regulations in four basic ways. First, the rules regarding most-favoured-nation treatment (Article I) and national treatment (Article III) apply to exports as well as imports. Second, GATT customs rules such as fees and formalities (Article VIII) and marks of origin (Article IX) apply to exports. Third, as we will see,[3] export promotional activity may implicate WTO rules concerning antidumping and countervailing duties. Fourth, export requirements, when used to condition foreign investment, may infringe the WTO Agreement on Trade Related Investment Measures.[4]

In most cases, however, the issue of the legality of export restrictions will involve GATT Article XI, which was broadly interpreted in the *Japan — Trade in Semi-Conductors* case to cover all trade "measures" whether affecting exports or imports.[5] Article XI contains some significant exceptions, however, and GATT Articles XX and XXI specify additional exceptions, both generally and for national security.

## 2. Export restraints

GATT Article XI:1 broadly prohibits export restraints other than duties, taxes or charges. Nevertheless, there are several important exceptions to this prohibition. Export restraints may be maintained:

1. temporarily to relieve "critical shortages" of foodstuffs[6];
2. where necessary to the application of standards or regulations relating to the classification, grading, or marketing of commodities in international trade[7];
3. where "necessary to protect human, animal or plant life or health"[8];

---

[2] Raj Bhala, *Mrs. WATU and International Trade Sanctions*, 33 INT'L LAW. 1, 5 (1999).

[3] *See* Chapters 12 and 13.

[4] *See* Chapter 19.

[5] *See Japan — Trade in Semi-Conductors*, adopted 4 May 1988, GATT B.I.S.D. (35th Supp.) at 116 (1989). *See also* Chapter 6.

[6] GATT Art. XI:2(a).

[7] *Id.* Art. XI:2(b).

[8] *Id.* Art. XX(b).

4. to restrict the exportation of gold or silver[9];
5. to protect "national treasures of artistic, historic, or archaeological value[10];
6. to conserve "exhaustible natural resources if such measures are made effective in conjunction with restrictions on domestic production or consumption"[11];
7. to comply with obligations under any intergovernmental commodity agreement.[12]

Many of these exceptions are relatively narrow and present little problem. Some of these exceptions present problems of interpretation that have not been addressed by any GATT/WTO case or decision (what is a "critical shortage", for example).[13] The most important exceptions are the two environmental provisions, Article XX(b) and (g). In the context of export restraints, these may be effectively used to prohibit exports of hazardous waste and hazardous goods or technology (Article XX(b) ) or to conserve natural resources such as forests (Article XX(g) ). These issues have been discussed in Chapter 19.

## 3. Export taxes

No provision of the GATT prohibits export taxes. As a result, Members are free to impose export taxes on products as long as they are not set at a level

[9] *Id.* Art. XX(c).
[10] *Id.* Art. XX(f).
[11] *Id.* Art. XX(g).
[12] *Id.* Art. XX(h).
[13] *See* Frieder Roessler, *GATT and Access to Supplies*, 9 J. World Trade L. 25, 30 (1975) (discussing three very early disputes over export restraints).

There appear to have been only three complaints against export controls in the history of GATT. In 1948, Pakistan complained that India did not refund excise duties on a number of commodities when they were exported to Pakistan while such refunds were granted for exports to all other destinations. In 1952, a similar complaint was discussed in GATT. This time the parties to the dispute were reversed. India complained that Pakistan discriminated in its taxation of jute exports against India. India explained that jute was exported from Pakistan in the form of wire-bound bales and loose bales and that Pakistan's export duties on loose bales were higher than those on wire-bound bales. Since India took most of its supplies in the form of loose bales it felt that it was the object of discrimination. Both these complaints were withdrawn following bilateral compromises. In 1949, Czechoslovakia brought a complaint against the United States arguing that its practice of export control licenses discriminated against Czechoslovakia. The Contracting Parties, however, formally

so as to amount to an export ban. GATT Article XI can be construed to apply where an export tax is effectively an export ban. In that case, the export tax would be considered illegal.

In theory, a Member could "bind" an export tax by including it in its schedule under GATT Article II. This would be achieved, however, since GATT Article II clearly was invented to apply solely to *import* duties and charges. Thus, there seems to be no way to "bind" export taxes effectively under the GATT rules.

Export taxes rarely have posed problems between GATT/WTO Members. Exceptionally, a Member may use an export tax to discourage exports of a commodity to give domestic producers the advantage of access to low cost supplies or to allow them to sell processed commodity products at a competitive advantage. An example of this was the case of Brazilian export taxes on coffee beans that favoured domestic processors of instant coffee, which could be exported tax-free. Thus, Brazilian coffee producers could buy coffee beans for less than foreign processors and undercut their prices for instant coffee.

This controversy, which was beyond the applicability of GATT rules, was resolved by a bilateral agreement.[14] This is a prototype as to the way such disputes must be handled under current law.

## 4. Security exceptions

GATT Article XXI contains "security exceptions" to the GATT rules that particularly affect export restraints.[15] Article XXI reads as follows:

> **Security Exceptions**
>
> Nothing in this Agreement shall be construed
>
> (a) to require any contracting party to furnish any information the disclosure of which it considers contrary to its essential security interests; or

---

decided that the United States had not "failed to carry out its obligation under the Agreement through its administration of the issue of export licenses".

*Id.*

[14] U.S. Controller General, The International Coffee Agreement, Report to the Senate Committee on Finance, 93d Cong., 1st Sess. (Comm. Print, 1973).

[15] For a comprehensive review of Article XXI, see Michael J. Hahn, *Vital Interests and the Law of GATT: An Analysis of GATT's Security Exception*, 12 Mich. J. Int'l L. 558 (1991).

(b) to prevent any contracting party from taking action which it considers necessary for the protection of its essential security interests
  (i) relating to fissionable materials or the materials from which they are derived;
  (ii) relating to the traffic in arms, ammunition or implements of war and to such traffic in other goods and materials as is carried on directly or indirectly for the purpose of supplying a military establishment;
  (iii) taken in time of war or other emergency in international relations; or

(c) to prevent any contracting party from taking any action in pursuance of its obligations under the United Nations Charter for the maintenance of international peace and security.

Article XXI has been invoked several times, but there is no definitive interpretation of its scope. The first invocation of Article XXI set the tone of the debate. In 1949, the United States cited Article XXI to justify export restraints against Czechoslovakia. The United States took the position that this Article could be invoked unilaterally as a *carte blanche* exception. The representative of Czechoslovakia disagreed, arguing that Article XXI should be interpreted closely. The GATT Contracting Parties rejected the Czechoslovakian complaint,[16] and the U.K. delegate expanded the U.S. position that "since the question clearly concerned Article XXI, the United States action would seem to be justified because every county must have the last resort relating to its own security".[17]

Subsequently, Article XXI was invoked by Ghana to restrict its trade with Portugal,[18] by the United States to boycott trade with Cuba,[19] by the European Community to restrict trade with Argentina during the Falklands/Malvinas War,[20] by Germany against Iceland,[21] by the United States against Nicaragua,[22] and by Sweden to justify import quotas for certain footwear.[23]

Because Article XXI has never been definitively interpreted, the issue presented is whether the subsections of the Article have objective content or present open-ended exceptions that can be invoked unilaterally. This

[16] GATT B.I.S.D. (2d Supp.) at 28 (1952).

[17] *Id.*

[18] GATT B.I.S.D. (5th Supp.) at 196 (1961).

[19] GATT Doc. Com. Ind/G Add.4 (Dec. 12, 1968).

[20] GATT Council, Minutes of Meeting Held on 7 May 1982, GATT Doc. C/B/157 (22 June 1982).

[21] GATT Council, GATT Doc. C/B/103 (18 February 1975).

[22] *United States — Trade Measures Affecting Nicaragua*, 15 July 1985, GATT Doc. L/5847 (1985).

[23] *Sweden — Import Restrictions on Certain Footwear*, 19 November 1975, GATT Doc. L/4250 (1975).

question should properly be asked with respect to each of the subsections of the Article.

Article XXI(a), first of all, is worded very broadly and appears to be an open-ended exception. The only criterion is whether the state concerned "considers" the disclosure of information contrary to its essential security interests. This obviously is a subjective judgment. The scope of Article XXI(a) is limited, however. It cannot be invoked to justify export restraints but merely to withhold information.

On the other hand, Article XXI(b) is worded in both a subjective and objective manner. Subjectively, a WTO Member must consider action "necessary" for the protection of its essential security interests. But the three subsections of the Article define objective circumstances. Article XXI(b)(i) requires the matter to relate to fissionable materials or the materials from which they are derived. This subsection is quite clear and uncontroversial. The export of fissionable materials or uranium may be banned, whether for civilian or military purposes. This subsection is rooted in preventing nuclear proliferation and protecting health and safety. Article XX(b)(ii) refers not only to "other goods and materials ... directly or indirectly for the purpose of supplying a military establishment". This certainly would include so-called "dual use" goods, those such as sophisticated computers and technology suitable for both civilian and military use; but the article does not define its scope. Thus as a practical matter, export controls in arms and "dual use" goods are left up to the discretion of each WTO Member.

Article XXI(b)(iii) is the most controversial subsection of this provision. It authorizes economic measures in two instances: in time of war or "other emergency in international relations". The first term, "war", should be considered to have objective content; war is a term of general international law and international relations and should be defined as such. War includes not only declared war, but also any situation involving armed conflict. War is a state of objective conditions that may cover legal as well as illegal use of arms. Export controls are justified in this situation.

A more difficult problem is posed by the term "other emergency in international relations". This obviously is broader than "war"; it also is *not* a term of art in public international law. Two major issues are presented in the interpretation of this term: (1) whether this is a self-judging provision in the discretion of the state that invokes it; and (2) whether the phrase has an objective content.

Some authors have concluded that Article XXI is a self-judging provision,[24] but this view seems untenable. The GATT rules are not designed to be self-judging, and unilateral action is specifically excluded in the Dispute Settlement Understanding. If any part of Article XXI were intended to be self-judging, the parties to the GATT or WTO would have specified this. The vague and ambiguous wording of parts of Article XXI(b), including the "emergency" provision, may constitute a loophole in the GATT,[25] but this does not mean that it is self-judging. In fact, the legislative history of the provision indicates the Article was not to be excluded from GATT dispute settlement procedures,[26] so that it was not conceived of as a self-judging provision.

Despite its ambiguity, the phrase "emergency in international relations" has a certain objective content. The term "emergency" requires a certain degree of seriousness as distinguished from routine tensions or disagreements. The phrase certainly would apply to international situations that could pose a threat of future, armed conflict. But clearly "emergency" can refer to an economic, social, or political situation as well. The best reading of this phrase would seem to allow it to apply to almost any situation, but to confine it to those of a serious nature. This implies a case-by-case judgment by WTO dispute settlement panels.[27]

Only two GATT panel reports dealt with Article XXI issues; both involved the United States and Nicaragua. In the first case,[28] the United States unilaterally reduced its import quota for Nicaraguan sugar. Although the U.S. action was in retaliation for the Nicaraguan government's support of subversive activities in the region and its military build-up, the United States did not invoke Article XXI as a defence. Instead, the United States took the position that it was "neither invoking any exception under . . . the General Agreement nor intending to defend its actions in GATT terms".[29]

[24] *E.g.*, Richard Sutherland Whitt, *The Politics of Procedure: An Examination of the GATT Dispute Settlement Panel and the Article XXI Defense in the Context of the U.S. Embargo of Nicaragua*, 19 LAW & POL'Y INT'L BUS. 604, 616 (1987). This was the U.S. position with respect to the Helms-Burton Act and similar legislation. *See* Hannes L. Schbennan and Stefan Ohlhoff, Comment, 93 AM. J. INT'L L. 424 (1999).

[25] *See* John H. Jackson, WORLD TRADE AND THE LAW OF GATT 748 (1969).

[26] *See* Hahn, above note 15, at 556–67.

[27] In 1996, the EC brought a claim against the United States over the application of U.S. trade sanctions against Cuba. *United States — The Cuban Liberty and Democratic Solidarity Act*, WT/DS38. This case was suspended on 22 April 1998 without a decision.

[28] *United States — Import of Sugar from Nicaragua*, 13 March 1984, GATT B.I.S.D. (31st Supp.) at 67 (1984).

[29] *Id.* para. 3.10, at 72.

The United States maintained that its dispute with Nicaragua was outside the ambit of the GATT. The panel did not analyse whether the reduction in Nicaragua's quota was justified under Article XXI.[30] In the second GATT case,[31] the terms of reference stated that Article XXI(b)(iii) was not within the ambit of the panel's examination. Thus, the panel concluded that "it could find the United States neither to be complying with its obligations under the [GATT] nor to be failing to carry out its obligations. . . ."[32]

It is unfortunate that the United States in the two Nicaragua cases was not willing to invoke Article XXI(b)(iii). The argument exists that the U.S. action restricting trade was a countermeasure under international law in response to a breach of the law by Nicaragua. Article XXI(b)(iii) should be interpreted to support trade measures enacted as countermeasures that are proportioned to an illegal act committed by the target state and are designed to secure compliance with international legal norms.[33]

Article XXI(c) ties the GATT into the UN Charter by providing that a WTO Member may take any action to fulfil its obligations under the Charter. This would permit trade sanctions authorized by the UN Security Council under Chapter VI of the Charter to maintain international peace and security.

## 5. Extraterritorial application of export controls

A frequently occurring issue with respect to U.S. export controls is the extent to which legislation passed by the U.S. Congress can be made binding upon non-U.S. companies and persons operating outside U.S. territory. This issue first arose in 1982 when the U.S. imposed export controls on oil and gas equipment destined for the Soviet Union to protest that country's repression of the Solidarity labour movement in Poland. U.S. export controls purported to regulate not only exports by U.S. persons but also exports by foreign subsidiaries of U.S. persons.

This type of regulation of exports contravenes fundamental principles of international law relating to jurisdiction. In international law, prescriptive

[30] *United States — Import of Sugar from Nicaragua*, above note 29, para. 4.4, at 74.

[31] *United States — Trade Measures Affecting Nicaragua*, 13 October 1986, Report of the Panel, GATT Doc. L/6053 (1986).

[32] *Id.* at 14.

[33] *See* Hahn, above note 15, at 603.

jurisdiction must be based upon certain recognized criteria to avoid conflicts with other states. These generally are:

1. *The territoriality principle.* A state may pass laws governing people and property in its own territory.
2. *The nationality principle.* A state may regulate its citizens in any part of the world.
3. *The objective territoriality principle.* A state may regulate conduct that has a direct and substantial effect within its territory even though the acts giving rise to the effects are undertaken abroad.
4. *The passive personality principle.* A state may prescribe conduct directed against the welfare of its own citizens.
5. *The protective principle.* A state may regulate conduct that targets its national security.
6. *The universality principle.* All states may exercise jurisdiction over certain criminal activity, notably piracy and slavery.

Although never tested in the WTO or by any international tribunal, it is doubtful at best that U.S. legislation extending to the activities outside U.S. territory of foreign subsidiaries of U.S. companies is consistent with any of the norms listed above.

The nationality principle is not applicable, because, under international law, a "state may not ordinarily regulate the activities of corporations organized under the laws of a foreign state on the basis that they are owned or controlled by nationals of the regulating state".[34] The United States has been unsuccessful in extending regulation to such entities as a practical matter. In *Freuhauf Corp. v. Massardy*,[35] the French Court of Appeals ordered the appointment of a short-term administrator in order to avoid the directive of a U.S. parent corporation to comply with U.S. export controls.

The "effects" doctrine also would not appear to be applicable. The sale of a product by a foreign subsidiary of a U.S. corporation would not have any substantial effect in the United States. The protective principle would not apply unless the export sale involved a secret document or an important weapons system.

[34] Restatement (Third) of the Foreign Relations Law of the United States § 4114(2) (1987).

[35] *Fruehauf Corp. v. Massardy*, 5 I.L.M. 476 (1966).

This same analysis is applicable to two recent U.S. laws, the Cuban Liberty and Democratic Solidarity Act of 1996[36] and the Iran and Libya Sanctions Act of 1996.[37] The Cuban Act strengthens the enforcement of the U.S. economic embargo against Cuba by creating a cause of action in U.S. federal courts in favour of any person whose property was nationalized by the Cuban government against any person guilty of "trafficking in the confiscated property"; trafficking is defined very broadly to include virtually any transaction or commercial benefit involving the property. The Cuban Act also excludes all traffickers and their relations from entering the United States. The Iran-Libya Sanctions Act requires economic sanctions against any foreign company that invests substantial sums for energy development in Iran or Libya.

Both of these Acts appear to exercise U.S. jurisdiction extraterritorially in violation of international law. Neither Act appears to be based upon the protective principle because neither "trafficking" in Cuban property nor investing in Iran or Libya could threaten U.S. security. The "effects" doctrine is not applicable because such acts cannot have any effect in the United States. In the case of Cuba, the trafficking does not substantially affect U.S. claimants, since their Cuban property already was nationalized by Cuba in the early 1960s. Foreign investment in Iran or Libya likewise would have no effect within the United States.

The WTO, however, has not rendered a definitive ruling on these issues. The European Community challenged both acts in 1996, but both disputes were settled by agreement in May 1998.[38]

## 6. Conclusions

The WTO/GATT regime regulatory export controls generally prohibit restraints while permitting export taxes. There are exceptions for many types of export controls for environmental purposes, to protect national security and for *bona fide* economic reasons. There are many unanswered legal questions involving the compliance of export controls with GATT/ WTO norms.

[36] Cuban Liberty and Democratic Solidarity Act of 1996, 22 U.S.C.A. § 6021 *et seq.*, reprinted in 35 I.L.M. 367 (1996).

[37] Iran and Libya Sanctions Act of 1996, 50 U.S.C.A. § 1701, reprinted in 35 I.L.M. 1273 (1996).

[38] *See* Current Developments, 93 AM. J. INT'L L. 227 (1999).

# 11

# TRADE IN SERVICES

## 1. Introduction

The agreement to liberalize trade in services is probably the single most important achievement of the Uruguay Round negotiations. At the domestic level, services represent the overwhelming majority of the GDP of OECD countries.[1] At the international level, however, services did not represent a majority of the GDP of most industrialized countries until after World War II. This explains why services were not on the ITO agenda in the 1940s. Before the Uruguay Round, liberalization of trade in services took place on a bilateral basis (the EC being the only full-fledged regional example before the NAFTA entered into force). Gradual liberalization of investment (mostly on a bilateral basis) led to liberalization of non-tradable service sectors, such as distribution. As a result, there was enough impetus to discuss liberalization of trade in services at the international level.

The Uruguay Round negotiations resulted in the first multilateral agreement on trade in services, namely, the General Agreement on Trade in Services (GATS). The GATS was inspired by the structure of the GATT but also displays elements of its own.

The GATS allows for negotiated exceptions to the rules: WTO Members can deviate from the non-discrimination obligations for political (*i.e.*, non-legal) reasons, provided they state their intention to do so when accepting

[1] *See* Bernard M. Hoekman, The General Agreement on Trade in Services (1994).

the GATS (with respect to the MFN obligation) or scheduling their commitments (with respect to the national treatment obligation).

Trade barriers for services are very different from trade barriers that affect goods. For services, border controls are minimal: there are no tariffs, and quotas are very difficult to maintain. Rather, services are subject to a myriad of domestic regulations, often very sector specific. Some service areas, such as telecommunications, are maintained as state monopolies. Some sectors are the subject of investment restrictions. For some professional services, such as doctors and attorneys, there are competency standards. In all areas, there are restrictions on immigration. Regulatory patterns differ greatly state by state.

Consequently, trade liberalization in services is largely a negotiation based on divergent domestic regulations. In a sense, the GATS story resembles that of the GATT after border protection had been substantially dismantled: if the process of liberalization requires first dismantling border controls and then negotiating regulatory barriers, the GATS did not miss much by coming into force 40 years after the GATT.

## 2. Overview of the General Agreement on Trade in Services

The GATS covers all manner of services except those supplied in the exercise of government authority.[2] Four modes[3] of trade in services are identified: (1) "cross border" services where both provider and user remain in their home territory (*e.g.*, services provided generally by facsimile, e-mail, phone, or other means of communication); (2) services provided to the user who travels to the territory of the provider (*e.g.*, tourism); (3) services provided where the provider establishes a commercial presence in the territory of the user (*e.g.*, a UK bank, insurance, or financial services company establishes a branch or subsidiary in Japan); and (4) services provided when a natural person provider temporarily travels to the territory of the user (*e.g.*, an attorney, interpreter, or teacher travels to another country to consult or lecture).

The GATS applies to any "measure" taken by governmental bodies or non-governmental associations exercising delegated authority affecting any of these modes of trade in services.[4]

[2] GATS Arts. I and XIII.
[3] *Id.* Art. I:2.
[4] *Id.* Art. I:1.

The broad scope of the GATS outlined above poses certain conceptual problems. First, the outer boundary of what is "services" for purposes of the GATS is not sharply defined. Services trade is defined more in terms of categories of transactions (the modes of supply) rather than substantive categories. Thus, although services can in most cases be distinguished from goods based upon the idea that services are simultaneously provided and consumed, whereas goods are storable for later use or enjoyment,[5] there may be overlap between the international rules for services and those for goods, especially given that GATS applies to all measures that "affect" services. Second, because trade in services is defined in terms of transactions, services trade under the GATS will inevitably involve more than just the bare services supplied. The transactional notion of services in the GATS means that services trade will also implicate in some instances certain international factor flows, notably (1) information; (2) technology; (3) capital or investment; and (4) labour or immigration.[6]

The core of the GATS is the national treatment provision.[7] As far as services are concerned, national treatment extends only to service sectors inscribed in an individual WTO Member's Schedule of Specific Commitments, and even commitments with respect to these service sectors can be conditioned and qualified.[8] Thus, so-called national treatment is distinctly limited under the GATS. A WTO Member may protect certain service sectors or modes of supply from national treatment by omitting it from its Schedule. However, with respect to market access[9] in those sectors liberalized under a particular Member's Schedule, six measures are, in principle, prohibited:

1. Limits on the number of service suppliers,
2. Limits on the value of transactions or assets,
3. Limits on the total quantity of service output,
4. Limits on the number of natural persons that can be employed,

[5] Jagdish Bhagwati, *Economic Perspective on Trade in Professional Services*, 1 Univ. Chi. Leg. F. 45, 45–46 (1986).

[6] While the GATS does not apply to immigration, it does require the negotiation of immigration commitments that will allow natural persons to exercise the rights accorded. GATS Annex on Movement of Natural Persons Supplying Services under the Agreement, Arts. 2 and 3.

[7] GATS Art. XVII.

[8] *Id.* Art. XVII:I.

[9] *Id.* Art. XVI.

5. Limits on the type of legal entity that can be used and
6. Limits on participation of foreign capital or investment.[10]

In addition, WTO Members may negotiate commitments with respect to service sectors not covered by national treatment or market access Schedule commitments.[11]

Most-favoured-nation treatment[12] is also highly qualified under the GATS. A WTO Member can list exemptions to MFN in the GATS Annex on Article II Exemptions. These exemptions can be maintained for up to ten years, although they are subject to periodic review and negotiation.[13] This means that MFN in the GATS is conditioned to prevent "free-riding" in the markets of more open WTO Members.

The GATS also contains a set of general obligations that apply to measures affecting trade in services. First, there is an obligation of transparency — the prompt publication of "all relevant measures"[14]; however, certain confidential information may be withheld.[15] Furthermore, WTO Members must administer domestic regulations affecting services in a "reasonable, objective and impartial manner".[16] A Council on Trade in Services is authorized to establish "disciplines" to ensure that regulations are objective, transparent and not more burdensome than necessary.[17] Mutual recognition (national agreements to recognize each others' approvals) and harmonization (adoption of similar standards) of domestic regulation are encouraged.[18] Service monopolies and exclusive service providers must not abuse their monopoly position or act inconsistently with a Member's commitments.[19] Business practices that restrain competition must be addressed through "full and sympathetic consideration" with a "view to eliminating" the practice.[20] Payments and transfers of capital must be open with respect to a Member's commitments.[21] Subsidies affecting services are subject to negotiation with a view to eliminating their trade distorting affects.[22]

GATS contains a number of qualifications and exemptions. Economic and market-to-market integration agreements are permitted to operate within the context of a Member's GATS commitments.[23] There is provision for

[10] *Id.* Art. XVI:2. [11] *Id.* Art. XVIII. [12] *Id.* Art. II.
[13] *Id.* Annex on Article II Exemptions, Arts. 3–5. [14] *Id.* Art. III.
[15] *Id.* Art. IV. [16] *Id.* Art. VI:1. [17] *Id.* Art. VI:4.
[18] *Id.* Art. VII. [19] *Id.* Art. VIII. [20] *Id.* Art. IX.
[21] *Id.* Arts. XI and XVI. [22] *Id.* Art. XV. [23] *Id.* Arts. V and VI.

emergency safeguard measures[24] and restrictions to safeguard balance of payments.[25] Government procurement is exempt,[26] and there are general exceptions[27] to protect public morals, human, animal, plant life, or health and to protect against fraud and invasion of privacy. There is also an exemption for certain issues of national security.[28]

The GATS also provides for progressive liberalization of services trade through future negotiations.[29] The increasing participation of developing countries is encouraged.[30] A Member's Schedule of Specific Commitments[31] is intended to be progressively liberalized, but commitments may also be modified and withdrawn.[32] Disputes are resolved according to the WTO Dispute Settlement Understanding.[33]

## 3. The relationship between GATT and GATS

The WTO Agreement provides no rules of conflict to assist WTO Members in understanding the relationship between the GATT and the GATS.[34] The issue of the relationship between the GATT and the GATS arises when a measure is challenged under both agreements. Several panels and the Appellate Body have had to define the boundaries between these two agreements.

In accordance with the principle of effective treaty interpretation, the GATT and the GATS must co-exist because they are both part of the WTO Agreement. The interpreter must ensure that each agreement has its own scope. The interpreter must also ensure that no confusion exists as to the scope of each agreement.

---

24 GATS Art. X.

25 *Id.* Art. XII.

26 *Id.* Art. XIII.

27 *Id.* Art. XIV.

28 *Id.* Art. XIV *bis.*

29 *Id.* Art. XIX.

30 *Id.* Art. IV.

31 *Id.* Art. XX.

32 *Id.* Art. XXI.

33 *Id.* Arts. XXII and XXIII.

34 *Cf.* Treaty Establishing the European Community, Art. 50 (providing that "[s]ervices shall be considered to be 'services' within the meaning of this Treaty where they are normally provided for remuneration, insofar as they are not governed by the provisions relating to freedom of movement of goods, capital and persons").

In defining the boundaries between the GATT and the GATS, one issue that arose was whether the GATT and the GATS overlap or whether the two agreements are mutually exclusive. In *Canada — Periodicals*, the Appellate Body agreed with the panel that the "obligations under GATT 1994 and GATS can co-exist and that one [agreement] does not override the other".[35] The Appellate Body did not, however, analyse the issue of whether there are overlaps between the two agreements, because the parties to the dispute agreed that the issue was not relevant to the appeal.[36] In *EC — Bananas*, the EC argued that a measure that falls within the scope of one of the two agreements cannot fall within the scope of the other.[37] The panel disagreed because, in the absence of overlap, WTO Members could easily circumvent their WTO obligations. The Appellate Body agreed with the panel that "the GATT 1994 and the GATS may overlap in application of a measure", but rejected the circumvention rationale.[38] The Appellate Body concluded that the GATT and the GATS "may or may not overlap, depending on the nature of the measures at issue".[39]

The Appellate Body identified three categories of measures.[40] The first category consists of measures that fall exclusively within the scope of GATT because they affect trade in goods as *goods*. The second category consists of measures that fall exclusively within the scope of GATS because they affect the supply of services as *services*. The third category consists of measures that fall within the scope of both the GATT and the GATS because they involve a service relating to or supplied in conjunction with a good. The Appellate Body found that, while a measure in the third category "could be scrutinized under both agreements, the specific aspects of that measure examined under each agreement could be different".[41] According to the Appellate Body, the issue of whether a measure affecting the supply of a service related to a particular good should be analysed "under the GATT 1994 or the GATS, or both, ... can only be determined on a case-by-case basis".[42] When a panel analyses such a measure under the GATT, it should focus "on how the measure affects the goods involved".[43] When a panel analyses

[35] Appellate Body Report, *Canada — Periodicals*, para. 20.

[36] *Id.* at para. 20.

[37] *See* Panel Report, *EC — Bananas, Complaint by the United States*, para. 7.283.

[38] *See* Appellate Body Report, *EC — Bananas*, paras 255(p).

[39] *Id.* para. 221.

[40] *Id.*

[41] *Id.*

[42] *Id.*

[43] *Id.*

such a measure under the GATS, it should focus "on how the measure affects the supply of the service or the service suppliers involved".[44] If both the GATT and the GATS apply to a given measure, the legal issues to be addressed will be different.

How does the overlap scenario apply? Imagine, for example, that a WTO Member has not made any commitments on transport (which, as will be shown below, is very much a possibility under the GATS). If it allows domestic products to be distributed by rail or truck, but allows imported products to be distributed only by one of these two forms of transportation, it will have violated GATT Article III:4. This is so because the national treatment obligation in the GATT context is independent of specific commitments, whereas in the GATS context it is conditioned on prior commitments in a Member's Schedule. Thus, GATT obligations may come into play even in the absence of commitments in GATS.[45]

## 4. The WTO model for liberalization of trade in services

### 4.1 When to negotiate in the context of GATS

During the Uruguay Round negotiations, WTO Members negotiated, in principle, on everything (with the notable exception of the difficult issue of rights in air transport).[46] There was, in principle, no decision to conduct negotiations on specific sectors. Sector-specific negotiations were, however, conducted on financial services, telecommunications, and maritime transport after the WTO Agreement entered into force because the negotiations in these sectors were not concluded in time. In the future, however, a decision to create sector-specific negotiating groups cannot be excluded.

The GATS is based on the principle that trade in services will be progressively liberalized. In this respect, the GATS echoes the GATT tradition. In the GATT, no date for the launching of a multilateral round of negotiations is specified. The GATT provides that "[t]he CONTRACTING PARTIES may therefore sponsor [tariff] negotiations *from time to*

[44] *See* Appellate Body Report, *EC — Bananas*, para. 221.

[45] GATT Art. III:4 has wide coverage because it applies to any measure affecting trade in goods.

[46] *See* Hoekman, above note 1; Michael J. Trebilcock and Robert Howse, The Regulation of International Trade (2d ed. 1999), Chap. 11 (trade in services).

*time*".[47] In the GATS, however, the point in time when new negotiations must start is specified. The GATS provides that "[i]n pursuance of the objectives of this Agreement, Members shall enter into successive rounds of negotiations, *beginning not later than five years from the date of entry into force of the WTO Agreement*".[48]

The GATS, therefore, required WTO Members to initiate negotiations on trade in services in January 2000.[49] It was not until March of 2001, however, that guidelines and procedures for the negotiations were adopted.[50] The obligation to negotiate at a particular time is hard to enforce due to lack of incentives and the absence of a meaningful remedy.

## 4.2 The concept of "services"

The GATS "applies to measures by Members affecting trade in services".[51] The term "services" is defined to include "*any service* in *any sector* except services supplied in the exercise of governmental authority".[52]

The scope of the GATS is, therefore, not limited to any list of covered sectors. There is, however, no agreement on an exhaustive list of services. This problem became apparent during the negotiations in the WTO on electronic commerce.[53] The legal implications of this lack of agreement are surmountable: the general obligations in GATS apply to all services, but WTO Members may impose restrictions when scheduling their specific commitments.

A "Services Sectoral Classification List"[54] was developed during the Uruguay Round and is largely based on the UN Central Product Classification System (CPC). The List classifies services by sector. Although the use of the Services Sectoral Classification List is not mandatory, most WTO

[47] GATT Art. XXVIII *bis*. 1 (emphasis added).

[48] GATS Art. XIX:1 (emphasis added).

[49] On the shaping of the agenda for the services negotiations, see Andre Sapir, *The General Agreement on Trade in Services: From 1994 to the Year 2000*, 33 J. World Trade, No. 1, 51 (1999).

[50] WTO, *Guidelines and Procedures for the Negotiations on Trade in Services*, S/L/93, 29 March 2001.

[51] GATS Art. I:1.

[52] *Id.* Art. I:3(b) (emphases added). The phrase "a service supplied in the exercise of governmental authority" is defined as "any service which is supplied neither on a commercial basis nor in competition with one or more service suppliers". *Id.* Art. I:3(c).

[53] *See* Marc Bacchetta et al., WTO, Electronic Commerce and the Role of the WTO (Special Study No. 2, 1998).

[54] *See* WTO, Services Sectoral Classification List, MTN.GNS/W/120, 10 July 1991.

Members have adopted it as basis for scheduling their commitments under the GATS.[55] This classification could be revised in the future.

In *EC — Bananas*, the panel noted that the EC had inscribed the CPC item number in its services Schedule. According to the panel, "any breakdown of the sector should be based on the CPC. Consequently, any legal definition of the scope of the EC's commitment in wholesale services should be based on the CPC description of the sector and the activities it covers".[56] Although the decision to follow the CPC is a sovereign decision of WTO Members not compelled by the WTO Agreement, the CPC authoritatively interprets the scope of national commitments.

## 4.3 Modes of supply

The term "trade in services" is defined in terms of so-called modes of supply of services[57]:

1. Mode 1 is the supply of a service "from the territory of one Member into the territory of any other Member".[58] Mode 1 is known as cross-border supply. Cross-border supply occurs when neither the service supplier nor the service consumer has to travel, such as a lawyer in Italy sends advice by facsimile to a person in Canada.
2. Mode 2 is the supply of a service "in the territory of one Member to the service consumer of any other Member".[59] Mode 2 is known as consumption abroad. Consumption abroad occurs when the consumer travels to the country where the service is supplied, such as with tourism.
3. Mode 3 is the supply of a service "by a service supplier of one Member, through commercial presence in the territory of any other Member".[60] Mode 3 is known as commercial presence.[61] The commercial presence mode of supply occurs when the service supplier establishes commercial presence in the country in which he supplies the service, such as when a U.S. bank establishes a subsidiary in Japan.

---

[55] GATS Arts. XVI, XVII and XVIII.

[56] *See* Panel Report, *EC — Bananas, Complaint by the United States*, para. 7.289.

[57] GATS Art. I:2. *See* Bernard M. Hoekman, *Market Access Through Multilateral Agreement: From Goods to Services*, 15 World Economy 707. (1992).

[58] GATS Art. I:2(a).

[59] *Id.* Art. I:2(b).

[60] *Id.* Art. I:2(c).

[61] The term "commercial presence" is defined in Article XXVIII(d) of the GATS.

4. Mode 4 is the supply of a service "by a service supplier of one Member, through presence of natural persons of a Member in the territory of any other Member".[62] Mode 4 is known as presence of natural persons. Presence of natural persons occurs when the service supplier (a natural person in this case and not a legal person as in mode 3) is established in a different country, such as when a lawyer who is a national of Costa Rica establishes himself as a lawyer in the United Kingdom.

The GATS disciplines, therefore, are relevant for not only services but also service suppliers (both natural and legal persons). Viewed from this angle, mode 3 essentially amounts to an international agreement to liberalize investment: by allowing foreign banks, for example, to sell banking services under mode 3, a WTO Member is *de facto* opening up to foreign investment in the banking sector.

## 4.4 Measures "affecting trade in services"

The question of whether a given measure constitutes a measure "affecting trade in services" is a threshold question because the GATS applies only to measures affecting trade in services. The Appellate Body, in *EC — Bananas*, stated that "the use of the term 'affecting' reflects the intent of the drafters to give a broad reach to the GATS. The ordinary meaning of the word 'affecting' implies a measure that has 'an effect on', which indicates a broad scope of application".[63] In the *Bananas* case, the Appellate Body upheld the panel's finding that there is no legal basis for excluding measures covered by the GATT from the scope of GATS. The *Canada — Automotive Industry* panel probably saw too much in the Appellate Body's statement. The panel noted that no measures are *a priori* excluded from the scope of application of the GATS and concluded that "[t]he determination of whether a measure affects trade in services cannot be done in abstract terms in isolation from examining whether the effect of such a measure is consistent with the Member's obligations and commitments under the GATS".[64] On appeal, the Appellate Body found that the determination of whether a measure affects trade in services and is, therefore, covered by the GATS "must be made *before* the consistency of that measure with any substantive obligation of the GATS can be assessed".[65]

---

[62] GATS Art. I:2.
[63] Appellate Body Report, *EC — Bananas*, para. 220.
[64] Panel Report, *Canada — Automotive Industry*, para. 10.234.
[65] Appellate Body Report, *Canada — Automotive Industry*, para. 151.

The Appellate Body set out the following two-part test for determining whether a measure is one "affecting trade in services": "first, whether there is 'trade in services' in the sense of Article I:2 [*i.e.*, in one of the four modes of supply]; and, second, whether the measure in issue 'affects' such trade in services within the meaning of Article I:1[, which covers measures taken by Members under the Agreement]".[66] The Appellate Body may have set out this test because it feared that an all-expansive interpretation of the term "affecting" could bring under the ambit of the GATS measures in sectors in which no specific commitments had been undertaken.

The first part of the test is satisfied if specific commitments have been negotiated in a given case. In the absence of specific commitments, this test is satisfied if the service falls under the ambit of the MFN obligation. In *Canada — Automotive Industry*, the Appellate Body determined that there was "trade in services" in mode 3 (commercial presence) because foreign service suppliers in Canada provided the services in question, namely, wholesale trade services of motor vehicles.[67] What if Canada had undertaken commitments with respect to mode 3, but at the time of the dispute, no foreign supplier had been established in Canada? Should the adjudicating body pay attention to the particular nature of the mode (investment) and accept, for example, that investment decisions can be influenced even in absence of actual trade? What is the appropriate test for other, less tangible modes of supply? These questions will await an answer in future experience.

The second part of the test is whether the measure in question "affects" trade in services in that mode of supply. The Appellate Body, in *Canada — Automotive Industry*, concluded that panels must explain how the measure in question affects the supply of the service or the service suppliers *in their capacity as service suppliers.*[68] The Appellate Body noted that the panel did not examine any evidence relating to the provision of wholesale trade services of motor vehicles in the Canadian market. The panel simply assumed a particular market situation without any actual review of the market.[69] In the Appellate Body's view, the panel should have examined *who* supplies such services and *how* such services are supplied. Because the panel did not conduct such a review, its findings were rejected as totally unsubstantiated. Assumptions are simply "not good enough".[70]

66 Appellate Body Report, *Canada — Automotive Industry*, para. 155.
67 *Id.* para. 157.
68 *Id.* paras 160, 164.
69 *Id.* paras 164–65.
70 *Id.* para. 166.

## 4.5 When are GATS commitments binding?

The issue of when GATS commitments are binding was put before the *EC — Bananas* panel when the EC argued that its import licensing regime predated the entry into force of GATS and, therefore, could not be reviewed by the panel. The panel disagreed. In its view, for a measure to be subject to review under the GATS, it has, independently of its entry into force, to exist after 1 January 1995 (of course, covered by the GATS).[71] The Appellate Body upheld this point of view.[72]

## 4.6 General obligations and specific commitments

The GATS model for liberalization of trade in services distinguishes between general obligations and specific commitments. General obligations apply to measures affecting trade in services regardless of whether a WTO Member has undertaken specific commitments in a sector. Two important general obligations are the obligation to grant MFN status to like services and like service suppliers from all WTO Members and the obligation of transparency.

Specific commitments refer to the degree of liberalization that each WTO Member deems optimal for its own market. WTO Members are free (subject of course, to negotiating pressure from their trading partners) to open their services market in the sectors where they wish to do so and with the caveats they deem appropriate. Specific commitments are, consequently, sector specific.

## 4.7 Institutional issues

The WTO Agreement provides for the establishment of a Council for Trade in Services (GATS Council), which operates under the general guidance of the General Council.[73] The mandate of the GATS Council is broad:

> The Council for Trade in Services shall carry out functions as may be assigned to it to facilitate the operation of this Agreement and further its objectives. The Council may establish such subsidiary bodies as it considers appropriate for the effective discharge of its functions.[74]

---

71 *See* Panel Report, *EC — Bananas, Complaint by the United States*, para. 7.308.

72 *See* Appellate Body Report, *EC — Bananas*, para. 237.

73 WTO Agreement Art. IV:2.

74 GATS Art. XXIV:2.

The GATS Council has established a series of subsidiary bodies to deal with sector-specific issues (*e.g.*, financial services, telecommunications) or horizontal issues (*e.g.*, the Working Party on GATS Rules established by the Council to pursue the mandate laid down in GATS Article X).

## 5. General obligations under the GATS

### 5.1 The GATS "positive list" approach

One of the most important characteristics of the GATS is the "positive list" approach: WTO Members must observe market access- and national treatment-related disciplines only to the extent they undertake specific obligations (by making the corresponding offer) in a given services sector. WTO Members must, however, respect the general obligations with respect to any services sector.

### 5.2 The MFN clause

WTO Members must accord "immediately and unconditionally" to any other WTO Member treatment no less favourable than the treatment they accord to like services and service suppliers of any other country.[75] This obligation to grant most-favoured-nation treatment is set forth in Article II of the GATS and is similar to the general MFN treatment obligation in Article I of the GATT.

There are several exceptions to the MFN obligation in GATS. Most of these exceptions correspond to exceptions in the GATT to the general MFN treatment obligation. There is an exception for preferential trade areas.[76] There are the usual general exceptions,[77] and there is an exception for security.[78]

The GATS regime, however, contains one unique provision: Article II:2 permits WTO Members to "maintain a measure inconsistent with para-

[75] GATS Art. II:1.

[76] GATS Arts. V and V *bis*. *See* Bernard M. Hoekman and Pierre Sauvé, *Regional and Multilateral Liberalization of Service Markets: Complements or Substitutes?*, 32 J. COMMON MKT. STUD. 283 (1994).

[77] GATS Art. XIV.

[78] *Id.* Art. XIV *bis*.

graph 1 provided that such a measure is listed in, and meets the conditions of, the Annex on Article II Exemptions".[79]

The lists of Article II exemptions are part of the Annex in the treaty copy of the WTO Agreement.[80] No new exemptions may be added to the original ones unless recourse has been made to the waiver provisions of the WTO Agreement.[81] During the Uruguay Round, because negotiations on financial services, telecommunications, and maritime transport did not conclude in time, a decision was made to extend the last date for MFN exemptions.[82] Following the successful conclusion of negotiations on financial services[83] and telecommunications,[84] the possibility exists to add MFN exemptions only in the field of maritime transport.

There is no analogue to GATS Article II:2 in the GATT. In the GATT context, exceptions to MFN have to be justified through recourse to one of the GATT provisions explicitly allowing departures from the MFN principle. In the GATS context, however, WTO Members can deviate from the MFN principle for reasons that are not spelled out in the GATS. In other words, GATS Article II:2 permits deviations from MFN not only for *legal* reasons but also for *political* reasons.

The MFN obligation has been the subject matter of both the *EC — Bananas* and the *Canada — Automotive Industry* disputes. Three issues were raised: (1) what is the scope of MFN; (2) what constitutes less favourable treatment; and (3) to what extent likeness of service suppliers is affected by the mode of supply. We take each issue in turn.

The panel report in *EC — Bananas* confirmed that the MFN obligation applies to all services sectors and suppliers regardless of whether specific commitments have been undertaken.[85]

The *EC — Bananas* panel noted that the term "less favourable treatment" appears in both Article II and Article XVII of the GATS. By striking a parallel

[79] *Id.* Art. II:2.

[80] Annex on Article II Exemptions, in WTO, The Legal Texts: The Results of the Uruguay Round of Multilateral Trade Negotiations 308 (1999).

[81] Annex on Article II Exemptions, above note 80, para. 2; WTO Agreement Art. IX:3.

[82] *See* WTO, *Decision on Commitments in Financial Services*, S/L/8, 24 July 1995; WTO, *Second Decision on Financial Services*, S/L/9, 24 July 1995.

[83] *See* Aaditya Mattoo et al., WTO, Opening Markets in Financial Services and the Role of the GATS (Special Study No. 1, 1997).

[84] *See* Bernard M. Hoekman et al., *Competition Policy & Market Access Negotiations: Lessons From the Telecommunications Sector, in* Competition and Trade Policies: Coherence or Conflict? 115–39, (Einar Hope and Per Maeleng eds., 1998).

[85] *See* Panel Report, *EC — Bananas, Complaint by the United States*, para. 7.298.

with GATT Article III (which like GATS Article XVII reflects the obligation to accord national treatment), the panel went on to state that the term must be interpreted in Article II GATS in the manner it is elaborated in GATS Article XVII:2 and :3.[86]

On appeal, the Appellate Body disagreed. In its view, "[t]he Panel would have been on safer ground had it compared the MFN obligation in Article II of the GATS with the MFN and MFN-type obligations in the GATT 1994".[87]

The Appellate Body went on to state:

> There is more than one way of writing a *de facto* non-discrimination provision. Article XVII of the GATS is merely one of the many provisions in the *WTO Agreement* that require the obligation of providing "treatment no less favourable".... we conclude that "treatment no less favourable" in Article II:1 of the GATS should be interpreted to include *de facto*, as well as *de jure*, discrimination. We should make it clear that we do not limit our conclusion to this case. We have some difficulty in understanding why the Panel stated that its interpretation of Article II of the GATS applied "*in casu*".[88]

The Appellate Body widened the ambit of the panel's ruling in this respect in two ways: first, by pointing out that all forms of *de facto* discrimination, and not only the one mentioned in GATS Article XVII, are covered by GATS Article II. Consequently, the Appellate Body's ruling holds for the proposition that *de facto* discrimination in Article II is more comprehensive than in Article XVII. Second, this ruling by the Appellate Body is not case-specific: all cases of *de facto* discrimination are covered in Article II cases.

Two panel reports, *EC — Bananas* and *Canada — Automotive Industry*, addressed the issue of likeness under the GATS. In *EC — Bananas*, the panel concluded that likeness concepts developed in the GATT jurisprudence may carry over to GATS.[89] In *Canada — Automotive Industry*, the panel confirmed this and added that services may be "like" even if delivered by different modes of supply.[90] In both cases, however, the Appellate Body reversed the panel without addressing the issue.

## 5.3 Transparency

The transparency obligation in the GATS operates on three levels: First, WTO Member must promptly publish all relevant measures of general

[86] *See* Panel Report, *EC — Bananas, Complaint by the United States*, para. 7.300 *et seq.*

[87] *See* Appellate Body Report, *EC — Bananas*, para. 231.

[88] *Id.* paras 233, 234 (italics in original).

[89] *See* Panel Report, *EC — Bananas, Complaint by the United States*, para. 7.300 *et seq.*

[90] *See* Panel Report, *Canada — Automotive Industry*, paras 10.247, 10.248.

application "which pertain to or affect the operation of this Agreement".[91] This obligation is of an absolute character and due diligence obliges WTO Members to publish more, rather than less, because the terms "relevant" and "affecting" invite a wide reading.

Second, WTO Members must periodically inform the GATS Council of all new "laws, regulations or administrative guidelines which significantly affect trade in services covered by its specific commitments under this Agreement".[92] The inclusion of the term "significantly" reduces the value of this provision in two ways. First, only some of the otherwise-published laws, regulations, and guidelines will be notified to the WTO. Second and more importantly, the wording seems to suggest that it will be up to the notifying WTO Member to choose which of its laws significantly affect its commitments and, hence, notify them. In case of disagreement, other WTO Members may contest a non-notification. WTO Members have little incentive to do so, however, because WTO remedies are customarily prospective.[93]

Finally, WTO Members must respond to any request by other Members for specific information on any of their measures of general application.[94] To this effect, they will have to establish inquiry points that will help provide specific information upon request.

There is institutional recognition of the possibility for cross-notifications.[95] To some extent, deficiencies in the notification to the WTO level can be supplemented through parallel actions such as the Trade Policy Review Mechanism (TPRM) reports. The problem with this alternative is that TPRM reports occur periodically and consequently, multilateral knowledge about services related measures will not be prompt.

## 5.4 Domestic regulation and mutual recognition

As a general obligation, Article VI of the GATS requires that domestic regulations concerning services be administered in a "reasonable, objective and impartial manner". A WTO Member must ensure this by providing oversight in the form of judicial, arbitral, or administrative review of regulatory decisions.[96] In addition, the Council on Trade in Services can establish and develop "necessary disciplines" for domestic regulations.[97]

[91] GATS Art. III:1.
[92] *Id.* Art. III:3.
[93] *See* Chapter 4.
[94] GATS Art. III.
[95] *Id.* Art. III:5.
[96] *Id.* Art. VI:2(a).
[97] *Id.* Art. VI:4.

The GATS also provides for mutual recognition among WTO Members of authorization, licensing or certification of services suppliers.[98] An unsettled question is to what extent such mutual recognition agreements, while desirable, may detract from or even violate MFN obligations.[99]

The only work in this field has been undertaken in the context of professional services and more specifically (on a priority basis) in the accountancy sector.[100] A Working Party was established to prepare guidelines for mutual recognition of accountancy qualifications. These guidelines are non-binding and do not preclude the use of alternative methods.[101]

The model advanced in the accountancy sector could be described as follows[102]:

1. Any WTO Member wishing to enter into a mutual recognition agreement (in accordance with Article VII GATS) with another WTO Member, whereby it will acknowledge that accountants from another WTO Member are fulfilling the criteria imposed by their domestic legislation, will have to promptly notify the GATS Council;
2. The WTO Member in question "shall afford adequate opportunity for other interested Members to negotiate their accession to such an agreement or arrangement or to negotiate comparable ones with it. Where a Member accords recognition autonomously, it shall afford adequate opportunity for any other Member to demonstrate that education, experience, licenses, or certifications obtained or requirements met in that other Member's territory should be recognized";
3. WTO Members whenever appropriate shall base their decisions on recognition on mutually agreed criteria.

This "soft-law" approach (non-binding character) might prove to be a very appropriate means to discuss regulatory cooperation in the future: it provides WTO Members with a forum to discuss their regulatory interventions and

[98] GATS Art. VII.

[99] *See* Aaditya Matoo, *MFN and the GATS, in* Regulatory Barriers and the Principle of Non-Discrimination 51 (Thomas Cottier and Petros C. Mavroidis eds. 2000).

[100] *See* WTO, Working Party on Professional Services, S/WPPS/W/1, 12, 12/Rev. 1, 14 and 14/Rev.1.

[101] At the time of this writing, the said guidelines had not been submitted for consideration to the GATS Council.

[102] *See* WTO, Working Party on Professional Services, S/WPPS/W/12/Rev. 1 9, and especially the Annex at 7.

the conditions under which they are willing to accept interventions by other WTO Members as "equivalent" to theirs.

The GATS Council also adopted *Disciplines on Domestic Regulation in the Accountancy Sector*,[103] a document laying out the obligations of WTO Members in the accountancy sector even if no specific commitments have been undertaken. The language in this document, too, is only hortatory.

## 5.5 Anticompetitive practices

Two provisions of the GATS speak to anticompetitive practices that may undermine services liberalization. Article VIII does not prohibit national service monopolies, but prohibits "abuse" of a monopoly position and requires WTO Members to ensure that national monopolies are not operated in a manner that is inconsistent with GATS obligations.

If "business practices" restrain or restrict trade in services, GATS Article IX requires "consultations" at the request of any WTO Member and "full and sympathetic consideration" to complaints.

## 5.6 Subsidies

The GATS did not come to any agreement concerning service subsidies. Article XV requires future negotiations on the matter and "consultations" for current complaints with regard to subsidies.[104]

## 5.7 Safeguards

Because of the limited nature of specific commitments under GATS, the matter of general safeguards was essentially left to future negotiation.[105] Import restrictions may be adopted, however, to safeguard a Member's balance of payments.[106]

[103] *See* WTO, *Disciplines on Domestic Regulation in the Accountancy Sector*, S/L/64, 17 December 1998.

[104] GATS Art. XV. *See also* Bernard M. Hoekman, *Safeguard Provisions and International Agreements Involving Trade in Services*, 16 World Economy 29 (1993).

[105] GATS Art. X.

[106] *Id.* Art. XII.

## 5.8 Developing countries

The concerns of developing countries are addressed in GATS through two requirements. First, Members must negotiate specific commitments to benefit developing countries[107]; second, developed Members must establish "contact points" to facilitate access of developing countries to information.[108]

## 5.9 Exceptions

Like the GATT, the GATS includes general exceptions[109] and security exceptions to the [general obligations].[110] The general exceptions GATS article breaks new ground, however, by specifically exempting measures "necessary" for the protection of the privacy of individuals with respect to data collection.[111] It also exempts measures aimed at preventing or reducing double taxation and inequitable imposition of taxes.[112]

Government procurement is also largely exempt from the [general obligations], but the GATS requires negotiations on this important matter.[113]

# 6. Specific commitments

## 6.1 The limits of general obligations

The general obligations assumed in the GATS do not, by themselves, guarantee market access: any WTO Member can, in principle, respect the MFN obligation and keep its market completely inaccessible to foreign services and service suppliers. The liberalizing aspect of the GATS, in the words of Patrick Low and Aaditya Mattoo, "depends on the extent and the nature of sector-specific commitments assumed by individual Members".[114]

---

[107] GATS Art. IV:1.

[108] *Id.* Art. IV:2.

[109] *Id.* Art. XIV.

[110] *Id.* Art. XV.

[111] *Id.* Art. XIV(c)(ii).

[112] *Id.* Art. XIV(d) and (e).

[113] *Id.* Art. XIII.

[114] Patrick A. Low and Aaditya Mattoo, *Reform in Basic Telecommunications and the WTO Negotiations: The Asian Experience* (WTO Working Paper, ERAD-98–01, 1998).

The relevant provisions of the GATS are as follows:

- Article XVI, which relates to market access;
- Article XVII, the national treatment obligation; and
- Article XVIII, which deals with additional commitments.

Sector-specific commitments do not operate in a regulatory vacuum. Domestic regulation can largely influence the effectiveness of specific commitments.

## 6.2 Market access (Article XVI)

Article XVI envisages a Schedule for each WTO Member concerning market access for services.[115] In its Schedule, the Member must specify by (1) service sector; and (2) mode of supply in its market access commitments. It must give services and service suppliers of any WTO Member "no less favourable" treatment than that provided in its Schedule.

Article XVI prohibits, in principle, six types of measures: (1) limitations on the number of suppliers; (2) limitations on the total value of service transactions or assets; (3) limitations on the total number of service operations or the total quantity of service output; (4) limitations on the total number of natural persons that may be employed; (5) measures that restrict or require specific types of legal entity or joint venture; and (6) limitations on the participation of foreign capital.

Exceptions to these prohibitions are permitted. WTO Members must indicate any of the above limitations or measures in their Schedule of Commitments and with respect to each mode of supply.[116]

## 6.3 The national treatment obligation (Article XVII)

Article XVII of the GATS requires WTO Members to place in their Schedules commitments with respect to service sectors and mode of supply for which it extends national treatment.[117] These commitments are separate from and additional to the market access commitments.[118] In accordance with the "positive list" approach of the GATS, national treatment is

[115] GATS Art. XX:1.
[116] *Id.* Art. XVI:2.
[117] *Id.* Art. XVII:1.
[118] *Id.* Art. XX:1.

required only for those sectors and modes of supply listed in a Member's Schedule.

The national treatment obligation covers both *de jure* and *de facto* discrimination.[119] GATS Article XVII:3 is inspired by the GATT case law. It serves as an interpretative note to Article XVII:2 and it states that "formally identical or formally different treatment shall be considered to be less favourable if it modifies the conditions of competition in favour of services or service suppliers of the Member compared to like services or service suppliers of any other Member".

The *United States — Superfund* panel report first made the point that for GATT Article III to be violated one need not show actual trade effects, since Article III (like GATT Articles II and XI) establish competitive conditions. Its findings have been incorporated in GATS Article XVII:3.

The *EC — Bananas* panel report dealt with the issue of whether the EC had breached its national treatment obligation with respect to wholesale services in the bananas sector. For GATS Article XVII to be breached, three elements must be cumulatively present:

1. The European Community must have undertaken a commitment in the relevant sector and mode of supply;
2. The European Community must have undertaken a measure that affected the supply of services in that sector or mode of supply;
3. The measure adopted accorded treatment less favourable to suppliers from non-EC countries than that accorded to their EC like counterparts.[120]

The first element is a factual one. The second element should be interpreted in accordance with the Appellate Body's subsequent ruling in *Canada — Automotive Industry*, that is, one should at least establish who provides the service concerned and how that service provider is affected by the measure adopted.

With respect to the third element, the *EC — Bananas* panel had first to establish whether the suppliers involved were like: it held that to the extent that services are like, those providing them are like service suppliers.[121]

Having established that the suppliers are like, the panel analysed to what extent the treatment accorded to non-EC wholesale traders was less favour-

[119] GATS Art. XVII:2. For a comprehensive analysis of the national treatment obligation in the field of GATS, see Mattoo, *MFN and the GATS*, above note 99.

[120] *See* Panel Report, *EC — Bananas, Complaint by the United States*, para. 7.314.

[121] *Id.* para. 7.322.

able than that accorded to their EC counterparts. The EC licensing scheme distinguished between Category A and Category B operators depending on whether they had marketed ACP or "dollar zone" bananas in a previous representative period. The panel report reflects that "the operator category rules apply to service suppliers regardless of their nationality, ownership or control".[122] The panel report further accepts that import licences are tradeable and transferable.[123] Category A operators are allocated 66.5 percent of the licences required for the importation of "dollar zone" bananas, and Category B operators are allocated 30 percent of these licences, regardless of whether they imported "dollar zone" bananas in the previous representative period. Licence transferees are usually Category A operators who are forced to pay a premium in order to be in a position to sell "dollar zone" bananas. In the panel's words, "given that license transferees are usually Category A operators who are most often service suppliers of foreign origin and since license sellers are usually Category B operators who are most often service suppliers of EC (or ACP) origin, we conclude that service suppliers of the Complainants' origin are subject to less favourable conditions of competition in their ability to compete in the wholesale services market for bananas than service suppliers of EC (or ACP) origin".[124] Consequently, in the panel's view, the allocation of the 30–percent quota constituted less favourable treatment.[125] The Appellate Body upheld the panel's findings in this respect.[126]

Nevertheless, the panel seems to confuse a goods issue with a services issue: the fact that a wholesale trader is of EC origin does not necessarily mean that he will trade EC (or ACP) bananas. Traders are rational human beings aiming to maximize their welfare: if the market is more favourable to EC (or ACP) bananas, this is what they will trade. Because access to Category A or Category B is unimpeded, as the panel report accepts, then where is the services issue?

It is true that the scheme operates in favour of EC (or ACP) bananas. There can be no doubt about that: access of non-EC (or ACP) bananas becomes even harder because traders will pay a premium to import them. This could drive non-EC (or ACP) bananas out of the EC market. It will not, however,

122 *Id.* para. 7.324.

123 *Id.* para. 7.336.

124 *Id.*

125 *Id.* para. 7.341.

126 Appellate Body Report, *EC — Bananas*, para. 244.

shut out non-EC (or ACP) traders who might decide to stay on and trade EC (or ACP) bananas.

To illustrate this point: what if the EC had a lawful quantitative restriction banning imports of all non-EC (or ACP) bananas? What would there be the services issue? By definition, one would have to question whether EC and non-EC wholesale traders can under equal conditions of competition trade EC (or ACP) bananas. In other words, the origin of the good must be immaterial when discussing a services issue; what we should care about is the origin of the supplier of the service.

## 6.4 The relationship between Article XVI and Article XVII

Imagine the following Schedule of Commitments: country A accepts only five banks in its territory (GATS Article XVI). It does not take an exemption from either GATS Article II or Article XVII. There is no doubt that with respect to the five banks, country A is bound by the obligation to accord national treatment. What if it decides to accept a sixth bank? Is it bound by the obligations laid down in Article II and Article XVII?

Various views have been presented in this respect.[127] It is submitted that the answer should be looked for in the terms of GATS Article XVI. Article XVI deals with "market access", which means that for the sake of our example, the overall number of incumbent service suppliers is not irrelevant: when country A states that it will accept only five banks and it already knows of three incumbents, this practically means that only two new banks will be allowed to establish themselves in its territory.

Article XVI:2(a) prohibits any limitation on the number of service suppliers in sectors where commitments have been undertaken, unless otherwise specified in the Schedule. The form of limitation prohibited concerns "the number of service suppliers" and not the "number of new service suppliers". What drafters of the Agreement obviously had in mind were examples where through regulatory intervention the number of suppliers is limited.[128] By adding a sixth bank, country A obviously forewent its right to take an exemption from GATS Article XVI:2(a). Its action constitutes a violation of this Article, because country A will be acting inconsistently with its international obligations. Moreover, since it did not take an

[127] *Compare* Hoekman, above note 1 with Aaditya Mattoo, *National Treatment in the GATS: Corner-Stone or Pandora's Box?*, 31 J. World Trade, No. 1, at 107 (1997).

[128] In some EC countries, for example, new pharmacies can be established only if no incumbent pharmacy exists within a specified geographical proximity.

exemption from either GATS Article II or Article XVII, as it could, it will be bound by both obligations when opening the sixth bank.

## 6.5 Additional commitments

Article XVIII GATS gives the possibility to WTO Members to negotiate additional commitments "with respect to measures affecting trade in services not subject to scheduling under Articles XVI or XVII".[129] Such additional commitments will typically include qualifications, standards and licensing matters, but other matters may be included as well.[130] If a WTO Member decides to exercise this option, additional commitments will be inscribed in its Schedule.

## 6.6 Modification of schedules

Article XXI GATS is the corresponding Article to Article XXVIII GATT. It includes some very welcome changes. First, when a WTO Member wants to modify its Schedule of Commitments, it will have to notify the GATS Council of its intent to do so. Contrary to what happens in the GATT, however, the notifying Member must negotiate not only with a select group of countries (namely, those holding initial negotiating rights, the so-called principal supplying interest countries, and those having a substantial interest in the modifying Member's market) but also with any affected WTO Member. This means that negotiations will by definition be multilateral. Second, compensation must be offered to all affected WTO Members for the modification of Schedules to be GATS-legal and such compensation must be granted on an MFN-basis. If there is disagreement as to the compensation, the matter must be referred to arbitration, and no modification can occur unless the modifying WTO Member has made compensatory adjustments in conformity with the findings of arbitration. Thus, one can avoid situations in which panels will be called to judge whether compensation offered was adequate.

WTO Members may modify their Schedules only after three years have elapsed from the date on which a commitment entered into force.[131]

---

[129] GATS Art. XVIII. [130] *Id.* [131] *Id.* Art. XXI:1.

## 7. Financial services, telecommunications, and maritime transport

### 7.1 What is so special about these agreements?

When the GATS entered into force, sector-specific negotiations had not been completed by that time, namely, financial services, telecommunications, and maritime transport. Agreements on financial services and telecommunications were subsequently concluded, but negotiations on maritime transport have not been concluded.

### 7.2 The Agreement on Financial Services

The Agreement on Financial Services provides a balance between trade liberalization and the need to regulate in this sensitive sector. The negotiations on financial services did not take place within the usual context of multi-sectoral negotiations. As a result, countries actively looking for trade-offs between services and other sectors were disadvantaged. Consequently, discussions focused on the regulation of conditions of competition in the domestic market. For Mattoo, this largely explains why, when looking at the outcome, one immediately notes that there has been less emphasis on the introduction of competition through new entrants.[132] Largely, what was negotiated was pre-existing liberalization, which sometimes was agreed at a bilateral level. Multilateralization of existing bilateral liberalization was not an easy task for negotiators. At the same time, even though the general picture is more or less a binding of the pre-existing liberalization, we note that some WTO Members made significant new commitments[133] whereas one should not overlook the fact that the WTO is an instrument of progressive liberalization. Even though the first step might not correspond to the original aspirations, WTO Members have "locked in" their policies with respect to financial services to the multilateral level and will eventually discuss further liberalization in the future.

The Agreement on Financial Services is reflected in the GATS, the Annex on Financial Services and the specific commitments of the parties to the Agreement. This agreement is the only multilateral agreement that was negotiated without the participation of the United States. For some, this

[132] *See* Aaditya Mattoo, *Financial Services and the WTO: Liberalization in the Developing and Transition Economies* (WTO Working Paper, TISD-98–03, 1998).

[133] *See* Mattoo et al., above note 83.

was deplorable, but this agreement proved that multilateralism can thrive even in cases where a major player is absent. The United States joined in later and deposited its Schedule of Commitments in February 1998.[134]

Commitments in the financial services sector concentrated on the first three modes of supply, the presence of natural persons being arguably less important in this sector.

This agreement was negotiated just before financial crisis hit the South East Asian markets (with its worldwide repercussions). The crisis made it plain once again that prudential regulation is necessary for the avoidance of similar problems. A central issue in the agreement is therefore the balance between trade liberalization and pursuit of legitimate regulatory objectives: in the field of financial services negative externalities are felt worldwide making the need to address this issue even more pressing.

Mattoo, examining the regulatory objectives advanced during the negotiations, concludes that "the commitments under GATS need not compromise the ability of governments to pursue sound macroeconomic and regulatory policies".[135] As far as prudential regulation is concerned, Paragraph 2(a) of the Annex on Financial Services reads:

> Notwithstanding any other provisions of the Agreement, a Member shall not be prevented from taking measures for prudential reasons, including for the protection of investors, depositors, policy holders or persons to whom a fiduciary duty is owed by a financial service supplier, or to ensure the integrity and stability of the financial system.

When it comes to macroeconomic policy in general, Mattoo points out that

> A Member may impose restrictions on current or capital transactions in certain circumstances. First, in the event of serious balance-of-payments and external financial difficulties or threat thereof, Article XII permits a member to introduce restrictions of a temporary nature on trade in services for which it has undertaken specific commitments . . . Secondly, the language of Paragraph 2 of the Annex on Financial Services would also seem to allow restrictions on international transactions if they were needed to ensure the integrity and stability of the financial system.[136]

Turning finally to other regulatory choices that governments often might make, we revert to our discussion of GATS Article VI. It is submitted that the disciplines of this Article provide the appropriate forum to entertain regulatory choices aiming at guaranteeing the stability of the financial system.

[134] GATS/SC/90/Suppl. 3, 26 February 1998.

[135] *See* Mattoo, *Financial Services and the WTO*, above note 132, at 6 *et seq*.

[136] Mattoo, *Financial Services and the WTO*, above note 132, at 7–8.

## 7.3 The Agreement on Telecommunications

The importance of telecommunications cannot be overstated. It is not simply that the sector as such is economically of colossal importance; telecommunications are a necessary means for other services to be provided.

On 30 April 1996, the GATS Council adopted the decision on Commitments in Basic Telecommunications[137] together with the Fourth Protocol to the GATS. The Fourth Protocol provides that the Agreement on Telecommunications would enter into force on 1 January 1998.[138] The final agreement had to wait a little more. In mid-February 1997, negotiators reached a final agreement on liberalization of trade in telecommunications. Sixty-nine governments signed the first multilateral agreement in this field.

The Agreement on Telecommunications consists of the GATS, the Annex on Telecommunications, the regulatory principles, and the Schedules of Commitments. The Annex and the specific commitments are integral parts of the GATS,[139] but the regulatory principles have been inscribed in Schedules of Commitments.[140]

The structure reflects a "new" reality that trade negotiators had to face when dealing with liberalization of the telecommunications sector.[141] The negotiators realized that the typical GATT process whereby elimination of government-induced barriers can guarantee market access would not always be suitable to the telecommunications context: incumbents, at times private entities, would be in a position to frustrate market access through a myriad of barriers that could not be always attributed to government behaviour (*i.e.*, lax enforcement of domestic antitrust laws).

This realization led the negotiators to conclude the Annex on Telecommunications, which is attached to the GATS. The Annex essentially imposes two obligations on WTO Members: on the one hand, an obligation to ensure transparency with respect to any relevant information affecting access to and use of public telecommunications transport networks and services (Paragraph 4) and, on the other, an obligation to guarantee access to and use of public telecommunications transport networks and services (Paragraph 5).

137 *See* WTO, *Decision on Commitments in Basic Telecommunications*, S/L/19, 30 April 1996.

138 *See* WTO, Council for Trade in Services, *Fourth Protocol to the General Agreement on Trade in Services*, S/L/20, 30 April 1996.

139 GATS Art. XXIX.

140 *Id.* Art. XVIII.

141 For a comprehensive recounting of the negotiating process, see Hoekman et al., above note 84; Low and Mattoo, above note 114; Trebilcock and Howse, above note 46.

The second obligation was the only response negotiators came up with to ensure that market access commitments will be meaningful. Paragraph 5 reads:

> Each Member shall ensure that any service supplier of any other Member is accorded access to and use of public telecommunications transport networks and services on reasonable and non-discriminatory terms and conditions, for the supply of a service included in its Schedule.

The paragraphs of the Annex following paragraph 5 make it plain that suppliers of such services are entitled to access to and use of any public telecommunications transport network or service offered within or across the border, including private leased circuits, the right to purchase or lease and attach terminal or other equipment to the network, and to interconnect private leased or owned circuits with public telecommunications transport network and services, or with circuits leased or owned by another service supplier.

Some negotiators felt that the Annex commitments were too general to guarantee new entrants adequate opportunity to compete. However, what is "reasonable terms" is not a self-interpreting term and future panels will deal with this issue on a case-by-case basis.

Proposals were made to define interconnection rights more specifically, including in terms of timeliness, cost-based pricing, and "unbundling" (that is, allowing a new entrant exactly which services to buy from the network operator, rather than being obliged to purchase a package that may raise costs and undermine competitiveness), and these were among the issues taken up in the subsequent discussions on regulatory principles.

This discussion finally found its way in the elaboration of regulatory principles. Approximately 30 governments made preliminary commitments to apply the regulatory principles agreed upon, pending confirmation and completion of the negotiations in February 1997. Six regulatory principles emerge: (1) competitive safeguards to prevent anti-competitive practices in telecommunications; (2) interconnection; (3) the right to require universal service; (4) public availability of licensing criteria; (5) establishment of independent regulatory bodies; and (6) the use of objective, transparent, and non-discriminatory allocation procedures for scarce resources such as frequency, numbers, and the right of way.

The drafting of the regulatory principles reflected the opinion of those negotiators who believed that the drafting of the Annex was too imprecise. Compare, for example, paragraph 2.2 of the Reference Paper dealing with interconnection with the already cited paragraph 5 of the Annex. Paragraph 2.2 reads:

> Interconnection with a major supplier will be ensured at any technically feasible point in the network. Such interconnection is provided under non-discriminatory terms, conditions (including technical standards and specifications) and rates and of a quality no less favourable than that provided for its own like services or for like services of non-affiliated service suppliers or for its subsidiaries or other affiliates;
>
> in a timely fashion, on terms, conditions (including technical standards and specifications) and cost-oriented rates that are transparent, reasonable, having regard to economic feasibility, and sufficiently unbundled so that the supplier need not pay for network components or facilities that it does not require for the service to be provided; and
>
> upon request, at points in addition to the network termination points offered to the majority of users, subject to charges that reflect the cost of construction of necessary additional facilities.

Beyond what was agreed in the Annex, negotiators managed to address in the context of interconnection, issues relating to the quality of the network, the price to pay, and also the term and conditions of interconnection ("unbundling" being one of the main concerns).

Although the regulatory principles constitute, as far as circumscription of the actual obligations is concerned, an advance in comparison to the Annex, there is room for interpretation of some of the terms included there. Terms like "reasonable rates" or "timely fashion" will have to be further interpreted in practice.

The most important element, however, describing the philosophy of the Agreement on Telecommunications has to do with the approach privileged by negotiators: markets will be integrated through regulatory action (the regulatory principles) and not through for example, enforcement of competition law. Was the latter really an option?

Mavroidis and Neven, drawing parallels from the EC experience, have argued that competition law was not an alternative.[142] Unlike WTO law, there is nothing like a world antitrust law, and hence, if competition law was the chosen means to integrate telecommunications markets, integration would occur in a context of regulatory diversity: domestic antitrust statutes differ.

The only harmonized component is of course provided in Articles VIII and IX GATS dealing with monopolies and restrictive business practices, respectively. Even the most ambitious reading of the two provisions however, leads to the unavoidable conclusion that one should not expect too much from them. The ambit of Article VIII GATS is limited to monopolies that have a

[142] Petros C. Mavroidis and Damien J. Neven, *The WTO Agreement on Telecommunications: It's Never Too Late*, in The Liberalization of State Monopolies in the European Union and Beyond 307 (Damien Geradin ed., 2000).

strong link to state, and hence other monopolies or dominant companies that are not monopolies are excluded from the application of Article VIII GATS. Article IX GATS, on the other hand, reflects an obligation to consult with respect to restrictive business practices and nothing more.

The issue will be faced in cases where, following strict enforcement of the regulatory principles, national markets have been opened to foreign suppliers of telecom services. Arguably, suppliers of telecom services installed around the world will be selling their services in a context of regulatory diversity. In some countries, it cannot be excluded that such suppliers will be operating in a context of antitrust vacuum: the WTO Agreement does not impose on its Members to adopt competition rules, never mind competition rules of a particular kind. Mavroidis and Neven have argued in this context that the regulatory principles have a "transitional" value.[143] After markets have been opened up, the behaviour of telecom operators in various national markets will largely depend on the reach of domestic antitrust laws. Arguably, there are gains from cooperation among antitrust authorities in this phase of market integration. Hence, in their view, telecom liberalization might as well give the impetus to WTO Members to discuss cooperation in the field of competition laws in the WTO.

## 7.4 The Agreement on Maritime Transport

When negotiators in the maritime transport sector realized that it would be impossible to conclude an agreement by the due date, they adopted a decision whereby they bound themselves to continue negotiations after the entry into force of the Uruguay Round agreements and to conclude such negotiations by no later than June 1996 (these negotiations have still not been completed). "Until the conclusion of the negotiations Article II and paragraphs 1 and 2 of the Annex on Article II Exemptions are suspended in their application to this sector, and it is not necessary to list MFN exemptions".[144] This essentially means that WTO Members through decisions can delay in time the deadline for MFN exemptions. So far, nothing of the sort has happened in any other sector-specific negotiation. A decision was finally adopted according to which negotiations on maritime transport will resume with the next round on services.[145]

143 *See* Mavroidis and Neven, above note 142, at 310.

144 *Id.* para. 5.

145 *See* WTO, *Decision on Maritime Transport Services*, S/L/24, 3 July 1996.

## 8. Conclusions

The GATS is best described as a forum of ongoing liberalization. Even though the argument could be made that existing Schedules of Commitments do not represent meaningful liberalization in the services sector, one should always keep in mind that the GATS is the first attempt to liberalize trade multilaterally in this field and that existing examples at the regional level (such as the EC) have not been immediately successful.

Scholars often point out that the GATS framework suffers from too many in-built safeguards.[146] Such safeguards include exemptions from the MFN obligation, exemptions from the obligation to accord national treatment, and, in addition, the right to have recourse to market access limitations (GATS Article XVI). The question then becomes whether one should add to the existing safeguards by negotiating additional ones? GATS Article X:1 obliges WTO Members to enter into "multilateral negotiations on the question of emergency safeguards based on the principle of non-discrimination". A Working Party was established that is still debating the issue.

The argument in favour of safeguards is the classical political economy argument that in absence of safeguards there will be no political will to continue liberalization: concessions depend on the possibility of evading them. It is quite difficult to counter this argument since it is almost impossible to construct the counterfactual.

Where does this all leave us? Liberalization will be a slow process. One should not expect too much too soon. The current attitude of WTO Members toward services is caution.

[146] *See*, for example, Hoekman, *Safeguard Provisions and International Agreements Involving Trade in Services*, above note 104; Hoekman and Sauvé, above note. 76.

# 12

# SUBSIDIES AND COUNTERVAILING DUTIES

## 1. Introduction

Broadly defined, a subsidy is a benefit that is not earned.[1] In economic terms, a subsidy is a "positive externality", that is, a benefit that comes from outside a business or firm. In lay terms, it is a "windfall".

[1] WEBSTER'S THIRD NEW INTERNATIONAL DICTIONARY (1993).

In the modern world, most important subsidies come from governments. Subsidies are widely used by governments as instruments of economic, social, and political policy.[2] Subsidies serve a variety of purposes, including benefiting underdeveloped regions, combating pollution, favouring particular constituents or economic sectors and developing new technologies and products. Governmental subsidies also take many forms; they can be direct or indirect, highly specific or extremely diffuse.

Subsidies often serve noble ends.[3] They may provide a means to raise standards of living for the poorest members of society. They may serve consumers. They may reverse environmental degradation. Subsidies can help realize public policy objectives that markets would not serve or would not pursue with the same intensity, such as public education and health, transport, and care for elderly and displaced workers. Of course, subsidies may serve lesser and even undesirable ends as well. Subsidies are widely used policy instruments that implicate wider considerations than trade policy.[4]

Subsidies are included in the regulation of international trade for several reasons. First, as far as trade is concerned, there is a key distinction between so-called export subsidies and domestic or production subsidies. An export subsidy is one that is paid to a firm with specific reference to the export of a product. In the crudest form, for example, a government may pay a firm a fee for every product it exports. An export subsidy has a direct impact on terms of trade because it counters, in whole or in part, the tariff levied on the product by the importing nation. A domestic or production subsidy, on the other hand, is one granted to a firm regardless of exports. This type of subsidy has less of an impact on trade. The impact may be very slight if the percentage of products exported by that firm is small. Even where exports are relatively high in proportion to the total production, however, the economic impact is reduced because the subsidy is spread over the entire amount produced. Thus, from a trade perspective, export subsidies are generally of greater concern than domestic or production subsidies.

Second, the economic impact of particular subsidy programmes and even subsidies in general, is a matter of great debate.[5] On the one hand, a subsidy can

---

[2] Bo Södersten and Geoffrey Reed, INTERNATIONAL ECONOMICS 299 (3d ed. 1994)

[3] *Id.* at 299–303.

[4] Alan O. Sykes, *Countervailing Duty Law: An Economic Perspective*, 89 COLUM. L. REV. 199, 200–201 (1989).

[5] *See generally* Alan O. Sykes, *Second Best Countervailing Duty Policy: A Critique of the Entitlement Approach*, 21 LAW & POL'Y INT'L BUS. 699 (1990).

be viewed as an economic "distortion" in international trade. Two distortions are prominent. For the country importing the subsidized product, there is unfair competition of imports with competing products of unsubsidized domestic producers. This unfair competition may injure domestic producers and workers. Moreover, even if subsidized products are sold by the subsidizing nation, A, to a third country, C, the domestic producers in country B may be injured because of a loss of export opportunities in country C. On the other hand, the "distortion" viewpoint of subsidies may be too narrow. From a global perspective or the viewpoint of the subsidizing country, the welfare gains from the subsidy may far outweigh the distortion or may actually compensate for other economic distortions.[6] Thus, ending the subsidy may, in some cases, reduce economic welfare. In any case, there are cost and benefit considerations in subsidy programmes that can only be dealt with on a case-by-case basis.

Third, there is controversy among trade theorists over the remedy for subsidization.[7] One remedy for a subsidy found to be a distortion is removal of the subsidy. Another remedy is known as a "countervailing" duty, which is "a duty imposed [on imports] to offset the advantage to foreign producers derived from a subsidy that their government offers for the production or export of the article taxed".[8] The economic rationale for a countervailing duty (CVD) is doubtful, at best, even in the case of a distorting subsidy because the effect of a CVD is to make the product more expensive for consumers in the *importing* country. A CVD may or may not be warranted. The best case for a CVD is when the subsidy is being used as an instrument of predatory pricing by the exporting nation. A second economic case for a CVD is where the subsidy is demonstrably causing serious injury to competing domestic producers in the importing country. In the absence of either of these scenarios, it may be best for the importing country simply to send a "thank-you" note to the government of the exporting country for the windfall received by its consumers.[9]

With all of these competing and highly controversial considerations, it is not surprising that the GATT contracting parties and WTO members have had a difficult time agreeing on the basics of a subsidies regime. Moreover,

[6] Sykes, *Countervailing Duty Law*, above note 4, at 205.

[7] John Barceló, *Subsidies and Countervailing Duties: Analysis and a Proposal*, 9 Law & Pol'y Int'l Bus. 779 (1977).

[8] Webster's Third New International Dictionary, above note 1.

[9] John Barceló, *The Two Track Subsidies Code: Countervailing Duties and Trade Retaliation, in* Non-Tariff Barriers After the Tokyo Round 121, 143 (John Quinn and Philip Slayton ed., 1982).

as we consider the WTO subsidies regime, an important, overarching point should be kept in mind: the legal concepts and norms devised to deal with subsidies are different from and coincide only approximately with economic considerations, let alone social and political norms. The actual and potential clashes between legal norms and socio-economic and political norms make the subject interesting and controversial.

## 2. The legal framework

### 2.1 Articles XVI and VI of GATT 1994

The GATT 1994 addresses the subject of subsidies in Article XVI. The original obligation of GATT 1947 was to report and "discuss" all subsidies that may affect trade, their estimated effect, and the reasons they are necessary.[10] Amendments[11] were later added to prohibit export subsidies, except that in the case of export subsidies on "primary products" — agricultural products — the obligation is not to apply them in a manner that results in the party applying them having "more than an equitable share" of world export trade.

This scheme was vague and unworkable. To make it more precise, the GATT contracting parties adopted an "illustrative list"[12] of prohibited export subsidies. This illustrative list of prohibited export subsidies was followed by the negotiation of special codes for subsidies, first in the Tokyo Round in 1979 and then in the Uruguay Round in 1994. Agricultural subsidies were addressed separately in the Uruguay Round, which resulted in a new Agreement on Agriculture.[13] Thus, for all practical purposes, two codes, the Subsidies and Countervailing Measures Agreement (SCM Agreement) and the Agreement on Agriculture, constitute the WTO law relating to subsidies.

Countervailing duties were originally addressed in GATT 1947 in Article VI. Article VI regulates the imposition of countervailing duties as well as that of antidumping duties. The general obligations contained in Article VI

---

[10] GATT Art. XVI:1.

[11] *Id.* Art. XVI:2 to :5.

[12] Provisions of Article XVI:4, 19 November 1960, GATT B.I.S.D. (9th Supp.) at 185 (1961).

[13] *See* Chapter 6.

were fully incorporated into Part V of the SCM Agreement, which is the current WTO law.[14]

## 2.2 The SCM Agreement

The SCM Agreement, which is binding on all WTO Members, is divided into 11 parts. Part I, General Provisions, sets out the definition of a subsidy and introduces the key concept of "specificity," the test of which is whether the subsidy is available only to an enterprise or industry or group of enterprises or industries.

Parts II, III and IV establish three categories of subsidies: (1) prohibited subsidies; (2) actionable subsidies; and (3) non-actionable subsidies. These subsidies are frequently termed "red," "yellow," and "green" light subsidies, respectively, because the first is forbidden *per se*, the second may be prohibited if they cause "adverse effects", and the third is permitted. A subsidy cannot fall into either the red or yellow light categories unless it meets the test of "specificity" in Part I.

Part V contains detailed provisions regulating the use of countervailing duties. This Part strictly disciplines their use and limits them in duration to five years unless it is established that there is a likelihood of continuation or recurrence of subsidization and injury.

Part VI establishes a Committee on Subsidies and Countervailing Measures (SCM Committee) to oversee the Agreement. Part VII requires notification of subsidies and authorizes their surveillance by the Committee. Part VIII contains special and differential treatment provisions applicable to developing country WTO Members. Part IX contains transitional arrangements, most importantly allowing seven years for WTO Members in the process of transformation to a market economy to comply with certain provisions of the Agreement. Part X on Dispute Settlement provides for the full applicability of the WTO dispute settlement regime. Part XI contains "Final Provisions," including the requirement that no action can be taken against the subsidy of a WTO Member except "in accordance with the provisions of GATT 1994, as interpreted by [the SCM] Agreement".[15]

---

[14] However, "the provisions of the SCM Agreement do not provide explicit assistance as to the relationship of the export subsidy provisions of the SCM Agreement and Article XVI:4 of the GATT 1994", Appellate Body Report, *United States — FSC*, para. 117.

[15] SCM Agreement Art. 32.1.

## 2.3 The SCM Agreement and agricultural subsidies

The SCM Agreement exempts most agricultural subsidies. The prohibition of subsidies under Article 3.1 is subject to exceptions "provided in the Agreement on Agriculture". Article 5 on "Actionable Subsidies" does not apply to subsidies maintained on agricultural products as provided in Article 13 of the Agreement on Agriculture.[16]

The Agreement on Agriculture, in turn, contains a "due restraint" provision, sometimes referred to as a "peace clause", regarding the SCM Agreement. Under Article 13 of the Agreement on Agriculture, domestic agricultural support measures and export subsidies that are consistent with the Agreement on Agriculture are exempt from the provisions of GATT 1994 and the SCM Agreement until 31 December 2004.[17]

## 2.4 Institutions and notifications

The SCM Agreement establishes a Committee on Subsidies and Countervailing Measures composed of representatives from each of the WTO Members.[18] The Committee elects its own chairman and meets at least twice a year. The WTO Secretariat is the secretariat to the Committee.[19]

The SCM Committee has two basic functions. First, the Committee has the primary responsibility of examining the reports of Members. Under Article 25, Members must notify all subsidies within their territories.[20] They must also notify the Committee of all cases of preliminary or final determinations of countervailing duties.[21] Second, the Committee must "afford members the opportunity of consulting on any matter relating to the operation of the Agreement".[22]

The SCM Committee must establish a Permanent Group of Experts (PGE) composed of five independent persons highly qualified in the field of subsidies and trade relations.[23] The SCM Committee elects the PGE

---

[16] *Id.* Art. 5.

[17] For discussion of the anti-subsidy provisions of the Agreement on Agriculture, *see* Chapter 6.

[18] SCM Agreement Art. 24.1.

[19] *Id.*

[20] *Id.* Art. 25.2.

[21] *Id.* Art. 25.11.

[22] *Id.* Art. 24.1.

[23] *Id.* Art. 24.3.

members.[24] One PGE member is replaced every year.[25] The function of the PGE is to assist panels, as required, with respect to prohibited subsidies.[26] The PGE may also render advisory opinions on subsidies at the request of the Committee or any Member.

### 2.5 Developing countries

Special and differential treatment for developing countries is provided in SCM Article 27. Such treatment generally takes the form of longer deadlines (eight years in most cases) for observance of SCM subsidy disciplines. During the phase-in period, developing countries must not increase their export subsidy levels.[27] Two additional benefits accrue to developing countries. First, with regard to actionable subsidies, there is no presumption of "serious prejudice" so that this will have to be proved by positive evidence.[28] Second, any countervailing duty investigation against a developing country Member must be terminated if it is determined by the country conducting the investigation that (a) the overall subsidy level of the product does not exceed 2 percent of its value, or (b) the volume of subsidized imports is less than 4 percent of the total imports of the like product (unless imports from developing countries cumulatively exceed 9 percent).[29]

## 3. The regulation of subsidies

### 3.1 Definition of subsidy

The SCM Agreement defines the term "subsidy" for the first time. One reason the term "subsidy" was not defined in the Tokyo Round Subsidies Code was that the EC and the United States were unable to come to agreement. The EC traditionally favoured an approach whereby a scheme must be attributed to a government to be characterized as subsidy. The United States, on the other hand, focusing on the effects rather than the source of the funding, took the

[24] SCM Agreement Art. 24.3.

[25] *Id.*

[26] *Id.*

[27] SCM Agreement Art. 27.4. This provision was held to be violated by Brazil in the *Brazil — Aircraft* case. Appellate Body Report, *Brazil — Aircraft*, para. 159.

[28] SCM Agreement Art. 27.8, applied in Panel Report, *Indonesia — Automobiles*, para. 14.158.

[29] SCM Agreement Art. 27.10.

position that a scheme can characterized as subsidy if it results in some benefit to recipients.

Shortly before the Uruguay Round, a GATT panel considered the meaning of the term "subsidy" in a dispute between the EC and the United States.[30] The issue was whether private bank debt forgiveness resulting in a benefit for the recipient steel industry was a subsidy. The case involved the imposition of countervailing duties by the United States on steel imports from the EC. The EC argued that the countervailed schemes did not constitute subsidies because they were the expression of private, rather than public, conduct. The United States argued that the private bank debt forgiveness was a subsidy because the recipient (Saarstahl, a German steel company) profited from the debt forgiveness. The EC countered that acts by private banks should not be attributed to governments. The panel essentially adopted the position advocated by the EC. The relevant passage of the panel report reads:

> The Panel therefore considered that, interpreted in the light of the object and purpose of the [Tokyo Round Subsidies] Agreement and in the context of other textual elements in the Agreement, the term "bounty or subsidy"...was to be interpreted to refer to measures of governments or public authorities of signatories.
>
> ...
>
> The Panel was of the view that under the Agreement a subsidy could not be considered to be provided indirectly when a government provided assistance to the production, manufacture or export by acting through a third party, on the condition that the relationship between the action of the private party and the government was such that the action of the private party could be qualified as a governmental measure.[31]

The panel report was not adopted, however, because the issues dealt with by the panel were being negotiated in the context of the SCM Agreement. The panel's interpretation apparently had a direct impact on the drafting of the SCM Agreement.

The SCM Agreement provides a definition of the term "subsidy" that acknowledges that some financial contribution by the government is necessary for a scheme to be a subsidy.[32] Pursuant to Article 1.1, government action that constitutes a subsidy "shall be deemed to exist" if:

---

[30] *See United States — Imposition of Countervailing Duties on Certain Hot-Rolled Lead and Bismouth Carbon Steel Products Originating in France, Germany and the United Kingdom,* 15 November 1984, GATT Doc. SCM/185 (unadopted) [hereinafter GATT Panel Report, *United States — CVDs*].

[31] *See* GATT Panel Report, *United States — CVDs,* above note 30, paras 390, 393.

[32] SCM Agreement Art. 1. For an excellent overview of the SCM Agreement, see Gary N. Horlick and Peggy A. Clarke, *The 1994 WTO Subsidies Agreement,* 17 J. World Trade, No. 4, at 41 (1994).

(a) (1) there is a financial contribution by a government [including "any public body"] . . . where:

(i) a government practice involves a direct transfer of funds (e.g. grants, loans, and equity infusion), potential direct transfers of funds or liabilities (e.g. loan guarantees);

(ii) government revenue that is otherwise due is foregone or not collected (e.g. fiscal incentives such as tax credits);

(iii) a government provides goods or services . . . or purchases goods;

(iv) a government makes payments to a funding mechanism . . . or directs a private body to carry out . . . (i) to (iii) above . . . ; *or*

(a) (2) there is any kind of income or price support in the sense of Article XVI of GATT 1994; *and*

(b) a benefit is thereby conferred.[33]

Thus, the definition of a subsidy in Article 1.1 has two discrete elements: (1) a financial contribution by government (Article 1.1(a)) and (2) a benefit (Article 1.1(b)).

WTO panels and the Appellate Body have issued several rulings interpreting Article 1.1(a)(1)(ii), which compels a finding of a financial contribution by government if "government revenue that is otherwise due is foregone". In *United States — FSC*,[34] the Appellate Body held that the provisions of U.S. tax law exempting "foreign sales corporations" (that is, foreign corporations responsible for the sale or lease with goods produced in the United States for export) from the payment of certain taxes constitutes the foregoing of revenue otherwise due for purposes of the SCM Agreement.

In the *FSC* case, the Appellate Body reasoned that the correct methodology to resolve the issue is to make a "comparison between the revenue due under the contested measure and revenues that would be due in some other situation".[35] The term "otherwise due" establishes in most cases a "but for" test, although this test may not work in all cases.[36] Rather, the essence of the legal test is to examine two comparable situations under the domestic laws of the Member and determine whether the contested measure results in the foregoing of revenue that would have been collected. In the subsequent *United States — ETI* case,[37] which involved legislation the United States passed to comply with the *FSC* ruling, the Appellate Body also applied this

[33] SCM Agreement Art. 1.1(a), (b) (footnote omitted).

[34] Appellate Body Report, WT/DS108/AB/R, 20 March 2000.

[35] *Id.* para. 90.

[36] *Id.* para. 91.

[37] Article 21.5 Panel Report, *United States — Tax Treatment under the Extraterritorial Income Exclusion Act of 2000.*

concept. In the *ETI* case, the Appellate Body ruled that the exclusion of so-called "qualifying foreign trade income" from tax, compared with U.S. taxation of other foreign-source income, coupled with giving taxpayers a right to elect the rules of taxation most favourable to them, results in foregoing revenue otherwise due.[38]

### *3.1.1 The financial contribution by a government must confer a benefit to the recipient*

To be characterized as a "subsidy" regulated under the SCM Agreement, a scheme must confer a "benefit".[39] The SCM Agreement does not, however, define the term "benefit".

The Appellate Body in *Canada — Aircraft* stated that "[a] 'benefit' does not exist in the abstract, but must be received and enjoyed by a beneficiary or a recipient. Logically, a 'benefit' can be said to arise only if a person, natural or legal, or a group of persons, has in fact received something".[40] The term "benefit" involves a "comparison"[41] with the marketplace: "the trade distorting potential of a 'financial contribution' can be identified by determining whether the recipient has received [the financial contribution] on terms more favourable than . . . the market".[42] Moreover, the economic analysis necessary to determine the existence of a "benefit" must relate to market conditions in the subsidizing country.[42a]

The Appellate Body has also clarified three important issues concerning the meaning of the term "benefit." The first issue is whether a benefit that a recipient could have obtained in the marketplace constitutes a "benefit" under the SCM Agreement. The Appellate Body in *Canada — Aircraft* found that "[a] 'benefit' arises under each of the guidelines [set forth in Article 14 of the SCM Agreement] if the recipient has received a 'financial contribution' on terms more favourable than those available to the recipient in the market".[43] The Appellate Body thus introduced into the WTO legal order the "private-investor" doctrine: government transactions that take place on market terms, even if they result in a benefit to a recipient, do not qualify as

[38] Appellate Body Report, *United States — ETI*, para. 104. For another application of this test, see Appellate Body Report, *Canada — Automotive Industry*, paras 87–94.

[39] SCM Agreement Art. 1.1(b).

[40] *See* Appellate Body Report, *Canada — Aircraft*, para. 154.

[41] *Id.* para. 157.

[42] *Id.*

[42a] *United States — Softwood Lumber*, Report of the Panel, paras 7.44–7.79.

[43] Appellate Body Report, *Canada — Aircraft*, para. 158.

subsidies. Moreover, even if a government were to loan money at a rate of interest more favourable than market conditions, only the difference between the market rate and that provided by the government would count as subsidy.

The second issue is whether a subsidy previously received by a government-owned entity passes through to the subsidized entity's private successor when the government-owned entity passes into private hands at market price. This issue was at the heart of the dispute between the EC and the United States concerning countervailing duties imposed by the United States on imports of steel from the EC.[44] The United States argued that EC companies that paid market prices for previously subsidized government enterprises continue to benefit from the past subsidies. In other words, the United States argued that market prices do not "exhaust" the effects of a subsidy.

The Appellate Body agreed:

> [t]he question whether a "financial contribution" confers a "benefit" depends . . . on whether the recipient has received a "financial contribution" on terms more favourable than those available to the recipient in the market. In the present case, the Panel made factual findings that UES and BSplc/BSES [the private British companies] paid fair market value for all the productive assets, goodwill, etc., they acquired from BSC [the British state-owned company] and subsequently used in the production of leaded bars imported into the United States in 1994, 1995 and 1996. We, therefore, see no error in the Panel's conclusion that, in the specific circumstances of this case, the "financial contributions" bestowed on BSC between 1977 and 1986 could *not* be deemed to confer a "benefit" on UES and BSplc/BSES [the private British companies].[45]

Thus, by applying the private-investor doctrine, the Appellate Body found that no pass-through of subsidies takes place if market prices were paid for the subsidized entity.[46]

The third issue is at what point in time may a subsidy be said to be "granted". In the *Brazil — Aircraft* case, the Appellate Body ruled that "payments may be 'granted' where the unconditional legal right of the beneficiary to receive the payments has arisen, even if the payments them-

---

[44] *See* Appellate Body Report, *United States — Imposition of Countervailing Duties on Certain Hot-Rolled Lead and Bismuth Carbon Steel Products Originating in the United Kingdom*, WT/DS138/AB/R, para. 68.

[45] *See* Appellate Body Report, *United States — Imposition of Countervailing Duties on Certain Hot-Rolled Lead and Bismuth Carbon Steel Products Originating in the United Kingdom*, above note 44, para. 68 (emphasis added).

[46] The same approach was followed in the U.S.-EC dispute on steel subsidies. *See* GATT Panel Report, *United States — CVDs*, above note 30.

selves have not yet been made".[47] This ruling permits anticipatory action to be taken against subsidies in the WTO.

### *3.1.2 The subsidy must be specific*

Even if a scheme meets the definition of "subsidy" in SCM Article 1.1, it must also be "specific" to be subject to the disciplines of the SCM Agreement.[48] SCM Article 2 defines specificity in terms of both *de jure* and *de facto* criteria.

A *de jure* specific subsidy exists when the granting authority "explicitly limits access to a subsidy to certain enterprises".[49] All prohibited subsidies are deemed to be *de jure* specific subsidies.[50] Finally, when the granting authority "establishes objective criteria or conditions governing the eligibility for, and the amount of, a subsidy, specificity shall not exist, provided that the eligibility is automatic and that such criteria and conditions are strictly adhered to".[51]

A subsidy that is *de jure* non-specific can still *de facto* be specific. SCM Article 2.1(c) provides a list of factors that can be used to make this assessment. The subsidy may be deemed specific if (1) the subsidy is used only by a limited number of "certain enterprises"; (2) the subsidy is predominantly used by "certain enterprises"; (3) disproportionate amounts of subsidy are granted to "certain enterprises"; or (4) the granting authority favours "certain enterprises" in exercising its discretion of authority. The first three factors seem to call for factual findings (although disagreements can exist as to what exactly amounts to "certain enterprises"). The last factor calls for an interpretation. These multiple tests demonstrate the will of the negotiators to include *a priori* as many subsidies as possible under the term "specific."

### *3.1.3 Subsidies are defined by reference to domestic law*

A scheme that constitutes a cost to government and results in an actual benefit to a recipient, if it is specific, is subject to the discipline of the SCM Agreement.[52] The last two elements are "universal", in the sense that the criteria for deciding these issues are the same in all situations.

The first element, namely, the cost to government, is a "local" element in the sense that the issue will be judged by reference to the relevant domestic legal regime. In the *United States — FSC* case, the panel ruled that what is

[47] Appellate Body Report, *Brazil — Aircraft*, para. 58.
[48] SCM Agreement Art. 1.2. [49] *Id.* Art. 2.1(a).
[50] *Id.* Art. 2.3. [51] *Id.* Art. 2.1(b). [52] *Id.* Art. 1.

income "otherwise due" must be decided by reference to the U.S. tax regime and rejected the U.S. argument that a scheme freeing private parties from tax obligations is not a subsidy if it is meant to level the playing field with foreign companies subjected to more lenient taxation.

The Appellate Body agreed, stating that

> [the] issue is *not*... whether a Member is or is not obliged to tax a particular category of foreign-source income. As we have said, a Member is not, in general, under any such obligation. Rather, the issue in dispute is whether, *having decided to tax a particular category of foreign-source income*, namely foreign-source income that is "effectively connected with a trade or business within the United States", the United States *is permitted to carve out an export contingent exemption from the category of foreign-source income that is taxed under its rules of taxation.*[53]

The Appellate Body ruled that subsidy obligations under the SCM Agreement will be applied against a background of domestic law. WTO Members are free to decide the optimal levels and forms of taxation. Once they have exercised this sovereign choice, they will be subjected to the obligations under the SCM Agreement.

## 3.2 The classification of subsidies

### *3.2.1 The "traffic light" approach*

One of the important innovations of the SCM Agreement is the classification of subsidies into three different categories: (1) prohibited; (2) actionable; and (3) non-actionable. Prohibited subsidies are so-called red light subsidies. Actionable subsidies are so-called yellow light subsidies, and non-actionable subsidies are so-called green light subsidies. Non-actionable subsidies are no longer permitted, however, because the relevant provision of the SCM Agreement expired at the end of 1999.[54]

### *3.2.2 Prohibited subsidies*

SCM Article 3 prohibits:

1. Subsidies contingent on export performance, including those illustrated in Annex I; and
2. Subsidies contingent on the use of domestic over imported goods.

[53] *See* Appellate Body Report, *United States — Foreign Sales Corporations*, para. 99 (italics in original).

[54] SCM Agreement Art. 31.

Export performance- and local content-related subsidies are, therefore, prohibited. Even subsidies that on their face (*de jure*) are not export subsidies will be deemed export subsidies if they are "in fact tied to actual or anticipated exportation or export earnings" (*de facto*).[55] By the same token, "the mere fact that a subsidy is granted to enterprises which export shall not for that reason alone be considered to be an export subsidy within the meaning of this provision".[56] Annex I contains an Illustrative List of Export Subsidies that, as the title itself indicates, is not an exhaustive list. In addition, the exemption or rebate of taxes on an exported product is not a subsidy even if taxes are collected on like products destined for domestic consumption.[57]

#### 3.2.2.1 Who determines whether a subsidy is a prohibited one?

If a WTO Member believes that a subsidy granted by another Member to its industry is prohibited, that Member can request consultations.[58] If bilateral consultations do not produce a mutually agreed solution within 30 days — which, however, can be extended by mutual agreement — the matter will be referred to a panel.[59] The panel will have to circulate its final report to all Members "within 90 days of the date of the composition and the establishment of the panel's terms of reference".[60]

The panel can decide whether the scheme at issue constitutes a prohibited subsidy or refer the matter for examination to the Permanent Group of Experts (PGE). Although reference to the PGE for consideration is optional,[61] the PGE's final decision binds the panel. The panel must accept, without modification, the PGE's conclusions on the issue of whether the measure in question is a prohibited subsidy.[62] The PGE may also provide advisory opinions to any WTO Member as to the character of measures introduced by them.[63] The PGE has adopted its own Rules of Procedure.[64]

---

[55] *Id.* Art. 3.1(a) note 4.

[56] *Id.*

[57] *Id.* Art. 1.1(a)(1)(ii) note 1.

[58] *Id.* Art. 4.1.

[59] *Id.* Art. 4.4.

[60] *Id.* Art. 4.6.

[61] Article 4.5 of the SCM Agreement states that "the panel may request the assistance of the Permanent Group of Experts".

[62] SCM Agreement Art. 4.5.

[63] *Id.* Art. 24.4.

[64] *See* WTO, Committee on Subsidies and Countervailing Measures, Rules of Procedures for the Permanent Group of Experts, G/SCM/W/365, 18 April 1996, revised by G/SCM/W/365/Corr.1, 24 April 1996; and G/SCM/W/365/Rev.1, 24 June 1996.

The panel's report must be adopted within 30 days of its issuance unless an appeal is filed.[65] If the case is appealed, the Appellate Body will have to provide its report within 60 days from the date the appeal is filed but must give reasons for delay if it cannot provide its report within 30 days.[66] These procedures cut the time for determination of a prohibited subsidy roughly in half compared to other dispute settlement cases.

#### 3.2.2.2 Remedies against prohibited subsidies

SCM Article 4.7 provides for a remedy against prohibited subsidies independent of the right of affected WTO Members to impose countervailing duties in accordance with Part V of the SCM Agreement:

> If the measure in question is found to be a prohibited subsidy, the panel shall recommend that the subsidizing Member withdraw the subsidy without delay. In this regard, the panel shall specify in its recommendation the time period within which the measure must be withdrawn.

SCM Article 4.7 provides for a more effective remedy than the usual WTO recommendation under DSU Article 19 because Article 4.7 provides a specific remedy, namely, the withdrawal of the illegal act, whereas Article 19 gives discretion to the losing party ("bring your measures into compliance"). In addition, the prohibited subsidy must be withdrawn "without delay".[67] If the subsidy is not withdrawn within the period specified by the DSB, countermeasures will be authorized.[68] A dispute over whether countermeasures are appropriate will be referred to binding arbitration.[69]

#### 3.2.2.3 WTO jurisprudence on prohibited subsidies

Most of the cases decided under the SCM Agreement have involved issues of prohibited subsidies. The *United States — FSC* and *United States — ETI* cases, discussed above, make clear that remission or deferral of direct taxes specifically related to exports will be condemned; however, a Member

[65] SCM Agreement Art. 4.8.

[66] *Id.* Art. 4.9.

[67] *Id.* Art. 4.7. In the *Brazil — Aircraft* case, the Appellate Body ruled that the provision of the DSU allowing 15 months for compliance does not apply to prohibited subsidies in view of the provision in Article 4.7 for removal "without delay". Thus, the Appellate Body upheld the panel's determination that Brazil had to withdraw its subsidy within 90 days. Appellate Body Report, *Brazil — Aircraft*, para. 194.

[68] SCM Agreement Art. 4.10.

[69] *Id.* Art. 4.11.

can make provision to prevent the double taxation of foreign source income.[70]

The most crucial determination in the prohibited subsidy cases has been whether the subsidy in question is "contingent"[71] on export performance. Contingent in this context means "conditional" or "dependent upon",[72] and this contingency can be either "in law or in fact".[73] Contingency in law (*de jure*) means that the "condition can be demonstrated on the basis of the very words of the relevant legislation [or] where the condition to export is clearly, though implicitly, in the instrument comprising the measure".[74] Contingency in fact (*de facto*), on the other hand, must be inferred on a case-by-case basis from the total configuration of facts constituting and surrounding the granting of the subsidy.[75] An example of a *de facto* export subsidy can be found in the *Australia — Leather* case, in which the panel concluded from the facts that the beneficiary (Howe) would be compelled to increase exports:

> [I]t is clear that the Australian market for automotive leather is too small to absorb Howe's production, much less any expanded production that might result from the financial benefits accruing from the grant payments, and the required capital investments, which were to be specifically for automotive leather operations. Therefore, we conclude that, in order to expand its sales in a manner that would enable it to reach the sales performance targets (interim targets and the aggregate target) set out in the grant contract, Howe would, of necessity, have to continue and probably increase exports. At the time the contract was entered into, the government of Australia was aware of this necessity, and thus anticipated continued and possibly increased exports by Howe. In our view, these facts effectively transform the sales performance targets into export performance targets.[76]

[70] See note 59 to Item (e) on the Illustrative List of Export Subsidies in Annex I of the SCM Agreement as interpreted by the Appellate Body in *United States — FSC*, paras 92 and 93, and *United States — ETI*, paras 121–186.

[71] SCM Agreement Art. 3.1(a).

[72] Article 21.5; Panel Report, *Canada — Aircraft, Recourse by Brazil to Article 21.5 of the DSU*, para. 7.79.

[73] SCM Agreement Art. 3.1(a).

[74] Appellate Body Report, *Canada — Automotive Industry*, para. 100 (holding that an import duty exemption was *de jure* contingent on export performance).

[75] Appellate Body Report, *Canada — Aircraft* (holding that Canadian regional aircraft assistance constitutes *de facto* export subsidy). *See also* Article 21.5 Appellate Body Report, *Canada — Aircraft* (finding that Brazil failed to establish that Canada's revised programme was *de facto* export subsidy).

[76] *See* Panel Report, *Australia — Leather*, para. 9.67 (footnote omitted).

One of the most controversial rulings of WTO adjudicating bodies involves Item (k) on the Illustrative List of Export Subsidies. Item (k) holds as a subsidy any government export credit that is "used to secure a material advantage in the field of export credit terms". Item (k) also contains a proviso, however, that a WTO Member that is a party to a multilateral agreement allowing export credits can apply the interest rate provisions of the agreement in giving export credits without this practice being considered a prohibited export subsidy. WTO adjudicating bodies have considered this proviso to be an affirmative defence and have uniformly rejected the argument that a party can "match" export credit terms despite that the OECD Export Credit Arrangement specifically allows a government to "match" officially supported export credit terms.[77] The Appellate Body ruled that such matching is not allowed under the Item (k) proviso.[78] This ruling has been adopted by the DSB over strong criticism of OECD members.[79]

*3.2.2.3.1 Punitive damages in the WTO?*

In the *Brazil — Aircraft* case, the Arbitrators considered a request by Canada to impose countermeasures against Brazil. The request came after a finding by a compliance panel that Brazil had not brought its measures into conformity with its WTO obligations. Consequently, under SCM Article 4.10, Canada was entitled to take "appropriate countermeasures".

The *Brazil — Aircraft* case highlights the fundamental problem of fashioning a remedy in a subsidies case. Should the "appropriate countermeasures" be based on the amount of the subsidy or the amount of the injury? Brazil argued that, even without the subsidy, many of the aircraft buyers would not have chosen Canadian aircraft.

The Arbitrators' final decision is not an example of clarity. Without any market analysis, the three Arbitrators decided that it was appropriate for Canada to take countermeasures up to the amount of the subsidy paid by Brazil, regardless of whether that amount corresponded to the injury suffered by Canada:

> [G]iven that export subsidies usually operate with a multiplying effect (a given amount allows a company to make a number of sales, thus gaining a foothold in a given market

[77] Appellate Body Report, *Brazil — Aircraft*, paras 180–87; Article 21.5 Panel Report, *Canada — Aircraft, Recourse to Article 21.5 by Brazil*, para. 5.114; Second Article 21.5 Panel Report, *Brazil — Aircraft, Second Recourse to Article 21.5 by Canada*, para. 5.118.

[78] Appellate Body Report, *Brazil — Aircraft*, para. 185.

[79] *U.S., EU Criticize WTO Ruling Against Canada's Aircraft Subsidies*, Inside U.S. Trade, 22 February 2002, at 8.

> with the possibility to expand and gain market shares), we are of the view that a calculation based on the level of nullification or impairment would, as suggested by the calculation of Canada based on the harm caused to its industry, produce higher figures than one based exclusively on the amount of the subsidy. *On the other hand, if the actual level of nullification or impairment is substantially lower than the subsidy, countermeasures based on the level of nullification or impairment will have less or no inducement effect and the subsidizing country may not withdraw the measure at issue.*
>
> . . .
>
> [W]e conclude that, when dealing with a prohibited export subsidy, an amount of countermeasures which corresponds to the total amount of the subsidy is appropriate.[80]

The Arbitrators did not quantify precisely the damage for Canada. Instead, they used a theory of questionable validity according to which subsidies have a multiplier effect.

This is a first in WTO law. The Arbitrators understood that the remedy for prohibited export subsidies was an exception to DSU Article 22.4, which calls for countermeasures equivalent to the damage suffered. Article 22.4 leaves no doubt that punitive damages are not an option in WTO law. Following this opinion of the Arbitrators, a door now appears to open to punitive damages for cases of prohibited subsidies.

In this case, no third party was injured. Suppose that, after Canada's claim, the EC brought a claim arguing that its own industry had been injured by Brazil's subsidies. Brazil, as noted, has already had countervailing duties imposed by Canada up to the amount of the subsidy paid. What would be the amount that the EC could countervail in case of a successful complaint? The arbitrators did not consider this interesting point.

#### *3.2.2.3.2 Retroactivity*

The *Australia — Leather* case is the first dispute that addressed the issue of whether retroactive remedies are possible in the WTO context. Chapter 4 contains a detailed discussion of the findings.[81] Suffice it to state here that the case holds for the proposition that retroactive remedies are not impossible in WTO law. In the view of its drafters, DSU Article 19 should not be interpreted as imposing an obligation always to recommend prospective remedies. Hence, an export subsidy can be found to be illegal as of the date it was introduced. In such case, the subsidy must be revoked as of that date (that is, the beneficiary

[80] Arbitrators' Report, *Brazil — Aircraft*, paras 3.54, 3.360 (emphasis added). In the *United States — FSC* case the Arbitrator also authorized countermeasures equal to the amount of the subsidy under the criteria of SCM Article 4.10. *See* Decision of the Arbitrator, paras 6.19–6.23.

[81] *See* Chapter 4, section 1.2.

must reimburse the benefit received through the years). Otherwise, the injured WTO Members can countervail up to the amount of the subsidy paid as of the date of its introduction. This is what stems from the *Australia — Leather* and *Brazil — Aircraft* case law.

Independently of the constitutional problems that such a remedy might pose in some domestic legal orders, from an international law perspective this remedy is consistent with re-establishing the *status quo ante*.

### *3.2.3 Actionable subsidies*

Actionable subsidies are defined by default: for a scheme to be deemed an actionable subsidy, two conditions must be met: (1) the scheme must represent a financial assistance by the government, confer a benefit to a recipient and be specific; and (2) the subsidy must not constitute either a prohibited subsidy or a non-actionable subsidy. In addition, for a scheme to be an actionable subsidy, it must cause "adverse effects" to the interests of other WTO Members.[82] The term "adverse effects" is defined as:

1. Injury to the domestic industry of another WTO Member;
2. Nullification or impairment of benefits accruing to other WTO Member(s); or
3. Serious prejudice to the interests of another WTO Member.[83]

The first term (namely, injury to the domestic industry of another Member) is used in the way the term appears in Part V of the SCM Agreement (*i.e.*, the Part dealing with the regulation of countervailing duties).[84] The term nullification or impairment is used in the way it is used in the relevant provisions of GATT 1994.[85] In the context of the GATT, recourse has been made to the nullification and impairment procedures of GATT Article XXIII:1(b) in non-violation cases where the following three conditions were fulfilled[86]:

1. First, a concession was negotiated under the GATT that resulted in a tariff binding;

[82] SCM Agreement Art. 5.

[83] *Id.* Art. 5.

[84] *Id.* Art. 5(a) note 11.

[85] *Id.* Art. 5(b) note 12.

[86] *See* Ernst-Ulrich Petersmann, *Violation and Non-Violation Complaints in Public International Trade Law*, 34 GERMAN Y.B. INT'L L. 225 (1991). *See also* Bernard M. Hoekman and Petros C. Mavroidis, *Competition, Competition Policy and the GATT*, 17 WORLD ECONOMY, at 121 (1994).

2. After the entry into force of the binding, a subsidy scheme was introduced in the territory of the country binding its tariff; which
3. Resulted in nullifying or impairing benefits of the country to which the promise of binding was addressed, because the subsidy scheme went against the legitimate expectations of the addressee of the promise.[87]

Essentially, the rationale behind this rule is the following: every time a tariff binding is negotiated and agreed on, WTO Members have reasonable expectations that they can profit from the conditions of competition established in the market of the Member binding its tariffs and gain market share. Moreover, Members have "paid" for the binding by promising to open up their market, that is, by binding their own tariffs. WTO Members may not then frustrate their promises by subsidizing the domestic industry producing the product for which a tariff binding has been previously offered. If this were allowed, frustrated WTO Members might lose the incentive to make concessions in the future.[88]

Article 6 of the SCM Agreement deals with the question of "serious prejudice". There is a rebuttable presumption that "serious prejudice" is present if any one of the following circumstances exists:

1. The total *ad valorem* subsidization of a product exceeds 5 percent;
2. The subsidy covers operating losses sustained by an industry;
3. The subsidy covers operating losses sustained by an enterprise except for one-time measures given merely to provide time for the development of long-term solutions and avoid acute social problems; or
4. Direct debt forgiveness.

However, these four circumstances of serious prejudice are no longer applicable because they expired by their terms at the end of 1999.[89]

Thus, "serious prejudice" now can arise only under Article 6.3. This provision is an innovation of the Uruguay Round allowing a WTO Member to complain if a subsidy is impeding its *exports* of a like product. This provision has become the essence of an "actionable" subsidy.

[87] The leading case is *European Economic Community — Payments and Subsidies to Processors and Producers of Oilseeds and Related Animal-Feed Proteins*, 25 January 1990, GATT B.I.S.D. (37th Supp.) at 86, para. 69 (1991) (finding that subsidy to seed processors was nullification and impairment).

[88] *See* Kyle Bagwell and Robert W. Staiger, *An Economic Theory of GATT*, 89 Am. Econ. Rev. 215 (1999).

[89] SCM Agreement Art. 31.

Serious prejudice under Article 6.3 arises in any of four circumstances:

1. Where the subsidy displaces or impedes the imports of a like product into the market of the subsidizing Member;
2. Where the subsidy displaces or impedes the exports of a like product into a third-country market;
3. Where the effect of the subsidy is significant price undercutting or significant price suppression of a like product; or
4. Where the effect of the subsidy is an increase in the world market share of the subsidizing Member in a particular primary product or commodity.

The last circumstance does not apply to any subsidy arrangement covered by the Agreement on Agriculture.[90] There are also several affirmative defences to a serious prejudice finding under Article 6.3 relating to *force majeure* and "unclean hands" by the complaining Member.[91]

The panel in the *Indonesia — Autos* case addressed the issue of "serious prejudice".[92] In this case, the EC and the United States contended that certain tariff and tax exemptions for cars manufactured in Indonesia or made abroad using Indonesian components displaced or impeded their exports of cars to Indonesia. The panel handed down several interesting rulings. First, it interpreted "like product" under Article 6.3 narrowly, holding that "like product" referred not to all passenger cars but only to cars with like characteristics to the subsidized cars.[93] Second, it ruled that unassembled cars shipped in "kit" form could be "like" to completed cars.[94] Third, the United States could not complain of serious prejudice where U.S. made products were not involved, even though U.S. companies suffered adverse affects.[95] Fourth, proof of a change in relative market share[96] is relevant only with respect to market displacement in a third country, not market displacement under Article 6.3(a) in the territory of the subsidizing Member.[97] Fifth, price undercutting must be "significant" and must be caused by the subsidy to be "serious prejudice" under Article 6.3(c).[98]

[90] SCM Agreement Art. 6.3(d) note 17.
[91] *Id.* Art. 6.7.
[92] Panel Report, *Indonesia — Automobiles.*
[93] *Id.* para. 14.178.
[94] *Id.* para. 14.197.
[95] *Id.* para. 14.204.
[96] SCM Agreement Art. 6.4.
[97] Panel Report, *Indonesia — Automobiles*, paras 14.210–14.222.
[98] *Id.* paras 14.254–14.255.

The *Indonesia — Auto* panel report was not appealed, so the interpretations of the panel stand untested, as do many other questions relating to "actionable" subsidies.

A dispute settlement procedure, specific to actionable subsidies, is provided for in Article 7 of the SCM Agreement. The provisions of Article 7 are "special or additional" rules to the DSU.[99] This means that the provisions of the DSU remain relevant to the extent that the provisions of Article 7 do not supersede them.

Article 7 of the SCM Agreement deviates in two respects from the DSU provisions of general applicability: first, with respect to deadlines and second, with respect to remedies. The deadlines in Article 7 are substantially shorter than those in the DSU:

1. The composition of panels will be decided within 15 days from their establishment[100];
2. The panel report will be circulated within 120 days from the date of the composition of the panel[101];
3. In case of appeal, the Appellate Body will circulate its report within 60 (exceptionally 90) days[102];
4. The DSB will decide on the adoption of the report within 20 days from its issuance to the Members[103]; and
5. If the Member concerned has not conformed to the DSB's rulings and recommendations within six months, the affected Member will have the right to request authorization to adopt countermeasures.[104]

Only practice can show the extent to which the deadlines set out in Article 7 can realistically be followed. The deadlines in the WTO are generally quite short compared to deadlines set by domestic and international jurisdictions.

The remedies issue is more complicated. Article 7.8 requires Members found to be granting actionable subsidies either to "take appropriate steps to remove the adverse effects or . . . withdraw the subsidy".

If the subsidizing Member does nothing, the affected Member can take countermeasures (after multilateral authorization has been granted, of course)

[99] *See* DSU Appendix 2 (providing that SCM Arts. 7.2 through 7.10 are special or additional rules or procedures to the DSU).
[100] SCM Agreement Art. 7.4.
[101] *Id.* Art. 7.5.
[102] *Id.* Art. 7.7.
[103] *Id.*
[104] *Id.* Art. 7.9.

"commensurate with the degree and nature of the adverse effects".[105] In case of disagreement as to the extent of the permissible countermeasures, an arbitrator will determine whether the countermeasures are commensurate with the degree and nature of the adverse effects found to exist.[106]

### *3.2.4 Non-actionable subsidies*

Three categories of subsidies were "non-actionable" during the first five years of the WTO: (1) research and development subsidies; (2) subsidies to disadvantaged regions; and (3) environmental subsidies.[107] The provisions regulating these non-actionable subsidies expired at the end of 1999.[108] These non-actionable subsidies are, nevertheless, described below.

#### 3.2.4.1 Research and development subsidies[109]

Article 8.2(a) of the SCM Agreement covers "assistance for research activities conducted by firms or by higher education or research establishments on a contract basis with firms". "Fundamental research", defined as "an enlargement of general scientific and technical knowledge not linked to industrial or commercial objectives" is not covered. Allowable assistance is limited to five cost categories: (1) personnel; (2) instruments, equipment, land and buildings; (3) bought-in research (patents) etc.; (4) additional overhead directly incurred; and (5) other running costs (like materials) directly incurred.

A distinction is made between industrial research and pre-competitive development activity. The term "industrial research" is defined as "planned search or critical investigation aimed at discovery of new knowledge, with the objective that such knowledge may be useful in developing new products, processes or services, or in bringing about a significant improvement to existing products, processes or services".[110] The maximum amount of government participation authorized is 75 percent of the costs of industrial research.[111] Pre-competitive development activity occupies the field between industrial research and commercial exploitation. It is defined as:

---

105 SCM Agreement. Art. 7.9.

106 *Id.* Art. 7.10.

107 *Id.* Art. 8.1, 8.2.

108 *Id.* Art. 31.

109 This sub-section draws on Bernard M. Hoekman and Petros C. Mavroidis, *Policy Externalities and High-Tech Rivalry: Competition and Multilateral Cooperation Beyond the WTO*, 9 LEIDEN J. INT'L L. 273 (1996).

110 SCM Agreement Art. 8.2(a) note 28.

111 *Id.* Art. 8.2(a).

> the translation of industrial research findings into a plan, blueprint or design for new, modified or improved products, processes or services whether intended for sale or use, including the creation of a first prototype which would not be capable of commercial use. It may further include the conceptual formulation and design of products, processes or services alternatives and initial demonstrations or pilot projects, provided these same projects cannot be converted or used for industrial application or commercial exploitation. It does not include routine or periodic alterations to existing products, production lines, manufacturing processes, services and other ongoing operations even though those alterations may represent improvements.[112]

The maximum amount of government participation is 50 percent of the cost of pre-competitive development activity. In case of programmes that span industrial research and pre-competitive development activity, the allowable level of non-actionable subsidization may not exceed the simple average of the allowable levels (62.5 percent) of the two categories.[113]

#### 3.2.4.2 Regional subsidies

As the EC experience shows, regional subsidies are not a shortcut to development of underdeveloped regions. They remain, however, an important instrument of industrial policy, because, notwithstanding the absence of effectiveness, they are easy to explain from a public choice perspective. Moreover, regional subsidies are, in principle, not targeted to specific enterprises (although, this could be the case were, for example, a declining region to be associated with the production of one good). Hence, political realism coupled with the relatively reduced threat that such schemes represent mandated their inclusion among the non-actionable category.

The regulation of regional subsidies in the WTO involves the following three areas:

1. "[R]egional subsidy programs [must be] part of an internally consistent and generally applicable regional development policy and . . . not granted in

[112] *Id.* Art. 8.2(a) note 29. Negotiating drafts referred to pre-competitive development activity as "applied R&D", implicitly defined as activities taking place before the industrial or commercial exploitation of the product. *See* Patrick McDonough, *Subsidies and Countervailing Measures, in* The GATT Uruguay Round: A Negotiating History (1986–1992), at 26 (Terence P. Stewart ed., 1993).

[113] SCM Agreement Art. 8.2(a) note 30. During the negotiations on the SCM Agreement, a number of proposals were tabled that would have subjected the use of subsidies to stricter rules. Although ultimately not retained, three proposals deserve mention: (1) a strictly defined time-limit for non-actionable programmes (a five-year review was included instead); (2) a requirement that the results of non-actionable schemes be generally available free of charges (this was the U.S. CVD rule prior to the WTO Agreement); and (3) significantly lower maximum allowable amounts of government support, see McDonough, above note 112.

isolated geographical points having no, or virtually no, influence on the development of a region".[114] Thus, the said footnote avoids targeting of specific industries under a nominal "regional" subsidy by emphasizing the genuine regional character of such schemes.

2. WTO Members must use neutral and objective criteria in determining whether a region constitutes a "disadvantaged region" which may receive subsidies under the SCM Agreement. Although the SCM Agreement does not provide for an exhaustive list of such criteria, two criteria are offered as an indication: the GDP *per capita* must not be above 85 percent of the average of the territory concerned, and the unemployment rate must be at least 110 percent of the average of the territory concerned. The two criteria need not be fulfilled: this means that WTO Members can grant regional subsidies if one of the two criteria is fulfilled.

3. The SCM Agreement does not provide for specific multilaterally agreed ceilings that may not be exceeded, and this is contrary to what is the case with respect to both R&D and environmental subsidies. However, WTO Members when notifying such schemes will have to provide a specific ceiling. They will further have to ensure that disproportionately large amounts are not absorbed by certain enterprises. This discipline, however, is rather loose for at least two reasons: (i) the wording of footnote 32 ("disproportionately large amounts") invites interpretation by a domestic constituency and gives little guidance to a WTO adjudicating body, which in most circumstances will find it difficult and maybe inopportune to second-guess domestic choices in this respect; and (ii) many disadvantaged regions end up being disadvantaged precisely because of the excessive association with the production of a particular product. There is ample empirical evidence suggesting that diversification of production can help avoid such declines. In such cases, it will be difficult to refuse a subsidy scheme to a region producing one particular product that otherwise qualifies as a disadvantaged region under the SCM Agreement.

### 3.2.4.3 Environmental subsidies

Non-actionability of environmental subsidies reflects the awareness at the international plane that environmental harm has not been avoided through private behaviour only. WTO Members can provide subsidies to firms wishing to protect the environment by upgrading their facilities provided that:

[114] SCM Agreement Art. 8.2(b) note 31.

1. The scheme is directed to existing facilities, that is, facilities that have been operational for at least two years;
2. It is a one-time measure, WTO Members being disallowed from re-subsidizing the same firm;
3. The assistance is limited to 20 percent of the cost of adaptation of existing facilities;
4. Costs related to replacing and operating the assisted investment must be fully borne by the subsidized firm;
5. It does not cover manufacturing cost savings; and
6. It is available to any firm that can adopt the new equipment or production process.

All conditions must be respected. A comparison of the criteria laid down for the three categories of non-actionable subsidies leads to the conclusion that the drafters of the SCM Agreement exhausted their rigour in the context of environmental subsidies.

#### 3.2.4.4 Who determines whether a subsidy is a non-actionable one?

WTO Members must notify their subsidy programmes to the SCM Committee.[115] Article 8.3 of the SCM Agreement requires WTO Members to notify to the Committee all subsidy programmes that they want to be classified as non-actionable. All such programmes must be notified before their implementation. In principle, those programmes that are not notified cannot profit from non-actionability. Cross-notification of subsidies is always possible.[116] Article 8.3 makes it clear that the consistency of the programme with the relevant provisions of the Agreement can only be established through recourse to the multilateral procedures established in Article 8. All three categories of subsidies addressed in Article 8 are specific and therefore, in principle, actionable; it is only on exceptional grounds, those mentioned in Article 8 of the SCM Agreement, that they are multilaterally tolerated as non-actionable. As stated above, the provisions regulating non-actionable subsidies, including Article 8, expired at the end of 1999.[117]

[115] *Id.* Art. 25.

[116] Article 8.3 of the SCM Agreement states that notifications will be effected in accordance with the provisions of Part VII. Part VII makes it clear that cross-notification of subsidies is possible. SCM Agreement Art. 25.10.

[117] SCM Agreement Art. 31.

#### 3.2.4.5 Can non-actionable subsidies become actionable?

Although by definition non-actionable subsidies are permissible if notified in advance to the SCM Committee, SCM Article 9 provides that, if a Member "has reason to believe" such subsidies are causing "serious adverse effects" to a domestic industry, "consultations" must be held. If no solution is reached within 90 days, the matter must be referred to the Committee, which can investigate and present "recommendations". If the recommendations are not followed within six months, the Committee can authorize countermeasures "commensurate with the nature and degree of the effects determined to exist".[118] As stated above, the provisions regulating non-actionable subsidies, including Article 9, expired at the end of 1999.[119]

## 4. The regulation of countervailing duties

### 4.1 Overview of procedural and substantive obligations

Countervailing duties may be imposed only in conformity with the SCM Agreement, that is, pursuant to an investigation, the object and purpose of which is "to determine the existence, degree and effect of any alleged subsidy".[120] Before imposing countervailing duties, a WTO Member must determine that (1) a countervailable subsidy exists; (2) injury to the domestic industry producing the like product exists; and (3) a causal link exists between the subsidized imports and the injury.[121] The subsidy and injury determinations are factual determinations. The only legal test is the causation requirement.

A certain administrative framework is called for under the SCM Agreement under the aegis of which the decision to impose countervailing duties will be carried out: a formal investigation must be initiated during which rights of affected parties will be protected essentially through the transparency of the whole exercise. The following sub-sections set forth a step-by-step presentation of the whole endeavour.

---

[118] SCM Agreement Art. 9.4. [119] *Id.* Art. 31. [120] *Id.* Arts. 10, 11.1.
[121] *Id.* Art. 11.2.

## 4.2 Investigation

### *4.2.1 Initiating an investigation*

An investigation can be initiated either (1) by, or on behalf of, the domestic industry producing the like product; or (2) by domestic authorities of their own accord.[122] In the first case, a petition is needed. In either case, the same information is required. In what follows, we focus on the information that must appear in the petition by the domestic industry.

The petition must include sufficient evidence that a subsidy has been granted that resulted in injuring the domestic industry producing the like product.[123] The Agreement does not provide for an exhaustive list of what must be included in the petition. It does, however, provide indications. All petitions must at least contain the following information: (1) the identity of the applicant; (2) a description of the subsidized product; (3) a description of the nature and the amount of the subsidy in question; and (4) evidence of injury caused to the domestic industry producing the like product.[124]

For an investigation to be initiated, producers accounting for no less than 25 percent of the total production of the like product produced by the domestic industry have to support the initiation.[125] The definition of the phrase "domestic industry producing the like product" is crucial: the narrower the definition, the easier to meet the threshold. Traditionally, voices have time and again been raised arguing that the definition of the term "like product" in both the countervailing and the antidumping fields is too narrow, and, as a result, duties have been imposed against imports representing a minimal share of a properly defined domestic market.[126]

Article 16 of the SCM Agreement refers to domestic industry as the industry producing the like product. The term "like product" is described in the SCM Agreement as follows:

> Throughout this Agreement the term "like product" ("produit similaire") shall be interpreted to mean a product which is identical, i.e. alike in all respects to the product

---

[122] *Id.* Art. 11.1, 11.6.

[123] *Id.* Art. 11.2.

[124] *Id.* Art. 11.2.

[125] *Id.* Art. 11.4.

[126] *See* Messerlin, above note 35; Bernard M. Hoekman and Petros C. Mavroidis, *Dumping, Antidumping and Antitrust*, 30 J. World Trade, No. 1, at 27 (1996).

under consideration, or in the absence of such a product, another product which, although not alike in all respects, has characteristics closely resembling those of the product under consideration.[127]

The term "like product" was interpreted in a dispute between Indonesia on the one hand, and the United States and the EC on the other. The dispute concerned subsidies paid by the Indonesian government to car producers.[128] This report is the first that dealt with the issue in the subsidies context. The panel constructed a standard inspired by the GATT panel report on *Japan — Alcoholic Beverages*, which accepted cross-price elasticity as the basic criterion for establishing whether two products are directly competitive, and established that "like products" are the inner circle of directly competitive products.[129]

The *Indonesia — Automobiles* report stands for the proposition that the GATT standard provides useful guidance for interpreting the term "like product" in the SCM context.[130] The panel adopted an approach dictated by a market survey,[131] and concluded that the car at issue competed with other cars that essentially served the same end-use and were offered within a comparable price range.[132] The panel also accepted that unassembled cars were still like products to assembled cars notwithstanding that they were being imported in kits.[133]

### *4.2.2 Evidentiary issues*

The application must contain "sufficient evidence" of the existence of a subsidy that causes injury to the domestic industry producing the like product.[134] The national authority investigating the matter determines whether the evidence submitted is sufficient to justify the initiation of an investigation. There are, however, limits imposed by the WTO: each Member must ascertain the adequacy and accuracy of the evidence presented "to determine whether the evidence is sufficient to justify the initiation of an investigation".[135] At any rate, "there shall be immediate termination in cases where the amount of a subsidy is *de minimis*, or where

[127] SCM Agreement Art. 15.1, note 46.
[128] *See* Panel Report, *Indonesia — Automobiles*.
[129] *See id.* para. 14.175.
[130] *See id.*
[131] *See id.* para. 14.177.
[132] *See id.* para. 14.192.
[133] *See id.* para. 14.197.
[134] SCM Agreement Art. 11.2.
[135] *Id.* Art. 11.3.

the volume of subsidized imports, actual or potential, or the injury, is negligible. For the[se] purpose[s] . . . , the amount of the subsidy shall be considered to be *de minimis* if the subsidy is less than 1 per cent ad valorem".[136]

Sufficient evidence does not, however, amount to full proof; "sufficient" in this context means there is probable cause for an investigation. Hence, a lesser than full proof standard must be understood to satisfy the requirement to provide sufficient evidence. Finally, the term "evidence" strongly suggests that speculative statements will have to be rejected.

### *4.2.3 The duties of the investigating authority*

Investigating authorities must review the accuracy of the submitted information and provide an assessment of whether such information constitutes sufficient evidence.[137] Investigating authorities must complete their investigations within 18 months.[138] During the investigation period, procedures of customs clearance may not be hindered.[139]

More importantly, investigating authorities are responsible for gathering and handling the evidence. They have a duty to invite all interested parties to participate in the hearings.[140] Interested parties have a right to express their views orally, but all decisions will be based on a written record.[141] This means that, in practice, oral statements will be reduced to written submissions. The term "interested parties" must include at least the exporter of the subsidized product and the domestic producer of the like product, and the investigating authority retains the authority to invite other parties as well.[142]

One of the novelties of the SCM Agreement is that parties who may be benefiting from the effects of the subsidy will also be heard by the investigating authority: investigating authorities must provide industrial users and consumer organizations with an adequate opportunity to present their views.[143]

The authorities must respect certain confidentiality requirements. They may not disclose any confidential information without specific permission

[136] *Id.* Art. 11.9. [137] *Id.* Art. 11.3.
[138] *Id.* Art. 11.11. [139] *Id.* Art. 11.10.
[140] *Id.* Art. 12.1. [141] *Id.* Art. 12.2.
[142] *Id.* Art. 12.9. [143] *Id.* Art. 12.10.

of the party submitting it,[144] but they may ask the latter to provide non-confidential summaries of confidential information that provides a reasonable understanding of the issue.[145]

In the absence of objections, investigating authorities may conduct investigations in the territory of other Members and even on the premises of the subsidized firm.[146] The purpose of this rule is to ensure that all interested parties will be heard and that the record before the investigating authority will be of such quality that it will enable the investigating authority to make an objective and unbiased assessment of the case. It may be the case that, notwithstanding the efforts of the investigating authority, the record cannot be established (or, it cannot be established within the limits set by the Agreement) due to the stance adopted by an interested party or parties.

To avoid such problems, the SCM Agreement allows investigating authorities to proceed on the basis of available information if interested parties refuse to cooperate.[147] This is an area, however, where practice, especially in the antidumping field, has shown abuses rather than uses of the possibility to have recourse to best information available.[148] After an application has been filed but before the investigation begins, investigating authorities must invite the subsidizing Member for consultations aimed at clarifying the situation.[149] Such consultations will carry on throughout the period of investigation.[150]

## 4.3 Provisional application

WTO Members can impose preliminary countervailing duties after first making a preliminary determination that a subsidy is causing or threatening to cause injury to a domestic industry, provided that:

1. Such duties are not applied sooner than 60 days after the initiation of the investigation[151];
2. Such duties are limited in time (not exceeding four months, roughly 120 days)[152]; and

[144] SCM Agreement Art. 12.4. [145] *Id.* Art. 12.4.1. [146] *Id.* Art. 12.6.
[147] *Id.* Art. 12.7. [148] See Chapter 13. [149] SCM Agreement Art. 13.1.
[150] *Id.* Art. 13.2. [151] *Id.* Art. 17.3.
[152] *Id.* Art. 17.4. For a case of violation of this provision and Article 17.3, *see United States — Softwood Lumber*, Report of the Panel, para. 7.103.

3. The relevant provisions of Article 19 of the SCM Agreement have been followed. This Article deals with the imposition of definitive countervailing duties.

## 4.4 Determination of subsidy

The SCM Agreement does not dictate a particular method of calculating a subsidy in terms of the benefit that the recipient has received. Regulatory diversity is condoned, imposing, however, the obligation to adopt "transparent and adequately explained" methods.[153]

The chosen method must be consistent with the guidelines set out in Article 14 of the SCM Agreement:

1. Equity infusions by the government will not automatically be considered as benefit to recipient if they correspond to a private investor's criteria[154];
2. When it comes to governmental loans, only the difference between commercial and governmentally paid loans will qualify as benefit;
3. The same is true for loan guarantees;
4. With respect to provision of goods or services or purchase of goods, the benefit will be the difference between the prevailing market conditions and the price paid by the governments.

## 4.5 Determination of injury

Under the SCM Agreement, injury means "material injury to the domestic industry, threat of material injury to the domestic industry or material retardation of the establishment of such an industry".[155] The term "material injury" is to be distinguished from the term "serious injury". The term "material injury" appears in both the Antidumping Agreement and the SCM Agreement, and the term "serious injury" appears in the Safeguards Agreement. The Appellate Body has concluded that the standard of "serious injury" is higher than that of "material injury".[156] As far as threat of injury

[153] *Id.* Art. 14.

[154] The unadopted panel report on *United States — CVDs* also adopted the private investor's criterion as the appropriate benchmark to judge whether a governmental equity infusion actually confers a benefit to the recipient. *See* GATT Panel Report, *United States — CVDs*, above note 30, para. 511 *et seq.*

[155] SCM Agreement Art. 15 note 45.

[156] Appellate Body Report, *United States — Lamb Safeguard*, para. 124.

is concerned, the SCM Agreement requests extra care by the authorities about to take corrective action through recourse to this ground.[157] The term "material retardation" is not interpreted any further in the SCM Agreement. It must be assumed that the analysis relevant for the determination of injury must also be relevant to show material retardation.

Investigating authorities must demonstrate injury based on "positive evidence" about both (1) the volume of subsidized imports and the effect of such imports on prices of the domestic like product; and (2) the impact of such imports on the domestic producers of such product.[158] The term "positive evidence" has not yet been interpreted in the SCM context.

This issue of positive information, however, was discussed in the GATT panel report, *United States — Antidumping Duties on Imports of Stainless Steel from Sweden.*[159] The panel report remains unadopted and therefore of limited legal value. In that case, Sweden claimed that the United States violated its obligations by failing to initiate a review of the duties as required by Article 9.2 of the Tokyo Round Antidumping Code. Article 9.2 required investigating authorities to "review the need for the continued imposition of the duty, where warranted, on their own initiative or if any interested party so requests and submits positive information substantiating the need for review".

"Positive information" is not, however, identical to "positive evidence". Positive evidence seems to set a higher standard. The United States did not accept the following items as positive information: negligible levels of imports as a result of decline in both absolute and relative exports of steel from Sweden; an increase of exports of Swedish steel to Europe mainly as a result of the entry into force of the EC-Sweden Free Trade Agreement; the changed strategy of Swedish producers who opted for direct investment in the United States (arguably, in order to avoid ever-recurring trade barriers); the reduced production capacity of the Swedish producer; and improvement in the condition of the U.S. domestic industry.[160] It is not surprising that the panel found that the United States had acted inconsistently with its international obligations.

[157] SCM Agreement Art. 15.8.

[158] *Id.* Art. 15.1.

[159] *United States — Antidumping Duties on Imports of Stainless Steel from Sweden*, ADP/117, 24 February 1994 [hereinafter GATT Panel Report, *United States — Antidumping Duties on Imports of Stainless Steel from Sweden*].

[160] *Id.* para. 246.

Most investigations concern subsidized imports from one source. At times, however, subsidized imports from several sources may be investigated. In such cases, cumulation will be permitted only to the extent that the disciplines laid down in Article 11.9 of the SCM Agreement are respected, that is, if the amount of subsidization does not exceed the *de minimis* benchmark (1 percent *ad valorem*) and to the extent that the volume of subsidized imports is not negligible.

### *4.5.1 Domestic industry*

The definition of "domestic industry" in the SCM Agreement is similar to the definition of the same term in the Antidumping Agreement. As a general rule, domestic industry includes domestic producers of like products as a whole or a "major proportion" of such producers.[161] Domestic producers that are related to exporters or importers may be excluded.[162] In exceptional cases, the domestic industry may be defined by a regional market, provided there is a concentration of imports into the market causing injury to "almost all" of the producers in that market.[163]

### *4.5.2 Causation*

Article 15.5 of the SCM Agreement requires a showing of causation between the subsidized imports and the injury to the domestic industry producing the like product:

> It must be demonstrated that the subsidized imports are, through the effects of subsidies, causing injury within the meaning of this Agreement. The demonstration of a causal relationship between the subsidized imports and injury to the domestic industry shall be based on an examination of all relevant evidence before the authorities. The authorities shall also examine any known factors other than the subsidized imports which at the same time are injuring the domestic industry, and the injuries caused by these other factors must not be attributed to the subsidized imports. Factors which may be relevant in this respect include, *inter alia*, the volumes and prices of non-subsidized imports of the product in question, contraction in demand or changes in the patterns of consumption, trade restrictive practices of and competition between the foreign and domestic producers, developments in technology and the export performance and productivity of the domestic industry.

[161] *See* Chapter 13.
[162] SCM Agreement Art. 16.1.
[163] *Id.* Art. 16.2.

Thus, WTO Members wishing to impose countervailing duties must:

1. Show that subsidized imports through their effects cause injury to the domestic industry. This means that, for a WTO Member to demonstrate that countervailing duties are lawfully imposed, it must demonstrate that an increase in subsidized imports through either price undercutting, price depression, or price suppression resulted in loss of market share or decline in return of investment or in any of the factors listed in Article 15.4 of the SCM Agreement;[164]
2. Not attribute to factors other than the subsidized imports any injury caused to the domestic industry.

Causation in the SCM Agreement is similar to that in the Antidumping and Safeguards Agreements, and the interpretations rendered by WTO adjudicating bodies under those agreements will undoubtedly carry over to the SCM Agreement.[165]

## 4.6 The imposition of definitive countervailing duties

WTO Members may impose definitive countervailing duties only after making a final determination that a countervailable subsidy exists and that such subsidy causes injury to the domestic industry.[166] The amount of countervailing duties may not exceed the amount of the subsidy found to exist.[167] It is desirable, however, that countervailing duties be limited to the amount necessary to counteract the injury caused if such amount is less than the amount of the subsidy found to exist.[168] Countervailing duties have to be collected on a non-discriminatory basis on imports from all sources found to be subsidizing. If duties are levied from exporters who were not investigated for reasons other than refusal to cooperate, such exporters will be entitled to an expedited review, the object of which will be for investigating authorities to demonstrate an individual CVD for the exporter concerned.[169]

[164] It could be that injury is demonstrated in a form other than mentioned in SCM Art. 15.4 because the list is not exhaustive. Arguably, though, it will have to perform a similar function to that of the factors mentioned in Article 15.4.

[165] *See* Chapters 9 and 13.

[166] SCM Agreement Art. 19.1.

[167] *Id.* Art. 19.4.

[168] *Id.* Art. 19.2.

[169] *Id.* Art. 19.3.

## 4.7 Duration and review

One of the novelties of the SCM Agreement is a "sunset clause" (Article 21), under which all countervailing duties will lapse at, the latest, five years after their imposition, unless the investigating authorities determine "that the expiry of the duty would be likely to lead to continuation or recurrence of subsidization and injury".[170]

The review of countervailing duties may take place before the five-year period on the initiative of the investigating authority or following a request by an interested party.[171] Interested parties can table a request only after a "reasonable period of time" has elapsed since the imposition of definitive countervailing duties.[172] The Agreement does not define the phrase "reasonable period of time".

Investigating authorities must review the need to continue imposing countervailing duties "where warranted".[173] The interpretation of the phrase "where warranted" is, therefore, crucial to circumscribe the ambit of the obligation imposed on WTO Members. The only panel report to deal with this issue is the unadopted GATT report, *United States — Antidumping Duties on Imports of Stainless Steel from Sweden.*[174] This report ruled that considerable deference must be accorded to investigating authorities.

The value of this GATT ruling is limited. The words "where warranted" suggest that a review will be conducted when information at the disposal of the investigating authority contradicts the information that formed the basis of the original imposition. Such information must be gathered in the context of an investigation process. Although Article 21 does not suggest that investigating authorities must conduct an on-going investigation, it can have meaning only if investigating authorities are required to check periodically whether a review is warranted.

## 4.8 Judicial review

All WTO Members that have national legislation allowing the imposition of countervailing duties must maintain judicial or administrative tribunals for

---

170 *Id.* Art. 21.3.

171 *Id.* Art. 21.2.

172 *Id.*

173 *Id.*

174 GATT Panel Report, *United States — Antidumping Duties on Imports of Stainless Steel from Sweden*, above note 159.

the "prompt review" of administrative action imposing or reviewing countervailing duties.[175]

## 4.9 Undertakings (suspension of countervailing duty investigations)

The proceedings leading to the eventual imposition of countervailing duties may be suspended or terminated if the parties involved agree to "undertakings". According to Article 18 of the SCM Agreement, undertakings can result when the subsidizing government agrees to eliminate or limit the amount of subsidy or when the exporter agrees to revise the price to eliminate the injurious effect of the subsidy. In practice, therefore, undertakings are a substitute for countervailing duties in that they constitute a different form of protection of the affected industry.

The initiative to conclude undertakings can originate with (1) the investigating authority; or (2) the subsidizing government or the exporter.[176] No matter where such an offer originates, the other party does not have to accept it. If the offer originates with the subsidizing government or the exporter and the investigating authority decides to reject it, reasons must be given.[177] If the offer originates with the investigating authority, and the subsidizing government or the exporters decide to reject it, the investigating authority must ensure that the ongoing investigation will not be prejudiced.[178]

Undertakings may be sought or accepted only after a preliminary affirmative finding of subsidization and injury.[179] This is because the function of undertakings is to provide for protection equivalent to that provided by countervailing duties.

The conclusion of undertakings does not automatically terminate the investigation. The investigation will continue and be completed if either the investigating authority or the subsidizing Member so desires. If the investigation concludes that there is either no subsidization or injury, the undertakings automatically lapse, except where such a determination is due in large part to the existence of an undertaking.[180] It seems that undertakings will also lapse where there is an affirmative finding of both subsidization and injury but

[175] SCM Agreement Art. 23.
[176] *Id.* Art. 18.3.
[177] *Id.* [178] *Id.* Art. 18.5.
[179] *Id.* Art. 18.2.
[180] *Id.* Art. 18.4.

no causal link between the two. Otherwise, one would have to accept that WTO Members may seek relief through recourse to undertakings under conditions different from those under which recourse to countervailing duties is legitimized. This, however, should not be the case because the function of undertakings is similar to that of countervailing duties.

## 4.10 Retroactivity

The concept of retroactivity in Article 20 of the SCM Agreement should be distinguished from that of revocation of illegal subsidies. In the context of Article 20, retroactivity has to do with two factual situations: first, when can duties be imposed and second, what should be done where there is a discrepancy between the provisional and the definitive duties imposed?

Duties may be applied retroactively only in exceptional circumstances, and they may not be applied to imports that took place more than 90 days prior to the application of provisional measures.[181]

With respect to cases of difference between the amounts of the provisional and the definitive duties, two situations can be distinguished: (1) the definitive duty is higher than the provisional one, in which case the difference may not be collected and[182]; (2) the definitive duty is lower than the provisional one, in which case the difference must be reimbursed.[183] Moreover, if the final determination is a negative one, any cash deposit must be refunded in an expeditious manner.[184]

## 4.11 The standard of review for subsidies and countervailing duties disputes

The SCM Agreement does not provide for a standard of review for subsidies or countervailing duty disputes. The Appellate Body report on *United States — CVDs on Steel* addressed the issue of whether the standard of review provided for in Article 17.6 of the Antidumping Agreement should be extended to the SCM Agreement as well.[185] The United States advanced this opinion based on (a) a Declaration by the Ministers during the conclusion of the Uruguay Round arguing in favour of a consistent resolution of disputes arising from antidumping and countervailing duties, and

[181] *Id.* Art. 20.6. Provisional measures cannot be applied retroactively. *United States — Softwood Lumber*, Report of the Panel, para. 7.94.

[182] *Id.* Art. 20.3. [183] *Id.* [184] *Id.* Art. 20.5.

[185] *See* Chapter 13.

(b) a Decision[186] to review whether the standard inscribed in Article 17.6 of the Antidumping Agreement should be of general application.

The Appellate Body rejected the argument on two grounds. First, the wording in the Declaration was merely hortatory and did not prescribe a standard of review to be applied.[187] Second, the contemplated review, which was scheduled within three years after the entry into force of the WTO agreements, never took place.[188]

As a result, the standard of review applied in disputes coming under the scope of the SCM Agreement is that provided for in DSU Article 11.

## 5. Conclusions

Compared to its Tokyo Round counterpart, the SCM Agreement is a step forward toward providing additional clarity in an area where clarity is badly needed. Compared to other WTO agreements, it is indeed an Agreement in which substantial changes occurred. Such changes are partly explained by the fact that, with the accession to power of the Clinton administration, the distance between the United States and the EC in this respect substantially shortened. Moreover, according to at least one source, the Clinton administration was even more in favour of subsidizing than the EC.[189] We now have a definition of subsidy. We know that subsidies that particularly distort international markets will be heavily sanctioned. We also know that more lenient forms of subsidization will be tolerated. There is, of course, room for improvement.

More than seven years after the entry into force of the SCM Agreement, it is remarkable that disputes in this area concerned, in principle, the most distorting subsidies — namely, export subsidies. The two disputes between Canada and Brazil, the dispute about leather export subsidies between Australia and affected countries, and the *FSC* and the *ETI* cases between the EC and the United States fall under this category. So far WTO practice has treated non-actionable subsidies as truly non-actionable. And very few cases

[186] Final Act Embodying the Results of the Uruguay Round of Multilateral Trade Negotiations, 15 April 1994, 33 I.L.M. 1140 (1994). The Decision is discussed by Croley and Jackson, 90 A.J.I.L. at 198.

[187] *See* Appellate Body Report, *United States — CVDs on Steel*, paras 48–50.

[188] *See* Appellate Body Report, *United States — CVDs on Steel*, paras 48–50.

[189] *See* Hugo Paemen and Alexandra Bensch, Du GATT à l'OMC: La Communauté européenne dans l'Uruguay Round 235 *et seq.* (1995).

have been brought over actionable subsidies. WTO practice consequently shows that Members are not willing to call into question domestic subsidies to the extent that their effects on export markets are not felt.

The SCM Agreement is the forum where the discussion on WTO remedies really took off. Following GATT case law in the field of anti-dumping and countervailing duties, the *Australia — Leather* report established that retroactive remedies are very much a possibility in the WTO. *Brazil — Aircraft* opened the door to punitive damages. For the time being, these two "advances" remain confined to the field of subsidies. This is in line with the fact that the WTO Agreement in large part has been negotiated to protect producers' interests: export subsidies (in the absence of predatory pricing) are a blessing for consumers worldwide. Yet, they are punished more heavily than any other deviation from the WTO Agreement. On the other hand, blatantly anti-consumer mechanisms (as is most of current antidumping practice) are let off the hook.

# 13

# ANTIDUMPING

## 1. What is dumping?

The term "dumping" has many meanings. It may mean exporting a product at an unduly low price to drive out competition in the importing country. It may also mean "social dumping", exporting a product from a country where wages are extremely low (and, therefore, where the export price is low) or where the level of working conditions is far below that of advanced countries. Whatever the term dumping means, it has the connotation of "unfair" or "predatory".[1] On the other hand, there is a view that "dumping" is merely legitimate price competition.

## 1.1 Dumping as sales below cost

Dumping may take the form of sales below cost. Sales below cost are defined in the legislation of many nations as sales of a product at prices below the cost of production (including indirect expenses). Sales below cost can occur in various circumstances.

First, intense competition in a market may result in sales below cost. If competition in a market is fierce, the mark-up tends to be small, below the marginal cost of production.

Second, a decline in demand in a market due to a recession may lead to sales below cost. This is true especially in industries, such as the steel industry, in which the fixed cost of production is high. When a recession hits the steel industry, the demand for steel declines, and the production capacity in the market becomes excessive in relation to that demand. When sales volume declines due to a recession, the average total costs increase due to an increase in the fixed cost per unit of products. This increase in the fixed cost per unit tends to push down the market price below the cost of production.

Third, forward pricing may result in sales below cost. Forward pricing is the practice of pricing goods below cost to increase sales volumes early in a product's life cycle and maximize profitability over the full life cycle of the product. In industries that require a huge amount of money to develop a product, the initial cost of production is so great that sales of the new product at prices above cost would be prohibitive. Under these circumstances, the only marketable price of the new product would be one below the cost of production. Enterprises therefore sell the product at prices below the cost of production expecting that the cost of production will sharply decline as the product is mass-produced and sold and that profit will be made later.[2]

[1] On predatory pricing, see generally Robert Bork, ANTITRUST PARADOX: A POLICY AT WAR WITH ITSELF (1978); Joseph Brodley and George A. Hay, *Predatory Pricing: Competing Economic Theories and the Evolution of Legal Standards*, 66 CORNELL L. REV. 739 (1981); Frank H. Easterbrook, *Predatory Strategies and Counterstrategies*, 48 U. CHI. L. REV. 263 (1981); Paul R. Krugman, STRATEGIC TRADE POLICY AND THE NEW INTERNATIONAL ECONOMICS (1986); Richard A. Posner, ANTITRUST LAW: AN ECONOMIC PERSPECTIVE (1976); and Laura D. A. Tyson, WHO'S BASHING WHOM: TRADE CONFLICT IN HIGH TECHNOLOGY INDUSTRIES (1992).

[2] *See* Tyson, *id.* at 57–59.

Finally, predatory pricing may cause sales below cost. Predatory pricing is the practice of an enterprise with market power engaging in sales below the cost of production to drive out the competition and to gain a monopoly. Predatory pricing may occur if an enterprise has a reasonable expectation that the profits lost to sales below cost can be recouped by raising prices after competitors have been driven from the market. An enterprise has this expectation only when it has market power, when the market is concentrated, and when other enterprises cannot easily enter the market to compete with it.

Predatory pricing is commonly illegal under national competition laws, but more than below-cost sales must be proved. For example, under U.S. antitrust laws, the requirements for a prima facie case of predatory pricing include: (1) proof that the enterprise engages in sales below cost; (2) proof that the sales below cost harm competition; and (3) proof that the enterprise engaging in predatory pricing has a reasonable prospect of recouping the money it lost by earning monopoly profits after driving competitors out, establishing market power and raising prices.[3] The rationale for the additional requirements is that an enterprise is presumed to behave rationally, *i.e.*, in such a way as to maximize profit. Moreover, the burden of proof of predatory pricing is on the party challenging the conduct.[4] Consequently, a case of predatory pricing is very difficult to prove.[5]

## 1.2 Dumping as international price discrimination

Another form of dumping is international price discrimination. International price discrimination occurs when an enterprise sells the same product at different prices in different areas or to different customers. In the international arena, price discrimination usually takes the form of selling the same or a similar product at different prices in the domestic market and an export market, *i.e.*, international price discrimination based on geography.

International price discrimination can occur when the markets of the exporting country and the importing country are relatively isolated (*e.g.*, by high tariffs, quotas or private restrictive business practices such as exclusive

[3] For major cases, see *In re Japanese Electronics Products Antitrust Litigation*, 513 F. Supp. 1100 (E.D. Pa. 1981), affirmed in part, reversed in part, 723 F.2d 238 (3d Cir. 1983), reversed and remanded, 475 U.S. 574 (1986); *Marsann Co. v. Brammall, Inc.*, 788 F.2d 611 (9th Cir. 1986); *A. A. Poultry Farms v. Rose Acre Farms*, 881 F.2d 1396 (7th Cir. 1989); *Liggett Group v. Brown & Williamson Tobacco*, 748 F. Supp. 344 (M.D.N.C. 1990), affirmed, 964 F.2d 335 (4th Cir. 1992), affirmed, 509 U.S. 209 (1993).

[4] *Japanese Electronic Products Antitrust Litigation*, above note 3, 475 U.S. at 585.

[5] *Id.* at 586.

dealing arrangements, tie-in contracts, boycotts, or other forms of anti-competitive practices). Products exported at a price lower than the price charged in the exporting country will be re-exported to the importing country unless (1) the market of the exporting country is insulated from that of the importing county; or (2) costs of transportation and other sales expenses are significant factors that prevent such a re-export from occurring.

International price discrimination can also occur when there are significant differences in elasticity of demand between different countries. If, for example, the demand for a product in the market of the exporting country is inelastic, a seller of the product in the market of the exporting country has incentive to charge higher prices in that market while charging lower prices to customers in the importing country, where demand for the product is elastic.

## 1.3 Duration

Dumping can be classified by duration into sporadic, intermittent, and continuous (persistent) activity. While sporadic dumping generally is not worrisome, intermittent or continuous dumping may produce adverse welfare effects if it is designed to be predatory, to drive competitors out of business. Dumping of longer duration also may result in a misallocation of resources, especially in the *exporting* country.

## 1.4 Cost analysis

Dumping may be analysed in terms of the relationship of prices to costs of production. Consider five cases of prices in the export market: (1) P1 is a price higher than average total cost as well as the equilibrium point of marginal revenue (MR) and marginal cost (MC); (2) P2 is the equilibrium of marginal revenue and marginal cost, above average total cost; (3) P3 is below average total cost but above average variable cost; (4) P4 is below average variable cost; and (5) P5 is below average fixed cost. In each case, the home market price is higher.

All five cases would meet the legal definition of dumping. Certainly, however, P1 and P2 can be defended as normal and rational behaviour; any price above average total cost is profitable. P2, which is equal to marginal cost, or short-run variable costs, is the proper basis for efficient output decisions and by definition is efficient pricing.

On the other hand, prices below average total cost cause the firm to incur losses. This may be rational, however, in periods of slack demand or for other economic reasons. Dumping below average total cost or marginal cost may be justified by uncertainties and the necessity to make decisions about production before prices can be determined. A firm also may be meeting competition, competing for market share, or trying to maximize sales rather than profits. In antitrust cases, prices above average total cost are legal *per se*, average variable cost is a marker of rebuttable presumptions, with the plaintiff holding the burden above and the defendant below.[6] Only P5, pricing below fixed cost, seems irrational, except where it occurs for very short periods.

## 1.5 Welfare effects

The welfare effects of dumping are mixed. Perhaps the greatest impact is in the exporting country, where consumers must pay more in an artificially segmented market. Some have called for antidumping duties to punish the exporting country for maintaining closed markets.[7]

In the importing country, consumers will be better off paying less, but producers will be disadvantaged. Third-country producers also will be at a disadvantage, as well as certain producers of products that are not directly competitive with the dumped imports through the misallocation of resources stimulated by artificially low prices. The seriousness and extent of the injuries may vary greatly.

## 1.6 Measures to counteract dumping

To counteract dumping, countries impose "antidumping" duties on imports of the products that are being dumped. As amplified below, an importing country may impose an antidumping duty on imported products if (1) products are sold at a certain price in the domestic market of the exporting country and such products or similar products are sold at a lower price in the market of the importing country; (2) a domestic industry in the importing country is materially injured; and (3) there is a causal relationship between dumping and the material injury. The maximum duty that may be imposed under WTO rules is the difference between those two prices.[8] Although WTO rules condemn dumping,[9] whether antidumping is a good policy is a controversial matter. Some argue that antidumping measures are

[6] *See Henry v. Chloride Inc.*, 809 F.2d 1334, 1346 (8th Cir. 1987).

[7] *See* Jeffrey E. Garten, *New Challenges in the World Economy: The Antidumping Law and U.S. Trade Policy*, 17 World Competition, No. 4, at 129 (1994).

[8] GATT 1994 Art. VI; Antidumping Agreement.

[9] GATT 1994 Art. VI.

necessary to counteract unfair trade on the part of exporters. Others argue that antidumping measures are often used to protect domestic industries from competition from imports and are themselves unfair. We will briefly review some of these arguments to determine whether antidumping is justified and, if so, under what conditions.[10]

# 2. The regulation of antidumping duties

## 2.1 The legal framework of antidumping in the GATT/WTO regime

It is quite remarkable that, despite a consensus among economists and lawyers that the antidumping laws are seriously flawed,[11] serious reform has proved difficult or impossible to achieve. The GATT Antidumping Code of 1979[12] introduced new procedural and substantive standards both for calculating dumping margins and for determining whether a domestic industry is materially injured, but abuses by protectionist interests increased in the 1980s.[13] The Uruguay Round of trade negotiations produced a new Antidumping Agreement, but since this latest "reform", the use and abuse of antidumping actions has continued unabated, especially in the United States and the European Union. There is evidence of increased use of antidumping duties, even by developing countries. This trend is cause for concern.

The legal framework of antidumping in the GATT/WTO regime consists of Article VI of the GATT 1994 and the Antidumping Agreement. Article VI of the GATT 1994 is the general provision and the Antidumping Agreement is an implementation of Article VI.

[10] For different views on antidumping, see S. P. Anderson et al., *Who Benefits from Antidumping Legislation?*, 38 J. Int'l Econ. 321 (1995); H. K. Gruenspecht, *Dumping and Dynamic Competition*, 25 J. Int'l Econ. 225 (1988); R. Pierce, *Antidumping Law as a Means of Facilitating Cartelization*, 67 Antitrust L.J. 725 (2000); U.S. Int'l Trade Comm'n, The Economic Effects of Antidumping and Countervailing Duty Order and Suspension Agreements, Investigation Nos. 332–344, USITC Publication 2900 (June 1995).

[11] *See generally* Down in the Dumps: Administration of the Unfair Trade Laws (Richard Botlick and Robert Litan eds., 1991); U.S. Trade Barriers: A Legal Analysis (Eberhard Grabitz and Armin von Bogdandy eds., 1991); Jagdish Bhagwati, Protectionism (1988).

[12] Agreement on the Implementation of Article VI of the General Agreement on Tariffs and Trade, GATT Doc.l MTN/NTM/W/232, GATT B.I.S.D. (26th Supp.) at 171 (1980).

[13] *See generally* Thomas J. Schoenbaum, *Antidumping and Countervailing Duties and the GATT: An Evaluation and a Proposal for a Unified Remedy for Unfair International Trade*, 30 German Y.B. Int'l L. 177 (1988).

### 2.1.1 GATT Article VI

Article VI of the GATT 1994 reads, in the relevant part, as follows:

> The contracting parties recognize that dumping, by which products of one country are introduced into the commerce of another country at less than the normal value of the products, is to be condemned if it causes or threatens material injury to an established industry in the territory of a contracting party or materially retards the establishment of a domestic industry.[14]

According to this provision, there are three requirements for dumping. First, the export price of a product must be lower than the price (normal value) of that product in the domestic market of the exporting country. Second, exports of such products must (1) cause or threaten to cause material injury to a domestic industry; or (2) materially retard the establishment of a domestic industry. Third, there must be a causal relationship between dumping and the injury or retardation. The GATT contracting parties, therefore, agreed that dumping is an unfair trade practice.

Article VI:6(a) of the GATT addresses the injury determination. Under this Article, national antidumping authorities may impose an antidumping duty only after first determining that the dumping causes or threatens material injury to an established domestic industry or materially retards the establishment of a domestic industry.

### 2.1.2 The Antidumping Agreement

Although Article VI of the GATT 1994 sets forth the basic principles to be followed by WTO Members when dealing with dumping issues, its terms are general and the content is rather sketchy. When trade negotiations took place in the Kennedy and Tokyo Rounds, the negotiators thought it necessary to conclude an additional agreement on antidumping issues to clarify the meanings of some of the key concepts of the GATT and to provide practical guides for the enforcers of antidumping legislation of Member countries and for exporters whose products may be subject to antidumping duty.

The Antidumping Agreement is formally titled "Agreement on Implementation of Article VI of the General Agreement on Tariffs and Trade 1994". For the sake of brevity, the term "Antidumping Agreement" is used in this work. It is clear from this title that the Antidumping Agreement is an agreement whose purpose is to implement (clarify and amplify) the provisions of the GATT. There follows an explanation of some of the important provisions of Article VI and the Antidumping Agreement.

14 GATT Art. VI:1.

### 2.1.3 *Institutions and notifications*

The Antidumping Agreement establishes a Committee on Antidumping Practices composed of representatives of all WTO Members. The function of the Committee is to seek information and provide a forum for consultation among Members. All preliminary and final antidumping actions taken by Members must be promptly notified to the Committee.

### 2.1.4 *Developing countries*

The interests of developing country Members are addressed in Article 15 of the Antidumping Agreement. Article 15 reads as follows:

> It is recognized that special regard must be given by developed country Members to the special situation of developing country Members when considering the application of anti-dumping measures under this Agreement. Possibilities of constructive remedies provided for by this Agreement shall be explored before applying anti-dumping duties where they would affect the essential interests of developing country Members.

This provision is vague and somewhat ambiguous. In the *EC — Bed Linen* case, the panel ruled that the EC violated Article 15 by failing to explore the possibility of "constructive remedies" in the form of price undertakings.[15]

Much could be done to improve "special and differential treatment" for developing countries in antidumping cases. There could, for example, be special rules for initiating an investigation, and special import share and *de minimis* thresholds for developing countries.[16]

## 2.2 Investigation

### 2.2.1 *Initiating an investigation*

National antidumping authorities may initiate an antidumping investigation when a domestic industry files a petition or on their own.[17] The petition must include evidence of dumping, material injury, and causation

[15] Panel Report, *EC — Bed Linen*, paras 65–69. In a recent antidumping dispute case (*United States — Anti-Dumping and Countervailing Measures on Steel Plate from India*, Report of the Panel, adopted 29 July 2002, WT/DS206/R), the Panel noted that, under Article 15 of the Antidumping Agreement, Members are under no obligation to take any action. As stated by the Panel, Article 15 of the Antidumping Agreement imposes on Members "no specific and general obligation" to take action, however, under this provision, Members are obligated to "explore" possibilities for constructive remedies when, in an antidumping dispute, a developing country is the target of an antidumping measure.

[16] *See* Adamantopoulous and De Notaris, below note 43, at 46, 58–59.

[17] Antidumping Agreement Art. 5.1.

that is "reasonably available" to the petitioner.[18] This requirement is set out in Article 5.2 of the Antidumping Agreement. WTO panels have concluded that, while Article 5.2 requires a petitioner to submit data that provides evidence of dumping, Article 5.2 does not require a petitioner to explain such data.[19]

To prevent abuse of antidumping duty proceedings, the Antidumping Agreement provides that national antidumping authorities may accept a petition only when there is evidence to show that a domestic industry or a person representing the industry has filed the petition.[20] If a petition is supported by domestic producers that account for more than 50 percent of domestic production of the domestic product of domestic producers that have expressed views on the petition, *either for or against the petition*, the petition is considered to have been made by a domestic industry or a person representing the industry.[21] If, however, domestic producers supporting the petition account for less than 25 percent of domestic production, national antidumping authorities may not initiate an investigation.[22]

These rules were incorporated into the Antidumping Agreement in the Uruguay Round to ensure that a petitioner properly represents the majority of the domestic industry. In the past, there were cases in which national antidumping authorities initiated antidumping investigations even though it was not clear whether the petitioner properly represented the domestic industry injured by dumping.[23]

### *2.2.2 Evidentiary issues*

The application must contain "sufficient evidence" of the existence of dumping that causes or threatens to cause injury to a domestic industry.[24]

Article 6 of the Antidumping Agreement addresses evidentiary issues that arise in antidumping cases. Interested parties (exporters, importers, and domestic producers) are guaranteed the opportunity to receive notice, produce evidence, and express their views on the matter in question. In general, evidence produced must be open to the public, but when

[18] Antidumping Agreement Art. 5.2.

[19] Panel Report, *Thailand — H-Beams*. A similar ruling was made by the panel in *Mexico — Corn Syrup (HFCS)*.

[20] Antidumping Agreement Art. 5.4.

[21] *Id.*

[22] *Id.*

[23] *See, e.g., United States Antidumping Duty on Stainless Steel Pipe from Sweden*, 20 August 1990, GATT Doc. ADP/47 (unadopted).

[24] Antidumping Agreement Art. 5.3.

the provider requests confidentiality, it is kept confidential, except that the provider must prepare a non-confidential summary of the confidential information.[25]

When persons from whom information is sought refuse to provide it or otherwise block the investigation, national antidumping authorities may proceed with the investigation and make decisions on the basis of "facts available", which includes information provided by the petitioner.[26] In *Guatemala — Cement*, an issue arose as to the meaning of "best information available", which is the same as "facts available".[27] In this case, the Mexican antidumping authority based its finding that products from Guatemala were dumped on the "best information available" because many key facts submitted by the parties could not be verified. According to the *Guatemala — Cement* panel, Article 6.8 of the Antidumping Agreement permits the use of facts available for determining dumping if an interested party (1) refuses access to necessary information; (2) otherwise does not provide necessary information; or (3) significantly impedes the investigation.[28] The panel found that a mere failure to cooperate on the part of a party to the investigation did not entitle the antidumping authority to resort to the "best information available" approach.[29]

"Facts available" was also an issue in *United States — Hot-Rolled Steel from Japan*.[30] In this case, one of the petitioners was a U.S. company jointly owned by a Japanese exporter (one of the respondents in the U.S. antidumping proceeding) and a Brazilian company. The U.S. antidumping authority asked the Japanese exporter to submit evidence that was in the possession of its U.S. joint venture. The Japanese exporter could not submit this evidence because the joint venture entity refused to supply it. The U.S. antidumping authority decided that the Japanese exporter was not cooperative in submitting evidence and therefore resorted to a "facts available" methodology. Japan appealed this determination, and the Appellate Body ruled that the U.S. antidumping authority was wrong in utilizing a fact available approach because the Japanese exporter could not be said to be

25 *Id.* Art. 6.5.

26 Antidumping Agreement Art. 6.8.

27 Antidumping Agreement Annex II, Art. 2.1.

28 *Guatamala — Definitive Antidumping Measures Regarding Grey Portland Cement from Mexico*, Report of the Appellate Body.

29 *Id.*

30 *See* Appellate Body Report, *United States — Hot-Rolled Steel from Japan.*

uncooperative in light of the joint venture's refusal to supply the information.[31]

Thus, national antidumping authorities must carefully adhere to WTO standards when assembling evidence. Parties can be required to produce evidence, but exporters and foreign producers must be given at least 30 days to reply to questionnaires.[32] The "facts available" approach allowing the use of evidence proffered by the domestic industry is a last resort. There must be specific findings of the conditions specified in Article 6.8 and Annex II of the Antidumping Agreement.[33] National antidumping authorities cannot utilize "facts available" solely because information was provided by the exporter after the deadline for response because Article 6.8 requires a "reasonable period" for response beyond the 30-day minimum.[34]

### *2.2.3 The duties of the investigating authority*

The Antidumping Agreement sets a maximum period for an antidumping investigation because prolonged investigations are burdensome to exporters and importers and impede imports unduly. Investigations must generally be conducted within one year and may not exceed 18 months.[35]

## 2.3 Determination of dumping

To determine whether a product is dumped, the antidumping authority of the importing country must determine whether there is a difference between the export price and the normal value (domestic price) of the product.[36] If the difference is slight (less than 2 percent of the export price), national antidumping authorities must terminate the investigation. Antidumping authorities must also terminate the investigation if the volume of imports

---

[31] Appellate Body Report, *United States — Hot Rolled Steel from Japan*. For recent panel rulings on facts available, *see* the following. *United States — Anti-Dumping and Countervailing Measures on Steel Plate from India*, Report of the Panel, 29 July 2002, WT/DS206/R; *Egypt — Definitive Anti-Dumping Measures on Steel Rebar from Turkey*, Report of the Panel, 1 October 2002, WT/DS211/R.

[32] Antidumping Agreement Art. 6.1.1.

[33] *See* Panel Report, *Argentina — Definitive Anti-Dumping Measures on Imports of Ceramic Floor Tiles from Italy*. The panel found a violation because the exporter's information was rejected without giving a reason.

[34] Appellate Body Report, *United States — Hot-Rolled Steel from Japan*.

[35] Antidumping Agreement Art. 5.3 and 5.10.

[36] Antidumping Agreement Art. 2.1.

of the dumped product is negligible (less than 3 percent of imports of the like product).[37]

Comparing the normal value and the export price is complicated. To be compared fairly, the normal value and the export price must be compared at the same "level of trade" or, if this is not possible, at levels as close as possible.[38] A comparison between the domestic price and the export price of the product in question should, in principle, be made at the same level of transaction (*e.g.*, at the ex-factory level).

In addition, various circumstances of sale affect the price level. For example, suppose a foreign purchaser pays for a product by letter of credit payable on sight, and a domestic purchaser pays for the same product by a promissory note payable after six months. The seller can get paid in cash from the foreign purchaser immediately after receiving the letter of credit, whereas he cannot get paid in cash until six months after receiving the promissory note. The seller is, therefore, justified in charging more to the domestic purchaser than the foreign purchaser, at least to the extent of interest that he would obtain if the domestic purchaser paid cash.

Other circumstances of sale may justify a difference in domestic and export prices. In comparing the domestic price and the export price of a product, national antidumping authorities must consider all such circumstances. GATT Article VI provides: "Due allowance shall be made in each case for differences in conditions and terms of sale, for differences in taxation, and for other differences affecting price comparability".

### 2.3.1 *Like product*

The "like product" issue is typically quite important in antidumping cases. The issue arises principally in three contexts. First, dumping involves a comparison of the prices of "like products" in the domestic market of the exporting country and the export market.[39] There may be some differences in the characteristics of the products sold in the two markets. These differences, in turn, may be due to various business purposes: (1) the product may be modified to suit individual markets; (2) the product may be modified for sale in the export market to circumvent a previous anti-dumping order or investigation; or (3) the product may be sold finished in

[37] *Id.* Art. 5.8. There is an exception to this rule if the volume of dumping imports from countries that individually account for less than 3 percent collectively account for more than 7 percent of imports of the like product into the importing country, the investigation may go ahead.

[38] Antidumping Agreement Art. 2.4.

[39] Antidumping Agreement Art. 2.1.

one market and in a "kit" for assembly by the buyer in another market. No WTO antidumping case has considered the "like product" issue, but from the consideration of this issue in other GATT 1994 contexts,[40] a determination would be made on a case-by-case basis. In all of the above contexts, the products would be considered "like" in the majority of cases by national antidumping authorities, and this determination would probably be upheld by the WTO.[41]

Second, the "like product" issue may come up in a context in which a foreign manufacturer buys product components at below-cost prices from an unrelated supplier and assembles them into a product for resale in domestic and export markets. This is known as "downstream dumping". Although no GATT or WTO case has arisen on this issue, it would seem that the "like product" issue would prevent the imposition of national antidumping duties in this case because the manufacturer selling below cost is not selling the product in the export market, and the manufacturer who is selling in the exporter market is not dumping with respect to the exported product. "Downstream dumping" may have to be considered by the Committee on Antidumping Practices.

Third, the "like product" issue may arise in the context of defining the domestic industry. Article 4 of the Antidumping Agreement states that the domestic industry includes domestic producers of "like products". Defining the domestic industry is also a case-by-case determination. If national antidumping authorities define the domestic industry broadly, they may decrease the dumping margin or the likelihood of finding dumping; but, if they use a narrow definition to focus on a particular sector that is hurt, this may allow future circumvention.

The term "like product" is defined in the Antidumping Agreement to mean "a product which is identical" or "has characteristics closely resembling the product under consideration".[42] Obviously, this is a vague definition that leaves the area largely unsettled. State practice concerning the "like product" issue varies widely.[43] For example, concerning polyester staple fibers (PSF), the EC antidumping authority consistently holds that

---

[40] See especially the national treatment cases in Chapter 8.

[41] In Article 2.6 of the Antidumping Agreement, a "like product" does not have to be identical but can be similar.

[42] Antidumping Agreement Art. 2.6.

[43] Specific examples are collected in Konstantinos Adamantopolous and Diego De Notaris, *The Future of the WTO and the Reform of the Anti-dumping Agreement: A Legal Perspective*, 24 FORDHAM INT'L LJ. 30, 36–38 (2000).

all PSF types are one product, while the U.S. antidumping authority divides PSF into different end-use categories.[44] The "like product" definition in Article 2.6 seems to be designed to allow such variations and to maximize discretion by national antidumping authorities. No WTO panel has yet considered in the issue, but the *Indonesia — Automobiles* case,[44a] which involved the SCM Agreement, interpreted "like product" to mean that similar physical characteristics is one criterion, but that other factors, such as tariff classification principles, whether the products are substitutable, and brand loyalty and reputation, may also be utilized by national antidumping authorities in making the "like product" determination. If this holding is carried over to antidumping, the discretion of national antidumping authorities on the "like product" issue would be the beneficiary.

The question arises whether the "like product" term should be more closely defined in order to limit this discretion and to increase legal certainty. For example, a market-based test could be used, grouping products as "like" that are in direct competition with each other. This question can be resolved only through future negotiations by WTO Members.

### *2.3.2 Comparison of third-country prices*

In two situations, the determination of dumping can be made by comparing the export price with the price of the like product when exported to an "appropriate third country", provided the third-country price is "representative".[45] These situations arise (1) when there are no sales of the like product in the ordinary course of trade in the home country; or (2) where there is a low volume of such sales.[46]

### *2.3.3 Constructed value*

In some situations, there is no domestic sale of the product in question or, if there is such a sale, the national antidumping authority cannot rely on the sale as the reference of comparison. For example, demand for a product in the domestic market may be so small that producers do not sell it domestically, but only export. It may be that the purchaser specially orders the product and that there cannot be any sale in the domestic market. This situation may happen, for example, if NASA (the U.S. space agency) purchases sophisticated equipment to be installed in a satellite. The details of specifications of this equipment are announced, and suppliers produce

[44] *Id.* at 36. [44a] Panel Report, *Indonesia — Automobiles*, paras 14.210–14.222.
[45] Antidumping Agreement Art. 2.2. [46] *Id.*

this product to meet the requirements of those specifications. Such equipment would be sold only to NASA, and there would be no sale in the domestic market.

If there is no domestic price or the domestic price is not suitable for comparison, national antidumping authorities may compare the export price with the constructed value of the product.[47] The term "constructed value" means the price of a product that is constructed by adding a reasonable amount of administrative expenses and a profit margin to the cost of the product.[48]

Constructed value is not a price that exists, but is calculated by adding costs, selling, general, and administrative (SG&A) costs, and profit. In calculating "constructed value," the amounts for SG&A costs and profit must be based on actual data pertaining to production and sales in the ordinary course of trade of the like product by the exporter or producer under investigation.[49] When such amounts cannot be determined on that basis, they may be determined based on the following[50]:

1. The actual amounts incurred and realized by the exporter or producer under investigation in respect of production and sales in the domestic market of the country of origin of the same general category of products;
2. The weighted average of the actual amounts incurred and realized by other exporters or producers subject to investigation in respect of production and sales of the like product in the domestic market of the country of origin; or
3. Any other reasonable method, provided the amount for profit so established shall not exceed the profit normally realized by other exporters or producers on sales of products of any of the same general category in the domestic market of the country or origin.[51]

When calculating constructed value, national antidumping authorities must use the actual data of the exporter or producer under investigation or, if this is not possible, the actual data of other exporters and producers producing and exporting like products.

In *EC — Bed Linen*, the EU antidumping authority used the constructed value of Indian bed linen and relied on the data of one firm in India that produced and exported like products. There was no other exporter or producer of like products.

[47] GATT Art. VI; Antidumping Agreement Art. 2.2.
[48] Antidumping Agreement Art. 2.2.
[49] *Id.* Art. 2.2.1.1.
[50] *Id.* Art. 2.2.2(i), (ii) and (iii).
[51] *Id.* Art. 2.2.2.

India objected on the ground that Article 2.2.2(ii) uses the term "weighted average" to calculate constructed value. The panel ruled that the wording of Article 2.2.2(ii), "weighted average", includes the singular and that, therefore, using data from one exporter or producer in the country of origin is permissible. India appealed this ruling to the Appellate Body. The Appellate Body reversed this ruling for the following reasons.

The Appellate Body stated that "weighted average" in Article 2.2.2(ii) precludes an interpretation that "other exporters or producers" in the plural can include a singular case. It concluded:

> We disagree with the Panel that the concept of weighted averaging is relevant only when there is information from more than one other producers or exporters available to be considered. We see no justification, textual or otherwise, for concluding that amounts for SG&A and profits are to be determined on the basis of the weighted average some of the time but not all of the time.[52]

### 2.3.4 *Arm's-length transactions and transactions between affiliated parties*

If an international trade transaction is carried out between two parties that are independent from each other, the agreed-upon price can be assumed to reflect the market price. If a transaction is made between affiliated parties, the agreed-upon price does not necessarily reflect the market price because the parties can manipulate the price. In the latter situation, national antidumping authorities must disregard the price paid by the affiliated party and use the price at which the product is first sold to an independent purchaser. Article 2.3 of the Antidumping Agreement states:

[52] Appellate Body Report, *EC — Bed Linen.* The question arises as to whether an interpretation that denies the possibility of calculating the normal value if there is only one other exporter or producer of like products in the country of origin is a reasonable one. This situation is not incomprehensible, and it is a duty of panels and the Appellate Body to formulate an interpretation that can deal with all situations that may arise. It appears that the interpretation adopted by the panel that the plural includes singular makes better sense. Can one not say that Article 2.2.2(i), (ii) and (iii) provide for representative cases and, as to situations not covered, an inference or analogy should be drawn from this provision?

As an alternative interpretation, one may propose that, while the conclusion of the Appellate Body' ruling is correct, its explanation is insufficient. This view would maintain that a constructed value is an artificial price and, when calculating constructed value, the antidumping authority should endeavour to arrive at a price which approximates market conditions as much as possible. If there is only one exporter or producer of like products in the market of the exporting country, there is insufficient evidence for the antidumping authority to draw an inference as to what the market would be like and to calculate what "would be SG & A". According to this interpretation, this is the reason why Article 2.2.2 (ii) of the Antidumping Agreement does not provide for a situation where there is only one other exporter or producer, and this absence should be interpreted to mean that under this circumstance a constructed value cannot be used.

> where it appears to the authorities concerned that the export price is unreliable because of association or a compensatory arrangement between the exporter and the importer or a third party, the export price may be constructed on the basis of the price at which the imported products are first resold to an independent buyer.

An example is the export of autos from a Japanese manufacturer to its U.S. subsidiary that sells them to independent dealers in the United States. The U.S. antidumping authority must compare the price at which autos are sold by the manufacturer to dealers in Japan and the price at which they are sold by the subsidiary to independent dealers in the United States.

### *2.3.5 Sales below cost*

When calculating the value of a product in the domestic market of the exporting country that will be compared with the export price of that product to be exported to the importing country, national antidumping authorities may disregard a sale of the product in the domestic market if such sale is below the cost of production. The rationale for this is that a sale below cost is not a transaction in the normal course of commerce and is not, therefore, appropriate for the standard of comparison. In the 1980s this rule was abused, however, and there were complaints among exporting countries that the rule was itself a trade barrier.

One such complaint was that of the Japanese government in relation to a U.S. Commerce Department investigation of alleged dumping of semiconductor chips. When semiconductor chips were sold, the Commerce Department decided to compare the export price and the "constructed value" of such semiconductor chips and concluded that there was dumping.

The Japanese government claimed that, in the semiconductor industry, the cost of research and development was so enormous that the initial cost of a semiconductor chip was very high. In the initial period of sale, however, the chips could not be sold if the price were set at the level at which the cost was recovered and a profit was gained, because such a price would not be competitive. Semiconductor producers, therefore, had to set the initial price at a level below the cost of production. Over an extended period, the cost would decline dramatically due to mass production and mass sales. If, therefore, the cost-price ratio were calculated for an extended period, such as six months or one year, there would be no sales at prices below the cost of production. It was claimed that a sufficient period should be taken into consideration when determining whether a domestic price was below the cost of production.

The negotiators in the Uruguay Round thought that it was necessary to address this issue, and the following new rules were incorporated into the Antidumping Agreement:

1. National antidumping authorities may disregard a sale below cost as the standard for comparison if such a sale is made (a) in an extended period, (b) in substantial quantity, and (c) at the price that would make recovery of all the cost in a reasonable period impossible.[53]
2. "Extended period" normally means one year, and in no case may it be less than six months.[54]
3. "Substantial quantity" means that the weighted average of the sales price of the product in question is below the weighted average of the cost of producing one unit of that product, or that the quantity of sale of the product at the price below cost is no less than 20 percent of the total sale of the product.[55]

### *2.3.6 Fair price comparisons*

When comparing the normal value and the export price, the former is often denominated in the domestic currency and the latter in a foreign currency. The problem is that the exchange rate between those two currencies fluctuates, and this fluctuation affects the price comparison. Suppose, for example, a Japanese auto company exports a car to the United States; the domestic sales price is ¥2,000,000; and the export price is $20,000 at the exchange rate of $1 = ¥100 that prevails when the auto is shipped from the factory. The auto company exports the auto to its subsidiary in the United States, and the subsidiary sells it to a dealer there. This sale may take place three months later, and the exchange rate may be $1 = ¥50.

If the price comparison is made when the auto is shipped from the factory, there is a parity of prices (¥2,000,000 (domestic price) = $20,000 (export price)). But if the price comparison is made when the car is sold to a dealer, the export price will still be 20,000 but the domestic sales price of ¥2,000,000 will be $40,000. There is no dumping in the former situation, but there is dumping in the latter. This is called "technical dumping". This hypothetical indicates that, for a fair price comparison, it is important to establish the exchange rate that is used when comparing prices.

In comparison of domestic and export prices, the exchange rates prevailing on the date of sale must be used.[56] The date of sale is defined as the date

---

[53] Antidumping Agreement Art. 2.2.1. [54] *Id.* Art. 2.2.1., note 4.
[55] *Id.* Art. 2.2.1, note 5. [56] Antidumping Agreement Art. 2.4.1.

of contract, date of purchase order, date of order confirmation, or date of invoice.[57] If a dumping margin is created through fluctuations of the exchange rate, exporters are allowed a six-month period in which to make adjustment of domestic and export prices.

One issue in connection with fluctuation of exchange rates is how to deal with a situation in which there is a sharp change in the exchange rate during the period of investigation. For example, if there is a sudden change of exchange rate at the end of the investigation period, the question arises whether national antidumping authorities should take an average of prices in this period or whether it should disregard prices in the period in which, due to a sharp drop of the value of the domestic currency in relation to the currency in which export prices are represented. This question was addressed in a case in which the U.S. antidumping authority imposed antidumping duty on steel imports from Korea.[57a]

### *2.3.7 Averaging*

Another important issue in a fair comparison of domestic and export prices is that of "averaging". In the past, antidumping authorities in the United States and the EU utilized the "averaging" method when comparing domestic and export prices.[58]

The following example illustrates the averaging method. Company A (a Japanese company) sells Product X in the domestic market and exports it to the EU market. In the domestic market, the average price of Product X is equivalent to $100 per unit. Company A exports Product X to the markets of the U.K., Germany, France and Italy. The price at which Product X is exported to the U.K. is $80; that at which it is exported to Germany is $90; that at which it is exported to France is $110; and that at which it is exported to Italy is $120. Assuming that the volume of sales is the same to each market, the weighted average of export price is equivalent to $100.

If the average prices were compared, there would be no difference between domestic prices and export prices and, therefore, no dumping. In the past, the antidumping authorities of the United States and the EU, however, compared the weighted average of the domestic price with each of the export prices before averaging. If an export price is lower than the averaged domestic

[57] Antidumping Agreement Art. 2.4.1, note 8.

[57a] *United States — Antidumping Measures on Stainless Steel Plate in Coils and Stainless Steel Sheet and Strip from Korea*, Report of the Panel, 1 February 2001, WT/DS179/R.

[58] *See* 2000 Report on the WTO Consistency of Trade Policies by Major Trading Partners, The Industrial Structure Council, The Ministry of International Trade and Industry (2000) at 53–54.

price, that export price is judged to be a dumping price. If, on the other hand, an export price is higher than the averaged domestic price, that export price is disregarded. There was, therefore, a non-symmetrical comparison between the domestic price and export prices and, consequently, dumping was artificially "created". There would be no dumping if there were a symmetrical comparison. The result was that there was dumping in almost all situations where there are a number of sales transactions both in the domestic market and the export market of a product.

To remedy this situation, the Antidumping Agreement provides that, in principle, an antidumping authority should compare either "a weighted average normal value with a weighted average of prices of all comparable export transactions" or "normal value and export prices on a transaction-to-transaction basis".[59] Antidumping authorities may, however, deviate from this rule when there is evidence that exporters manipulate domestic and export prices so that there is no dumping margin if a comparison of prices is made on a weighted-average basis.[60]

### *2.3.8 Zeroing*

Zeroing is a variation of the averaging issue. Zeroing refers to a method by which national antidumping authorities count as zero the dumping margin for which the weighted average difference between normal value and the export price is negative. In the *EC — Bed Linen* case,[61] the EC imposed an antidumping duty on imports of cotton-type bed linen from India. In calculating the dumping margin, the EC compared weighted average export prices and the weighted average normal value for each of several models (product types of bed linen). In some cases, the export price was lower than the normal value, and, in others, the export price was higher than the normal value. In each of the latter cases, there was a "negative" margin of dumping. The EC then calculated a weighted average dumping margin for cotton linen based on the results obtained in the comparisons. The EC calculated the dumping amounts by multiplying the value of the imports of each model by the margin of price difference for each model and counted as zero the dumping amount for those models where the margin was negative. The EC then divided the total dumping amount by the value of the exports involved, counting all negative dumping margins as zero.

[59] Antidumping Agreement Art. 2.4.2. [60] *Id.*

[61] Appellate Body Report, *EC — Bed Linen*; Panel Report, *EC — Bed Linen. See also* Panel Report, *United States — Antidumping Measures on Stainless Steel Plate in Coils and Stainless Steel Sheet and Strip from Korea*, 1 February 2001, WT/DS179/R.

In short, the EC computed the dumping margin by comparing a weighted average of export prices and the normal value of each model of the product in question but, when it came to calculating the dumping margin for the totality of the product by averaging the whole of dumping margins, the EC disregarded the "negative dumping margin" that accrued with respect to some models. This was a device to inflate dumping margin by disregarding the portion of export price which was higher than the normal value (the domestic price) and treating the excess by which export price exceeded the domestic value as zero. Therefore, the dumping margin was calculated to be larger than it would have been if "negative dumping" had been taken into consideration. India argued that such a "zeroing" of negative dumping was contrary to Article 2.4.2 of the Antidumping Agreement.

The following hypothetical further illustrates this zeroing practice. Suppose the product in question can be categorized as Product A, Product B, Product C, and Product D. The domestic value of Product A is $115 and the export price is $96. The dumping margin is 20. The domestic value of Product B is $80 and the export price is $70. The dumping margin is 10. The domestic value of Product C is $100 and the export price is $150. The dumping margin is minus 50. The domestic value of Product D is $105 and the export price is $85. The dumping margin is 20. If all of the dumping margins are taken into account and averaged out, the dumping margin would be zero. However, if the minus dumping margin (minus 50) is treated as zero, there would be a dumping margin of 12.5 percent.

The panel in the *EC — Bed Linen* case recognized that a dumping margin should be established on the basis of a comparison of a weighted average normal value with a weighted average of prices of all comparable export transactions or on the basis of a comparison of individual transactions, and then noted that Article 2.1 of the Antidumping Agreement states that "a product is to be considered as being dumped" when that product is imported at less than its normal value. The panel noted that Article 2.4.2 of the Antidumping Agreement specifies that the weighted average normal value shall be compared with a weighted average of "all" comparable export transactions. In this case, however, the EC did not compare the prices of all comparable export transactions, but counted as zero the results of comparison showing a negative margin. The panel ruled that this was an impermissible change of the results of an otherwise proper comparison. The practice of the EC amounted to counting the weighted average export price to be equal to the weighted average normal value for those models for which negative margins were found in the comparison, although it was, in fact, higher than the weighted average normal value. For these reasons, the panel ruled that the zeroing used by the EC was inconsistent with Article 2.4.2 of the Antidumping Agreement.

This finding of the Panel was upheld by the Appellate Body. The Appellate Body reasoned that, under Article 2.4.2 of the Antidumping Agreement, an administering authority is called upon to determine whether there is dumping with regard to "a product" but not a type or a model of the product, and it was incumbent on the EC to calculate the dumping margin of the product in question.[62]

## 2.4 Determination of injury

### *2.4.1 Material injury or threat of material injury*

Before imposing an antidumping duty, WTO Members must make a determination of material injury or threat thereof to a domestic industry or material retardation of the establishment of a domestic industry.[63] The term "material injury" is, however, not defined. The Appellate Body has concluded that the "material injury" standard for antidumping measures is lower than the "serious injury" standard for safeguard measures.[64] It reasoned that the degree of injury to a domestic industry should be something less for antidumping measures than for safeguard measures because antidumping measures counteract "unfair" trade whereas safeguard measures counteract "fair" trade.[65] The terms "threat" of material injury and "material retardation" are also not defined.

Determination of material injury to a domestic industry must be based on evidence regarding (1) the quantity of dumped product and its effect on the price of like domestic products; and (2) its effect on producers of such domestic products.[66] With regard to the quantity of dumped import, the national antidumping authority must examine whether there is significant increase of the quantity of dumped product. An increase of import can be absolute (*e.g.*, the quantity of import increases) or relative (*e.g.*, the quantity of import remains the same as before, but the supply of domestic products is reduced and, consequently, the market share of imports increases). With

[62] *EC — Bed Linen*, paras 46–58.

[63] GATT Art. VI; Antidumping Agreement Art. 3, note 9.

[64] Appellate Body Report, *United States — Lamb Safeguard*, para. 124.

[65] *Id.; see also* Appellate Body Report, *Argentina — Footwear Safeguard*, para. 94.

[66] Antidumping Agreement Art. 3.1. For an application, *see Egypt — Definitive Antidumping Measures on Steel Rebar from Turkey*, Report of the Panel, 1 October 2002, WT/DS211/R.

respect to price, the antidumping authority must investigate whether the dumped product undercuts the like domestic products, depresses the domestic price, or prevents the domestic price from rising.[67]

### *2.4.2 Factors to be considered when determining injury*

In determining whether material injury exists, Article 3.4 requires national antidumping authorities to consider:

> all relevant economic factors and indices having a bearing on the state of the industry, including actual and potential decline in sales, profits, output, market share, productivity, return on investments, or utilization of capacity; factors affecting domestic prices; the magnitude of the margin of dumping; actual and potential negative effects on cash flow, inventories, employment, wages, growth, ability to raise capital or investments.

The Appellate Body has concluded that national antidumping authorities must evaluate all of the factors listed in Article 3.4 when examining whether there is a material injury due to dumping.[68] The impact of these rulings on national antidumping authorities appears to be that specific findings have to be made with respect to all the factors listed in Article 3.4.

### *2.4.3 Factors to be considered when determining threat*

In determining whether a threat of material injury exists, Article 3.7 requires national antidumping authorities to consider specific factors. One question of interpretation is whether antidumping authorities must consider the impact of the dumped imports on the domestic industry (Article 3.4) as well as the Article 3.7 factors in determining whether a threat of material injury exists. In *Mexico — Corn Syrup (HFCS)*, the Mexican antidumping authority based its finding of a threat of injury on Article 3.7.[69] The United States argued before the panel that it was wrong for Mexico to rely solely on Article 3.7 in determining a threat of injury, because Article 3.4 is the general provision for finding injury and applies to both injury and threat thereof. The panel concluded that national antidumping authorities must also consider the Article 3.4 factors in making a threat of injury determination.[70]

---

[67] Antidumping Agreement Art. 3.2.

[68] *See, e.g.*, Appellate Body Report, *Thailand — H-Beams*, para. 128; Appellate Body Report, *EC — Bed Linen*, para. 168; Appellate Body Report, *United States — Hot-Rolled Steel from Japan*, para. 194.

[69] Panel Report, *Mexico — Corn Syrup (HFCS)*, para. 7.131.

[70] *Id.* para. 7.32.

Under Article 3.7, the national antidumping authorities must determine whether, in the absence of protective action, material injury would occur. Thus, consideration of the Article 3.4 factors is required in a case involving threat of injury in order to make a determination consistent with the requirements of Articles 3.1 and 3.7.

### *2.4.4 Cumulation of injuries*

National antidumping authorities may cumulate injuries when (1) more than one exporting country is involved; and (2) exporters from all of the exporting countries are engaged in dumping.[71] An example of cumulation of injuries is as follows. Product X is dumped into the market of Country A from several countries (B, C, and D). Imports from B and C occupy 90 percent of the dumped product and those from D share only 10 percent. Imports from D, standing alone, would not cause a material injury to a domestic industry. The question is whether the antidumping authority of the importing country may cumulate injuries caused by imports from B, C, and D and decide that there is material injury to a domestic industry caused by dumped imports from B, C, and D.

National antidumping authorities may make such a cumulation as long as (1) an import from each country is more than *de minimis*; and (2) a cumulation is appropriate in light of the competitive relationship between imports from those countries and between imported product and domestic product.[72]

### *2.4.5 Causation*

There may be factors other than dumping that cause injury to a domestic industry. Before a WTO Member may impose an antidumping duty on imports, a causal link between dumping and injury must be established. Under Article 3.5 of the Antidumping Agreement, national antidumping authorities must take into consideration all of the relevant factors causing material injury to a domestic injury, including those other than dumping (*e.g.*, domestic competition, decline of demand, change of consumers' preference, restrictive business practices) in assessing injury to a domestic industry, and the injury caused by those other factors must not be attributed to the dumped imports.

Article 3.5 of the Antidumping Agreement requires that national antidumping authorities "shall examine any known factors other than the

[71] Antidumping Agreement Art. 3.3. [72] *Id.*

dumped imports which at the same time are injuring the domestic industry..." In *Thailand — H-Beams*,[73] one of the issues was the meaning of "any known factors". Poland, the petitioner, argued that the government applying an antidumping measure must on its own look for any factor other than dumping that may have caused material injury to a domestic industry. The panel, however, found that the term "any known factors" includes only causal factors that are raised before the national antidumping authorities by interested parties in the course of an investigation. It is not, therefore, incumbent on national antidumping authorities to "seek out and examine" in each case on their own initiative the effects of all possible factors other than imports that may be causing injury to the domestic industry.

In *Thailand — H-Beams*,[74] another issue was whether national antidumping authorities can base their determination on confidential evidence not disclosed to the parties. The Appellate Body ruled that national antidumping authorities are not required to base an injury determination only on evidence disclosed to or discernible by the parties to the investigation. It considered that an antidumping investigation involves the commercial behaviour of firms and involves the collection and assessment of both confidential and non-confidential information. The Appellate Body concluded that an injury determination must be based on the totality of evidence and that nothing in Article 3.1 of the Antidumping Agreement requires national antidumping authorities to base an injury determination only on non-confidential information.[75]

The antidumping agreement concluded in the Kennedy Round of trade negotiations in 1967 contained a provision that stated that, in determining the causation between a dumping and an injury, there should be evidence to show that the dumping was demonstrably the major cause of the injury. This provision, however, was regarded as too strict and, when the Tokyo Round concluded in 1979, a provision in a new antidumping agreement stated that injuries caused by factors other than dumping should not be attributed to the dumping. Article 3.4 of the Antidumping Agreement adopted wording that is essentially the same as in the Tokyo Round antidumping agreement.

---

[73] Panel Report, *Thailand — H-Beams.*

[74] Appellate Body Report, *Thailand — H-Beams.*

[75] A question, however, arises under this ruling as to whether the rights of parties to an antidumping proceeding can be properly protected. If national antidumping authorities are authorized to base their determinations on undisclosed evidence, how can parties present their views on the evidence and, if necessary, produce counter-evidence?

## 2.5 Domestic industry

An antidumping duty is imposed when there is a dumping that causes a material injury to a domestic industry and the causation between the dumping and injury. The meaning of a domestic industry is defined as:

> the domestic producers as a whole of the like products or . . . those of them whose collective output of the products constitutes a major proportion of the total domestic production of those products.[76]

If a domestic producer is related to or affiliated with exporters or importers of the product in question or the domestic producer is an importer of the product, national antidumping authorities may decide that such a domestic producer should be excluded from the category of domestic industry. This is because a domestic producer that is related to exporters or importers of the dumped product or is itself an importer of that product and, thereby, presumably benefits from such relationship does not need protection by an antidumping measure. The term "related", rather than the term "affiliated", is used in the Antidumping Agreement. Domestic producers will be considered "related" to exporters or importers if: (1) a domestic producer directly or indirectly controls an exporter or vice versa; (2) both are directly or indirectly controlled by a third person; and (3) it is likely that the domestic producer acts differently from what it would if there were no such relationship.[77]

In *United States — Hot-Rolled Steel*,[78] the Appellate Body dealt with the question of whether or not production of hot-rolled steel by the domestic industry for "in-house consumption" can be excluded from the scope of domestic industry. The Appellate Body ruled that an injury determination must be based on the totality of the domestic industry and not simply on one part of the domestic industry.[79]

[76] Antidumping Agreement Art. 4.1.

[77] *Id.* Art. 4.1(i), note 11.

[78] Appellate Body Report, *United States — Hot-Rolled Steel.*

[79] It seems, however, that this ruling is valid only on the premise that there is cross-elasticity of demand between the captive market and the merchant market, *i.e.*, there is a condition that the product in question flows into the captive market if the cost of production there becomes high. As long as there is condition that the product can shift back and forth between the captive market and the merchant market, both markets can be regarded as an integrated market.

## 2.6 The imposition of antidumping measures

### *2.6.1 Provisional measures*

After an antidumping investigation is initiated, imports of the products under investigation may suddenly increase in anticipation of the imposition of an antidumping duty. Such a sudden increase in imports may cause damage to a domestic industry. When such an increase is likely to occur, national antidumping authorities may impose a provisional measure. Article 7 of the Antidumping Agreement regulates the imposition of provisional measures by national antidumping authorities. National antidumping authorities may apply provisional measures only after making a preliminary affirmative determination of dumping and determining that provisional measures are necessary to prevent damage that may occur during the period of investigation. In general, provisional measures may be applied for no more than four months. Provisional measures may be applied for six months, however, if requested by exporters that account for a substantial portion of the transactions in question.[80]

### *2.6.2 Definitive measures*

The maximum amount of antidumping duty is the difference between the domestic price and the export price. If a duty less than this can effectively eliminate the harm of dumping to a domestic industry, a lesser duty is regarded as desirable.[81] Under the Antidumping Agreement, the lesser duty rule is hortatory rather than mandatory.

The following hypothetical example illustrates the lesser duty rule. The normal value (domestic price) of Commodity X in Country Y is $150 and its export price to Country Z is $100. Therefore, the dumping margin is 50. The price of the domestic industry in Country Z producing and selling a like product (competing product) in the domestic market of Country Z is $120. In this situation, if the antidumping authority of Country Z imposes on imports of Commodity X from Country Y an antidumping duty equal to $20, the price of dumped Commodity X in the market of Country Z is $120 ($100+$20=$120) and the parity of the export price and the domestic price is restored. In this approach, the antidumping authority imposes an antidumping duty equal to "injury margin" and, for this reason, it can be called the injury margin rule.

[80] Antidumping Agreement Art. 7.4. [81] *Id.* Art. 9.

### 2.6.3 Retroactivity

As a general rule, antidumping duties cannot be imposed retroactively, but may be applied only after all requirements for the imposition of antidumping duties have been fulfilled.[82] However, where, a final determination of injury (but not threat or material retardiation) is made, duties may be applied retroactively to the date of provisional measures.[83] Where a final determination is negative, any cash and bonds deposited must be refunded.[84]

### 2.6.4 Duration and review

An antidumping duty shall remain in force only so long as and to the extent necessary to counteract the dumping that is causing injury.[85] This determination of "necessary" is made in conjunction with a finding of whether the continued imposition of the duty is needed to offset dumping and whether the injury would be "likely to recur" if the duty were removed.[86] There is also an obligation to review the need for continued antidumping duties after "a reasonable period of time".[87]

Under a general "sunset" clause[88] in the Antidumping Agreement, antidumping duties must be terminated in any event on a date not later than five years after their imposition or after the date of their most recent review unless it is determined that the expiry of the duty would be likely to lead to a continuation or recurrence of dumping and injury.[89]

## 2.7 Price undertakings (suspension of antidumping duty investigations)

Antidumping investigations are costly and burdensome to exporters, importers, and national antidumping authorities. Settlements between exporters and national antidumping authorities can save time and resources. For this reason, the Antidumping Agreement permits a "price undertaking", whereby an exporter subject to an antidumping investigation offers a price undertaking to the national antidumping authority to the effect that there would be an increase of export price to eliminate the dumping margin or otherwise cease the alleged dumping.[90] If the antidumping authority accepts

---

82 *Id.* Art. 10.1 and 10.4.

83 *Id.* Art. 10.2.

84 *Id.* Art. 10.5.

85 *Id.* Art. 11.1.

86 *Id.* Art. 11.2. Appellate Body Report, *United States — Anti-dumping Duty on Dynamic Random Access Memory Semi-Conductors (DRAMS) from Korea*, para. VI. 751–752.

87 Antidumping Agreement Art. 11.2.

88 *Id.* Art. 11.3.

89 *Id.*

90 *Id.* Art. 8.

this offer, the investigation is suspended. National antidumping authorities may accept a price undertaking only after making an affirmative preliminary determination of dumping and injury caused by such dumping.[91] The party requesting a price undertaking may request that the dumping and injury investigation be continued.[92] If the antidumping authority determines that there is neither injury nor threat thereof, the price undertaking will have no effect.[93] If there is a violation of the terms of the price undertaking, the antidumping authority may resume the investigation.[94]

## 2.8 Anti-circumvention

"Anti-circumvention" measures aim at preventing foreign producers or exporters subject to an antidumping duty from circumventing that duty. For example, a company subject to an antidumping duty order in country A might decide to establish a factory in country A and assemble the same product from imported parts and components. Another example of circumvention is that a company subject to antidumping may shift production to one or more third countries.

Thus, exporters may try to avoid paying antidumping duties by shifting their sites of production or exporting the product from different countries. The question is whether the country that imposed the antidumping duty on imports is justified in taking measures to counter such a move.

On the one hand, the importing country may be justified in imposing anti-circumvention measures because circumvention nullifies or reduces the effectiveness of antidumping duty. On the other hand, circumvention actions are nothing more than direct investment in the importing country or a third country. Direct investment helps the local economy by creating employment and paying local taxes. One may argue that such a move on the part of an exporter is a legitimate business action.

The WTO Antidumping Agreement does not speak to circumvention because there was no agreement on this issue in the Uruguay Round. Some countries, such as the United States and the EC, enforce anti-circumvention measures; others, such as Japan, do not.

Only one pre-WTO case dealt with the issue. In 1990, a GATT panel[95] considered a case in which the EC had imposed an antidumping duty on

---

[91] Antidumping Agreement Art. 8.2. [92] *Id.* Art. 8.4.
[93] *Id.* [94] *Id.* Art. 8.6.
[95] *EEC — Regulation of Imports of Parts and Components*, 16 May 1990, GATT B.I.S.D. (37th Supp.) at 132 (1990).

imported parts and components that were used to assemble a product in a factory in the EC. The EC found that there was little value added in the EC assembly operation and that the scheme was a circumvention of antidumping duties previously imposed on the importer. The GATT panel disagreed, ruling that the EC measure was a discriminatory internal tax imposed on foreign-made components contrary to the national treatment obligation of GATT Article III:2.

The legality of anti-circumvention measures under the GATT and the Antidumping Agreement is uncertain. The Committee on Antidumping Practices has examined the issue, but no proposal has been forthcoming. This is an important issue, and an early resolution is desirable.

## 2.9 Dispute settlement

Any WTO Member that believes that a benefit accruing to it under the Antidumping Agreement or that the achievement of any objective of the Agreement is being impeded can refer the matter to the WTO's Dispute Settlement Body (DSB). The DSB will establish a panel to hear the case if a satisfactory solution cannot be reached through consultations with the parties.[96] A threshold question is whether WTO review is proper. In *Guatemala — Cement*, the Appellate Body concluded that it lacked jurisdiction to review Mexico's claim that Guatemala violated the Antidumping Agreement. Interpreting Article 17.4 of the Antidumping Agreement, the Appellate Body ruled that it had jurisdiction to review only (1) a definitive antidumping duty; (2) a price undertaking; or (3) a provisional measure. Mexico's request for review focused on actions taken by Guatemala during the course of the antidumping investigation.

Article 17.6 provides for a standard of review in WTO antidumping cases:

> (i) in its assessment of the facts of the matter, the panel shall determine whether the authorities' establishment of the facts was proper and whether their evaluation of those facts was unbiased and objective. If the establishment of the facts was proper

[96] A 1988 GATT panel decision (unadopted) on the U.S. application of antidumping duties on imports of Swedish stainless steel pipe and tube products became a cause celebre for U.S. negotiations at the Uruguay Round seeking to negotiate a standard of review in dumping cases that would be deferential to national authorities. *See* Minutes of Meeting held on 24, 25, and 26 Oct. 1988, GATT Doc. ADP/M/24 9, 9 Jan. 1989. What resulted was a standard of review that says that if analysis under international law norms produces ambiguity, the national antidumping authority's interpretation prevails.

and the evaluation was unbiased and objective, even though the panel might have reached a different conclusion, the evaluation shall not be overturned;

(ii) the panel shall interpret the relevant provisions of the Agreement in accordance with customary rules of interpretation of public international law. Where the panel finds that a relevant provision of the Agreement admits of more than one permissible interpretation, the panel shall find the authorities' measure to be in conformity with the Agreement if it rests upon one of those permissible interpretations.

Subsection (i) of this provision articulates a standard of deference to national antidumping authorities regarding review of the facts of an antidumping case.[97] Subsection (ii) is properly less deferential when it comes to review of the law. International standards under the Antidumping Agreement should prevail over inconsistent national laws. Under subsection (ii), the Agreement is to be interpreted according to the norms of customary international law; this can be taken to refer to the Vienna Convention on the Law of Treaties,[98] which codifies those norms. Article 31 of the Vienna Convention requires that a treaty be interpreted in accordance with "the ordinary meaning [of the] terms of the treaty in their context and in the light of its object and purpose". Article 32 of the Convention allows recourse to supplementary means of interpretation, such as preparatory work of the relevant agreement where the ordinary meaning is obscure or ambiguous.

The premise of Article 17.6(ii) is that there can be at least two permissible interpretations of a provision of the Antidumping Agreement. Panels, however, are required to interpret provisions of any WTO Agreement according to Articles 31 and 32 of the Vienna Convention. Article 17.6 of the Antidumping Agreement, however, requires deference to national antidumping authorities in such a case, which is a derogation from the Vienna Convention rule. Thus, Article 17.6(ii) contains an inherent contradiction.

Article 11 of the Dispute Settlement Understanding states that panels shall engage in objective assessments of facts of the matter. In the *United States — Hot-Rolled Steel* case,[99] the Appellate Body stated that Article 17.6 of the Antidumping Agreement and Article 11 complement each other. On the other hand, Article 13 of the DSU confers broad authority on panels to request information from the parties as well as from third persons. This

[97] Antidumping Agreement Art. 17.

[98] U.N. Doc. A/Conf. 39/27, 23 May 1969, available at http://www.un.org/law/ilc/texts/treatfra.htm. *See generally* Steven P. Crowly and John H. Jackson, *WTO Procedures, Standard of Review, and Deference to National Governments*, 90 Am. J. Int'l L. 193 (1996).

[99] *See* Appellate Body Report, *United States — Hot-Rolled Steel from Japan.*

authority seems to be at odds with Article 17.6(i) and (ii) of the Antidumping Agreement, which restrict the power of panels with regard to fact-finding. If there is a conflict between Article 13 of the DSU and Article 17.6 of the Antidumping Agreement, Article 17.6 should prevail as it is special to the Antidumping Agreement compared with the more general rules of the DSU.

Article 17.6 states a deference principle in fact-finding and legal interpretation of the Antidumping Agreement that panels should observe when examining a national antidumping authority's disposition of antidumping cases. The intent is to circumscribe the discretion of panels in reviewing establishment of facts and legal interpretations by the national antidumping authority. Panels must still decide, however, whether the establishment of facts by the antidumping authority is "proper, unbiased and objective".

## 3. Criminal penalties and private remedies

Typically, antidumping legislation authorizes the government of a country to counteract dumping. National antidumping legislation of WTO Members must conform to the requirements of Article VI of the GATT 1994 and the Antidumping Agreement. In the United States, however, the U.S. Antidumping Act of 1916 provides for criminal penalties and private treble damage actions when a dumping causes injury to a domestic industry. Moreover, competition laws provide for the control of predatory pricing and price discrimination that may involve dumping. Should WTO rules apply to these laws?

### 3.1 The U.S. 1916 Antidumping Act

The 1916 Act provides for (1) criminal penalties and (2) private damage actions brought by private parties. It states that it is unlawful for any person importing any articles to do so at a price substantially less than the actual market value of such articles in the markets of the country of their production if done with the intent of destroying or injuring an industry in the United States. It also states that any person who violates this provision is guilty of a misdemeanour and may be subject to a fine of up to $5,000 or imprisoned for up to one year. With regard to private remedies, it states that any person injured may sue in a U.S. court and recover threefold the damages sustained and costs.

This Act has never been applied but could be used (1) by the U.S. Department of Justice to combat predatory pricing; or (2) by U.S. domestic industries to sue foreign exporters and domestic importers of competing products. In 1999, the European Communities and Japan brought petitions to the WTO on the ground that the very existence of the Act was contrary to Article VI of the GATT 1994 and the Antidumping Agreement.

The panel held that the Act was inconsistent with the requirements of both GATT Article VI and the Antidumping Agreement.[100] The United States appealed to the Appellate Body. The European Communities and Japan cross-appealed on other grounds. The Appellate Body upheld the rulings of the panel.[101] Two principal issues were considered: (1) whether the U.S. Antidumping Act of 1916 comes within the scope of GATT Article VI and the Antidumping Agreement; and (2) whether the U.S. Antidumping Act of 1916 is discretionary legislation that, unless applied, cannot infringe GATT Article VI or the Antidumping Agreement.

As to the first issue, the Appellate Body stated that, according to GATT Article VI:2, there is dumping when a product of one country is introduced to another at a price below that at which the same or like product is sold in the domestic market of the exporting country and a domestic industry of the importing country is materially injured by reason of the dumping. It held that "any" measure dealing with dumping as defined in Article VI:2 is covered by this definition.

The Appellate Body read Article 1 of the Antidumping Agreement to provide that an antidumping measure could only be applied under the conditions stipulated in Article VI and only in accordance with the procedure established in the Antidumping Agreement. It stated that Article 18.1 of the Antidumping Agreement makes antidumping duties the only antidumping remedy permitted under WTO law. Thus, the U.S. Antidumping

[100] Panel Report, *United States — Antidumping Act of 1916.*

[101] Appellate Body Report, *United States — Anti-Dumping Act of 1916. See also* Mitsuo Matsushita and Douglas E. Rosenthal, *Was the WTO Mistaken in Ruling on Antidumping Act of 1916?,* International Trade Reporter Vol. 18, No. 36 (13 September 2001). *See also,* Hiroko Yamane, The Antidumping Act of 1916: A Victory at What Cost? Vol. 7, International Trade Law and Regulation, ISSN, 12–18 (February 2001). In 2002 a WTO panel relied upon the Appellate Body's decision to find that another provision of U.S. antidumping law, the Byrd Amendment, which allows duties assessed in antidumping and countervailing duty cases to be distributed to injured domestic producers, was inconsistent with Article 18.1 of the AD Agreement and Article 32.1 of the SCM Agreement. United States — Continued Dumping and Subsidy Offset Act, Report of the Panel, paras 7.7–7.46.

Act of 1916, which provides for criminal penalties and damages, is inconsistent with GATT Article VI and the Antidumping Agreement.

With regard to the distinction between "mandatory legislation" and "discretionary legislation", the Appellate Body stated that the 1916 Act does not fall within the category of "discretionary legislation". In upholding the ruling of the panel on this issue, the Appellate Body held that "the discretion enjoyed by the United States Department of Justice is not discretion of such a nature or of such breadth as to transform the 1916 Act into discretionary legislation".[102]

There are two principal problems with this ruling. First, Article 17.6 of the Antidumping Agreement is interpreted to mean that a challenge to an antidumping measure at the WTO cannot be taken unless there is (1) a provisional antidumping measure; (2) a final antidumping measure; or (3) a price undertaking settlement.[103] All of these relate to the imposition of antidumping duties. A logical conclusion from this is that a challenge to an antidumping measure at the WTO should be sustained only if one of the above three antidumping duty measures is involved. In this sense, a WTO challenge to the remedies under the 1916 Act is questionable.

Second, the 1916 Act covers not only a situation where a low-priced import injured a national market, but also one in which trade is restrained and monopolized by that import. There is no language in Article VI and the Antidumping Agreement suggesting coverage of "restraints of trade" and "monopolization". The Appellate Body chose to ignore this part of the 1916 Act. It relied on some of the wording in the 1916 Act being similar to language in Article VI and the Antidumping Agreement but ignored its uniquely antitrust language.

## 3.2 Future implications of the panel and the Appellate Report on the 1916 Act case

Regardless of what measure the U.S. government takes to remedy the inconsistency of the 1916 Act with Article VI of the GATT 1994 and the Antidumping Agreement, the rulings of the panel and Appellate Body reports will have wide implications with respect to legislation of trading nations which deal with price discrimination. The Appellate Report states that the 1916 Act is legislation covered by Article VI and the Antidumping Agreement for the

[102] Appellate Body Report, paras 90–91.

[103] See Appellate Body Report, *Guatemala — Cement.*

reason that the 1916 Act deals with the control of differentiated pricing of a product between the domestic market and a foreign market, *i.e.*, charging a higher price of a product domestically and a lower price when the same or like product is exported to another country and this is within the scope of coverage envisaged by Article VI of the GATT 1994.

Many WTO Members have competition law of one kind or another, including the United States, the European Communities, Canada, Japan, and Members of the European Union. In each body of competition law, there are provisions for the control of price discrimination. The question arises whether, under the ruling of the panel and the Appellate Body in the *1916 Act* case, all such domestic legislation is amenable to challenge under Article VI of the GATT and the Antidumping Agreement. To state that all such legislation must meet the requirements of Article VI of the GATT and the Antidumping Agreement (especially Article 17.4), and a private remedy (collection of damages sustained by a private party due to an international price discrimination or predatory pricing) is not permitted simply because it is not provided for in Article VI of the GATT 1994 and the Antidumping Agreement seems to create a vacuum in the sense that a private party which suffers from international price discrimination is left without a remedy.[104]

## 4. Conclusions

Antidumping is defined as a measure to counteract dumping, which is a type of "unfair export". Dumping, as defined in GATT Article VI and the Antidumping Agreement, however, can include conduct involving only price differences, and not all such conduct is unfair. Dumping is so broadly defined in Article VI and the Antidumping Agreement that conduct that is normal behaviour may be regarded as dumping. It may be rational behaviour for an enterprise to set a high price in the domestic market if the elasticity of demand for a product is small, and to set a lower price in an export market where elasticity is greater. Moreover, sales below cost may occur during a recession when the market price of a product is below the cost of production.

[104] In a case in which the nature of the 1916 Act was at issue, a U.S. court held that the 1916 Act was designed to supplement Section 2 of the Clayton Act, which prohibits price discrimination and is part of U.S. antitrust laws. *See In re Japanese Electronics Products Antitrust Litigation*, 494 F. Supp. 1190 (E.D. Pa. 1980).

Of course, there are times when sales below cost or price discrimination can be regarded as predatory. As noted above, a predatory dumper could use dumping to drive competitors out of the market in anticipation of raising prices later and reaping monopoly profits.

One might argue that antidumping should be replaced by measures developed in competition law, such as the control of predatory pricing. In the long run, this should be the goal.[105] In the short term, however, we must live with differences of market conditions and of competition policies among trading nations. There are many imperfections in both national and international markets. Politically, the constituency for antidumping is different from that for competition law. Accordingly, a proposal that antidumping be abolished is probably not possible.

In light of this situation, we propose that the Antidumping Agreement be amended to incorporate concepts that have developed in competition law. Several ideas are given below.

1. To offset or prevent dumping, national antidumping authorities may levy on any dumped product an antidumping duty not greater in amount than the margin of dumping in respect of such product.[106] Therefore, the maximum amount of antidumping duty should be equal to the dumping margin. Article 9.1 of the Antidumping Agreement states: "It is desirable . . . that the duty be less than the margin if such lesser duty would be adequate to remove the injury to the domestic industry". In addition, Article 3.4 of the Antidumping Agreement lists factors to be examined when determining injury to a domestic industry, which include "the magnitude of the dumping margin". The spirit of this provision is that an antidumping duty should be less than the antidumping margin if such a lesser duty accomplishes the purpose of removing the injury to the domestic industry. The language, however, is exhortative rather than mandatory. It is recommended that this lesser duty rule be made mandatory.

The lesser duty rule would allow the collection of an antidumping duty that is equal to "injury margin." In fact, the lesser duty rule is the practice of the European Communities when it enforces its antidumping rule. An example of the lesser duty rule would be as follows: Suppose the domestic

[105] See Bernard M. Hoekman and Petros C. Mavroidis, *Dumping, Antidumping and Antitrust*, 30 J. World Trade, 27 (1996).

[106] GATT Art. VI:2.

value of a product is $100 per unit, the export price of this product is $50, and the domestic price of the competing industry in the country of importation is $70. In this case, the injury margin is $20. If an antidumping duty equal to $20 is imposed, then the difference between the dumped price and the domestic price of the competing domestic industry in the country of importation is removed, and parity is established.

The principle of the lesser duty rule is akin to the "meeting competition" defence in U.S. antitrust laws.[107] The meeting competition defence permits an enterprise to set a lower price in an area where there is competition than the price the enterprise sets in other areas, provided the low price does not undercut the price of competitors. The meeting competition defence thus authorizes an enterprise to set a lower price in an area where there are competitors so that its price matches those of competitors. If the lesser duty rule is applied, and the antidumping duty collected is equal to the injury margin, the price of the dumped product in the market of the importing country would be equal to that of the domestic industry, and the result would be similar to the meeting competition situation.

2. There is no provision in GATT Article VI or the Antidumping Agreement for a public interest requirement, *i.e.*, a requirement that national antidumping authorities consider whether the imposition of antidumping duty serves the public interest. "Public interest" in this context would involve a multitude of factors, such as the interests of domestic producers that are affected by dumped imports, importers of the product, and domestic consumers. Article VI and the Antidumping Agreement protect only one interest, namely that of domestic producers. The imposition of an antidumping duty may, however, have a far-reaching effect on other interests in society, such as consumers of the product subject to the antidumping duty. In light of this, it seems reasonable to argue that there should be a provision in Article VI or in the Antidumping Agreement that domestic antidumping legislation contain the requirement that the public interest be considered when deciding whether to impose an antidumping duty.

3. Antidumping duties may have the effect of stifling competition in the importing country. Indeed, a market-dominating enterprise in the

[107] *See FTC v. A. C. Staley Mfg. Co.*, 324 U.S. 746 (1945); *Standard Oil Co. v. Brown*, 238 F.2d 54 (5th Cir. 1956); *FTC v. National Lead Co.*, 352 U.S. 419 (1957); *In re Minneapolis-Honeywell Regulator Co.*, 44 F.T.C. 351 (1948); *FTC v. Standard Oil Co.*, 355 U.S. 396 (1958); *Standard Oil Co. v. FTC*, 340 U.S. 231 (1951); *Sunshine Biscuit, Inc. v. FTC*, 306 F.2d 48 (7th Cir. 1962); *Balian Ice Cream Co. v. Arden Farms Co.*, 104 F. Supp. 796 (S.D. Cal. 1952).

importing country may utilize antidumping measures to ward off competition from abroad. Members of a cartel may likewise use antidumping to prevent the cartel from being undermined by competition from abroad. In any event, the imposition of antidumping duties may implicate competition policy. There should be a mechanism through which national antidumping authorities and competition authorities consult with respect to an antidumping measure. In the past, the U.S. competition authorities have engaged in "competition advocacy" before trade authorities. Although this advocacy seems to have had little effect, it seems that the time has come to consider a bridge between national antidumping authorities and competition authorities, now that the introduction of competition policy into the framework of the WTO is being discussed.

4. Advocates of antidumping legislation often argue that antidumping measures are necessary to counteract unfair exports from a country in which the domestic market is closed. There is an element of plausibility to the argument that, if the domestic market is closed to foreign imports through governmental barriers or private anti-competitive practices, the exporters in question possess market power in the domestic market of the exporting country, and they may use monopoly profits to cross-subsidize lower export prices to the market of the importing country. Such export behaviour is indeed unfair.

A logical consequence of the latter argument would be that Article VI of the GATT 1994 or the Antidumping Agreement should require that national antidumping authorities find that the market of the exporting country is relatively closed to imports before determining that an antidumping duty should be imposed. This requirement seems necessary to establish that the export of dumped product is "unfair". However, who should decide whether a market of the exporting country is closed, the antidumping authority of the importing country or the competition authority of the exporting country? What if there is no competition authority in the other exporting country? Difficult questions arise in this situation. In any case, there should be close communication and cooperation between competition authorities and antidumping authorities of both exporting and importing countries.

# 14

# REGIONAL TRADE AGREEMENTS

## 1. Introduction

When the WTO was established, all but three of its original 120 Members were parties to at least one of the 62 regional trade agreements then in force (the three exceptions being Japan, Korea, and Hong Kong).[1] This widespread participation in regionalism is paradoxical in two ways. First, countries that have liberalized trade through the GATT would seemingly not have much to gain through regional trade liberalization. Second, there is policy tension between participation in regional trade arrangements and the GATT/WTO because regionalism involves preferential treatment, which is, in principle, inimical to the WTO. Why, then, do countries simultaneously pursue regional and global trade policies?

The principle reason is that non-economic, political interests usually motivate economic regionalism.[2] The political reasons for economic regionalism vary but range from ending a cycle of war and enmity to enhancing political and economic clout on the international scene. While economic concerns are always present, the actual motives are mixed and may be difficult to fathom.[3]

[1] *See, e.g.*, Andre Sapir, *The Political Economy of EC Regionalism*, 42 Eur. Econ. Rev. 717, 718 (1998).

[2] In a unique study, Walter Mattli, a political scientist at Columbia University, using tools of political economy, considered why certain integration schemes in nineteenth- and twentieth-century Europe, Latin America, North America and Asia since the 1950s have succeeded while many others have failed. Walter Mattli, The Logic of Regional Integration: Europe and Beyond (1999).

[3] Mattli, above note 2, at 50ff.

In any case, regionalism is a widespread phenomenon. The best known and most successful of the regional trade agreements are the EU/EC and the North American Free Trade Agreement (NAFTA). Relatively successful regional agreements exist on every continent, and more are contemplated. Some regional agreements may, in fact, become multi-regional. NAFTA, for example, could be transformed into a Free Trade Agreement of the Americas consisting of the whole western hemisphere. The Asia-Pacific Economic Cooperation (APEC) forum could evolve into a free-trade area. Regionalism, now and in the future, poses challenges and difficulties for the WTO.[4]

Economic analysis of economic regionalism focuses on the welfare effect of preferential trade areas (PTAs)[5] which differ widely and change over time. The point of departure is that PTAs both create and divert trade. Trade is created within a preferential trade area, but trade is also diverted because more-efficient suppliers outside the preferential trade area lose business to less-efficient suppliers within the area.

The net welfare effect of this combination of trade creation and trade diversion varies.[6] The key is ensuring that trade diversion is minimized. Economists differ on the tendency of PTAs in this regard. On the one hand, PTAs may tend to use their economic size to construct optimal external tariffs that are higher than pre-union rates to improve their terms of trade.[7] On the other hand, PTAs may, because of increased growth and prosperity, facilitate external trade liberalization.[8] In any case, these economic findings demonstrate the need for discipline of PTAs by GATT/WTO rules.

PTAs are an exception to the most-favoured-nation obligation because, by definition, they involve preferential treatment for participants not

[4] *See* Sapir, above note 1, at 620ff. *See, e.g.*, Jagdish Bhagwati and Arvind Panagariya, *Preferential Trading Areas and Multilateralism: Strangers, Friends or Foes?*, in FREE TRADE AREAS OR FREE TRADE? THE ECONOMICS OF PREFERENTIAL TRADING AGREEMENTS (Jagdish Bhagwati and Arvind Panagariya eds., 1996); Alan L. Winters, *Regionalism Versus Multilateralism*, Centre for Economic Policy Research, Discussion Paper No. 1525 (1996).

[5] In this work, the term "preferential trade areas" refers to regional as well as multi-regional trade areas.

[6] *See generally* Jacob Viner, THE CUSTOMS UNION ISSUE (1950); A. El-Algraa and A. Jones, THEORY OF CUSTOMS UNION (1981). For detailed economic analysis, see Richard Pomfret, THE ECONOMICS OF REGIONAL TRADE AGREEMENTS 375–80 (1997).

[7] Paul R. Krugman, *Is Bilateralism Bad?*, in INTERNATIONAL TRADE AND TRADE POLICY 9 (Elhanan Helpmann and Assaf Razin eds., 1991).

[8] Robert Z. Lawrence, *Emerging Regional Arrangements: Building Blocks or Stumbling Blocks?*, in FINANCE AND THE INTERNATIONAL ECONOMY 23 (Richard O'Brien ed., 1991).

granted to all WTO Members. This exception is set out in GATT Article XXIV, which applies to both customs unions and free-trade areas. A customs union creates common external tariffs and trade policies and eliminates internal tariffs and trade barriers.[9] A free-trade area eliminates internal tariffs and trade barriers, but participants retain autonomy with respect to their external trade policy.[10]

The role that GATT Article XXIV, as well as the corresponding provision in the General Agreement on Trade in Services (GATS Article V), are called on to play is captured in GATT Article XXIV:4:

> The contracting parties recognize the desirability of increasing freedom of trade by the development, through voluntary agreements, of closer integration between the economies of the countries parties to such agreements. They also recognize that the purpose of a customs union or of a free-trade area should be to facilitate trade between the constituent territories and not to raise barriers to the trade of other contracting parties with such territories.

This policy applies no matter what degree of trade liberalization exists before the creation of the PTA. For example, imagine two cases: in the first case, the constituent WTO Members have very high external tariffs; in the second, external trade barriers are very low. GATT Article XXIV and GATS Article V test each case on its own terms, and after the creation of the PTA, the allowable protectionism in the first would be greater than in the second.

The substantive components of the legal test for a qualifying PTA are ambiguous. GATT Article XXIV merely requires (1) that the "general incidence" of protection after the creation of a PTA must not be "higher or more restrictive" (the so-called external trade requirement); and (2) that "substantially all the trade" must be liberalized within the customs union or free-trade area (the so-called internal trade requirement).[11]

The WTO and its predecessor, the GATT, have not been successful in clarifying this test. During the GATT years, a working party was typically formed to review the consistency of a notified PTA with the GATT rules. Such review is known as Track I review. Track I review leaves much to be desired because of the mode of voting, namely, consensus. Moreover, as Frieder Roessler, a prominent participant in such reviews, has pointed out,

---

[9] The General Agreement on Tariffs and Trade [hereinafter GATT], Art. XXIV:8, reprinted in WTO, The Legal Texts: The Results of the Uruguay Round of Multilateral Trade Negotiations 424 (1999).

[10] *Id.*

[11] GATT, above note 9, Art. XXIV:5(a), XXIV:8(a)(i) (for customs unions); *id.* Art. XXIV:5(b), XXIV:8(b) (for free-trade areas).

countries entrusted with enforcing the legal test have no incentive to do so and sometimes have an incentive not to do so, especially with respect to the internal trade requirement.[12] In 1996, the WTO Committee on Regional Trade Agreements replaced the GATT working parties.[13] The voting mode and the incentive structure, however, remain the same.

Multilateral review of the consistency of PTAs can also take place through submission of PTA-related disputes to WTO adjudicating bodies. Review by WTO adjudicating bodies is known as Track II review. In practice, PTA-related disputes have rarely been submitted to adjudicating bodies for review. As a result, PTAs have been left largely unchallenged. This does not mean, however, that all regionalism is bad. Unchallenged regionalism essentially means that the WTO has not been instrumental in taming regionalism. Taming regionalism, however, is not a plausible objective *per se*. PTAs are a permanent and prominent feature of the multilateral trading system. The goal should be to integrate them more fully into the WTO system.

## 2. Must preferential trade agreements (PTAs) cover both goods and services in the WTO era?

Before the WTO entered into force, in the GATT years, only trade in goods was regulated at the world level. Naturally, the rules on PTAs applied only to trade in goods. The WTO Agreement, however, applies not only to trade in goods but also to trade in services. One legal issue that arises is whether WTO Members may enter into PTAs that cover only trade in goods (or only trade in services, as the case may be) or whether PTAs must cover trade in both goods and services. In practice, WTO Members have entered into PTAs confined to either goods or services.

This approach is of questionable legality (not to mention desirability). WTO panels have interpreted the WTO Agreement as one agreement to

---

[12] Frieder Roessler, *The Relationship Between Regional Integration Agreements and the Multilateral Trade Order*, in REGIONAL INTEGRATION AND THE GLOBAL TRADING SYSTEM 311, 323–324 (Kym Anderson and Richard Blackhurst eds., 1993).

[13] *See* WTO, Committee on Regional Trade Agreements, *Decision of 6 February 1996*, WT/L/127, 7 February 1996 [hereinafter *Decision Establishing the CRTA*].

which the GATT, the GATS and the TRIPS Agreement are annexed.[14] The Appellate Body endorsed this point of view, stating that,

> [u]nlike the previous GATT system, the *WTO Agreement* is a single treaty instrument which was accepted by the WTO Members as a "single undertaking". Article II:2 of the *WTO Agreement* provides that the Multilateral Trade Agreements in Annexes 1, 2 and 3 are "integral parts" of the *WTO Agreement*, binding on all Members.[15]

To what extent is non-discriminatory trade a WTO principle rather than a GATT or GATS principle? If one accepts that the principle of non-discrimination is a WTO principle, the legal consequence would be a WTO exception for PTAs, that is, an exception covering trade in both goods and services. The opposite would be the case were one to answer the question in the negative.

The WTO Agreement (excluding the agreements annexed thereto) does not mention the principle of non-discrimination. The preamble, however, states that WTO Members desire "the elimination of discriminatory treatment in international trade relations".[16] Although the preamble is not legally binding, it is part of the context of the relevant provisions. Consequently, contextual arguments could be advanced in favour of a "unitary" approach whereby a WTO-compatible PTA would have to cover both goods and services.[17]

Such arguments are of limited value until WTO Members clarify the matter through legislative action. Thus, the unavoidable legal conclusion is that, under the WTO Agreement, WTO Members may enter into PTAs that cover either goods or services. WTO Members may also enter into PTAs that cover both goods and services; if they do so, they must notify the WTO and be subjected to a control of consistency under both GATT Article XXIV and GATS Article V.

---

[14] This interpretation accords with the Final Act Embodying the Results of the Uruguay Round of Multilateral Trade Negotiations where it is stated that "[t]he representatives *agree* that the WTO Agreement shall be open for acceptance as a whole". Final Act Embodying the Results of the Uruguay Round of Multilateral Trade Negotiations, reprinted in THE LEGAL TEXTS, above note 9, at 2 (emphasis in original).

[15] *See* Appellate Body Report, *Brazil — Measures Affecting Desiccated Coconut*, WT/DS22/AB/R, adopted 20 March 1997, at 12.

[16] Marrakesh Agreement Establishing the World Trade Organization [hereinafter WTO Agreement], 3d recital in the preamble, reprinted in THE LEGAL TEXTS, above note 9, at 4.

[17] Messerlin seems to be sympathetic to this idea. *See* Patrick Messerlin, LA NOUVELLE OMC (1995).

## 3. When is a PTA compatible with WTO rules?

### 3.1 The GATT test

Article XXIV of the GATT sets out rules with which WTO Members must comply in establishing a PTA covering trade in goods. Article XXIV applies to customs unions (CUs) and free-trade areas (FTAs). There is an overlap between a CU and an FTA: in both forms of regional integration, parties to the agreement must liberalize substantially all the trade between them. The difference is that a CU has a common external policy, but an FTA does not.

Regional integration is an exception to the basic obligation to treat international trade in a non-discriminatory manner. It follows that WTO Members wishing to enter into a PTA have the burden of proving that they have complied with the WTO rules.

Article XXIV imposes three basic obligations on WTO Members wishing to enter into a PTA covering trade in goods:

1. An obligation to notify the PTA to the WTO;
2. An obligation not to raise the overall level of protection and make access to products of third parties not participating in the PTA more onerous (the so-called external trade requirement); and
3. An obligation to liberalize substantially all the trade among constituents of the PTA (the so-called internal trade requirement).

WTO Members may go further than the CU level. The EC, which has evolved into a part of a political union, the EU, is a perfect example. Article XXIV, consequently, has a function similar to a minimum threshold: WTO Members wishing to integrate have at least to comply with what it dictates.

WTO Members can also enter into interim agreements to form a CU or an FTA within a "reasonable period of time".[18] In such a case, the agreement must include a plan or schedule for the CU or FTA.[19] A "reasonable period of time" is construed as not more than 10 years unless a full explanation is given for a longer period.[20]

Until recently, it was assumed, perhaps naively, that an economic and monetary union by definition encompasses a CU, or at the very least an

[18] GATT, above note 9, Art. XXIV:5(c).

[19] *Id.*

[20] Understanding on the Interpretation of Article XXIV of the General Agreement on Tariffs and Trade 1994 [hereinafter Understanding on the Interpretation of Article XXIV of the GATT 1994], para. 3, reprinted in THE LEGAL TEXTS, above note 9, at 26.

FTA. Hence, by examining the CU or FTA component of an economic and monetary union, the GATT test for consistency of a PTA would have been satisfied. As the Asian financial crisis shows, however, this is not necessarily the case. WTO Members might be willing to unify their economic regulations without entering into a CU or an FTA. It is still too soon to pronounce on the consistency of such an agreement with the WTO. This issue may have to be faced in the future, however.

## 3.2 The obligation to notify

WTO Members deciding to enter into a PTA covering trade in goods must notify the Council for Trade in Goods, which adopts the terms of reference and transfers the PTA to the Committee on Regional Trade Agreements (CRTA) for examination.[21] The CRTA will examine the compatibility of the notified PTA with the multilateral rules.

The CRTA is the successor to GATT Article XXIV working parties. The WTO General Council established the CRTA in 1996.[22] All WTO Members can participate in the CRTA. The mandate of the CRTA is as follows:

> (a) to carry out the examination of agreements in accordance with the procedures and terms of reference adopted by . . . and thereafter present its report to the relevant body for appropriate action;
>
> . . . .
>
> (d) to consider the systemic implications of such agreements and regional initiatives for the multilateral trading system. . . .[23]

The CRTA decides by consensus. The relevant procedural rules provide that "[w]here a decision cannot be arrived at by consensus, the matter at issue shall be referred, as appropriate, to the General Council, the Council for Trade in Goods, the Council for Trade in Services or the Committee on Trade and Development".[24]

### *3.2.1 From GATT working parties to the Committee on Regional Trade Agreements (CRTA): just a cosmetic change?*

The fact that the CRTA decides by consensus does not mean that the change from GATT working parties to the CRTA is without effect. The establish-

[21] Understanding on the Interpretation of Article XXIV of the GATT 1994, para.3, above note 20.

[22] *See Decision Establishing the CRTA*, above note 13.

[23] *See id.* para. (1)(a), (d) (citation omitted).

[24] *See* WTO, Committee on Regional Trade Agreements, *Rules of Procedure for Meetings of the Committee on Regional Trade Agreements*, Rule 33, WT/REG/1, 14 August 1996.

ment of a permanent committee in lieu of *ad hoc* working parties provides a focus and "crystallization" that contributes to greater expertise and consistency. The members of the CRTA will be confronted with their own "jurisprudence", and more likely than not, they will have before them recurring themes. They cannot easily hide behind the argument "it was someone else's working party". The passage from *ad hoc* working parties to the CRTA can consequently contribute to a more coherent "jurisprudence" in the field of regional integration.

### *3.2.2 The timing of the notification*

GATT Article XXIV:7(a) reads as follows:

> Any contracting party *deciding to enter* into a customs union or free-trade area, or an interim agreement leading to the formation of such a union or area, shall *promptly* notify the CONTRACTING PARTIES and shall make available to them such information . . . as will enable them to make such reports and recommendations to contracting parties as they may deem appropriate.[25]

This provision requires WTO Members to notify a PTA covering trade in goods to the GATT/WTO in advance, but stops short of requiring advance approval to form or join a PTA. In other words, WTO Members are free to form or join a PTA if they satisfy the requirements of Article XXIV.

Political reality, however, has moved in the opposite direction. Most PTAs have been notified, contrary to the wording of Article XXIV:7(a), after their establishment. For example, NAFTA was signed on 17 December 1992 and entered into force on 1 January 1994. A working party to examine its consistency with the GATT was established on 23 March 1994.[26]

Working parties and the CRTA thus commonly have been presented with a *fait accompli*: what was originally supposed to an *ex ante* review slowly became an *ex post* review with all the problems that such a shift might entail. What is the appropriate remedy in case a notified PTA, which meanwhile has entered into force, does not comply with the WTO rules? This question is purely theoretical because the CRTA decides by consensus, which means

[25] GATT, above note 9, Art. XXIV:7(a) (emphasis added).

[26] For information on this issue, on all notified PTAs, see the table in 2 Guide to GATT Law and Practice 858–72 (6th ed. 1995) [hereinafter GATT Analytical Index]. *See also* WTO, Committee on Regional Trade Agreements, *Basic Information on Regional Trade Agreements*, WT/REG/W/44, 7 February 2002. The information in this document is available on the WTO website (http://www.wto.org/English/tratop_e/ region_e/ region_e.htm) and will be updated every two months.

that the WTO Members participating in the notified PTA will, in all likelihood, argue in favour of the compatibility of their PTA with the multilateral rules.

Although the possibility now exists to have recourse to voting in case of absence of consensus (Article IX of the WTO Agreement), this has not yet happened. Working parties (and now the CRTA) will simply agree to disagree and decline to make a formal decision. In a 1989 study, Jeffrey Schott found only four cases in which there was an agreement at the end of the process.[27] After 1989, the only case in which members of a working party by consensus agreed that a notified PTA was consistent with the GATT is in the context of the *Working Party on the Customs Union Between the Czech Republic and the Slovak Republic.*[28]

Consequently, GATT practice shows remarkable tolerance when it comes to sanctioning belated notifications. This is a very important point: taking into account that the WTO system does not in practice allow retroactive remedies,[29] belated notification essentially amounts to tolerance of GATT/WTO-incompatible PTAs.

### *3.2.3 The powers of the CRTA*

In principle, the CRTA has broad powers. The relevant provision of GATT Article XXIV requires WTO Members to "make available to [the Contracting Parties] such information... as will enable them to make *such reports and recommendations to contracting parties as they may deem appropriate*".[30]

This wording suggests that the CRTA can make any recommendation it deems appropriate. It may even conclude that a notified PTA is inconsistent with the GATT. When it comes to notified, interim agreements leading to the establishment of a CU or an FTA, the CRTA enjoys especially broad power. GATT Article XXIV:7(b) reads as follows:

> If... the CONTRACTING PARTIES find that such agreement is not likely to result in the formation of a customs union or of a free-trade area... the CONTRACTING PARTIES shall make recommendations to the parties to the agreement. *The parties shall not maintain or put into force, as the case may be, such agreement if they are not prepared to modify it in accordance with these recommendations.*[31]

[27] Jeffrey J. Schott, *More Free Trade Areas?*, in FREE TRADE AREAS AND U.S. TRADE POLICY 1, 25 (1989).

[28] WTO Doc. L/7501, 15 July 1994.

[29] *See* Chapter 4, section 2.

[30] GATT, above note 9, Art. XXIV:7(a) (emphasis added).

[31] *Id.* Art. XXIV:7(b) (emphasis added).

In such cases, the CRTA can effectively strike down a proposed CU or FTA. The GATT Contracting Parties, however, never exercised their authority in such a drastic way. Little has changed in the WTO era.

### *3.2.4 The CRTA in the context of the GATS*

WTO Members that are parties to a PTA covering trade in services must "promptly" notify the PTA to the Council on Trade in Services.[32] The Council on Trade in Services may decide to form a working party or pass the agreement to the CRTA for examination. Unlike the case of PTAs notified under GATT Article XXIV, such examination is optional, not mandatory.[33]

## 3.3 The external trade requirement

### *3.3.1 Free-trade areas*

As stated above, the difference between a CU and an FTA is the presence in the former and the absence in the latter of a common external policy. This difference has direct implications in the regulation of the external requirement described in GATT Article XXIV:5.

Article XXIV:5(b), which applies to free-trade areas, reads in the relevant part as follows: "duties and other regulations of commerce . . . shall not be higher or more restrictive than the corresponding duties and other regulations of commerce existing in the same constituent territories prior to the formation of the free-trade area. . . ."[34]

Article XXIV:5(b) states that WTO Members participating in a PTA may not modify their external protection when joining an FTA. This approach is dictated by the very nature of FTAs, because an FTA aims only at liberalizing trade within its constituents without addressing the question of protection external to the FTA.[35] Although WTO Members that join an FTA make no changes to their external protection, internal regulations such as rules of origin can dramatically affect external protection. Rules of origin are particularly "appropriate" in an FTA context: unless goods circulating through an FTA are accompanied by a "certificate of origin", exporters will have an incentive to the cheapest port of entry (because external protection remains an issue of national

[32] General Agreement on Trade in Services [hereinafter GATS] Art. V:7(a), reprinted in THE LEGAL TEXTS, above note 9, at 286.

[33] *Id.* Art. V:7(b).

[34] GATT, above note 9, Art. XXIV:5(b).

[35] This is why goods originating in a non-FTA state are in practice accompanied by a certificate of origin when moving from one FTA member to another.

sovereignty, and it could very well be the case that there are asymmetries as to the level of customs duties among members of an FTA). The first best would be that the national systems conferring origin at the pre-FTA stage remain in force unchanged post-FTA. This is almost never the case, however. Members of the FTA renegotiate "regional" rules of origin that, from an empirical perspective, are, more often than not, stricter after the creation of an FTA.[36] In the absence of a WTO Agreement on Rules of Origin, "regionalisation" of rules of origin can be challenged only under GATT Article XXIV:5(b).

### *3.3.2 Customs unions*

With respect to CUs, the external trade requirement is distinguished into two specific obligations: an obligation not to raise the overall level of protection above a certain threshold and a specific obligation to compensate in cases where customs duties in some constituents of a CU had to be raised to match the CU-level.

In addition to liberalizing trade among members of the PTA, CUs aim to provide for a common external protection. In case of asymmetrical external protection between the prospective members of the CU (some being more and some being less open to foreign products) adjustments will have to be made. Only in exceptional circumstances (cases of perfect symmetry) are no adjustments needed. In practice, however, such cases are hard to find.

Consequently, the external trade requirement can pose problems in the context of a CU. Article XXIV:5(a) reads:

> duties and other regulations of commerce . . . shall not *on the whole* be higher or more restrictive than *the general incidence* of the duties and regulations of commerce applicable in the constituent territories prior to the formation of such union . . . (emphasis added).

The italicized words mark the difference between the text of GATT Article XXIV:5(b) and that of GATT Article XXIV:5(a). At first, the words seem to suggest, in practice, the inevitable need for adjustment. "On the whole" and "general incidence" invite for a comparison of the general (and not item by item) picture before with the picture after the formation of the CU.[37]

[36] *See* Serra Jaime et al., CARNEGIE ENDOWMENT FOR INTERNATIONAL PEACE, REFLECTIONS ON REGIONALISM: REPORT OF THE STUDY GROUP ON INTERNATIONAL TRADE (1997).

[37] Incidentally, this seems to have been the intention of the drafters. Quoting from the preparatory materials: "[T]he phrase 'on the whole' . . . did not mean that an average tariff should be laid down in respect of each individual product, but merely that the whole level of tariffs of a

Subsequent practice seems to accept that, in principle, an item-by-item approach is unwarranted in the context of GATT Article XXIV:5(a), but there is disagreement as to the precise level on which comparisons will take place. The 1983 working party report on "Accession of Greece to the European Communities" contains the view expressed by the EC that "Article XXIV:5 required only generalized, overall judgment on this point",[38] but it failed to reach a consensus among its members on this point. By the same token, the 1988 working party report on "Accession of Portugal and Spain to the European Communities" contains the view of the EC that "Article XXIV:5 only required an examination on the broadest possible basis".[39] The same report though contains the view of a member of the working party, which "could not accept the Communities' contention that the extension of the tariff of the EC/10 to the EC/12 was compatible with their obligations under Article XXIV:5(a), regardless of the effect on the tariffs of Spain and Portugal. Article XXIV:5(a) required a comparison with the pre-accession tariffs of the constituent territories, and the relative size of those territories was not a relevant factor".[40]

Moreover, disagreements appeared often among working party members as to whether bound or applied rates should be used in the context of GATT Article XXIV:5(a).[41]

The picture seems much clearer now with the entry into force of the "WTO Understanding on the Interpretation of Article XXIV of the General Agreement on Tariffs and Trade 1994".[42] Panels have yet to pronounce

customs union should not be higher than the average overall level of the former constituent territories", see EPCT/C.II/38 at 9, reproduced in GATT ANALYTICAL INDEX, above note 26, at 803; "The Sub-Committee recommended that the words 'average level of duties' be replaced by 'general incidence of duties' in paragraph 2(a) of the new Article. It was the intention of the Sub-Committee that this phrase should not require a mathematical average of customs duties but should permit greater flexibility so that the volume of trade may be taken into account," Havana Reports, reproduced in GATT ANALYTICAL INDEX, above note 26, at 803.

[38] *See* Accession of Greece to the European Communities, 9 March 1983, GATT B.I.S.D. (30th Supp.) at 168, para. 42, at 184 (1984).

[39] *See* Accession of Portugal and Spain to the European Communities, 19–20 October 1988, GATT B.I.S.D. (35th Supp.) at 293, para. 6, at 295–96 (1989).

[40] *Id.* para. 36, at 311.

[41] *See, e.g.*, the discussions in the working party examining the compatibility of the EEC with Article XXIV, GATT Doc. SR.18/4 at 46–54 and also in C/M/8, SR.19/6–7; *see* Accession of Greece to the European Communities, above note 38; *see also* Working Party on the Free-Trade Agreement Between Canada and the United States, 12 November 1991, GATT B.I.S.D. (38th Supp.) at 47, para. 62, at 66 (1992).

[42] Above, note 20.

on the legal nature of the WTO Understandings. It seems reasonable to conclude, however, that such Understandings constitute international agreements concluded by WTO Members and that they should, therefore, be interpreted in accordance with the Vienna Convention on the Law of Treaties (Vienna Convention).[43] The Understanding is self-explanatory:

> The evaluation under paragraph 5(a) of Article XXIV of the general incidence of the duties and other regulations of commerce applicable before and after the formation of a customs union shall in respect of duties and charges be based upon an overall assessment of weighted average tariff rates and of customs duties collected. This assessment shall be based on import statistics for a previous representative period to be supplied by the customs union, on a *tariff-line basis* and in values and quantities, broken down by WTO country of origin. The Secretariat shall compute the weighted average tariff rates and customs duties collected in accordance with the methodology used in the assessment of tariff offers in the Uruguay Round of Multilateral Trade negotiations. For this purpose, the duties and charges to be taken into consideration shall be the applied rates of duty. It is recognized that for the purpose of the overall assessment of the incidence of other regulations of commerce for which quantification and aggregation are difficult, the examination of individual measures, regulations, products covered and trade flows affected may be required.[44]

Moving to tariff-lines in itself provides the necessary precision to the terms "on the whole" and "general incidence". Hence, with respect to GATT Article XXIV:5(a), it seems appropriate to conclude that the test for consistency post-Understanding is precise enough for interpreters.

There is an additional provision relevant only to the formation of CUs. GATT Article XXIV:6 reads as follows:

> If, in fulfilling the requirements of subparagraph 5(a), a contracting party proposes to increase any rate of duty inconsistently with the provision of Article II, the procedure set forth in Article XXVIII shall apply. In providing for compensatory adjustment, due account shall be taken of the compensation already afforded by the reduction brought about in the corresponding duty of the other constituents of the union.

Article XXIV:6 deals only with customs duties. In that, it is *lex specialis* to Article XXIV:5(a). An example can help best illustrate the function of Article XXIV:6. Countries A, B, and C decide to enter into a CU. Assume that before the formation of the CU, the tariff protection (bound rates)[45] of the automotive sector in the three countries was the following:

[43] Vienna Convention on the Law of Treaties, 11 U.N.T.S. 331 (1969), available at http://www.un.org/law/ilc/texts/treatfra.htm.

[44] Understanding on the Interpretation of Article XXIV of the GATT 1994, above note 20, para. 3

[45] GATT Art. XXIV:6 refers to bound and not to applied duties.

A 20 percent
B 30 percent
C 40 percent

When the CU is formed, A, B, and C decide to bind customs duties at 30 percent for the automotive sector for the CU as a whole. Arguably, they have met their obligations under GATT XXIV:5(a). They have not, however, necessarily met their obligations under GATT XXIV:6. As will be shown, if Article XXIV:5(a) is violated, Article XXIV:6 will be *ipso facto* violated. Compliance with Article XXIV:5(a) does not, however, automatically lead to compliance with Article XXIV:6.

GATT Article XXIV:6 comes into play because A had to raise its pre-CU duty from 20 to 30 percent. In such cases, according to GATT Article XXIV, GATT Article XXVIII negotiations will begin. This means that WTO Members that have "initial negotiating rights", "principal supplying interest" or "substantial interest" will participate in the negotiations with the members of the CU; such negotiations aim at compensating those WTO Members which will have more difficult access to A's market as a result of the formation of the CU.

The second sentence of Article XXIV:6 GATT makes it clear that built-in compensation will be taken into account, that is new market opportunities in those constituents of the CU that were forced to lower their pre-CU duties in order to comply with GATT Article XXIV:5(a).

First scenario: A is a low *per capita* income small country, whereas C is a high *per capita* large income country. Neither A nor C produce cars, or their domestic production allows for a substantial amount of imports. The fact that C lowers its duties from 40 to 30 percent in all likelihood over-compensates the fact that A raised its own duties from 20 to 30 percent. This is the notion of built-in compensation: C will import more cars, and hence exporters will be compensated for their losses due to the fact that they will export less to A.

Second scenario: A is the high *per capita* income large country, whereas C is the low *per capita* small income country. In this case, the amount of trade lost because A had to raise its duties is, most likely, not compensated by the fact that C lowered its own duties. In such cases, there is nothing like built-in compensation in the formation of the CU for exporters. Hence, something has to be done. GATT Article XXIV calls for compensation, which will be offered to the WTO Members in accordance with an Article XXVIII-type of procedure.

### *3.3.3 PTAs in the GATS context*

The GATS regime does not deal with external protection. Article V:5 of the GATS, however, makes it plain that compensation analogous to that offered in the GATT context under GATT Article XXIV:6 will be offered in the GATS context if a WTO Member entering into an PTA has to modify its Schedule.

## 3.4 The internal trade requirement

WTO Members wishing to enter into a CU or an FTA are required under Article XXIV:8 to eliminate "duties and other restrictive regulations of commerce" with respect to "substantially all the trade" in products originating in the PTA.[46] Unlike GATT Article XXIV:5(a), no clarification of Article XXIV:8 took place during the Uruguay Round negotiations. Over the years, major controversies have arisen because working party members could not agree on the meaning of the key terms "substantially all the trade" and "other restrictive regulations of commerce" contained in Article XXIV:8.

### *3.4.1 Substantially all the trade*

The GATT contracting parties were reluctant to submit the interpretation of the term "substantially all the trade" to dispute settlement panels. No case is reported in the GATT years although dozens of PTAs came into being.

Thus, 50 years of GATT practice later, the term "substantially all the trade" remains unclear. To interpret this term, we observe the constraint imposed by Article 3.2 of the Dispute Settlement Understanding (DSU) that any interpretation advanced has to be in conformity with the customary rule of interpretation in Article 31 of the Vienna Convention.

Article 31 of the Vienna Convention obliges the interpreter to examine: the ordinary meaning of the terms; in their context; in light of their object and purpose; taking into account any subsequent decision; and taking into account subsequent practice.

If the interpreter still finds the meaning of the term to be manifestly ambiguous or unreasonable, recourse may be made to supplementary means of interpretation (Article 32 of the Vienna Convention), the preparatory

[46] GATT, above note 9, Art. XXIV:8.

work (*travaux préparatoires*) of an international treaty (in our case, the GATT).

#### 3.4.1.1 The ordinary meaning of the terms

The term "all the trade" is qualified by the word "substantially". The word "substantially" indicates that not all trade between members of a customs union (CU) or a free-trade area (FTA) has to be included for a CU or an FTA to be judged compatible with GATT Article XXIV:8. But the question remains *how much* trade can be included (or omitted) for a CU or an FTA to pass the Article XXIV:8 test.

The term "substantial" has both quantitative and qualitative aspects. Thus, to determine whether "substantially all the trade" is included, both the quantity and the sectors included (or omitted) must be considered. The word "all" indicates a comparison must be made between what is included (or omitted) and 100 percent of the trade among the constituencies of the PTA. Beyond this, there is ambiguity.

#### 3.4.1.2 The context

The context of an Article of an international treaty is at least the remaining Articles of the same agreement and, sometimes, other agreements dealing with the same (or even comparable) subject matter. We have already presented the relevant sub-paragraphs of GATT Article XXIV (4, 5, 6 and 7). None of them, however, sheds any light on the interpretation of the term "substantially all the trade".

Consequently, we turn to the rest of the GATT. GATT Article XXIV must be read in the context of Article I GATT, which lays down the basic obligation imposed on WTO Members not to discriminate between products of other WTO Members (the MFN-clause).[47] This assertion is mandated by the second sentence of GATT Article XXIV:4, which reads in the relevant part as follows: "They also recognize that the purpose of a customs union or a free-trade area should be to facilitate trade between the constituent territories and not to raise barriers to the trade of other contracting parties with such territories".

[47] As Andre Sapir often remarks, in rather colloquial terms, in conferences on Regionalism, there must be some reason why the founding fathers of the GATT placed the non-discrimination principle in Article I GATT and the possibility to form PTAs 23 Articles later.

Thus, there is a recognition that a PTA can subvert the fundamental GATT obligation not to discriminate. The discrimination element is included in GATT Article XXIV:8, which serves two purposes:

1. On the one hand, it allows members of a PTA to treat other members of a PTA more favourably than they treat other WTO Members, since obstacles to substantially all trade between members of the PTA are eliminated (and this is not the case for the other WTO Members which do not participate in the PTA); and
2. On the other, it sets a threshold which must be complied with, that is for a PTA to be compatible with the GATT, it must guarantee the elimination of duties and other restrictive regulations of commerce with respect to substantially all the trade between the members of the PTA.

GATT Article XXIV:8 is an exception to GATT Article I only to the extent that Article XXIV:8 has been complied with. Acknowledging that a treaty provision is of exceptional character has only one legal consequence: the burden of proof to demonstrate compatibility rests with the party invoking the exception. No additional light is shed on the meaning of the term.

#### 3.4.1.3 The object and purpose of the agreement

The object and purpose of the GATT are to liberalize international trade. Such liberalization should occur on a non-discriminatory basis. Any deviation, consequently, from the non-discrimination principle must be well justified and should be kept to the minimum possible so as not to subvert the object and purpose of the GATT.

The "complementarity" between non-discrimination and regional trade is, as stated above, institutionally acknowledged in Article XXIV: the pursuit of one goal does not necessarily make the other redundant; if this were the case, the interpreter would have a hard time achieving effective treaty interpretation in accordance with the Vienna Convention.

The object and purpose of the GATT, consequently, because of the "complementarity" of regional and multilateral trade, do not offer guidance as to the meaning of the term.

#### 3.4.1.4 Subsequent decisions

This term refers to any formal amendment or interpretative note concluded between the WTO Members. No such decision exists. The GATT Contracting Parties never adopted an interpretation of the term "substantially all the trade". Unadopted proposals have no legal significance.

### 3.4.1.5 Subsequent practice

When the GATT Contracting Parties adopted a working party report on the compatibility of a notified PTA with GATT Article XXIV, they were acting under the authority of GATT Article XXV, which authorizes joint action. Consequently, adopted working party reports constitute subsequent practice in accordance with Article 31 of the Vienna Convention. However, GATT working party reports are inconclusive on this issue. For example, in the working party report on "*EC — Agreements with Portugal*",[48] the EC noted that "there is no exact definition of the expression referring to the term 'substantially all the trade'". Another working party expressed the opinion that it is "inappropriate to fix a general figure of the percentage of trade which would be subjected to internal barriers".[49] EC Member States expressed the view that "a free-trade area should be considered as having been achieved for substantially all trade when the volume of liberalized trade reached 80 percent of total trade", but this was not accepted by the working party.[50]

The working party report on "EFTA", on the other hand, records the view that "the percentage of trade covered, even if it were established to be 90 percent, was not considered to be the only factor to be taken into account".[51] Other working party reports reflect the view that the exclusion of a whole sector, no matter what percentage of current trade is contrary to the spirit of both Article XXIV and the GATT.[52]

In 1997, Australia proposed a clarification of the term that is worth discussing.[53] In Australia's view, only a quantitative element (not a qualitative element) can define "substantially all the trade", and future negotiations should concentrate on putting a number next to the concept. Australia proposed that "substantially all the trade" should be defined as coverage of

[48] *See European Communities — Agreements with Portugal*, 19 October 1973, GATT B.I.S.D. (20th Supp.) at 171 (1974).

[49] *See* The European Economic Community, 29 November 1957, GATT B.I.S.D. (6th Supp.) at 70, section D, para. 34.

[50] *See id.* para. 30.

[51] *See* European Free Trade Association, 4 June 1960, GATT B.I.S.D. (9th Supp.) at 70, para. 48 (1961).

[52] *See* Working Party Report on *EEC — Agreements with Finland*, GATT B.I.S.D. (29th Supp.) at 77, para. 12 (1983); Free Trade Area between Canada and the United States, above note 41, para. 83.

[53] *See* WTO, Committee on Regional Trade Agreements, *Communication from Australia*, WT/REG/W/18, 17 November 1997.

95 percent of all the six-digit tariff lines listed in the Harmonized System. Australia conceded that the 95-percent figure is an arbitrary figure intended to move negotiations out of a deadlock and to provide a rule of thumb.[54] Mindful of the fact that if trade is concentrated in only a few products, the 95-percent figure could exempt sizeable trade flows, Australia proposed an assessment of prospective trade flows under an arrangement at various stages. If accepted, this proposal would replace the never-ending discussion on the meaning of "substantially all the trade" with a more specific criterion. This has not yet happened, however.

#### 3.4.1.6 Preparatory work

Having exhausted recourse to Article 31 of the Vienna Convention, one will have to concede that the meaning of the term is obscure and, therefore, recourse to supplementary means of interpretation is warranted. However, the preparatory work on Article XXIV is also inconclusive.

In a series of papers the WTO Secretariat prepared for the Committee,[55] the conclusion was reached that the drafters of the treaty used the term "substantially all the trade" loosely.

#### 3.4.1.7 Conclusion

Neither the GATT nor the WTO has provided a workable legal definition of "substantially all the trade", a key element of the internal trade requirement of GATT Article XXIV. GATT contracting parties and WTO Members that were outsiders with respect to particular PTAs had neither the incentive nor the political will to enforce this element. Not surprisingly, the precise meaning of this term remains elusive.

Non-action on this issue may in fact accord with the wishes of most WTO Members. Clarification of this term would inevitably limit the discretion of both the CRTA and WTO adjudicating bodies, which may not be welcome.

### *3.4.2 "Other restrictive regulations of commerce"*

GATT Article XXIV:8 requires the elimination not only of duties but also "other restrictive regulations of commerce" ("except, where necessary, those

[54] *See* WTO, Committee on Regional Trade Agreements, *Communication from Australia*, WT/REG/W/22/Add.1, 24 April 1998.

[55] *See* WTO, Committee on Regional Trade Agreements, *Systemic Issues Related to "Other Regulations of Commerce"*, WT/REG/W/17, 31 October 1997, revised by WT/REG/W/17/Add.1, 5 November 1997; WT/REG/W/17/Corr. 1, 15 December 1997; and WT/REG/W/17/Rev. 1, 5 February 1998.

permitted under [GATT] Articles XI, XII, XIII, XIV, XV and XX") between constituencies of a PTA. This rule applies to both CUs and FTAs.[56] The term "other restrictive regulations of commerce" is not further defined. The ordinary meaning of the term, however, seems to prohibit any regulation that restricts commerce other than those mentioned in the parenthesis.

#### 3.4.2.1 The context

The items mentioned in the parenthesis pose interpretative problems. In fact, what poses problems is what is not mentioned in the parenthesis. Does this mean that other restrictive regulations of commerce (like Articles VI (antidumping), XVIII (government assistance to economic development), XIX (safeguard), or XXI (security exceptions) ) cannot be invoked, or is this simply a regrettable omission?

On its face, it seems that anything not mentioned in the parenthesis is not tolerated after the formation of a CU or an FTA. This would essentially mean that no antidumping action can take place between members of a PTA, and that for a PTA to be judged compatible with Article XXIV:8, it must abolish imposition of antidumping duties between its members. To our knowledge, however, only two of the numerous PTAs (the EC and the ANZCERTA between Australia and New Zealand) have eliminated antidumping duties between their members.[57] PTAs like NAFTA continue to provide for the possibility that one member can impose antidumping duties against another.

Moreover, whereas good arguments can be advanced with respect to the elimination of antidumping duties or safeguard actions among members of a PTA, this is hardly the case with respect to measures based on security exceptions. It is not sustainable to argue that by agreeing to form an FTA, members acknowledge that their security will never again be threatened by actions of their partners. Thus, the listed exceptions do not appear to be exhaustive.

#### 3.4.2.2 Subsequent practice

Subsequent practice is an illustration of divergent opinions. Starting with the 1970 working party report on "*EEC—Association with African and Malgasy*

[56] GATT, above note 9, Art. XXIV:8(a), (b).

[57] *See* Petros C. Mavroidis, *The Treatment of Dumping, Subsidies and Anti-Competitive Practices in Regional Trade Agreements*, in REGIONALISM AND MULTILATERALISM AFTER THE URUGUAY ROUND 389–96 (Paul Demaret et al. eds., 1997).

*States*", one notes, on the one hand, the opinion of members of the working party which were not members of the notified PTA to the effect that "free trade within the meaning of Article XXIV:8(b) did not exist" in view of the continued imposition by certain parties to the Convention of fiscal charges on imports from other members; at the same time the members of the PTA were declaring that "the provisions of Article XXIV, concerning the concept of a free-trade area concerned only protective measures. The taxes referred to were of a fiscal character, not protective. . . ."[58]

There were also discussions on the issue whether resort to GATT Article XXI (security exceptions) should be precluded under GATT Article XXIV in the working party report on the EEC. The view of the EEC Member States reflected that "it would be difficult, however, to dispute the right of contracting parties to avail themselves of that provision which related, among other things, to traffic in arms, fissionable materials, etc., and it must therefore be concluded that the list was not exhaustive".[59] Other working party reports reflect a series of discussions on this issue.[60]

During the Uruguay Round negotiations, a draft decision was tabled to clarify the relationship of GATT Article XIX with GATT Article XXIV. It read as follows:

> When an Article XIX action is taken by a member of a customs union or free-trade area, or by the customs union on behalf of a member, it [need not] [shall not] be applied to other members of the customs union or free-trade area. However, when taking such action it should be demonstrated that the serious injury giving rise to the invocation of Article XIX is caused by imports from non-members; any injury deriving from imports from other members of the customs union or free-trade area shall not be taken into account in justifying the Article XIX action.[61]

Had this proposal been accepted, it would have provided a much-needed clarification, but most importantly would have led to a more general discussion on what is and what is not permitted between members of a PTA. The proposal was rejected, however, and the possibility to engage in meaningful discussion of these issues ends.

In fact, subsequent practice has developed in the contrary way. On three occasions, the Appellate Body examined whether a party to a PTA (a CU in

---

[58] *See* GATT B.I.S.D. (18th Supp.) at 133, 135–37.

[59] *See* The European Economic Community, above note 49, para. 26.

[60] *See* GATT Analytical Index, above n. 26, at 820 *et seq.*

[61] *See Systemic Issues Related to "Other Regulations of Commerce,"* above note 55, at 4.

the case of Argentina[62] and an FTA in the case of the United States[63]) could impose safeguards against other parties to the PTA. These cases involved interpretations of the WTO Safeguards Agreement, but these interpretations also answer the question of whether the items figuring in the parenthesis of GATT Article XXIV:8 form an exhaustive list. On every occasion, the WTO adjudicating bodies held that parties to a PTA may impose safeguards against other parties to the PTA.[64]

Thus, the parenthetical list described above is not an exhaustive one. Safeguards are now included. What else, however, is included? Should one by analogy be brave enough and apply the stated reasoning in all forms of "contingent protection"? Only future experience will tell. The odds, however, are that WTO adjudicating bodies are willing to adopt a "pragmatic" attitude and re-design GATT Article XXIV according to modern reality. A textualist approach that does not keep up with modernity[65] is certainly not envisaged by the Vienna Convention system. Subsequent practice is probably the single most important factor listed in Article 31 of the Vienna Convention. Subsequent practice in the present discussion suggests that one can imagine other forms of contingent protection to be soon added to the list in the parenthesis of Article XXIV:8.

#### 3.4.2.3 Preparatory work

Recourse to preparatory work is meaningful here only to see whether the precise scope of the term is anywhere reflected in the records. This is not the case.

#### 3.4.2.4 Conclusion

The conclusion we can draw with respect to the term "other restrictive regulations of commerce" is two-fold:

1. In principle, any regulation of commerce that can restrict trade is caught by GATT Article XXIV:8;

[62] *See* Appellate Body Report, *Argentina — Safeguard Measures on Imports of Footwear*, WT/DS121/AB/R, adopted 12 January 2000 [hereinafter Appellate Body Report, *Argentina — Footwear Safeguard*].

[63] *See* Appellate Body Report, *United States — Wheat Gluten Safeguard*, Appellate Body Report, *United States — Line Pipe Safeguard*.

[64] Appellate Body Report, *Argentina — Footwear Safeguard*, para. 107–108; Appellate Body Report, *United States — Wheat Gluten Safeguard*, para. 98–100; Appellate Body Report, *United States — Line Pipe Safeguard*, para. 181–194.

[65] *See* Michael C. Dorf, *The Supreme Court 1997 Term, Foreword: The Limits of Socratic Deliberation*, 112 Harv. L. Rev. 4 (1998).

2. However, the current tendency of WTO adjudicating bodies is to interpret GATT Article XXIV:8 in light of state practice that has evolved to modify the standard in Article XXIV:8. By extending the list of items in the parenthesis of Article XXIV:8, WTO adjudicating bodies show a "conciliatory attitude" vis-à-vis reality and a willingness to keep up with modern times.[66] The impact, of course, will be an easier standard for aspiring PTAs.

## 4. The GATS regime

Unlike GATT Article XXIV, Article V of the GATS fails to distinguish between a CU and an FTA. It is entitled "Economic Integration" and addresses only one form of regional integration. From the wording and the spirit of Article V, one can deduce that regional integration in the context of GATS closely resembles a GATT FTA.

GATS Article V seems to set a looser standard than GATT Article XXIV. The GATS essentially imposes two conditions for a PTA to be judged consistent with the GATS:

1. That it has "substantial sectoral coverage"; and
2. That it abolishes discrimination.

The term "substantial sectoral coverage" is understood "in terms of number of sectors, volume of trade affected and modes of supply".[67] The GATS provides that, "[i]n order to meet this condition, agreements should not provide for the *a priori* exclusion of any mode of supply".[68]

Liberalization in the GATS context is not of the same width and breadth as in the GATT context. It probably was considered politically untenable to request from WTO Members aspiring to enter into PTAs covering trade in services to include sectors that they have not previously liberalized on an MFN-basis. On the other hand, had such a requirement been introduced, regionalism in GATS could prove to be a vehicle for liberalization.[69]

In the absence of relevant practice,[70] it is reasonable to conclude, therefore, that while some service sectors can be excluded without calling into question

[66] See the discussion of the *United States — Line Pipe Safeguard* case, below section 5.1.

[67] GATS, above note 32, Art. V, note 1.

[68] *Id.*

[69] Bhagwati's "open regionalism" apsiration could gain full effect in this context.

[70] The only working party that has made substantial progress in examining the consistency of a notified PTA with GATS Article V is the working party on NAFTA. *See* WTO Doc. S/C/N/4.

the consistency of a PTA with GATS Article V, no exclusion of one of the four specified modes of supply[71] is permitted for the sectors covered.[72]

## 5. The WTO: less tolerance for PTAs?

Along with the other Uruguay Round agreements, negotiators concluded and adopted an Understanding on the Interpretation of Article XXIV of the GATT 1994.[73] The Understanding reads, in the relevant part, as follows:

> The provisions of Articles XXII and XXIII of GATT 1994 as elaborated and applied by the Dispute Settlement Understanding may be invoked with respect to *any* matters arising from the application of those provisions of Article XXIV relating to customs unions, free-trade areas or interim agreements leading to the formation of a customs union or a free-trade area.[74]

On its face, this Understanding seems to grant a large review power to WTO adjudicating bodies: their power extends to any matter arising from the application of GATT Article XXIV. Roessler has argued, however, that the terms of the Understanding lean towards a restrictive understanding of its scope: the reference made is to the application of Article XXIV and not to Article XXIV as such.[75] But this argument does not sufficiently address the fact that the reference is to Article XXIV in a horizontal manner and not to any particular CU or FTA. The application of Article XXIV from a horizontal perspective seems to cover anything that can come within the ambit of Article XXIV.

Any matter relating to the application of Article XXIV, thus, signals the willingness of negotiators to affirm their intention that WTO panels deal with PTA-related issues. Although GATT practice suggests that panels are competent to adjudicate PTA-related claims, the 1994 Understanding marks the first time that such an acknowledgement is made explicitly.

### 5.1 Dispute settlement

To date, no WTO case has attempted to use GATT Article XXIV as a sword to invalidate a PTA. Several interesting cases have, however, raised

[71] For discussion of the four modes of supply under the GATS, see Chapter 11.

[72] Compare the discussions in the GATT Art. XXIV working party reports, in which it was often stated that no sector should be excluded.

[73] Understanding on the Interpretation of Article XXIV of the GATT 1994, above note 20.

[74] *Id.* para. 12 (emphasis added).

[75] Frieder Roessler, Are the Judicial Organs Overburdened?, Paper presented in the *Conference in the Honour of Raymond Vernon*, Harvard, Kennedy School, 2–3 June 2000.

the issue of whether Article XXIV can be used as a shield, to protect otherwise WTO-inconsistent trade practices.

The first instance of this arose under the GATT in late 1994. A GATT panel in the *EEC — Bananas* case[76] ruled in passing on the question whether the EC's discriminatory import regime for bananas that favoured ACP (African-Caribbean-Pacific) countries could be shielded by the Lomé Convention between the EC and these countries. The panel ruled that the Lomé Convention did not qualify as an Article XXIV customs union or free-trade area:

> This lack of *any* obligation of the sixty-nine ACP countries to dismantle their trade barriers, and the acceptance of an obligation to remove trade barriers only on imports into the customs territory of the EEC, made the trade arrangements set out in the Convention substantially different from those of a free trade area, as defined in Article XXIV:8(b).[77]

Under the WTO, the Appellate Body has echoed this approach by construing the requirements of Article XXIV relatively strictly. In *Turkey — Textiles*,[78] Turkey attempted to use Article XXIV to justify quotas on textiles and clothing. In ruling on this matter, the Appellate Body focused on the "chapeau" of Article XXIV:5 and the wording that the provisions of GATT 1994 "*shall not prevent* ... the formation of a customs union" (or a free-trade area).[79] Thus, the Appellate Body concluded, Article XXIV can justify a measure "only if it is introduced upon the formation of a customs union, and only to the extent that the formation of the customs union would be prevented if the introduction of the measure were not allowed".[80] The Appellate Body went on to give guidance as to how these issues should be approached.

---

[76] *EEC — Import Regime for Bananas*, GATT Doc. DS38/R, 11 February 1994 (unadopted) [hereinafter GATT Panel Report, *EEC — Bananas*]. Two other GATT cases were inconclusive on Article XXIV issues. *See EC — Tariff Treatment on Imports of Citrus Products from Certain Mediterranean Countries*, GATT Doc. L/5776, 7 February 1985 (unadopted), (finding the legal status of the alleged Article XXIV PTAs "remain open"). In 1974, Canada brought a challenge in connection with the accession of Denmark, Ireland, and the United Kingdom to the EC; this challenge was withdrawn by mutual agreement. *See* GATT Doc. C/W 250 and GATT Doc C/W/259.

[77] GATT Panel Report, *EEC — Bananas*, above, para. 159. *See id.* paras 159–64.

[78] Appellate Body Report, *Turkey — Restrictions on Imports of Textile and Clothing Products*, WT/DS34/AB/R, adopted 19 November 1999 [hereinafter Appellate Body Report, *Turkey — Textiles*].

[79] *Id.* para. 45–46 (emphasis in original).

[80] *Id.*

The first level of analysis is to determine, in any particular case, whether there is a customs union (or free-trade area).[81] This determination involves consideration of the elements of Article XXIV:8(a), which defines the term "customs union", specifically the internal trade requirement of Article XXIV:8(a)(i) and the external trade requirement of Article XXIV:8(a)(ii).[82]

As to the internal trade requirement, the Appellate Body stated that the term "substantially all the trade" involves some flexibility: it is "not the same as *all* the trade . . . but considerably more than some of the trade".[83] The Appellate Body cautioned that the flexibility of this requirement is limited by the call for "duties and other restrictive regulations of commerce" to be "eliminated" with respect to internal trade.[84]

As to the external trade requirement, the Appellate Body stated that it could examine the issue of whether "substantially the same" duties and other regulations of commerce are applied with respect to external trade with third countries.[85] The Appellate Body, construing this term, agreed with the panel that the word "substantially" refers to both qualitative and quantitative elements.[86] And while there is flexibility here too, this flexibility is limited because "substantially" qualifies "same". Thus, something closely approximating sameness is required.[87]

The second level of analysis is to examine the requirements of Article XXIV:5(a). This involves a consideration of whether "duties and other regulations of commerce" imposed on external trade with WTO members are "not on the whole . . . higher than the general incidence" of the duties imposed by the constituent members of the customs union before its formation.[88]

In interpreting the above-quoted phrase, the Appellate Body relied upon paragraph 2 of the Understanding on the Interpretation of Article XXIV of the GATT 1994. Paragraph 2 requires that the before-and-after evaluation "shall be based upon an overall assessment of weighted average tariff rates and of customs collected".[89] Thus, the valuation compares the *applied* rates of duty

81 *Id.* para. 58.
82 *Id.* para. 47.
83 *Id.* para. 48 (emphasis in original).
84 *Id.* para. 48.
85 *Id.* para. 49.
86 *Id.*
87 *Id.* para. 50.
88 *Id.* para. 51.
89 *Id.* para. 53. Understanding on the Interpretation of Article XXIV of the GATT 1994, above note 20, para. 2.

not merely the *bound* rates. Moreover, with respect to the "other regulations of commerce" issue, paragraph 2 states that because quantification and aggregation of these may be difficult, "the examination of individual regulations, products covered and trade flows affected may be required".[90] This, the Appellate Body pointed out, is an *economic* test for assessing the compatibility of a particular customs union with Article XXIV.[91]

This two-level analysis is required to satisfy the *first* condition to justify a WTO-inconsistent measure. To defend such a measure conclusively, a *second* condition must be met, namely, the chapeau of Article XXIV, paragraph 5, which requires proof that the formation of the customs union would be prevented if the measure were not allowed.[92] Applying this test, the Appellate Body determined that the quotas maintained by Turkey would not have prevented Turkey and the EC from forming a customs union.[93] Specifically, through adopting rules of origin, Turkey could ensure that the EC would distinguish between Turkish-origin clothing and textile products (which enjoy free access to the EC market) and third country clothing and textile products.[94]

Finally, the Appellate Body referred to Article XXIV:4, stating that the purpose of a customs union is to facilitate trade, as setting forth the "overriding and pervasive purpose for Article XXIV". This "informs" the chapeau of paragraph 5 and other relevant provisions of Article XXIV.[95]

The *United States — Line Pipe Safeguard* panel faced an argument by the United States that, as a party to NAFTA, it was entitled to treat imports from NAFTA countries differently from imports from non-NAFTA countries when imposing a safeguard in the form of a tariff quota. The panel addressed the issue of burden of proof: "As the party seeking to rely on an Article XXIV defense . . . the onus is on the United States to demonstrate compliance with these conditions".[96]

The panel addressed the issue of the quantum of proof that the party carrying the burden of proof has to provide to establish a prima facie case of consistency of a PTA with the multilateral rules:

---

[90] As quoted in Appellate Body Report, *Turkey — Textiles*, above note 78, para. 54.

[91] *Id.* para. 55.

[92] *Id.* para. 58.

[93] *Id.* para. 62.

[94] *Id.* para. 62.

[95] *Id.* para. 57.

[96] Panel Report, *United States — Definitive Safeguard Measures on Imports of Circular Welded Carbon Quality Line Pipe*, 29 October 2001, para. 7.142.

> In our view, the information provided by the United States in these proceedings, the information submitted by the NAFTA parties to the Committee on Regional Trade Agreements ("CRTA") (which the United States has incorporated into its submissions to the Panel by reference), and the absence of effective refutation by Korea, establishes a prima facie case that NAFTA is in conformity with Article XXIV:5(b) and (c), and with Article XXIV:8(b).[97]

The information provided by the United States in the proceedings essentially consisted of a statement that duties on 97 percent of the NAFTA-parties' tariff lines will be eliminated within ten years, whereas with respect to "other restrictive regulations of commerce", the United States referred to "the principles of national treatment, transparency, and a variety of other market access rules" contained in NAFTA.[98]

As to the legal significance of the fact that the CRTA had not issued its report at the time the dispute was submitted to the panel, the panel report stated:

> Concerning Article XXVIII:8(b), we do not consider the fact that the CRTA has not yet issued a final decision that NAFTA is in compliance with Article XXIV:8 is sufficient to rebut the prima facie case established by the United States. Korea's argument is based on the premise that a regional trade arrangement is presumed inconsistent with Article XXIV until the CRTA makes a determination to the contrary. We see no basis for such a premise in the relevant provisions of the Agreements Establishing the WTO.[99]

Thus, the WTO adjudicating bodies have made a significant beginning in interpreting Article XXIV in various contexts.

## 5.2 How will PTAs fare in the WTO?

There is every indication that, in the future, the WTO will inject greater discipline into the formation and maintenance of PTAs, as well as derogations based upon Article XXIV of the GATT. In the *Turkey — Textiles* case, the WTO Appellate Body laid the foundation for this effort. Based on the *Turkey — Textiles* analysis, it will be very difficult in the future to use Article XXIV as a shield for WTO-inconsistent measures. In addition, the Appellate Body set out a new interpretative framework for the Article XXIV substantive characteristics of customs unions and free-trade areas. Because the Uruguay Round Understanding on the Interpretation of Article XXIV

97 *Id.* para. 7.144. 98 *Id.* para. 7.142. 99 *Id.* para. 7.144.

of the GATT 1994 specifically subjects even the question of their formation to WTO dispute settlement, the CRTA (Track I) and the Appellate Body (Track II) may be expected to be more active on these issues in the future. The interpretation in *Turkey — Textiles* also more closely aligns the legal analysis of a PTA to economic analysis.

The question may be raised which Track, I or II, will be used to test PTAs in the future?

If a PTA is simultaneously before a panel and the CRTA and the CRTA first rules on the consistency of the PTA with the WTO rules, the panel will most likely follow the opinion reflected in the CRTA. The panel report on *India — Quantitative Restrictions on Imports of Agricultural, Textile and Industrial Products,*[100] which dealt with a similar issue (*i.e.*, to what extent a panel dealing with an issue where the Balance of Payments Committee has already decided), provides that "we see no reason to assume that the panel would not appropriately take those conclusions into account. If the nature of the conclusions were binding[,] . . . a panel should respect them".[101]

The same should be true for panels dealing with PTA-related issues. This, of course, raises the question whether panels should stop short of deciding PTA-related disputes if the CRTA has not pronounced on the overall consistency of the given PTA. Such a "peace clause" does not, of course, exist. Panels could, through their rulings, effectively insert such a peace clause by exercising judicial restraint. Such an approach is hardly recommendable. For if panels were to indeed exercise restraint and avoid ruling on PTA-related issues (in the name of an ill-defined institutional balance), they would be effectively depriving WTO Members of their MFN rights: the CRTA will invariably take a long time to reach consensus and the "consensus" will invariably reflect a disagreement.[102]

Should one view the issue of reviewing a PTA as tantamount to a political question that escapes the judicial review by WTO panels? Are in other ways PTA-related questions not justiciable? Again, the answers should be in the negative.

First, the Understanding on the Interpretation of Article XXIV of the GATT 1994 specifically entrusts adjudicating bodies with the possibility of reviewing PTA-related disputes. Second, the only way one could conceiv-

[100] *See* Panel Report, *India — Quantitative Restrictions on Imports of Agricultural, Textile and Industrial Products,* WT/DS90/R, 6 April 1999.

[101] *Id.* para. 5.94.

[102] For a relatively recent expression of a typical disagreement, see Working Party report on the Free Trade Agreement between EFTA and Turkey, 17 December 1993, L/7336, paras 31–38.

ably make the argument that in this context we are dealing with a political question is by highlighting the rationale for going regional. But the rationale for going regional is the one element that panels cannot put into question. The wording of Article XXIV in itself makes the rationale for going regional a non-concern for subsequent interpretations. In other words, independently of the reasons why a WTO Member decides to opt for regionalism, it must always abide by Article XXIV. Finally, the question of a political question doctrine was raised by India in the balance-of-payments-related dispute mentioned above and was rejected by the Appellate Body essentially on textual grounds.[103] Textual grounds argue in favour of a similar outcome in the PTA context as well: whenever drafters of the GATT wanted to reflect in a legal text their intention to see a relaxed standard of review, they did so in unambiguous terms. It is not accidental that GATT Article XXI, which deals with the security exception (the only genuine political question), reads in a manner that makes it obvious that the margin of discretion rests primarily with the state invoking the exception. This is not the case in Article XXIV, which acknowledges the discretion of multilateral organs to decide whether a given PTA is in conformity with WTO law.

[103] *See* Appellate Body Report, *India — Quantitative Restrictions on Imports of Agricultural, Textile and Industrial Products*, WT/DS90/AB/R, adopted 22 September 1999, paras 98–100.

# 15

# DEVELOPING COUNTRIES



## 1. The developing world

The participation of developing countries in the WTO has increased greatly compared with their participation in the GATT. A majority of the WTO Membership consists of developing countries. During the period of 1980–2000, the share of developing country trade was almost unchanged — 28.8 percent in 1999 compared to 27.4 percent in 1980.[1] Service trade is, however, growing even more rapidly for developing countries than merchandise trade.[2] Yet, developing countries differ greatly in the degree to which

[1] Constantine Michalopoulos, DEVELOPING COUNTRIES IN THE WTO 7–16 (2001).
[2] *Id.* at 15–16.

their economies are integrated into the international trading system. While some have made enormous progress, others still trade largely in a few primary commodities.[3]

It is commonplace to speak rather loosely about "developing" countries, but most people, including many who use the term, do not have a clear idea of its meaning. The World Bank uses a classification system to differentiate between countries based on income.[4] So-called developing countries are divided into *low-income economies* ($755 or less per capita in 2000) and middle-income economies (between $756 and $9,265 per capita). The latter group is divided into *lower-middle-income economies* (between $756 and $2,995 per capita) and *upper-middle-income economies* (between $2,995 and $9,265 per capita). Many upper-middle-income economies also are called "newly industrialized" economies or countries. The fourth group is *high-income economies*, primarily members of the Organisation for Economic Co-operation and Development (OECD), with incomes of $9,266 or more per capita.[5]

The term "developing country" is not defined in the WTO Agreement nor was it defined in the GATT regime. As a result, developing country designation is made on an *ad hoc* basis and primarily through self-selection. The WTO Agreement does, however, provide a reference for "least-developed" countries,[6] namely, those recognized as such by the United Nations.[7]

The term "developing country" is vague because (1) there is a lack of international consensus; and (2) the term is used for different purposes in various international contexts. This ambiguity has caused controversy in the WTO, most notably in the negotiations for the accession of China, which wanted developing country status. At the conclusion of the Uruguay

[3] Constantine Michalopoulos, Developing Countries in the WTO (2001) at 17–20.

[4] World Bank, World Development Indicators 2001 (2001). For more information about the World Bank's classification of economies, see the World Bank's web page on Country Classification (under the Data & Statistics section), http://www.worldbank.org/data/countryclass/countryclass.html.

[5] There are some anomalies in this system of classification. Certain Middle Eastern countries have high per-capita incomes because of oil resources but are not really industrialized. Other economies, such as Singapore and Israel, are considered developing by some international organizations, but have high per-capita incomes. The economies of Eastern Europe, including Russia, are middle-income economies but have many of the characteristics of industrialized countries.

[6] WTO Agreement Art. XI:2.

[7] The UN Committee for Development Planning periodically makes this determination by reference to four criteria: per capita income, population size, quality-of-life index, and economic diversification. UNESCOR, 29th Sess. Supp. No. 2, at 64, 67, U.N. Doc. E/1994/22 (1994).

Round, the United States and the European Union declared that they would not consider certain countries, such as Singapore, Hong Kong, and South Korea, to be developing countries.[8] Both the United States and the EU have adopted their own definitions of developing countries for purposes of their national preference programmes.[9]

## 2. A bit of history

Developing countries played only a small role in the founding of the GATT. Only ten of the original 23 GATT contracting parties were in this category,[10] and developing countries continued to be in the minority until the late 1960s. By May 1970, 52 of the 77 GATT contracting parties could be classified as developing countries. The proportion of developing countries has continued to increase, and developing countries now constitute a large majority of the WTO Membership.

The history of developing countries and the GATT has been written in excellent fashion and will not be repeated here except to note the landmarks that continue to have influence.[11] Historically, developing countries were very critical of the GATT. One of the major challenges has been how to integrate the developing world into the multilateral trading system.

Perhaps the first major initiative was a GATT ministerial decision in November 1957 that cited "the failure of the trade of less developed countries to develop as rapidly as that of industrialized countries" as a major problem.[12] This decision, in turn, produced a study called the Haberler Report,[13] which supported the perception that the export earnings of developing countries were not satisfactory.

---

[8] Alice Alexandra Kipel, *Special and Differential Treatment for Developing Countries, in* The World Trade Organization 617, 624 (Terence P. Stewart ed., 1996).

[9] *See* Report by the Secretary-General of the OECD, The Generalised System of Preferences, Review of the First Decade (1983).

[10] The ten original developing country GATT contracting parties were Brazil, Burma, China, Ceylon, Chile, Cuba, India, Pakistan, Syria, and Lebanon. In the first few years of the GATT, China, Lebanon, and Syria withdrew from the GATT.

[11] *E.g.*, Robert E. Hudec, Developing Countries in the GATT Legal System (1987).

[12] Trends in International Trade, 29 November 1957, GATT B.I.S.D. (6th Supp.) at 18, 2d recital in preamble (1958).

[13] Gottfried Haberler et al., Contracting Parties to the GATT, Trends in International Trade (1958).

In late 1961, Uruguay filed a legal complaint against virtually the entire developed-country membership listing 576 restrictions that allegedly nullified and impaired Uruguayan exports. This litigation, which ended inconclusively in three panel reports,[14] accomplished its main purpose, which was to dramatize the shabby treatment of developing countries. Out of this same milieu, spiced additionally with Cold War rivalries, came the formation of a "rival" organization of sorts, the United Nations Conference on Trade and Development (UNCTAD), which began as a conference but became a permanent UN organization in 1964.[15] The formation of UNCTAD spurred several initiatives within the GATT. First, in 1965, the GATT contracting parties adopted Part IV of the GATT to demonstrate a new concern for the interests of developing countries. Part IV, however, contains no legal obligations. Second, in 1971, the GATT adopted two waivers for two types of preferences to favour developing countries: (1) a set-aside of the MFN obligation to permit a "generalized system of preferences"; and (2) permission for developing countries to exchange tariff preferences among themselves. In 1979, both waivers were made permanent through the so-called Enabling Clause.[16]

The Enabling Clause continues to guide WTO policy:

GATT CONTRACTING PARTIES, DECISION OF NOVEMBER 28, 1979 ON DIFFERENTIAL AND MORE FAVOURABLE TREATMENT, RECIPROCITY AND FULLER PARTICIPATION OF DEVELOPING COUNTRIES

Following negotiations within the framework of the Multilateral Trade Negotiations, the Contracting Parties *decide* as follows:

1. Notwithstanding the provisions of Article I of the General Agreement, contracting parties may accord differential and more favourable treatment to developing countries, without according such treatment to other contracting parties.

[14] Uruguay v. 15 Developed Countries: Recourse to Article XXIII, L/1923 (15 Nov. 1962), GATT B.I.S.D. (11th Supp.) 95; L/2074 (30 Oct. 1963), GATT B.I.S.D. (13th Supp.) 35; L/2278 (27 Oct. 1964), GATT B.I.S.D. (13th Supp.) 45.

[15] UNCTAD, Final Act, United Nations Document E/CONF. 46/141 91964. UNCTAD was established by a subsequent resolution of the UN General Assembly, UN Doc., General Assembly Resolution 1995 (1964).

[16] GATT Contracting Parties, Decision of November 28, 1979 on Differential and More Favourable Treatment, Reciprocity and Fuller Participation on Developing Countries, GATT B.I.S.D. (26th Supp.) at 203 (1980) [hereinafter Enabling Clause]. *See generally* Abdulqawi A. Yusuf, "*Differential and More Favorable Treatment": The GATT Enabling Clause,* 14 J. World Trade L. 488 (1980); General M. Meir, *The Tokyo Round of Multilateral Trade Negotiations and Developing Countries,* 13 Cornell Int'l L.J. 249 (1980).

2. The provisions of paragraph 1 apply to the following:

   (a) Preferential tariff treatment accorded by developed contracting parties to products originating in developing countries in accordance with the Generalized System of Preferences,
   (b) Differential and more favourable treatment with respect to the provisions of the General Agreement concerning non-tariff measures governed by the provisions of instruments multilaterally negotiated under the auspices of the GATT;
   (c) Regional or global arrangements entered into amongst less-developed contracting parties for the mutual reduction or elimination of tariffs and, in accordance with criteria or conditions which may be prescribed by the Contracting Parties for the mutual reduction or elimination of non-tariff measures, on products imported from one another;
   (d) Special treatment of the least developed among the developing countries in the context of any general or specific measures in favor of developing countries.

3. Any differential and more favourable treatment provided under this clause:

   (a) shall be designed to facilitate and promote the trade of developing countries and not raise barriers to or create undue difficulties for the trade of any other contracting parties;
   (b) shall not constitute an impediment to the reduction or elimination of tariffs and other restrictions to trade on a most-favored-nation basis;
   (c) shall in the case of such treatment accorded by developed contracting parties to developing countries be designed and, if necessary, modified, to respond positively to the development, financial and trade needs of developing countries.

. . .

5. The developed countries do not expect reciprocity for commitments made by them in trade negotiations to reduce or remove tariffs and other barriers to the trade of developing countries, i.e., the developed countries do not expect the developing countries, in the course of trade negotiations, to make contributions which are inconsistent with their individual development, financial and trade needs. Developed contracting parties shall therefore not seek, neither shall less-developed contracting parties be required to make, concessions that are inconsistent with the latters' development, financial and trade needs.
6. Having regard to the specific economic difficulties and the particular development, financial and trade needs of the least-developed countries, the developed countries shall exercise the utmost restraint in seeking any concessions or contributions for commitments made by them to reduce or remove tariffs and other barriers to the trade of such countries, and the least-developed countries shall not be expected to make concessions or contributions that are inconsistent with the recognition of their particular situation and problems.
7. The concessions and contributions made and the obligations assumed by developed and less-developed contracting parties under the provisions of the General Agreement should promote the basic objectives of the Agreement, including those embodied in the Preamble and in Article XXXVI. Less-developed contracting parties expect that their

> capacity to make contributions or negotiated concessions or take other mutually agreed action under the provisions and procedures of the General Agreement would improve with the progressive development of their economies and improvement in their trade situation and they would accordingly expect to participate more fully in the framework of rights and obligations under the General Agreement.[17]

The Enabling Clause settled a debate within the GATT and established the policy of special and preferential treatment for developing countries. At the same time, the Enabling Clause contains a so-called graduation clause,[18] which is the policy that eventually preferential treatment should end. Implementation of this policy remains controversial.

The Uruguay Round continued the policy of special and preferential treatment for developing countries. Most WTO agreements contain exceptions, longer phase-in periods, or special provisions for developing countries. Some agreements, such as the agreements on textiles and agriculture, adopt policies long sought by developing countries. Others, such as the TRIPS Agreement, the TRIMs Agreement, and the GATS, were viewed as concessions. Overall, the Uruguay Round was mixed in terms of benefits for developing countries.[19]

Nevertheless, under the WTO, there is a new concern for developing countries. This concern is not only recognition of their political power now that they comprise a majority of WTO Members, but also new recognition that, overall, trade liberalization is beneficial rather than detrimental to economic development.

Developing countries now play a key role in the WTO and have cast aside their past reluctance to use dispute settlement procedures.[20] They see increasing benefit in an effective rule-based system that can protect small or weak countries, but they still hold the view that developed countries have not lived up to their commitments to provide special and preferential treatment to developing countries.

The WTO has retained the viewpoint prevalent during the Uruguay Round negotiations that trade liberalization within a framework of internationally agreed rules benefits developed and developing countries alike. The WTO has called for special attention to developing countries to

---

[17] Enabling Clause, above note 16.

[18] *Id.* para. 7.

[19] In a decision taken at Cologne in June 1999, the Group of Eight (G8) major industrialized countries agreed to provide debt relief to developing countries. G8 Cologne Communique 1999.

[20] Michalopoulos, above note 1, at 167–70.

increase trade and investment and for a common Africa initiative.[21] The first WTO Ministerial Conference, held in Singapore in 1996, adopted the following declaration:

> **Developing Countries**
>
> 13. The integration of developing countries in the multilateral trading system is important for their economic development and for global trade expansion. In this connection, we recall that the WTO Agreement embodies provisions conferring differential and more favourable treatment for developing countries, including special attention to the particular situation of least-developed countries. We acknowledge the fact that developing country Members have undertaken significant new commitments, both substantive and procedural, and we recognize the range and complexity of the efforts that they're making to comply with them. In order to assist them in these efforts, including those with respect to notification and legislative requirements, we will improve the availability of technical assistance under the agreed guidelines. We have also agreed to recommendations relative to the decision we took at Marrakesh concerning the possible negative effects of the agricultural reform programme on least-developed and net-food-importing developing countries.
>
> **Least-Developed Countries**
>
> 14. We remain concerned by the problems of the least-developed countries and have agreed to . . . a Plan of Action, including provision for taking positive measures, for example duty-free access, on an autonomous basis, aimed at improving their overall capacity to respond to the opportunities offered by the trading system; . . .[22]

In 1997, as a follow-up to the First Ministerial Conference, there was a high-level meeting in Geneva to adopt an Integrated Framework for trade-related assistance to least-developed countries (LDCs). The participants, which included the IMF, the World Bank, UNCTAD, and the UN Development Program, undertook to provide technical and financial assistance for institution building in LDCs.[23]

At the Doha Ministerial Conference in 2001, the WTO continued its concerns for developing country Members. The Declaration[24] and the Implementation Decision[25] adopted at the Ministerial Conference call for

[21] WTO Focus, No. 11 (June–July 1996).

[22] WTO, Ministerial Conference, Singapore, 9–13 December 1996, *Singapore Ministerial Declaration*, WT/MIN(96)/DEC, 18 December 1996, paras 13, 14.

[23] Michalopoulos, above note 1, at 96–97.

[24] WTO, Ministerial Conference, Fourth Session, Doha, 9–14 November 2001, *Ministerial Declaration*, WT/MIN(01)/DEC/1, 20 November 2001 [hereinafter *Doha Ministerial Declaration*].

[25] WTO, Ministerial Conference, Fourth Session, Doha, 9–14 November 2001, *Implementation-Related Issues and Concerns*, WT/MIN(01)/DEC/17, 20 November 2001.

new WTO initiatives in three areas: (1) initiatives to provide market access in product areas of particular concern to developing countries, such as agriculture and textiles; (2) additional special and differential treatment provisions in WTO agreements to benefit developing countries; and (3) technical assistance to increase the capacity of developing countries to implement WTO obligations and to participate more fully in the WTO.

## 3. GATT Article XX(h)

Article XX(h) of the GATT provides a general exception to GATT rules for International Commodity Agreements conforming to criteria set out by the UN Economic and Social Council.[26] International Commodity Agreements, which are essentially producer cartels, have been established at the urging of UNCTAD[27] for several commodities such as cocoa, tin, oil, cotton, coffee, and copper. With the possible exception of OPEC (the Organization of Petroleum Exporting Countries), the oil cartel, none has been very successful, and most are moribund.[28]

## 4. GATT Article XVIII

Article XVIII of the GATT was the original GATT privilege accorded to developing countries. Article XVIII permits developing countries to raise tariffs and use other means to protect so-called infant industries.[29] The infant industry idea is one of the oldest arguments in favour of protectionism. Modern economic analysis has shown, however, that there are costs associated with such protectionism, and that application of the infant industry idea should be preceded by careful analysis on a case-by-case basis.[30] The GATT accepts infant industry protection, albeit reluctantly, and sets out general criteria and a procedure for its application.

---

[26] Resolution 30 (IV) of 28 March 1947.

[27] Michael J. Trebilcock and Robert Howse, The Regulation of International Trade 379 (2d ed. 1999).

[28] Michalopoulos, above note 1, at 32–33.

[29] For example, Ceylon (Sri Lanka) was found to have met these criteria. *See* Report of the Panel on Article XXIII Applications by Ceylon, GATT B.I.S.D. (6th Supp.) at 14, 112 (1958).

[30] *See* Robert Gilpin, The Political Economy of International Relations 184–87 (1987).

WTO Members whose economy "can only support low standards of living and is in the early stages of development" may invoke Section A, B, or C of Article XVIII.

Under Section A, a developing country may withdraw or modify a schedule concession "to promote the establishment of a particular industry with a view to raising the general standard of living of its people". To do so, it must (1) notify the WTO (formerly the GATT), (2) negotiate with affected parties, and (3) agree on a compensatory adjustment. If agreement cannot be reached on a compensatory adjustment, the matter can be referred to the WTO Council (formerly the GATT contracting parties) for a ruling on the adequacy of the adjustment.

Under Section B, a developing country may impose quotas for balance-of-payments reasons under slightly different criteria than the more general Article XII.[31] This matter is considered in Chapter 2.

Under Section C, a developing country may grant governmental assistance "to promote the establishment of a particular industry with a view to raising the general standard of living of its people". Granting governmental assistance requires a finding by the contracting parties that no such measure consistent with the GATT "is practicable". Although the applicant party may implement the measure without the concurrence of the contracting parties upon the passage of 90 days after notification to the contracting parties, affected parties may withdraw equivalent concessions. There can be no exemption from the discipline of GATT Articles I, II, or XIII under this Section. Thus, most-favoured-nation and bound tariff obligations must be respected in implementing this concession.

Under Section D, a country that is in the process of development, but that does not meet the criterion of low living standards, may apply for permission to deviate from GATT rules to establish a particular industry. Section D would seem to apply to countries like Saudi Arabia.

Article XVIII has, overall, proved to be an inadequate vehicle for lifting poor countries out of poverty. Despite the GATT Council's practice of granting sweeping concessions without requiring compensation, allowing developing countries to pursue import substitution and infant industry protection under Article XVIII, Section A (as well as through GATT waivers),[32] economic benefits were limited. First, empirical evidence shows that liberal trade policies are usually better than import substitution

[31] GATT Arts XVIII and XII were redrafted in 1954–55.

[32] Hudec, above note 11, Ch. 2.

policies.[33] Second, even if infant industry protection achieves a modicum of success, there is no guarantee of access to export markets,[34] and the internal market of most developing countries will be too small to achieve economies of scale in most cases.

The other Sections of Article XVIII are likewise of limited value. Section B of Article XVIII comes into play, if at all, only to avert disaster, not to spur economic growth. Sections C and D may be marginally useful, but history has failed to show (putting it mildly) that government assistance is effective to stimulate economic growth, and developing countries do not have the means for such assistance in any event. Thus, Article XVIII is a poor and ineffective way to integrate developing countries into the international trading system.

## 5. Part IV of the GATT

Part IV of the GATT was added in 1965 as a result of the 1958 Haberler Report and the political initiatives of developing countries in the 1960s.[35] Part IV consists of Articles XXXVI, XXXVII, and XXXVIII.

Article XXXVI is a hortatory provision of "Principles and Objectives" stating the need to raise standards of living in developing countries, the need for "rapid and sustained expansion" of their export earnings, and increased access to world markets for their products. Article XXXVI sets out the principle that developed countries "do not expect reciprocity" for their commitments to remove or reduce tariffs and other trade barriers.[36] This principle is repeated in the Enabling Clause.[37] Developing countries have relied on this principle in trade negotiations and application for waivers.[38] Article XXXVI also sets out the principle that developed countries should

[33] *See* Trebilcock and Howse, above note 27, at 370–71, 394.

[34] *Id.*

[35] Protocol Amending the General Agreement on Tariffs and Trade to Introduce a Part IV on Trade and Development and to Amend Annex I, done at Geneva, 8 February 1965, 17 U.S.T. 1977, T.I.A.S. No. 6139, 572 U.N.T.S 320 (entered into force 27 June 1966).

[36] GATT Art. XXXVI:8.

[37] *See* Enabling Clause, above note 16, para. 5.

[38] *See* 2 Guide to GATT Law and Practice 1057 (6th ed. 1995) [hereinafter GATT Analytical Index].

collaborate with developing countries by consulting with them before taking action that would adversely affect their interests.[39]

Article XXXVII is entitled "Commitments" but has had little direct effect. The commitments of paragraph 1 are quite general and are qualified by the phrase "except when compelling reasons, which may include legal reasons, make it impossible...." Paragraphs 2 and 5 contain obligations to consult and report. Paragraph 3 reflects the aspirations of developing countries to obtain a "standstill" on tariff increases on their products and exemption from actions otherwise permitted under the GATT such as antidumping, countervailing duties, and safeguards.[40] These commitments are qualified, however, by the phrases "make every effort", "give active consideration", and "have special regard". These qualifications render the obligations nugatory.

Article XXVIII requires "Joint Action" by the parties to further the objectives of Article XXXVI. Paragraph 2(f) requires the establishment of "such institutional arrangements as may be necessary". Part IV has very limited effect without the additional measures contemplated by these provisions.

## 6. The generalized system of preferences

Part IV of the GATT was a disappointment for many developing countries that had hoped to get new provisions allowing preferences. The demand for preferences was finally granted in 1971 when the GATT contracting parties adopted waivers authorizing the Generalized System of Preferences (GSP)[41] and tariff preferences among developing countries.[42] These two waivers became permanent policy through the adoption of the Enabling Clause in 1979.[43] Between 1971 and 1976, most OECD countries, including the

[39] GATT Art. XXXVI:6 and :7. *See European Communities — Refunds on Exports of Sugar — Complaint by Brazil*, 10 November 1980, GATT B.I.S.D. (27th Supp.) at 69, para. 25 (1981); *European Economic Community — Restrictions on Imports of Dessert Apples — Complaint by Chile*, 22 June 1989, GATT B.I.S.D. (36th Supp.) at 93, para. 12.32 (1990) (noting that consultations between the EEC and Chile, a less-developed country, had not related specifically to the interests of less-developed countries in terms of Part IV, but declining to make a finding under Part IV because the panel found the import restrictions to be inconsistent with obligations under Part II).

[40] *See* GATT Analytical Index, above note 38, at 1059–62.

[41] Decision of 25 June 1971, GATT B.I.S.D. (18th Supp.) at 24 (1969).

[42] Decision of 26 November 1971, GATT B.I.S.D. (18th Supp.) at 26.

[43] *See* Enabling Clause, above note 16, para. 2.

United States and the EU/EC, implemented the GSP by adopting national legislation authorizing tariff preferences for developing countries.[44] These GSP programmes generally provide duty-free treatment for industrial products and reduced tariffs for agricultural products.[45] The United States has implemented GSP through Title V of the Trade Act of 1974[46] as well as programmes to benefit certain geographical areas.[47] The EU/EC supplements its GSP programmes with an international convention, the Cotonou Agreement, conferring broad benefits on 77 (including 55 WTO Members) associated nations from Africa, the Caribbean, and the Pacific (so-called ACP countries).[48]

The predecessor to the Cotonou Agreement, known as Lomé IV,[49] was the subject of extensive litigation in the WTO in the famous *Bananas* case.[50] In this case, the EU/EC's scheme for giving a preference to bananas from ACP countries was found to be inconsistent with Article I of the GATT as well as several other WTO agreements.[51] The Appellate Body also ruled that the GATT waiver in connection with Lomé IV did not justify derogations from fundamental WTO obligations.[52] This unfortunate dispute pitted developing countries from Latin America against developing countries from the Caribbean as well as the United States against the EU/EC. After much acrimony, the matter was settled by a waiver adopted at the Doha Ministerial Conference in 2001.[53]

These GSP programmes have had limited impact on the economic development of beneficiary countries. The range of products allowed duty-free treatment is limited by political considerations, and the list of beneficiary countries is often arbitrary. Rule-of-origin criteria are strictly applied to exclude even bona fide products: U.S. courts have held that a double substantial transformation is required before goods made from imported parts

[44] Michalopoulos, above note 1, at 29–33.

[45] See the UNCTAD website (unctad.org) for updated GSP systems in various countries.

[46] 19 U.S.C.A. §§ 2461–2467.

[47] Caribbean Basin Trade Partnership Act, 19 U.S.C.A. §§ 2707–2707; Andean Trade Preferences Act, 19 U.S.C.A. §§ 3201–3206; African Growth and Opportunity Act; 19 U.S.C.A. §§ 3701–3741.

[48] Cotonou Agreement (2000) text available at http://europa.eu.int/comm/development/cotonou/agreement_en.htm.

[49] 17 August 1991, O.J. (L 229) 3.

[50] Panel Report, *EC — Bananas*; Appellate Body Report, *EC — Bananas*.

[51] Appellate Body Report, *EC — Bananas*.

[52] *Id.*

[53] Inside U.S. Trade, 15 November 2001, at 10.

qualify.[54] In addition to at least 35-percent value added, the constituent materials of the eligible article must be "wholly the growth, product or manufacture of the beneficiary developing country".[55] Rules such as these render GSP treatment very technical and uncertain for developing country exporters.

As Constantine Michalopoulos, a senior official at the World Bank, has stated, "the GSP turned out to be less than it has been touted to be at its inception. It was important for some products, for some countries, for some of the time. But it [has not] served to strengthen the integration of developing countries into the world trading system".[56]

## 7. The Global System of Trade Preferences

A second UNCTAD initiative authorized by both the 1971 GATT waivers and the Enabling Clause[57] is the so-called Global System of Trade Preferences (GSTP), which allows developing countries to maintain preferences in trade with each other on a global basis. The GSTP Agreement,[58] which has been signed by 46 developing countries, provides for most-favoured-nation treatment between the signatories.[59] The GSTP has not, however, had much effect, and increased trade among developing countries has failed to materialize.[60]

## 8. Special and differential treatment provisions for developing countries in the Uruguay Round

Virtually all WTO agreements contain special provisions with respect to developing country Members. The WTO has classified the so-called special

[54] *Torrington Co. v. United States*, 764 F.2d 1563 (Fed. Cir. 1985).

[55] 19 U.S.C.A. § 2463(b)(1) overruling *Madison Galleries Ltd. v. United States*, 870 F.2d 627 (Fed. Cir. 1989).

[56] Michalopoulos, above note 1, at 30.

[57] Enabling Clause, above note 16.

[58] Text available at http://www.g77.org/gstp/gstptext.htm.

[59] Robert E. Hudec, *The Structure of South-South Trade Preferences in the 1988 GSTP Agreement: Learning to Say MFMFN*, *in* 1 Developing Countries and the Global Trading System 53 (J. Whalley ed., 1989).

[60] Trebilcock and Howse, above note 27, at 378.

and differential (S&D) provisions into the following six categories: (1) "provisions aimed at increasing the trade opportunities of developing country Members"; (2) "provisions under which WTO Members should safeguard the interests of developing country Members"; (3) "flexibility of commitments, of action, and use of policy instruments"; (4) transitional time periods; (5) technical assistance; and (6) "provisions relating to least-developed country Members".[61]

Using this typology, the WTO Secretariat has identified 145 separate provisions for S&D treatment contained in the WTO agreements.[62]

1. *Increasing Trade Opportunities.* Twelve S&D provisions in four WTO agreements require action by Members to increase trade opportunities for developing countries.
2. *Safeguarding Interests.* Forty-nine S&D provisions in 13 WTO agreements require Members to take or avoid taking actions to safeguard the interests of developing countries.
3. *Flexibility Provisions.* Thirty S&D provisions in nine WTO agreements allow developing countries exemptions or a reduced level of commitments.
4. *Transitional Periods.* Eighteen S&D provisions in eight WTO agreements allow developing countries transition periods to comply with WTO commitments.
5. *Technical Assistance.* Fourteen provisions in six WTO agreements provide for technical as well as financial assistance to developing countries.
6. *Least-Developed Countries.* Twenty-two provisions in seven WTO agreements cover one or more of the previous five areas but apply only to least-developed country Members.

As far as specific agreements are concerned, there follows a brief summary of the most important S&D provisions:

1. *WTO Agreement.* The WTO Agreement establishes a Committee on Trade and Development that will report periodically on special treatment for least-developed country Members and recommend appropriate action to the WTO Council (Article IV:7). Least-developed country Members

[61] WTO, Committee on Trade and Development, *Implementation of Special and Differential Treatment Provisions in WTO Agreements and Decisions*, WT/COMTD/W/77, 25 October 2000, at 3.

[62] *Id.*

will be required to undertake trade concessions only to the extent consistent with their individual development, financial and trade needs, or their administrative and institutional capabilities (Article XI:2).

2. *Dispute Settlement Understanding.* Developing country Members are granted additional time for consultation and to answer a complaint (Article 12.10). Special procedures apply to least-developed countries: Members must exercise "due restraint" in raising disputes and asking for compensation (Article 24).

3. *The SCM Agreement.* Developing countries may retain subsidies critical to their economic well being and development (Article 27). These include exemptions, extensions of time, and grace periods. For example, least-developed countries are exempt from the ban on export subsidies.

4. *The Agriculture Agreement.* There are transition time periods (Article 15.2), special exemptions, such as for domestic support reduction commitments (Article 6), and special consideration is required for the effect of the Agreement on least-developed and net-food-importing developing countries (Article 16).

5. *The Agreement on Textiles and Clothing (ATC).* The ATC is intended to benefit least-developing countries as well as developing countries (Preamble and Article 1.2). There are special exemptions from safeguard measures in favour of least-developing countries (Article 6).

6. *The TBT Agreement and the SPS Agreement.* The TBT and SPS Agreements accord similar special treatment to developing countries. This includes provision for technical assistance, special phase-in allowances and particularized notification of other countries' standard-setting and regulatory activities.

7. *The TRIMs Agreement.* The TRIMs Agreement contains an exemption for balance-of-payments measures of developing countries (Article 4) and an expanded transitional period (Article 5).

8. *The Safeguards Agreement.* There are special favourable rules concerning the imposition of safeguard measures against developing countries and the duration of such safeguard measures (Article 9).

9. *The Antidumping Agreement.* WTO Members must explore "constructive remedies" before the application of antidumping duties that would affect "the essential interests" of developing country Members (Article 15).

10. *The GATS.* The General Agreement on Trade in Services (GATS) provides for increased participation of developing countries and flexibility and exemptions regarding liberalization measures.

11. *The TRIPS Agreement.* The TRIPS Agreement accords longer periods for compliance to developing countries (Articles 65 and 66).
12. *The Customs Valuation Agreement.* When joining the WTO, developing country Members may delay the implementation of the Valuation Agreement for up to five years (Article 20).

## 9. Trade and economic development

Developing countries continue to regard it in their interests to be WTO Members to facilitate their economic development. No single factor is responsible for under-development. No one policy can set in motion the complex process of economic development, but trade is considered one important component of any development policy.[63]

Yet, tensions and disagreements between developed and developing countries continue; the latter expect a greater degree of special treatment than industrialized countries have afforded them. This demand was expressed comprehensively in the New International Economic Order and the Charter of Economic Rights and Duties of States[64] promoted by UNCTAD in the 1970s. Although the Charter was never accepted by developing countries and is now dead, the political, economic, and social concerns that inspired it are still present. The Charter called for restitution for the economic and social costs of colonialism, racial discrimination, and foreign domination.[65] It would have imposed a duty on all states to adjust

[63] At the first session of UNCTAD in 1964, Secretary General Raol Prebisch presented a report that first broached the idea that preferential tariff rates were a key to economic development in the "Third World".

[64] The New International Economic Order was the subject of two UNGA resolutions: (a) a Declaration; and (b) an Action Programme. *See* G.A. Res. 3201, 3202 (S–IV) May 1, 1974 (adopted without vote) and G.A. Res. 3281 (XXIX) Dec. 12, 1974 (vote of 120–6, ten abstentions). *See* 14 I.L.M. 251. *See generally* Mohammed Bedjaoui, Towards a New International Economic Order (1979); The New International Economic Order: Commercial, Technological and Cultural Aspects (René-Jean Dupuy ed., 1981); Marthinus Gerhardus Erasmus, The New International Economic Order and International Organizations (1979); Legal Aspects of the New International Economic Order (Kamal Hossain ed., 1980); Oswaldo de Rivero, New International Order and International Development Law (1982); Pieter Verloren Van Themaat, The Changing Structure of International Economic Law (1981); Abdulqawi A. Yusuf, Legal Aspects of Trade Preferences for Developing States (1982).

[65] Art. 16.

the prices of exports to their imports.[66] The realization of the New International Economic Order was an impetus for developing country support for the Tokyo Round of trade negotiations.[67] Critics of the WTO continue to state that little of substance for developing countries came out of either the Tokyo or Uruguay Rounds.[68]

Second, states continue to disagree on trade policy issues relating to developing countries. Traditionally, developing countries wanted to obtain preferential access for their exports while pursuing restrictive import substitution policies and controls on investment in their home markets. While many developing countries have become more open to trade and investment, a degree of the older policy persists. There also are differences regarding the effect of including environmental and labour policies into trade concerns. Developing countries generally regard these policies as devices to limit their exports.

While developing countries are in the majority, they do not yet play a key role in many WTO initiatives and institutions, often because they lack the administrative and institutional capacities to participate fully in the WTO organizational structures. As this is remedied, developing countries are sure to be stronger voices within the WTO.

## 10. Trade and the right to development

The United Nations has proclaimed the existence of a human right to development.[69] This right refers not only to economic growth but also to human welfare, including health, education, employment, social security, and a wide-range of other human needs.[70] This human right to development is vaguely defined as a so-called third-generation human right that cannot be implemented in the same way as civil and political human

---

[66] Art. 28.

[67] GATT B.I.S.D. (20th Supp.) at 21 (1974).

[68] *See* the speeches by world leaders at the WTO Second Ministerial Conference in Geneva held in May 1998, reprinted in WTO Focus, No. 31 (June 1998), available at http://www.wto.org/english/res_e/focus_e/focus31_e.pdf.

[69] *See* UN Declaration on the Right to Development, Res. 41/128 (1986), available at http://www.unhchr.ch/html/menu3/b/74.htm; UN General Assembly Resolutions 2542 and 2586 (XXIV 1969) and 2626 (XXV 1970).

[70] *See* Oscar Schachter, International Law in Theory and Practice 348–52 (1991).

rights.[71] Rather, it is the obligation of states and intergovernmental organizations to work within the scope of their authority to combat poverty and misery in disadvantaged countries.[72]

There is common ground between this human right to development and WTO initiatives concerning developing countries. The human right to development is best understood as a "right to a particular process of development" and "eliminating obstacles to development".[73] The WTO's contribution to this process consists of (1) preferential treatment for developing countries based on the concept of non-reciprocity; and (2) special and differential treatment for developing countries. Special and differential treatment requires WTO Members to safeguard the interests of developing countries and allows flexibility to developing countries in meeting WTO commitments.

## 11. Enhancing market access

In the almost 25 years since the developing country initiatives of the 1970s culminated in the Enabling Clause, a radical shift has overtaken the developing country debate. Almost without exception, developing countries now espouse outwardly oriented economic policies: they seek to promote exports, reduce trade barriers, and attract foreign investment.[74] The successful conclusion of the Uruguay Round was possible because of this change in policy. Yet, developing countries contend that the results of the Uruguay Round do little to benefit developing countries.[75] They argue that economic sectors of particular interest to developing countries, such as textiles, clothing, and agricultural products, remain outside the WTO's drive towards economic liberalization. With respect to services, they con-

[71] *See* Oscar Schachter, above note 70.

[72] Isabella D. Bunn, *The Right to Development: Implications for International Economic Law*, 15 AM. U. INT'L L. REV. 1425, 1467 (2000).

[73] *Study on the Current State of Progress in the Implementation of the Right to Development*, U.N. Doc. E/CN. 4/1999/WG. 18/2, 27 July 1999. *See generally* Hoe Lim, *Trade and Human Rights*, 35 J. WORLD TRADE, No. 2, at 275 (2001); F. V. García-Amador, THE EMERGING INTERNATIONAL LAW OF DEVELOPMENT (2000).

[74] Robert Z. Lawrence et al., EMERGING AGENDA FOR GLOBAL TRADE: HIGH STAKES FOR DEVELOPING COUNTRIES 4 (1996).

[75] Asoke Mukerig, *Developing Countries and the WTO*, 34 J. WORLD TRADE, No. 6, at 33, 39–40 (2000).

tend that sectors and modes of supply of potential benefit to developing countries have been ignored.[76]

Thus, enhanced market access is one of the key needs and demands of developing countries.[77] There are three aspects to this market access problem. The first is to dismantle overt tariffs and other border measures maintained by developed countries on products of vital concern to developing country exporters.[78] The second is to examine market access barriers to developing countries in existing WTO agreements and to consider whether special and differential treatment measures are needed to enhance market access potential. The third is to consider carefully developing countries' market access problems when addressing new issues, such as rules of origin, investment competition, the environment, and labour. Any agreements in these areas must be drafted with developing countries and the potential impact on their market access in mind.

## 12. New initiatives

Developing countries in the WTO have three categories of special needs. First, they often lack the technical and financial resources to participate fully in and implement fully WTO agreements. Thus, the WTO should make available financial and technical assistance. Second, special attention should be given to improving market access for developing countries in certain key economic areas, such as agriculture and textiles. Third, although virtually all WTO agreements contain "Special and Differential" provisions for developing countries, further attention should be given to such matters. These provisions should be evaluated carefully and, if necessary, extended.

Freer trade under the aegis of the WTO has and will continue to benefit developing countries. Trade and investment boost economic growth, and developing countries currently are very active in the dispute settlement process and other WTO forums.

At the Fourth WTO Ministerial Conference in Doha in November 2001, several initiatives were approved to benefit developing countries. First, in the Doha Round of trade negotiations, special attention must be given to provide market access for both agricultural and non-agricultural

[76] *Id.*

[77] Michalopoulos, above note 1, at 208–14.

[78] *Id.* at 214–15.

products from developing countries. The WTO Members reaffirmed that preferences granted to developing countries under the Enabling Clause should be generalized, non-reciprocal, and non-discriminatory. For the category of least-developed countries, WTO Members committed themselves to the objective of duty-free, quota-free market access for products originating in such countries.

Second, the WTO created a Working Group to examine the relationship between trade, debt and finance. This Working Group will enable the WTO to work with the World Bank, the International Monetary Fund, and the Group of Eight (G8) major industrialized countries on debt reduction of developing countries.[79]

Third, the WTO approved a broad initiative offering technical and financial assistance to developing countries to enable them to participate meaningfully in WTO activities. The WTO Secretariat was further instructed to work in coordination with other agencies to support domestic efforts for mainstreaming trade into national plans for economic development and strategies for poverty reduction.

Fourth, the WTO reaffirmed the provisions for Special and Differential Treatment (SDT) for developing countries and agreed to investigate the feasibility of concluding an SDT Framework Agreement to make Special and Differential Treatment "more precise, effective and operational".[80] SDT will be an agenda item on all WTO implementation issues and concerns. These issues range from investment to technical barriers to trade to subsidies and antidumping.

Fifth, in the area of intellectual property (IP) protection, developing country concerns are to be given special attention:

1. The WTO will examine the relationship between TRIPS and the IP provisions of the UN Convention on Biological Diversity;
2. New incentives will be proposed to facilitate transfer of technology to developing countries;
3. Developing countries will have freedom to use compulsory licensing and undertake other initiatives to combat national health emergencies without being impeded by TRIPS obligations;
4. The deadline for compliance with key provisions of the TRIPS Agreement is extended to 1 January 2016 for least-developed countries.

[79] *See* the web site of the Trade and Development Centre, a joint venture of the World Bank and the World Trade Organization at http://www.itd.org/.

[80] *Doha Ministerial Declaration*, above note 24, para. 44.

Finally, there is a need for greater coherence between trade policies and other policies aimed at promoting economic growth in developing countries. Article III:5 of the WTO Agreement mandates greater coherence in global economic policy making, but this has been lacking in the past. For example, the World Bank and the UN Development Program reduced their assistance for trade-related capacity building in developing countries in 1995, just when these countries were called on to take complex and costly implementation of their Uruguay Round commitments.[81] In 1998, discussions among the WTO, World Bank, and the IMF finally led to cooperative agreements by these three institutions.[82] This should lead to greater coherence among the three Bretton Woods institutions, so they may become the focal point for coherence with other international and national agencies concerned with the developing world.

[81] Michalopoulos, above note 1, at 240.
[82] *Id.* at 239.

# 16

# INTELLECTUAL PROPERTY

## 1. Introduction

The link between intellectual property and trade in the WTO calls for explanation.[1] Unlike most other Uruguay Round agreements, the Agreement on Trade-Related Aspects of Intellectual Property Rights (TRIPS

[1] For a critical view of the trade and intellectual property link, see generally R. Michael Gadbaw, *Intellectual Property and International Trade: Merger or Marriage of Convenience?*, 22 VAND J. TRANS L. 223 (1989).

Agreement) is not an elaboration of a subject covered in GATT 1947. In fact, the GATT is devoid of any mention of intellectual property (IP) rights.

Historically, the link between IP and trade was forged under the leadership of the United States.[2] After the close of the Tokyo Round in 1979, the United States became concerned and frustrated by the reluctance of developing countries to adopt high normative standards and strict enforcement measures for IP rights. Initiatives under the auspices of the World Intellectual Property Organization (WIPO) and the principal international conventions on IP came to no avail, so the United States successfully placed IP on the negotiating agenda for the Uruguay Round.[3] The linkage between IP and trade was based on two points. First, widespread piracy, counterfeiting and infringement of IP rights constitute a barrier to trade in that the availability of such goods diminishes market access for legitimately traded goods. This point has merit, but the premise on which it is based — strong IP rights — appeals to developed countries, which will benefit, but does not necessarily appeal to developing countries. Second, there is a link between trade and IP through IP rights transfer agreements. National regulation of such agreements is common and is generally of two types: (1) notification; and (2) registration and approval. U.S. negotiators were concerned that burdensome registration and approval requirements in certain countries inhibited investment and IP licensing and, therefore, trade. This position is controversial and may be disagreeable to developing countries. Thus, the negotiation of the TRIPS Agreement was primarily one between developed and developing countries of the GATT. The latter accepted the TRIPS Agreement reluctantly as part of the Uruguay Round package deal.[4]

The Agreement on Trade-Related Aspects of Intellectual Property Rights (TRIPS Agreement),[5] which entered into force on 1 January 1995 along with the other WTO agreements, is largely an affirmation of the position of the industrialized world in the trade and IP debate. The TRIPS Agreement provides relatively high minimum standards for each of the main categories of intellectual property rights, establishes standards of protection and

---

[2] *See generally* Daniel Gervais, The TRIPS Agreement: Drafting History and Analysis (1998).

[3] Paul Goldstein, International Intellectual Property Law 110 (2001).

[4] Michael Trebilcock and Robert Howse, The Regulation of International Trade (2nd edn., 1999), 320–321.

[5] Agreement on Trade-Related Aspects of Intellectual Property Rights in WTO, The Legal Texts: The Results of the Uruguay Round of Multilateral Trade Negotiations 321 (1999) [hereinafter TRIPS Agreement].

enforcement, and provides for the application of the WTO dispute settlement mechanism to resolve disputes between WTO Members. The TRIPS Agreement does, however, not resolve many issues resulting from different intellectual property regimes in different countries. For example, the United States employs a first-to-invent criterion for priority in patent applications,[6] while the rest of the world uses a first-to-file system.[7] This discrepancy was not harmonized under the TRIPS Agreement.

One of the first international agreements for the protection of intellectual property rights was the Paris Convention,[8] signed in 1883 and the subject of successive revisions. The Paris Convention requires national treatment, but lacks provisions for effective enforcement or dispute settlement. In the field of copyright, the Berne Convention[9] also lacks effective enforcement provisions.

The World Intellectual Property Organization,[10] a specialized agency of the United Nations whose mandate is to promote the protection of intellectual property, administers the Paris and Berne Conventions and other intellectual property treaties. WIPO administers some 23 intellectual property treaties,[11] including the following:

- The Madrid Agreement for the Repression of False and Deceptive Indications of Source on Goods,[12]
- The Madrid Agreement Concerning the International Registration of Marks,[13]

---

[6] 35 U.S.C.A. § 102(g) (2001).

[7] *See* Harold C. Wegner, *TRIPS Boomerang: Obligations for Domestic Reform*, 29 VAND. J. TRANSNAT'L L. 535 (1996).

[8] Paris Convention for the Protection of Industrial Property, 20 March 1883, as last revised at Stockholm, 14 July 1967, 21 U.S.T. 1538 [hereinafter Paris Convention].

[9] Berne Convention for the Protection of Literary and Artistic Works, 9 September 1886, as last revised at Paris, 24 July 1971 (amended 1979), 828 U.N.T.S. 221 [hereinafter Berne Convention].

[10] Convention Establishing the World Intellectual Property Organization, 14 July 1967, 8 U.N.T.S. 3 [hereinafter WIPO].

[11] The treaties administered by WIPO are available on the WIPO web page entitled Treaties and Contracting Parties, http://www.wipo.org/treaties/index.html. A good general reference work is Frederick Abbott, Thomas Cottier, and Francis Gurry, *The International Intellectual Property System*, Parts One and Two (1999).

[12] 14 April 1891, revised at Washington (1911), The Hague (1925), London (1934), and Lisbon (1958).

[13] Madrid Agreement Concerning the International Registration of Marks, 14 April 1891, 828 U.N.T.S. 389 [hereinafter Madrid Agreement]. States that are parties to the Madrid Agreement "constitute a Special Union for the international registration of marks, known as the Madrid Union." *Id.* Art. 1. States that are parties to the Madrid Agreement Protocol are also members of the Madrid Union. *See* Madrid Agreement Protocol, below note 14, Art. 1.

- The Madrid Agreement Protocol (for the further development of the international registration of marks),[14]
- The Patent Cooperation Treaty (for cooperation in the filing, searching, and examining of international applications for the protection of inventions where such protection is sought in several countries),[15]
- The Rome Convention for the Protection of Performers, Producers of Phonograms and Broadcasting Organizations,[16]
- The Washington Treaty on intellectual Property in Respect of Integrated Circuits,[17]
- The International Convention for the Protection of New Varieties of Plants (UPOV Convention),[18]
- Locarno Agreement Establishing an International Classification for Industrial Designs,[19] and
- Hague Agreement Concerning the International Deposit of Industrial Designs.[20]

## 2. Types of intellectual property rights addressed in the TRIPS Agreement

The TRIPS Agreement addresses seven categories of intellectual property rights: (1) copyright and related rights; (2) patents; (3) trademarks and

[14] Protocol Relating to the Madrid Agreement Concerning the International Registration of Marks, 28 June 1989, WIPO Pub. No. 204(E) [hereinafter Madrid Agreement Protocol].

[15] Patent Cooperation Treaty, 19 June 1970, amended 2 October 1979 and modified on 3 February 1984.

[16] International Convention for the Protection of Performers, Producers of Phonograms and Broadcasting Organizations, 26 October 1961, 12 U.S.T. 2377 [hereinafter Rome Convention].

[17] Treaty on Intellectual Property in Respect of Integrated Circuits, 26 May 1989, 28 I.L.M. 1477 (1989) [hereinafter Washington Treaty].

[18] International Convention for the Protection of New Varieties of Plants, 2 December 1961, 815 U.N.T.S. 89 (amended in 1972, 1978 and 1991) [hereinafter UPOV Convention]. Under a cooperation agreement between the International Union for the Protection of New Varieties of Plants (UPOV) and WIPO, the Director General of WIPO is the Secretary-General of UPOV. UPOV is derived from the French name of the organization: "Union internationale pour la protection des obtentions végétales". As of 7 December 2001, 50 states, including the EU Member States and the United States, were parties to the UPOV Convention.

[19] In force 27 April 1971. This provides a system of classifying designs to expedite novelty and infringement searches.

[20] 6 November 1925, revised 28 November 1960. This enables nationals of Hague Union member countries to make a single design deposit with the International Bureau of WIPO in Geneva to gain protection in all member countries.

service marks; (4) geographical indications; (5) undisclosed information or trade secrets; (6) industrial designs; and (7) layout designs of integrated circuits. There are overlaps between these categories. For example, a computer program may be patentable and is protected by copyright. It is useful, however, to keep in mind the general categories of IP rights. Because the moving force behind TRIPS was the United States, we will often refer to U.S. laws as well as the international conventions that have shaped IP concepts.

*Copyright* protects the literary, musical, graphic, or other artistic form in which the author (the creator) expresses intellectual concepts. The key concept of copyright is originality. Copyright can extend to any tangible form, including literary works, dramas, pantomimes and choreography, pictorial, graphic and sculptural works, motion pictures and audiovisual works, musical works (including sound recordings), and architectural works.[21] Copyright can also extend to computer programs as well. Copyright does not, however, extend to ideas or facts.[22]

Two concepts associated with copyright were developed in the civil law tradition and have made their way into the TRIPS Agreement. Civil law countries developed the concept of "neighbouring rights" to extend privileges of copyright to creative works, such as sound recordings and radio and television broadcasts, that were not by personal authors.[23] The more pragmatic legal culture of the United States, a common law country, easily folds these rights into copyright without drawing this distinction, but the TRIPS Agreement contains a separate provision (Article 14) on neighbouring rights. Civil law countries also developed the concept of "moral rights" of authors. Moral rights recognize that a work of art is an expression of the author's personality. Moral rights include the right of the artist to have his work associated with his name, the right that his work not be distorted or falsified, and the right to decide when and how to divulge his work to the public.[24] Moral rights were included in international law by the 1971 Berne Convention (Article 6 *bis*). At U.S. insistence, the TRIPS Agreement (Article 9.1) excludes recognition of these moral rights by excluding "rights conferred under Article 6 *bis*" of the Berne Convention.

---

[21] *E.g.*, 17 U.S.C.A § 102(a) (1996 & Supp. 2001).

[22] *E.g.*, 17 U.S.C.A § 102(b) (1996 & Supp. 2001).

[23] Paul Goldstein, COPYRIGHT'S HIGHWAY: FROM GUTENBERG TO THE CELESTIAL JUKEBOX 189–95 (1994).

[24] *See* Adolf Dietz, *The Moral Right of the Author: Moral Rights and Civil Law Countries*, 19 COLUMBIA-VLA J.L. & ARTS 199, 213–27 (1995).

In the past, many jurisdictions required either notice or registration as a prerequisite for copyright protection. For example, in the United States, notice was required. Notice was given by including the following on the form of expression: the symbol © or the word copyright (copr.) followed by the year of first publication and the name of the claimant. To adhere to the Berne Convention, the United States abolished the notice requirement for works published on or after 1 March 1989.[25] The Berne Convention is incorporated into Article 9 of the TRIPS Agreement; thus, neither notice nor registration is needed to obtain copyright protection. The United States, like many WTO Members, administers a voluntary copyright registration office.[26] As a practical matter, however, copyright notice and registration are still important in establishing and proving copyright.

*Patent* law protects inventions of all kinds; national laws require an "invention" to be novel, useful, and non-obvious.[27] To encourage new inventions, patent laws typically grant the inventor a monopoly on commercial exploitation for a limited period. Patents can be granted for inventions categorized as machines, processes, compositions of matter, articles of manufacture, or new uses of any of these. In the United States, by decision of the Supreme Court, computer programs that involve mathematical formulas can be protected by patent.[28]

In all jurisdictions, patents are obtained by filing a patent application, and the right exists when the appropriate government office issues the patent. In the United States, patents are granted to the first person to invent. In most other countries, patents are granted to the first person to file the patent application (in the United States, the first-to-file is presumed to be the first inventor).

Patents are territorial, and a patent holder has rights only in the territory in which the patent was issued. To gain rights in other countries, the inventor must file a patent application in those countries under their laws. International conventions[29] help this application process by establishing

[25] 17 U.S.C.A § 401 (1996 & Supp. 2001).

[26] 17 U.S.C.A § 408 (1996 & Supp. 2001).

[27] *See, e.g.*, the U.S. Patent Law, 35 U.S.C.A § 100 *et seq.* Article 27 of the TRIPS Agreement uses the European definition of patents as new, involving an inventive step and being capable of industrial application.

[28] *Diamond v. Diehr*, 450 U.S. 175 (1981). *See also, e.g., State St. Bank & Trust Co. v. Signature Fin. Group, Inc.*, 149 F.3d 1368 (Fed Cir. 1998) (holding that computer programs are patentable).

[29] The Paris Convention, above note 8, and the Patent Cooperation Treaty, above note 15, are the principal international patent conventions.

principles of national treatment and non-discrimination for foreign applicants. Under the Paris Convention, an inventor obtains the benefit of the filing date in his home country provided he files in another convention country within one year of the home-country filing date.[30] Under the Patent Cooperation Treaty, the inventor can file in multiple countries by one application and obtain the benefit of his home country's filing date.[31] In Europe, the European Patent Convention[32] created a European Patent Office to serve EU Member States, and one filing is sufficient to obtain patents in all EU countries.

*Trademark* law protects any word, name, symbol, logo, or device used to identify, distinguish, or indicate the source of goods or services. Trademark includes trade dress (the total image and overall appearance of a product) and product configuration (the shape, if non-functional). The purpose of this protection is to safeguard the integrity of products and to prevent product confusion and unfair competition (known as "passing off").

In most countries, trademark rights arise through registration, on a first-come, first-served basis, and there is no requirement of prior use of the mark. In the United States, trademark rights arise under the common law through use of the mark, but protection is limited to the geographical area of the use.[33] Registration is also possible under state law, but protection is limited to the territory of the state or states involved.[34] Thus, the most practical alternative is to register the trademark under federal law, the Lanham Act, which allows the registered holder to identify the mark with the symbol ® or wording noting federal registration.[35] A trademark holder under the Lanham Act must file periodic affidavits of use of the mark; however, under Section 44 of the Act, a foreign mark may be registered in the United States without a showing of use.

Trademark rights are territorial. To obtain rights in other countries, separate applications must be filed. The Paris Convention aids the application process by giving priority to anyone in a Convention country who files a foreign registration application within six months of filing in his home

[30] Paris Convention, above note 8, Art. 4.

[31] This must be followed up, however, by national application within 30 months in all Patent Cooperation Treaty countries in which patents were sought.

[32] European Patent Convention, 5 October 1973, T.S. No. 20 (1978), 13 I.L.M. 270 (1974).

[33] *See* Margreth Barrett, Intellectual Property 678–79 (2001).

[34] Richard Stim, Intellectual Property: Patents, Trademarks and Copyrights 268 (2d ed. 2001).

[35] 15 U.S.C.A. § 1051 *et seq.* (1997 & Supp. 2001).

country. Moreover, in the EU, a single registration can be filed to gain a Community trademark valid in all EU countries. Another convention, the Madrid Agreement Protocol, allows a home-country trademark office to forward an application to WIPO, which can issue an international registration for the mark.

*Geographical indications* are denominations that identify a good as originating in a region or locality, where the reputation or quality of the good is essentially attributable to its geographical origin. Whether protection should be afforded for *geographical indications* has provoked controversy. Many argue that geographical indications must be policed to prevent confusion and unfair competition. In the United States, however, geographical indications were long considered descriptive and, thus, not capable of trademark protection without proof they had acquired a secondary meaning. After the TRIPS Agreement, the United States amended the Lanham Act to outlaw false designation of origin,[36] and products bearing false indications can be barred from importation.[37]

*Trade secrets*, broadly defined, are information (such as a formula, pattern, compilation, program, method, technique, process, or device) that has economic value and with regard to which reasonable efforts are made to keep confidential. In most countries, trade secrets are not subject to registration but are protected through laws against unfair competition. In the United States, trade secrets are protected through common law and state statutes.[38] Trade secrets laws primarily protect against business espionage and disclosure of information by former employees.

*Industrial design* laws protect works of applied art that have industrial application, such as the design of a chair or a pair of running shoes. Many countries have separate registration systems for industrial design[39]; in the United States, the Design Patent Act[40] authorizes design patents for anyone "who invents any new, original and ornamental design for an article of manufacture".[41] The Hague Agreement Concerning the International Deposit of Industrial Designs authorizes nationals of member countries to make a single design application with the International Bureau of WIPO in Geneva in lieu of individual state application. The Locarno Agreement

[36] 15 U.S.C.A. § 1125(a) (1997 & Supp. 2001).
[37] 15 U.S.C.A. § 1124 (1997 & Supp. 2001).
[38] *See* The Uniform Trade Secrets Act, available at http://hsi.org/Library/Espionage/usta.htm.
[39] Goldstein, above note 3, at 552.
[40] 35 U.S.C.A. §§ 171–173.
[41] 35 U.S.C.A. § 171.

Establishing an International Classification for Industrial Design aids novelty and infringement searches by establishing an agreed system of classification for designs. The minimum term of protection under the TRIPS Agreement is ten years.[42]

*Layout designs of integrated circuits* refer to mask works (topographies) of integrated circuits, the stencils used to etch or encode an electrical circuit on a semiconductor chip. These are usually protected under copyright or under a special law.[43] The minimum term of protection under the TRIPS Agreement is ten years from the date of first commercial exploitation.[44]

## 3. Overview of the TRIPS Agreement

The question presents itself: given the existence of WIPO in Geneva and the multitude of longstanding international IP conventions, why was the TRIPS Agreement desirable or necessary?

Two considerations led to the creation of the TRIPS Agreement. First, the United States and other developed countries failed in their attempts to increase normative standards of protection for IP through WIPO and the Paris and Berne Conventions. Second, these two conventions leave enforcement of IP through judicial and administrative remedies to local decisions.

With the coming of globalization, higher standards of IP protection and international enforcement became increasingly important. Yet, IP enforcement is restricted to national territories. Even the United States, accustomed in certain fields such as antitrust to enforcing its laws extraterritorially,[45] has difficulty establishing extraterritorial enforcement of its IP laws.

In *Subafilms, Ltd. v. MGM-Pathe Communications Co.*,[46] the U.S. Court of Appeals for the Ninth Circuit held that acts occurring outside the United States do not constitute infringement under the U.S. Copyright Act. In the field of patent law, the U.S. Supreme Court in *Deepsouth Packing Co. v. Laitram Corp.*[47] held that U.S. patent laws do not reach conduct abroad. In

---

[42] TRIPS Agreement Art. 26.3.

[43] In the United States, mask works are protected under the Semiconductor Chip Act of 1984, 17 U.S.C.A. § 901 et seq. (1996 & Supp. 2001). This Act is administered by the U.S. Copyright Office. The term of protection is ten years.

[44] TRIPS Agreement Art. 38.2.

[45] *See* Chapter 20 § 3.2.

[46] 24 F.3d 1088 (9th Cir. 1994) (*en banc*).

[47] 406 U.S. 518 (1972).

1984, this holding was legislatively overruled,[48] but no case has arisen, largely because of the difficulty of obtaining personal jurisdiction. In trademark cases, the courts apply balancing tests to determine jurisdiction.[49] However, lack of subject matter jurisdiction will be the result in most cases.[50] Thus, as a rule, intellectual property right holders are not able to rely on their home countries for international enforcement of their rights.

The TRIPS Agreement establishes rights and obligations between WTO Members, not private individuals or firms. Nevertheless, it is crucially important for four reasons: (1) it establishes an international law of substantive minimum standards for national IP laws; (2) it establishes minimum international criteria for national enforcement of IP rights through civil, criminal, and administrative proceedings; (3) it subjects national IP standards and enforcement to the WTO dispute settlement system, thereby providing an international forum for enforcement of rights and resolution of disputes; and (4) it establishes certain common procedural requirements that each national government must meet concerning the administration and maintenance of IP rights. The TRIPS does not unify IP, but it stipulates a certain harmonization on a worldwide basis.

The TRIPS Agreement contains general non-discrimination obligations, most importantly a national treatment obligation for WTO Members to afford nationals of all Members the opportunity to protect IP rights to the same extent as a Member's own nationals. There is also a most-favoured-nation (MFN) obligation to accord the same rights to nationals of all WTO Members.

The TRIPS Agreement contains minimum substantive standards for IP protection for all of the categories of IP: copyright and neighbouring rights, patents, trademarks, geographical indications, trade secrets, industrial designs, and layout designs of integrated circuits. The TRIPS Agreement incorporates the substantive standards of IP conventions, such as the Berne Convention and the Paris Convention, but goes beyond them to establish even higher and more specific norms of protection for IP.

---

[48] 35 U.S.C.A. § 271(f).

[49] Compare, *e.g.*, *Steele v. Bulova Watch Co.*, 344 U.S. 280 (1952) (holding that the Lanham Act applies extraterritorially if defendant's conduct had a substantial effect on U.S. commerce); *Nintendo of America, Inc. v. Aeropower Co.*, 34 F.3d 246 (4th Cir. 1994) (holding that the Lanham Act applies to conduct abroad that has significant effect on U.S. commerce); *Wells Fargo & Co. v. Wells Fargo Express Co.*, 556 F.2d 406 (9th Cir. 1977) (holding that extraterritorial effect of the Lanham Act depends on principles of comity).

[50] *Wells Fargo*, above note 49.

The TRIPS Agreement also sets out standards of enforcement of IP rights by foreign rights holders as well as national rights holders. Enforcement must be effective as well as fair and equitable. There must be judicial review of final administrative decisions. Civil and administrative enforcement procedures must conform to certain standards regarding matters such as evidence and proof and due process matters and must offer a full range of remedies including injunctions and damages. Members must adopt border procedures that allow an IP rights holder to block the import of infringing goods. Parties must also provide appropriate criminal penalties for wilful violators of IP rights.

The TRIPS Agreement requires WTO Members to establish an adequate IP office and procedures to facilitate the acquisition and maintenance of IP rights. Procedures for grant and registration of IP rights must operate within reasonable periods, and the law must allow *inter partes* proceedings of opposition, revocation, and cancellation. Final administrative decisions must be subject to judicial review.

## 4. Institutional arrangements

A Council for Trade-Related Aspects of Intellectual Property Rights is established to monitor the operation of the TRIPS Agreement.[51] The Council is composed of representatives of each of the WTO Members, who meet regularly in Geneva. Each WTO Member must make available to the Council, as well as to other WTO Members on request, copies of its IP laws, regulations, judicial decisions, and administrative rulings. The Council monitors and reviews these laws, regulations, decisions, and rulings for each WTO Member and may ask questions and demand answers.[52] The records of each review, including any questions and answers, are made available publicly on the WTO web site.[53] This review allows deficiencies to be identified and differing interpretations of the TRIPS Agreement to be identified and discussed.

The TRIPS Council cooperates fully with WIPO under a 1995 Cooperative Agreement between WIPO and the WTO.[54] There is a common

[51] TRIPS Agreement Art. 68.

[52] *See* Adrian Otten, *Implementation of the TRIPS Agreement and Prospects for Its Further Development*, 1 J. INT'L ECON. L. 523–30 (1998).

[53] http://www.wto.org.

[54] Agreement Between the World Intellectual Property Organization and the World Trade Organization (1995), reprinted in INTERNATIONAL LEGAL MATERIALS ON INTELLECTUAL PROPERTY 681 (Paul Goldstein ed., 2002). *See* Otten, above note 52, at 528.

register of IP laws and regulations, and the two organizations cooperate in these areas: (1) notification and translation of national laws and regulations; (2) communication of national emblems as called for by the Paris Convention; and (3) technical assistance.

The TRIPS Council is also charged with reviewing new developments and recommending modifications or amendment of the TRIPS Agreement itself.

## 5. Provisions relating to developing countries

The TRIPS Agreement makes relatively few concessions to developing countries. Developing countries and countries in the process of transformation to a market economy were given until 2000 to comply with the Agreement, four years more than developed country members.[55] In addition, if a developing country is required by the TRIPS Agreement to extend patent protection to new product and technology areas heretofore not covered by its IP laws, it can delay compliance until 1 January 2005.[56] Least-developed country members have until 2006 to comply with all of the TRIPS Agreement, with the exception of the general obligations of national treatment and MFN treatment.[57] With respect to pharmaceuticals, the 2006 deadline for least-developed countries was extended to 1 January 2016 by the Doha Ministerial Conference.[58]

Developed country members are obligated to provide (1) incentives for transfer of technology to least-developed countries[59]; and (2) technical assistance and financial help to developing countries in preparing laws and regulations on the protection and enforcement of IP rights.[60]

Even though developing countries benefit from certain grace periods for full compliance with the TRIPS Agreement, Article 70.8 and 70.9 require that they must establish an administrative means for preserving novelty and

[55] TRIPS Agreement Art. 65.2 and .3.

[56] *Id.* Art. 65.4.

[57] *Id.* Art. 66.

[58] WTO, Ministerial Conference, Fourth Session, Doha, 9–14 November 2001, *Declaration on the TRIPS Agreement and Public Health*, WT/MIN(01)/DEC/2, 20 November 2001, para. 7.

[59] TRIPS Agreement Art. 66.2.

[60] *Id.* Art. 67.

priority for patent applications during the transitional period.[61] They must also provide a system for granting exclusive marketing rights for such products.[62]

## 6. Public policy criticisms

There are five essential public policy criticisms of the TRIPS Agreement. All involve the relationship between developed and developing countries and issues fundamental to globalization:

1. Is the TRIPS Agreement a "marriage of convenience"[63] between trade and IP to further exacerbate the divide between rich and poor countries? Are poor countries being forced to protect IP rights against their fundamental self-interest in order to serve the welfare of transnational businesses based in rich countries?
2. Does the TRIPS Agreement, by ignoring the interests of poor countries, allow "reverse piracy", that is, the appropriation by transnational companies in rich countries of valuable "traditional knowledge" and cultural works, such as music, art, and dance, in poorer, less-developed societies?
3. Does the TRIPS Agreement undermine the UN Convention on Biological Diversity,[64] which specifies that people in developing countries have the right to control access to the biological resources within their borders?
4. Does the TRIPS Agreement endanger human health in poor countries by providing pharmaceutical companies in rich countries an IP monopoly over medicines essential to fight health crisis and pandemics such as HIV? Such medicines are prohibitively expensive in poor countries.
5. Does the TRIPS Agreement threaten food production rich countries to gain IP rights over food plants and seeds, denying them to farmers in developing countries too poor to pay the prices demanded for them?

[61] Appellate Body Report, *India — Patent Protection for Pharmaceutical and Agricultural Chemical Products*, WT/DS50/AB/R, para. 97. An identical complaint was filed by the EC, WT/DS79/R, para. 1.1.

[62] Appellate Body Report, *India — Patents*, para. 84. See also Panel Report, *Indonesia — Automobiles*, para. 14.263 (in which Indonesia successfully defended its right to apply the grace period in TRIPS Art. 65.2).

[63] *See* Gadbaw, above note 1, at 223–25.

[64] Convention on Biological Diversity, UNEP/Bio. Div./Conf./L.2, 22 June 1992, 31 I.L.M. 818 (1992).

## 6.1 Benefits and costs of higher IP standards for developing countries

The first policy objection, namely, benefits and costs of higher IP standards for developing countries, to the TRIPS Agreement has a long history. Put as a general, abstract proposition, a definitive answer is elusive.[65] The arguments pro and con must be carefully and objectively evaluated.[66]

The case against IP protection is that, simply put, for developing countries the costs of protection outweigh the benefits. This is the traditional view,[67] namely, that developing countries receive little or nothing for the price they pay in granting foreign monopolies over technology and industry within their borders. According to this view, IP rights stifle domestic innovation and impede the diffusion of technology in poor countries. Protecting IP means that using technology will involve higher prices and paying royalty payments to foreign companies. Why should a developing country spend administrative costs to process thousands of IP applications filed primarily by U.S., Japanese, and European companies? Patent statistics show that people from developing countries hold less than 1 percent of patents.[68] These arguments hold that developing countries should offer only minimum protection to IP, should discriminate in favour of their own nationals, and should carefully scrutinize technology transfer agreements with foreign companies.[69]

In the 1970s, as part of the New International Economic Order,[70] developing countries sought an International Code of Conduct on the Transfer of Technology. This Code, the adoption of which was blocked primarily by the United States, would have affirmed the right of nations to

[65] For an illuminating essay on the theoretical bases of protection, see A. Samuel Oddi, *TRIPS: Natural Rights and a "Polite Form of Economic Imperialism"*, 29 Vand. J. Transnat'l L. 415 (1996).

[66] *See* Alan S. Gutterman, *The North-South Debate Regarding the Protection of Intellectual Property Rights*, 28 Wake Forest L. Rev. 89 (1993).

[67] Edith Tilton Penrose, The Economics of the International Patent System 233 (1951).

[68] OECD, "Economic Agreements for Protecting Intellectual Property Rights Effectively", TC WP (88) (1989) at 21.

[69] Douglas F. Greer, *The Case Against Patent Systems in Less-Developed Countries*, 8 J. Int'l L. & Econ. 223 (1973).

[70] For a discussion of the New International Economic Order, see Chapter 15, section 9.

review technology transfer contracts and object to restrictive clauses favouring transnational foreign companies.[71]

On the other side of the ledger, World Bank economists cogently expressed the case for increased protection for IP during the TRIPS negotiations: worldwide welfare suffers because of less than socially optimal R&D investment. Weak protection of IP in developing countries aggravates this problem.[72] Are there benefits for developing countries?

Several specific benefits may be argued, but their extent is hard to measure. First, there is evidence that IP protection will mean increased investment and technology transfer and diffusion in developing countries.[73] Second, IP protection will mean increased investment, trade, and opportunity for capital formation.[74] Third, there will be positive benefits on a micro level in the form of training, the productivity of research, and international interactions with foreign business and universities.[75] Fourth, protection for IP may foster more creativity and "an inventive habit of mind" in the population and, more specifically, in the work force.[76]

Which side has the stronger case? In a very real sense this is now an academic question, for TRIPS represents the victory of those who believe in strengthened IP rights. The fact that developing countries, the majority in the WTO and even in the old GATT, were willing to accept TRIPS represents the trend, evident since the 1980s, in developing countries' willingness to accept a more liberal, less regulatory approach to international trade and investment.

Thus, the debate has shifted to identifying and dealing with problems, including social, economic, and environmental difficulties that developing countries may have in implementing TRIPS. Developing countries certainly need financial and technical assistance in setting up and operating IP offices.

[71] Hans Peter Kunz-Hallstein, *The United States Proposal for a GATT Agreement on Intellectual Property and the Paris Convention for the Protection of Intellectual Property*, 22 VAND J. TRANS. L. 265 (1989).

[72] Edwin Mansfield, *Intellectual Property Rights, Technological Change and Economic Growth*, in INTELLECTUAL PROPERTY RIGHTS OF CAPITAL FORMATION IN THE NEXT DECADE 29 Walker and Bloomfield eds., 1988).

[73] Carlos Prima Braga, *The Developing Country Case for and Against Intellectual Property Protection*, in STRENGTHENING PROTECTION OF INTELLECTUAL PROPERTY IN DEVELOPING COUNTRIES 69-87, 112 (W. E. Siebeck ed., 1990).

[74] *Id.*

[75] Robert M. Sherwood, INTELLECTUAL PROPERTY AND INTERNATIONAL DEVELOPMENT 138 (1990).

[76] *Id.*

This is already a feature of TRIPS. Beyond this, TRIPS must be examined with a view to what possible new "special and differential" treatment provisions are needed, if any.

## 6.2 Protection of traditional knowledge and culture

Does the TRIPS Agreement adequately protect "traditional knowledge and culture"? "Traditional knowledge and culture" covers a lot of ground, ranging from knowledge that certain plants have health benefits, to stories, songs, music, dance, carvings, designs, pottery, sculpture, woodwork, mosaics, costumes, and metal ware — the list is endless.

Many developing nations have legislation defining and protecting "folklore", an appellation for traditional knowledge and culture. Ghana defines folklore as "all literary, artistic and scientific work belonging to the cultural heritage of Ghana which were created, preserved and developed by ethnic communities of Ghana or by unidentified Ghanaian authors. . . ."[77] Similarly, Nigeria defines folklore as "a group-oriented and tradition-based creation of groups of individuals reflecting the expectation of the community as an adequate expression of its cultural and social identity, its standards and values as transmitted orally, by imitation or by other means".[78]

There seems to be a consensus in WIPO[79] and the TRIPS Council that TRIPS should contain protection for traditional knowledge, culture, and folklore.[80] The UN Convention on Biological Diversity already mandates protection for traditional knowledge associated with biological resources.[81] Yet, key issues remain regarding the manner and scope of such protection. First, should these items be protected in traditional IP categories or should a separate category be recognized? Second, folklore is often the creation of a group or an unknown (and forgotten) person or persons. Who should receive payment? How should the price be determined? Third, what should the scope of protection encompass? It appears that the rationale

[77] Copyright Law (Ghana) § 53 (21 March 1985), as quoted in Paul Kuruk, *Protecting Folklore Under Modern Intellectual Property Regimes*, 48 Am. Univ. L. Rev. 769, 778 (1999).

[78] Copyright Decree (Nigeria) § 28(5) (19 December 1988), as quoted in Kuruk, above note 77, at 778.

[79] *WTO Debates Geographical Indications, Traditional Knowledge*, Inside U.S. Trade, 15 March 2002.

[80] Thomas Cottier, *The Protection of Genetic Resources and Traditional Knowledge: Towards More Specific Rights and Obligations on World Trade Law*, 1 J. Int'l Econ. L. 555, 581–84 (1998).

[81] Convention on Biological Diversity, above note 64, Arts. 8( j) and 10(c).

for protecting folklore is very different from that for other categories of IP. Unlike other IP, the rationale for protecting folklore would seem to be rooted in human rights. The scope of protection of folklore should be determined by precise identification of why protection is important. Careful consideration should also be given to whether too much protection would negate or stifle creativity and cultural expression.

## 6.3 Biological diversity

The TRIPS Agreement guarantees recognition and enforcement of intellectual property rights backed by the authority of the WTO's dispute settlement mechanism. The Convention on Biological Diversity provides that the genetic resources of plants and animals are under the sovereignty of the state in which they are located, and developing countries have a right to benefit from the development of these resources as well as from the transfer of technology relevant to the development and use of genetic resources. These two agreements contain the seeds of potential conflicts[82] with vast implications not only for the environment, but also for the biotechnology, pharmaceutical, and agricultural industries.

The TRIPS Agreement and the Convention on Biological Diversity were developed, albeit at the same time, by different delegations, in different fora, with different objectives and with almost no consultation or communication between the two groups of negotiators. Even now, years after both negotiations have been completed, there has been little or no systematic analysis of the potential conflicts between the two agreements. Conflicts are most likely to arise between nations that have accepted both the Convention on Biological Diversity, which is in force and has been adopted by over 160 nations, and the WTO Agreement, which has been adopted by 144 states.

In the event of a dispute between parties to both agreements, the Convention on Biological Diversity adopts the following rule of priority:

> 1. The provisions of this Convention shall not affect the rights and obligations of any Contracting Party deriving from any existing international agreement, except where the exercise of those rights and obligations would cause a serious damage or threat to biological diversity.

[82] *See* generally Graham Dutfield, INTELLECTUAL PROPERTY RIGHTS, TRADE AND BIODIVERSITY (2000).

2. Contracting Parties shall implement this Convention with respect to the marine environment consistently with the rights and obligations of States under the law of the sea.[83]

This "serious damage or threat" standard is vague and difficult to apply because it is subject to interpretation. This flawed priority rule highlights the importance of dispute settlement when concrete issues arise.

### 6.3.1 *Access to genetic resources*

Industries such as biotechnology, pharmaceuticals, and agriculture are dependent on worldwide access to genetic resources. These and other industries use wild plants and animals in three basic ways. First, a natural species can be used directly as a source of natural chemicals or compounds for the production of drugs, or other products. An example is the use of the Pacific yew tree to produce an anti-cancer drug. Second, a natural species' chemicals can provide information and ideas that can lead to the production of useful synthetic chemicals, drugs, or other products. An example is aspirin, a drug developed as a synthetic modification of salicylic acid, which is found in plants. Third, a natural species can be a source of a gene or genetic sequence that can be used to develop new varieties through breeding or a genetically modified organism through implantation. The former process is essential to modern agriculture. Because crops and animals are susceptible to disease and adverse climatic conditions, it is critical to have access to natural gene pools (germ plasm) to develop more productive and disease-resistant plants and animals. The latter process is critical to the biotech industry, which develops new products through genetic modification and incorporation of genetic materials.

Article 15 of the Convention on Biological Diversity authorizes states to limit or place conditions on access to genetic resources. How states will implement this provision is unclear, but the vague language of Article 15 could provide the basis for a range of actions, from an export ban to market pricing.

Although Article 15 itself is virtually open-ended in its authority, WTO Members must observe GATT 1994 norms and the TRIPS Agreement in its implementation. Most notably, export bans or conditions must comply with GATT Article XX(g), which requires that export restrictions must relate to the conservation of the resource and must be applied in conjunction with restrictions on domestic production or consumption. In addition,

[83] Convention on Biological Diversity, above note 64, Art. 22.

under GATT Article XX(g), an export restriction must not employ "arbitrary or unjustifiable discrimination between countries" or be a "disguised restriction on international trade". Article 15 is subject to the discipline of the GATT and the TRIPS Agreement.

The most notable exercise of Article 15 rights is the regime adopted by Costa Rica, which passed amendments to its Wildlife Conservation Law in 1992 declaring wildlife to be in the "public interest" and requiring advance governmental approval for the export of genetic materials and for biogenetic research.[84] This law was designed to give the Costa Rican government broad discretion in negotiating contracts with foreign firms that wish to employ genetic resources for research.

An example of the contractual regime Costa Rica is using to implement this policy is the 1989[85] contract signed by Merck & Company, the largest U.S. pharmaceutical company, and the Instituto de Biodiversidad Nacional (INBIO), a non-profit institution created by the Costa Rican government. In this arrangement, Merck advanced $1 million to INBIO for the right to develop drugs from Costa Rican plants, insects, or microbes supplied by INBIO, and INBIO and the Costa Rican government agreed to share an amount, reportedly between 1 and 3 percent, of the revenues from any products developed from INBIO-supplied genetic resources.

The TRIPS Agreement would not bar this arrangement or any other that requires compensation in the form of payment or royalties in return for resource use.[86] The TRIPS Agreement does not regulate pricing. Any payment arrangement would, therefore, be permissible. If, however, a state-trading enterprise is involved, GATT Article XVII requires that purchases and sales must be in accordance with commercial considerations and must be made on a non-discriminatory basis.[87] Thus, the TRIPS Agreement and Article 15 of the Convention on Biological Diversity are *prima facie* compatible.

A troublesome question likely to arise in legislation and contracts implementing Article 15 is whether countries may discriminate against foreign

---

[84] Costa Rica Strengthens Wildlife Protection Law, Envtl. Watch Latin Am., November 1992, available in Lexis, News Library, Zevl File.

[85] *See* Michele A. Powers, *The United Nations Framework Convention on Biological Diversity: Will Biodiversity Preservation be Enhanced Through Its Provisions Concerning Biotechnology Intellectual Property Rights?*, 12 Wis. Int'l L.J. 103, 117–20 (1993).

[86] For a review and analysis of contractual arrangements, see Edgar J. Asebey and Jill D. Kempenaar, *Biodiversity Prospecting: Fulfilling the Mandate of the Biodiversity Convention*, 28 Vand. J. Transnat'l L. 703 (1995).

[87] GATT Art. XVII:1 and :2.

firms by charging them for resource use while exempting domestic firms. The answer depends on whether the charge is levied as a customs charge or an internal tax or charge. A true customs charge must comply only with the MFN requirement of GATT Article I, while an internal charge must comply not only with Article I, but also with GATT Article III, which requires national treatment.[88] In the latter case, it would be illegal under the GATT to exempt domestic firms. Thus, foreign firms that establish and carry on research activities in the country of origin of the biological materials could not be subjected to a discriminatory pricing arrangement.

While Article 15 is, in principle, compatible with the GATT and the TRIPS Agreement, it may be difficult for developing countries to derive substantial revenues from Article 15 unless they illegally control exports and discriminate against foreign firms. First, only rarely will biological materials be limited to one country. Availability from multiple sources will reduce the price. For example, Eli Lilly Company produced two anticancer drugs (namely, vinblastine and vincristine) from periwinkle leaves first obtained in Madagascar. The periwinkle plant, however, grows wild in many areas of the world including Texas, where it is grown commercially. Although Eli Lilly has been criticized[89] for failing to compensate Madagascar, it is not difficult to see why it did not do so. Second, few new drugs or products are made from unmodified biological sources; more often they will be derivatives or produced purely synthetically.[90] Thus, Article 15 seems to be flawed as a mechanism for sustainable development.[91]

[88] It is not always easy to distinguish between a customs charge and an internal charge. Resolution of this issue can often only be made on a case-by-case basis considering the particular facts and circumstances involved.

[89] *See* Richard Stone, *The Biodiversity Treaty: Pandora's Box or Fair Deal?*, 256 SCIENCE 1624 (1992).

[90] Office of Technology Assessment, U.S. Cong., Biotechnology in a Global Economy 75–76 (1991).

[91] Another arrangement to provide compensation to developing countries is being carried on by three U.S. governmental agencies, the National Science Foundation, the Agency for International Development, and the National Institute of Health. These agencies encourage academic and commercial organizations in the United States to sign cooperative agreements with developing countries called International Cooperative Biodiversity Groups (ICBG), to inventory native species in the developing country to screen them for potential value, and to establish joint research and training. The arrangement typically provides for "best efforts" to negotiate with a pharmaceutical company that may produce a drug commercially for a percentage of royalties to the developing country partner. *See* Karen Anne Goldman, *Compensation for the Use of Biological Resources under the Convention on Biological Diversity: Compatibility of Conservation Measures and Competitiveness of Biotechnology Industry*, 25 LAW & POL'Y INT'L BUS. 695, 707 (1994).

### 6.3.2 Patentability

Patentability is important for the development of both beneficial biotechnologies and marketable environmental technologies that generate less waste and pollution. The TRIPS Agreement, by strengthening global intellectual property protection, will have a positive effect on both categories by providing incentives for research and development. Under the TRIPS Agreement, Article 27.1, patents must be available for both products and processes in all fields of technology. TRIPS Article 8.1 permits "measures necessary to protect public health and nutrition, and to promote the public interest in sectors of vital importance to . . . socio-economic and technological development", but requires that such measures must be "consistent with . . . this Agreement". Thus, Article 8.1 cannot derogate from the patentability requirement of Article 27. Article 27.2 allows WTO Members to exclude from patentability inventions that endanger human, animal, or plant life or health or the environment, but the exclusion must be "necessary", not "merely because the exploitation is prohibited by their law".[92] Plants, animals, and essential biological processes may also be excluded from patentability, but micro-organisms, microbiological processes, and non-biological processes are patentable.[93]

This formulation assures that most biotechnological, pharmaceutical, and agricultural biotechnical inventions are patentable. Although naturally occurring plants and animals are not patentable, genetically modified micro-organisms, animal genes, human DNA sequences, human proteins, and human genes have all been patented in the United States and in Europe.[94] Although transgenic animals such as the "Harvard mouse",[95] an experimental animal developed for the study of breast cancer, would not be patentable under the TRIPS Agreement, the transgenic process by which

[92] TRIPS Agreement Art. 27.2.

[93] TRIPS Agreement Art. 27.3(b).

[94] In *Diamond v. Chakrabarty*, 447 U.S. 303 (1980), the U.S. Supreme Court held that a genetically altered micro-organism was patentable under U.S. law either as a "manufacture" or a "composition of matter". For European patent cases, *see* Michael Bowman and Catherine Redgwell, International Law and the Conservation of Biological Diversity 171 (1996).

[95] Genetically altered animals are patentable under U.S. law. For example, the U.S. Patent and Trademark Office issued U.S. Patent No. 4,736,866 in 1988 to the inventors of a transgenic mouse with cancer-sensitive characteristics known as the "Harvard mouse". *See* Thomas Traian Moga, *Transgenic Animals as Intellectual Property (or the Patented Mouse That Roared)*, 76 J. Pat. & Trademark Off. Soc'y 511 (1994).

such animals are developed would be, either as a microbiological or non-biological process.

### *6.3.3 Transfer of technology*

Perhaps the most difficult potential conflict between the TRIPS Agreement and the Convention on Biological Diversity concerns the transfer of technology. The TRIPS Agreement mandates a private, free-market system for the transfer of rights to intellectual property. Patent owners have the exclusive right to assign, transfer, or license their patents. The Convention on Biological Diversity, in contrast, requires that the contracting parties provide for (1) priority or concessional access for developing countries; (2) preferential terms for such countries; and (3) joint research and development efforts by firms that develop the intellectual property rights and the country supplying the genetic resources.[96]

All of these requirements potentially conflict with the TRIPS regime, which would leave matters to the private sector to decide without government interference. There appear to be two ways of dealing with this potential conflict. First, Articles 20 and 21 of the Convention on Biological Diversity provide for a "financial mechanism" to facilitate transfer of technology to developing countries on favourable terms. Nothing in the TRIPS Agreement would prohibit the use of an international financial mechanism to assure access and the transfer of technology. Articles 15, 16, and 19 of the Convention can be interpreted to mean that transfer of technology should be left to negotiations between parties, supplemented where needed by the financial mechanism.

A second method available under the TRIPS Agreement to implement the Convention on Biological Diversity might be compulsory licensing. The Convention contains no specific authorization for compulsory licensing, but it does authorize "legislative, administrative or policy measures as appropriate"[97] to give developing countries access to technology. Compulsory licensing by WTO Members would be controlled by the TRIPS Agreement, which has specific provisions on this issue. Article 30 of the TRIPS Agreement permits "limited exceptions to the exclusive rights conferred by a patent, provided [the exceptions] do not unreasonably prejudice the legitimate interest of the patent owner . . . " These conditions almost certainly would

[96] *See* Convention on Biological Diversity, above note 64, Arts. 15(7), 16(2) and (3), and 19(1) and (2).

[97] *Id.* Arts. 15(4), 16(3) and 19(1).

not apply to a technology transfer agreement. This leaves TRIPS Article 31, which authorizes compulsory licensing, subject to highly restrictive conditions that would seem impractical to achieve the aims of the Convention on Biological Diversity. Thus, amendment of the Convention, the TRIPS Agreement, or both may be necessary to reconcile the two regimes.

## 6.4 Health

The argument that the TRIPS Agreement blocks developing country access to medicine is a favourite of critics of the WTO.[98] Infectious diseases such as HIV/AIDS, tuberculosis, and malaria are the scourge of the developing world, but few people in developing countries have access to effective treatment at affordable prices.[99] Many blame this lack of access on the TRIPS Agreement.[100]

The claim that the TRIPS Agreement and the WTO are blocking access to medicines in poor countries is demonstrably false. There are enormous political economic, and structural problems that must be solved to make such access a reality. The TRIPS Agreement is *not* the culprit, though it is an easy scapegoat because the real, underlying problems are hidden, complex, and perhaps intractable.

As a point of departure, the TRIPS Agreement and the WTO are *essential* to even begin to tackle health in the developing world. The TRIPS Agreement provides global patentability, which is part of the solution because it gives private pharmaceutical companies an incentive to develop medicines for diseases in tropical and other developing areas. Of course, instruments of flexibility are needed, but the TRIPS Agreement is essential in this respect as well. Flexibility must not be random but must keep to rules. Rules create and fulfil expectations on all sides. The TRIPS Agreement provides the rules, which are essential to dealing with the problems.

At the 2001 WTO Ministerial Conference in Doha, the Declaration on the TRIPS Agreement and Public Health addressed health in developing countries in the following ways:

1. It affirmed the TRIPS Agreement and the importance of IP protection for the development of new medicines.

[98] Lori Wallach and Michelle Sforza, The WTO: Five Years of Reasons to Resist Corporate Globalization 48–49 (1999).

[99] *A War Over Drugs and Patents*, Economist, 10 March 2001, at 43.

[100] *E.g.*, Wallach and Sforza, above note 98.

2. It agreed that the TRIPS Agreement does not and should not prevent Members from taking action to protect public health.
3. It recognized the freedom of Members to grant compulsory licences and determine the grounds for such licences.
4. It affirmed that each Member has the right to determine what disease conditions constitute a national emergency under TRIPS Article 31(b).
5. It reaffirmed TRIPS Article 6, which allows each Member to establish a regime for exhaustion of IP rights "without challenge".
6. It recognized that some developing nations cannot use compulsory licensing effectively and called on the TRIPS Council to "find an expeditious solution" to this problem.
7. It agreed that least-developed countries will not be obliged to comply with the patent and trade secret parts of TRIPS until 2016 at the earliest.

The Doha TRIPS Declaration requires the amendment of the TRIPS Agreement in certain respects, but the two techniques specifically affirmed by the TRIPS Declaration (namely, compulsory licensing, and parallel imports) are flexibility measures already present in TRIPS without amendment. These measures can be used right away.

### *6.4.1 Compulsory licensing*

Article 31 of TRIPS permits a WTO Member to pass a national law providing use of the subject matter of a patent without the authorization of the right holder if certain conditions are met. Four of the Article 31 conditions are most relevant.

First, the proposed user must have made efforts to obtain authorization from the rights holder on "reasonable commercial terms", and these efforts must have not been successful "within a reasonable period of time".[101] A Member can waive this condition "in the case of a national emergency".[102] In the light of the Doha TRIPS Declaration, this condition would seem easy to meet because that Declaration recognizes that each Member "has the right to determine what constitutes a national emergency".[103]

Second, the scope and duration of the licence must be limited to the purpose for which it was authorized.[104] This condition, too, would seem easy to meet.

[101] TRIPS Agreement Art. 31(b).
[102] *Id.*
[103] *See* Doha Declaration, above note 58.
[104] TRIPS Agreement Art. 31(c).

Third, the licence must be "predominantly" for the supply of the Member's domestic market.[105] This would be the case if the compulsory licence was to deal with the *Member's* health crisis. This condition would present problems for parallel importing, which is discussed below.

Fourth, the right holder must be paid "adequate remuneration in the circumstances of each case, taking into account the economic value of the authorization".[106] Although this condition presents some interpretative issues, it is flexible enough not to be an obstacle, especially in the light of the Doha Declaration.

A final issue is presented by TRIPS Article 27.1, which provides that "patents shall be available and patent rights enjoyable without *discrimination* as to . . . the field of technology". It may be argued that singling out pharmaceuticals is discriminatory. However, as Professor Fred Abbott has pointed out,[107] the WTO panel in the *Canada — Generic Pharmaceuticals* case[108] read Article 27.1 flexibly, stating that it "does not prohibit *bona fide* exceptions to deal with problems that may exist only in certain product areas".[109]

### *6.4.2 Parallel imports*

Another method available under the TRIPS Agreement for dealing with health crises in poor countries is parallel importing. Parallel importing is the term used for importing a legally produced product from a low-priced distributor instead of buying directly from the manufacturer. Parallel importing would enable a developing country to import needed medicines at the lowest world prices, bypassing authorized distributors. This tool is particularly useful for poor countries that have no capacity to build their own pharmaceutical plants to produce medicines under compulsory licences. Parallel importing allows such countries to import generic versions of patented drugs produced legally in countries like Brazil or India under compulsory licences. Thus, parallel importing must be combined with compulsory licensing to serve the poorest nations. The goods subject to

---

[105] TRIPS Agreement Art. 31(f).

[106] *Id.* Art. 31(h).

[107] Frederick M. Abbot, *The TRIPS-Legality of Measures Taken to Aldren Public Health Crises: A Synopsis*, 7 Widener L. Symp. J. 71, 75–76 (2001).

[108] Panel Report, *Canada — Protection of Pharmaceutical Products*, WT/DS114/R, 7 April 2000.

[109] *Id.* para. 7.92.

parallel importing are known as "gray market" goods because, while they are not counterfeit, they are sold without the authority of the IP owner.

The TRIPS Agreement allows parallel importing. Article 6 of the TRIPS Agreement states that exhaustion of intellectual property rights is a matter left to Members to determine.[110] Exhaustion means that once a patented product has been sold anywhere under the authority of the patent holder, the patent holder has no right to prevent further sale or importation anywhere in the world.

WTO Members deal with parallel importation in different ways. For example, in the United States parallel importation of patented goods generally is allowed,[111] but neither the Supreme Court nor the Court of Appeals for Federal Circuit, the two most important courts, have addressed the issue.[112] As for goods under trademark, parallel importation is allowed if the foreign authorized manufacturer and the domestic owner of the mark are under common control (parent, subsidiary, or sister corporation). If the foreign entity is independent and operating under licence of the trademark owner, parallel imports may be blocked.[113] Moreover, even goods sold by a foreign affiliate may be blocked on importation if they are different physically from domestic goods subject to the mark.[114] The status of parallel importation of goods subject to copyright is unclear.[115] In the EU, parallel imports are permitted freely throughout the territory of EU Member States as well as the European Economic Area (EEA).[116] The exhaustion principle

---

110 *See* Marco C. E. J. Bronckers, *The Exhaustion of Patent Rights Under World Trade Organization Law*, 32 J. World Trade, No. 1, at 137, 142 (1998).

111 *Curtiss Aeroplane & Motor Corp. v. United Aircraft Eng'g Corp.*, 266 F. 71 (2d Cir. 1920).

112 *See* Margreth Barrett, *The United States' Doctrine of Exhaustion: Parallel Imports of Patented Goods*, 27 N. Ky. L. Rev. 911 (2000).

113 *K-Mart Corp. v. Cartier, Inc.*, 486 U.S. 281 (1988).

114 *Lever Brothers Co. v. United States*, 981 F.2d 1330 (D.C. Cir. 1993); *Gamut Trading Co. v. U.S. Int'l Trade Comm'n*, 200 F.3d 775 (Fed. Cir. 1999). In contrast, in the *Duracell* case, gray market goods were blocked by the U.S. International Trade Commission under 19 U.S.C. § 1337 (Section 337 of the Trade Act of 1974), but President Reagan vetoed the ruling under § 1337(j). *See* Disapproval of the Determination of the United States International Trade Commission in Investigation No. 337–TA–165, Certain Alkaline Batteries, 50 Fed. Reg. 1655 (1985). There were no physical differences in this case. For a case in which gray market goods were successfully blocked under Section 337, see *Gamut Trading Co. v. U.S. Int'l Trade Comm'n*, 200 F.3d 775 (Fed. Cir. 1999).

115 *See Quality King Distributors, Inc. v. L'Anza Research Int'l, Inc.*, 523 U.S. 135 (1998).

116 Case 78/70, *Deutsche Grammophon Gesellschaft GMBH v. Metro-SB-Grossmarkte GMBH & Co.*, 1971 E.C.R. 487; Cases C–267–268/95 *Merck & Co. v. Primecrown Ltd.*, 1996 E.C.R. I–6285.

operates, however, only as to goods sold within the EU and EEA, and Member States may block parallel imports from outside.[117]

The Doha Ministerial Declaration, as an official interpretation of Article 6, removes all doubt that parallel importing of pharmaceuticals is permitted under the TRIPS Agreement.[118]

There is, however, a problem with respect to combining compulsory licensing in country A with parallel importing by country B, which may be necessary to combat health crises in poor countries with no pharmaceutical industry.[119] TRIPS Article 31(f), as stated above, requires that a compulsory licensee produce the product "predominantly" for the supply of its domestic market. This wording would permit some parallel exports, but not on a large scale. It seems advisable, therefore, that Article 31(f) be modified.

### *6.4.3 Beyond the TRIPS Agreement*

Obviously, the TRIPS Agreement will not solve health problems in poor countries, but it should not stand in the way. Many elements are necessary for even a modicum of effective action. Funding by UN organizations and the World Bank is being solicited from member countries. This finding must be supplemented by two techniques that may involve WTO agreements: (1) subsidies; and (2) tiered pricing by pharmaceutical countries to make medicines available at lower prices in poor countries. The first may necessitate WTO action to amend the SCM Agreement, and the second may call for an exception from antidumping rules. Most difficult, however, will be establishing the necessary political will, training, education, and medical infrastructure in poor countries to do the job.[120]

---

[117] Case C-355/96, *Silhouette International Schmied GmbH v. Hartlauer Handelsgesellschaft mbH,* 1998 E.C.R. I–3682.

[118] Only the WTO Ministerial Conference and the General Council have the power to issue official interpretations of the TRIPS Agreement. WTO Agreement Art. XI:2

[119] WTO, Ministerial Conference, Fourth Session, Doha, 9–14 November 2001, *Ministerial Declaration,* WT/MIN(01)/DEC/1, 20 November 2001, para. 6 [hereinafter *Doha Ministerial Declaration*].

[120] A major tool in combating disease in developing countries is The Global Fund to Fight AIDS, Tuberculosis and Malaria, a private corporation based in Geneva. In April 2002, the Fund awarded $616 million to more than 40 countries for prevention and treatment of the three diseases. David Brown, *$616 Million to Fight Scourges: Global Fund Awards Programs Treating AIDS, TB, Malaria,* WASH. POST, 26 April 2002, at A12.

## 6.5 Food

Will IP rights protected by the TRIPS Agreement deny developing countries the seed stock necessary to grow their own food?

The TRIPS Agreement requires plant breeders' rights to be given worldwide IP rights protection. Although naturally occurring plants cannot be patented, the TRIPS Agreement provides that "Members shall provide for the protection of plant varieties either by patents or by an effective *sui generis* system or by any combination thereof".[121] The *sui generis* system refers to the UPOV Convention. States adhering to the UPOV Convention undertake to create a system of granting plant breeders' rights under their domestic laws. The TRIPS Agreement supplements the UPOV Convention by requiring all WTO Members to grant IP rights status to plant breeders' rights, either through the UPOV Convention or by admitting their patentability.

Yet, the TRIPS Agreement contains balancing provisions that may be sufficient to allow developing countries full access to food and seed resources. Article 8.1 allows Members "to protect public health and nutrition, and to promote the public interest in sectors of vital importance to their socio-economic and technological development". However, the measures chosen under this provision must be consistent with the TRIPS Agreement.

Fortunately, the TRIPS Agreement provides two ways of securing seed supplies. First, under Article 27.2, Members may exclude from patentability inventions "necessary to protect human, animal or plant life or health". A case that a particular exclusion is "necessary" could be made on the basis of the *EC — Asbestos* ruling[122] and in the light of TRIPS Article 8.1. Second, Article 30 allows "limited exceptions" to patent rights as long as these exceptions do not (1) unreasonably conflict with the normal exploitation of the patent; or (2) unreasonably prejudice the legitimate interests of the patent owner. It would seem that Article 30 might be invoked by developing countries to provide seed stock for family and small cooperative farming operations.

The Convention on Biological Diversity calls for respect and preservation of the knowledge, innovations, and practices of indigenous and local communities in developing countries.[123] Such knowledge, practices, and

[121] TRIPS Agreement Art. 27.3(b).
[122] Appellate Body Report, *E.C. — Asbestos*, para. 172. *See* also Chapter 17.
[123] Convention on Biological Diversity, above note 64, Arts. 8(j) and 10(c).

innovations should be explicitly recognized under the TRIPS Agreement and given IP protection. This recognition would further ensure that the TRIPS Agreement will not endanger food security or agricultural production in poor countries.

## 7. The general principles of the TRIPS Agreement

### 7.1 The relationship between the TRIPS Agreement and other intellectual property treaties

The TRIPS Agreement provides that WTO Members must respect the standards under the Paris Convention regardless of whether they are parties to the Paris Convention.[124] In addition, the TRIPS Agreement requires compliance with certain other multilateral conventions administered by WIPO.[125] The incorporation of WIPO conventions into the TRIPS Agreement subjects them to the TRIPS Agreement dispute settlement regime and allows WTO panels to interpret WIPO conventions. This authority has the potential to create conflicts between WIPO and the WTO.

### 7.2 Acquisition and maintenance of intellectual property rights

WTO Members must create and operate governmental offices for the acquisition and maintenance of all forms of IP rights. Procedures for granting and registration of IP rights must be reasonable,[126] and a Member's law must provide appropriate *inter partes* procedures, such as opposition, revocation, and cancellation.[127] Members may adopt measures to protect public health and the public interest that are consistent with TRIPS obligations.[128]

---

124 TRIPS Agreement Art. 2.1.

125 *See id.* Arts. 1, 2, 3, 4, 5, 9, 10, 14, 15, 16, 22, 35 and 39.

126 TRIPS Agreement Art. 62.1–.2.

127 *Id.* Art. 62.4.

128 *Id.* Art. 8.1.

## 7.3 National treatment and most-favoured-nation treatment

WTO Members must generally accord both national treatment and most-favoured-nation treatment to individuals and enterprises in connection with the acquisition, maintenance, and enforcement of IP rights.[129] This general rule is subject to exceptions recognized in existing international IP conventions.[130]

# 8. Minimum substantive standards

The TRIPS Agreement provides minimum substantive standards that must be observed by all WTO Members for each category of IP rights. The TRIPS Agreement contains minimum standards for the following categories of IP rights: (1) copyright and related rights; (2) patents; (3) trademarks (as well as service marks); (4) geographical indications; (5) undisclosed information or trade secrets; (6) industrial designs; and (7) layout designs of integrated circuits.

## 8.1 Copyright and related rights

The TRIPS Agreement requires WTO Members to give full recognition to the copyright regime of the Berne Convention.[131] Computer programs must be copyrightable as literary works, as the term is used in the Berne Convention.[132] The minimum term of copyright protection must be 50 years from the end of the calendar year of making or publication.[133] A limited exception to copyright protection is provided in Article 13 of the TRIPS Agreement for "certain special cases which do not conflict with a normal exploitation of the work and do not unreasonably prejudice the legitimate interests of the right holder". Article 13 was narrowly interpreted in the *United States — Section 110(5) of the U.S. Copyright Act*[134] case

[129] *Id.* Arts. 3 and 4. In *United States — Section 211 Omnibus Appropriations Act*, the Appellate Body ruled that by not according protection to trademarks of businesses confiscated by the Cuban government, the United States was in violation of both of these obligations. Appellate Body Report, *United States — Section 211 Omnibus Appropriations Act*, WT/DS176/AB/R.

[130] TRIPS Agreement Arts. 3.1, 4.1(a), (b), (c) and (d), and 5.

[131] *Id.* Art. 9.

[132] *Id.* Art. 10.

[133] *Id.* Art. 12.

[134] Panel Report, *United States — Section 110(5) of the U.S. Copyright Act.*

involving an exception in U.S. copyright law to allow the playing of music by small retail establishments and restaurants. The panel ruled that Article 13 did not apply because its conditions were not fulfilled.[135]

## 8.2 Patents

WTO Members must extend patent protection to all inventions, whether products or processes, in all fields of technology.[136] The term of patent protection must be at least 20 years from the date of filing the application.[137] Moreover, patent rights must also be available without *discrimination* as to the place of invention, the field of technology, and whether products are imported or produced locally.[138] Three important deregations exist from these broad requirements: (1) exclusions; (2) limited exceptions; and (3) compulsory licensing.

### *8.2.1 Patent excludability*

The TRIPS Agreement allows WTO Members to exclude inventions from patentability on several grounds:

1. inventions that are necessary "to protect *ordre public* or morality, including to protect human, animal or plant life or health or to avoid serious prejudice to the environment..."[139]
2. "diagnostic, therapeutic and surgical methods from the treatment of humans or animals".[140]
3. "plants and animals other than micro-organisms, and essentially biological processes for the production of plants or animals other than non-biological and microbiological processes".[141]

None of these exclusions has been definitively interpreted, and the first and third exclusions are particularly ambiguous and thus susceptible to different interpretations. The first exclusion is potentially a broad exception to allow Members to protect public health and the environment. The phrase

---

[135] Panel Report, *United States — Section 110(5) of the U.S. Copyright Act*, para. 6.133.

[136] TRIPS Agreement Art. 27.

[137] *Id.* Art. 33. Thus rule was applied in *Canada — Term of Patent Protection.* Panel Report, *Canada — Term of Patent Protection*, WT/DS170/R (holding that certain patents were subject to 20–year minimum term).

[138] TRIPS Agreement Art. 27.1.

[139] *Id.* Art. 27.2.

[140] *Id.* Art. 27.3(a).

[141] *Id.* Art. 27.3(b).

"*ordre public*" indicates that this exclusion may even reach beyond these concerns to exclude inventions from patentability on political, cultural and religious grounds. This exclusion is narrowed considerably, however, because of the additional requirement that the exclusion must be "necessary" to prevent "commercial exploitation" within a Member's territory. A Member relying on this provision may have to show that all commercial exploitation of the invention is harmful within its territory. This would be a rare case, indeed, and the exception would thus seem to be extremely narrow.

The third exclusion allows Members to exclude animals and plants as well as biological processes for their production from patentability. This exclusion would seem to include even genetically altered animals and plants, which are patentable under the law of the United States.[142] This exclusion is, however, qualified by three exceptions: WTO Members may patent (1) non-biological processes; (2) micro-organisms, and microbiological processes and (3) plant varieties.[143]

### 8.2.2 *Limited exceptions*

Article 30 of the TRIPS Agreement allows "limited exceptions" to the exclusive rights conferred by patent. Three requirements must be met to invoke this section.[144] First, the exception must be "limited". Second, it must not "unreasonably conflict with normal exploitation of the patent". Finally, it must not "unreasonably prejudice the legitimate expectations of the patent owner".[145] In the *Canada — Patents* case, the WTO panel ruled that a provision allowing stockpiling of generic pharmaceuticals in anticipation of the expiration of the patent term could not be considered "limited" because it was a "substantial curtailment" of the patent holders' rights. On the other hand, an exception to allow regulatory review of the generic drug during the term of the patent so that the generic drug could be marketed quickly was held to meet the Article 30 requirements.[146] Curiously, however, the panel ruled that this exception was invalid because it violated the non-discrimination requirement of Article 27.1, which the panel held applied even to exceptions.[147] This

[142] *See* above note 95.

[143] *See* above note 93. For plant varieties, a *sui generis* system such as the UPOV Convention is allowable.

[144] *See* Panel Report, *Canada — Patent Protection of Pharmaceutical Products*, WT/DS114/R, 7 April 2000.

[145] *Id.* para. 7.20.

[146] *Id.* para. 7.84.

[147] *Id.* paras 7.93–7.105.

ruling appears wrong on two grounds. First, the non-discrimination prohibition in Article 27.1 qualifies only that subsection by its terms, and there is no textual basis for transporting it to Article 30. Second, a limited exception, specifically allowed in Article 30, would by its very terms be discriminatory in some way; if it were not, it would not be *limited.*

### *8.2.3 Compulsory licensing*

#### 8.2.3.1 Differing views on compulsory licensing

In some countries, patent law provides for compulsory licensing under certain conditions. There are divergent views on the question of under what conditions there should be compulsory licensing of a patent. In the United States, the importance of intellectual properties is emphasized, and compulsory licensing is done only in extreme situations, generally in cases of violations of the antitrust laws. Japan allows compulsory licensing under similar conditions, although these have never been invoked.

On the other hand, many developing countries take the view that compulsory licensing should be required if the public interest is injured due to an abuse of patent monopoly. For example, if a company that owns a patent in an area in which there is no competing technology deprives society of its benefit or unduly raises the price of the patented product, a national authority should be able to order compulsory licensing.

The problem boils down to whether the conditions under which compulsory licensing of a patent may be ordered should be indicated clearly by law or whether compulsory licensing may be ordered if doing so is justified and patent law should enumerate the conditions for such a licence. In the Uruguay Round trade negotiations that led to the conclusion of the TRIPS Agreement, advanced countries, such as the United States, took the former position, and the latter was asserted by developing countries, such as India.

#### 8.2.3.2 Provisions in the TRIPS Agreement

In the Uruguay Round, the above issues were discussed and, as the result of negotiation, the TRIPS Agreement incorporates Article 31, which provides the requirements that must be met when ordering compulsory licensing. There are 11 principles listed in Article 31:

1. Whether ordering compulsory licensing shall be judged on a case-by-case basis.
2. When ordering compulsory licensing, there shall be consultation with the owner of the right in advance. However, compulsory licensing

ordered for public and non-commercial use is exempted from this requirement.

3. The scope of the license and its period shall be determined on the basis of the objective of compulsory licensing. With regard to technology relating to semiconductors, compulsory licensing shall be given only for the purposes of utilizing public non-commercial use or the remedy for restrictive business practices.

4. Compulsory licensing shall be non-exclusive.

5. Rights derived from compulsory licensing cannot be transferred to a third party except for those cases in which the two parties jointly engage in business.

6. The purpose of compulsory licensing shall be, in principle, limited to the supply to the domestic market of the country concerned.

7. When the situation that led to the setting of compulsory licensing has ceased to exist and there is no likelihood of recurrence, the compulsory licensing shall be terminated, provided the legitimate benefit of the licensee shall be protected.

8. The owner of the right shall be given an appropriate compensation.

9. There shall be the opportunity for judicial review as regards the setting of compulsory licensing.

10. If a compulsory license is ordered as a remedy to restrictive business practices, (2) and (6) above do not apply.

11. Where a compulsory license is given for exploiting a patent (the second patent), which cannot be exploited without infringing another patent (the first patent), the invention claimed in the second patent shall involve an important technical advance. The owner of the first patent is entitled to a cross-license on reasonable terms of the second patent and the authorized use for the first patent shall be non-assignable without including assignment of the second patent.

Issues of compulsory licensing of patents are those of balancing two opposing interests: namely, the interests of inventors and of technologically advanced countries and those of licensees and of technologically less-advanced countries. Article 31 attempts to strike this balance. Nevertheless, many ambiguities and issues of interpretation remain.

## 8.3 Trademarks and service marks

Trademarks and service marks must be given full protection by WTO Members; however, registration may be made dependent on use.[148] The initial registration of a trademark shall be for a term of no less than seven years, and it must be renewable indefinitely.[149] If use is required to maintain registration, the mark may be cancelled only after an uninterrupted period of three years of non-use.[150] Trademarks are assignable and compulsory licensing of trademarks is not permitted.[151]

## 8.4 Geographical indications

WTO Members must create a legal system of protection for geographical indications where the reputation or quality of a good is "essentially attributable" to its geographical origin.[152] This is especially necessary for wines and spirits.[153] Negotiations are ongoing to determine the precise framework of protection for geographical indications.[154]

An example of geographic indications would be the use of the term "Bordeaux", which indicates the name of a place in France and is associated with a high quality of wine produced therein. A wine producer in another country may use this name to promote the sale of its wine as "Bordeaux-style wine". The TRIPS Agreement allows WTO Members to prohibit the use of geographic indications in such a way as to cause deception and provides for injunctive relief, the refusal of trademark registration, and invalidation of trademark registration when there is an authorized use of geographical indications causing deception. In addition, the TRIPS Agreement allows WTO Members to prohibit the use of geographical indications with regard to wine and spirits even if they do not cause a deception.

## 8.5 Undisclosed information or trade secrets

WTO Members must protect undisclosed information (or trade secrets). Undisclosed information that is secret and has commercial value is sometimes called "know-how". The requirements for being qualified as undisclosed information under the TRIPS Agreement are that it is a secret (*i.e.*, it is not in general circulation) and that it has commercial value. Primary examples include industrial know-how, which is undisclosed technology not

[148] TRIPS Agreement Art. 15. [149] *Id.* Art. 18.
[150] *Id.* Art. 19.1. [151] *Id.* Art. 21.
[152] *Id.* Art. 22. [153] *Id.* Art. 23.
[154] *Id.* Arts. 23.4 and 24.

patented but useful for industrial purposes and not in general circulation. The wording of provisions relating to undisclosed information does not exclude other types of undisclosed information such as know-how in marketing and distribution (*e.g.*, a list of customers).

### 8.6 Industrial designs

WTO Members must provide IP protection for independently created industrial designs.[155] Design protection extends to aesthetic aspects not dictated by technical or functional considerations.[156] The duration of protection shall amount to at least 10 years.[157] The owner of a protected design must have the right to prevent third parties from making, selling, or importing products bearing or embodying a design that is a copy of a protected design.[158]

### 8.7 Layout designs of integrated circuits

WTO Members must give IP protection to layout designs (topographies) of integrated circuits (semi-conductor chips).[159] The minimum term of such protection must be ten years from the date of filing an application for registration or from the first commercial exploitation anywhere in the world.[160]

## 9. Enforcement of intellectual property rights under the TRIPS Agreement

The TRIPS Agreement provides minimum standards for the enforcement of intellectual property rights. As explained below, these enforcement measures must include civil and administrative remedies, criminal remedies, and border (customs) measures.

### 9.1 General principles

WTO Members must enact and maintain domestic laws and regulations that can deal effectively with infringements of intellectual property rights.

[155] *Id.* Art. 25.1.
[156] *Id.*
[157] *Id.* Art. 26.3.
[158] *Id.* Art. 26.1.
[159] *Id.* Art. 35.
[160] *Id.* Art. 38.1.

The process of enforcement of intellectual property rights must be fair and equitable and not be unnecessarily complex and expensive. The period of investigation should not be unduly limited or delayed. With regard to the administrative decisions, Members must provide opportunities for judicial review concerning such decisions.[161]

## 9.2 Civil and administrative procedures and remedies

WTO Members must provide for civil and administrative procedures for the enforcement of intellectual property rights to holders of such rights.[162] The United States was held to violate Article 42 by denying protection for trademarks such as "Havana Club Rum", linked with properties confiscated by the Castro government in Cuba.[163] Courts must be authorized to issue injunctive relief to stop infringement and order the payment of damages sustained by parties whose rights have been infringed.[164]

## 9.3 Criminal procedures

WTO Members must impose criminal penalties on at least wilful infringement of trademark and copyrights committed on a commercial scale.[165]

## 9.4 Border measures

The TRIPS Agreement permits WTO Members to exclude imports that infringe intellectual property rights.[166] With regard to trademark rights and copyrights, Members must adopt procedures whereby a party can petition an administrative or judicial body for an injunction preventing an importation when it reasonably suspects that a product that infringes a trademark or copyright is being imported.[167] Members may adopt such a procedure in respect to the other intellectual property rights, such as patent rights, but are not obligated to do so.[168] The rationale is that, whereas an infringement of a trademark right and copyright is clear on the surface, whether an import-

[161] TRIPS Agreement Art. 41.1 and .2.

[162] *Id.* Art. 42.

[163] Appellate Body Report, *United States — Section 211 Omnibus Appropriations Act*, (AB 2001–7), 2 January 2002, WT/DS176/AB/R.

[164] TRIPS Agreement Arts. 44, 45, and 46.

[165] *Id.* Art. 61.

[166] *Id.* Art. 51.

[167] *Id.*

[168] *Id.*

ation of a commodity infringes a patent cannot be determined until after detailed examination of the matter.[169]

In addition, it is provided that a claimant has the burden of proof that an imported article infringes its intellectual property rights.[170]

The United States has long had a procedure, Section 337 of the Tariff Act,[171] for excluding imports of goods that violate intellectual property laws. In 1989, a GATT dispute settlement panel ruled that Section 337 violated the national treatment provision (Article III:4) of the GATT.[172] After the Uruguay Round, the United States amended Section 337, ostensibly to correct the offending provisions.[173]

## 9.5 Provisional measures

Enforcement authorities of Members can impose provisional measures to stop importation of a commodity when it determines that an importation of such a commodity infringes a right granted by law and there is urgency to take a prompt measure.

## 9.6 Dispute settlement

The dispute settlement process, as provided for in the Dispute Settlement Understanding (the DSU) of the WTO Agreement, applies to the settlement of disputes arising under the TRIPS Agreement.[174]

Non-violation complaints could not be brought under the TRIPS Agreement until 2000,[175] and the Doha Ministerial Conference agreed that such complaints cannot be brought before the next Ministerial Conference meets in 2003.[176]

---

[169] *Id.* Art. 53.

[170] *Id.* Art. 52.

[171] 19 U.S.C.A. § 1337 (1999 & Supp. 2001).

[172] *United States — Section 337 of the Tariff Act of 1930*, 7 November 1989, GATT B.I.S.D. (36th Supp.) at 345 (1990) [hereinafter *United States — Section 337*].

[173] For an argument that the amended section 337 violates Article 3 of the TRIPS Agreement, see N. David Palmeter, *Section 337 and the WTO Agreements Still in Violation?*, 20 World Competition 27 (1996).

[174] TRIPS Agreement Art. 64.1.

[175] *Id.* Art. 64.2 and .3.

[176] WTO, Ministerial Conference, Fourth Session, Doha, 9–14 November 2001, *Implementation-Related Issues and Concerns*, WT/MIN(01)/DEC/17, 20 November 2001, para. 11.1.

## 10. Exhaustion of intellectual property rights

There are two competing theories of exhaustion of intellectual property rights. Under the universal or international exhaustion theory, an IP right holder's rights are exhausted on the first sale of the protected product anywhere in the world. Under this theory, the protected product can be resold and even exported to or imported into other countries where the original rights holder has a protected interest. Under the domestic or territorial exhaustion theory, however, the right holder's IP rights are not exhausted until after the first sale of the product in the territory in which he holds the rights. Under this theory, the rights holder can prevent the export or import of the protected product. Thus, "parallel" or "gray market" imports — the sale of a legally produced product in a different territorial market — are allowed under the international exhaustion theory but prohibited under the domestic exhaustion theory. Furthermore, different exhaustion theories may be applicable to different forms of IP; thus, parallel imports of patented products may be prohibited, while parallel imports of trademarked products are permitted.

In the negotiation of the TRIPS Agreement, the parties were unable to reach agreement on the issue of exhaustion. This disagreement is reflected in TRIPS Article 6: "For the purposes of dispute settlement under this Agreement, subject to the provisions of Article 3 and 4, nothing in this Agreement shall be used to address the issue of the exhaustion of intellectual property rights".[177] The international exhaustion doctrine is, therefore, outside the scope of the TRIPS Agreement. Thus, the resolution of exhaustion issues is left to national laws. There are no international or customary law norms in this area. The various positions of WTO Members differ widely. At the Doha Ministerial Conference in 2001, the Members reaffirmed that each Member is free to establish its own regime on exhaustion.[178]

[177] TRIPS Agreement Art. 6.

[178] *Doha Ministerial Declaration*, above note 119, at para. 5(d).

# 11. Restrictive business practices

## 11.1 Types of restrictive business practices involved in technology licensing agreements

International technology licensing often takes the form of a patent or know-how licensing agreement. When a firm owns a patent covering a certain area of production in a country and grants a licence to another firm, the technology incorporated into the patent is transferred. If the patent owner is a foreign firm and the licensee a domestic firm, the licensing agreement provides for international transfer of technology. The same applies to a licensing agreement of know-how.

Restrictive conditions are often attached to a patent or know-how agreement whereby the licensee is prevented from engaging in certain activities. Some examples follow with respect to patent licensing agreements:

1. The licensor may require the licensee to observe a minimum price when it sells the product produced using the licensed patent.
2. The licensor may require the licensee to purchase parts and components necessary to produce a product covered by the patent from the licensor or a party designated by the licensor.
3. The licensor may require the licensee not to handle a commodity that competes with the product covered by the licensed patent.
4. The licensor may require the licensee not to engage in the research and development of a competing product during the period of the licence.

The above are but a few of many examples of restrictive business covenants incorporated into patent or know-how licensing agreements. Some restrictive covenants are necessary and reasonable for protecting the interests of the licensor. For example, it is legitimate for a licensor of a patent to limit the field of use of the patent that the licensee can exploit. Other restrictive covenants may be excessively restrictive and deprive licensees of the benefit they are entitled to enjoy. For example, if a licensor of a patent requires that a licensee must transfer to the former any improvement technology that it develops on the basis of the licensed technology, the licensee is deprived of any incentive to develop new technology.

Different countries have different attitudes to restrictive conditions attached to patent or know-how licensing agreements. In many countries, restrictive conditions are regarded as issues of competition law or foreign investment law. The United States generally takes a lenient attitude to conditions attached to licensing agreements, whereas the European Community and Japan take a more stringent attitude to them. Developing countries are generally critical of restrictive conditions attached to patent or know-how licensing agreements because, in many cases, an enterprise of an advanced country imposes such conditions on an enterprise of a developing country that licenses the intellectual property.

## 11.2 Article 40 of the TRIPS Agreement

Article 40.1 of the TRIPS Agreement recognizes that some licensing practices or conditions pertaining to intellectual property rights that restrain competition may have adverse effects on trade and may impede the transfer and dissemination of technology. The TRIPS Agreement specifies only three examples of licensing practices or conditions that restrain competition and allows WTO Members to enact domestic legislation on restrictive business practices incorporated in licensing arrangements. Licensing practices or conditions listed in Article 40.2 of the TRIPS Agreement as examples of those that restrain competition are: (1) exclusive grantback conditions; (2) conditions preventing challenges to validity; and (3) coercive package licensing. This is an illustrative, not an exhaustive list.

In exclusive grant back conditions, the licensor of technology requires that the licensee must grant back an improvement technology that the latter has developed on the basis of the licensed technology. This grant back may take the form of transfer of rights, such as a transfer of patent on this improvement technology or of an exclusive licence to be given to the former whereby everyone except the former is excluded from utilizing this technology. An exclusive grant back (or assign back) of improvement technology is regarded as an unfair business practice in some jurisdictions, such as the European Community, where this is a prohibited practice, and Japan, where the guidelines designate this as an unfair business practice.

Conditions preventing challenges to validity sometimes are referred to as "non-contestability clauses", which means that the licensee of patent cannot challenge the validity of the licensed patent. Although, in the United States a non-contestability clause is regarded as not enforceable, there are jurisdictions, including the European Community, in which a non-contestability clause is regarded not necessarily as an unfair business practice. The rationale behind the inclusion of this category in Article 40.2 is not clear.

A coercive package licensing agreement generally is regarded as unlawful as long as a package licensing is imposed on the licensee in the major jurisdictions. However, a package licensing may be reasonable if patents or know-how combined in the package are inextricably linked with each other or the combination of those patents or know-how guarantees the effective use of technology. This suggests that a judgment must be made on a case-by-case basis.

It should be observed that these three types of restrictive business practices are by no means representative of conditions in licensing agreements which hinder free flows of technology, and the rationale behind the inclusion of only those three categories in Article 40.2 of the TRIPS Agreement, even as examples, is not clear. Therefore, the scope of legislation which Members enact to combat restrictive business practices incorporated in licensing agreements should be greater. It is desirable that Article 40.2 be modified to include more practices or guidelines to indicate what practices may fall under such legislation.

## 12. Conclusions

The TRIPS Agreement is a highly innovative document that breaks new ground to cover a field tangentially related to international trade that is not covered in the GATT 1994. Overall, the TRIPS Agreement has worked well, and the WTO has established a working relationship with WIPO to upgrade significantly intellectual property rights protection around the world.

In the coming years, WTO Members must continue to implement the wide-ranging provisions of the TRIPS Agreement. Significant public policy questions have arisen with regard to the TRIPS Agreement that must be addressed in the future. The Ministerial Declaration adopted at Doha, Qatar in 2001 signals that the TRIPS may be significantly modified.

# 17

# ENVIRONMENTAL PROTECTION AND TRADE

## 1. Introduction

The "link" between international trade and protection of the environment bears explanation. In the popular mind, and even among some specialists, the topic of the WTO and the environment dominates discussion. One finds criticism such as the following:

> The WTO has been a disaster for the environment. Threats — often by industry but with government support — of WTO-illegality are being used to chill environmental innovation and to undermine multilateral environmental agreements. Already WTO threats and challenges have undermined or threatened to interfere with U.S. Clean Air rules, the U.S. Endangered Species Act, Japan's [sic] Kyoto (global warming) Treaty implementation, a European toxics and recycling law, U.S. longhorned beetle infestation policy, EU ecolabels, U.S. dolphin protection legislation and an EU humane trapping law.
>
> Things only stand to get worse . . .[1]

This criticism implies that the link between trade and the environment is one of overlap and opposition. Upon analysis, this is not the case.

First, international trade and protection of the environment are both essential for the welfare of mankind. In the vast majority of cases, these two values do not come into conflict. On the contrary, they are mutually supportive. As stated in Agenda 21, adopted at the UN Conference on Environment and Development in 1992,

> Environment and trade policies should be mutually supportive. An open multilateral trading system makes possible a more efficient allocation and use of resources and thereby contributes to an increase in production and incomes and to lessening demands on the environment. It thus provides additional resources needed for economic growth . . . and improved environmental protection. A sound environment, on the other hand, provides the ecological and other resources needed to sustain growth and underpin continuing expansion of trade.[2]

[1] Lori Wallach and Michelle Sforza, The WTO: Five Years of Reasons to Resist Corporate Globalization 27 (1999).

[2] Agenda 21, § 2.19, UN Doc. A/CONF. 151/4 (1992), reprinted in 31 I.L.M. 881.

Second, taking active steps to protect the environment is beyond the scope of authority allotted to the WTO under international law. The WTO's function is limited to administering the WTO agreements.[3] Thus, the WTO deals only with trade, not protection of the environment. The WTO agreements apply to measures protecting the environment only where and insofar as they have an impact on international trade. Relatively few environmental measures fall into this category.

Third, nothing in the WTO Agreements requires that free trade be accorded priority over environmental protection. Rather, the preamble to the WTO Agreement acknowledges that expansion of production and trade must allow for "the optimal use of the world's resources in accordance with the objective of sustainable development, seeking both to protect and preserve the environment and to enhance the means for doing so in a manner consistent with their respective needs and concerns at different levels of economic development".[4]

Thus, what is sought is balance between the two objectives of free trade and environmental protectionism. In addition, the WTO is sensitive to uncovering measures that purport to be for environmental reasons but are a subterfuge for serving other interests, such as protection of domestic producers.

Accordingly, many WTO agreements contain conditional exceptions for environmental measures.

The GATT 1994 states as follows in Article XX:

> Subject to the requirement that such measures are not applied in a manner which would constitute a means of arbitrary or unjustifiable discrimination between countries where the same conditions prevail, or a disguised restriction on international trade, nothing in this Agreement shall be construed to prevent the adoption or enforcement by any contracting party of measures:
>
> ...
>
> (b) necessary to protect human, animal or plant life or health;
>
> ...
>
> (g) relating to the conservation of exhaustible natural resources if such measures are made effective in conjunction with restrictions on domestic production or consumption.

The General Agreement on Trade in Services (GATS) contains an identical exception to GATT Article XX(b).[5] The Agreement on Trade-Related Aspects of Intellectual Property Rights (TRIPS Agreement) states that

[3] WTO Agreement Art. III:1.

[4] WTO Agreement, 1st recital in the preamble.

[5] GATS Art. XIV(b).

"Members may exclude from patentability inventions, the prevention within their territory of the commercial exploitation of which is necessary ... to protect human, animal or plant life or health or to avoid serious prejudice to the environment".[6] The Agreement on Subsidies and Countervailing Measures (SCM Agreement) contains an exemption for certain environmental subsidies.[7] The Agreement on Technical Barriers to Trade (TBT Agreement) states that protection of the environment is a "legitimate objective" that allows a WTO Member to enact high standards of protection.[8] The Agreement on the Application of Sanitary and Phytosanitary Measures (SPS Agreement) sets out criteria to supplement GATT XX(b) to govern the validity of national measures passed to protect humans, plants and animals from contaminants, disease-carrying organisms, and pests.

The latter agreements are the subjects of separate chapters and will be discussed only briefly here. This chapter concentrates on GATT Article XX, which has produced the liveliest discussion and the most interesting interpretations.

The WTO established a Committee on Trade and Environment (CTE) in 1995. The CTE was charged with making appropriate recommendations on "the need for rules to enhance the positive interaction between trade and environment measures for the promotion of sustainable development". The CTE was asked to address the following matters:

1. "the relationship between the provisions of the multilateral trading system and trade measures for environmental purposes, including those pursuant to multilateral environmental agreements";
2. "the relationship between environmental policies relevant to trade and environmental measures with significant trade effects and the provisions of the multilateral trading system";
3. "the relationship between the provisions of the multilateral trading system and: (a) charges and taxes for environmental purposes[,] (b) requirements for environmental purposes relating to products, including standards and technical regulations, packaging, labelling and recycling";
4. "the provisions of the multilateral trading system with respect to the transparency of trade measures used for environmental purposes and environmental measures and requirements which have significant trade effects";

[6] TRIPS Agreement Art. 27.2.

[7] SCM Agreement Art. 8.2(c).

[8] SPS Agreement Art. 2.2.

5. "the relationship between the dispute settlement mechanisms in the multilateral trading system and those found in multilateral environmental agreements";
6. "the effect of environmental measures on market access, especially in relation to developing countries, in particular to the least developed among them, and environmental benefits of removing trade restrictions and distortions";
7. "the issue of exports of domestically prohibited goods";
8. "the relevant provisions of the Agreement on Trade-Related Aspects of Intellectual Property Rights";
9. "the work programme envisaged in Decision on Trade in Services and the Environment"; and
10. "input to the relevant bodies in respect of appropriate arrangements for relations with inter-governmental and non-governmental organizations".[9]

However, no significant decision has been taken by the CTE, which is open to participation by all members. Consequently, the Final Declaration of the Doha Ministerial Conference in November 2001, adopted a Trade and Environment Work Programme, which includes the following:

1. The relationship between WTO rules and trade restrictions in multilateral environmental agreements;
2. Criteria for granting observer status and information exchange;
3. reduction and elimination of trade barriers for environmental goods and services; and
4. Fisheries subsidies.[10]

In addition, the CTE was instructed to give particular attention to (1) the effect of environmental measures on market access, especially for developing countries; (2) environmental aspects of TRIPS; and (3) labelling requirements for environmental purposes.

Thus, the accommodation of protection of the environment and trade is incomplete and ongoing.

---

[9] Decision on Trade and Environment, in WTO, THE LEGAL TEXTS: THE RESULTS OF THE URUGUAY ROUND OF MULTILATERAL TRADE NEGOTIATIONS 411 (1999).

[10] WTO, Ministerial Conference, Fourth Session, Doha, 9–14 November 2001, *Ministerial Declaration*, WT/MIN(01)/DEC/1, 20 November 2001, paras 31–33.

## 2. Environmentalist trade demands: a critical analysis

What is the basis of the environmentalist objection to the rules of the multilateral trading system? Daniel Esty, a distinguished critic, has identified the following four environmentalist critiques:

- Without environmental safeguards, trade may cause environmental harm by promoting economic growth that results in the unsustainable consumption of natural resources and waste production.
- Trade rules and trade liberalization often entail market access agreements that can be used to override environmental regulations unless appropriate environmental protections are built into the structure of the trade system.
- Trade restrictions should be available as leverage to promote worldwide environmental protection, particularly to address global or transboundary environmental problems and to reinforce international environmental agreements.
- Even if the pollution they cause does not spill over into other nations, countries with lax environmental standards have a competitive advantage in the global marketplace and put pressure on countries with high environmental standards to reduce the rigour of their environmental requirements.[11]

## 3. The environmental impact of trade

Some environmentalist opposition to trade is based on the notion that international mobility of goods, services, and capital is fundamentally anti-environmental. Herman Daly, an economist, for example, has stated that free trade:

> sins against allocative efficiency by making it difficult for nations to internalize external costs; it sins against distributive justice by widening the disparity between labor and capital in high wage countries; it sins against community by demanding more mobility and by further separating ownership and control; [and] it sins against sustainable scale [by offering] a way to loosen local constraints by importing environmental services (including waste absorption) from elsewhere.[12]

[11] Daniel C. Esty, THE GREENING OF THE GATT 42 (1994).

[12] Herman E. Daly, *From Adjustment to Sustainable Development: The Obstacle of Free Trade*, 15 LOY. L.A. INT'L & COMP. L. REV. 33, 41–42 (1992).

The facts, however, belie these charges. It is wrong to blame failure to internalize environmental costs of trade. First, there is little empirical evidence that companies relocate to take advantage of lax pollution controls.[13] Second, countries like Brazil, with very protectionist trade policies, still fail to preserve natural resources. Commercial logging for export, for example, plays little part in the destruction of the Amazon rain forest. Instead, the basic causes are the demand for land and local agriculture and forestry practices.[14]

A 1994 OECD study[15] on the impact of trade on the environment found that the direct effects of trade on the environment are generally small because only a limited share of ecologically sensitive goods enter into trade and because trade is only one of many factors affecting the environment. It found:

> In general, trade is not the root cause of environmental problems, which are due to market and intervention failures. Market failures occur when markets do not reflect environmental values. Intervention failures occur when public policies do not correct for, create or exacerbate market failures. Such failures can distort the incentives for protecting the environment and can drive a wedge between the private and socially optimum rates and modes of production and consumption. Environmental economics has focused on understanding and correcting these failures at the domestic level, but such failures also occur at the international level and increasingly have global impacts. International trade can help correct market and intervention failures through providing increased funds and incentives for environmental protection and promoting efficient resource use. But, at times, international trade may exacerbate the environmental problems in the presence of market and intervention failures.[16]

The impact of trade on the environment is complex; it may be positive, negative or neutral, depending on the economic sector and the circumstances. The OECD framework for analysis is to consider trade-related environmental impacts from two perspectives (1) market failures and (2) intervention failures. The chief categories of market failure leading to environmental degradation are (1) failure to externalize environmental costs[17];

---

[13] Judith Dean, *Trade and Environment: A Survey of the Issues,* in INTERNATIONAL TRADE AND THE ENVIRONMENT 15, 27 (Patrick Low ed., 1992).

[14] *See* Brian F. Chase, *Tropical Forests and Trade Policy: The Legality of Unilateral Attempts to Promote Sustainable Development Under the GATT,* 17 HAST. INT'L & COMP. L. REV. 349, 356–57 (1994).

[15] OECD, The Environmental Effects of Trade (1994) [hereinafter OECD Report].

[16] *Id.* at 8.

[17] The OECD Report (at 8) states as follows:

In other words, the environmental costs are externalities rather than internalised in the prices of goods and services. Environmental externalities stem from the consumption of products which impose costs on others which are not compensated through the market. The divergence of the

(2) improper valuation of ecosystems[18]; and (3) ill-defined or open property rights regimes[19] for certain resources. Two categories of intervention failure are (1) subsidies[20] and (2) trade barriers.[21]

apparent costs of an activity from its total cost is reflected in the loss of clean air and water and the degradation of environmental resources. Examples are the pollution resulting from excess use of fertilizers and chemicals in the agricultural sector or the pollution associated with intensive aquaculture in the fisheries sector and congestion in the transport sector. Failure to internalise environmental costs at the national level can contribute to transboundary and global environmental problems, such as acid rain, river pollution and climate change.

[18] According to the OECD Report (at 9):

**Improper valuation of ecosystems**

Market failures also result from the failure to take into account the total economic value derived by society from the structural features and environmental functions of ecosystems. This total economic value can be categorised into different components, namely direct use value of an environmental asset, which is the most easily quantified, relates to the actual output of goods and services from the asset....

The indirect use value of an environmental asset relates to its functional role in supporting economic activity and may best be measured in terms of the benefits derived from its contribution to the avoidance of environmental damage. For example, forests and wetlands provide both atmospheric and microclimatic support functions, such as carbon retention, flood control and groundwater recharge. ...

Economists have also identified existence values, relating to the benefits derived from the mere knowledge that an environmental asset exists and plays a functional role in maintaining ecosystems, and option values, associated with the future use of a resource. For example, it is estimated that closed tropical forests hold between 50 and 60 percent of the world's diversity essential to future pharmaceutical and crop-breeding research; this is an option value, part of the total economic value of forests.

[19] The OECD Report (at 9):

Market failures can stem from lack of property rights for environmental assets and the difficulties of defining and enforcing regimes for governing their use. The non-excludable nature of environmental goods, such as air and water, may lead to over-exploitation or over-consumption of a resource due to lack of incentives to protect it against actions that would diminish its supply. For example, the lack of direct ownership of many fisheries resources complicates fisheries management and may contribute to the over-exploitation or depletion of certain world fish stocks. Open access to forested areas in certain regions may contribute to environmentally damaging deforestation.

[20] The OECD Report (at 10):

While most production subsidies are directed to achieving domestic policy goals, they carry implications for both trade and the environment; export subsidies have more direct impacts on trade flows and can also have environmental effects. Distortions caused by production and export subsidies are believed to occur in the **agricultural sector** to a greater extent than in most other sectors. Subsidy policies, which in many countries influence the prices received by farmers and the cost of the inputs they use, can reinforce rather than mitigate market failures. In developed countries, output prices may be supported above market-clearing levels and, in some cases, input prices (for water, fertilizers, etc.).

[21] The OECD Report cited two examples (at 10):

Using these analytical tools, the positive or negative effects of trade may be identified and measured. With respect to products, trade may make a significant positive contribution by providing the opportunity for the global spread of environmental technologies and services to address particular environmental problems. Traded products may also have a negative environment effect if hazardous wastes or harmful chemicals are involved or through the sale of products from endangered species.

Trade may foster economic efficiency and growth, raising incomes and providing more money for environmental protection. If there is market or intervention failure, however, trade may lead to degradation and depletion of natural resources.

All WTO Members should keep the environmental impacts of trade and trade agreements under review.[22] Positive and negative impacts of trade should be identified, the positive impacts enhanced, and the negative aspects eliminated. For example, in the United States, the tariff-quota on sugar imports leads to greater production of sugar by American farmers. One of the principal sugar growing areas is in south Florida, where the high water use and fertilizers necessary for the production of sugar cane have an adverse impact on the Everglades, one of the most valuable and productive U.S. ecosystems.[23] Such trade distortions should be removed.

---

In the **fisheries sector**, the important tariffs applied to unprocessed products by most developed countries are lower than the tariffs on semi-processed and processed products. For example, the difference in the nominal tariff rates for fresh cod and cod fillets is 10 per cent in some countries, and the effective difference when taking into account weight loss may be nearly 50 per cent. These tariff differentials can contribute to overexploitation and fish stock depletion when exporting countries increase their fresh and frozen fish exports to maximise foreign exchange receipts without implementing proper fisheries management policies.

...

In the **forestry sector**, trade protectionism affects resource use and possibly contributes to forest degradation. Developing countries often face lower tariffs on unprocessed wood products and higher relative tariffs on processed products, which could be a factor in unsustainable industrialisation in low income countries. Tariff and quotas on imported forest products may provide protection to domestic forest industries and contribute to unsustainable forestry practices in importing countries.

[22] In the United States, the basis for doing this exists in the National Environmental Policy Act (NEPA), 42 USC.A. § 4331 *et seq.* Regrettably, the courts have held that negotiating a trade treaty is not "agency action", which is the trigger for the application of NEPA. *See Public Citizen v. U.S. Trade Representative*, 5 F.3d 549 (D.C. Cir. 1993) (no environmental impact statement required for NAFTA).

[23] For further discussion, see Thomas T. Ankerson and Richard Hamann, *Ecosystem Management and the Everglades: A Legal and Institutional Analysis*, 11 J. LAND USE & ENVTL. L. 473 (1996).

## 4. The *Tuna Dolphin* cases: a false start

Before 1991, the relationship between protection of the environment and international trade was an arcane specialty that attracted little attention.[24] In 1971, the GATT Council established a Working Group on Environmental Measures and International Trade.[25] This group did not even meet for over 20 years.

Everything changed with the decision in the *Tuna Dolphin I* case, in which a GATT panel declared a U.S. embargo on tuna caught by fishing methods causing high dolphin mortality to be illegal.[26] The *Tuna Dolphin I* decision produced an explosion of rhetoric in both learned journals[27] and the popular press.[28] It was also a very interesting clash of highly different "cultures": trade specialists versus environmentalists.

Acting under the U.S. Marine Mammal Protection Act (MMPA), the United States had adopted a unilateral ban on imports of yellowfin tuna

[24] Concern over the issue of trade and environment was expressed by several observers beginning in the early 1970s. *See generally* William J. Baumol, ENVIRONMENTAL PROTECTION, INTERNATIONAL SPILLOVERS AND TRADE (1971); C. Fred Bergsten, THE FUTURE OF THE INTERNATIONAL ECONOMIC ORDER: AN AGENDA FOR RESEARCH 42 (1973); Wolfgang E. Burhenne and Thomas J. Schoenbaum, *The European Community and the Management of the Environment*, 13 NAT. RESOURCES J. 494 (1973) (analysing problem of harmonizing different environmental standards for products that move in international trade in the context of Community law); Frederic L. Kirgis, Jr., *Effective Pollution Control in Industrialized Countries: International Economic Disincentives, Policy Response and the GATT*, 70 MICH. L. REV. 859 (1972) (analysing legality under the GATT of various environmental taxes on imports).

[25] Decision of the GATT Contracting Parties, GATT Doc. C/M/71 (1971).

[26] *United States — Restrictions on Imports of Tuna*, GATT B.I.S.D. (39th Supp.) at 155 (1993), reprinted in 30 I.L.M. 1594 (1991) (unadopted) [hereinafter *Tuna Dolphin I*].

[27] The literature is too voluminous to cite here. Among the most prolific and vocal commentators have been, on the environmentalist side, Steve Charnovitz, and on the trade side, Jagdish Bhagwati. *See especially* Steve Charnovitz, *Free Trade, Fair Trade, Green Trade: Defogging the Debate*, 27 CORNELL INT'L L.J. 459 (1994); Steve Charnovitz, *A Taxonomy of Environmental Trade Measures*, 6 GEO. INT'L ENVTL. L. REV. 1 (1993); Jagdish Bhagwati, *Trade and Environment: The False Conflict?*, in TRADE AND THE ENVIRONMENT: LAW, ECONOMICS AND POLICY 159 (D. Zaelke et al. eds., 1993). A leading book on the subject is Esty, above note 11. For a synthesis of the opposing views, see Ernst-Ulrich Petersmann, *International Trade Law and International Environmental Law: Prevention and Settlement of International Disputes in GATT*, 27 J. WORLD TRADE 43 (1993).

[28] *E.g.*, Patricia Dodwell, *Trade Row Looms over U.S.'s Dolphin-Friendly Trade Policy*, FIN. TIMES (London), 30 January 1992, at 22. From time to time, environmental groups have taken full-page ads in national newspapers to oppose the GATT. *E.g.*, *Sabotage!*, N.Y. TIMES, 20 April 1992, at A9 (nat'l ed.).

using methods that also kill dolphins, a protected species under the MMPA. Upon Mexico's complaint to the GATT, a dispute settlement panel found that the U.S. tuna embargo violated GATT Article XI:1, which forbids measures prohibiting or restricting imports or exports. The United States sought to justify the embargo under GATT Article III:1 and III:4 because U.S. fishermen were subject to the same MMPA rules. The GATT panel rejected the U.S. argument on the grounds that Article III:1 and Article III:4 permit only regulations relating to products as such. Because the MMPA regulations concerned harvesting techniques that could not possibly affect tuna as a product, the ban on tuna could not be justified. This holding was reiterated by a second GATT panel in the *Tuna Dolphin II* decision, which involved the legality of a secondary embargo of tuna products from countries that processed tuna caught by the offending countries.[29] The *Tuna Dolphin II* panel condemned the unilateral boycott in even stronger terms.[30]

Both *Tuna Dolphin* panels also concluded that neither GATT Article XX(b) nor XX(g) could justify the U.S. tuna import ban. As to Article XX(b), both panels held that the ban failed the "necessary" test. They rejected the U.S. argument that "necessary" means "needed", stating that "necessary" means that no other reasonable alternative exists and that "a contracting party is bound to use, among the measures available to it, that which entails the least degree of inconsistency" with the GATT.[31] A trade measure taken to force other countries to change their environmental policies, and that would be effective only if such changes occurred, could not be considered "necessary" within the meaning of Article XX(b).[32] Both panels similarly concluded that Article XX(g) was not applicable; they found that the terms "relating to" and "in conjunction with" in Article XX(g) meant "primarily aimed at", and held that unilateral measures to force other countries to change conservation policies cannot satisfy the "primarily aimed at" standard.[33]

---

[29] *United States — Restrictions on Imports of Tuna*, DS29/R, 16 June 1994, reprinted in 33 I.L.M. 839 (1994) (unadopted) [hereinafter *Tuna Dolphin II*].

[30] *Id.* paras 5.38–5.39.

[31] *Tuna Dolphin I*, above note 26, para. 5.27; *Tuna Dolphin II*, above note 29, para. 5.35.

[32] *Tuna Dolphin I*, above note 26, para. 5.27; *Tuna Dolphin II*, above note 29, paras 5.36–5.38.

[33] *Tuna Dolphin I*, above note 26, para. 5.33; *Tuna Dolphin II*, above note 29, para. 5.26. The *Tuna Dolphin I* panel's reasoning was that the U.S. requirement linking maximum incidental kills of dolphins by other countries to U.S. records and experience was so unpredictable that it

The GATT panels in the two *Tuna Dolphin* cases came to different conclusions regarding the territorial application of Article XX(b) and (g). The *Tuna Dolphin I* panel concluded that the natural resources and living things protected under these provisions were only those within the territorial jurisdiction of the country concerned.[34] This view, which was based on the belief that the drafters of Article XX had focused on each contracting party's domestic concerns, has been widely criticized.[35] The *Tuna Dolphin II* panel, in contrast, "could see no valid reason supporting the conclusion that the provisions of Article XX(g) apply only to . . . the conservation of exhaustible natural resources located within the territory of the contracting party invoking the provision".[36] Nevertheless, the panel ruled that governments can enforce an Article XX(g) restriction extraterritorially only against their own nationals and vessels.[37]

---

would not be primarily related to the conservation of dolphins. Article XX(g) was held inapplicable in several previous cases for similar reasons. In 1983, a GATT panel ruled that a U.S. embargo of tuna from Canada could not be justified under Article XX(g) because there were no U.S. correlative restrictions on the U.S. domestic production or consumption of tuna. (The U.S. had adopted the ban in retaliation against Canada's seizing U.S. fishing vessels). *United States — Prohibition of Imports of Tuna and Tuna Products from Canada*, 22 February 1982, GATT B.I.S.D. (29th Supp.) at 91 (1983).

In *Canada — Measures Affecting Exports of Unprocessed Herring and Salmon*, a Canadian export ban was held illegal since it was found not to be primarily aimed at or relating to conservation or rendering domestic production or consumption restrictions effective. *Canada — Measures Affecting Exports of Unprocessed Herring and Salmon*, 22 March 1988, GATT B.I.S.D. (35th Supp.) at 98 (1989) [hereinafter *Canada Herring*]. Subsequent to this decision, Canada adopted new regulations requiring salmon and herring caught in Canadian waters to be landed in Canada prior to exportation. A NAFTA dispute panel declared that this could not be justified under GATT Article XX(g) since the landing requirement did not "relate to" the conservation of natural resources. *In re Canada's Landing Requirement for Pacific Coast Salmon and Herring*, CDA–89–1807–01 (U.S.-Canada FTA Ch. 18 decision), 3 Can. Trade & Commodity Tax Cas. (CCH) 7162 (1989).

[34] *Tuna Dolphin I*, above note 26, paras 5.26, 5.31.

[35] *See, e.g.*, William J. Snape III and Naomi B. Lefkovitz, *Searching for GATT's Environmental Miranda: Are "Process Standards" Getting "Due Process"?*, 27 Cornell Int'l L.J. 777, 782–90 (1994); Alison Raina Ferrante, *The Dolphin/Tuna Controversy and Environmental Issues: Will the World Trade Organization's "Arbitration Court" and the International Court of Justice's Chamber for Environmental Matters Assist the United States in Furthering Environmental Goals?*, 5 J. Transnat'l L. & Pol'y 279, 297 (1996).

[36] *Tuna Dolphin II*, above note 29, para. 5.20.

[37] *Id.*

## 5. The WTO approach under GATT 1994

These two *Tuna Dolphin* GATT panel decisions represent the first tentative steps of the multilateral trading system to come to terms with protection of the environment. Neither decision was binding under the GATT because neither was adopted by the contracting parties. Even if they were, they would have little force as precedents because their reasoning was partially inconsistent and the decisions of prior GATT or WTO panels are not binding on future panels.[38] In addition, the WTO Appellate Body is fashioning its own approach to Article XX that makes significantly greater allowance for legitimate measures of environmental protection. Much of the reasoning in the *Tuna Dolphin* cases has been effectively overruled.

### 5.1 GATT Article XX(g)

A consistent theory of interpretation of Article XX(g) has been advanced by the Appellate Body in two important cases, the *United States — Reformulated Gasoline* case[39] and the *Shrimp/Turtle*[40] case. The latter case is particularly relevant because it involved a trade measure similar to those employed in the *Tuna Dolphin* cases, a ban on imported shrimp from countries that do not require their fishermen to harvest shrimp with methods that do not pose a threat to sea turtles. The first issue that must be addressed under Article XX(g) is whether the particular trade measure[41] concerns the conservation of exhaustible natural resources.[42] The Appellate Body has taken a generous view of this matter: a "resource" may be living or non-living, and it need not be rare or endangered to be potentially "exhaustible". Thus, dolphins, clean air, gasoline, and sea turtles qualify. Under this expansive interpretation, virtually any living or non-living resource, particularly those addressed by multilateral environmental agreements, would qualify.

---

[38] Appellate Body Report, *Japan — Alcoholic Beverages*, at 14.

[39] Appellate Body Report, *United States — Reformulated Gasoline.*

[40] Appellate Body Report, *Shrimp/Turtle.* For discussion of the case, *see, e.g.*, Howard Mann, *Of Revolution and Results: Trade Law and Environmental Law in the Afterglow of the* Shrimp-Turtle *Case*, 9 Y.B. INT'L ENVTL. L. 28 (1998); Thomas J. Schoenbaum, *The Decision on the* Shrimp-Turtle *Case*, 9 Y.B. INT'L ENVTL. L. 35 (1998); David A. Wirth, *Some Reflections on Turtles, Tuna, Dolphin and Shrimp*, 9 Y.B. INT'L ENVTL. L. 40 (1998).

[41] By "measure" is meant the law or rule challenged as inconsistent with WTO/GATT norms. Appellate Body Report, *United States — Reformulated Gasoline*, at 19.

[42] Appellate Body Report, *Shrimp/Turtle*, para. 127.

The second "relating to" element of Article XX(g) has proved more difficult to apply. Although a trade measure does not have to be "necessary" (as in Article XX(b)) to natural resource conservation, the GATT panels have interpreted "relating to" to mean that it must be "primarily aimed at" conservation.[43] Thus phrased, this requirement has proved a difficult obstacle. The question arises whether the "primarily aimed at" interpretation of "relating to" is correct. Certainly, these phrases are not synonymous. The "primarily aimed at" requirement seems to be an unwarranted amendment of Article XX. As the Appellate Body in *United States — Reformulated Gasoline* pointed out, "the phrase 'primarily aimed at' is not, itself, treaty language and was not designed as a simple litmus test" for Article XX.[44]

A third requirement of Article XX(g) is that the measure in question must be "made effective in conjunction with restrictions on domestic production or consumption". The Appellate Body in the *United States — Reformulated Gasoline* case gave the definitive interpretation of this phrase:

> [T]he basic international law rule of treaty interpretation . . . that the terms of a treaty are to be given their ordinary meaning, in context, so as to effectuate its object and purpose, is applicable here. . . . [T]he ordinary or natural meaning of "made effective" when used in connection with a measure — a governmental act or regulation — may be seen to refer to such measure being "operative," as "in force," or as having "come into effect." Similarly, the phrase "in conjunction with" may be read quite plainly as "together with" or "jointly with." Taken together, the second clause of Article XX(g) appears to us to refer to governmental measures like the baseline establishment rules being promulgated or brought into effect together with restrictions on domestic production or consumption of natural resources. . . . [W]e believe that the clause "if such measures are made effective in conjunction with restrictions on domestic product[ion] or consumption" is appropriately read as a requirement that the measures concerned impose restrictions, not just in respect of imported gasoline but also with respect to domestic gasoline.[45]

As the Appellate Body further pointed out, however, the "in conjunction with" element requires a certain amount of even-handedness, but not identity of treatment, and restrictions on either domestic production or consumption will be satisfactory.[46]

A similar approach was used in the *Shrimp/Turtle* case.[47] The Appellate Body found that the design of the measure or means used in the import ban

[43] *See Canada Herring*, above note 33, para. 6.39; Appellate Body Report, *United States — Reformulated Gasoline*, at 19.

[44] Appellate Body Report, *United States — Reformulated Gasoline*, at 19.

[45] *Id.* at 20.

[46] *Id.* at 21.

[47] Appellate Body Report, *Shrimp/Turtle*, paras 138–142.

on shrimp was reasonably related to the end or purpose of protecting sea turtles (just as the Appellate Body in the *United States — Reformulated Gasoline* case found that there was a reasonable relationship between the baseline establishment rules and clean air). Moreover, the "in conjunction with" requirement was satisfied because the United States required all shrimp trawlers to use turtle excluder devices in areas and at times when there is a likelihood of intercepting sea turtles. Thus, there are correlative restrictions on the domestic harvesting of shrimp.[48]

The approach to Article XX(g) now mandated by the Appellate Body is substantially different from the restrictive and somewhat illogical interpretations of GATT panels, particularly the *Tuna Dolphin* decisions. In fact, the U.S. restrictions on the harvesting of tuna would now pass Article XX(g) with flying colours. Dolphins clearly are an exhaustible natural resource; the import ban on tuna harvested by methods that kill dolphins clearly is related to the purpose of cutting dolphin mortality; and the requirements protecting dolphins also apply to U.S. vessels and fishermen. Importantly also, the Appellate Body in the *Shrimp/Turtle* case gave clear extraterritorial scope to Article XX(g): It applies without distinction to exhaustible resources beyond areas of national jurisdiction as well as to domestic resources.[49]

## 5.2 GATT Article XX(b)

The Appellate Body has fashioned a new approach to consider the GATT-compatibility of health measures "necessary to protect human, animal or plant life or health" under Article XX(b). The *EC — Asbestos* case[50] involved a Canadian complaint against a French regulation that prohibits the manufacture, sale, and import of all asbestos products subject to limited exceptions where no substitute product exists. The Appellate Body upheld the ban, and pointed to two separate ways such national health or environmentally protective measures can be approved under GATT 1994. First, when considering whether the banned product or substance is a "like product" to permissible products for purposes of applying the national treatment standard of GATT Article III:4, the Appellate Body stated that a crucial factor is evidence that consumers' behaviour is influenced by the health or environmental risks associated with a product.[51] Thus, the fact

[48] *Id.* paras 143–145.
[49] *Id.* paras 132–133.
[50] Appellate Body Report, *EC — Asbestos.*
[51] *Id.* para. 122.

that a product entails health or environmental risks may justify different treatment from otherwise similar products, and an import ban coupled with a ban on domestic manufacture and sale may satisfy GATT Article III:4.

Second, the Appellate Body in the *EC — Asbestos* case provided a new interpretation of GATT Article XX(b) that provides more flexibility to national governments in enacting measures to protect health and the environment. Article XX(b) has two requirements: (1) a showing that a measure is intended to protect human, animal, plant life or health; and (2) proof that the measure is "necessary".[52] Under GATT 1947, the "necessary" criterion was interpreted very restrictively.[53] In the *EC — Asbestos* case, however, the Appellate Body emphasized the interpretation of "necessary" as "reasonably available".[54] This approach shows deference and gives flexibility to national authorities.

Upholding a French ban on imports of asbestos under Article XX(b), the Appellate Body held that where there is a scientifically proven risk to health, "WTO members have the right to determine the level of protection of health that they consider appropriate ... ", based *either* on the quality of the risk (*i.e.*, is it regarded as socially acceptable) or on the quantity of the risk (*i.e.*, how likely is it). The more vital the common interests or values pursued, the easier it would be to accept as "necessary" measures designed to achieve those ends. In this case, it found that there was no alternative means of eliminating the risk. The Appellate Body's approach to the application of Article XX(b) thus brings it closer to the proportionality or balancing analysis applied by the European Community and the United States[55] when testing the necessity of restrictions on trade for environmental purposes.

## 5.3 The chapeau of Article XX

All of the Article XX exceptions are qualified by the chapeau, which sets out the tests for the manner in which a trade measure is applied. Three standards are stated in the chapeau: (1) arbitrary discrimination; (2) unjusti-

[52] *Tuna Dolphin* II, above note 29, para. 5.29.

[53] *See* Thomas J. Schoenbaum, *International Trade and Protection of the Environment: The Continuing Search for Reconciliation*, 91 Am. J. Int'l L. 268, 276–77 (1997).

[54] Appellate Body Report, *EC — Asbestos*, para. 172.

[55] *See* Case 302/86, *Commission v. Denmark* [1988] E.C.R. 4607 [hereinafter the *Danish Bottles* case] (applying a proportionality analysis); *Minnesota v. Clover Leaf Creamery Co.*, 449 U.S. 456 (1981) (applying a balancing test).

fiable discrimination; and (3) a disguised restriction on international trade. In the *Shrimp/Turtle* case, the Appellate Body stated that the chapeau is (1) a balancing principle to mediate between the right of a member to invoke an Article XX derogation and its obligation to respect the rights of other members; (2) a qualification making the Article XX exemptions "limited and conditional"[56]; (3) an expression of the principle of good faith in international law; and (4) a safeguard against *abus de droit*, the doctrine that requires the assertion of a right under a treaty to be "exercised bona fide, that is to say reasonably".[57] According to the Appellate Body, the chapeau protects "both substantive and procedural requirements".[58]

In the *Shrimp/Turtle* case, the unilateral measures applied by the United States to protect sea turtles were found to violate the chapeau's criteria against arbitrary and unjustifiable discrimination. The Appellate Body's reasoning focused on the manner of application of the U.S. regulations. First, it found that there was "arbitrary discrimination" because U.S. law required a "rigid and unbending . . . comprehensive" regulatory programme that is essentially the same as the U.S. programme, without inquiring into the appropriateness of that programme for the conditions, prevailing in the exporting countries.[59] Arbitrary discrimination was found to exist separately because the U.S. authorities, in their certification process for shrimp imports, did not comply with basic standards of fairness and due process with regard to notice, the gathering of evidence, and the opportunity to be heard. The Appellate Body found that the GATT requires "rigorous compliance with the fundamental requirements of due process" with respect to exceptions to treaty obligations.[60]

Second, the U.S. regulations were "unjustifiable"[61] because they required (1) a duplication of the U.S. programme without considering conditions in other countries; and (2) applied differing phase-in periods for countries similarly situated and impacted by the import ban. Most importantly, the Appellate Body held that it was unjustifiable discrimination for the United States not to have negotiated seriously with some of the affected countries: the subject matter — protection of sea turtles — demanded international cooperation, the U.S. statute recognized the importance of seeking international

[56] Appellate Body Report, *Shrimp/Turtle*, para. 157.
[57] *Id.* para. 158.
[58] *Id.* para. 160.
[59] *Id.* para. 177.
[60] *Id.* para. 182.
[61] *Id.* para. 182.

agreements, and the United States had, subsequent to imposing its own restrictions, entered into the 1996 Inter-American Convention for the Protection and Conservation of Sea Turtles. The Appellate Body concluded: "The Inter-American Convention thus provides convincing demonstration that an alternative course of action was reasonably open to the USA".[62]

In response to the Appellate Body's decision in the *Shrimp/Turtle* case, the United States retained the ban on shrimp from countries that do not protect sea turtles, but substantially revised its regulations to allow imports of shrimp harvested under specified conditions in which sea turtles are not harmed. The United States also entered into negotiations with the countries adversely affected and offered them technical assistance in conserving sea turtles. In 2001, the Appellate Body ruled that these U.S. measures satisfied the conditions of the chapeau.[63] It ruled that the U.S. regulatory scheme no longer was discriminatory. First, putting in place a regulatory programme that is comparable in effectiveness to the domestic programme "gives sufficient latitude to the exporting Member".[64] Second, the Appellate Body rejected the argument that the chapeau requires the conclusion of an international agreement on the conservation and protection of sea turtles. Rather, "serious, good faith efforts" to negotiate an agreement are sufficient to satisfy the chapeau.[65]

Taken together, the *Shrimp/Turtle* case and the *EC — Asbestos* case have overturned the *Tuna Dolphin* decisions' reasoning and transformed Article XX of GATT 1994 into an adequate tool for a balanced approach to the trade and environment controversy.[66]

## 6. Multilateral and bilateral environmental agreements

A question of paramount importance is how the WTO/GATT system will accommodate multilateral environmental agreements (MEAs) that employ

[62] Appellate Body Report, *Shrimp/Turtle*, para. 171.

[63] WT/DS58/AB/RW, 21 November 2001.

[64] Paras 122 and 144.

[65] Para. 134.

[66] *But see* Sanford Gaines, *The WTO's Reading of the GATT Article XX Chapeau: A Disguised Restriction on Environmental Measures*, 22 U. Pa. J. Int'l Econ. L. 739, 743–745 (2001).

trade restrictions.[67] Leading examples of such MEAs include the Montreal Protocol on Substances that Deplete the Ozone Layer,[68] which adopts trade controls that are more restrictive as to non-parties than parties; the Convention on International Trade in Endangered Species (CITES),[69] which regulates imports and exports in certain species of animals and plants and allows punitive trade restrictions to be imposed on non-complying parties; and the Basel Convention on the Control of Transboundary Movements of Hazardous Wastes,[70] which prohibits exports and imports of hazardous and other wastes by parties to the Convention to and from non-party states.

As a general matter, both the WTO Committee on Trade and Environment and the Appellate Body favour MEAs. The CTE has endorsed "multilateral solutions based on international cooperation and consensus as the best and most effective way for governments to tackle environmental problems of a transboundary or global nature".[71] The GATT panel in the *Tuna Dolphin I* case stated that dolphins could be protected through "international cooperative arrangements".[72] The WTO dispute settlement panel and the Appellate Body in the *Shrimp/Turtle* case expressed strong favour for MEAs as well.[73] However, it is difficult to predict how a WTO panel would rule on particular MEAs. Thus, there is an urgent need to clarify their legal status.

The WTO could address the relationship between GATT and multilateral environmental agreements in one of four ways. First, each MEA could

[67] *See* James Cameron and Ian Robinson, *The Use of Trade Provisions in International Environmental Agreements and Their Compatibility with the GATT*, 2 Y.B. INT'L ENVTL. L. 3 (1991); Richard G. Tarasofsky, *Ensuring Compatibility Between Multilateral Environmental Agreements and the GATT/WTO*, 7 Y.B. INT'L ENVTL. L. 52 (1996); Duncan Brack, *The* Shrimp-Turtle *Case: Implications for the Multilateral Environmental Agreement*, 9 Y.B. INT'L ENVTL. L. 13 (1998).

[68] Montreal Protocol on Substances that Deplete the Ozone Layer, 16 September 1987, 26 I.L.M. 1550 (1987), amended by 30 I.L.M. 539 (1991).

[69] Convention on International Trade in Endangered Species of Wild Fauna and Flora, 3 March 1973, 993 U.N.T.S. 243, 22 June 1979 and 30 April 1983, available at http://www.cites.org/eng/disc/text.shtml [hereinafter CITES].

[70] Basel Convention on the Control of Transboundary Movements of Hazardous Wastes, 22 March 1989, UN Doc. EP/IG.80/3 (1989), reprinted in 28 I.L.M. 649 (1989).

[71] WTO, Committee on Trade and Environment, Report (1996) of the Committee on Trade and Environment, WT/CTE/1, 12 November 1996, at para. 171 [hereinafter 1996 CTE Report].

[72] *Tuna Dolphin I*, above note 26, para. 5.28.

[73] Panel Report, *U.S. — Import Prohibition of Certain Shrimp and Shrimp Products*, WT/DS58/R (1998), para. 50; Appellate Body Report, *Shrimp/Turtle*, paras 68–69.

be examined on a case-by-case basis using Article IX:3 of the WTO Agreement. This provision allows waiver of any obligation under "exceptional circumstances" by vote of a three-fourths majority of the member states. For several reasons, this solution seems unsatisfactory. The WTO would abdicate from setting criteria to influence MEAs and, thus, states would have no prior guidance when framing them. Moreover, the test of "exceptional circumstances" is unduly vague. Approval under the waiver provision would be a political decision rather than one on the substance of the case. Furthermore, the status of MEAs would be doubtful until they had received the *ex post* blessing of a waiver.

A second possible solution is to follow the approach of the North American Free Trade Agreement (NAFTA), which provides that certain MEAs (such as the Montreal Protocol, CITES, and the Basel Convention) take precedence over NAFTA obligations.[74] This clarifies the status of certain MEAs but does not provide a process for the approval of future MEAs. Furthermore, an *ad hoc* approach such as this may be workable for an organization of three states, but may not be for the WTO.

Two additional alternatives are to amend Article XX by adding a provision on MEAs or to adopt an interpretation[75] of Article XX that would validate existing MEAs and provide for notification of future MEAs as well as set out criteria, a "safe harbour", they would have to fulfil to receive approval.[76] A model for MEAs might be GATT Article XX(h), which creates an exception for trade measures imposed pursuant to obligations in international commodity agreements that otherwise are illegal under the GATT. Article XX(h) sets out two methods of approval. First, commodity agreements that conform to specified criteria are valued automatically. Second, other commodity agreements can be evaluated on an *ad hoc* basis if they are submitted to the GATT contracting parties and not disapproved. Robert E. Hudec advocates a similar GATT amendment for MEAs.[77] Such an amendment[78] might provide that (1) negotiation of the MEA shall be under the auspices of the United

[74] North American Free Trade Agreement, 17 December 1992, 32 I.L.M 289, 296 and 605 [hereinafter NAFTA].

[75] An interpretation can be adopted by a three-quarters majority vote of the WTO Ministerial Conference. WTO Agreement Art. IX:2.

[76] These ideas are discussed in Vinod Rege, *GATT Law and Environment-Related Issues Affecting the Trade of Developing Countries*, 28 J. World Trade, No. 3, at 95, 124–28 (1994).

[77] *Id.* at 125–45.

[78] A similar proposal was put forward by the European Union. *See* 1996 CTE Report, above note 71, at 5–6.

Nations Environment Programme (UNEP) or a similar organization, and accession shall be open to all states that have a legitimate interest in the environmental problem addressed; (2) the problem dealt with must relate to serious environmental harm; (3) there be a reasonable relationship between the trade restrictions adopted and the object and purposes of the MEA; and (4) the MEA must be formally notified to the WTO. This would effectively immunize current and future MEAs from attack under WTO/GATT rules.

Finally, there is a way to validate MEAs without resorting to waiver or a GATT amendment. Article 31.3 of the Vienna Convention on the Law of Treaties requires that, in the interpretation of any treaty, there shall be "taken into account" (a) any subsequent agreement between the parties; (b) any subsequent practice; and (c) any relevant rules of international law. This provision brings MEAs into the WTO/GATT legal system.

## 7. Unilateral measures

The *Shrimp/Turtle* case is a well-reasoned decision of great importance for the trade and environment controversy. The Appellate Body, unlike prior GATT panels, did not totally condemn unilateral action or declare it illegal *per se*. The Appellate Body stated only that "[T]he unilateral character . . . heightens the disruptive and discriminatory influence of the import prohibition and underscores its unjustifiability".[79] This leaves room for unilateral measures to protect the environment beyond national jurisdiction. If, for example, the U.S. measures in the *Shrimp/Turtle* case had been tailored carefully to meet due process concerns, were suited to conditions in other countries, and especially if the countries concerned had spurned offers of negotiation or refused to negotiate in good faith, it is probable that unilateral measures to protect turtles would have been upheld. Of particular interest is the Appellate Body's emphasis on good faith as a principle of international law. If, in a given case, a state were to spurn environmental controls and refuse to enter into negotiations over the depletion of resources beyond national jurisdiction, it would be in breach of the principle of good faith, and unilateral measures may be justified.

## 8. Protection of natural resources

The issue arises whether a country may ban or restrict exports of natural resource products on the grounds that it is necessary for conservation

[79] Para. 172.

purposes. Natural resources export bans would have to qualify either under GATT Article XI:2(a), which permits an export prohibition or restriction to relieve temporary domestic "critical shortages", or under Article XX(g), as a measure related to conservation of exhaustible natural resources. The limits of these sections can be illustrated best by examining a specific case, the U.S. export ban on unprocessed logs from federal and state lands. Section 488 of the U.S. Forest Resources Conservation and Shortage Relief Act of 1990 states that timber is essential to the United States; that forests, forest resources, and the forest environment are exhaustible natural resources that require efficient and effective conservation efforts; that there is evidence of a shortfall in the supply of unprocessed timber in the United States; that any existing shortfall may worsen unless action is taken; and that conservation action is necessary with respect to exports of unprocessed timber. Among the stated purposes of the Act are to take action necessary under the GATT Article XI:2(a) to ensure sufficient supplies of certain forest resources or products that are essential to the United States and to effect measures aimed at meeting these objectives in conformity with U.S. obligations under the GATT.[80]

It is doubtful, however, whether this Act would survive the scrutiny of a WTO dispute resolution panel. Neither possible justification under the GATT seems to apply. Article XI:2(a) would not be applicable since there is no evidence that timber or timber products are in "critical" short supply in the United States. Article XI(g) would not apply because the export restrictions must be "in conjunction with restrictions on domestic production or consumption". There are no such domestic restrictions on timber in the United States. In fact, there is ample evidence that timber production is subsidized by low government prices for standing timber on federal and state lands. It is more likely that the real purpose of the ban, then, is to create jobs in the domestic wood products industry by giving domestic mills the right to perform value-added processing.

In contrast, a ban on timber exports for true conservation purposes would be consistent with Article XX(g). For example, if a U.S. ban on unprocessed logs over a certain diameter were accompanied by the elimination of domestic subsidies for timber cutting and restrictions on the cutting of old growth forests,[81] it almost certainly would be upheld by the WTO.

---

[80] 16 USC. § 620 (1994).

[81] Old growth or ancient forests denote forest habitat where trees vary considerably in age and size and there is a multilevel canopy that supports a rich ecosystem.

## 9. Environmental standards and process and production methods

Both environmental standards and regulation of their related processes and production methods are covered by one of two agreements, the TBT Agreement or the SPS Agreement. The Appellate Body has defined standards very broadly as including any mandatory regulation relating to the characteristics of a product.[82] Processes and production methods, which are covered by the TBT and SPS Agreements, are even more controversial than standards because they relate to how a product is made or produced in its country of origin.

### 9.1 Standards and technical regulations

Standards and technical regulations subject imported products to administrative scrutiny to determine whether their characteristics comply with set mandatory criteria.[83] All standards and technical regulations must comply with the disciplines of the TBT or SPS Agreements. Such regulations that are higher or different from internationally accepted norms carry a special burden of justification. The TBT and SPS Agreements are mutually exclusive,[84] so the first step in analysis is to determine which Agreement applies to any particular measure.

The matter of what is needed to comply with each of the two Agreements is covered in Chapter 18.

### 9.2 Process and production methods

In addition to placing environmental trade measures on products, import restrictions may also regulate how a product is produced, manufactured, or obtained, commonly referred to as process and production methods (PPMs). Some PPMs are related directly to the characteristics of the products concerned. For example, pesticides used on food crops produce residues on food products; cattle raised on growth hormones produce meat with hormone residues; and unsanitary conditions in slaughterhouses result in meat that may be contaminated with disease-causing organisms. The TBT and SPS Agreements cover PPMs such as these. Other PPMs, however, are

[82] Appellate Body Report, *EC — Asbestos*, paras 66–75.
[83] *Id.* para. 75.
[84] TBT Agreement Art. 1.5.

not reflected in the characteristics of the associated product. For example, whether a polluting or non-polluting process produces steel is irrelevant to its specifications, although it may be very important for environmental protection.

The latter type of PPM probably cannot be justified under either the SPS or TBT Agreements. The SPS Agreement, by its terms, covers only PPMs designed to protect humans, animals, and plants within the territory of the trade-restricting state.[85] This would exclude PPMs designed to improve the environment of the exporting state. Similarly, the TBT Agreement states that PPMs in the form of technical regulations must be justified as necessary to the fulfilment of a legitimate objective,[86] including protection of the environment, but the context is clear that this refers to the environment of the trade-restricting member, not the territory of the exporting member.

The GATT ruling opposed to PPMs comes from the now infamous *Tuna Dolphin* cases. In these cases, the PPM involved catching tuna by setting fishing nets on schools of dolphins without requiring precautions to spare the dolphins. When the United States banned imports of tuna caught by such methods, two GATT dispute settlement panels declared this action inconsistent with GATT norms on the ground that it discriminated between "like" products.[87] Thus, a state cannot adopt different treatment for two products with the same physical characteristics based on how the products have been produced or harvested.[88]

Two different groups have opposed these controversial rulings. Environmentalists regard them as a setback to the goal of protecting ecosystems all over the world as well as the global commons. Others fear unfair competition from pollution havens, countries that maintain different conditions of production, particularly with respect to environmental, health and safety laws, and workers' rights and pay. This group wants the ability to "level the playing field" by prohibiting imports from any country that refuses to adopt laws and regulations mirroring those of the importing country.

Scholars sympathetic to one or both of these views have called on the WTO to repudiate the *Tuna Dolphin* rulings by (1) redefining "like product" in GATT Article III so that products could be considered

---

[85] SPS Agreement Annex A, para. 1.

[86] TBT Agreement Art. 2.2.

[87] *See Tuna Dolphin I*, above note 26; *Tuna Dolphin II*, above note 29.

[88] Another example of a PPM controversy is the EU proposal to prohibit the import of pelts and manufactured goods of certain animal species caught or killed by methods using leg-hold traps. *See* Council Regulation 3254/91, 1991 O.J. (L 308) 1.

"unlike" on the basis of how they are made, produced, or harvested[89]; (2) adopting countervailing or "eco-dumping" duties on products from countries that some believe constitute "pollution havens" where products are made without adequate environmental controls[90]; or (3) employing a new method of balancing trade and environmental interests by analysing the intent or effect of the measure, the legitimacy of the environmental policy, and the justification for the disruption to trade.[91] The first and second of these proposals could be implemented only by amendments to the GATT.[92] There are powerful arguments — both political and legal — against these ideas. Allowing trade restrictions on the basis of PPMs, however well intended, would allow trade to be restricted willy-nilly on the basis of any Member's pet peeve and ultimately would favour only large countries able to throw their weight around. Although the term "like product" is defined flexibly on a case-by-case basis,[93] it would be a radical shift to differentiate products based on how they are produced, manufactured, or harvested.

The enforcement of PPMs in other countries also could be encouraged by replacing the current legal tests with a more lenient test that would allow WTO dispute settlement panels to balance the legitimacy of the protected environmental value with the disruption to trading interests.[94] However, this proposal, which is derived from the way the U.S. Supreme Court decides Commerce Clause cases,[95] may be unsuited to international tribunals like WTO panels whose *ad hoc* judges would, thereby, be delegated extraordinary discretion. Under this scheme, many PPM regulations undoubtedly would be upheld, but in the international context, this would encourage nations to violate fundamental principles of public international

---

89 *See* Snape and Lefkovitz, above n. 35, at 788–92.

90 *See* Esty, above note 11, at 163–68.

91 *Id.* at 114–16. Steve Charnovitz, "The Law of Environmental 'PPMs' in the WTO: Debunking the Myth of Illegality", 27 YALE J. INT'L L. 59 (2002).

92 Eco-dumping and countervailing duties are not authorized under the WTO Subsidies and Countervailing Duty Agreement or current U.S. law. For analysis of whether low environmental standards can be treated as subsidies or dumping, see Robert E. Hudec, *Differences in National Environmental Standards: The Level-Playing-Field Dimension,* 5 MINN. J. GLOBAL TRADE 1, 14–21 (1995).

93 *See* Appellate Body Report, *Japan — Alcoholic Beverages.*

94 *See* Esty, above note 11, at 114–18.

95 *See, e.g., Huron Cement Co. v. Detroit,* 362 U.S. 440 (1960); *see also* Daniel Farber and Robert E. Hudec, *Legal Restraints on Domestic Environmental Standards,* in 1 FAIR TRADE AND HARMONIZATION 59, 64–88 (Robert E. Hudec and Jagdish Bhagwati eds., 1996).

law, which, for the sake of harmony among nations, restrict the exercise of jurisdiction to accepted normative concepts.[96]

Fortunately, the GATT rule taking a hard line against all PPM import restrictions that are not based on product characteristics has been modified under the WTO. This is one of the most important aspects of WTO jurisprudence.

There are two theoretical ways of permitting PPM trade restrictions under the GATT. One is to allow them under Article III, the national treatment provision. Important scholarship[97] has contended that Article III provides no support, by its terms, for the PPM distinction or the proposition that Article III precludes process measures. But this is the very argument that was considered and rejected in the *Tuna Dolphin* cases. The major problem with interpreting Article III in this fashion is that it opens the door too wide. Every kind of PPM, no matter how irrational or silly, may be permitted.

The WTO Appellate Body has developed a more limited, but principled, way of permitting PPMs based on GATT Article XX. As Charnovitz[98] has carefully argued, the *Shrimp/Turtle* case crafted a tailored exception based on GATT Article XX for environmental PPMs. In this case the Appellate Body built upon the foundation established in the *U.S. Reformulated Gasoline* case. As detailed above,[99] a PPM (such as requiring turtle excluder devices when fishing for shrimp) will be permitted if it meets the tests for the application of Article XX. This Article embodies two categories of test. The first is *substantive*. The standards for the application of Article XX(g) and XX(b) involve meeting specific substantive criteria.[100] The second — the criteria of the chapeau of Article XX — is *procedural*. In addition to the substantive tests of Article XX, a PPM, to be permitted, must not be discriminatory or arbitrary.[101] WTO jurisprudence has cut the Gordian knot — to permit certain environmental PPMs without creating an exception that would swallow other GATT rules.

[96] *See generally* Ian Brownlie, PRINCIPLES OF PUBLIC INTERNATIONAL LAW (5th ed. 1998), Ch. 15.

[97] Robert Howse and Donald Regan, "The Product/Process Distinction — An Illusory Basis for Disciplining Unilateralism" in TRADE POLICY 11 EJIL 249 (2000).

[98] Steve Charnovitz, "The Law of Environmental 'PPMs' in the WTO: Debunking the Myth of Illegality", 27 YALE J. INT'L L. 59 (2000).

[99] Section 5.1, above.

[100] Sections 5.1 and 5.2, above.

[101] *See* the discussion in section 5.3, above.

Instead of allowing unilateral regulation of PPMs to deal with environmental protection/pollution haven problems, other approaches might be considered, such as environmental agreements, environmental management systems, and investment standards.

### *9.2.1 Environmental agreements*

The PPM/pollution haven problem can be dealt with directly by encouraging countries to negotiate environmental agreements. First, if PPMs are causing transboundary pollution, the states concerned, relying on well-established principles of state responsibility under international law, may enter into an agreement to abate the pollution and compensate for its damage.[102] Where the problem is serious, as in the border region between the United States and Mexico, new institutions may be required both to deal with the pollution and to upgrade the environmental enforcement of the lax country concerned. Thus, the United States and Mexico have created a U.S.-Mexican International Boundary Water Commission,[103] a Border Plan, and a Border Environmental Cooperation Agreement.[104] Mexico, Canada, and the United States have created a trilateral Commission for Environmental Cooperation to promote enforcement of environmental laws in the three countries.

Second, a specific problem may be addressed either through a bilateral or multilateral agreement designed to deal with it. An example is the tuna-dolphin dispute itself, which was addressed by the 1992 Agreement for the Reduction of Dolphin Mortality in the Eastern Pacific Ocean.[105] The Agreement has been implemented so successfully that scientists say that the eastern Pacific is now the "world's safest tuna fishery for dolphins".[106]

Third, regional pollution control agreements could be adopted following the model of the UNEP Regional Seas Programme.[107] Under that

[102] *See, e.g., Train Smelter Arbitration*, 33 Am. J. Int'l L. 182 (1939); *Train Smelter Arbitration*, 35 Am. J. Int'l L. 684 (1941); 1991 Canada-U.S. Agreement on Air Quality, 30 I.L.M. 676.

[103] 22 USC. §§ 277–78b (1994). *See* Stephen Mumme, *Innovation and Reform in Transboundary Resource Management: A Critical Look at the International Boundary and Water Commission, United States and Mexico*, 3 Nat. Resources J. 93 (1993).

[104] *See* Robert Housman, Reconciling Free Trade and the Environment: Lessons from the North American Free Trade Agreement (1994).

[105] Agreement for the Reduction of Dolphin Mortality in the Eastern Pacific Ocean, 33 I.L.M. 936 (1994).

[106] *Dolphin Slaughter Ended*, Int'l Herald Trib., 26 June 1996, at 5.

[107] *See* Matthew Hulm, A Strategy for the Seas: The Regional Seas Programme, Past and Future (1983).

programme, "framework" conventions have been concluded to preserve marine ecosystems in the Persian Gulf, the Red Sea and the Gulf of Aden, the South Pacific, and the Caribbean; and the East African side of the Indian Ocean, the Latin American side of the southeast Pacific, and the West African side of the South Atlantic. These agreements are comprehensive in their regulation of all sources of marine pollution; they are models for facilitation cooperation and technical assistance, and new protocols can be added as needed to focus on particular pollution problems. A similar system of regional treaties could foster higher environmental PPMs, as well as control pollution on an appropriate regional basis.

Fourth, appropriate international organizations can encourage the transfer of environmentally friendly technology[108] through development assistance or foreign direct investment. Thus, countries would upgrade PPMs in return for assistance in acquiring environmentally enhancing technology. In this way, as countries develop particular industrial sectors, they would acquire the means to control the environment consequences. The transfer of technology also would promote voluntary standardization of PPMs. To some extent, this already is happening under international treaty regimes for the control of ozone-depleting substances and climate change.

### *9.2.2 Environmental management systems*

Many environmentalists saw the *Tuna Dolphin* decisions as an obstacle to the maintenance of high environmental standards because these decisions invalidated efforts to require environmentally protective PPMs in other countries. How should the WTO respond to these concerns? Should international minimum PPM standards be required?

The term "environmental standards" has various meanings. It can refer to the characteristics of products, PPMs, the cleanliness of the ambient environment or procedural requirements. There are three general approaches to the international treatment of product standards: (1) national treatment, where each country determines its own standards and applies them to imported products; (2) mutual recognition, where countries agree to recognize each other's standards; and (3) harmonization, where, through negotiation, countries agree to adopt identical or similar standards, which therefore become international.

[108] This idea, advanced by Rege, above note 76, at 113–16, already is occurring to some extent through environmental agreements and the Global Environmental Facility.

The WTO/GATT system, through the TBT and SPS Agreements, relies primarily on the first and third approaches, encouraging harmonization and the adoption of international standards, but permitting national treatment. Empirical studies evaluating WTO/GATT harmonization of product standards find that, other than "interface" harmonization (*e.g.*, weights and measures), it has had very limited success, because the costs and benefits of harmonization are incommensurable, so that most countries perceive it as a lose-lose exchange.[109] If harmonization of product standards on a worldwide basis has proved difficult, harmonizing PPMs would be impossible. There also are valid economic and environmental reasons why process standards should not be identical on a worldwide basis.[110] In addition, the putative international race to the bottom has been much exaggerated. Actually, there is much evidence that trade between nations improves environmental standards of all kinds.[111]

If requiring worldwide PPM harmonization is not the answer, what can be done to ameliorate the PPM/pollution haven problem? PPMs can be upgraded through private efforts to protect the environment by means of corporate responsibility programmes and widespread adoption of environmental management systems such as the ISO 14000 Series.[112] ISO 14001 was developed by the International Standards Organization to identify the core elements of a voluntary environmental management system that would call on organizations to conduct their environmental affairs within a structured system integrated with ordinary management activity. The elements of such a corporate system are (1) adoption of a senior management level environmental policy; (2) identification of the key environmental aspects of a company's operations; (3) identification and implementation of legal requirements; (4) identification of quantifiable environmental targets and objectives; (5) establishments of an environmental management system that allocates responsibility for environmental improvement; (6) training of

[109] *See* David W. Leebron, *Laying Down Procrustes: An Analysis of Harmonization Claims*, in 1 FAIR TRADE AND HARMONIZATION, above note 95, at 41 (1996).

[110] *See* Richard B. Stewart, *Environmental Regulation and International Competitiveness*, 102 YALE L.J. 2039, 2051–57 (1993).

[111] *See* Alessandra Casella, *Fair Trade and Evolving Standards*, in 1 FAIR TRADE AND HARMONIZATION, above note 95, at 119; John Douglas Wilson, *Capital Mobility and Environmental Standards: Is There a Theoretical Basis for the Race to the Bottom?*, in 1 FAIR TRADE AND HARMONIZATION, above note 95, at 393.

[112] *See* Naomi Roht-Arriaza, *Shifting the Point of Regulation: International Organization for Standardization and Global Lawmaking on Trade and the Environment*, 22 ECOLOGY L.Q. 479 (1995).

employees; (7) establishment of monitoring, auditing, and corrective action; and (8) establishment of management review and responsibility. The ISO 14001 EMS is not limited to compliance but focuses on pollution prevention as well.

ISO 14001 is becoming established as the internationally accepted voluntary standards system of environmental management. Many companies are moving to adopt this system, and there is every indication that adherence to it will become a prerequisite for access to international markets. ISO 14001 does not establish specific PPMs or standards for pollution control. Rather, it requires companies to commit themselves to continual improvement of their environmental management systems' compliance with applicable laws and pollution prevention, but it leaves each company free to implement individual solutions to pollution and negative externality problems. Although adoption of ISO 14001 is voluntary, governments can provide incentives for its use through relief from "command and control" regulation, enforcement policies that impose reduced penalties, and environmental privilege guarantees for companies that implement it.

### *9.2.3 Investment*

An important aspect of the pollution haven problem is the charge that countries with lax pollution standards attract industry and jobs away from countries with high standards. Empirical studies, however, fail to show much evidence of this loss of jobs.[113] The United States and other OECD countries enforce similar environmental standards and spend about the same to control pollution, about 2 percent of gross domestic product.[114] Even though certain developing countries have lower pollution standards and there is anecdotal evidence of job losses, empirical evidence again suggests cost differences in environmental standards play little role in company location decisions.[115] Environmental compliance costs in most industries are only a small percentage of production costs. Thus, cost differences in raw materials and wages probably are more significant.[116]

---

[113] *See* Robert Carbaugh and Darwin Wassink, *Environmental Standards and International Competitiveness*, 16 World Competition, No. 1, at 81 (1992).

[114] *Id.* at 87–88.

[115] Jeffrey Leonard, Pollution and the Struggle for World Product (1988); Charles Pearson, Down to Business: Multinational Corporations, the Environment and Development (1985).

[116] Carbaugh and Wassink, above note 108, at 88–90.

Nevertheless, it may be wise for the WTO to counter this concern by adopting an amendment to the Agreement on Trade Related Investment Measures[117] or a broader Multilateral Agreement on Investment, if one is negotiated.[118] A model might be the NAFTA provision on Environmental Measures:

> The Parties recognize that it is inappropriate to encourage investment by relaxing domestic health, safety or environmental measures. Accordingly, a Party should not waive or otherwise derogate from, or offer to waive or otherwise derogate from, such measures as an encouragement for the establishment, acquisition, expansion or retention in its territory of an investment of an investor. If a Party considers that another Party has offered such an encouragement, it may request consultations with the other Party and the two Parties shall consult with a view to avoiding any such encouragement.[119]

Such a provision would not require any specific level of pollution control in the country where the investment is located, but it would set up a channel of complaint if environmental laxity is used to attract investment.

## 10. Recycling and packaging

Several countries have taken bold steps to introduce mandatory recycling of products and packaging to reduce the generation of waste and the resulting pollution and need for landfills. Germany has led the way, passing the *Verpackungsverordnung* (*Packaging Ordinance*)[120] in 1991, which regulates the packaging of products and sets mandatory recycling requirements for packaging waste. The Packaging Ordinance requires the manufacturers of products to take back packaging wastes and to arrange for their recycling. They fulfil this duty by participating in a private waste collection system, which, for a fee, will handle this obligation by collecting waste from consumers. Participating manufacturers may mark their products with a

[117] The TRIMs Agreement was one of the key agreements of the GATT Uruguay Round.

[118] A proposed OECD Multilateral Agreement on Investment was abandoned in 1998. *See* Chapter 19 section 4 and Yoshi Kodoma, *The Multilateral Agreement on Investment and Its Legal Implications for Newly Industrialising Economies*, 32 J. World Trade 21 (1998). However, trade and investment is on the tentative agenda for a future WTO negotiating round.

[119] NAFTA, above note 74, Art. 1114(2).

[120] 20 August 1991 BGBl I S 1234, translated in 21 I.L.M. 1135 (1992). For commentary, see Stephanie A. Goldfine, *Using Economic Incentives to Promote Environmentally Sound Business Practices*, 7 Geo. Int'l Envtl. L. Rev. 309 (1994).

green dot. The Packaging Ordinance applies to all products distributed within Germany.[121]

Largely because of this German initiative and in order to harmonize Member State legal regimes, the European Union adopted a Packaging Directive in December 1994.[122] The European Union directive sets target ranges for packaging waste recovery and recycling, standardizes methods of analysing product lifecycles and measuring toxicity of packaging components and waste, and sets maximum concentration levels for heavy metals in packaging. The directive applies to the packaging of all products sold in the European Union, including imports.[123]

These laws are part of an increasing trend in many industrialized countries to consider the environmental impact of products throughout their lifecycles to the point of their ultimate disposal. The purpose of these laws is to weaken this impact by (1) minimizing packaging waste; (2) prohibiting the use of toxic and hazardous materials in packaging; and (3) creating incentives or requirements for recycling, reuse, or proper disposal of both the packaging and the products themselves. Such laws have the potential to disrupt international trade. Manufacturing groups are alarmed that the spread of such lifecycle or producer responsibility laws will have a protectionist effect, isolating national markets. Developing countries are especially concerned that their exporters will be unable to comply with these laws.

Nevertheless, lifecycle laws serve important purposes and the international trading system should be adjusted to accommodate them. Two separate sets of issues arise. The most serious problems come from the proliferation of such laws rather than their substantive requirements. If every country adopts its own national (or sub-national) system, trade will be disrupted by the burden of satisfying many different national bureaucracies. Moreover, though well intentioned, some packaging or product regulations may be environmentally harmful. The problems stemming from proliferation could be alleviated through international harmonization of product lifecycle regulation. This should be encouraged by the WTO Committee on Trade and Environment, but probably is best left to private groups like the International Standards Organization that can work with

[121] Bundesministerium für Umwelt, Naturschutz, and Reaktorsicherheit, *The Packaging Ordinance and International Trade* § 1(1), 23 June 1993.

[122] Council Directive 94/62, 1994 O.J. (L 365) 10. *See generally* Alexandra Haner, *Will the European Union's Packaging Directive Reconcile Trade and the Environment?*, 18 FORDHAM INT'L L.J. 2187 (1995).

[123] Council Directive 94/62, above note 117, para. 2(1).

national governments, industry and environmental interest groups. Harmonization efforts should emphasize environmental protection, but should screen carefully the current array of laws for effectiveness, and eliminate those that are not working. The second problem with such laws is that they may be more restrictive than necessary or may discriminate intentionally or unintentionally against foreign producers. To ensure that this does not happen, they should be held to scrutiny under international trade law norms that recognize the necessity of environmental protection for national governments to have some flexibility in the remedies they adopt.

In principle, product lifecycle and producer responsibility laws are permitted under GATT Article III as long as they apply equally to domestic and foreign producers. These laws are also subject to the discipline of the TBT Agreement, which imposes the additional requirements that they must not create "unnecessary obstacles to international trade" and not be "more restrictive than necessary to fulfil a legitimate objective", including, of course, protection of the environment.[124] These tests assure that a proper balancing process will be applied so that restrictive measures are not out of proportion to their benefits.[125]

## 11. Eco-labels

Another method of raising environmental standards is through eco-labelling. The theory behind eco-labels is that if consumers are informed, the market and consumer choice can be relied on to stimulate the production and consumption of environmentally friendly products.[126] A great variety of eco-labelling schemes exist, sponsored by governments, private groups, or a combination of the two. They take several forms: mandatory negative content labelling, mandatory content neutral labelling, and voluntary multi-criteria

[124] TBT Agreement Art. 2.2 and Annex I, para. 1.

[125] A useful balancing test that might be employed is the concept of proportionality. *See* the *Danish Bottles* case, above note 55. The ECJ upheld a ban on non-returnable beverage containers, but held that a limitation on the sale of non-approved containers was discriminatory against foreign producers and out of proportion to the benefits served.

[126] *See* H. Ward, *Trade and Environmental Issues in Voluntary Eco-Labelling and Life Cycle Analysis*, 6 RECEIL 139 (1997); S. Subedi, *Balancing International Trade and Environmental Protection*, 2 BROOKLYN J. INT'L L. 373 (1999). For a skeptical view, see H. Mennell, *The Uneasy Case for Eco-labelling* 4 RECIEL 304 (1995).

labelling.[127] Eco-labels can show product characteristics or process and production methods (PPMs). They can operate as a seal of approval or objectively impart information. Well-known examples of eco-labelling plans include Germany's Blue Angel programme and the White Swan mark launched by the Scandinavian countries.[128] In the United States, a private organization operates a Green Seal programme. Increasingly, governments are adopting such programmes.[129] In 1992, the European Union established an eco-label scheme to "promote the design, production, marketing, and use of products which have a reduced environmental impact during their entire lifecycle, and provide consumers with better information on the environmental impact of products".[130]

Eco-labelling must comply with WTO/GATT requirements. Even mandatory eco-label requirements on products would be permissible if they are applied on a non-discriminatory basis, adhering to the GATT 1994 MFN and national treatment requirements. For example, under the U.S. Energy Policy and Conservation Act,[131] corporate average fuel economy standards for automobiles must be calculated for domestic manufacturers and importers, and new automobiles sold in the United States must bear a label stating the estimated miles-per-gallon rate for city and highway use.[132] This programme was the subject of a GATT panel report in the *United States — Taxes on Automobiles* case,[133] which upheld the standards except for the separate foreign fleet accounting aspects, which discriminated unfairly against foreign manufacturers.

Even eco-label schemes that pertain to PPMs may be upheld if they adhere to MFN and national treatment norms. In the *Tuna Dolphin I* case, the panel accepted the voluntary dolphin safe labelling scheme for tuna products sold in the United States:

> [T]he labelling provision of the [U.S. law] do not restrict the sale of tuna products; tuna products can be freely sold both with and without the "Dolphin Safe" label. Nor

[127] U.S. Environmental Protection Agency, Status Report on the Use of Environmental Labels Worldwide (1993).

[128] *See* Elliott B. Staffin, *Trade Barrier or Trade Boon: A Critical Evaluation of Environmental Labeling*, 21 COLUM. J. ENVTL. L. 205, 225 (1996).

[129] *Id.* at 230–32.

[130] Commission Regulation 880/92, Art. I, 1992 O.J. (L 99) 1.

[131] 17 USC. § 4001 (1994).

[132] 40 C.F.R. pt. 600 (1996).

[133] *United States — Taxes on Automobiles*, DS31/R, 11 October 1994, reprinted in 33 I.L.M. 1397, para. 5.10 (1994) (unadopted) [hereinafter *United States — Taxes on Automobiles*].

> do these provisions establish requirements that have to be met in order to obtain an advantage from the government. Any advantage which might possibly result from access to this label depends on the free choice by consumers to give preference to tuna carrying the "Dolphin Safe" label. The labelling provisions therefore did not make the right to sell tuna or tuna products, conditional upon the use of tuna harvesting methods.[134]

In contrast, a discriminatory PPM labelling scheme would not be upheld. One that singled out wood products made from tropical forests might fail if like products from temperate forests were not included.[135]

Mandatory eco-labelling schemes also must comply with the TBT Agreement, which applies to any technical regulation that deals with a product characteristic, including "terminology, symbols, packaging, marking or labelling requirements as they apply to a product, process or production method".[136] The Agreement requires that eco-labels "fulfil a legitimate objective", not be "more trade-restrictive than necessary", and comply with notice and transparency requirements, including the TBT Code of Good Practice.[137]

Additional steps should be taken by the WTO Committee on Trade and Environment to ensure that eco-labelling does not become a barrier to trade. First, eco-label schemes might be required to be registered with the WTO so that transparency is guaranteed. National eco-label systems should also be open to all producers on a non-discriminatory basis, not contain requirements that favour domestic producers or be too costly or difficult to meet. Environmental labelling has been a designated subject of negotiation since the Doha Ministerial Conference.

## 12. The export of hazardous substances and wastes

### 12.1 Domestically prohibited goods

Domestically prohibited goods are products whose sale and use are restricted in a nation's domestic market on the grounds that they present a

[134] *Tuna Dolphin I*, above note 26, para. 5.42. For a dissenting view that PPM labels would pass GATT muster, see Bartenhagen, 17 VA. ENVTL. L.J. 1 (1997).

[135] *See* Chase, above note 14.

[136] TBT Agreement Annex 1, para. 1.

[137] TBT Agreement Annex 3.

danger to human, animal, or plant life, health, or the environment. They include unregistered pesticides, expired pharmaceuticals, alcohol, tobacco, dangerous chemicals, and adulterated food products. For example, in the United States, the export of unregistered pesticides is permitted only under a system of notice that requires prior informal consent.[138]

Clearly, a state may bar imports of a product that is banned for domestic sale or consumption. Can exports of such products also be restricted? A GATT working group addressed this issue in 1991,[139] but there was no consensus on its report; the issue was transferred to the agenda of the Committee on Trade and Environment (CTE). This was followed in 1998 by the negotiation of a treaty[140] establishing a prior informed consent (PIC) regime for banned or restricted chemical products and hazardous pesticide formulations that may cause health or environmental problems. The international shipment of these products would be barred without the prior notice and explicit consent of a designated national authority in the destination country. Do these export control and PIC regimes for dangerous products conform to WTO rules? Would it be permissible for a state to go beyond PIC and adopt a total ban on the export of certain categories of domestically prohibited goods?

A PIC restriction or a total ban may be carried out within current established legal limits. GATT Article XX(b) allows trade measures (affecting either imports or exports) that are "necessary to protect human, animal, plant life or health". Moreover, according to the *Tuna Dolphin II* and *Shrimp/Turtle* cases, nothing in Article XX prevents a state from imposing a trade measure to protect the health or safety of persons or the environment located outside the territory of that state. Under this interpretation, a PIC export regime or a total export ban would be justified.

However, further clarification by the CTE would remove any remaining uncertainty by reaffirming the requirements of current law and stating explicitly that they apply to domestically prohibited goods. The CTE also

[138] 7 USC. § 1360 (1994).

[139] *See* Report by the Chairman of the GATT Working Group in Export of Domestically Prohibited Goods and Other Hazardous Substances, GATT Doc. L/6872 (1991). This group recommended a code that would allow individual member states to decide whether their domestic restrictions should be carried over to exports.

[140] 1998 Rotterdam Convention on the Prior Informed Consent Procedure for Certain Hazardous Chemicals and Pesticides in International Trade, 38 I.L.M. 1 (1999). The 2001 Stockholm Convention on Persistent Organic Pollutants (POPS) further prohibits or restricts trade in a variety of pesticides and chemicals, available at UNEP web site, unep.ch/pops.

could adopt transparency requirements that would compel trade-restricting states to notify the WTO and publish in full all laws, regulations, and decisions relating to the products concerned. The WTO would thus provide a clearinghouse for the notification and publication of domestically prohibited goods restrictions, and they would be fully subject to the WTO dispute resolution regime.

## 12.2 Waste

Export of hazardous wastes has received great attention from the international community. The Basel Convention on the Control of Transboundary Movements of Hazardous Wastes and Their Disposal requires prior notification and informed consent of the receiving country as a precondition for authorizing international waste shipments. Furthermore, the Convention provides that parties must prohibit the export of the waste whenever there is reason to believe that it will not be managed in an environmentally sound manner.

Two aspects of the Basel Convention raise problems with respect to WTO rules. First, the Conference of the Parties adopted an amendment to ban the export of hazardous wastes from industrialized countries (the OECD, the European Union, and Liechtenstein) to developing countries. The ban applies both to hazardous waste intended for disposal and, from the end of 1997, to hazardous waste intended for reuse or recycling. Second, Article 4(5) of the Convention prohibits export and imports of hazardous and other wastes between parties and non-party states. These trade restrictions on wastes are based on experience and future fears concerning the exploitation of developing countries. They also reflect certain principles adopted at the 1992 UN Conference on Environment and Development, notably Principle 14 of the Rio Declaration, which provides that states should cooperate to prevent the movement of materials harmful to the environment and humans, and Principle 19, which requires prior notice to potentially affected states with regard to potentially harmful activities.

The international regime for the transboundary movement of hazardous wastes is in marked contrast to that in effect domestically in the United States, where the Supreme Court has struck down state-imposed limitations on the import of hazardous waste as violating constitutional norms under the Commerce Clause.[141] On the other hand, the European Court of

[141] *E.g., City of Philadelphia v. New Jersey*, 437 U.S. 617 (1978).

Justice in the *Belgian Waste* case[142] stated that waste can be a threat to the environment because of the limited capacity of each region or locality to receive it. Accordingly, the Court ruled that it is permissible under Articles 30 and 36 of the EC Treaty for a locality to adopt an import ban unless this is inconsistent with EC legislation.[143] The Court based its decision on the proximity principle — that wastes should be treated at their sources — and the importance of self-sufficiency regarding waste. The Court's ruling would seem to allow export as well as import restrictions on waste.

An export ban on hazardous wastes may be justified under GATT Article XX(b) on the same basis as export restrictions on domestically prohibited goods. Hazardous wastes have the potential to endanger human health and the environment; thus, Article XX(b) may be interpreted to allow export bans to protect areas outside the territory of the trade restricting country. Even a discriminatory export ban may be upheld under Article XX(b) if the discrimination is not "arbitrary or unjustifiable... between countries where the same conditions prevail". A ban that distinguishes between OECD and developing countries, arguably at least, could pass this test because of the very different conditions in developing countries. Thus, emerging international hazardous waste regimes seem reconcilable under the WTO/GATT system.

## 13. Environmental taxes

Many commentators have called on governments and public authorities to use market-based economic incentives[144] rather than command-and-control regulation to improve environmental quality. As a result, taxes may be used more frequently in the future, both to raise revenue and to achieve environmental goals. Environmental taxes are based on the principle that many resources are underpriced and, therefore, overused. Environmental taxes, in effect, raise the price of the use of these resources. They have three purposes:

[142] Case C-2/90, *Commission v. Belgium* [1992] E.C.R. I-4431, 1 C.M.L.R. 365.

[143] The Court upheld the ban as regards the importation of non-hazardous waste not covered by a Council directive. However, the Court ruled that to the extent that the ban related also to hazardous waste, Belgium had failed to fulfil its obligation to comply with Council Directive 84/631. *Id.* para. 38–39.

[144] There are four basic types of economic incentives: (1) taxes on charges; (2) transferable pollution permits; (3) deposit-and-return systems; and (4) information strategies. *See* Stewart, above note 105, at 2093–94.

(1) to discourage the consumption of goods and services that create environmental costs; (2) to encourage producers to develop alternative production methods and products that are less harmful to the environment; and (3) to implement the polluter pays principle (PPP), which holds that the polluter should bear the expenses imposed on society of ensuring that the environment is in an acceptable state.[145] In the *United States — Superfund* case, a GATT panel stated: "The General Agreement's rules on tax adjustment... give the contracting party the possibility to follow the polluter-pays principle, but they do not oblige it to do so".[146]

Despite their attractiveness, environmental taxes are not yet widespread for several reasons. First, many people are opposed in principle to raising taxes. Second, analysis shows that some environmental taxes would be regressive, falling most heavily on the poor. Third, there is concern that countries employing them would no longer be competitive in the global marketplace, as their industries would suffer in comparison to industries in countries without such taxes. There are, in general, two solutions to this problem. Countries can cooperate and enter into an international agreement that requires all to levy environmental taxes on their producers; or countries that tax their own producers can levy a similar charge on like imported products. Moreover, even if environmental taxes are imposed by international agreement, import taxes may be needed to even out unequal taxation. Charges on imports raise the issue of their consistency with the WTO system and GATT 1994.

There are three different categories of environmental taxes that governments may use. First, taxes can be imposed directly on the sale of a product that has potentially adverse environmental consequences. This category includes deposit-and-return systems, where tax is rebated, and unrebated taxes on environmentally unfriendly products such as cigarettes, certain types of energy, and certain chemicals. Second, the tax can be levied on the use of an environmental resource itself. Examples include charges for the emission of pollutants into the air, discharges into rivers or sewer systems, the congestion of highways, and the use of landfills or hazardous waste disposal facilities. Third, environmental taxes may be imposed on product inputs.

[145] On the polluter pays principle, see OECD, Recommendations (C(72)128 on Guiding Principles Concerning International Economic Aspects of Environmental Policies, 11 I.L.M. 1172 (1972); C(74)223 on the Implementation of the *Polluter Pays* Principle, 14 I.L.M. 234 (1974).

[146] *United States — Taxes on Petroleum and Certain Imported Substances*, 17 June 1987, GATT B.I.S.D. (34th Supp.) at 136, para. 5.2.2 (1988) [hereinafter *United States — Superfund*].

Here, two kinds of measures may be distinguished: taxes on inputs that are incorporated physically into the final product (such as chemical feedstock incorporated into a plastic or petroleum product), and taxes on inputs that are completely consumed during production (such as fuel or energy used in making a manufactured product).

GATT distinguishes two principal categories of taxes and charges and submits them to different controls.[147] Article II:1, which applies to customs duties and import charges, prohibits WTO members from imposing higher charges than those specified in their agreed schedules of concessions. Article III, which applies to internal taxes and charges, requires national treatment. To distinguish between the two, Article II:2(a) provides:

> Nothing in this Article shall prevent any contracting party from imposing *at any time* on the importation of any product:
>
> (a) a charge equivalent to an internal tax imposed consistently with the provisions of paragraph 2 of Article III in respect of an article *from which* the imported product has been manufactured or produced *in whole or in part.* (Emphasis added)

To further clarify the distinction, an interpretive note (*Ad* Article III) states that "[a]ny internal tax . . . which applies to an imported product and to the like domestic product and is collected or enforced in the case of the imported product at the time of importation, is nevertheless to be regarded as an internal tax".

This pattern of GATT regulation makes clear that the distinction between customs charges (Article II) and internal taxes (Article III) is not based on when or where the taxes are levied. Internal taxes can be adjusted at the border or anywhere else in the distribution process. The difference is that internal taxes on imports are equalizing taxes for the purpose of subjecting imports to the equivalent tax regime for domestic like products. Environmental taxes are internal taxes subject to the discipline of Article III, not Article II. Thus, environmental taxes theoretically can be imposed on imports and be adjusted at the border.[148] Which kinds of environmental taxes can be applied to imports depends on the GATT's border tax adjustment rules.

---

[147] *See generally* Ole Kristian Fauchald, ENVIRONMENTAL TAXES AND TRADE DISCRIMINATION (1998); ENVIRONMENTAL TAXATION (O'Riordan ed., 1995).

[148] Of course, the requirements of Article III:2 must be met, which means that imports cannot be charged more than domestic products. In *Japan — Alcoholic Beverages*, however, the Appellate Body held that Article III:2 embodies two standards. *See* Appellate Body Report, *Japan — Alcoholic Beverages*, at 17–25.

Border tax adjustment (BTA) is the mechanism invented to harmonize the international taxation of products in accordance with the destination principle, which holds that goods should be taxed where they are used or consumed. BTA, which can be traced to the eighteenth century,[149] allows each nation to implement its own regime of domestic taxation while assuring that goods that move in international trade are neither exempt from taxation nor subject to double taxation. BTA allows (1) an internal tax to be imposed on imported products; and (2) the remission of internal taxes on domestic products destined for export.

What kinds of domestic taxes are eligible for BTA? From its origin in 1947, the GATT has maintained a fundamental distinction between taxes on products (so-called indirect taxes) and taxes on various forms of income and the ownership of property (so-called direct taxes).[150] Only taxes on products, indirect taxes, are eligible for BTA. For example, as to taxes remitted on export, Article VI:4 provides:

> No product of the territory of any contracting party imported into the territory of any other contracting party shall be subject to an anti-dumping or countervailing duty by reason of the exemption of such product from duties or taxes borne by the like product when destined for consumption in the country of origin or exportation, or by reason of the refund of such duties or taxes.

*Ad* Article XVI also makes this point: "The exemption of an exported product from duties or taxes borne by the like product when destined for domestic consumption, or the remission of such duties or taxes in amounts not in excess of those which have accrued, shall not be deemed to be a subsidy". In 1970, the GATT Working Party on Border Tax Adjustments made the distinction explicit, agreeing that "taxes directly levied on products were eligible for tax adjustment", and that "certain taxes that were not directly levied on products were not eligible for adjustment [such as] social security charges . . . and payroll taxes".[151]

The economic distinction between direct and indirect taxes originally was based on the idea that indirect taxes generally were passed on to the ultimate consumer, while direct taxes were not. It is now recognized that this distinction is too simplistic; producers absorb many indirect taxes and direct

[149] *See* Paul Demaret and Raoul Stewardson, *Border Tax Adjustments under GATT and EC Law and the General Implications for Environmental Taxes*, 28 J. World Trade, No. 4, at 5, 6–7 (1994).

[150] For the history of this distinction, see *id.* at 9–12.

[151] *Border Tax Adjustments*, 2 December 1970, GATT B.I.S.D. (18th Supp.) at 97, para. 14 (1972).

taxes can be passed on in the price of a product.[152] Thus, today the distinction rests on tradition and practicality. It is fundamentally a political compromise that allows equalization of some, but not all, of the differences in internal tax regimes; it is based on administrative practicality in that BTA would be much more difficult to apply to direct taxes; and also is based on the fact that taxes on products can be abused more easily for protectionist purposes.

## 13.1 Taxes on products

Environmental taxes levied on products are eligible for BTA as long as they are consistent with the national treatment standards of GATT Article III. In the *United States — Superfund* case, the panel made the point that the GATT "does not distinguish between taxes with different policy purposes".[153] The GATT requires only that "like" imported and domestic products be taxed the same. Moreover, there is some flexibility in this national treatment standard. As stated above, when products are "like" only in the sense of being "substitutable or competitive" with each other, a higher tax on imports is allowable.[154] In addition, in *United States — Taxes on Automobiles*,[155] the GATT panel upheld the validity of U.S. taxes that fell more heavily on imported cars. This ruling seems to justify *de facto* (but not *de jure*) discrimination against imports as long as a tax has a valid environmental purpose. This decision is thrown into doubt, however, by the WTO Appellate Body's ruling in *Japan — Alcoholic Beverages* that the purpose of a tax is not a legitimate inquiry under GATT Article III.[156]

A deposit-and-return system of taxes on products is also permissible under GATT rules. In the *Canada Beer* cases,[157] panels upheld the Canadian deposit/return system on beer containers as applied to imports; to meet the national treatment standard, however, the system had to be applied

[152] Gary Clyde Hufbauer and Joanna Shelton Erb, Subsidies in International Trade 23 (1984).

[153] *United States — Superfund* case, above note 141, at para. 5.2.8.

[154] Appellate Body Report, *Japan — Alcoholic Beverages*.

[155] *United States — Taxes on Automobiles*, above note 128.

[156] Appellate Body Report, *Japan — Alcoholic Beverages*.

[157] *Canada — Import, Distribution and Sale of Alcoholic Drinks by Canadian Provincial Marketing Agencies*, 22 March 1988, GATT B.IS.D. (35th Supp.) 37 (1989) [hereinafter *Canada Beer I*]; *Canada — Import, Distribution and Sale of Certain Alcoholic Drinks by Provincial Marketing Agencies*, 18 February 1992, GATT B.I.S.D. (39th Supp.) at 27 (1993) [hereinafter *Canada Beer II*].

equally without different systems of delivery to points of sale for imported and domestic beer.[158] Thus, GATT norms freely permit BTA with respect to environmental taxes on products.

## 13.2 Taxes on resource use

Environmental taxes and charges on resource use, such as effluent and emission charges, are not subject to BTA under GATT rules. Such taxes are not on products as such, even though they are incurred in connection with the manufacture of products. The GATT would classify these charges as direct taxes paid out of gross revenues not eligible for BTA.

## 13.3 Taxes on inputs

The leading case on environmental taxation of physically incorporated inputs is *United States — Superfund*, which ruled that taxes on articles used for the manufacture of domestic products may be taken into account in BTA of imported like products. In coming to this conclusion, the panel relied on an example provided by the 1947 drafting committee to explain the word equivalent in Article II:2(a): "If a charge is imposed on perfume because it contains alcohol, the charge to be imposed must take into consideration the value of the alcohol and not the value of the perfume, that is to say the value of the content and not the value of the 'whole' ".[159] The panel concluded that the tax met the requirements of Article III:2 because the chemical feed stocks taxed were "used as materials in the manufacture or production" of the final product. "[T]he tax is imposed on the imported substances because they are produced from chemicals subject to an excise tax in the USA and the tax rate is determined in principle in relation to the amount of these chemicals used and not in relation to the imported substance".[160] The *United States — Superfund* panel also upheld the method U.S. authorities used in assessing the tax, which was to charge 5 percent of the appraised value of the final product unless the importer furnished the information necessary to determine the exact amount to impose. This method was permissible[161] because the importer, by furnishing proper information, could avoid the penalty tax.

[158] *Canada Beer II*, above note 152, para. 5.33.

[159] GATT Doc. EPCT/TAC/PV/26, at 21 (1947), quoted in *United States — Superfund*, above note 141, para. 5.2.7.

[160] *United States — Superfund*, above n. 141, para. 5.2.8.

[161] *Id.* para. 5.3.9.

Thus, environmental taxes on inputs that are physically present in some form in the final imported product are properly subject to BTA. This means that BTA can be made, for example, for a tax on chlorofluorocarbons (CFCs) and other ozone-depleting substances with respect to the export/import of refrigerators in which they are incorporated.

The status of inputs consumed in the production process is more problematic, as is shown by the example of the UN Framework Convention on Climate Change. Although the Convention merely requires parties to work toward the modest goal of reducing greenhouse gas emissions to 1990 levels by the year 2000,[162] the 1997 Kyoto Protocol[163] obliges most developed state parties to make binding reductions of the main greenhouse gases by the year 2012. The parties' implementation of greenhouse gas reductions may call for taxes on carbon emissions or energy.[164] Although proposals to tax energy in both the United States[165] and the European Community[166] proved politically unacceptable, their allure to policymakers is undeniable: such taxes produce more governmental revenues while improving environmental quality. If energy taxes are to become politically palatable, many concerns must be addressed, such as their impact on poorer members of society, how the revenue produced will be used (for reduction of other forms of taxation, deficit reduction, or new programmes), and their impact on international competitiveness. To deal with the latter problem, BTA is essential.[167]

---

[162] Art. 4.

[163] 37 I.L.M. 22 (1998)

[164] *See generally* OECD/IEA, TAXING ENERGY: WHY AND HOW (1993).

[165] In 1993, President Clinton proposed a broad-based energy tax that would have applied to all fuels at a basic rate in proportion to their energy content as measured in British Thermal Units (BTUs). The Senate substituted a 4.3-cent per gallon increase in the tax on motor fuels, which became law. *See* H.R. Rep. No. 103–111, 103d Cong., 1st Sess. (1993).

[166] In 1992, the European Commission proposed a hybrid carbon/energy tax to limit carbon dioxide emissions and to improve energy efficiency. *See Commission Proposal for a Council Directive Introducing a Tax on Carbon Dioxide Emissions and Energy*, 1992 O.J. (L 196) 1; Amy C. Christian, *Designing a Carbon Tax: The Introduction of a Carbon Burned Tax (CBT)*, 10 UCLA J. ENVTL. L. & POL'Y 332, 342 (1992). This and modified versions of an energy tax have not been enacted, although a few member states have adopted their own energy taxes, including the U.K. and Denmark.

[167] Another environmental tax of this kind is § 4681 of the U.S. Internal Revenue Code, which provides for a tax on "any product (other than an ozone-depleting chemical) entered into the USA. for consumption, use, or warehousing if any ozone-depleting chemical was used as material in the manufacture or production of such product". This would cover such products even if the ozone-depleting chemicals were completely consumed in the production process.

But the GATT is ambiguous about BTA for taxes on inputs consumed during the production process. Article III does not deal with this issue, but Article II:2(a) appears to preclude BTA, since it allows a tax with respect to Article III only on inputs "from which", *not* "with the help of which", the imported and the like domestic product were produced. Hence, energy taxes apparently cannot be imposed on imported products because energy is consumed and is not physically incorporated into the product during its production. The 1970 GATT Working Party on Border Tax Adjustments noted a divergence on views on taxes occultes, that is, taxes on energy, advertising, machinery, and transport.[168] Thus, this point needs clarification.

## 14. Conclusions

After a difficult start, the WTO has laid a foundation for reconciling actual and potential conflicts between international trade and protection of the environment. The new accommodation that has occurred since 1995 is almost wholly the work of the Appellate Body. Now it is time for other institutions, such as the CTE and the Ministerial Conference, to address additional aspects of the trade and environment agenda.

Two aspects bear mentioning that have not been addressed at all. First, the matter of environmental regulations and their effect on market access problems of developing countries, one of the tasks given to the CTE in 1995, has not received enough attention. This needs to be corrected. A second area that has been overlooked is subsidies that have the effect of impairing environmental quality. Fishing subsidies are now on the negotiating agenda; this is long overdue. The WTO should tackle other subsidy programmes as well, such as the U.S. sugar subsidy programme that encourages sugar farming in south Florida to the great detriment of Everglades National Park.[169]

We should realize, however, that there will be no grand synthesis of the trade and environment conflict. Rather, the process of accommodation will be ongoing, demanding continual concern at the WTO as work proceeds on the built-in agenda of the Uruguay Round as well as possible new trade and

[168] Border Tax Adjustments, 2 December 1970, GATT B.I.S.D. (18th Supp.) at 92, para. 14, at 100–101 (1972).

[169] Aaron Schwaback, *How Free Trade Can Save the Everglades*, 14 Geo. Int'l Envtl. L. Rev. 301 (2002).

investment agreements. New trade and environment conflicts are on the horizon, especially in the areas of food safety, intellectual property, trade in services, and subsidies. Other important tasks facing the WTO are the careful monitoring of the impact of new environmental initiatives and protection of developing countries' access to global markets. Finally, the WTO should adopt thoroughgoing procedural reforms to improve the transparency of its decision-making process to both the public and non-governmental organizations.

# 18

# TECHNICAL BARRIERS, STANDARDS, TRADE AND HEALTH

## 1. Introduction

One of the most serious charges against the WTO is that it endangers food, safety and environmental standards, and public health. The essence of this charge is that the WTO readiness to invalidate trade restrictions means that national laws and regulations enacted to protect food, safety, and the environment will be struck down.[1] In this chapter, we examine the force of this charge and the WTO criteria for setting standards that protect human, animal or plant life or health.

Although the most important WTO agreement for the trade and health link is the Agreement on the Application of Sanitary and Phytosanitary Measures (SPS Agreement), the Agreement on Technical Barriers to Trade (TBT Agreement), Article XX of the GATT and Article XIV of the GATS are also relevant. WTO case law with respect to health-related issues now exists under the GATT and the SPS Agreement but not under the TBT Agreement. There are still many interpretive uncertainties with respect to these Agreements.

## 2. The GATT, the SPS Agreement, and the TBT Agreement

The GATT permits measures that are "necessary to protect human, animal or plant life or health".[2] The SPS Agreement applies only to sanitary and phytosanitary measures and permits WTO Members to use such measures "to protect human, animal or plant life or health".[3] The TBT Agreement applies only to technical regulations and recognizes that the "protection of human health or safety, animal or plant life or health" may be a legitimate objective of such regulations.[4] What is the relationship between these three Agreements?

[1] Lori Wallach and Michelle Sforza, The WTO: Five Years of Reasons to Resist Corporate Globalization 39–45 (1999).

[2] GATT Art. XX(b). An identically worded provision is contained in Article XIV(b) of the GATS. GATT Art. XX(b) interpretations will undoubtedly shed light on interpretations of GATS Art. XIV(b).

[3] SPS Agreement Art. 2.1.

[4] TBT Agreement Art. 2.2.

The SPS Agreement defines the term "sanitary or phytosanitary measure" as follows:

> [a]ny measure applied:
>
> (a) to protect animal or plant life or health within the territory of the Member from risks arising from the entry, establishment or spread of pests, diseases, disease-carrying organisms or disease-causing organisms;
> (b) to protect human or animal life or health within the territory of the Member from risks arising from additives, contaminants, toxins or disease-causing organisms in foods, beverages or feedstuffs;
> (c) to protect human life or health within the territory of the Member from risks arising from diseases carried by animals, plants or products thereof, or from the entry, establishment or spread of pests; or
> (d) to prevent or limit other damage within the territory of the Member from the entry, establishment or spread of pests.[5]

The TBT Agreement defines a "technical regulation" as a

> [d]ocument which lays down product characteristics or their related processes and production methods, including the applicable administrative provisions, with which compliance is mandatory. It may also include or deal exclusively with terminology, symbols, packaging, marking or labelling requirements at they apply to a product, process or production method.[6]

The term "technical regulation" was interpreted in the *EC — Asbestos* case between Canada and France.[7] The measure at issue, a French decree, prohibited the sale in France of asbestos and products containing asbestos fibres because of dangers to human health but provided certain exceptions to those prohibitions. The dispute settlement panel first examined the part of the decree containing the prohibitions and concluded that it was not a technical regulation because it did not define the "characteristics" of specific products.[8] The panel then examined the part of the decree containing the exceptions and concluded that it *was* a technical regulation because it was product specific.[9] The panel did not, however, analyse the decree under the TBT Agreement because Canada made no claims under the part of the decree containing the exceptions.[10]

[5] SPS Agreement Annex A:1.

[6] TBT Agreement Annex 1.1.

[7] Appellate Body Report, *EC — Asbestos*; Panel Report, *EC — Asbestos.*

[8] Appellate Body Report, *EC — Asbestos*; paras 8.33–8.58, specifically 8.33, 8.52, 8.57 and 8.58.

[9] *Id.* paras 8.64–8.72.

[10] *Id.*

The Appellate Body, however, concluded that the French decree should have been "examined as an integrated whole".[11] It ruled that the decree was a "technical regulation" because the products covered by the measure are identifiable, compliance with the prohibitions is mandatory and the exceptions set out " 'applicable administration provisions, with which compliance is mandatory' for products with certain objective 'characteristics' ".[12]

The relationship between GATT Article XX(b) and the TBT Agreement is somewhat unclear. As the Appellate Body stated, "the *TBT Agreement* imposes obligations on Members that seem to be *different* from and *additional* to the obligations imposed on Members under the GATT 1994".[13] In the *EC — Bananas* case, the Appellate Body observed that, when both the GATT and another agreement in Annex 1A to the WTO Agreement appear to apply to the measure at issue, the measure should be examined under the agreement that deals "specifically" and "in detail" with that class of measures.[14] This supports the idea that, if a measure qualifies as a technical regulation, it should first be examined under the TBT Agreement; then, if it also concerns health, it should, as in *EC — Asbestos*, be scrutinized under GATT Article XX(b).

The relationship between GATT Article XX(b) and the SPS Agreement is also somewhat unclear. When presented with a health or safety measure that is a sanitary or phytosanitary measure and is challenged under both the GATT and the SPS Agreement, it is unclear whether WTO adjudicating bodies will analyse the measure under the SPS Agreement or the GATT or both. In *Japan — Agricultural Products (Apples)*, the panel did not evaluate the phytosanitary measure at issue under the GATT because the measure was ultimately challenged under only the SPS Agreement.[15] This approach presumes that the SPS Agreement is consistent with GATT Article XX(b) and is an elaboration of its more general norms. This presumption appears to be correct because the preamble of the SPS Agreement states that its purpose is to "elaborate rules for the *application* of... Article XX(b)".[16]

[11] Appellate Body Report, *EC — Asbestos*, para. 64.

[12] *Id.* paras 66–75.

[13] Appellate Body Report, *EC — Asbestos*, para. 80 (emphasis in original).

[14] Appellate Body Report, *EC — Bananas*, para. 204 (finding that the panel should have applied the Agreement on Import Licensing Procedures, an Annex 1A agreement, before applying the GATT, because the licensing agreement "deals specifically, and in detail" with the administration of the class of measures at issue).

[15] Panel Report, *Japan — Agricultural Products (Apples)*, para. 8.12.

[16] SPS Agreement, Preamble, last sentence.

There are both similarities and differences between GATT Article XX(b) and the SPS Agreement. Both require that a nationally pursued health or safety policy be "necessary".[17] The SPS Agreement, however, contains additional requirements, including the requirement that SPS measures must be based on scientific principles[18] and the so-called consistency requirement.[19] Measures challenged under the SPS Agreement as opposed to the GATT will be subjected to additional scrutiny.

The relationship between the TBT Agreement and the SPS Agreement appears to be addressed by the TBT Agreement, which provides that the TBT Agreement does not apply to sanitary and phytosanitary measures as defined in the SPS Agreement.[20] Sanitary or phytosanitary measures that are also technical regulations should, therefore, be analysed under the SPS Agreement rather than the TBT Agreement.

The precise relationships between the three Agreements will ultimately have to be worked out on a case-by-case basis by dispute settlement panels and the Appellate Body. Because these Agreements appear to be complimentary, there do not appear to be direct conflicts between them. Rather, the key question will be overlap, particularly in the case of GATT Article XX(b) and one or the other of the Agreements. In most cases of overlap, however, the panel or the Appellate Body is likely to apply either the SPS Agreement or TBT Agreement alone because these Agreements appear to be special applications of the Article XX(b) principles.[21] Article XX(b), then, will apply, in most cases, as a supplement to either the SPS Agreement or the TBT Agreement.[22]

---

[17] GATT Art. XX(b); SPS Agreement Art. 2.1.

[18] SPS Agreement Art. 2.2.

[19] SPS Agreement Art. 5.5. See the discussion of this requirement, below.

[20] TBT Agreement Art. 1.5.

[21] *E.g.*, Panel Report, *Japan — Agricultural Products (Apples)* (reviewing the phytosanitary measure at issue under the SPS Agreement but not under the GATT because the claims originally made under the GATT were not pursued).

[22] *E.g., EC — Asbestos.* This approach is consistent with the General Interpretive Note of Annex 1A of the WTO Agreement. General Interpretive Note to Annex 1A, Multilateral Agreements on Trade in Goods, of the WTO Agreement, in WTO, THE LEGAL TEXTS: THE RESULTS OF THE URUGUAY ROUND OF MULTILATERAL TRADE NEGOTIATIONS 16 (1999) [hereinafter General Interpretive Note]. The General Interpretive Note deals with the relationship between the various WTO agreements in Annex 1A (to which the GATT, the SPS Agreement and the TBT Agreement belong). The General Interpretive Note reads as follows:

> In the event of conflict between a provision of the General Agreement on Tariffs and Trade 1994 and a provision of another agreement in Annex 1A to the Agreement Establishing the World Trade Organization (referred to in the agreements in Annex 1A as the "WTO Agreement"), the provision of the other agreement shall prevail to the extent of the conflict.

## 3. Health and safety standards under the three agreements

What are the WTO norms that national measures protecting human, animal and plant health and safety must meet? Are these norms adequate? These questions can best be addressed by analysing each of the three Agreements, together with relevant WTO jurisprudence.

### 3.1 The GATT

The GATT subjects national health and safety measures to two levels of analysis. First, is there a violation of Article III:4 (the national treatment obligation) because "like products" produced domestically are granted treatment that is more favourable? Second, if so, is the health or safety measure justified as a general exception under Article XX(b)? The leading case to rule on these issues is the *EC — Asbestos* case. This case involved a challenge by Canada to a French regulation that broadly prohibited the manufacture, processing, sale, and importation of products containing asbestos fibres. Canada argued that the ban was too broad and that France could have protected health by less-stringent measures, such as by using standards for asbestos products developed by the International Organization for Standardization (ISO), a private standards-setting body based in Geneva.

The *EC—Asbestos* case first considered the issue of the ban on the basis of the first level of analysis, the national treatment obligation. Because the French asbestos ban covered both domestic and imported asbestos, the determination of an Article III:4 violation depended upon finding, as the WTO panel did,[23] that asbestos products and certain competing non-asbestos containing products were "like" products. If so, the asbestos ban would violate the national treatment obligation of Article III:4. The Appellate Body, ruling that asbestos and non-asbestos products were not "like" products, reversed the Panel's finding.[24] The Appellate Body reasoned that health risks could differentiate products. Health risks may be considered in assessing whether products are "like" because (1) they are important in the competitive relationship between the products in the marketplace[25]; and (2) they influence

[23] Panel Report, *EC — Asbestos*, paras 361–378; *see also id.* para. 175.

[24] Appellate Body Report, *EC — Asbestos*, paras 88–141. *See* the discussion of the "like" products issue in Chapter 7.

[25] *Id.* para. 115.

consumers' tastes and habits.[26] Thus, the national treatment obligation of Article III:4 did not prevent France from banning asbestos-containing products.

The Appellate Body's decision is an important ruling. It established the proposition that objective health or safety factors associated with a product may be sufficient to distinguish it from otherwise closely associated products such that the two products are not "like" under GATT Article III:4.[27] If so, imports of the dangerous product may be banned under GATT rules. Of course, this determination must be made on a case-by-case basis, and the dangerous product must be banned domestically as well.

A second level of analysis can be used to justify a national health or safety measure even if it fails the national treatment test of Article III:4. A measure that conflicts with Article III:4 can be upheld under GATT Article XX(b).

Article XX(b) reads as follows:

> Subject to the requirement that such measures are not applied in a manner which would constitute a means of arbitrary or unjustifiable discrimination between countries where the same conditions prevail, or a disguised restriction on international trade, nothing in this Agreement shall be construed to prevent the adoption or enforcement by any contracting party of measures:
>
> . . .
>
> (b) necessary to protect human, animal or plant life or health;

To meet the criteria of Article XX(b), two elements must be proved. First, objective evidence of the health or safety risk must be demonstrated. The party claiming the exception must submit at least *prima facie* evidence of the risks associated with the product.[28] In *EC — Asbestos*, the panel and the Appellate Body consulted a committee of four scientific experts and accepted their views.[29] Scientific reports can also be consulted.[30]

The second issue in an Article XX(b) case is historically the most difficult: proving that the ban or other measure is "necessary". In prior cases under the GATT,[31] the term "necessary" was construed very strictly. GATT

---

[26] *Id.* para. 122.

[27] *Id.* para. 115.

[28] *Id.* para. 157.

[29] *Id.* para. 162.

[30] *Id.*

[31] *E.g., Thailand — Restrictions on Importation of and Internal Taxes on Cigarettes*, DS10/R, 7 November 1990, reprinted in 1990 GATTPD LEXIS 6, paras 73–75 (1990) [hereinafter *Thai Cigarette* case]; *United States — Restrictions on Imports of Tuna*, GATT B.I.S.D. (39th Supp.) at

panels inquired very closely into whether a measure was truly necessary and whether it was the least trade-restrictive measure available.[32]

In *EC — Asbestos*, the panel and Appellate Body took a more flexible, less restrictive approach, emphasizing that "necessary" means "reasonably available".[33] The Appellate Body noted that the issue of whether a measure is "necessary" should be determined in a "weighing and balancing process" and that what is "reasonably available" can depend on the end pursued.[34] The more vital and important the interests or values being pursued, the easier it is to stretch the "necessary" concept.[35] In the case of asbestos, the Appellate Body accepted the French asbestos ban as "necessary".

Thus, health and safety import measures are subject to GATT criteria, but these do not seem unduly burdensome. Of course, under Article XX(b), the conditions of the "chapeau" must also be met,[36] but meeting these conditions will not be a problem in the absence of arbitrary or unjustifiable discrimination.

### *3.1.1 "Necessary": a sliding scale*

An extremely important difference between the GATT and the WTO is the interpretation of the word "necessary" in GATT Article XX. The concept "necessary" is critical because this word qualifies three major Article XX exceptions: measures "(a) necessary to protect public morals; (b) necessary to protect human, animal or plant life or health; [and] (d) necessary to secure compliance with laws or regulations".

Under the GATT, the word "necessary" in Article XX was given a rigid, strict interpretation:

> [A] contracting party cannot justify a measure ... as "necessary" ... if an alternative measure which it could reasonably be expected to employ and which is not inconsistent with other GATT provisions is available to it....

---

155 (1993), reprinted in 30 I.L.M. 1594 (1991) (unadopted) [hereinafter *Tuna Dolphin I*]; *United States — Restrictions on Imports of Tuna*, DS29/R, 16 June 1994, reprinted in 33 I.L.M. 839 (1994) (unadopted) [hereinafter *Tuna Dolphin II*].

[32] In the *Thai Cigarette* case, the GATT panel found that discriminatory taxes on foreign cigarettes were not "necessary" under Article XX(b) because non-discriminatory taxes could be used to discourage smoking. *Thai Cigarette* case, above note 31, para. 81.

[33] Appellate Body Report, *EC — Asbestos*, paras 169–173.

[34] *Id.* para. 172.

[35] *Id.* para. 172.

[36] The chapeau of Article XX is considered in Chapter 17 § 4.3.

> [A] contracting party is bound to use, among the measures reasonably available to it, that which entails the least degree of inconsistency[37] with other GATT provisions.

However, under the WTO the rigid interpretation of "necessary" became untenable. Even on its face, a strict view of what is "necessary" cannot be reconciled with the object and purpose of Article XX. This is so because, while "necessary" qualifies exceptional measures to protect human health (Article XX(b)), exceptional measures to conserve natural resources are permitted (Article XX(g)) without being "necessary". Thus, a strict and rigid interpretation would result in a higher standard to protect health than to protect resources.

The solution to this dilemma in the WTO was to keep the GATT formulation of the test for "necessary", but to radically alter its interpretation. Two cases decided by the Appellate Body accomplished this revolution. In the *Korea — Beef* case the Appellate Body announced that to interpret the word "necessary", "we look first to the ordinary meaning of the word . . . in its context and in the light of the object and purpose of Article XX, in accordance with Article 31(1) of the Vienna Convention".[38] The Appellate Body noted that the word "necessary" has a "continuum" of meanings, ranging from "indispensable" to "making a contribution to".[39] Then, importantly, the Appellate Body ruled that to apply the "reasonably available" GATT test of "necessary", a "weighing and balancing" process should be employed.[40] This balancing process must "take into account the relative importance of the common interests or values that the [measure] is intended to protect".[41]

Applying this to the case at hand, the Appellate Body in the *Korea — Beef* case held that Korea had not shown that a separate distribution system for imported beef products was "necessary" in the sense that no alternative measure to deal with misrepresentation in the retail market for beef was reasonably available.[42] In the context of Article XX(d) the word "necessary" has a relatively strict meaning.[43] In contrast, in the *EC — Asbestos*[44] case a

[37] *Thailand — Restrictions on Importation of and Internal Taxes on Cigarettes*, Report of the Panel, para. 75; United States — Section 337 of the Tariff Act of 1930, Report of the Panel, para. 5.26.

[38] *Korea — Beef*, Report of the Appellate Body, para. 159.

[39] *Id.* para. 161.

[40] *Id.* paras 162–166.

[41] *Id.* para. 162.

[42] *Id.* para. 167–168.

[43] *Id.* para. 162.

[44] *EC—Asbestos*, Report of the Appellate Body, para. 172

few months later, the Appellate Body used a balancing approach to "necessary" that favoured the measure, a ban on asbestos-containing products. In the case of Article XX(b), the Appellate Body ruled, the value pursued — protection of public health — is "both vital and important in the highest degree".[45] Thus, it was relatively easy for the EC to prove that there was no reasonable alternative.[46]

These cases demonstrate that the term "necessary" in Article XX (and perhaps in other WTO contexts) carries a sliding scale of meaning dependent upon the value which the contested measure strives to protect. In the context of protection of public health, "necessary" carries a very flexible meaning that is relatively easy to meet.

## 3.2 The Sanitary and Phytosanitary Agreement (SPS Agreement)

The SPS Agreement, as noted above,[47] applies to trade measures adopted to protect against risks associated with diseases, pests, additives, contaminants, toxins, and disease-causing organisms in foods, beverages, and feedstuffs.

The SPS Agreement provides three methods of adopting trade restrictions against these risks. First, a WTO Member can choose measures that "conform to international standards".[48] International standards are developed in many important areas by international bodies, such as the Codex Alimentarius Commission, the UN standard-setting body for food safety that is recognized under WTO rules. This category of standards does not present problems under the SPS Agreement because the SPS Agreement grants a presumption of consistency to national SPS measures that "conform to international standards".[49] Second, a national measure can be based on international standards, guidelines, or recommendations; these national standards are so-called harmonized standards,[50] in which there are minor variations from the international standards. No national SPS measures that conform to or are based on international standards, guidelines, or recommendations have been contested at the WTO.

45 *EC—Asbestos*, Report of the Appellate Body, para. 172.

46 *Id.* para. 175

47 *See* above note 5 and accompanying text, which contains the definition in the SPS Agreement of sanitary or phytosanitary measures.

48 SPS Agreement Art. 3.2.

49 *Id.* Art. 3.2.

50 *Id.* Art. 3.1.

Only the third category of SPS standards has been the subject of disputes in the WTO. This category consists of national standards that introduce or maintain a distinctively higher level of protection than international or harmonized norms.[51] These standards have been the subject of three dispute settlement decisions by the Appellate Body.[52]

National health and safety standards that are SPS measures must meet several requirements. First and foremost, the Appellate Body ruled in the *EC — Hormones* case that national health and safety standards must be based on a "risk assessment", which, in turn, must be based on "scientific principles" and "sufficient scientific evidence".[53] Each of these terms needs definition.

### *3.2.1 Assessing risks on the basis of scientific principles and evidence*

As to the term "risk", the Appellate Body stated in *Australia — Salmon* that "the 'risk' evaluated in a risk assessment must be an ascertainable risk; theoretical uncertainty is 'not the kind of risk which, under Article 5.1, is to be assessed' ".[54] The Appellate Body also stated that "it is not sufficient that a risk assessment conclude that there is a *possibility* of entry, establishment or spread of diseases and associated biological and economic consequences".[55] Hence, a risk in the context of Article 5.1 of the SPS Agreement is more than a mere possibility. This does not mean, however, that the Appellate Body believed that there should be a minimum level of risk for a definitive measure to be lawful: "To the extent that the Panel purported to require a risk assessment to establish a minimum magnitude of risk, we must note that imposition of such quantitative requirement finds no basis in the SPS Agreement".[56]

The term "risk assessment" is defined in Annex A of the SPS Agreement as follows:

> The evaluation of the likelihood of entry, establishment or spread of a pest or disease within the territory of an importing Member according to the sanitary or phytosanitary

---

[51] *Id.* Art. 3.3.

[52] Appellate Body Report, *EC — Hormones*; Appellate Body Report, *Australia — Salmon*; Appellate Body Report, *Japan — Agricultural Products (Apples). See* Joost Pauwelyn, *The WTO Agreement on Sanitary and Phytosanitary (SPS) Measures as Applied in the First Three SPS Disputes*, 2 J. Int'l Econ. L. 641 (1999) (providing an excellent account of the first three SPS-related cases treated by the Appellate Body).

[53] Appellate Body Report, *EC — Hormones*, paras 179, 180 (construing Articles 2.2 and 5.1 of the SPS Agreement together to define the basic obligation).

[54] Appellate Body Report, *Australia — Salmon*, para. 125 (citing Appellate Body Report, *EC — Hormones*, para. 186).

[55] *Id.* para. 123 (emphasis in original).

[56] Appellate Body Report, *EC — Hormones*, para. 186.

measures which might be applied, and of the associated potential biological and economic consequences; or the evaluation of the potential for adverse effects on human or animal health arising from the presence of additives, contaminants, toxins or disease-causing organisms in food, beverages or feedstuffs.

The *EC — Hormones* panel understood the term "risk assessment" to mean, "at least for risks to human life or health, a *scientific* examination of data and factual studies; it is not a policy exercise involving social value judgments made by political bodies".[57]

The *EC — Hormones* panel distinguished "risk assessment", as defined above, from "risk management", which is a decision by a WTO Member to enact an SPS measure.[58] After a risk assessment has been carried out and provided there is an ascertainable risk, WTO Members can choose their appropriate level of sanitary or phytosanitary protection.[59] As the panel implied, WTO Members, if they respect the disciplines laid out in Article 5.4 to 5.6, are free to choose the level of protection that seems appropriate to them. This finding is in line with the finding of the Appellate Body that WTO Members can legitimately pursue a zero-risk policy.[60]

The Appellate Body, however, reversed, stressing that the SPS Agreement uses the term "risk assessment" but not the term "risk management".[61] This finding has legal implications but did not change the outcome of the case. The notion of appropriate risk management should be understood as equivalent to the notion of maintaining the appropriate level of sanitary or phytosanitary protection. The operative consequence is that, if proper risk assessment has been made, WTO Members are free to choose their optimal level of protection (for instance, Members might have different attitudes to risk reduction). "Risk management" reflects the fact that we live in a world of regulatory diversity. The Appellate Body rejected the use of the term "risk management",[62] but did not cast any doubt on the proposition that we live in a world of regulatory diversity.[63]

[57] Panel Report, *EC — Hormones, Complaint by the United States*, para. 8.94 (emphasis in original); Panel Report, *EC — Hormones, Complaint by Canada*, para. 8.97 (emphasis in original).

[58] *Id.* para. 8.98.

[59] *Id.* para. 8.101.

[60] *Id.* para. iv.83.

[61] Appellate Body Report, *EC — Hormones*, para. 181.

[62] The distinction between "risk assessment" and "risk management" is not unknown, for example, in European Community law. Indeed, the EC argued along the lines of this distinction before the panel.

[63] Subsequent Appellate Body decisions, like *United States — Shrimp* and *United States — FSC*, made this point clear.

The Appellate Body clarified the concept of risk assessment in *Australia — Salmon*. In that case, the Appellate Body held for the following proposition:

> [W]e consider that, in this case, a risk assessment within the meaning of Article 5.1 must:
>
> 1. *identify* the diseases whose entry, establishment or spread a Member wants to prevent within its territory, as well as the potential biological and economic consequences associated with the entry, establishment or spread of these diseases;
> 2. *evaluate the likelihood of entry*, establishment or spread of these diseases, as well as the associated potential biological and economic consequences; and
> 3. evaluate the likelihood of entry, establishment or spread of these diseases *according to the SPS measures that might be applied*.[64]

According to this interpretation, a risk assessment involves the establishment of a likelihood of entry of an identified disease and a causal relationship between the SPS measure at stake and the occurrence of the disease, in the sense that the measure will reduce the identified risks.

For an SPS measure to be compatible with the SPS Agreement, it must be *based on* a risk assessment. In *EC — Hormones*, the panel and the Appellate Body interpreted two aspects of the term "based on": the time dimension and the question of overlap between the SPS measure enacted and the risk assessment. We take each issue in turn.

The *EC — Hormones* panel held that "the Member imposing a sanitary measure needs to submit evidence that at least it actually *took into account* a risk assessment when it enacted or maintained its sanitary measure in order for that measure to be considered as *based on* a risk assessment".[65] According to this view, the lawfulness of a measure depends on the *decision-making process* leading to the measure: scientific evidence not used in the decision-making process is irrelevant even if it would support the measure.[66]

The Appellate Body, however, reversed the panel's finding that WTO Members must take into account a risk assessment when enacting or maintaining an SPS measure. The operative consequence of the Appellate Body's ruling is that a WTO Member can show, for the first time, that it based a measure on a risk assessment when the measure is challenged before a WTO adjudicating body.[67] According to this view, a WTO Member can

[64] Appellate Body Report, *Australia — Salmon*, para. 121.

[65] Panel Report, *EC — Hormones, Complaint by the United States*, para. 8.113 (emphasis in original); Panel Report, *EC — Hormones, Complaint by Canada*, para. 56 (emphasis in original).

[66] *See id.* para. 8.116.

[67] *See* Appellate Body Report, *EC — Hormones*, paras 188–191.

lawfully enact a measure even when it cannot offer a basis of risk assessment when the measure is enacted, provided a basis can be offered if the measure is challenged before a WTO adjudicating body.[68]

The *EC — Hormones* Appellate Body, again reversing the panel, made it clear that "based on" should not be understood to mean that the SPS measure must conform to the risk assessment. A certain margin of discretion in favour of the WTO Member enacting legislation must be acknowledged. The relevant passage reads as follows: "A measure, however, based on the same standard might not conform to that standard, as where only some, not all, of the elements of the standard are incorporated into the measure".[69]

As to the scientific evidence that must be taken into account in a risk assessment, the Appellate Body had this to say:

> Article 5.1 does not require that the risk assessment must necessarily embody only the view of a majority of the relevant scientific community. In some cases, the very existence of divergent views presented by qualified scientists who have investigated the particular issue at hand may indicate a state of scientific uncertainty. Sometimes the divergence may indicate a roughly equal balance of scientific opinion, which may itself be a form of scientific uncertainty. In most cases, responsible and representative governments tend to base their legislative and administrative measures on "mainstream" scientific opinion. In other cases, equally responsible and representative governments may act in good faith on the basis of what, at a given time, may be a divergent opinion coming from qualified and respected sources.[70]

It follows that minority scientific opinions may suffice for a WTO Member to meet its burden under the SPS Agreement. We are still in the dark, however, as to the meaning of the term "scientific evidence". Indirectly, the Appellate Body shed some light on this issue. When examining an oral statement by an expert (Dr. Lucier) invited to testify before it, the Appellate Body noted that:

> th[e] opinion by Dr. Lucier does not purport to be the result of scientific studies carried out by him or under his supervision focusing specifically on residues of hormones in meat from cattle fattened with such hormones. Accordingly, it appears that the single divergent opinion expressed by Dr. Lucier is not reasonably sufficient to overturn the contrary conclusions reached in the scientific studies referred to by the European Communities that relate specifically to residues of the hormones in meat from cattle to which hormones had been administered for growth promotion.[71]

[68] *See* Appellate Body Report, *EC—Hormones*, para. 189. [69] *Id.* para. 163.
[70] *Id.* para. 194. [71] *Id.* para. 198.

Nevertheless, the Appellate Body cautioned that "based on" a risk assessment means that there must be a rational relationship between the trade measure and the risk assessment.[72] The lack of such a relationship was the primary failing in the *EC — Hormones* case. The scientific evidence and reports marshalled by the EC as its risk assessment were found insufficient to support the ban on hormone-fed meat.

### *3.2.2 Factors to consider when assessing risks*

Article 5.2 of the SPS Agreement provides that "[i]n the assessment of risks, Members shall take into account available scientific evidence; relevant processes and production methods; relevant inspection, sampling and testing methods; prevalence of specific diseases or pests; existence of pest- or disease-free areas; relevant ecological and environmental conditions; and quarantine or other treatment". Thus, in carrying out the risk assessment required by Article 5.1, WTO Members must take into account the factors listed in Article 5.2.

In *EC — Hormones*, the Appellate Body interpreted the objective function of this list:

> Some of the kinds of factors listed in Article 5.2 such as "relevant processes and production methods" and "relevant inspection, sampling and testing methods" are not necessarily or wholly susceptible of investigation according to laboratory methods of, for example, biochemistry or pharmacology. Furthermore, there is nothing to indicate that the listing of factors that may be taken into account in a risk assessment of Article 5.2 was intended to be a closed list. It is essential to bear in mind that the risk that is to be evaluated in a risk assessment under Article 5.1 is not only risk ascertainable in a science laboratory operating under strictly controlled conditions, but also risk in human societies as they actually exist, in other words, the actual potential for adverse effects on human health in the real world where people live and work and die.[73]

By allowing WTO Members to view the factors listed in Article 5.2 not necessarily from a strict scientific angle, the Appellate Body seems to have opted for a hands-free attitude vis-à-vis national SPS measures. The Appellate Body adopted the position that the factors listed in Article 5.2 are not exhaustive and that other factors can be taken into account when a WTO Member assesses a risk.

This interpretation by the Appellate Body also is particularly confusing because it blurs the line between risk assessment and risk management. Risk assessment, as the panel found, normally means technical scientific analysis,

[72] *Id.* para. 193. [73] *Id.* para. 187.

while risk management adds economic and social value judgments. The Appellate Body confuses the two and brings risk management into the picture after formally rejecting it earlier in its opinion.

### 3.2.3 The precautionary principle

The precautionary principle[74] was a central issue in the *Hormones* case because it was invoked by the EC to justify the hormones ban despite minimal scientific evidence. The EC argued that the precautionary principle had become customary international law or a general principle of law that must be applied by the WTO adjudicating bodies to supplement the specific wording of WTO agreements. The EC argued that the application of the precautionary principle relieved it from adducing specific scientific evidence and a risk assessment.[75]

The Appellate Body rejected this argument. It refused to rule on the general status of the precautionary principle in international law, stating that it is "less than clear",[76] but, regardless, the principle cannot override the specific provisions of the SPS Agreement.[77] Nevertheless, the precautionary principle may be invoked in connection with SPS measures, most notably in Article 5.7, which allows provisional SPS measures.[78] Thus, the precise bounds of the precautionary principle remain unsettled, but in connection with SPS measures, the specific mandates of the SPS Agreement are unaffected. It appears that the precautionary principle may be used to justify time-limited SPS measures, but is not an alternative to risk assessment and scientific evidence for a definitive standard.

### 3.2.4 Economic factors to consider when assessing risks to animal or plant life or health

Article 5.3 of the SPS Agreement requires Members to take into account relevant economic factors when assessing the appropriate level of protection.[79]

---

[74] The precautionary principle appears in a number of international law instruments, but has never been definitively codified. The formulation contained in Principle 15 of the Rio Declaration is the following: "When there are threats of serious or irreversible damage, lack of full scientific certainty shall not be used as a reason for postponing cost-effective measures to prevent environmental degradation". United Nations Conference on Environment and Development: Rio Declaration on Environment and Development, 14 June 1992, Principle 15, 31 I.L.M. 874, 879 (1992).

[75] Appellate Body Report, *EC — Hormones*, paras 118–122.

[76] Appellate Body Report, *EC — Hormones*, para. 123.

[77] Appellate Body Report, *EC — Hormones*, paras 123–125.

[78] *Id. See* the discussion, below.

[79] SPS Agreement Art. 5.3.

Relevant economic factors are defined to include potential loss of production or sales from disease, the costs of control or eradication of the disease, and the relative cost-effectiveness of alternative measures to limit risk.[80]

Article 5.3 seems to open a wide range of possibilities to rationalize beggar-thy-neighbour type measures. Article 5.3, however, is circumscribed by Article 5.6, which requires Members to avoid regulatory distinctions that result in a disguised restriction of international trade. Article 5.3 has not yet been interpreted by WTO adjudicating bodies.

The possibility to consider economic factors when enacting SPS measures exists only with respect to risks to animal or plant life or health. No reference to economic factors is reflected in Article 5.2, which covers risks to human health. Does this mean that economic factors are not a concern when it comes to human health-related SPS measures? So far, there has been no response to this question in the Appellate Body case law.

### *3.2.5 Taking into account the objective of minimizing negative trade effects*

Article 5.4 of the SPS Agreement states that Members "should, when determining the appropriate level of sanitary or phytosanitary protection, take into account the objective of minimizing negative trade effects". None of the Appellate Body reports contains specific rulings on this provision. However, an explicit reference to this Article can be found in the *Hormones* panel report, which, in pertinent part, reads:

> Guided by the wording of Article 5.4, in particular the words "should" (not "shall") and "objective", we consider that this provision of the SPS Agreement does not impose an obligation. However, this objective of minimizing negative trade effects has nonetheless to be taken into account in the interpretation of other provisions of the SPS Agreement.[81]

This statement, read in conjunction with the statement that WTO Members can legitimately pursue a zero-risk policy, leads to the conclusion that the Appellate Body case law does not impose a limit on the appropriate level of protection sought by individual WTO Members.

### *3.2.6 The objective of achieving consistency in the protection against risk*

Article 5.5 concerns the obligation to adopt consistent measures to deal with SPS risks. The *Hormones* Appellate Body acknowledged that "the objective

[80] *Id.*

[81] Panel Report, *EC — Hormones, Complaint by the United States*, para. 8.59; Panel Report, *EC — Hormones, Complaint by Canada*, para. 8.166.

of Article 5.5 is formulated as the "achieving [of] consistency in the application of the concept of appropriate level of sanitary or phytosanitary protection".[82]

This objective should not, however, be equated with a requirement that SPS policies must be consistent over time. The same report a few lines later explains:

> we agree with the Panel's view that the statement of that goal does not establish a *legal obligation* of consistency of appropriate levels of protection. We think, too, that the goal set is not absolute or perfect consistency, since governments establish their appropriate levels of protection frequently on an *ad hoc* basis and over time, as different risks present themselves at different times. It is only arbitrary or unjustifiable inconsistencies that are to be avoided.[83]

Three elements must be demonstrated cumulatively for a violation of Article 5.5 SPS to exist:

1. The WTO Member imposing the measure must have "adopted its own appropriate levels of sanitary protection against risks to human life or health in several different situations".[84]
2. Those levels of protection must "exhibit arbitrary or unjustifiable differences ('distinctions' in the language of Article 5.5) in their treatment of different situations".[85]
3. The arbitrary or unjustifiable differences must "result in discrimination or a disguised restriction of international trade". In other words, the "*measure* embodying or implementing a particular level of protection" must result, "in its application, in discrimination or in a disguised restriction on international trade".[86]

The *Hormones* Appellate Body concluded that prohibiting the use of some hormones for beef production while permitting the use of others for pig production was compatible with Article 5.5 of the SPS Agreement, even though this difference of treatment was found to be arbitrary or unjustifiable.[87] The Appellate Body found that the third element had not been met because the "arbitrary or unjustifiable differences" did not "result in discrimination or a disguised restriction of international trade".

[82] Appellate Body Report, *EC — Hormones*, para. 213.
[83] *Id.* (emphasis in original).
[84] *Id.* paras 214–215.
[85] *Id.* paras 214–215.
[86] *Id.* paras 214–215 (emphasis in original).
[87] *Id.* para. 246.

The motivation of the Appellate Body is to be found in the following passage:

> We do not attribute the same importance as the Panel to the supposed multiple objectives of the European Communities in enacting the EC Directives that set forth the EC measures at issue. The documentation that preceded or accompanied the enactment of the prohibition of the use of hormones for growth promotion and that formed part of the record of the Panel makes clear the depth and extent of the anxieties experienced within the European Communities concerning the results of the general scientific studies (showing the carcinogenicity of hormones), the dangers of abuse (highlighted by scandals relating to black-marketing and smuggling of prohibited veterinary drugs in the European Communities) of hormones and other substances used for growth promotion and the intense concern of consumers within the European Communities over the quality and drug-free character of the meat available in its internal market.[88]

The *Australia — Salmon* Appellate Body applied the same three-pronged test when it examined the compatibility of an Australian measure with Article 5.5 SPS.[89] It further confirms the finding of the *Hormones* Appellate Body report that differences in levels of protection are a "warning signal" that the implementing measure in its application might be discriminatory.[90] It thus confirms that different levels of protection as such are not enough to satisfy the third element of the three-prong test: they are a necessary, but not sufficient condition to this effect.

In the *Australia — Salmon* case, the Appellate Body noted that the panel had identified two warning signals and three additional factors.[91] The two warning signals were substantial differences in levels of protection and inconsistency of the SPS measure at hand with Article 5.1.[92] The three additional factors were discrimination between salmon and herring used as bait, the substantial but unexplained difference in conclusions between two reports recommending the SPS measures, and the absence of controls on the internal movement of salmon products within Australia.[93]

The Appellate Body agreed with Australia that the first additional factor was a mere restatement of the first warning signal and hence should not be taken into account separately.[94] The Appellate Body accepted the remaining part of the panel's analysis and concluded as follows:

---

88 *Id.* para. 245.
89 Appellate Body Report, *Australia — Salmon*, para. 140.
90 *Id.* para. 161.
91 *Id.* paras 167–174.
92 *Id.* paras 163–165.
93 *Id.* paras 167–174.
94 *Id.* para. 169.

> We have only reversed the Panel's finding on the first "additional factor". We consider, however, that this reversal does not affect the validity of the Panel's conclusion . . . that the "warning signals" and "other factors", considered cumulatively, lead to the conclusion that the distinctions in the level of protection imposed by Australia result in a disguised restriction on international trade.[95]

At first glance, a discrepancy appears to exist between the *EC — Hormones* case and the *Australia — Salmon* case although the same standard was applied. There are two distinguishing factors between the two cases, however, which probably explain the difference in the outcome. First, the *Australia — Salmon* panel stated that "the protection of human life or health is not at issue in this dispute".[96] Second, the anxieties of consumers mentioned in the *Hormones* Appellate Body report were reflected in the EC Directive, but not in the Australian SPS measure. It thus appears that the Appellate Body will use a more deferential standard when human life or health is at stake.

### *3.2.7 SPS measures may not be more trade restrictive than necessary*

Article 5.6 of the SPS Agreement essentially reproduces the so-called necessary test from the GATT case law under Article XX(b). Article 5.6 is in close relationship with Article 5.4. The latter refers to the objective sought by WTO Members whereas the former deals with the issue of means applied to reach the stated objective. As mentioned above,[97] WTO adjudicating bodies will not call into question the level of the objective sought; all they can do is examine whether the means used are the least restrictive means that a WTO Member could use to reach its objective.

The logical link between means and ends prejudges the standard of review to be applied by WTO adjudicating bodies: if the end is a zero-risk policy, the means will be adjusted to that end. Hence, adjudicating bodies will have less leeway to examine whether the means used are indeed the least-restrictive option than in a case where the objective sought is more flexible than a zero-risk policy.

These issues have already been explored in WTO case law. Consider first the issue of whether WTO Members are unrestricted as to the determination of appropriate level of protection. The *Australia — Salmon* Appellate Body report reads:

[95] Appellate Body Report, *Australia — Salmon*, para. 177.

[96] Panel Report, *Australia — Salmon*, para. 8.32.

[97] See the text accompanying notes 49 and 50, above.

> The determination of the appropriate level of protection . . . as "the level of protection deemed appropriate by the Member establishing a sanitary . . . measure" is a *prerogative* of the Member concerned and not of the panel or of the Appellate Body.
>
> The "appropriate level of protection" established by a Member and the "SPS measure" have to be clearly distinguished. They are not one and the same thing. The first is an *objective*, the second is an *instrument* chosen to attain or implement that objective.[98]

The closely related question in a case where a WTO Member has enacted an SPS measure, but has not clearly identified the appropriate level of protection sought, was dealt with in the same report, which reads, in the relevant part, as follows:

> [If] a Member does not determine its appropriate level of protection, or does so with insufficient precision, the appropriate level of protection may be established by panels on the basis of the level of protection reflected in the SPS measure actually applied. Otherwise, a Member's failure to comply with the implicit obligation to determine its appropriate level of protection — with sufficient precision — would allow it to escape from its obligations under this Agreement and, in particular, its obligations under Articles 5.5 and 5.6.[99]

The test to be applied when reviewing the means used is whether the means are appropriate to reach the objective sought. The *Australia — Salmon* Appellate Body determined that Article 5.6 requires "an examination of whether possible alternative SPS measures meet the appropriate level of protection *as determined by the Member concerned*".[100]

Upholding the panel's findings in this respect, the Appellate Body provided a test for determining whether the means are the least restrictive to reach the ends sought:

> the three elements of this test under Article 5.6 are that there is an SPS measure which: [1] is reasonably available taking into account technical and economic feasibility; [2] achieves the Member's appropriate level of sanitary or phytosanitary protection; and [3] is significantly less restrictive to trade than the SPS measure contested.[101]

If each of these three elements is demonstrated, the SPS measure in question will be deemed to be the least restrictive means to reach the ends sought. In subsequent case law, the Appellate Body confirmed this test.[102]

The next question is the course of action that a WTO adjudicating body will adopt to persuade itself that a less-restrictive option exists that would

[98] Appellate Body Report, *Australia — Salmon*, paras 199–200 (emphasis in original).

[99] *Id.* para. 207.

[100] *Id.* para. 204 (emphasis in original).

[101] *Id.* para. 194.

[102] *See* Appellate Body Report, *Japan — Agricultural Products (Apples)*, para. 95

permit WTO Members to reach their objectives without calling into question the level of protection sought. During the *Japan — Agricultural Products (Apples)* panel proceedings,[103] the United States argued that Japan could reach its stated objective by using less-restrictive means. The panel examined and rejected the U.S. argument because no evidence was presented, and the Appellate Body upheld the result.[104]

If presented with evidence by a party to the dispute that the means chosen by a WTO Member to reach a health objective are not the least restrictive, WTO adjudicating bodies will have to entertain the argument and decide accordingly.

The WTO case law provides some answers in this respect. We discuss them when we address the burden of proof issue (below at § 3.2.9).

### *3.2.8 Provisional measures*

Article 5.7 of the SPS Agreement reflects the precautionary principle. Absence of scientific evidence is not, however, tantamount to a statement that WTO Members are completely unconstrained when enacting SPS measures under Article 5.7. The *Japan — Agricultural Products (Apples)* Appellate Body report explains that:

> a Member may provisionally adopt an SPS measure if this measure is: imposed in respect of a situation where "relevant scientific information is insufficient"; [and] adopted "on the basis of available pertinent information".
>
> Pursuant to the second sentence of Article 5.7, such a provisional measure may not be maintained unless the Members which adopted the measure: "seek to obtain the additional information necessary for a more objective assessment of risk"; and "review the . . . measure accordingly within a reasonable period of time".
>
> These four requirements are clearly cumulative in nature and are equally important for the purpose of determining consistency with this provision. Whenever *one* of these four conditions is not met, the measure at issue is inconsistent with Article 5.7.[105]

Because the *Japan — Agricultural Products (Apples)* panel did not interpret the first sentence of Article 5.7, the Appellate Body did not have the opportunity to interpret the first sentence.[106]

With respect to the second sentence, the Appellate Body observed:

[103] *See* Panel Report, *Japan — Agricultural Products (Apples)*, paras 8.78–8.84.

[104] Appellate Body Report, *Japan — Agricultural Products (Apples)*, paras 96–100.

[105] Appellate Body Report, *Japan — Agricultural Products (Apples)*, para. 89 (emphasis in original).

[106] *Id.* para. 91.

> Article 5.7 states that the additional information is to be sought in order to allow the Member to conduct "a more objective assessment of risk". Therefore, the information sought must be germane to conducting such a risk assessment, i.e., the evaluation of the likelihood of entry, establishment or spread of, *in casu*, a pest, according to the SPS measures which might be applied.[107]

And later:

> what constitutes a "reasonable period of time" has to be established on a case-by-case basis and depends on the specific circumstances of each case, including the difficulty of obtaining the additional information necessary for the review and the characteristics of the provisional SPS measure. In the present case, the Panel found that collecting the necessary additional information would be relatively easy. Although the obligation "to review" the varietal testing requirement has only been in existence since 1 January 1995, we agree with the Panel that Japan has not reviewed its varietal testing requirement "within a reasonable period of time".[108]

What emerges from this case law is that the additional information must be pertinent and that, if it is relatively easy for a WTO Member to collect the additional information, such collection must have taken place within four years.

We are still in the dark, however, as to the interpretation of the term "available pertinent information", which appears in the first sentence of Article 5.7. This term is the cornerstone of Article 5.7 because it is, by definition, less authoritative than scientific evidence; we need to know how much less is necessary for the precautionary principle to be invoked.

### *3.2.9 Burden of proof*

The WTO (like public international law generally) employs a decentralized system of enforcement. This means that, in principle, parties to a dispute carry the burden of proof of their arguments. On the other hand, WTO adjudicating bodies administer the process and are obliged under DSU Article 11 to conduct an objective assessment of the dispute before them.

The *Hormones* Appellate Body report establishes the rule to be followed when allocating burden of proof:

> The initial burden lies on the complaining party, which must establish a *prima facie* case of inconsistency with a particular provision of the *SPS Agreement* on the part of the defending party, or more precisely, of its SPS measure or measure complained about. When the *prima facie* case is made, the burden of proof moves to the defending party, which must in turn counter or refute the claimed inconsistency.[109]

[107] *Id.* para. 92. [108] *Id.* para. 93.
[109] Appellate Body Report, *EC — Hormones*, para. 98 (emphasis in original).

Thus, the Appellate Body interprets Article 3 of the SPS Agreement to require that the Member employing a standard that is different from or higher than an international standard bears a rebuttal burden of proving that its level of protection is consistent with the norms in Article 5 of the SPS Agreement.

### *3.2.10 The role of expert witnesses*

Article 13 DSU and Article 11.2 SPS allow WTO adjudicating bodies to select outside experts in consultation with the parties to the dispute. In the context of the SPS Agreement, seeking outside expertise is routine because panellists are rarely well versed in scientific matters.

In the *Hormones* litigation, the panel first asked parties to the dispute to name one outside expert each. It then named two experts from a list prepared by the Codex Alimentarius Commission and the International Agency for Research on Cancer and one additional expert in the area of carcinogenic effects of hormones.[110] The European Community appealed the fact that one of the experts was a national of a party and had links with the pharmaceutical industry. The Appellate Body, distinguishing the selection of expert witnesses in the context of SPS from expert review groups (Appendix 4 of the DSU), dismissed the EC argument and held that "once the panel has decided to request the opinion of individual scientific experts, there is no legal obstacle to the panel drawing up, in consultation with the parties to the dispute, *ad hoc* rules for those particular proceedings".[111]

In *Australia — Salmon*, the panel chose four experts after consultations with the Office International des Epizooties (OIE), a recognized international scientific body that deals with food contamination issues.[112] Finally, in the *Japan — Agricultural Products (Apples)* dispute, the panel chose three experts after soliciting suggestions from the Secretariat of the International Plant Protection Convention.[113]

Thus, WTO panels may, in consultation with the parties to the dispute, seek expertise from outside sources following suggestions by the organizations mentioned in the SPS Agreement.[114] In the *Hormones* litigation, the parties themselves were given the opportunity to name one expert each.[115]

[110] Panel Report, *EC — Hormones, Complaint by the United States*, para. 8.7; Panel Report, *EC — Hormones, Complaint by Canada*, para. 8.7.

[111] *Id.* para. 148.

[112] Panel Report, *Australia — Salmon*, para. 6.1.

[113] Panel Report, *Japan — Agricultural Products (Apples)*, para. 6.2(c).

[114] The organizations mentioned in the SPS Agreement include OIE, IPCC and Codex.

[115] Panel Report, *EC — Hormones, Complaint by the United States*, para. 8.59; Panel Report, *EC — Hormones, Complaint by Canada*, para. 6.2.

Panels may also receive and consider unsolicited expertise in the form of *amicus* briefs or scientific reports. Following the Appellate Body Report on *United States — Shrimp*, Article 13 DSU has been interpreted in a rather "liberal" manner: outside sources can forward their opinions to WTO adjudicating bodies and the latter have the right either to take into account or to ignore such unsolicited expertise. In other words, following this report, panels lost their monopoly on the initiative to seek expertise.

### *3.2.11 Summary of obligations under the SPS Agreement*

This sub-section is a re-writing of the SPS Agreement in the light of the aforementioned case law. The following seems to correspond to such a re-writing:

1. WTO Members can enact definitive SPS measures if a risk assessment has taken place.
2. WTO Members can enact provisional SPS measures in the absence of a risk assessment in the light of available pertinent information.
3. When WTO Members enact definitive SPS measures, their risk assessment must be based on scientific evidence.
4. For evidence to be considered scientific, some minimum methodological requirements must be met.
5. SPS measures can be enacted following a risk assessment based on minority scientific opinions.
6. Scientific evidence does not have to be provided to the WTO at the moment an SPS measure is enacted. Scientific evidence must, however, be provided to the WTO when an SPS measure is challenged before a WTO panel.
7. The scientific evidence supplied must support the view that there is a probability (not merely a possibility) that a given disease will enter the territory of a WTO Member unless the SPS measure in question is enacted.
8. WTO Members are free to set the level of risk they are willing to undertake at any level they deem appropriate. When deciding on risk management measures, WTO Members may take into account economic factors as well.
9. WTO adjudicating bodies can examine to extent to which the means chosen to achieve the level of protection sought are the least-restrictive option.
10. To examine whether an SPS measure is in accordance with the SPS Agreement, WTO adjudicating bodies can have recourse to outside experts.

WTO adjudicating bodies select expert witnesses from the organizations mentioned in the SPS Agreement in consultation with the parties to the dispute. They may also allow parties to the dispute to name their own experts. WTO adjudicating bodies can take into account unsolicited expertise.

11. WTO Members challenging an SPS measure carry the original burden of proof to show that the WTO Member whose measure is being challenged has not complied with the WTO Agreement (inconsistency of an SPS measure with any of the points mentioned above).

12. WTO adjudicating bodies can seek outside expertise to inform themselves about the arguments presented by a party but not to evaluate arguments that have not been presented by a party.

13. When a WTO Member invokes the precautionary principle, it must nevertheless show a rational relationship between the measure it enacts and the risk it wants to avoid.

14. When a WTO Member invokes the precautionary principle for provisional measures, it must seek any additional information within a reasonable period, which in one case was deemed to be four years.

15. If an SPS measure is found to be inconsistent with the WTO, it need not be revoked *ab initio.* Remedies in the SPS context are prospective.

## 3.3 The Technical Barriers to Trade Agreement (TBT Agreement)

The TBT Agreement comes into play in connection with health and safety regulations that meet the definition of "technical regulation". The TBT Agreement defines this term broadly as including mandatory standards for characteristics of products and their processes and production methods. The term also includes matters such as terminology, symbols, packaging, marking, and labelling requirements.[116] In the *EC—Asbestos* case, the Appellate Body ruled that the prohibition of a product (namely, asbestos) could be a technical regulation because it lays down mandatory product characteristics.[117] This is an expansive interpretation of the definitional section.

The definition of "technical regulation" under the TBT Agreement was further developed by the Appellate Body in the *EC Sardines* case.[118] This

[116] *See* above note 6 and accompanying text, which contains the definition in the TBT Agreement of technical regulation.

[117] Appellate Body Report, *EC — Asbestos,* para. 75.

[118] *European Communities — Trade Description of Sardines,* Report of the Appellate Body, 26 September 2002.

case involved an EC regulation that "canned sardines" required use of the species "sardina pilchardus" and excluded by implication the species "sardinops sagax" from being marketed as preserved sardines. The Appellate Body stated that three criteria must be fulfilled for a technical regulation under the TBT Agreement[119]:

1. application to an identifiable product or group of products;
2. specification of one or more characteristics of the product;
3. mandatory compliance.

Applying these criteria, the Appellate Body held that the EC regulation for sardines was a technical regulation subject to the TBT Agreement.[120] Even though sardinops sagax was not mentioned in the regulation, "a product need not be expressly referred to for it to be identifiable".[121] Thus, the Appellate Body took a broad view of what is a technical regulation under the TBT Agreement.

The TBT Agreement places *three* major substantive obligations on technical regulations. First, Members must "ensure that technical regulations are not prepared, adopted or applied with a view to or with the effect of creating unnecessary obstacles to international trade".[122] This embodies a purpose and effect test.

Second, the regulation may not be more trade restrictive than necessary to fulfil a "legitimate objective".[123] Such objectives include: "national security requirements; the prevention of deceptive practices; protection of human health or safety, animal or plant life or health, or the environment".[124]

Third, the technical regulation may not be maintained if the objectives or circumstances change or if the objectives can be addressed in a less-trade restrictive manner.[125]

The core of the TBT Agreement is Article 2.4, which states that "where international standards exist . . . , Members shall use them . . . as a basis for their technical regulations except when such international standards would be an ineffective or inappropriate means for the fulfillment of the legitimate objectives pursued . . . ". Thus, Article 2.4 refers to the legitimate objectives enumerated in Article 2.2.[126]

[119] TBT Agreement, Annex 1.1. [120] Report of the Appellate Body, paras. 138–195.
[121] *Id.* para 138. [122] TBT Agreement Art. 2.2. [123] *Id.*
[124] *Id.* [125] *Id.* Art. 2.3. [126] *EC — Sardines*, Report of the Appellate Body, para. 286.

The burden of proof of compliance with Article 2.4, according to the Appellate Body, is allocated first to the complaining WTO member, who must establish a *prima facie* case of violation; this raises a presumption of invalidity that must be rebutted by the respondent.[127]

In the *EC — Sardines* case the Appellate Body examined compliance with Article 2.4 by considering four issues. First, is there a relevant international standard? In this case there was a Codex standard that the Appellate Body found to be "relevant".[128] It stated that "relevant" does not mean that product coverage has to be identical.[129] Second, the Appellate Body examined whether the Codex was used as a "basis" for the EC regulation. "Basis" was stated to mean a "strong and very close relationship".[130] It found that the EC regulation contradicts the Codex so that the Codex was not used as a "basis".[131] Third, the Appellate Body considered the legitimate objectives of the EC regulation, which were (1) market transparency; (2) consumer protection; and (3) fair competition.[132] Fourth, Peru, the complaining member, was found to have the burden of showing that the Codex standard was ineffective or inappropriate. The Appellate Body recognized that to do this the complaining member would have to obtain information, but this could be done since, under the TBT Agreement, a member applying a technical regulation must "explain the justification"[133] and establish an "enquiry point"[134] to answer questions. The Appellate Body agreed with the panel that Peru had carried its burden of showing that the Codex was effective and appropriate, and this point was not adequately rebutted by the EC.[135] The Appellate Body recognized that, under the "objective assessment" standard of DSU Article 11, the panel could exercise a "margin of discretion" in ruling on the issues.[136]

This important case establishes the first fully-developed interpretation of the TBT Agreement by the Appellate Body. Although the technical regula-

[127] *EC — Sardines*, Report of the Appellate Body, paras. 264–274. This burden is similarly allocated in the case of the SPS Agreement as interpreted by the Appellate Body in the *Hormones* case. *Id.*

[128] *Id.* paras 226–227.

[129] *Id.* paras 228.

[130] *Id.* para. 245. The Appellate Body rejected the meaning "rational relationship" argued by the EC.

[131] *Id.* paras 256–257.

[132] *Id.* para. 263.

[133] TBT Agreement, Art. 2.5.

[134] *Id.* Art. 10.1.

[135] Report of the Appellate Body, paras 287–291.

[136] *Id.* para 292.

tion in question was ruled to be inconsistent with Article 2.4 of the Agreement, it is significant that the burden of proof of showing inconsistency falls largely on the complaining WTO member. This is true for both the TBT and SPS Agreements. This should make national regulations easier to uphold in the face of a WTO challenge.

## 4. The Cartagena Biosafety Protocol

New technologies bring new problems as well as benefits. New technologies also involve unknown dangers and fears. So it is with biotechnology and living modified organisms (LMOs).

Living modified organisms, also called genetically modified organisms (GMOs), are living organisms that contain novel combinations of genetic material as a result of the application of biotechnology. Thus far, the principle introduction of LMOs has been in agriculture. Dozens of agricultural biotechnology products are on the market and more are on the way.[137] Over 30 varieties of biotech crops have been approved for sale in the United States, and U.S. and Canadian farmers planted 81 million acres of bio-engineered seed in 1999. This acreage accounted for 47 percent of the U.S. soybean harvest and 37 percent of the U.S. corn crop.[138] Virtually every processed food sold in the United States today contains LMOs of some kind.[139]

Of course, the manipulation of genetic traits of agricultural plants is not new. Natural selection and breeding techniques have long been used to develop favourable plant varieties. What is new is that through genetic bioengineering desirable traits can now be directly implanted into organisms using genes derived from totally different varieties of living organisms.

So far, the purpose of most genetic alterations has been to enhance traits useful in the production or marketing of goods. Examples are tolerance of weed-killing herbicides, resistance to insects, improvement in taste, colour,

137 *See To Plant or Not to Plant*, ECONOMIST, 15 January 2000, at 30.

138 Biotechnology Industry Association, Washington, D.C.

139 *Sticky Labels*, ECONOMIST, 1 May 1999, at 75–76. In the United States, three governmental agencies regulate the introduction of genetically modified plants and foods: the U.S. Department of Agriculture has responsibility for protecting plants and U.S. agriculture under the Federal Plant Pest Act, 7 U.S.C. §§ 150aa190jj; the Food and Drug Administration regulates novel foods under the Federal Food, Drug and Cosmetic Act, 21 U.S.C. §§ 301–395; and the U.S. Environmental Protection Agency regulates genetic techniques to develop plants that produce their own pesticides under the Federal Insecticide, Fungicide and Rodenticide Act, 7 U.S.C. §§ 136–136y.

and lengthened shelf life. However, a new generation of LMOs could provide medical or nutritional benefits to consumers, such as foods with less saturated fat and more vitamin and nutritional value. LMOs could also benefit the environment by allowing greater production per acre, freeing rural lands for parks, natural areas, and green space, and reducing the need for environmentally destructive pesticides and chemical fertilizers. Thus, we may be at the dawn of an agricultural revolution that will benefit society.

Nevertheless, controversy over LMOs is increasing. Criticism began in Europe, where food safety was an important issue because of several unrelated incidents, such as mad cow disease (bovine spongiform encephalopathy) that resulted in an EU ban on imports of beef from Britain and the chicken dioxin problem in Belgium in 1999. Recently, unease over LMOs has spread to the United States and other countries.

Critics make several points: first, although there is no scientific evidence of any danger to consumers of genetically modified foods, some urge caution and demand that GM foods be labelled or marketed separately. Second, environmental groups argue that LMOs may pose a danger for the environment if LMO plants invade native ecosystems, cross-pollinate with native plants or prove toxic to native species of animals, birds or, butterflies. Again, there is little evidence of this apart from a study on monarch butterflies[140] and a flawed British study over the effects of GM potatoes on experimental animals.[141] Third, critics argue that widespread LMO technology in agriculture will benefit a few large multinational companies and allow them to establish a global cartel to the detriment of the world's consumers and farmers. An antitrust suit has already been filed on this ground in the United States.[142] In developing countries, critics argue that using GM seeds will disrupt traditional family farming practices and raise

[140] An entomological study indicated that monarch butterfly caterpillars could be killed by pollen from GM corn crops planted in the vicinity of the milkweed plants on which the caterpillars feed. This conclusion was debated at a Monarch Butterfly Research Symposium hosted by the U.S. Environmental Protection Agency in Chicago, on 2 November 1999. Peer reviewers minimized the problem, but research is continuing on possible "sub-lethal" effects on caterpillars. Current Developments, 22 INT'L ENVT. REPORTER (BNA) 822, 10 November 1999.

[141] A study carried out in the United Kingdom that concluded that GM potatoes have negative impacts on the health of rats was criticized by scientists as "half- baked" and "hopelessly confused" because of procedural flaws. The ECONOMIST, 16 October 1999, at 85.

[142] *See Bruce Pickett et al. v. Monsanto Co.*, Case No. 1: 99CVO3337 (Antitrust), U.S. District Court for the District of Columbia.

costs to farmers.[143] Thus, the issue of LMOs raises serious health, environmental, economic, and social issues, but the nature and extent of these problems are ill defined.[144]

International trade in LMOs is most importantly addressed outside the context of the WTO in the Cartagena Protocol on Biosafety of 29 January 2000.[145] This instrument, which governs that transboundary movement of most bio-engineered products, will come into force 90 days after the 50th ratification is received.[146]

The Biosafety Protocol divides LMOs into two groups for the purpose of international regulatory action. First, the transboundary movements of LMOs are subject to an "Advance Informed Agreement" (AIA) procedure, under which the transboundary movement may proceed only after advance written consent by the competent national authority of the putative importing state.[147] The AIA procedure involves several steps: (1) notification by the party of export[148]; (2) acknowledgement of receipt of notification by the party of import[149]; (3) a decision procedure[150]; and (4) possible review of decisions in light of new scientific information. Decisions regarding importation must be made using scientifically sound risk assessment procedures and recognized risk assessment techniques.[151] Importantly, however, lack of scientific certainty due to insufficient scientific evidence can be resolved in favour of banning importation.[152] Risk management techniques may also be used by the importing state.[153]

There are several exceptions to the AIA procedure: (1) LMOs contained in pharmaceuticals[154]; (1) transit LMOs[155]; (3) contained-used

[143] *See* Susan Boensch Meyer, *Genetically Modified Organisms*, 1998 Y.B. Colo. J. Int'l Envt. L. & Pol'y 102, 111 (1998).

[144] For perhaps the most comprehensive view to date of the issues and problems as well as recommendations for future research, see U.S. National Academy of Sciences, Genetically Modified Pest-Protected Plants: Science and Regulation (2000).

[145] Cartegena Protocol on Biosafety to the Convention on Biological Diversity, 29 January 2000, 39 I.L.M. 1027 (2000) [hereinafter Biosafety Protocol].

[146] *Id.* Art. 37.

[147] *Id.* Art. 10.

[148] *Id.* Art. 8.

[149] *Id.* Art. 9.

[150] *Id.* Art. 10.

[151] *Id.* Art. 15.

[152] *Id.* Art. 10.6

[153] *Id.* Art. 16.

[154] *Id.* Art. 5.

[155] *Id.* Art. 6.

LMOs[156]; and (4) LMOs "intended for direct use as food, feed or processing".[157] In addition, the Conference of the Parties may exempt other LMOs from the AIA procedure.[158]

LMOs intended for direct use as food, feed or for processing agricultural commodities are subject to a less rigorous regulatory scheme. This is appropriate because most such LMOs are also subject to the WTO's SPS Agreement. Food, feed, and process LMOs (FFP LMOs) are not subject to the AIA procedure, but a party may decide to ban or limit imports of FFP LMOs under its "domestic regulatory framework" as long as it is "consistent with the objective of the [Biosafety] Protocol".[159]

Obviously, this opens the door to import regulation, and Article 11.8 of the Biosafety Protocol explicitly adopts the precautionary principle for the regulation of FFP LMOs, allowing import regulation even in the face of "lack of scientific certainty due to insufficient scientific information".[160] This undoubtedly will result in future conflict with the SPS Agreement, which allows the precautionary principle only for preliminary regulatory decisions.[161]

The Biosafety Protocol also breaks new ground compared with the SPS Agreement in subjecting LMOs to international standards regarding transport, packaging, and labelling.[162] FFP LMOs, in particular, are subject to labelling and identification in three respects: (1) that they "may contain" LMOs; (2) that they are not intended for intentional introduction into the environment; and (3) that they specify a contact for further information.[163]

The Biosafety Protocol also envisages the development of a standard international labelling system. LMOs intended for introduction into the environment are subject to a different labelling regime that identifies them as LMOs, specifies their identity and relevant traits, requirements for safe handling, storage, transport and use, a contact point for further information, the name of the exporter, and a declaration of compliance with regulatory requirements.[164]

If the Biosafety Protocol enters into force, there are several points of potential conflict with the SPS Agreement. First, does Article 11.8 of the Biosafety Protocol extend the precautionary principle to protect human as well as animal and plant life and health? The wording of Article 11.8 is clumsy: "adverse effects of a living modified organism on the conservation and sustainable use of biological diversity in the party of import, taking into

156 Biosafety Protocol, Art.6. 157 *Id.* Art. 7.1–7.2. 158 *Id.* Art. 7.4.
159 *Id.* Art. 11. 160 *Id.* Art. 11.8. 161 See the discussion in section 3.2.1.
162 Biosafety Protocol, above note 125, Art. 18. 163 *Id.* Art. 18(b). 164 *Id.*

account risks to human health". This applies the precautionary principle to biological diversity, but it is less direct regarding human health concerns. Yet it would be extraordinary to interpret Article 11.8 as protecting only animal and plant life and health. Surely the phrase "taking into account" is intended to allow the precautionary principle to be applied to human health as well.

Second, what is the relationship between the two treaties? This relationship is addressed in the preamble to the Biosafety Protocol as follows:

> *Emphasizing* that this Protocol shall not be interpreted as implying a change in the rights and obligations of a Party under any existing international agreements.
> *Understanding* that the above recital is not intended to subordinate this Protocol to the other international agreements.[165]

These two recitals appear to cancel one another out to some degree. The matter may be resolved with reference to the Vienna Convention on the Law of Treaties.[166] Article 30 on the application of successive treaties relating to the same subject matter[167] would not seem to apply in light of the preamble, which intends both agreements to be regarded on the same level; neither is intended to be superior to the other. Thus, the applicable rule of interpretation would be Article 31.3 of the Vienna Convention. Article 31.3 provides that "[t]here shall be taken into account, together with the context, any subsequent agreement between the parties regarding the interpretation of the treaty or the application of its provisions".

The application of this rule of interpretation would appear to mean that the statement of the precautionary principle in Article 11.8 of the Biosafety Protocol is intended to supplement the risk assessment requirements of the SPS Agreement. This interpretation is the only one that gives maximum effect to both the Biosafety Protocol and the SPS Agreement so that neither cancels out the other. This interpretation, however, has a great impact: it creates a potential conflict with the Appellate Body's reasoning in the

---

[165] *Id.* 10th and 11th recitals in the preamble.

[166] U.N. Doc. A/Conf. 39/27 (1969), 23 May 1969, 8 I.L.M. 679 (entered into force 27 January 1980), available at http://www.un.org/law/ilc/texts/treatfra.htm [hereinafter Vienna Convention].

[167] Article 30 of the Vienna Convention reads in relevant part as follows: "2. When a treaty specifies that it is subject to, or that it is not to be considered incompatible with, an earlier or later treaty, the provisions of that other treaty will prevail. 3. When all parties to the earlier treaty are also parties to the later treaty but the earlier treaty is not terminated or suspended in operation under article 59, the earlier treaty applies only to the extent that its provisions are compatible with those of the later treaty". Vienna Convention, above note 146, Art. 30.2 and 30.3.

*Hormones* case. Specifically, import restrictions on GM foods would seem to be permitted in the face of insufficient scientific evidence as long as a risk assessment was carried out using available scientific evidence and areas of scientific uncertainty were identified and addressed.

Still another point of potential conflict between the Biosafety Protocol and the SPS Agreement will come to the fore when mandatory labelling for GM foods is developed. Labelling under the "may contain" standard was agreed in the Biosafety Protocol. However, mandatory labels as a food safety measure would be subject to the "scientific principles" and "sufficient scientific evidence" standards of the SPS Agreement.[168]

Who will decide these questions and other interpretative disputes over the two agreements? The Biosafety Protocol has no dispute settlement provision but refers to the dispute settlement mechanisms of the Convention on Biological Diversity.[169] Under the Convention on Biological Diversity, dispute settlement is largely optional.[170] Thus, disputes over these two regimes are likely to be resolved through the WTO dispute settlement mechanism.

---

[168] SPS Agreement Annex A, definition 1. *See* Sara Pardo Quintillán, *Free Trade, Public Health Protection and Consumer Information in the European and WTO Context: Hormone-Treated Beef and Genetically Modified Organisms*, 33 J. World Trade, No. 6, at 147, 171–72 and 190–91 (1999).

[169] Biosafety Protocol, above note 145, Art. 34; Convention on Biological Diversity, UNEP/Bio. Div./Conf./L.2, 31 I.L.M. 818 (1992).

[170] Convention on Biological Diversity, above note 169, Art. 27. Article 27 of the Convention on Biological Diversity reads as follows:

1. In the event of a dispute between Contracting Parties concerning the interpretation or application of this Convention, the parties concerned shall seek solution by negotiation.

2. If the parties concerned cannot reach settlement by negotiation, they may jointly seek the good offices of, or request mediation by, a third party.

3. When ratifying, accepting, approving or acceding to this Convention, or at any time thereafter, a State or regional economic integration organization may declare in writing to the Depositary that for a dispute not resolved in accordance with paragraph 1 or paragraph 2 above, it accepts one or both of the following means of dispute settlement as compulsory.

(a) arbitration in accordance with the procedure laid down in Part 1 of Annex II;

(b) submission of the dispute to the International Court of Justice.

4. If the parties to the dispute have not, in accordance with paragraph 3 above, accepted the same or any procedure, the dispute shall be submitted to conciliation in accordance with Part 2 of Annex II unless the parties otherwise agree.

5. The provisions of this Article shall apply with respect to any protocol except as otherwise provided in the protocol concerned.

## 5. Health and safety: a reprise and synthesis

The anti-globalist charge that the WTO rules invalidate national health and safety standards is manifestly untrue. National standards that are higher or different in content and scope from international standards can be maintained consistently with WTO norms. However, these norms have bite. National standards that significantly restrict trade must be developed, adopted, and operated according to WTO rules. National authorities that develop these standards must realize that they must, from the inception of their work, consciously plan courses of action that will lead to a favourable outcome if their work is challenged at the WTO. This requires new thinking on the part of governments and people who work for standard-setting agencies. Heretofore, national standards have been developed and set only with a view to solving *national* problems and serving *national* constituencies. These can no longer be the only considerations. WTO norms have real impact, and national governments and authorities must learn to satisfy *international* norms and *international* constituencies. In this respect, the WTO has accomplished a revolution.

An evaluation of the WTO rules on setting standards is in order. On the negative side, four main problems are evident. First, standards are governed by three different agreements, each with its own complexities, and the scope of application of each is less than clear. This is a source of confusion. Second, many of the important concepts and criteria used in the Agreements are ill defined. This includes fundamentally important matters such as risk assessment, risk management (a fundamental concept that is not even mentioned in the Agreements), scientific evidence, the burden of proof and the burden of coming forward with evidence. In the future, the WTO must do a better job of defining these concepts and their interrelationship. Third, the WTO agreements provide a basis for international review of national standards without setting a standard of review. Is it really intended that WTO dispute settlement panels review standards *de novo* without any deference to national authorities? This is how review has proceeded up to now. This is tolerable only because relatively few cases have been considered. But in the future, many more cases could arise. The WTO should consider adopting a deferential standard of review: the "arbitrary and capricious" and "substantial evidence" standards of U.S. administrative law come to mind as possibilities. Fourth, the precautionary principle should be given a greater role in the WTO criteria for standards, and that role should be more precisely defined. In *EC — Asbestos*, the Appellate Body stated that "necessary" in GATT Article XX(b) is a function of how vital or important are the interests being pursued,[171] which sounds very much like the precautionary principle. Yet, this principle remains undefined and controversial. Under *EC — Asbestos*, it seems to be applicable on a case-by-case basis.

On the positive side of the ledger, the main point is that the balance the WTO has struck in judging national standards seems to be fundamentally correct. All three Agreements achieve essentially the same balance, that is, a mandate of transparency and a trade-restricting Member must be prepared to produce objective evidence and demonstrate the reasonable relationship between the means chosen and legitimate national ends.

A final, all-important point must be made. In the three Agreements discussed, the WTO has achieved the basis for broad international review of the standards, including health and safety standards, of most of the nations of the world. This power is essentially dormant and unexercised at present. If, however, even a modicum of this authority is exercised, further fundamental changes in the regime will be necessary. First, because it is intolerable for the WTO always to act after the fact, new WTO rules will have to be formulated for the standard-setting process itself. The formulation of new rules will amount to nothing less than a body of international administrative law. Such a body of law, if it is developed, must include provision for significant public participation in standard setting as well as "judicial" review by the WTO.

[171] Appellate Body Report, *EC — Asbestos*, para. 172.

# 19

# TRADE AND INVESTMENT

## 1. Introduction to the trade and investment debate

International trade and investment go hand in hand.[1] Market access through trade can lead to foreign investment, which can, in turn, lead to additional trade. Global sourcing of components means that multinational companies may wish to establish operations in many different markets or countries. Investment can be for exporting as well as for selling in a domestic market. Businesses established with foreign investment can, in turn, import components in the course of their operations. In some cases, too, investment can substitute for trade as companies establish in a market to circumvent trade barriers. Investment can go hand in hand with trade in services as well, as one of the modes of delivering services is through a commercial presence in a foreign country.[2]

Despite the close linkage between trade and investment, there is no comprehensive multilateral agreement on investment. Investment liberalization has been carried out primarily through bilateral agreements, regional economic organizations, and in certain economic sectors. Bilaterally, trading partners commonly enter into so-called bilateral investment treaties (BITS), whereby agreement is reached on the conditions of foreign investment, the standards of compensation in case of expropriation, and investor remedies, which are often sought through investment-state arbitration.[3] At the regional level, the EC/EU integration process has emphasized complete liberalization of investment and free movement of capital as one of the fundamental economic "freedoms" agreed by Member States.[4]

The North American Free Trade Agreement (NAFTA) liberalizes investment and movement of capital between Mexico, the United States and

[1] *See, e.g.*, WTO, Working Group on the Relationship Between Trade and Investment, *The Relationship Between Trade and Foreign Direct Investment*, WT/WGTI/W/7, 18 September 1997.

[2] GATS Art. I:2(c). *See* Chapter 12.

[3] *See generally* The Valuation of Nationalized Property in International Law (Richard B. Lillich and Burns H. Weston eds., 1972); Richard B. Lillich, The Protection of Foreign Investment: Six Procedural Studies (1965); Rudolf E. Dolzer, Eigentum, Enteignung und Entschädigung im geltenden Völkerrecht (1985); Richard B. Lillich and Burns H. Weston, International Claims: Their Settlements by Lump-Sum Agreements (1975); Georges R. Delaume, *ICSID Arbitration and the Courts*, 77 Am. J. Int'l L. 784 (1983).

[4] George Berman, Roger J. Goebel, William J. Davey, and Eleanor M. Fox, European Union Law 451 (2002).

Canada.[5] As far as economic sectors are concerned, the leading example is the Energy Charter Treaty,[6] which liberalizes investment in the energy sector among the parties to the treaty.

In the 1990s, a serious effort was made to negotiate a comprehensive treaty on investment, known as the Multilateral Agreement on Investment (MAI). Negotiated by the OECD, the MAI was intended for transfer to the WTO, where it would have completed triumvirate global liberalization agreements covering goods, services, and investment. The MAI would have removed barriers to investment, provided protection against expropriation and measures diminishing its value, and instituted a dispute settlement system. Yet, the MAI negotiations failed in late 1998 and were abandoned. This defeat was due to an unprecedented coalition of anti-globalists who feared the impact of the MAI on society, including workers and the environment. Over 600 non-governmental organizations (NGOs) from 70 countries were reportedly involved in opposing the MAI.[7]

The debate involving the MAI focused on several issues. First, although investment creates jobs, foreign firms can, it is charged, exert too much influence on or dominate economic sectors, especially in developing countries, unless they are subject to some controls. Second, there are fears that investment liberalization can lead to economic crisis when, in times of trouble, foreign investors pull their money out. However, empirical research has shown that the withdrawal of foreign investment is a problem only with portfolio investment, bank deposits, and loans, not with foreign direct investment (FDI). For example, during both the Mexican peso devaluation of 1994–95 and the Asian economic crisis of 1997–98, FDI was largely stable; there was little capital flight in this sector.[8]

Third, investment liberalization is opposed because NGOs argue that multilateral companies will use FDI to exploit workers in low-wage countries with inadequate labour standards.[9] Similarly, NGOs charge that companies will invest in countries with low environmental standards and use their influence to attack efforts in these countries to improve environmental

[5] North American Free Trade Agreement, Ch. 11, 17 December 1992, 32 I.L.M 289 (1993).

[6] December 1994, 34 I.L.M. 360 (1995).

[7] Kenneth W. Dam, THE RULES OF THE GLOBAL GAME 175 (2001).

[8] Assaf Razin et al., *Social Benefits and Losses from FDI, in* REGIONAL AND GLOBAL CAPITAL FLOWS 310, 311 (Ito Takatosh and Anne O. Krueger eds., 2001).

[9] Michael J. Trebilcock and Robert Howse, THE REGULATION OF INTERNATIONAL TRADE 363 (2d ed. 1999).

standards.[10] As evidence, they cite the impact of NAFTA, Chapter 11, which has been used by companies to recover damages when new, higher environmental standards frustrate investment expectations.[11]

At the Ministerial Conference in November 2001, WTO Members agreed to undertake negotiations on trade and investment beginning in 2003.[12] However, the scope of these negotiations was not defined. The WTO must do a better job than the OECD did in addressing the societal issues implicit in investment. Although the MAI is over, the trade and investment debate remains.

## 2. The legal framework of trade-related investment measures in the GATT/WTO regime

### 2.1 Introduction to the TRIMs Agreement

The TRIMs Agreement applies to investment measures related to trade in *goods*.[13] The TRIMs Agreement prohibits Members from applying any such investment measure that is inconsistent with GATT Article III (national treatment) or Article XI (prohibition on quotas and other measures prohibiting or restricting the importation, exportation or sale for export of any product, except for duties, taxes and other charges).[14] An Illustrative List annexed to the TRIMs Agreement provides examples of measures that are inconsistent with Article III:4 or Article XI:1. This List cites the following as examples of host-country investment measures that either restrict imports or exports or require imports or exports: local content requirements, export performance requirements, trade balancing requirements, foreign exchange balancing restrictions, and restrictions on an enterprise's export or sale for export of products. Such measures are prohibited, but a transition period allows WTO Members to phase out WTO-inconsistent measures that were notified to the WTO under the TRIMs Agreement. A different transition

[10] *See Environmentalists' Letter on MAI*, 13 February 1997, reprinted in INSIDE U.S. TRADE, 21 February 1997 at 12–13.

[11] *E.g.*, *Metalclad Corp. v. United Mexican States*, 40 I.L.M. 36 (2001) (awarding damages when company's investment in a hazardous waste treatment facility approved by the federal government of Mexico was blocked by local Mexican authorities).

[12] WTO, Ministerial Conference, Fourth Session, Doha, 9–14 November 2001, *Ministerial Declaration*, WT/MIN(01)/DEC/1, 20 November 2001, para. 20.

[13] TRIMs Agreement Art. 1.

[14] *Id.* Art. 2.1.

period is stipulated for developed and developing countries. During the transition period, the TRIMs Agreement imposes a "standstill" obligation.

## 2.2 TRIMs against the background of the GATT

Article III:4 and Article XI:1 of the GATT are worded broadly enough to cover investment-related measures. Article III:4 of the GATT applies to "all laws, regulations and requirements affecting . . . internal sale, offering for sale, purchase, transportation, distribution or use". Article III:4 has been found to apply to investment-related measures that require the investor to use a certain amount of "domestic content" in manufacturing operations.[15] Article XI:1 applies to "prohibitions or restrictions" other than duties, taxes or other charges on the importation, exportation or sale for export of any product. By definition, any measure that conditions investment upon export performance operates as a restriction.

The TRIMs Agreement adds value to the GATT/WTO system by describing types of trade-related investment measures that are considered to be inconsistent with GATT Article III or XI. The Illustrative List is annexed to the TRIMs Agreement and "provides additional guidance as to the identification of certain measures considered to be inconsistent with Articles III:4 and XI:1 of the GATT 1994".[16] As the *Indonesia — Automobiles* panel observed: "An examination of whether the measures [in question] are covered by Item (1) of the Illustrative List . . . will not only indicate whether they are trade-related but also whether they are inconsistent with Article III:4 and thus in violation of Article 2.1 of the TRIMs Agreement".[17]

Another way in which the TRIMs Agreement adds value to the GATT/WTO system is by including a transition period during which WTO Members agreed to phase out WTO-inconsistent measures that were notified to the WTO under the TRIMs Agreement. Properly notified measures should not be found to be inconsistent with the GATT during the transition period. In this respect, the TRIMs Agreement is a "one-stop shop". Any other reading of the legal texts would lead to manifestly absurd results because the interpreter would have to conclude that a measure properly notified to the WTO and, therefore, permissible under the

[15] *See Canada — Administration of the Foreign Investment Review Act (FIRA)*, 7 February 1984, GATT B.I.S.D. (30th Supp.) at 140 adopted 7 February 1984.

[16] Panel Report, *India — Auto Sector*, para. 7.157.

[17] Panel Report, *Indonesia — Automobiles*, para. 14.83.

TRIMs Agreement during the transition period is, nevertheless, prohibited under the GATT.

## 2.3 The legal relationship between the GATT and the TRIMs Agreement

The issue of the legal relationship between the GATT and the TRIMs Agreement arises when a measure is challenged under both agreements. Several panels have dealt with measures challenged under both provisions of the GATT and Article 2.1 of the TRIMs Agreement.

In analysing the legal relationship between the GATT and the TRIMs Agreement, one issue is whether there is a "conflict" between the two agreements. The term "conflict" appears in the General Interpretive Note to Annex 1A of the WTO Agreement.[18] The General Interpretive Note provides that, when a conflict exists between a provision of the GATT and a provision of another agreement in Annex 1A, which includes the TRIMs Agreement, the provision of the other agreement "shall prevail to the extent of the conflict". In the event of a "conflict" between provisions of the GATT and the TRIMs Agreement, the provisions of the TRIMs Agreement would, therefore, prevail. The term "conflict" is not defined, but has been interpreted quite narrowly.[19] WTO jurisprudence suggests that a conflict will be found (1) where obligations under the GATT and obligations under another Annex 1A agreement are "*mutually exclusive* in the sense that a Member cannot comply with both obligations at the same time"; or (2) where a provision in one agreement prohibits what a provision in another agreement explicitly permits.[20] If a WTO panel were faced with the question of whether there is a conflict between the GATT and the TRIMs Agreement, it would probably have to conclude that there is no such conflict.

Panels have analysed whether measures should be examined under the TRIMs Agreement before being examined under the GATT, based on the principle that, where two agreements apply, the more specific agreement should be examined before the more general agreement.[21] The first panel to

[18] General Interpretive Note to Annex 1A, Multilateral Agreements on Trade in Goods, of the WTO Agreement, in WTO, THE LEGAL TEXTS: THE RESULTS OF THE URUGUAY ROUND OF MULTILATERAL TRADE NEGOTIATIONS 16 (1999) [hereinafter General Interpretive Note].

[19] *E.g.*, Panel Report, *Guatemala — Cement.*

[20] Panel Report, *EC — Bananas (ECU)*, para. 7.159 (emphasis added).

[21] In a different context, the Appellate Body, in *EC — Bananas*, suggested that a panel would normally be expected to examine the more specific agreement before the more general, where two

analyse the issue was the *Indonesia — Automobiles* panel. That panel "first examine[d] the claims under the TRIMs Agreement since the TRIMs Agreement is more specific than Article III:4 [of the GATT] as far as the claims under consideration are concerned".[22] The panel may have done so because the measures in question were local content requirements, which fall within one category of WTO-inconsistent TRIMs set out in the Illustrative List annexed to the TRIMs Agreement. Subsequently, in *Canada — Automotive Industry*, the panel recognized "that a claim should be examined first under the agreement which is the most specific with respect to that claim".[23] The panel concluded, however, that the TRIMs Agreement could not be "properly characterized as being more specific than Article III:4 in respect of the claims raised by the complainants in the present case".[24] The panel may have first analysed the measures in question under the GATT because the parties disagreed "not only on whether the measures at issue can be considered to be 'trade-related investment measures', but also on whether the Canadian value-added requirements and ratio requirements are explicitly covered by the Illustrative List annexed to the TRIMs Agreement".[25] Most recently, in *India — Auto Sector*, the panel stated that

> [a]s a general matter, even if there was some guiding principle to the effect that a specific covered Agreement might appropriately be examined before a general one where both may apply to the same measure, it might be difficult to characterize the TRIMs Agreement as necessarily more "specific" than the relevant GATT provisions.[26]

In *India — Auto Sector*, the panel analysed the measures in question under the GATT first, partly because India, the responding party, encouraged the panel to refrain from analysing the measures under the TRIMs Agreement.[27] The order of analysis should not affect the outcome but may have an impact on the potential for panels to apply the principle of judicial economy.[28]

---

agreements apply simultaneously. *See* Appellate Body Report, *EC — Bananas*, para. 204; *see also* Panel Report, *India — Auto Sector*, para. 7.152. The principle that a "special" law prevails over a general law on the matters specifically addressed in the special law (*lex specialis derogat lex generali*) is an accepted legal principle in many jurisdictions.

[22] Panel Report, *Indonesia — Automobiles*, para. 14.63.

[23] Panel Report, *Canada — Automotive Industry*, para. 10.63.

[24] *Id.*

[25] *See id.*

[26] *See* Panel Report, *India — Auto Sector*, para. 7.157.

[27] *See id.* para. 7.158.

[28] *See id.* para. 7.158–7.161.

Some panels have analysed measures under one agreement and determined that, based on the principle of judicial economy, it was not necessary to analyse them under the other agreement.[29] In *Indonesia — Automobiles*, after finding that the measures in question were inconsistent with Article 2.1 of the TRIMs Agreement, the panel determined that, based on the principle of judicial economy, it did not have to address the claims under Article III:4 of the GATT. The panel described the principle of judicial economy as one in which "a panel only has to address the claims that must be addressed to resolve a dispute or which may help a losing party in bringing its measures into conformity with the WTO Agreement".[30] In *India — Auto Sector*, the panel noted "that it is permitted to apply judicial economy in considering matters before it, so that 'a panel need only address those claims which must be addressed in order to resolve the matter in issue in the dispute' ".[31] After finding that the measures in question violated Articles III:4 and XI:1 of the GATT, the panel applied the principle of judicial economy and concluded that it was not necessary to analyse the measures under the TRIMs Agreement.[32]

Other panels have first analysed measures under the GATT and determined that it was not necessary to analyse them under the TRIMs Agreement because the TRIMs Agreement does not add to or subtract from the GATT obligations. In *EC — Bananas*, after finding that the measure in question was inconsistent with Article III:4 of the GATT, the panel determined that it was not necessary to examine whether the measure was inconsistent with Article 2.1 of the TRIMs Agreement because,

> with the exception of its transition provisions, the TRIMs Agreement essentially interprets and clarifies the provisions of Article III (and also Article XI) where trade-related investment measures are concerned. Thus the TRIMs Agreement does not add to or subtract from those GATT obligations, although it clarifies that Article III:4 may cover investment-related matters.[33]

The *EC — Bananas* panel may have analysed the measure under the GATT because it did not fall squarely within any category set out in the Illustrative List annexed to the TRIMs Agreement. Subsequently, in *Canada — Automotive Industry*, the panel found that the measures in question were

[29] While nothing in the WTO agreements bars a panel from exercising judicial economy, the wording of Article 17.12 of the DSU suggests that the Appellate Body may not do so.

[30] Panel Report, *Indonesia — Automobiles*, para. 14.93 (citing Appellate Body Report, *United States — Shirts and Blouses*, 17–20).

[31] Panel Report, *India — Auto Sector*, para. 7.152.

[32] *See id.* para. 7.324.

[33] Panel Report, *EC — Bananas (ECU)*, para. 7.185 (footnote omitted).

inconsistent with Article III:4 and determined that it was not necessary to determine whether the measures were inconsistent with Article 2.1 of the TRIMs Agreement because the reasoning of the *EC — Bananas* panel applied to the present case.[34]

After the transition period, WTO Members challenging a trade-related investment measure will most likely invoke both the GATT and the TRIMs Agreement. WTO jurisprudence suggests that panels finding a violation of one of the agreements will consider that action taken to remedy the inconsistencies under one agreement would necessarily remedy any inconsistencies under the other agreement.[35]

## 2.4 The legal relationship between the TRIMs Agreement and other WTO Annex 1A agreements

The issue of the legal relationship between the TRIMs Agreement and another agreement in Annex 1A of the WTO Agreement arose in a case involving a measure challenged under the TRIMs Agreement and the Agreement on Subsidies and Countervailing Measures (SCM Agreement).

In that case, *Indonesia — Automobiles*,[36] the panel concluded that measures challenged under both the TRIMs Agreement and the SCM Agreement must be reviewed under both agreements. The panel examined whether there is conflict between the two agreements. The panel stated that the General Interpretive Note does not apply to the relationship between the TRIMs Agreement and the SCM Agreement.[37] One can hardly disagree with this statement because the General Interpretive Note applies only when a provision of the GATT conflicts with a provision of another Annex 1A agreement. The panel noted that only in cases of "conflict" between the two agreements

[34] Panel Report, *Canada — Automotive Industry*, para. 10.91.

[35] *See id.*; Panel Report, *Indonesia — Automobiles*, para. 14.93; Panel Report, *EC — Bananas (ECU)*, para. 7.186.

[36] A cautious approach as to the potential impact of the *Indonesia — Automobile* panel's ruling is recommended for two reasons. First, the panel report was not appealed, so we do not know whether the Appellate Body would uphold the panel's reasoning. Second, the panel dealt only with the relationship between the TRIMs Agreement and SCM Agreement and stopped short of any general statements as to the relationship between any two "horizontal" agreements in Annex 1A of the WTO Agreements. This report is, however, the only report analysing the relationship between the TRIMs Agreement and another Annex 1A agreement, and for this reason, its conclusions merit review.

[37] *See* General Interpretive Note, above note 18; Panel Report, *Indonesia — Automobiles*, para. 14.49.

would it have to choose which agreement to apply. The panel even stated that "there is no general conflict between the SCM Agreement and the TRIMs Agreement".[38] The issue, however, is not whether there is a conflict between the two agreements, but whether a given measure can come under the scope of both. The panel's response was to review the measure under both agreements.

The *lex specialis* maxim[39] is not of much help in analysing the relationship between the SCM Agreement and the TRIMs Agreement. TRIMs can take the form of regulatory subsidies. Such TRIMs may or may not constitute "subsidies" under the SCM Agreement.

The principle of effective treaty interpretation can help to distinguish the coverage of the two agreements, when a measure is challenged under both. Every measure that is both a TRIM and a subsidy must be reviewed under the SCM Agreement rather than the TRIMs Agreement because the SCM Agreement reflects a more elaborate legal regime dealing with subsidies. This approach does not, however, relegate the TRIMs Agreement to a redundancy. Not all TRIMs could be considered subsidies as defined in the SCM Agreement. Although the TRIMs Agreement would not apply to most export performance schemes because they would qualify as subsidies, it would apply to local content requirements that do not represent a cost to the government, such as a requirement that the more local steel a firm uses to produce cars, the more TV advertising time it can buy at market prices.

## 2.5 Investment issues in the GATS

Although the GATS does not deal with investment, it covers foreign direct investment through its commercial presence mode of supply. Commercial presence occurs when a service supplier establishes commercial presence in the country in which it supplies the service.[40] The commercial presence mode of supply is, in fact, an agreement to open up markets to foreign investment. WTO Members opened up their markets in an asymmetric way reflecting their perceptions about how open (or, conversely, how closed) an economy should be to foreign investment. Moreover, they can always impose restrictions with respect to commercial presence. They can, for example, limit the number of economic operators.[41] They can take exceptions from the obligation to accord MFN treatment to foreign service

[38] Panel Report, *Indonesia — Automobiles*, para. 14.55.
[39] *See* above note 21.
[40] For an explanation of the commercial presence mode of supply, *see* Chapter 12 section 3.3.
[41] GATS Art. XVI.

suppliers or from the obligation to accord national treatment.[42] Hence, the commercial presence mode of supply is, for all practical purposes, a multilateral agreement on investment.

## 2.6 Investment issues in the TRIPS Agreement

The TRIPS Agreement contains no provisions on investment, but it helps to open up economies to foreign investment by protecting technology. The protection of technology is important because transfers of technology accompany "the great majority of foreign investment from multinational enterprises in home countries to their subsidiaries in host countries".[43] The protection of technology "removes another source of insecurity for foreign investors and promotes the transfer of technology between countries, in particular between developed and developing countries".[44]

# 3. The regulation of trade and investment

## 3.1 Analysing whether TRIMs are inconsistent with GATT Article III:4 under the TRIMs Agreement

The TRIMs Agreement prohibits WTO Members from applying TRIMs that are inconsistent with Article III of the GATT.[45] The Illustrative List annexed to the TRIMs Agreement sets out two categories of "TRIMs that are inconsistent with the obligation of national treatment provided for in [Article III:4 of the GATT]".[46] TRIMs that are inconsistent with Article III:4 include TRIMs that are:

> mandatory or enforceable under domestic law or under administrative rulings, or compliance with which is necessary to obtain an advantage, and which *require*:
>
> (a) the purchase or use by an enterprise of products of domestic origin or from any domestic source . . . or

[42] *See* GATS Art. II:2 and Art. XVII; *see also* Chapter 12.

[43] Riyaz Dattu, *A Journal from Havana to Paris: The Fifty-Year Quest for the Elusive Multilateral Agreement on Investment*, 24 Fordham Int'l L.J. 275, 294–95 (2000) (citation omitted); *see also* Eric M. Burt, *Developing Countries and the Framework for Negotiations on Foreign Direct Investment in the World Trade Organization*, 12 Am. U. Int'l L. Rev. 1015, 1039 (1997).

[44] Dattu, above note 43, at 294–95; *see also* Burt, above note 43, at 1039.

[45] *See* TRIMs Agreement Art. 2.1.

[46] *Id.* Annex, para. 1.

(b) that an enterprise's purchases or use of imported products be limited to an amount related to the volume or value of local products that it exports.[47]

In *Indonesia — Automobiles*,[48] the WTO panel ruled on the legality of an Indonesian "car programme" linking tax benefits for cars manufactured in Indonesia to domestic content requirements and linking customs duty benefits for imported components of cars manufactured in Indonesia to similar domestic content requirements. The panel found that these local content requirements were "investment measures" because they had a significant impact on investment in the automotive sector[49] and that they were "trade-related" because they affected trade.[50] The panel also found that compliance with the requirements for the purchase and use of products of domestic origin was necessary to obtain the tax and customs duty benefits and that such benefits were "advantages" within the meaning of the Illustrative List.[51] As a result, the panel ruled that the local content requirements violated the TRIMs Agreement.[52]

## 3.2 Analysing whether TRIMs are inconsistent with GATT Article XI:1 under the TRIMs Agreement

The TRIMs Agreement prohibits WTO Members from applying TRIMs that are inconsistent with Article XI of the GATT.[53] The Illustrative List annexed to the TRIMs Agreement sets out three categories of "TRIMs that are inconsistent with the obligation of general elimination of quantitative restrictions provided for in [Article XI:1 of the GATT]".[54] TRIMs that are inconsistent with Article XI:1 include TRIMs that are:

mandatory or enforceable under domestic law or under administrative rulings, or compliance with which is necessary to obtain an advantage, and which *restrict*:

(a) the importation by an enterprise of products used in or related to its local production, generally in an amount related to the volume or value of local production that it exports;
(b) the importation by an enterprise of products used in or related to its local production by restricting its access to foreign exchange to an amount related to the foreign exchange inflows attributable to the enterprise; or

(c) the exportation or sale for export by an enterprise of products . . . .[55]

[47] TRIMS Agreement (emphasis added).
[48] Panel Report, *Indonesia — Autos*.
[49] *Id.* para. 14.80.
[50] *Id.* para. 14.82.
[51] *Id.* paras 14.89–14.91.
[52] *Id.* para. 14.91.
[53] TRIMs Agreement Art. 2.1.
[54] *Id.* Annex, para. 2.
[55] *Id.* (emphasis added).

The *India — Auto Sector* case involved a TRIM requiring "trade balancing". Domestic auto manufacturers were allowed to import components and parts conditioned on a certain FOB (free on board) value of exports of cars and components over the same period. The panel addressed this measure in the following manner:

> [As of the date of the establishment of the trade balancing condition,] there would necessarily have been a practical threshold to the amount of exports that each manufacturer could expect to make, which in turn would determine the amount of imports that could be made. This amounts to an import restriction. The degree of effective restriction which would result from this condition may vary from signatory [of a memorandum of understanding with the Indian government] to signatory depending on its own projections, its output, or specific market conditions, but a manufacturer is in no instance free to import, without commercial constraint, as many kits and components as it wishes without regard to its export opportunities and obligations.
>
> The Panel therefore finds that the trade balancing condition[,] ... by limiting the amount of imports through linking them to an export commitment, acts as a restriction on importation, contrary to the terms of Article XI:1.[56]

After finding that the trade balancing requirements violate GATT Article XI:1, the *India — Auto Sector* panel invoked the principle of judicial economy and concluded that it was not necessary to analyse the measures under the TRIMs Agreement.[57]

## 3.3 Notification of existing WTO-inconsistent TRIMs

WTO Members have an obligation to notify all TRIMs that are not in conformity with the TRIMs Agreement to the Council for Trade in Goods within 90 days of the entry into force of the WTO Agreement or the date of their acceptance of the WTO Agreement.[58] Article 2.1 of the TRIMs Agreement and the Illustrative List of WTO-inconsistent TRIMs annexed to the TRIMs Agreement provide the guidance needed in this respect. It is up to WTO Members to first judge whether one of their TRIMs is WTO-inconsistent.

## 3.4 Transparency

WTO Members also have an obligation to "notify the Secretariat of the publications in which TRIMs can be found, including those applied by

[56] Panel Report, *India — Auto Sector*, paras 7.277–7.278. [57] *Id.* paras 7.323–7.324.
[58] TRIMs Agreement Art. 5.1.

regional and local governments and authorities within their territories".[59] The purpose of this obligation is to ensure transparency. This transparency obligation covers both WTO-consistent and WTO-inconsistent TRIMs. Consequently, if the obligation to notify WTO-inconsistent TRIMs is implemented in a meaningful way, the shortcomings stemming from this transparency obligation could be avoided.

The problem with this notification provision is that it depends on the good will of Members. WTO Members have no incentive to notify because notification does not amount to an exemption; the notification requirement is a mere transparency requirement. Moreover, failure to notify can be largely left unpunished because most WTO remedies are prospective.

## 3.5 The obligation to eliminate TRIMs within a transition period

The TRIMs Agreement provides for three different transition periods during which WTO Members, according to their level of development, must phase out WTO-inconsistent TRIMs that were notified to the Council on Trade in Goods.[60]

1. Developed country Members were required to eliminate such TRIMs by 1 January 1997.
2. Developing country Members were required to eliminate such TRIMs by 1 January 2000.
3. Least-developed country Members were required to eliminate such TRIMs by 1 January 2002.

When it comes to characterizing a country as developing, the WTO system is undisciplined. In principle, "self-election" is observed in the WTO, that is, a country claiming to be a developing country is accepted as such.[61] The self-election principle is an expression of the principle of sovereignty.

When it comes to characterizing a country as least developed, the situation is as follows: Although the TRIMs Agreement does not provide for any elaboration in this respect, the SCM Agreement includes a UN list containing the least-developed countries.[62] Although no such reference to the UN list is

[59] TRIMS Agreement Art. 6.2.

[60] *Id.* Art. 5.2.

[61] Interestingly, the WTO Trade Policy Review Mechanism does not exclude graduation from developing country status. There have been no reported cases of graduation as of the time of writing.

[62] SCM Agreement Annex VII.

included in the TRIMs Agreement, one would reasonably expect to view the same group of countries as least developed throughout the WTO system.

Some developing countries were unable to eliminate WTO-inconsistent measures within the transition period. The TRIMs Agreement permits the Council for Trade in Goods to extend the deadline for compliance for developing or least-developed countries that demonstrate particular difficulties in implementing the Agreement.[63]

## 3.6 The "standstill" obligation

During the transition period, a WTO Member may not modify the terms of any WTO-inconsistent TRIM notified to the WTO from those prevailing on the date of entry into force of the WTO Agreement.[64] This is a "standstill" provision prohibiting additional WTO-inconsistent TRIMs during the transition period.

Moreover, new TRIMs introduced within 180 days after the entry into force of the Agreement may not profit from the transition period.[65]

## 3.7 The review of the TRIMs Agreement

The Council for Trade in Goods was required to review the TRIMs Agreement by 1 January 2000.[66] It was to "consider whether the Agreement should be complemented with provisions on investment policy and competition policy".[67] As of the time of writing, this review has not taken place.

## 3.8 Institutional issues

A Committee on Trade-Related Investment Measures (TRIMs Committee) was established.[68] The main task of the TRIMs Committee is to monitor the operation and implementation of the TRIMs Agreement. The Committee reports annually to the Council for Trade in Goods.

A Working Group on the Relationship Between Trade and Investment was established in December 1996 at the Ministerial Conference in Singapore.[69]

[63] TRIMs Agreement Art. 5.3.
[64] *Id.* Art. 5.4.
[65] *Id.* Art. 5.5.
[66] *Id.* Art. 9.
[67] *Id.* Art. 9.
[68] *Id.* Art. 7.
[69] WTO, Ministerial Conference, Singapore, 9–13 December 1996, *Singapore Ministerial Declaration*, WT/MIN(96)/DEC, 18 December 1996, paras 20 and 21.

At the Ministerial Conference in Doha, the WTO General Council decided that the Working Group on the Relationship between Trade and Investment should continue its work on the topics identified in the Checklist of Issues Suggested for Study. These topics are: "the scope and definition of investment; transparency; non-discrimination; the modalities for pre-establishment commitments based on a GATS-type positive list approach; development provisions; exceptions and balance of payments safeguards; consultation and the settlement of disputes between members".[70] The Ministerial Conference recognized the need for a multilateral framework on investment and agreed to begin negotiations in 2003.[71]

## 4. The MAI: a short-lived story

In 1992, the OECD Investment Committee started the preparatory work of a very ambitious project, that is, drafting of a Multilateral Agreement on Investment.[72] The MAI was supposed to become the first truly global agreement on liberalization of investment. The negotiations formally began in September 1995, continued until April 1998 and extended into the fall of 1998.

The mandate for the negotiations was to achieve a multilateral framework for investment with high standards of investment liberalization and protection. Moreover, negotiators aimed at providing an effective dispute settlement system that would be accessible to non-OECD Members as well as OECD Members.

The 29 OECD Members as well as the Commission of the European Community participated in the negotiations. Eight non-OECD Members participated as observers: Argentina; Brazil; Chile; Estonia; Hong Kong, China; Latvia; Lithuania; and the Slovak Republic. Other non-OECD Members were informed on a regular basis about the status and substance of the negotiations.

[70] Doha Declaration, para. 22.

[71] *Id.* para. 21.

[72] Negotiating Text of 24 April 1998, available on the OECD web site (www.oecd.org). For a comprehensive presentation of the MAI, see Joachim Karl, *Das Multilaterale Investitionsabkommen (MAI)*, 44 Recht der internationalen Wirtschaft 432 (1998); Michael Daly, *Investment Incentives and the Multilateral Agreement on Investment*, 32 J. World Trade, No. 2, at 5 (1998); Andrew W. A. Berkeley, *The Multilateral Agreement on Investment: Progress?*, 1 Int'l Trade L.Q. 96 (1998).

The negotiators felt the time was ripe for a global framework for investment mainly because FDI grew 14 times between 1973 and 1996 (from $25 to $350 billion), largely faster than growth in international trade.[73]

Unlike the regime envisaged by most bilateral investment treaties, the MAI purported to cover the pre-establishment phase as well.[74] Hence, the MAI included provisions on privatization, behaviour of monopolies, and the temporary entry and stay of key personnel, such as investors, managers, and experts.

The MAI had three pillars: investment liberalization, investment protection, and dispute settlement. With respect to the first and the second pillars, the MAI advances the principle of non-discrimination. First, the MAI parties committed to treat foreign investors and their investments no less favourably than they treat their own (national treatment). Second, the MAI parties agreed not to distinguish between investors and investments of other MAI parties (most-favoured-nation treatment). With respect to the third pillar, the MAI contained provisions on cross-border transfer of funds, fair and equitable treatment, and the standard of compensation in case of expropriation.

The coverage of the MAI was quite broad: FDI, portfolio investment, and rights under contract formed part of its subject matter. Its negotiations, however, provoked a series of negative reactions. Early on, developing countries disputed its global character because they did not participate[75] in the negotiations. Some developed countries argued that the MAI must take into account environmental concerns or the so-called cultural exception.

The project was abandoned in late 1998.[76] At this stage, it is impossible to predict whether the work done will be used in future negotiations on the issue.

---

[73] OECD; Trebilcock and Howse, above note 9, at 357–58.

[74] *See* Giorgio Sacerdotti, *Bilateral Treaties and Multilateral Instruments on Investment Protection*, 269 RECEUIL DES COURS, TOME 255 (1997).

[75] *See, e.g.*, Corinne Vadcar, *Le projet d'Accord multilatéral sur l'investissement: Problématique de l'adhésion des pays du Sud*, 125 JOURNAL DU DROIT INTERNATIONAL 9 (1998).

[76] According to Jan Huner, Secretary to the Chair of the OECD committee that led the MAI negotiations, the reasons for the failure are political: the negotiators were not prepared to "sell" the whole project politically, when this is what they were called to do. *See* Jan Huner, TRADE, INVESTMENT AND THE ENVIRONMENT (1998).

# 20

# COMPETITION POLICY AND TRADE

# 1. WTO and competition policy

## 1.1 Introduction

Both competition policy and the WTO regime aim at establishing and maintaining a free market where the optimal allocation of economic resources is achieved through the price mechanism and competition among enterprises. Therefore, competition policy and the WTO share the same objective, namely, an economic system based on a market economy. Indeed, competition policy is an integral principle of the WTO regime, even though there is no WTO agreement on competition policy.

Competition policy is concerned with governmental barriers to competition and private anti-competitive conduct. Governmental barriers to competition and private restraints of competition are closely related. Governmental barriers to competition impose restrictions on the freedom of enterprises to compete. Private anti-competitive conduct restricts competition by abusive conduct of a monopolist or collusive behaviour of enterprises. Even if governmental barriers to competition have been removed or reduced, private anti-competitive conduct may offset the benefit of the liberalization of economy afforded by the removal or reduction of such barriers. Therefore, as the liberalization of trade progresses through trade negotiations sponsored by the GATT/WTO regime, it becomes increasingly important to take measures to control anti-competitive conduct of private enterprises that will counteract the results of liberalization. In light of this, the introduction of competition policy into the WTO regime is a necessity if the effectiveness of the regime is to be maintained. There are differences of views on if, when and how the introduction of competition policy into the WTO framework should be made. Eventually, however, the issue of how to incorporate an agreement on competition policy will become an important agenda item for the WTO.

## 1.2 Anti-competitive conduct that adversely affects international trade

### *1.2.1 International cartels, export cartels, and import cartels*

Enterprises of different nations may enter into an agreement to fix the prices of products, control the amount of production, or divide markets. Such an agreement is an international cartel. An international cartel affects international trade and offsets the benefit of trade liberalization achieved by the WTO. If the price of a product is fixed by an agreement entered into among enterprises of different nations and made uniform in the different national markets in which they operate, movement of that product across the boundaries of those nations is hindered. If national markets are divided among the enterprises of different nations, negative impacts on the flow of international commerce are obvious.

In the history of competition policy, there are a number of well-known cases, notably in the United States and more recently in the European Community, in which international cartels were the target of challenge. Examples include the *National Lead* case,[1] the *ICI* case,[2] the *Uranium Cartel* case,[3] the *Sugar Cartel* case,[4] and the *Wood Pulp* case.[5] U.S. antitrust law prohibits anti-competitive conduct not only in interstate commerce but also in foreign commerce including export and import. In the European Communities, international cartels are under Article 81 of the Treaty of Amsterdam if they impede competition among the Member States. Under the Japanese Antimonopoly Law, there are cases in which the Japanese Fair Trade Commission proceeded against international cartels in which Japanese and European enterprises divided markets among themselves.[6]

There are a number of cases in which import cartels were challenged either under the competition law of the importing country or the exporting country. In the *Soda Ash* case,[7] the Japanese Fair Trade Commission, upon a request from the U.S. government, proceeded against an import cartel arrangement whereby Japanese importers controlled the quantity of soda ash imported from the United States. In the *Tanner Crab* case,[8] the United States proceeded against an import cartel in Japan whereby Japanese importers of tanner crabs from the United States exchanged information regarding the price of tanner crabs. The United States regarded this arrangement as price fixing and, after negotiation between the importers and the U.S. government, the case was settled by consent decree.

International cartels, export cartels and import cartels are antithetical to the objective of the WTO, and any attempt of either a WTO Member or the WTO to control such activities is not only compatible with the basic purpose of the WTO, but also highly commendable.

[1] *United States v. National Lead Co.*, 63 F. Supp. 513 (S.D.N.Y. 1945).

[2] *United States v. Imperial Chemical Indus.*, 100 F. Supp. 504 (S.D.N.Y 1951).

[3] *In re Uranium Antitrust Litigation*, 480 F. Supp. 1138 (N.D. Ill. 1979).

[4] *Cooperatieve Vereinigung "Suiker Unie" UA and Others v. Commission* [1975] E.C.R. 1163.

[5] *Commission Decision of 19 December 1984*, 1985 O. J. (L 85); Joined Cases 89, 104, 114, 116–117 and 125–129/85, *A. Ahlström Osakeyhtiö v. Commission* [1988] E.C.R. 5193 [hereinafter *Wood Pulp* case].

[6] For those cases, see Mitsuo Matsushita, *Application of the Japanese Antimonopoly Law to International Transactions*, in New Directions in International Economic Law 559–69 (Marco C. E. J. Bronckers and Reinhard Quick eds., 2000).

[7] *In re Asahi Glass Co.*, Decision of the Fair Trade Commission of Japan, 31 March 1983, 29 Shinketsushū [Fair Trade Commission] 104.

[8] *United States v. C. Itoh & Co.*, 1982–83 Trade Cas. (CCH) para. 65,010 (W.D. Wash. 1982).

### *1.2.2 Boycotts, tie-in contracts, and vertical restraints*

A boycott is a collective refusal to deal where a number of enterprises agree that they will not deal with a party or parties. Boycotts may adversely impact access to international markets. If, for example, a group of manufacturers or a manufacturer with market power in a domestic market prevents its distributors and retailers from dealing in imported goods that compete with the goods supplied by the manufacturers, the adverse trade effect is clear. In the 1980s and the early 1990s, a huge trade imbalance between the United States and Japan was a serious trade issue between the countries. Both governments engaged in a trade negotiation called the Structural Impediments Initiative (SII). An important issue in this negotiation was anti-competitive conduct by Japanese companies that inhibited imports of U.S. products into Japan. Because of this negotiation, the Japanese government (the Fair Trade Commission) published Distribution Guidelines,[9] in which it described conduct that would be regarded as constituting unfair business practices and would, therefore, be prohibited. Among such conduct, boycotts were named as the most serious offence. This action shows that the Japanese government was keenly aware that boycotts of Japanese companies of foreign products had a great negative impact on access into the domestic market.

A tie-in contract is a contract whereby the supplier of one product (the tying product) conditions the sale of that product on the purchase of another product (the tied product). If, for example, the supplier of an operating system (the tying product) that is the basic software for computers imposes a condition on the purchaser or licensee that the latter must purchase or receive a licence for other software (for example, browser software and a tied product), this is a tie-in arrangement. A tie-in contract may exclude imports, because foreign suppliers are deprived of the opportunity to sell competing products. A tie-in contract is regarded as unlawful in many jurisdictions if the supplier has sufficient economic power with regard to the tying product.[10]

---

[9] The Fair Trade Commission of Japan publishes a translation of the Guidelines in English. *See* The Executive Office, Fair Trade Commission, The Anti-Monopoly Act Guidelines Concerning Distribution System and Business Practices (11 July 1991). For an analysis of the Guidelines, see Mitsuo Matsushita, *Japanese Anti-trust Law in the Context of Trade Issues, in* JAPANESE COMMERCIAL LAW IN AN ERA OF INTERNATIONALIZATION 15 (Hiroshi Oda ed., 1994).

[10] *E.g., Jefferson Parish Hospital District No. 2 v. Hyde,* 466 U.S. 2 (1984).

Vertical restraints restrict competition on different levels of trade. Examples include exclusive dealing arrangements, sole agency agreements, resale price maintenance, and vertical territorial allocation. Not all such restraints directly affect international trade, but some may adversely affect it. A typical exclusive dealing arrangement is a contract between (a) a manufacturer or supplier of a product; and (b) a dealer or distributor of the product, whereby the dealer or distributor is obligated to refrain from handling products of the manufacturer's competitors. If this contract is enforced by a powerful manufacturer or supplier in the domestic market, it will have a negative impact on the import of competing products.

Vertical restraints cannot automatically be presumed to have a negative impact on international trade. Some vertical restraints may have an anti-competitive effect and hinder foreign products from coming into the market. On the other hand, other vertical restraints may be neutral or even have a positive effect on trade, either in the short run or in the long run. For the above reasons, therefore, impacts of vertical restraints on international trade are more complex and need a case-by-case analysis.

### *1.2.3 Mergers and acquisitions*

Mergers and acquisitions are primarily a domestic competition law issue. In some cases, however, mergers and acquisitions affect international trade. An enterprise may acquire a foreign competitor to block the importation of competing products. If this happens there is an impact on international trade. For example, Gillette (a U.S. razor manufacturer) acquired stocks of Braun (a German razor manufacturer), a potential competitor of Gillette. The effect of this acquisition was to control exports of Braun to the U.S. market. The U.S. Justice Department proceeded against this acquisition and this was deemed to be a violation of Section 7 of the Clayton Act.[11]

Another case involved a merger between two Swiss pharmaceuticals manufacturers, Ciba and Geigy. These two companies had a large market share in the United States with regard to pharmaceutical products such as Valium. Both had subsidiaries in the United States, but due to the merger, those subsidiaries were to be controlled by one entity in Switzerland, Ciba/Geigy, and competition in the U.S. market would cease to exist. The U.S. Department of Justice proceeded against this merger and, a consent decree was entered whereby Ciba/Geigy and its U.S. subsidiaries agreed to estab-

[11] *United States v. Gillette Co.*, 406 F.Supp. 713, 1 Trade Reg. Rep. para. 4,345.19 (D. Mass. 1975).

lish another company, invest it with assets, technology, and other management resources, keep it for some time, and later sever the relationship with this company with the consent of the court. The idea was to create competition between the U.S. subsidiary of Ciba/Geigy and a newly created entity in the United States.[12]

In the *Brunswick* case,[13] a U.S. company, Brunswick, which manufactured and sold outboard engines for motor boats, entered into a joint venture with a Japanese company, Yamaha, that manufactured and sold the same product in order to prevent Yamaha from exporting outboard engines to the U.S. market. The Federal Trade Commission issued a cease-and-desist order that required the cancellation of this agreement. The purpose of this joint venture was to stifle import competition.

Thus, mergers and acquisitions may have a significant impact on international trade. On the other hand, many mergers and acquisitions have no trade effect and belong to the realm of domestic regulation. In addition, mergers and acquisitions may be an important corporate strategy and governmental policy for industrial reorganization. Therefore, the regulation of mergers and acquisitions is primarily the matter of domestic policy of national governments and municipal laws. However, in situations in which the trade impact of mergers and acquisitions is clear, international review may be warranted.

## 2. Provisions on competition policy in the WTO agreements

Although a comprehensive agreement on competition policy is yet to come into the WTO regime, there are several provisions in the existing WTO agreements that deal with competition matters. In this respect, competition policy is already an integral part of the WTO. These provisions have not been utilized much so far. If used effectively, however, they may serve as an important tool to enhance competition policy within the framework of the WTO. A brief review of such provisions follows.

---

[12] *United States v. CIBA Corp.*, 50 F.R.D. 507, 514, 1970 Trade Cas. (CCH) para. 73,319 (S.D.N.Y. 1970).

[13] *Brunswick Corp.*, 94 F.T.C. 1174 (1979), aff'd as modified sub.non; *Yamaha Motor Co. v. FTC.*, 657 F.2d 971 (8th Cir. 1981), *cert. denied*, 456 U.S. 915 (1982).

## 2.1 Agreement on technical barriers to trade (TBT Agreement)

The TBT Agreement provides that "Members shall not take measures which have the effect of, directly or indirectly, requiring or encouraging such bodies [non-governmental bodies assessing conformity of products to technical regulations and standards] to act in a manner inconsistent with the provisions of Articles 5 and 6".[14] Articles 5 and 6 of the TBT Agreement provide that, in the assessment of conformity by central government bodies, the principle of national treatment must be observed, technical regulations must not be more trade restrictive than necessary, and mutual recognition of technical regulations must be promoted. WTO Members may not, therefore, require or encourage private bodies that perform product tests or issue certificates that products meet technical regulations and standards to discriminate against foreign products vis-à-vis domestic products or impose undue restrictions on imported products.

Standard setting has been recognized as a competition policy matter when it is performed by private enterprises. Often private enterprises form trade associations that perform product tests and issue certificates confirming that products meet technical regulations and standards. Such trade associations may discriminate against non-members' products and imported products. Such discrimination may violate competition laws. In the United States, there are a series of cases in which standard setting and testing practices of trade associations were held to be violations of the Sherman Act.[15]

This has been an important competition and trade issue in the U.S.-Japan trade relationship. The United States argued that trade associations in Japan applied testing procedures in a manner that discriminated against foreign products and favoured domestic products. Because of the Structural Impediments Initiative, a trade negotiation between the two governments, the Fair Trade Commission revised the Guidelines on the Activities of Trade Associations. The Guidelines state that, although standard setting by private associations may perform an important public function, restrictive activities of private associations setting product standards violate provisions of the Anti-

[14] TBT Agreement Art. 8.1.

[15] *See National Macaroni Manufacturers Ass'n v. FTC*, 345 F.2d 421 (7th Cir. 1965); *United States v. Automobile Mfrs. Ass'n, Inc.*, 307 F.Supp. 617, 1969 Trade Cas. (CCH) para. 721,907 (C.D. Cal 1969); *United States v. Southern Pine Ass'n*, indictment returned Feb. 16, 1940, Cr. 19, 903, E.D. La., civil complaint filed Feb. 21, 1940, Civ. 275, E.D. La., consent decree entered

monopoly Law if they restrict access to conformity assessment procedures in a situation in which the utilization of such conformity assessment procedures is essential to carry on business.[16] The utilization of conformity assessment services should be open to any enterprise. In addition, the Guidelines state that, in situations in which private bodies are entrusted by the government to perform conformity assessment, their conduct will be subject to scrutiny under the Antimonopoly Law and, if they discriminate against certain enterprises, they are in violation of the relevant provisions of the Antimonopoly Law.

Thus, if a WTO Member encourages private conformity assessment bodies to discriminate against foreign enterprises, this constitutes a violation of the TBT Agreement (Article 8.1), and in many jurisdictions, a violation of their national competition laws.

## 2.2 Trade in services

Article VIII:1 of the General Agreement on Trade in Services (GATS) provides that each Member shall ensure that any monopoly supplier of a service in its territory does not, in the supply of the monopoly service in the relevant market, act in a manner inconsistent with that Member's obligations under Article II and specific commitments. Article II of the GATS provides for most-favoured nation treatment. Therefore, a Member must ensure that a monopoly enterprise operating in its territory accords persons from any Member treatment no less favourable than that which it accords to persons from any other Member. If, for example, a Member grants a monopoly to one enterprise in telecommunication in its territory, that

Feb. 21, 1940, 1940–43 Trade Cas. (CCH) para. 56,007; *United States v. Western Pine Ass's*, indictment returned Sept. 18, 1940, Cr. 14, 522, S.D. Cal., civil complaint filed Feb. 6, 1941, Civ. 1389–RJ, S.D/.Cal., consent decree entered Feb. 6, 1941, 1940–43 Trade Cas. (CCH) para. 56,107; *United States v. West Coast Lumbermen's Ass'n*, indictment returned Sept. 25, 1940, Cr. 14,532, S.D. Cal., civil complaint filed Apr. 16. 1941, 1940–43 Trade Cas. (CCH) para. 56,122; *United States v. National Retail Lumber Dealers Ass'n*, indictment returned Apr. 14, 1941, Cr. 9,337, D. Colo., civil complaint filed Jan. 3, 1942, Civ. 406, D. Colo., consent decree entered Jan. 3, 1942, 1940–43 Trade Cas. (CCH) para. 56,181; *United States v. National Lumber Mfrs. Ass'n*, civil complaint filed May 6, 1941, Civ. 11, 262, D.D.C., consent decree entered May 6, 1941, 1940–43 Trade Cas. (CCH) para. 56,123; *United States v. Retail Lumbermen's Ass'n*, civil complaint filed Oct. 24, 1941, Civ. 378, D/ Colo., consent decree entered Oct. 24, 1941, 1940–43 Trade Cas. (CCH) para. 56,166.

[16] Guidelines on Activities of Trade Associations, Art. 7.1 issued by the Fair Trade Commission of Japan (1995) (Jigyoshadantai no katsudonikansuru dokusenkinshihojono shishin).

Member must ensure that the enterprise accords equal treatment to all persons who wish to all utilize the service of that enterprise.

Article VIII:2 of the GATS provides that, where a Member's monopoly supplier competes, either directly or through an affiliated company, in the supply of a service outside the scope of its monopoly rights and which is subject to that Member's specific commitments, the Member shall ensure that such a supplier does not abuse its monopoly position to act in its territory in a manner inconsistent with such commitments. If, for example, a Member grants a monopoly to one enterprise in the area of railway transportation and has made a commitment in the area of trucking that it would accord the national treatment to enterprises of any other Member, it must ensure that that monopoly enterprise does not abuse its monopoly power by engaging in predatory pricing in the area of trucking.

Article VIII:3 provides for the consultation procedure to be used by Members when there is reason to believe that a monopoly supplier in a Member engages in conduct which is inconsistent with the above two provisions. Article VIII:4 provides for a notification procedure by which a Member must notify the Council of Trade in Services when it grants a monopoly to an enterprise in its territory which supplies services covered by its specific commitments.

Article VIII:5 of the GATS states that the provisions of this Article apply to cases of exclusive service suppliers, where a Member, formally or in effect, (a) authorizes or establishes a small number of service suppliers; and (b) substantially prevents competition among those suppliers in its territory.

Furthermore, Article IX:1 of the GATS, entitled "Business Practices", states that Members recognize that certain business practices other than those falling under Article VIII may restrain competition and thereby restrict trade in services. Article IX:2 provides for a consultation procedure whereby a Member is obligated to enter into consultation with other Members at the request of any other Member with the view to eliminating such practices.

In April 2002, the United States filed a complaint with the DSB against Mexico with regard to anticompetitive conduct in telecommunications. Generally the United States complains that Mexico authorizes its telecommunications entity called Telmex to charge an excessively high connection charge to foreign telecommunications companies desiring to make connections into Mexico from abroad. Among various claims, the United States argues that Mexico is in violation of provisions of the GATS for not effectively controlling abusive conduct on the part of Telmex vis-à-vis foreign telecommunications companies. At the time of writing, this case has just begun. This is the first case to challenge the regulatory system of a Member of the WTO with regard to abusive conduct of a dominant business entity in trade in services. The outcome of this case will be important.[17]

Conduct that is specifically prohibited under the GATS is also subject to control under the competition laws of Members. Article 82 of the Treaty of Amsterdam prohibits abuses of dominant positions of enterprises. An enterprise which enjoys a monopoly in a specific service area and engages in predatory pricing by using the monopoly profit earned in that monopolized area as a subsidy can come under Article 82 of the Treaty of Amsterdam and Section 2 of the Sherman Act in the United States.[18]

## 2.3 Intellectual property and trade-related investment measures

Article 40 of the TRIPS Agreement (Agreement on Trade-Related Aspects of Intellectual Properties) authorizes Members to enact legislation prohibiting restrictive conditions attached to licensing agreements regarding intellectual properties. Article 40 provides, by way of examples, exclusive grant back conditions, non-contestability clauses, and coercive package licensing. This list, of course, does not exhaust restrictive conditions that may be attached to licensing agreements and that may come under the prohibition of competition laws of Members. Competition laws of Members can cover other conditions such as excessive royalties, tie-in arrangements, and resale price maintenance. Although Article 40 is rather sketchy in specifying restrictive conditions that may be prohibited by the national legislation of Members, this provision is a link between the TRIPS Agreement, one of the WTO agreements, and competition policy and law.

Article 9 of the TRIMS Agreement (Agreement on Trade-Related Aspects of Investment Measures) provides that, within five years after entering into force, the Council for Trade in Goods shall conduct a review of the operation of this agreement and propose to the Ministerial Conference

[17] *See* U.S. Set To Move To Panel Over Alleged Mexico Telecom Violations, Inside U.S. Trade, 2002/04/19; U.S. Panel Request In Mexico Telecom Fight, Inside U.S. Trade, 2002/05/03.

[18] For U.S. cases, *see Inglis & Sons Baking, Inc. v. ITT Continental Baking Co.*, 668 F.2d 1014 (9th Cir. 1981); *Liggett Group v. Brown & Williamson Tobacco*, 744 F. Supp. 344 (M.D.N.C. 1990); *Liggett Group v. Brown & Williamson Tobacco*, 964 F.2d 335 (4th Cir. 1992); *Brooke Group, Ltd. v. Brown & Williamson Tobacco*, 509 U.S. 209, 113 S. Ct. 2578, 1993–1 Trade Cas. (CCH) para. 70,277 (1993). For EC cases, see Commission Decision of 14 December 1985 Relating to a Proceeding Under Art. 86 of the EEC Treaty, 1985 O.J. (L 374) 1 [hereinafter *ECS/AKZO*] (1985); Commission Decision of 24 July 1991 Relating to a Proceeding Under Art. 86 of the EEC Treaty, 1992 O.J. (L 72) 1 [hereinafter *Tetra Pak II*].

amendments to its text. It continues to provide that: "In the course of this review, the Council for Trade in Goods shall consider whether the Agreement should be complemented with provisions on investment policy and competition policy". Although nothing has happened in this regard since the inauguration of the WTO in 1995, the existence of this provision indicates that there was an awareness among the framers of the agreement that there is a close link between subject matters covered by the TRIMS Agreement and competition policy.

### 2.4 Safeguards and antidumping

As discussed in the chapter dealing with safeguards,[19] Article 11.1 of the Safeguards Agreement prohibits voluntary restraints of trade and orderly marketing agreements. Article 11.3 forbids Members to "encourage or support the adoption or maintenance by public and private enterprises of non-governmental measures equivalent to those referred to in paragraph 1". "Adoption or maintenance by public and private enterprises of non-governmental measures equivalent to those referred to in paragraph 1" refers to export, import, and international cartels entered into among enterprises and encouraged by governments (or sometimes coerced *de facto* by governments) whereby markets of different nations are divided, quantities of exports and imports are fixed, and export and import prices are rigged. Such cartels are prohibited by competition laws of many Members. This issue is dealt with in the chapter dealing with safeguards, and readers are advised to consult that chapter.

The relationship between antidumping and competition policy is discussed in the chapter that deals with dumping issues. Readers are, therefore, advised to consult that chapter.

## 3. Extraterritorial application of domestic competition laws

### 3.1 In general

At present, there is no worldwide competition code. The OECD has engaged in mutual assistance and cooperation among the Member States

[19] *See* Chapter 9 section 6.

regarding the enforcement of competition policy, and the role of the OECD is essentially to promote cooperation among the member states in competition law areas.[20] More recently, a Working Group was established at the WTO in which the relationship between trade and competition policy is being discussed. At present, it is not certain whether there will be any new agreement on competition policy within the framework of the WTO. The task of prohibiting and controlling anti-competitive conducts of enterprises that affect international trade is left to national competition laws.

A question arises as to how much the competition law of a state (which is national law) can exert control on business activities that cut across international boundaries. Transnational enterprises operate in a "twilight zone" of national jurisdictions, and it is difficult for a national authority to control activities that extend beyond the boundary of that state. For example, a transnational enterprise with many international connections may be able to transfer evidence easily to another country when an investigation is initiated in one jurisdiction. As mentioned earlier, a merger may occur in a foreign country that has the serious impact of eliminating competition within a national jurisdiction.

In response to the situations described above, the competition authorities in some nations have engaged in "extraterritorial application" of their national competition laws. Generally, an extraterritorial application of a national competition law means that the national law applies to conduct that occurs in a foreign country. The theory and rationale behind this application varies from jurisdiction to jurisdiction, *i.e.*, from "the effect doctrine" in the United States to "the implementation doctrine" in the European Community. However, what is common to any extraterritorial application of national competition laws is that conduct subject to the application of national law is wholly or partly performed in a foreign country.

With regard to the question of how to resolve conflicts of jurisdictions caused by extraterritorial application of national competition laws, there have been studies and proposals for almost 50 years, and there still is no final solution to this problem.[21] In the following pages, a brief survey will be

[20] Centre for Competition with Non-Members, OECD, OECD Global Forum on Trade, Trade Policy Issues: The Labour, Environmental and Competition Issues, CCNM/GF/TR/M (2001)3 (Summary by Rapporteur Jean-Pierre Cling 2001) reprinted at http://www.oecd.org (visited 25 April 2002).

[21] Numerous books and articles have been published on this subject matter. Probably the most comprehensive work on this subject is: Spencer W. Waller, 1 & 2 ANTITRUST AND AMERICAN BUSINESS ABROAD (3d ed. 1997).

made into extraterritorial application of national competition laws. Examples are taken from the United States, the European Community, Germany, and Japan. This does not suggest that national laws are applied extraterritorially only in those countries. Our purpose, however, is not to engage in a comprehensive study of extraterritorial application of domestic competition laws, but merely to highlight some important jurisdictional issues.

## 3.2 The United States

In the *Alcoa* case,[22] which was decided in 1945, Judge Learned Hand stated the jurisdictional doctrine that Section 1 of the Sherman Act could be applied to a conduct which occurred in a foreign country if that conduct produced a substantial "effect" in the United States, and if such effect was intended, and that this was a recognized principle of international law. In this doctrine, the application of domestic competition law is justified on the ground of the "effect" within the United States of a conduct that occurred abroad. Therefore, this jurisdictional doctrine is often referred to as "the effect doctrine".

Since the *Alcoa* decision, there are many examples in which U.S. national competition laws were applied to conduct in a foreign country. This has led to conflicts of laws and jurisdiction. This is touched on below.

In the 1970s and 1980s, U.S. courts somewhat modified the effect doctrine and established "the jurisdictional rule of reason" whereby courts dealing with cases of extraterritorial application of U.S. domestic competition law take into consideration a variety of factors: the proportion of the conduct which occurs domestically as opposed to that which occurs abroad; conflicts with foreign law and policy; effectiveness of enforcement measures, whether or not the conduct is unlawful in the country in which it occurs; the relative importance of the conduct to the U.S. market and to the foreign country in which it occurs; and related matters.

Under this doctrine, although the effect test is still the basic principle, U.S. courts may refrain from exercising extraterritorial jurisdiction if such application is unreasonable when the totality of factors enumerated above is taken into account.[23]

---

[22] *United States v. Aluminum Co. of America*, 148 F.2d 416 (2d Cir. 1945).

[23] *Timberlane Lumber Co. v. Bank of America*, 549 F.2d 597 (9th Cir. 1976); *Mannington Mills, Inc. v. Congoleum Corp.*, 595 F.2d 1287 (3d Cir. 1979).

In 1995, the U.S. Justice Department announced Antitrust Enforcement Guidelines for International Operations.[24] These guidelines set out Justice Department policy regarding conduct that occurs abroad but harms the domestic economy. One feature of these guidelines is the emphasis on access to foreign markets. In a number of hypothetical examples used to explain the policy of the Justice Department, it is stated that the Justice Department may assert jurisdiction over conduct abroad that impedes market access of U.S. enterprises. One such hypothetical example is a case in which enterprises in a foreign country engage in a boycott to block importation of U.S. products. In this way, it seems that these guidelines take into account "export interests" of U.S. enterprises.

Another aspect of extraterritorial application of U.S. domestic competition laws is the personal jurisdication issue. Although conduct of a foreign enterprise produces an "effect" in the United States, and such effect is intended, U.S. courts cannot initiate a proceeding unless the foreign enterprise, the prospective defendant, is present in the United States through its subsidiaries and agents. This aspect of jurisdiction is referred to as "personal jurisdiction", "enforcement jurisdiction", or "procedural jurisdiction". All are concerned with the application of legal process vis-à-vis a foreign enterprise located abroad.

This is an enormously complex issue, and we have no space to engage in detailed discussions of this subject matter. However, it is necessary to touch on the essentials. The key concept here is "minimum contacts".[25] If a foreign enterprise has a branch or a wholly-owned subsidiary and, through such domestic entities, carries out business in the country, generally the host state is justified in asserting personal jurisdiction over the foreign enterprise. If the contact of a foreign enterprise is less than the existence of a branch or wholly-owned subsidiary, it does not automatically exclude national courts from exercising jurisdiction over the foreign enterprise. However, there is need for evidence to show that the foreign enterprise has minimum contacts with the jurisdiction.

---

[24] United States Department of Justice and Federal Trade Commission, Antitrust Enforcement Guidelines for International Operations, 68 Antitrust & Trade Reg. Rep. (BNA) 462 (1995), available at 34 I.L.M. 1080 (1995). For a detailed analysis of the Guidelines, see Joseph P. Griffin, United States International Antitrust Enforcement: A Practical Guide to the Agencies' 1995 Guidelines, Number 53–2d, The Bureau of National Affairs, Inc., 1995.

[25] *International Shoe Co. v. Washington*, 326 U.S. 310 (1945); *Asahi Metal Indus. Co. v. Superior Court*, 480 U.S. 102 (1987); *Helicopteros Nacionales de Columbia, S.A. v. Hall*, 466 U.S. 408 (1984).

## 3.3 The European Community

In the European Community, case law has not developed as much as in the United States with regard to the jurisdictional doctrine. There are, however, instances in which the extraterritorial application of European Community competition law was a contested issue.[26] The best known case is the *Wood Pulp* case,[27] in which the claim was that U.S. enterprises exporting wood pulp to the European Community agreed to fix prices. The European Commission proceeded against this alleged cartel, and the case went to the European Court of Justice. The ECJ ruled that, even if the conduct occurred abroad, European Community competition law would be applicable if that conduct was "implemented" within the Community.

The meaning of the term "implement" is not quite clear. If, for example, a cartel fixing the export price sells the product in question at that price within the Community, the cartel agreement is implemented within the Community. A question arises as to whether there is jurisdiction in the following situation:

Suppose a group boycott whereby the participants agree not to purchase a product from European producers is carried out in a foreign country. Is this boycott agreement "implemented" within the European Community? The answer is probably no. Implementation in the domestic market seems to require some actions in the domestic market such as selling products. Conduct which merely affects the opportunity of European enterprises abroad does not seem to constitute "implementation" under European Community competition law.

Therefore, the doctrine of extraterritorial application of domestic competition law in the European Community seems to be somewhat more restrained as compared with the United States.

Nevertheless, in early 1970, the European Commission published an announcement that an export cartel entered into among foreign enterprises (Japanese enterprises) and designed to restrain competition among exporters would come under the prohibition of Article 85(1) of the Treaty of Rome.[28] Although the main focus of this announcement was that an export cartel agreement encouraged or suggested by the Japanese government would not be held immune from the application of European Community competi-

[26] Article 81 and Article 82 of the Treaty of Amsterdam and the Merger Regulation.

[27] *Wood Pulp* case, above note 5.

[28] The Franco-Japanese Ball Bearing Agreement [1974] O. J./L 343/ 19.

tion law, the premise was that an export cartel would come under the jurisdiction of European Community competition law even if it was formed in Japan if the intent was to restrain export from Japan to the European Community.

## 3.4 Germany

Article 98(2) of the German Law against Restraint of Competition states that provisions of that law apply to conduct that is initiated in a foreign country and brings about "effects" (Auswirkungen) in the territory of Germany. In theory at least, the extraterritorial reach of this law is even wider than under the *Alcoa* case in the United States; the former applies to any conduct that occurs abroad and produces effect within Germany, whereas, in the latter, "intent" to affect the territory of the United States as well as "effect" are required.

There are a number of cases in which the German Cartel Authority proceeded against conduct that occurred outside the territory of Germany.

In the *Philip Morris* case,[29] a U.S. company engaged in the production and sale of cigarettes, acquired control of a South African company engaged in the same business, and the South African company owned a subsidiary in the United Kingdom. The U.K. company, in turn, owned a subsidiary in Germany and the U.S. company owned a subsidiary in Germany. The result of this acquisition was that there would be no competition in Germany between the two subsidiaries because they would be controlled by the consolidated entity to be formed as the result of this acquisition. The Germany Cartel Authority proceeded against this acquisition, although it was made abroad, and held this to be a violation of German law.

In another case, German and Japanese textile producers entered into an agreement whereby the German participants would refrain from exporting to Japan, and the Japanese participants would refrain from exporting to Germany. The German Cartel Authority imposed administrative fines on the German participants, and the Fair Trade Commission of Japan proceeded against the Japanese participants and prohibited them from continuing the international cartel.[30]

[29] *Rothmann/Philip Morris*, 24 February 1982, WuW/E BkartA 1983.

[30] Decision of the Fair Trade Commission of Japan, 27 December 1972, 19 SHINKETSUSHŪ [Fair Trade Commission Reporter] 140. For the decision of the German Cartel Authority, *see* WuW/E Bkart A, 1393, 1411, 1413, 1415.

## 3.5 Japan

Although there is no explicit statutory authorization for an extraterritorial application of the Antimonopoly Law in Japan (the AML) such as Article 98(2) of the Law against Restraint of Competition in Germany, several recent developments indicate that the AML will be applied extraterritorially. In 1998, Articles 10 and 15 of the AML (as well as some other provisions) were amended which took effect on 1 January 1999. Article 10 prohibits acquisitions by a company of stocks or assets of another company if such acquisitions tend to restrain competition substantially in a particular field of trade. Article 15 prohibits mergers of companies under the same condition. Before the amendment, both Article 10 and Article 15 provided that an acquisition or a merger, as the case may be, would come under these Articles if a "domestic company" was acquired or a merger took place between "domestic companies". The amendment deleted the term "domestic" from both Articles.

The purpose of the amendment was to change the law to control mergers and acquisitions that take place abroad if they substantially restrain competition in a particular field of trade in Japan. An immediate target of this amendment may be as follows:

Japanese Company A and Japanese Company B are engaged in the production and sale of Product X and hold a large market share in Japan. Due to high costs in Japan, both of them established their subsidiaries or affiliated companies in Country Y, which produce Product X in Country Y and export them to Japan. The subsidiaries and affiliated companies of Company A and Company B in Country Y decide to merge under the law of Country Y. This eliminates competition between Company A and Company B through the activities of their subsidiaries and affiliated companies in Japan.

Together with an amendment of substantive provisions, the notice requirements of mergers and acquisitions were changed. Under the current rule, a merger and acquisition that occurs abroad is required to be notified if a party to the merger or acquisition owns assets in Japan amounting to ¥1 billion or more.

Before the amendment, this merger could not be challenged unless it was a clear evasion of domestic regulation on the part of Company A and Company B. Now that the new merger control is in effect, it can be proceeded against.

A merger or acquisition between two or more parties which are foreign companies and which takes place entirely abroad is, in theory, liable to challenge under the AML according to this amendment, as long as it brings about the situation that competition in a particular field of trade is substantially restrained. Therefore, a merger between Exxon and Mobil, both U.S. companies that hold a large market share in Japan, would now be subject to the control of the AML.

In 1990, the Fair Trade Commission published a report on the extraterritorial application of the AML that was the result of a task force commissioned by it to investigate this subject.[31] Although views expressed in this report are not officially those of the Commission, they are considered to represent the policy of the Commission. The report stated that conduct that occurred abroad would be subject to the application of the AML as long as it produced an anti-competitive result in Japan. For example, if a foreign export cartel fixing the export price in Japan sells the product at that price, the result is that competition in Japan is substantially restrained.

In 1998, the Fair Trade Commission proceeded against Nordion Company, a Canadian company that is a dominant enterprise in the production and sale of molibudenum 99 (a substance used for medical purposes) on the ground of a violation of Article 3 of the AML (the prohibition of private monopolization). The conduct accused of was that it required Japanese purchasers of this substance to cancel purchases from competing companies in Europe and thereby eliminated competition from the Japanese market. Because Nordion decided to accept the recommendation of the Fair Trade Commission to cease and desist from enforcing this requirement and cancel the restrictive agreement, the decision was handed down against this foreign respondent without administrative hearings.[32]

It is not clear whether this case can be characterized as an extraterritorial application of the AML. In this case, the party in violation is a foreign company and has no points of contact in Japan such as branch, subsidiary, or office. However, the contracts containing restrictive provisions were negotiated and signed in Japan, the unlawful contracts were put into effect in Japan, and the restraint of competition occurred in Japan. In this respect, it may be argued that the challenged conduct took place and was executed in

[31] Secretariat of the Fair Trade Commission of Japan, Antidumping and Competition Policy/ Extraterritorial Application of the Antimonopoly Law (Danpingu Kisei to Kyoso Seisaku/ Dokusen Kinshiho no Ikigai Tekiyo) (1990).

[32] On the Nordion case, see Matsushita, above note 6, at 564–565.

Japan. Nevertheless, this case illustrates that the Fair Trade Commission is increasingly interested in enforceing the law against violations that cut across national boundaries.

Given the state of globalizing economies today and the tremendous expansion of transnational business activities together with the increasing importance of competition law and policy among the major trading nations, the extraterritorial application of domestic competition laws, to a certain extent, is inevitable. However, the assertion of jurisdiction on the part of the enforcement agency and courts in one nation generates conflicts of jurisdiction with other nations. The ultimate solution of this issue should be found in international cooperation in the enforcement of competition law and policy among nations.

## 4. Conflict of jurisdictions

### 4.1 In general

Extraterritorial application of domestic competition law has created conflicts of jurisdictions and tensions among the nations concerned. This has been true with the application of U.S. antitrust laws. Although there is a possibility of such conflicts and tensions with regard to the application of competition laws of other jurisdictions such as the European Community, a serious case of conflicts so far has not been reported. In the following pages, a review will be made of a few of the cases where such conflicts and tensions arose.

### 4.2 The ICI case[33]

The *ICI* case, an early 1950s case, is a classical example of extraterritorial application of domestic competition laws and conflicts of jurisdictions that resulted. The facts of this case are enormously complex, but the essential facts are as follows.

DuPont (a U.S. manufacturer of chemical products, including nylon) and ICI (Imperial Chemical Industries, Ltd., a U.K. manufacturer of chemical products including nylon) owned patents covering the manufacture of nylon in the United States and the United Kingdom, respectively. Before World War II, they had engaged in a series of negotiations to divide

[33] *Imperial Chemical Indus.*, above note. 2, 100 F. Supp. at 504; *United States v. Imperial Chemical Indus.*, 105 F. Supp. 215 (S.D.N.Y. 1952).

markets between them. Generally, the division of markets was agreed so that the North American market was allocated to DuPont and the European market was assigned to ICI. To implement this basic agreement for the division of markets, both companies cross-licensed their patents in such a way that patents on nylon owned by ICI in the United States were licensed exclusively to DuPont and those owned by DuPont in the United Kingdom were licensed exclusively to ICI. In this way, DuPont could effectively exclude imports of nylon products from the United Kingdom to the United States, and ICI could prevent imports of nylon products from the United States to the United Kingdom.

The U.S. Justice Department regarded this as an illegal division of the market between DuPont and ICI and proceeded against them under Section 1 of the Sherman Act. After a long and elaborate examination of pieces of evidence, the District Court in the United States handed down a decision holding that this amounted to an agreement to divide the international market and was a violation of Section 1 of the Sherman Act.

The court order required DuPont not to block imports of patented products (nylon) from the United Kingdom by using the patents owned by DuPont and licensed to DuPont under the licence agreement, which the court regarded as part of the unlawful agreement to divide the market. Although ICI was a foreign company, it had a substantial point of contact in the United States in the form of the ownership of a subsidiary so the court in the United States had personal jurisdiction. The court ordered ICI to give "immunity" to imports of patented products (nylon) from the United States to the United Kingdom.

When the case was in progress, DuPont assigned its patents in the United Kingdom to ICI. This move was apparently made for the purpose of removing the patents in question from the reach of U.S. antitrust laws. Furthermore, ICI entered into contract with its U.K. subsidiary, British Spinners (BNS), to give it an exclusive licence to the patents in question. Again, the purpose of this licence apparently was to remove the patents as far away as possible from the reach of U.S. antitrust laws.

The U.S. court ordered ICI to reassign the patents back to DuPont. If ICI had reassigned the patents to DuPont in compliance with the order of the court, it would have been unable to give the exclusive patent licence to BNS. BNS initiated proceedings in a U.K. court against ICI, its parent, and sought an injunction to prohibit ICI from reassigning the patents to DuPont in compliance with the court order in the United States.

The English court handed down a decision,[34] in which it stated that the court order in the United States was an undue extraterritorial application of its domestic laws, the licence agreement in question was duly entered into between the two parties in England, and it would be wrong to recognize and enforce the order of the U.S. court.

This case gave rise to two types of conflicts between English and U.S. laws. First, the U.S. court ordered ICI to give "immunity" when nylon products covered by the patents in question were imported from the United States to England. However, under English patent law, if a product covered by a patent registered in England was imported (which would infringe the patent), and the owner of the patent did not take any action against this infringement, this patent was regarded as abused and the patent authority could give a licence to a third party. Therefore, this constituted a conflict between the U.S. court order and the patent law of England.

Second, the English court in the *ICI/BNA* case stated that the application of the U.S. court decree amounted to an extraterritorial application of domestic law and could not be given recognition in England. This was a conflict between U.S. antitrust laws and English contract law.

## 4.3 The Swiss Watch case[35]

The Swiss government had a policy of promoting the watch industry as one of its key industries and, for this purpose, enacted "The Watch Law" (Uhrengesetz), which authorized agreements among enterprises in the watch industry to engage in the control of production and sale of watches. U.S. companies joined the industry agreement in Switzerland through their subsidiaries in Switzerland. The industry agreement concluded among Swiss watch companies within the framework of this law included control of watch production in the United States and countries other than Switzerland.

The U.S. Justice Department initiated an antitrust lawsuit against U.S. and foreign watch companies, including Swiss watch companies. The Swiss government reacted to this lawsuit strongly and argued that the U.S. government's legal challenge to the industry agreements was an infringement of Swiss sovereignty.

[34] *British Nylon Spinners, Ltd. v. Imperial Chemical Indus.* [1953] 1 Ch. 19 (C.A. 1952).

[35] *United States v. Watchmakers of Switzerland Info. Center*, 1965 Trade Cas. (CCH) para. 71,352 (S.D.N.Y. 1965).

The U.S. Justice Department requested that a decree be entered which would order the defendants to cancel industry agreements controlling production of watches "anywhere outside Switzerland". Again, the government of Switzerland protested that the scope of the decree was too broad, and threatened that it would bring a petition to the International Court of Justice and challenge the jurisdiction of U.S. laws.

A compromise was made among the parties to the dispute to the effect that the scope of decree be limited to the territory of the United States, and an outright conflict was avoided.

This case represents a clash between U.S. competition policy and Swiss industrial policy as well as a clash of legal jurisdictions. Often a nation promotes its industries through industrial policies, and this may include private measures to control production and the sale of products. Often foreign enterprises join such agreements indirectly through subsidiaries and agencies.

Although the enforcement agency of competition law of a nation cannot directly challenge actions of the government of a foreign country, it can bring an action, under domestic competition law, against conduct of private enterprises which were authorized by law in the foreign country and even encouraged through governmental assistance, if anti-competitive effects occur within the territory of the nation. Possibilities for the resolution of jurisdictional conflicts are discussed below.

## 4.4 The Laker case[36]

In this case, Laker Airways Ltd. (Laker), a British airline, sold low-cost tickets for air travel between the United States and the United Kingdom. Major international airlines that formed the International Air Transport Association (IATA) (British Airways, British Caledonian, Lufthansa, Pan American, TWA, and others) responded to Laker's competition by conspiring to cause the bankruptcy of Laker.[37] Laker brought an antitrust suit against the IATA airlines in a U.S. court. The IATA airlines sued in an English court and asked the court to enjoin Laker from continuing the antitrust proceeding in the United States, and an interlocutory injunction was issued.

The IATA airlines took an appeal to the English Court of Appeal and, while this was in progress, the English government invoked a statute

[36] *British Airways v. Laker Airways*, [1983] 3 W.L.R. 592.

[37] *Id.*

(a blocking statute) prohibiting any person doing business in the United Kingdom from complying with requirements or prohibitions under U.S. antitrust laws and providing documents and information to foreign authorities without approval by a U.K. minister. The English court then handed down a decision restraining Laker from continuing the antitrust suit in the United States because the IATA airlines could not comply with a U.S. court decision under the English blocking statute. Laker appealed to the House of Lords.

The House of Lords granted the appeal, stating that English courts had no power to block the exercise of judicial power by U.S. courts as long as U.S. courts had jurisdiction.[38]

Laker brought an antitrust action against those IATA airlines which had not procured injunctive relief restraining Laker from continuing antitrust suits in the United States and sought a preliminary injunction which would prohibit the defendants from taking action in the United Kingdom for blocking the exercise by Laker of lawsuit in the United States. A U.S. court granted this request. In its decision, the U.S. court stated that English courts could issue an injunction to restrain private parties from carrying out proceedings in U.S. courts only under "the most extraordinary circumstances".[39]

Upon appeal by some of the IATA airlines, a court of appeals in the United States handed down a decision upholding the decision of the lower court.[40] The rationale of the decision contained, among other things, the following points: (a) U.S. courts were empowered to exercise jurisdiction over private parties as long as their activities affected the United States; (b) the proceeding in England was pursued for the only purpose of blocking the proceeding in the United States; and (c) the international comity would not be recognized if this was contrary to the public policy of the United States.

The controversy between Laker and the IATA airlines was resolved through settlement. Although the legal consequence in this case was an anticlimax, the series of decisions in the United Kingdom and the United States shows that legal battle between U.S. courts and English courts resulted in victory on the side of the U.S. courts.

---

[38] *British Airways v. Laker Airways* [1984] 3 W.L.R. 413.

[39] *Laker Airways Ltd. v. Pan American World Airways*, 559 F. Supp. 1124 (D.D.C. 1983).

[40] *Laker Airways Ltd. v. Sabena, Belgian World Airlines*, 731 F.2d 909 (D.C. Cir. 1984).

## 4.5 The GE/Honeywell case[41]

In this case the European Community prohibited a proposed merger between two American companies, GE (General Electric) and Honeywell, which was to take place in the United States. GE was a leading producer of jet engines for large commercial and regional aircraft. Honeywell was a leading supplier of non-avionics products as well as engines for corporate jets and engine starters, an important input in the manufacturing of engines. The United States antitrust agencies, the Department of Justice, and the Federal Trade Commission, approved this merger. However, the European Community considered that this merger would create or strengthen the dominant position of GE and would severely reduce competition in the aerospace industry and result ultimately in higher prices for customers.

GE and Honeywell notified their merger agreement to the European Commission on 5 February 2001, and the Commission initiated an investigation to see if, after the merger, GE would have a dominant position in the markets for jet engines for large commercial and large regional aircraft. There was a proposal on the part of GE/Honeywell to restructure the merger plan, but the Commission rejected this proposal. The Commission concluded that the strong market position of GE, combined with its financial strength and vertical integration, assured the dominance of GE in the relevant markets. For this reason, the Commission refused to approve the merger.

A high-ranking official of the U.S. Justice Department stated that this merger would have been pro-competitive and beneficial to consumers. He is reported to have said that this difference in attitude between the European Commission and the authorities in the United States "reflects a significant point of divergence".[42]

This recent case is an important example of extraterritorial application of the competition law of the European Communities and of policy conflict between the United States and the European Communities with regard to merger control.

---

[41] *Antitrust Division Chief Reacts to EU Decision to Prohibit GE/H Deal*, Antitrust & Trade Regulation Report, Vol. 81, No. 2015 (BNA 6 July 2001) at 15; Daily Report for Executives, No. 128 (BNA 5 July 2001).

[42] *Antitrust Division Chief Reacts to EU Decision to Prohibit GE/H Deal*, above note 41, at 15.

## 4.6 Summary

Efforts have been made in the past several decades to clarify and establish a set of principles that would govern extraterritorial application of competition laws.[43] However, to date, there are no firmly established principles of international law that would effectively resolve the issues arising from extraterritorial application of competition laws. Efforts will continue to establish jurisdictional principles. It is not certain, however, that any such attempt will produce a set of principles which would be accepted by the majority of nations and which would resolve such issues. It seems that the promotion of international cooperation in the field of competition law and policy will mitigate, if not eliminate, the severity of conflicts that may arise from the application of domestic competition law extraterritorially.

When one examines competition cases in which extraterritorial application was an issue, one can see that, in those cases, international trade was restrained either by international cartel arrangements, technology licensing arrangements or mergers and acquisitions. Competition authorities attempted to liberalize trade through unilateral applications of domestic competition laws. Although such attempts on the part of national competition authorities to exercise jurisdiction over transnational restrictive business practices created tensions and conflicts among trading nations, such attempts show that competition policy shares the same goals as the trade liberalization efforts of the WTO, *i.e.*, the elimination of barriers to trade. Trade barriers reduce trade among nations whether they are governmental barriers or private barriers.

At the same time, the above situation suggests that a unilateral extraterritorial application of competition laws is an imperfect and incomplete way of coping with international anti-competitive conduct that extends beyond national boundaries. A better way would be to construct an international programme for a cooperative scheme through which competition authorities of trading nations can rally their efforts to combat anti-competitive conducts which occur in international arenas. This suggests that the inclusion of competition policy in the WTO framework is an important agenda item for future WTO negotiations.

[43] *See, e.g.*, The Resolution of the International Law Association on Extraterritorial Application of Restrictive Trade Legislation adopted in the 55th Conference of the International Law Association held in New York in August 1972, reported in Report of the Fifty-fifth Conference (1974), 107–75.

# 5. Trade policy and competition policy

## 5.1 Trade policy and competition

Trade policies of nations are sometimes oriented to protecting their domestic industries from import competition. A trading nation may engage in restrictions of trade, such as the imposition of high tariffs and import quotas. In addition, as discussed in the chapter on antidumping, trade remedy laws such as antidumping may be "abused" so that the effect is to restrain competition in imported products. Such matters are of concern to competition policy because they may reduce market openness, which forms the basis upon which competition among enterprises occurs among the trading nations, and they are of immediate concern to the WTO, which deals with trade restrictions imposed by members. From a competition-policy viewpoint, one may criticize the enforcement of such trade remedy laws. This issue, however, should be dealt with in a broader context of how to construct a proper balance between trade policy and competition policy.

In the safeguards chapter, we reviewed VER cases in which tension and conflict between competition policy and trade policy was revealed, such as the Automobile VER case and the Steel VER case (the Consumers Union Case). Readers are advised to refer to the relevant parts of that chapter. In the following paragraphs, one more such case is reviewed, that is, the Semiconductor case.

## 5.2 The Semiconductor case[44]

The semiconductor case arose from a series of trade measures applied by the U.S. government to imports of Japanese semiconductor chips into the United States and the U.S. demand for market access to the Japanese market of semiconductor chips. The U.S. government initiated an antidumping investigation on imports of semiconductor chips from Japan. At the same time, the U.S. government requested that the Japanese government take measures to increase the market access of foreign-made semiconductor chips in the Japanese market.

---

[44] See generally Symposium — Prevention and Settlement of Economic Disputes Between Japan and the United States: Part II: Application of Framework to Specific Sectors and Issues: Lessons from the United States–Japan Semi-Conductor Dispute, 16 ARIZ. J. INT'L & COMP. L. 91 (1999); Charles S. Kaufman, The U.S.-Japan Semi-Conductor Agreement: Chipping Away at Free Trade, 12 U.C.L.A. PAC. BASIN L. J. 329 (1994).

In 1986 the U.S./Japanese Semiconductor Agreement was agreed between the two governments to resolve these issues. Within the framework of this agreement, Japanese semiconductor manufacturers/exporters entered into suspension agreements whereby they promised to the U.S. antidumping authority that their export prices of semiconductor chips would not be lower than fair value (the domestic price). With respect to market access, both governments informally agreed that the Japanese government would ensure that the market share of foreign-made semiconductor chips would be 20 percent or more. There was no official statement or any other evidence that such an agreement was entered into between the two governments. However, the U.S. government believed that there was such a promise on the part of the Japanese government.

To ensure that the suspension agreements entered into between Japanese manufacturers/exporters and the U.S. government regarding the export price of semiconductor chips would not be circumvented by Japanese exporters through exporting semiconductor chips to third countries at lower prices and then shipping them to the United States, the agreement contained a provision that the Japanese government monitor export prices of semiconductor chips shipped from Japan to third countries.

Subsequently the U.S. government invoked Section 301 of the Trade Act of 1974 and decided that the Japanese government had violated the pact by allowing export of semiconductor chips to third-country markets at lower prices and by not securing the 20 percent market share for foreign-made chips in the Japanese market.

Meanwhile, the European Community complained to the GATT that the requirement that the Japanese government monitor and control export prices to third country markets, which included the EC, was a violation of Article 11 of the GATT prohibiting export/import restrictions, and the GATT panel decided the case in favour of the European Community.[45]

In 1991, the Second U.S./Japanese Semiconductor Agreement was signed. With regard to dumping issues, the suspension agreements were maintained. In addition, a provision was incorporated into the agreement to the effect that foreign-made chips were expected to occupy a 20 percent market share in the Japanese market. It also said, however, that this 20 percent market share was not a promise or commitment on the part of the Japanese government, but was merely an "expectation".

---

[45] *Japan — Trade in Semi-Conductors*, 4 May 1988, GATT B.I.S.D. (35th Supp.) at 116 (1989).

Export control of chips to be exported from Japan to third countries was abolished and replaced by a provision which stated that, in case dumping of Japanese chips to a third country occurred, the United States would request that country to invoke its antidumping law and prevent dumped products from entering that country at dumped prices. This agreement was continued for five years and was replaced by a Third Semiconductor Agreement in which the restrictive features were largely eliminated.

## 5.3 Competition policy implications of the Semiconductor Agreement

Although the Semiconductor Agreement did not present a case of direct conflict between competition laws and trade remedies, this also reflects tension between those two sets of policy and law. The suspension agreement, which was part of the Semiconductor Agreement, required Japanese chip manufacturers not to lower the export price to the United States below the level of fair value (the domestic price in Japan). This necessitated Japanese chip manufacturers to issue instructions to their U.S. subsidiaries to maintain the price of chips in the United States at a certain level, and there was a potential conflict between this pricing policy and U.S. antitrust laws. Under U.S. antitrust laws, resale price maintenance is regarded as a *per se* offence. If Japanese manufacturers directed their U.S. subsidiaries and affiliated companies to maintain a certain level of price when they sold chips, this could be regarded as resale price maintenance.

Under U.S. antitrust laws, a transaction between a parent company and its subsidiary is regarded as an intra-corporate transaction and is given immunity if the latter is 100 percent owned by the parent.[46] The case law is not, however, clear regarding a transaction between a company and its subsidiary or a related company if the former merely owns the majority of the stock of the latter.[47] Moreover, if a company owns a minority of the stock of another company, a transaction between them would probably not be deemed an intra-corporate transaction, and the prohibition on resale price maintenance would presumably apply. Yet, under U.S. antidumping law, if a foreign exporter owns even a minority of the stock of an importer in the United States, these two companies are regarded as related companies, and the resale price of the importer is regarded as the export price of the commodity

[46] *Copperweld Corp. v. Independence Tube Corp.*, 467 U.S. 752 (1984).

[47] *See* Stephen F. Ross, Principles of Antitrust Law 179–82 (1993).

involved. Therefore, in order to avoid a dumping charge the exporter has to direct the importer not to lower that price below the domestic price of the commodity in the domestic market in the home country.

The Japanese government asked the U.S. Attorney General whether there was a possibility of an antitrust violation if Japanese exporters directed their U.S. subsidiaries to maintain their sales prices in the United States as indicated by the directive of the exporters when they sold the imported products. The U.S. Attorney General responded that he believed that any conduct which would be regarded as an implementation of antidumping legislation would be regarded as immune from antitrust liability.[48] However, there is no statutory authority or case law that endorses this position.

In addition, the Semiconductor Agreement had the same effect as an international cartel dividing international markets and fixing prices. Japanese exports of chips to the United States slowed. Competition thus decreased, and consumers paid high prices for chips. Meanwhile, outside parties to the Agreement, such as Korean manufacturers, grew to be important players in this field.

## 6. International cooperation in competition policy

### 6.1 Globalizing economy and the need for convergence[49] of competition law and policy

In an era when economies are open to globalization and business activities are more transnational, differences in national competition policy and law among major trading nations are an impediment to effective enforcement of competition laws and also to the predictability of law enforcement essential for the smooth operation of business activities. In addition, differences in competition law and policy often create disparity in the degree of accessibility to national markets of major trading nations. For example, if, in Country A, boycotts to exclude foreign products are prohibited under its competition

[48] *See* Letter from Charles F. Rule, Acting Assistant Attorney General, Antitrust Division, Department of Justice, to Makoto Kuroda, Vice-Minister for International Affairs, Japanese Ministry of International Trade and Industry, dated 30 July 1986, cited in U.S. Department of Justice and Federal Trade Commission, Antitrust Enforcement Guidelines for International Operations, April 1995, at 28 note 103.

[49] For an overview of convergence issues, *see* Mitsuo Matsushita, Basic Principles of the WTO and the Role of Competition Policy, The Journal of World Investment, Vol. 3, No. 4 (August 2002), pp. 567–584.

law, but they are allowed under competition law in Country B, enterprises in Country B are at an advantage over their counterparts in Country A. This is because, in Country B, enterprises can engage in exclusive activities vis-à-vis foreign competing products with impunity, while those in Country A are at a disadvantage since they cannot lawfully engage in such exclusive activities as against competing products coming from Country B. This creates a sense of unfairness and may lead to trade friction. Such situations call for a convergence of competition policy and law among trading nations.

An issue of this type was raised in *Japan — Film*, in which the United States argued that the Japanese government took measures to cause a private enterprise in the film industry in Japan to construct exclusive distribution networks and thereby exclude foreign film from the Japanese market. Although the panel ruled that the United States did not adduce sufficient evidence to sustain either a violation or a non-violation complaint, this case shows that restrictive business practices engaged in by private enterprises and supported by governmental policy can be an impediment to international trade and a subject matter of dispute settlement at the WTO if sufficient evidence is provided.

Since the time of the Havana Charter, issues of international competition policy have been discussed in various international fora, such as the GATT, the OECD, the UNCTAD, the EC and, more recently, the WTO, as well as in private circles. The framers of the ITO Charter (the Havana Charter) included Chapter V which dealt extensively with restrictive business activities such as price-fixing and division of markets. However, as the result of the failure of the ITO Charter, Section V was put into limbo and never revived.

More recently, attention has been focused again on the need for introducing some form of competition policy in the international trade order. This is because globalizing economies require that competition policy and law be enforced not only domestically but also internationally. In addition, there is a growing awareness that the international trading system requires competition policy not only at the national level but also at international level to guarantee the effectiveness of trade liberalization achieved through series of trade negotiations.

## 6.2 International cooperation in competition policy

### *6.2.1 Types of cooperation in competition policy*

There are different types of cooperative relationships with regard to the enforcement of competition policy and law among nations. One is a bilateral agreement between two nations; another is a regional agreement; the third is a plurilateral agreement; and the forth is a multilateral agreement. There may be others, but these seem to be the major types of agreement among nations concerning the cooperative relationship on competition laws.

There are a number of bilateral agreements for cooperation in the enforcement of competition laws. Examples include agreements between the United States and the European Union,[50] between the United States and Canada,[51] between the United States and Germany,[52] and between Australia and New Zealand.[53] A number of others are contemplated, including between the European Union and Japan.

Bilateral agreements on competition policy have several advantages. First, it is easier for two parties to reach an agreement than for many parties to agree on a plurilateral or multilateral agreement. Second, a bilateral agreement can address issues that are unique to the two parties concerned. Third, a proliferation of bilateral agreements may pave the way for a plurilateral or multilateral agreement in the future by accumulating experience in international cooperation in competition law matters and creating a spirit of cooperation among the officials of enforcement agencies.

On the regional level, the most highly developed system of competition law is, of course, the European Union, which has many characteristics of a state, including strong antitrust enforcement. In addition, many regional free trade arrangements, such as the North American Free Trade Agreement (NAFTA) address competition law and provide for regional cooperation on competition policy. Even the loose regional grouping known as APEC (Asian Pacific Economic Cooperation) includes a cooperative scheme concerning competition policy.

[50] Agreement Between the Government of the United States of America and the Commission of the European Communities concerning the Application of their Competition Laws, 23 Sept. 1991, 30 I.L.M. 1487 (1991).

[51] Memorandum of Understanding Between the Government of the United States of America and the Government of Canada as to Notification, Consultation, and Cooperation with Respect to the Application of National Antitrust Laws, 9 Mar. 1984, U.S.-Can., 23 I.L.M. 275.

[52] Agreement Between the Government of the United States of America and the Federal Republic of Germany Relating to Unilateral Cooperation on Restrictive Business Practices, 23 June 1976, U.S.-F.R.G., 27 U.S.T. 1956, T.I.A.S. No. 91.

[53] Australia-New Zealand Closer Economic Relations Trade Agreement and Exchange of Letters, 1983 Austl. T.S. No. 2.

In a plurilateral agreement the membership is not as comprehensive as a multilateral agreement in which all or the majority of nations with competition laws would be parties. The membership of a plurilateral agreement may be few or many. A plurilateral agreement could be formulated within the framework of the WTO Agreement, Annex 4. Members could therefore have the option of joining, but adherence would not be required. A plurilateral agreement in the area of international competition policy was proposed by the Munich Group (the Draft International Antitrust Code).[54]

A plurilateral agreement on competition may be more practical than a comprehensive multilateral agreement. For example, one can envisage a plurilateral agreement among major industrial nations or an agreement among the Quad (the United States, the EC, Canada, and Japan) plus Australia, New Zealand, Korea, Taiwan, and some Latin American nations. If properly tailored, a plurilateral agreement may be a useful instrument for a cooperative relationship among nations concerning international competition policy. For such an agreement to be successful, it is important that the number of nations which join the agreement is not too many, that there are sufficient common interests among the participants, and that the membership is voluntary.

A multilateral agreement on competition was originally proposed as Chapter V of the Havana Charter. Due to the abortion of the Havana Charter, Chapter V has never come into existence. It is not presently foreseeable that anything resembling Chapter V of the Havana Charter would be formulated and implemented. However, this may serve as an ultimate goal for framers of any agreement on international competition policy. There may be some time in the future at which globalization of economies has progressed so much that a multilateral agreement on international competition policy is not just a dream.

### 6.2.2 *Positive comity*

Positive comity has been incorporated into a number of bilateral agreements, including that between the United States and the EU. In positive comity, upon request, a party invokes its domestic competition law to prohibit anti-competitive practices that occur in its jurisdiction that adversely affect another party. This is a way to control anti-competitive international activities

[54] The text of the Draft International Antitrust Code (The DIAC) is found in: International Antitrust Code Working Group, Antitrust & Trade Regulation Report (BNA), No. 1628 at S-9-22 (Special Supplement, 19 August 1991)

without resorting to extraterritorial application of competition laws that may result in conflicts of laws and jurisdictions.

Although positive comity can play an important role, there is a limit to its usefulness. This approach is effective when the anti-competitive conduct that adversely affects the jurisdiction of the requesting nation also affects that of the requested nation. When the conduct complained of adversely affects only the jurisdiction of the requesting nation, but not that of the requested nation, the latter has little incentive to invoke its domestic law to control those activities. It may be that the conduct complained about is permitted in the jurisdiction of the requested nation. For example, an export cartel is exempt from the application of antitrust laws in the United States under the Webb–Pomerene Act[55] and the Export Trading Company Act[56] and, in Japan, under the Export and Import Transactions Law. Export cartels are allowed in other jurisdictions as well.

Suppose Japan requests the United States that a Webb–Pomerene association of wood pulp exporters be prosecuted in the United States because it fixes the price of wood pulp to be exported to Japanese paper mills and causes injury to Japanese interests. Will the United States authority prosecute it? The answer will be "no" because an export association is exempt from the application of U.S. antitrust laws. If the U.S. government asks the Japanese government to prosecute a Japanese export cartel organized under the Export and Import Transactions Law because it fixes the export prices of a commodity exported to the United States and thereby burdens the foreign commerce of the United States, the only legal answer seems to be that such a prosecution is not possible since it is exempted from the application of the Antimonopoly Law.

However, despite its limited effectiveness, positive comity is a useful concept. It is most effective when the competition laws of participating nations are harmonized. In addition, a positive comity approach may prompt parties to harmonize their competition laws.

### *6.2.3 Cooperation in investigation*

When an antitrust authority applies domestic competition law to conduct that occurs abroad, the key issue is how to obtain evidence of a suspected violation. In a number of cases in which the U.S. applied antitrust laws to conduct abroad, an extraterritorial investigation was conducted. This created conflict

[55] The Webb-Pomerene Act of 1918, 15 U.S.C.A. §§ 61–88.

[56] The Export Trading Company Act of 1982, 15 U.S.C.A. §§ 4011–4021.

with other nations, including the invocation of blocking statutes. In this respect, cooperation in investigation between the parties to an international agreement on competition policy is useful in avoiding such conflicts, and brings to bear the competition law of the parties vis-à-vis conduct that occurs in the jurisdiction of one of the parties that brings about harm to the other.

A number of bilateral agreements incorporate provisions for cooperation in investigation. Generally, such provisions state that a party to the agreement endeavours to provide evidence to the other when requested without making the provision of information obligatory. The question is whether providing evidence and information can be made obligatory, and whether such evidence and information may include confidential information. In many jurisdictions, provision of confidential information obtained through the investigation to any outside person, including a foreign government, is contrary to the confidentiality law of that state. Presently, therefore, a provision in an international agreement that provides that parties provide evidence and information on a voluntary basis and are not obligated to provide confidential evidence is the most that can be achieved.

Under the International Antitrust Enforcement Assistance Act,[57] the U.S. authority may investigate conduct that occurs in the U.S. that adversely affects another state and transfer the evidence obtained through such an investigation, including confidential evidence, to that state on the condition that that state agrees to reciprocate with regard to anti-competitive conduct that affects the U.S. This enhances the effectiveness of domestic competition laws against anti-competitive conduct that cuts across national boundaries. Although the possibility of this type of agreement is remote, this should be kept in mind as a future goal. It is noteworthy also that Article 26 of the Tax Treaty between the United States and Japan provides that the parties provide information and evidence, including confidential evidence, to each other. If this is possible in tax law, it may be possible in competition law.

### 6.2.4 *Convergence of competition policy and law*

No matter how closely states cooperate with each other in the enforcement of competition laws, there is a limit to the effectiveness of such cooperation if there is great divergence in the substance of competition laws of the states involved. Cooperation may be hampered if there is inconsistency between provisions of competition laws of different states. In light of this,

[57] The International Antitrust Enforcement Assistance Act of 1994, 15 U.S.C.A. § 46.

convergence of competition laws is, to a degree, necessary in order to effectuate the cooperative relationship among states in the enforcement of competition laws.

One should bear in mind that, in regulating trade and investment, each state has sovereignty in regulating its own domestic affairs. Although, with the advance of globalization, economic boundaries between nations are becoming blurred compared with the time when the "nation-states" were in their heyday, it still is true that each nation-state jealously safeguards its sovereign right to control business activities within its own territory.

This issue arises in discussions whether to introduce a competition policy agreement within the framework of the WTO. This is so because the WTO system is backed up by the dispute settlement procedures, which can subject a Member government in violation of a WTO agreement to economic retaliation at a request of a Member government. Excessive intervention on the part of the WTO in the domestic affairs of a Member will be met with strong resistance. In light of this state of affairs, any proposal for convergence of competition policy within the framework of the WTO should aim at reducing or eliminating harmful effects of anti-competitive conducts that adversely affect international trade without unduly encroaching upon purely domestic competition matters. Therefore, the primary objective of convergence of competition policy and law should be to establish and declare principles that are essential for the maintenance of a liberal trading order. The following items may be worth thinking about.

Looking around the world of competition policy and law, there seem to be two major systems of competition laws: that of the United States and that of the European Union (also representing the Member States). There are others that are a mixture of the two. For example, the Japanese enforcement system, which originally was based on the U.S. system, has deviated somewhat from the American model and has come closer to the European Union system. The U.S. system is characterized by heavy emphasis on criminal prosecution of cartels, litigation by the government and private parties in courts, and treble damage suits. The European system is characterized by an emphasis on administrative process, such as the imposition of administrative fines and orders restraining unlawful conduct.

The enforcement system of competition law of a national jurisdiction reflects the legal history and tradition of the nation in which it operates. Hasty transplantation of an enforcement system developed in one nation to another nation with a different legal system has little chances of success. Any attempt to harmonize the enforcement process should not be focused on enforcement system uniformity without regard for the national enforcement tradition. In this sense, a convergence of enforcement systems is even more difficult than that of substantive laws.

For the time being, an effort to harmonize the enforcement process should be concentrated on such matters as procedural due process of law and transparency of the process. An international agreement on competition policy would provide that parties guarantee that the due process principle will be observed whether it is an administrative process, civil process, or criminal process; that a well-founded complaint filed by a private party which suffers from a violation will not be rejected without a good reason; that there shall be no distortion and disregarding of evidence duly filed; and that proceedings will generally be open to the public.

In addition to the above, it may be useful to establish an international forum in which penalty issues are discussed among nations. The forms and magnitude of penalties, whether criminal, civil or administrative, reflect the national tradition of the jurisdiction concerned and are not easily amenable to change. However, reduction of the great disparity in the magnitude of penalties among different jurisdictions is essential to guarantee that enterprises operate under competition law systems that guarantee that there is no great difference in the deterrent effect of competition laws among different jurisdictions.

### *6.2.5 The ICPAC Report* [58]

In the United States, the International Competition Policy Advisory Committee (the ICPAC Committee) was set up in 1997 in order to study the relationship between trade and competition. This committee was appointed by the Attorney General of the United States and was commissioned to report to the Attorney General and the Assistant Attorney General. In 1999, the ICPAC Committee reported to the Attorney General and recommended proposals for international cooperation in competition policy matters. The recommendation covers a variety of issues including (1) multi-jurisdictional mergers; (2) strategies for facilitating substantive convergence and minimizing conflict; (3) rationalizing the merger review process through targeted reform; (4) international cartel enforcement; (5) interagency enforcement cooperation where trade and competition intersect; and (6) preparing for the future.

[58] U.S. Department of Justice, Antitrust Division: Final Report, International Competition Policy Advisory Committee to the Attorney General and Assistant Attorney General for Antitrust (2000), available at www.usdoj.gov/atr/ipac/finalreport.htm.

Chapter 5 (Where Trade and Competition Intersect) and Chapter 6 (Preparing for the Future) of the ICPAC Report are especially relevant to the discussion of this chapter. In Chapter 6, the Report recommends the position that the United States government should take in respect to international competition policy.

The Report is sceptical about a hasty introduction of a comprehensive agreement on competition policy into the WTO. This scepticism is based on the concern that the premature introduction of a comprehensive competition agreement may result in, among other things, (1) the possible distortion of competition standards through the *quid pro quo* nature of WTO negotiations; (2) the potential intrusion of WTO dispute settlement panels into domestic regulatory practices; and (3) the inappropriateness of obliging countries to adopt competition law. The Report takes the position that national authorities are best suited to address anti-competitive practices of private firms that are occurring in their territory.

The Report emphasizes the importance of positive comity through which a trading nation requests another trading nation that the latter take measures under its own domestic law to deal with anti-competitive conducts that occur in the latter's territory but affect adversely competition in the former's territory. It recognizes, however, that there is a limit to the effectiveness of positive comity. The Report does not rule out extraterritorial application of domestic competition laws to deal with anti-competitive conduct that occurs outside the territory but brings about adverse impacts inside the territory of a trading nation.

The Report recommends that there should be a "Global Competition Initiative" toward a greater convergence of competition law and analysis, common understandings, and common culture. To accomplish this purpose, the Global Competition Initiative should include the programmes to: (a) multilateralize and deepen positive comity; (b) agree on developing consensus principles in the practices for merger control laws; (c) consider the scope of governmental exemptions and immunities; (d) consider approaches to multinational merger control; (e) consider frontier subjects such as e-commerce and competition; (f) undertake collaborative analysis of such issues as global cartels; and (g) possible mediation of dispute and technical assistance. The Report emphasizes that a Global Competition Initiative does not require a new international bureaucracy or substantial funding. It can be accomplished by informal understandings among the trading nations after the model of the Group of Seven (G-7).

The Report advocates a "soft" convergence of competition policy and law among trading nations and states no formal organization or institution is necessary. In addition, there should be no mandatory requirement that trading nations must comply. Cooperation can be accomplished through exchanges of views and the experience of working together.

Based upon the recommendations and proposals of the ICPAC Report, the United States government initiated the "International Competition Network" (the ICN) in which about 60 trading nations join and work together in informal ways.[59]

## 7. The competition policy debates in the WTO

### 7.1 Activities of the working group on trade and competition policy in the WTO

WTO Members established a Working Group on the Interaction between Trade and Competition Policy at the WTO Ministerial Conference held in Singapore in December 1996. The Singapore Ministerial Declaration states that an agreement was reached to establish a working group to study issues raised by Members relating to the interaction between trade and competition policy, including anti-competitive practices, in order to identify any areas that may merit further consideration in the WTO framework. However, it adds that: "It is clearly understood that future negotiations, if any, regarding multilateral disciplines in these areas, will take place only after an explicit consensus decision is taken among WTO Members regarding such negotiations".[60]

The Working Group issued reports in 1997, 1998, 1999, 2000, and 2001.[61] In 1997 and 1998, the Group concentrated on issues listed in "Checklist of Issues Suggested for Study" developed at the first meeting of the Group. The work centred on the following items in the Checklist:

---

[59] *See* website of the ICN (http://www.internationalcompetitionnetwork.org).

[60] WTO, Ministerial Conference, Singapore, 9–13 December 1996, *Singapore Ministerial Declaration*, WT/MIN(96)/DEC, 18 December 1996, para. 20.

[61] WTO, Report (2000) of the Working Group on the Interaction between Trade and Competition Policy to the General Council, 30 November 2000, WT/WGTCP/4; WTO, Report (1999) of the Working Group on the Interaction between Trade and Competition Policy to the General Council, 11 October 1999, WT/WGTCP/3; WTO, Report (1998) of Working Group on Interaction between Trade and Competition Policy to the General Council,

- The relationship between the objectives, principles, concepts, scope, and instruments of trade and competition policy; and their relationship to development and economic growth.
- Stocktaking and analysis of existing instruments, standards and activities regarding trade and competition policy, including experience with their application.
- The interaction between trade and competition policy, including consideration of the following sub-elements:
    - The impact of anti-competitive practices of enterprises and associations on international trade;
    - The impact of state monopolies, exclusive rights and regulatory policies on competition and international trade;
    - The relationship between the trade the trade-related aspects of intellectual property rights and competition policy;
    - The relationship between investment and competition policy;
    - The impact of trade policy on competition.

In December 1998, a detailed report was published on the Group's discussions on the above items. In 1999, the Group concentrated on the following three additional topics:

- The relevance of the fundamental WTO principles of national treatment, transparency and most-favoured nation treatment to competition policy and vice versa;
- Approaches to promoting cooperation and communication among Members, including in the field of technical cooperation; and
- The contribution of competition policy to achieving the objectives of the WTO, including the protection of international trade.

In the discussions of the Group, there was a consensus that WTO principles and competition policy were closely related to each other and would complement each other. There was a general agreement that cooperation among Members in addressing anti-competitive practices needed to be enhanced. However, there was diversity of views as to the need for action at the level of the WTO to enhance the relevance of competition policy to the

8 December 1998, WT/WGTCP/2; WTO, Working Group on Interaction between Trade and Competition Policy — Report (1997) to the General Council, 28 November 1997, WT/WGTCP/1; Report (2002) of the Working Group on the Interactions between Trade and Competition Policy to the General Council, 8 October 2001, WT/WGTCP/5.

multilateral trading system. Some Members supported the development of a multilateral framework on competition policy in the WTO, the implementation of effective competition policies by Members and the reduction of the potential for conflicts in this area. However, some others questioned the desirability of such a framework and favoured bilateral and/or regional approaches to cooperation in this field.

The next step would have been to introduce an agenda regarding a multilateral framework on competition policy to the Seattle Ministerial Conference. However, due to the failure of the Seattle Ministerial Conference, this agenda was never submitted to the Ministerial Conference. In the WTO Ministerial Conference held in Doha in November 2001, Members decided to initiate a negotiation of competition policy within the framework of the WTO if a consensus is achieved on the modalities of negotiation. This is touched upon below.

The Group continued to work on issues of trade and competition policy and, in December 2000, it published a Report. The major areas covered in this report are largely the same as those in the 1998 and 1999 Reports. However, there are a few additions. The Report reflects deliberations of the members of the Group during the period of 1999 to 2000 on: (1) the relevance of fundamental WTO principles of national treatment, transparency, and most-favoured nation treatment to competition policy and vice versa; (2) approaches to promoting cooperation and communication among Members, including in the field of technical cooperation; (3) the contribution of competition policy to achieving the objectives of the WTO, including the promotion of international trade; and (4) other issues raised by Members relating to the Group's mandate to study the interaction between trade and competition policy. As in the 1998 and 1999 Reports, there was general agreement that the fundamental principles of the WTO (national treatment, transparency, and most-favoured-nation treatment) are relevant to the cause of competition policy, but the views of Members differed with regard to the ways in which the WTO should handle competition policy matters.

## 7.2 Review of the working group's reports

Numerous papers and so-called non-papers were submitted to the Group, and many oral presentations were made in the Group's discussions. In these papers and presentations, a tremendous number of issues were taken up and a great diversity of views were expressed on major issues. It is not possible to take up every issue discussed nor is it necessary to do so. In the following paragraphs, only a few of the issues dealt with in Group's discussions that seem to be relevant to the purpose of this chapter will be considered.

### *7.2.1 Consensus*

The similarity between the objective of the WTO (promotion of free trade) and that of competition policy is generally recognized. In fact, the whole scheme of the WTO is designed to establish the framework of free trade and guarantee the operation of the market mechanism in international trade. Competition policy is aimed at establishing and maintaining a free and open market. In this respect, the philosophical orientations underlying both are quite similar. It should probably be said that both are the same.

The basic principles of the WTO are: (a) most-favoured-nation treatment; (b) national treatment; and (c) transparency. The first two boil down to the principle of non-discrimination. Non-discrimination is certainly an essential element in competition policy and is a cornerstone for free and open markets.

There is also a consensus that anti-competitive practices engaged in by private enterprises in international trade are harmful to the international trading system. Special mention is often made of the harmfulness of international cartels which divide markets of different trading nations, import cartels which restrict imports, export cartels which restrict exports, unreasonable exclusive dealing arrangements which limit market access, and an abuse of dominant positions in which a dominant enterprise excludes competing products from markets.

### *7.2.2 Divergent views*

There are divergent views on specific issues. There are so many different views expressed in the reports that it is difficult to touch on every one of them. The following are but a few illustrations of the divergent views.

Views regarding the relationship between antidumping and competition policy are diverse and sometimes opposed to each other. Some argue that competition policy and antidumping are designed to control unfair practices. On the other hand, there are views that antidumping is much easier to invoke than provisions in competition laws on predatory pricing. Whereas, in predatory pricing, one needs to prove not only below-cost pricing but also the possibility that the wrongdoer is expected to recoup the loss that it incurs by below-cost selling through the exercise of a market power that results from the predatory pricing, there is no such requirement either in the

Antidumping Agreement or in domestic antidumping legislation. All that is required in antidumping is that there is a differential between export and domestic prices, that there is a material injury to a domestic industry, and that there is causation between the two. Some argue that it is a mistake to try to replace antidumping with competition policy since antidumping and competition policies are based on different objectives, have different constituencies, and are designed to serve different purposes.

Some suggest that, if trade barriers are substantially eliminated in international trade, there may be no need for antidumping legislation. They cite the example of the trade agreement between Australia and New Zealand[62] in which antidumping legislation was abolished with regard to the relationship between those two countries and was replaced by competition policy type legislation.

There are many views and arguments regarding bilateral, regional, and multilateral trade agreements regarding competition policy. Although there are views that bilateral and regional arrangements on competition policy serve useful purposes, there are others who argue that bilateral and regional arrangements do not have sufficient geographical coverage and could provide advantages only to the participants.

Developing countries argue that there are about 60 nations without competition laws. Important WTO members, such as Singapore and China, for example, have a competition policy but no competition law. In their view, the best competition policy is an open market and the pressure of foreign competition to correct any distortions caused by the anti-competitive activities of private enterprises domestically.

Some developing countries argue that they need flexibility in the employment of their industrial policies for their economic development, and the imposition of a competition agreement in the WTO of a straightjacket type would be counter-productive to their economic development. They emphasize that there are differences in the degree of economic developments and in competition culture among the Members of the WTO, and any sensible international competition policy should consider them.

Although there is no consensus (or convergence) of views as to whether there should be an international agreement on competition policy within the framework of the WTO, there are some striking features in many views expressed on this subject matter. The view that there should be a comprehensive international agreement on competition policy and law that is

[62] Treaty between Australia-New Zealand, above note 49.

binding on Members of the WTO is, at the best, a minority opinion. Most Members express the view that any comprehensive agreement on competition policy which binds all Members of the WTO is still premature.

This point is expressed in the 2000 report: "a number of delegations remained of the view that there was no need for any global rules on competition policy and/or that the call for a multilateral agreement might be too ambitious at the moment. It is difficult to consider multilateral rules in this area since, in the case of many developing countries, such rules could require revisiting and possibly re-designing laws which have only recently been adopted by legislatures".[63]

It seems, therefore, that the main current of thoughts expressed in discussions of the Group is directed toward establishing a non-binding and "soft law"-type agreement. This multilateral scheme of competition policy would include programmes such as technical assistance, notification of actions in competition law which would have some international implications, exchange of non-confidential information, and mutual cooperation in the enforcement of competition laws, including positive comity.

## 7.3 The Ministerial Declaration on Competition Policy adopted at the Doha Ministerial Conference in November 2001

The Ministerial Conference held in Doha, Qatar in November 2001 adopted the Ministerial Declaration in which WTO Members agreed to initiate trade negotiations with the view to establishing new rules and clarifying existing rules. Three paragraphs of the Declaration are devoted to competition policy. The title of these paragraphs is "Interaction between Trade and Competition Policy", and it consists of Paragraphs 23, 24, and 25:

> 23. Recognizing the case for a multilateral framework to enhance the contribution of competition policy to international trade and development, and the need for enhanced technical assistance and capacity-building in this area as referred to in paragraph 24, we agree that negotiations will take place after the Fifth Session of the Ministerial Conference on the basis of a decision to be taken, by explicit consensus, at that Session on modalities of negotiations.
> 24. We recognize the needs of developing and least-developed countries for enhanced support for technical assistance and capacity building in this area, including policy analysis and development so that they may better evaluate the implications of closer multilateral cooperation for their development policies and objectives, and

[63] WTO Report para. 88.

human and institutional development. To this end, we shall work in cooperation with other relevant intergovernmental organizations, including UNCTAD, and through appropriate regional and bilateral channels, to provide strengthened and adequately resourced assistance to respond to these needs.
25. In the period until the Fifth Session, further work in the Working Group on the Interaction between Trade and Competition Policy will focus on the clarification of: core principles, including transparency, non-discrimination and procedural fairness; and provisions on hardcore cartels; modalities for voluntary cooperation; and support for progressive reinforcement of competition institutions in developing countries through capacity building. Full account shall be taken of the needs of developing and least-developed country participants and appropriate flexibility provided to address them.

Paragraph 23 states that "we agree that negotiations will take place after the Fifth Session of the Ministerial Conference on the basis of a decision to be taken, by explicit consensus, at that Session on modalities of negotiations". The initiation of negotiation on competition policy depends upon an explicit consensus regarding modalities of negotiations. The meaning of "modalities" is not clearly spelled out, and there is ambiguity with regard to the exact meaning of this term. If "modalities" is defined broadly to include some substantive issues such as the mode of agreement (whether an agreement on competition should be binding and mandatory and what types of anti-competitive conduct should be made the subject matter of the agreement), difficulty in reaching consensus should be expected. In light of this, it is not certain at this time whether there will be future negotiations on competition policy in the Doha Development Round.

Paragraph 24 stresses the important of capacity-building in competition policy matters for developing and least-developed countries. Capacity-building for developing and least-developed countries is the thread which runs through the Doha Ministerial Declaration, and programmes for capacity-building will be made and carried out in many WTO matters including competition policy. Therefore, it is likely that some form of agreement will be reached for the promotion of technical assistance and capacity building for developing and least-developed countries in competition policy.

Paragraph 25 declares that, in the meantime, the Working Group on the Interaction between Trade and Competition will be engaged in the study of core issues, including transparency, non-discrimination and procedural fairness, provisions on hardcore cartels, modalities for voluntary cooperation, and support for progressive reinforcement of competition institutions in developing countries through capacity-building. Transparency, non-discrimination and procedural fairness, modalities for voluntary cooperation, and support for progressive reinforcement of competition institutions in developing countries through capacity-building are likely items for the adoption if an agreement on competition policy is included in the WTO. There will be divergent views regarding what are "hardcore cartels" and whether or not they should be limited to international cartels, export and import cartels which affect international trade directly, or should also include domestic cartels.

## 8. Conclusions

It seems clear that the introduction into the WTO of a comprehensive agreement on competition policy as envisaged by the Chapter V of the Havana Charter or even a plurilateral agreement as proposed by the Munich Group is premature. In this state of affairs, the following options are advanced for consideration.

### 8.1 Option 1: A declaration that competition policy is an integral part of the WTO regime

This option is merely to suggest that the WTO declare, in the form of Ministerial declaration, that competition policy is an integral part of the WTO regime. It would state that, through the eight rounds of trade negotiations conducted under the auspices of the GATT, governmental trade barriers have been reduced, that there are still considerable governmental trade barriers, that, in due course, such barriers will be further reduced and, as governmental barriers are reduced, private barriers are recognized as becoming more and more serious impediments to trade.

It would further state that, under these circumstances, it is important for the WTO to establish principles of competition policy within the framework of the WTO in order to deal with both governmental and private trade barriers.

### 8.2 Option 2: A plurilateral agreement

This option would be a plurilateral agreement on competition policy within the framework of the WTO. There should be a two-stage implementation of this option. The first stage would be the implementation of rules that prohibit private anti-competitive conduct that directly injures the objectives of the WTO, such as international cartels, import cartels, and export cartels. In the second stage, the WTO would consider the negotiation of an international agreement on competition policy that would cover a wider area including vertical restraints and mergers and acquisitions.

Such a plurilateral agreement on competition policy might be called the Plurilateral Agreement on Competition and Trade (PACT). PACT would contain rules regarding transparency, objectivity, and due process of law, as well as the principles of most-favoured-nation and national treatment in the application and enforcement of competition laws of Members.

In its initial stage, PACT should incorporate rules that deal with matters directly affecting trade between Members of the WTO, such as international cartels. Such rules should state that public and private measures that restrict trade among Members are contrary to the purpose of the WTO and can undermine the benefits of liberal trade achieved through trade negotiations.

The WTO might also consider introducing rules of competition regarding mergers and acquisitions, the regulation of which primarily belongs to the realm of domestic policy. In this event, the WTO should take into account whether rules of competition policy on such matters will enhance the objectives of the WTO and promote the effectiveness of the WTO system.

The WTO should formulate additional rules regarding the implementation of Article 40 of the TRIPS Agreement in order to give more guidance to Members seeking to introduce legislation on restrictive business practices involved in the licensing of technology. The WTO should clarify the requirements contained in provisions of WTO agreements which relate to competition policy, such as Article 8 of the TBT Agreement, Article VII of the GATT, Article 9 of the TRIMS Agreement, Articles VIII and IX of the GATS, and Article 11(b) of the Safeguards Agreement, in order to assist Members to implement such provisions.

The WTO should also consider whether some principles of competition policy might be incorporated into agreements regarding trade remedies, such as the Antidumping Agreement and the SCM Agreement.

Finally, the WTO should consider establishing a permanent group of experts on competition and trade (such as the Permanent Group of Experts on Subsidies and Trade Relations as provided for in Article 24 of the SCM Agreement) that would advise WTO bodies on competition policy matters.

## 8.3 Option 3: A non-binding multilateral framework for cooperation in competition policy

This option is aimed at establishing a multilateral framework for cooperation in competition policy among WTO Members. The provisions of this agreement would be hortatory rather than binding as "a covered agreement" so that a violation could not be invoked by a Member against another Member of the WTO. This option would provide for notification of legal action taken under the competition law of a Member when such an action provokes international implications, exchange of information, cooperation among enforcement agencies, coordination of policies, mutual assistance in investigation and enforcement, including "positive comity", and technical assistance, education and dissemination of information regarding the competition laws and policies of Members.

Option 3 is modelled after the bilateral agreements on competition policy that have been signed by a number of countries, such as the United States, the European Community and some of its members, Canada, Japan, Australia, and New Zealand. In spite of their narrow coverage, bilateral agreements have worked quite well in promoting cooperation among participants. One of the reasons for this success may be their informal and non-binding nature of such agreements. Although some may argue that this type of multilateral agreement has no "teeth", this is probably the most realistic approach for today. An agreement such as this, which is non-binding, is unusual for the WTO, which is essentially a rule-oriented system. However, there is no reason that the WTO must reject agreement simply because it is non-binding.

In 1980, the UNCTAD (The United Nations Conference on Trade and Developments) announced "The Set of Multilaterally Agreed Equitable Principles and Rules for the Control of Restrictive Business Practices".[64] In Part IV — Section E, the UNCTAD stated, inter alia, that states should, at the national level or through regional groupings, adopt, improve and effectively enforce appropriate legislation and implementing judicial and administrative procedures for the control of restrictive business practices including those of transnational corporations. However, this was a non-binding recommendation.

[64] http://www.unctad.org/en/subsites/cpolicy/docs/CPSet/cpsetsp4.htm.

On 15 August 2002, the UNCTAD submitted to the Working Group on the Interaction between Trade and Competition Policy a new proposal in which it raises the possibility for creating a multilateral competition framework.[65]

In this document, the UNCTAD explores different possibilities for developing the concept of multilateral framework for competition policy which may be included in the WTO. However, as to the issues such as whether it is "binding", whether it should be enforced through a dispute settlement mechanism and whether exchanges of information should include confidential information, no definitive position is taken. This may indicate that views of developing countries which compose the UNCTAD are diverse and consensus has not yet been achieved.

## 8.4 Option 4: A partly-binding multilateral framework

This was proposed by the European Community in the position paper it submitted to the WTO in 2000.[66] In the proposed framework, several core principles are incorporated such as non-discrimination, transparency, and due process of law in enforcing competition law. The European Community proposes that such core principles should be regarded as binding on Members. Besides the binding core principles, there would be arrangements with regard to technical assistance and capacity-building for developing countries to increase their ability to implement and enforce competition policy and law. Also there would be agreement with respect to promotion of mutual assistance in the enforcement of competition laws and policies. This would include such matters as notification of measures that Members take with regard to anticompetitive conduct that may affect the interests of other Members, exchange of information, and positive comity.[67]

The European Community submitted another communication on 22 April 2002 to the Working Group on the Interaction between Trade and Competition Policy[68] in which it states its new position.

[65] The World Trade Organization, Communication from UNCTAD, WT/WGTCP/W/197 (15 August 2002).

[66] Communication from the European Community and its Member States, WT/WGTCP/W/152, 25 September 2000

[67] However, positive comity is not mentioned in this position paper.

[68] World Trade Organization, Communication from the European Community and its Member States, WT/WWTTCP/W/184 (22 April 2002).

In this position paper, the EC emphasizes the importance of proposals which meet the needs of developing countries and argues that any WTO competition agreement should include modalities for international cooperation whereby developing countries and their recently established competition authorities could also benefit from the advantages of international cooperation while at the same time not be required to become full fledged parties to more traditional and resource-demanding bilateral cooperation agreements. The EC focuses on (a) modalities for international cooperation between competition authorities and (b) technical assistance for capacity-building purposes.

With regard to (a), the EC emphasizes the importance of provisions to facilitate voluntary, case-specific cooperation on anti-competitive practices having an impact on international trade, and provisions relating to general exchanges of information and experiences and joint analysis of global trade-related competition issues. The EC argues that this latter function can be undertaken by a Competition Policy Committee to be established once a WTO framework agreement has been concluded.

With respect to (b), the EC suggests that technical assistance should include support for the drafting of laws and the establishment of competition authorities, building expertise in the area of enforcement, training staff and support for general information policies, and integrated technical assistance programmes including relevant international organizations and other donors.

# 21

# FUTURE CHALLENGES



## 1. Three crises

At the beginning of the twenty-first century, the WTO is facing three fundamental challenges. First, it must reform its own internal structures and decision-making to address adequately the needs of the future. Second, it must respond to the demands of civil society and integrate broader social concerns into its agenda. Third, it must address the problem of poverty and become more responsive to the needs of developing countries. That these problems have arisen and the WTO has become controversial is a mark, not of failure, but of the organization's remarkable accomplishments. The WTO has evolved into a unique intergovernmental body, an essential part of the architecture of contemporary international relations.

Through lengthy negotiations, the spectacular successes of the Tokyo and Uruguay Rounds were achieved, creating the WTO of today. Two characteristics stand out. The WTO administers a vast body of processes and substantive legal norms. The shallow integration of the GATT has given way to integrated political and legal structures that project deeply into traditional realms of national sovereignty and concern. The WTO also has a dispute settlement system that is unprecedented in international law, complete with mandatory jurisdiction, binding determinations, and sanctions that bite.

The metamorphosis of the GATT into the WTO occurred not according to any theoretical model but as a response to practical concerns and needs. Many theoretical models are proposed for reform of the WTO,[1] but these are unlikely to be followed regardless of their merit. Rather, the WTO will be shaped in the future and will succeed or fail based on how it responds to the three principal challenges mentioned above.

## 1.1 Internal decision-making

The first challenge concerns the WTO's internal system for administration and taking decisions. There are three aspects to the decision-making problems in the WTO: there is an imbalance and a strange dichotomy between the fast-paced, legalistic, even draconian, dispute settlement process administered by the DSB and the tepid, deadlock-plagued political decision-making process employed by other WTO bodies. Furthermore, there are no explicit links between the two. Thus, what happens is that, although the WTO Agreement (Article IX:2) gives the Ministerial Conference and the General Council "exclusive authority" to interpret the multilateral trade agreements, in practice, definitive interpretations are issued by dispute settlement bodies.[2] An egregious example of this has already been detailed in the

[1] Three theoretical models put forth are: (1) the Trade Stakeholders Model put forth by Professor Richard Shell; (2) the Global Subsidiary Model advocated by Professors Robert Howse and Kalypso Nicolaides; and (3) the Libertarian Model, created by Professor John McGinnis. *See* Claude E. Barfield, Free Trade, Sovereignty, Democracy, the Future of the World Trade Organization 163–73 (2001).

[2] Barfield, above note 1, at 172.

chapter on Environmental Protection and Trade, where the Appellate Body in the *Shrimp/Turtle* case stepped in to reform GATT Article XX, although the WTO Committee on Trade and Environment was deadlocked. A more negative example is the way that the EU and the United States have, for several years, used the judicialized dispute settlement process to play a game of "gotcha" and as leverage in trade disputes. Each side has used the dispute settlement to attack the other's most vulnerable points in feuds over bananas, taxes, hormones, and safeguards. In May 2002, in meetings in Washington between President Bush and EU Commission President Romano Prodi, this process continued: to forestall a threatened retaliation over U.S. steel safeguards by the EU, the American side threatened to bring a WTO complaint against the EU over trade in genetically-modified foods.[3] This transatlantic one-upsmanship has damaged both participants as well as the WTO.[4]

Three changes should be considered by WTO Members to deal with these problems. First, it is evident, as Dr. Claude Barfield of the American Enterprise Institute has cogently argued,[5] dispute settlement in the WTO has become too judicialized and should be modified to return somewhat to the negotiation/diplomacy model that predominated under the GATT. Some suggested ways of accomplishing this are (1) to provide a greater role in the WTO for alternative dispute resolution techniques, such as conciliation, mediation, and arbitration; (2) to allow a specified minority of the DSB to block or defer the adoption of a dispute settlement report in lieu of the present "negative consensus" rule; and (3) to modify the sanctions in case of non-compliance with a dispute settlement decision so that a monetary fine or trade compensation is the usual remedy instead of retaliation.[6]

Second, the cumbersome political decision-making process in the WTO needs improvement. Some sort of weighted voting scheme might be fashioned according to shares of world trade or an executive committee could be created to trade certain specified decisions. Such an executive committee could consist, perhaps, of several permanent Members such as the EC, the United States, China, Japan, Brazil, India, South Africa and Nigeria, and rotating non-permanent members. Another "constitutional" change that

[3] WASH. POST, 3 May 2002, at H1.

[4] *See* C. Fred Bergsten, *The Transatlantic Century*, WASH. POST, 30 April 2002, at H2.

[5] Barfield, above note 1, at 111–31.

[6] *Id.*

might be helpful is to change Article X of the WTO Agreement to make amendments to the multilateral trade agreements easier to pass. Under current law, the agreements are written as if in stone because amendment is too difficult. This is unwarranted. Many agreements contain errors, gaps, and ambiguities.

Third, there should be explicit links between dispute settlement and the political processes in the WTO so that controversies can move from judicialized dispute settlement to a political and diplomatic process. Two such links come to mind. WTO adjudicating bodies (panels and the Appellate Body) could be specifically authorized in the DSU to declare what international lawyers call a *non-liquet* (a "no decision") in a given case that seems very political or where existing law seems inadequate. These controversies could be referred to political bodies for decision. Another mechanism would be to allow a "political appeal" of a legal question. This could take the form of an amendment to Article 11 of the DSU to allow any party to appeal to the WTO's General Council or Ministerial Conference the question of whether the WTO adjudicating body made an "objective assessment" of the matter before it. Negotiation and diplomacy could then be used to settle the dispute as well as legal arguments.[7]

In summary, more needs to be done so that political and diplomatic decision-making in the WTO catches up with legal determinations. Nothing is gained by subjecting what are essentially political controversies, such as trade in genetically modified foods, to strictly legal determinations.

## 1.2 Civil society

Although the tactics and excesses of the protestors at Seattle and elsewhere are subject to criticism and despite the incoherence of their message, there is no doubt that the WTO must formulate a response to the criticism of the larger civil society in many countries. What is called for is not the adoption of substantive norms protecting workers or the environment, which would deeply divide the WTO membership, but rather the introduction into WTO law and political practice of meaningful processes of participation for groups and interests that presently consider themselves outside the system. Three such suggestions come to mind.

[7] In only one case was there a successful appeal based on Article 11. *See* Appellate Body Report, *United States — Wheat Gluten Safeguard*, para. 161.

First, much can still be done to interject transparency and information into the system.[8] The WTO should establish rules for the publication of most dispute settlement reports and official documents. Provision should be made for public access to dispute settlement proceedings, and appropriate rules freely allowing the submission and consideration of *amicus* briefs.[9]

Second, the WTO should explore ways to allow NGOs (non-governmental organizations) and other non-governmental institutions meaningful participation in the system. A great deal of work has been done on how to do this,[10] which will not be restated here. Suffice it to say that "participatory democracy" among non-traditional international law participants is a movement that cannot be denied. The WTO should work out procedures for NGOs and corporate observer status and participation. However, the rules for selection and modes of participation must be carefully considered and drafted. NGO participation, as many observers have pointed out,[11] does not guarantee democratic legitimacy in international organizations.

Third, the WTO might consider special procedures for interjecting social concerns into the multilateral trading system's rules.[12] One suggestion made by Professor Dani Rodrik of the Kennedy School of Government, Harvard University, is the conclusion by the WTO of a regime for social safeguards.[13] This would be instituted by a new WTO Social Safeguards Agreement similar to the Safeguards Agreement. This new regime would allow any domestic public interest group or organization to petition a designated national authority asking for a trade measure to foster a social concern such as workers' rights, human rights, or protection of the environment. An appropriate procedure would require investigation and public debate among interest groups, NGOs, corporations, and individuals regarding costs, benefits, effectiveness, and other issues. If a national decision is taken to impose the trade measure, affected WTO Members would have a right to compensation. The right to compensation would differ, however, depending on whether the affected Members are constituted

[8] *See* Bernard M. Hoekman and Michael M. Kostecki, The Political Economy of the WTO 371–72 (2d ed. 2001).

[9] *See* Barfield, above note 1, at 15–16.

[10] This work is summarized and synthesized in Barfield, above note 1, at 97–110.

[11] Barfield, above note 1, at 105–10.

[12] *See Symposium: Boundaries of the WTO*, 96 Am. J. Int'l L. 1–158 (2002) (edited by José E. Alvarez).

[13] Robert Z. Lawrence et al., Emerging Agenda for Global Trade: High Stakes for Developing Countries 62–67 (1996).

democratically. WTO Members with democratic institutions would be allowed compensation because a presumption would obtain that the social conditions targeted are the result of legitimate political or economic policy differences. Authoritarian regimes would, however, be denied compensation because they would be unable to claim their offending policies are reflective of democratic social choice.

## 1.3 Developing countries

A third challenge for the WTO is to do a better job of serving the needs of developing countries. Despite the special and differential treatment of developing countries in the WTO multilateral trading agreements, developing countries are not fully integrated into the world trading system.[14] At present, developing countries comprise 73 percent of the Membership of the WTO.[15] Another 28 countries are applying for accession, and these are mostly developing countries.[16] Although a few developing countries have made giant strides[17] in recent years, more can be done.

Several policy developments are important if developing countries are to be brought more fully into the system. First, technical and financial assistance should be made available so that developing countries can fully participate in WTO affairs. Second, the specific market access problems of developing countries should be identified and negotiated. Often, a lack of policy coherence prevents developing countries' access to markets although access is formally given. For example, the huge agricultural subsidies in developed WTO Members effectively prevents poor countries that may have comparative advantage in commodities from agricultural export markets.[18] Moreover, high tariff-rate quotas for certain products, such as textiles and sugar, effectively exclude developing countries from markets. Third, the particular concerns of developing countries should be respected in the field of intellectual property. Specifically, provision should be made to allow developing countries to respond to health emergencies, traditional knowledge should be given IP protection, and poor countries

[14] *See* Constantine Michalopoulos, Developing Countries in the WTO 17–21 (2001).

[15] *Id.* at 154.

[16] *Id.*

[17] *Id.* at 244.

[18] Carmen G. Gonzalez, *Institutionalising Inequality: the WTO Agreement on Agriculture, Food Security and Developing Countries*, 27 Col. J. of Envt'l L. 433 (2002).

should share in the economic benefits of patents derived from their natural resources. Fourth, the WTO should cooperate more closely with other intergovernmental organizations such as the IMF and the World Bank in plans to aid poor countries.

The Doha Ministerial Conference of 2001 adopted a work programme that is a good foundation for considering many of these points.

## 2. The multilateral trading system at a crossroads

Since its inception in 1947, the GATT has contributed significantly to stability in international economic relations. By focusing on a specialized and esoteric agenda, the GATT persuaded its signatories to entrust it with growing responsibilities. GATT's often criticized pragmatism was the main reason for its success, for pragmatism ensured that all changes were "internalized" by the GATT signatories, and behavioural regularity through the GATT was established and respected. To start with, despite the fact that unilateral liberalization has obvious economic benefits, countries are seldom, if ever, ready to embark on such an exercise, and on most occasions need an "outside" excuse. The term "concession" used in the GATT to describe the process of liberalization illustrates this point: countries "concede" but in fact are the prime beneficiaries from their "concessions" in terms of cheap imports. For "concessions" to take place, however, a multilateral instrument as well as reciprocity was necessary. Giving up discretion with respect to tariff policy (*i.e.*, by binding tariffs) was far from obvious in the late 1940s. The GATT managed to reduce tariffs substantially, to almost insignificant levels, with the exception of certain well-known peaks.

Reducing tariffs, however, is only part of the effort to reduce protection. The negotiators are well aware of that; and since the Tokyo Round of negotiations, the GATT started attacking non-tariff barriers: that is, domestic regulation. The pattern continued during the Uruguay Round. In a sense, however, the logic of the Uruguay Round negotiations was substantially different from that of previous negotiations. The qualitatively different element was the conclusion of "positive" integration-type agreements, like the TRIPS Agreement.

The GATT further managed to maintain a dispute settlement system that, without eliminating altogether bilateral efforts to resolve disputes, promoted third-party adjudication. Between 1947 and 1989, the possibility to block third-party adjudication was open, as was and still is the case in public international law in the absence of an explicit agreement to the contrary. As Robert Hudec's 1993 study shows,[19] however, this discretion was seldom used. *De facto*, the GATT dispute settlement system was the largest multilateral system of binding third-party adjudication.

The WTO system is at a crossroads. It addresses both the width (by adding multilateral legislative new agreements, such as the GATS and the TRIPS Agreement) and the depth (by adding "positive" integration-type agreements to the existing multilateral framework) of the integration process. This seems to be the case in the presence of the ongoing negotiations (or attempts to negotiate) on "trade and..." issues, such as environment, investment, competition, or labour standards.

The current picture of the WTO most likely reflects deliberate choices by the influential players. Trade liberalization in the GATT/WTO is not a linear process; significant "back and forths" proved necessary for the overall cooperative game to continue. Moreover, trade liberalization in the WTO is not characterized by a sense of priority. Discussions do take place and new issues are introduced in fields in which most likely no significant gains will be reported, while trade barriers persist in areas in which high gains can be expected from liberalization. This is so because the WTO is part of an overall cooperation scheme among sovereign nations, not a single-minded entity trying to achieve rapid integration in a specified area. Perhaps the most important contribution of the GATT/WTO integration process is reflected in the fact that international trade relations since 1947 are integral parts of the overall cooperation scheme among sovereign nations, and, arguably, this overall cooperation is the *raison d'être* of the WTO.[20]

Two additional points seem pertinent. First, trade liberalization has an implicit limit: the more a country liberalizes, the less is left to liberalize. Furthermore, at some time, there will be no need to liberalize: the world will

[19] *See generally* Robert E. Hudec, Enforcing International Trade Law: The Evolution of the Modern GATT Legal System (1993).

[20] In 1947, the GATT preamble mentioned that the objective of the signatories was to ensure "full employment", "a large and steadily growing volume of real income", "developing the full use of the resources of the world". And how to do that? Again, quoting from the GATT preamble, "by entering into reciprocal and mutually advantageous arrangements directed to the elimination of discriminatory treatment in international commerce". Signatories of the WTO Agreement eagerly retained these objectives and only slightly modified it (instead of referring to "developing the full use," they now refer to "optimal use of the world's resources").

be one free-trade area in which factors of production will move without restriction. Is the WTO final objective, therefore, the establishment of a world free-trade area?

It is legally unrealistic, however, in the realm of public international law to speculate about such a transfer of competence. The principle of sovereignty obliges that one must be sure about the quantity and the quality of sovereignty transferred. Hence, a world free-trade area is not the WTO objective: at least, not for the time being. Its objective is trade liberalization in the fields brought under the auspices of the WTO.

Second, experience shows that trade liberalization is not a linear process. Whenever the GATT/WTO liberalizing process went too far (according to the point of view of influential constituencies), it had to readjust.[20a] In other words, the GATT/WTO negotiating process is not merely aimed at eliminating trade protection. This may be largely the case with respect to tariff negotiations (the possibility being institutionally retained for WTO Members to re-raise their tariff protection, in accordance with GATT Article XXVIII), but it definitely is not true with respect to non-tariff barriers. Three examples can illustrate this point: safeguards, TRIMs, and antidumping.

According to the original regulation of safeguards (GATT Article XIX), countries were free to impose safeguard measures, provided of course that the substantive conditions laid down in Article XIX were met on a non-discriminatory basis. The wording of Article XIX was clear in this respect, and no legislative amendment took place in the GATT years. However, practice developed in a drastically different way. Beginning in the 1960s, there was ample empirical evidence pointing to the existence of voluntary export restraints (VERs), which are selective safeguard measures that are inconsistent with the principle of non-discrimination. GATT parties, for reasons that have been adequately explained elsewhere,[21] concluded VERs with targeted exporters. Legally, VERs are in violation of Article XIX, but

[20a] Does this mean that the originally assigned objective has not been reached? The right question seems to be what exactly is the originally assigned objective?

Economic theory teaches that optimality has to be defined relative to constraints. What are they in the present context? Do we talk about maximization of world income, given technology, resources, and preferences, as in the most simple trade theory paradigm? Do we require, as we move to the "optimum," that no country be worse off? Do we take into account political feasibility constraints? The concept of optimality is empty if we do not state both what objective function is to be maximized, and the constraints under which it is maximized.

[21] Chapter 9, section 6.

no one brought a complaint against them. In the absence of *ex officio* complaints, no one had the incentive to do so: importers requested them and exporters were reaping monopoly rents thanks to their conclusion. During the Uruguay Round, almost 50 years after the entry into force of Article XIX, the negotiators reinstated the obvious: that VERs are illegal under the WTO Safeguards Agreement and, hence, have to be eliminated with immediate effect. This time, however, they pronounced the illegality of VERs after first securing the legality of quota modulation, a scheme that *de facto* permits a "mild" VER-type arrangement. In this respect, the WTO Safeguards Agreement is a step back in comparison to GATT Article XIX: the precision and the level of detail now introduced took away a substantial part of the non-discriminatory element which formed the quintessence of Article XIX. More importantly, what does it mean to outlaw VERs when the incentive to conclude them is still there? In the absence of overall effective remedies, can one plausibly make the argument that VERs will vanish from the face of the earth by a sentence that outlaws them in the relevant Agreement? This would be the case only if the law reflected the incentive structure in this respect. Practice, however, shows that this is not the case.

The TRIMs Agreement provides another useful example. The Agreement contains no new disciplines. It outlaws two categories of TRIMs: local content and export performance-related requirements. Both measures were outlawed in the GATT era as well; GATT Article III:5 and GATT Article XI apply to the former and the latter respectively. Neither Article III:5 nor Article XI reserved special treatment for developing countries. Now, however, Article 4 of the TRIMs Agreement allows developing Members to deviate temporarily. Consequently, the new Agreement is a step back. Did the prolific use of TRIMs, especially by developing countries, dictate the setback? At any rate, such practices, previously outlawed, now will be tolerated.

A third example is the Antidumping Agreement. Although this Agreement did provide clarifications to the previous Agreement, traditional users of antidumping protection managed to get into the Agreement a novel standard of judicial review to be used by the WTO adjudicating bodies when examining the legitimacy of impositions of antidumping duties by national authorities. This new standard, the overall legitimacy of which under public international law has been questioned, is a huge step back in comparison to the standard used in the GATT years, since it substantially reduces the bite of judicial review. It is still too early to pronounce on its impact, but one can safely argue that, if the standard laid down in

Article 17.6 of the WTO Antidumping Agreement stays in place, it will give national authorities the incentive to use antidumping, more than any other instrument to protect their domestic industry.

Cynics will state that without such concessions further trade liberalization will not be politically feasible. Instead of speaking of trade liberalization in the WTO, one should speak of "practicable" trade liberalization.

## 3. Societal issues

In the last decade of the twentieth century, a rising tide of protest has swirled around the GATT/WTO as agents of globalization. This came to a head in 1999 with the disruption of the WTO Ministerial Conference in Seattle. In the last few years, exaggerated and often wildly inaccurate attacks[22] have been levelled at the WTO. At the same time, serious studies of some of the negative aspects of globalization have been published.[23] These have caused those concerned with the WTO to consider, for the first time, the impact of WTO standards on the broader society beyond the world of trade. These are the so-called "linkage" issues, also referred to as "trade and" problems.

Specific criticisms of the WTO fall into eight categories: (1) the environment; (2) health; (3) workers' rights; (4) human rights; (5) the poor; (6) intellectual property; (7) transparency; and (8) governance. These topics will be considered in turn.

### 3.1 The environment

The relationship of trade and the WTO to environmental protection can be analysed from four perspectives. First, increased trade and investment do not directly cause environmental degradation, which is caused by polluting production processes, over-exploitation of resources, certain kinds of consumption, and the disposal of wastes. Empirical studies have established that the competitive effects of environmental regulations are minor, and there is

[22] *See, e.g.*, Marjorie Cohn, *The World Trade Organization: Elevating Property Interests Above Human Rights*, 29 GA. J. INT'L & COMP. L. 427 (2001); Geoffrey Lean, *The Hidden Tentacles of the World's Most Secret Body*, INDEPENDENT ON SUNDAY, 18 July 1999, at 13.

[23] *See* John Gray, FALSE DAWN (1998); Friedl Weiss et al., INTERNATIONAL ECONOMIC LAW WITH A HUMAN FACE (1998); Robert Gilpin, THE CHALLENGE OF GLOBAL CAPITALISM (2000); Jerry Mander and Edward Goldsmith, THE CASE AGAINST THE GLOBAL ECONOMY (1996).

little evidence that polluting industries migrate to pollution havens to reduce environmental compliance costs.[24]

Second, although the WTO properly is not an environmental protection agency, it should not be allowed to interfere with legitimate efforts at the national or international levels to deal with environmental problems. Moreover, the WTO has no authority to help formulate environmental policy; its primary role is to stay out of the way.

On this point, the GATT got off to a bad start with the panel decisions (which never were adopted by the GATT Council) in *Tuna/Dolphin I and II.* These decisions, which caused environmentalists to "discover" the GATT and brought them out on the streets to demonstrate, were subjected to heavy criticism by scholars as well.[25]

However, as analysed in Chapter 17, the effect of these decisions was overturned after the WTO was established in 1995. Specifically, the GATT general exceptions in Article XX(b) for measures necessary to protect human, animal, or plant life or health, was flexibly interpreted in the *EC — Asbestos* case to uphold any national trade restriction that is reasonably related to such protection.

Moreover, the Appellate Body in the *Shrimp/Turtle* case issued an environmental interpretation of the GATT Article XX(g) general exception which allows trade restrictions in order to protect natural resources even if located in areas beyond national jurisdiction. Although there is an obligation to seek international cooperation for such an endeavour, a WTO compliance panel upheld limited unilateral regulation by the U.S. in the *Shrimp/Turtle* case. After *Shrimp/Turtle*, Article XX(g) permits protection of natural resources within a WTO Member's territory as well as global resources. International environmental regimes that employ trade restrictions have never been challenged by the WTO, and, on the basis of the *Asbestos* and *Shrimp/Turtle* rulings, would pass muster unless they involve arbitrary or unjustifiable discrimination between WTO Members.

Thus, despite the fears of environmentalists, the WTO does not pose any future threat against the implementation of either national or international

[24] WTO, Trade and Environment 1–8 (Special Study No. 4, 1999); Gene M. Grossman and Alan B. Krueger, Environmental Impacts of a North American Free Trade Agreement 6 (1991); J. J. Leonard, Pollution and the Struggle for World Product (1988).

[25] *E.g.*, Thomas J. Schoenbaum, Free International Trade and Protection of the Environment: Irreconcilable Conflict?, 86 Am. J. Int'l L. 700 (1992); Edith Brown Weiss, *Environment and Trade as Partners in Sustainable Development: A Commentary*, 86 Am. J. Int'l L. 728 (1992).

environmental protection measures as long as they are not blatantly disguised protectionism.

Third, the WTO can aid in the fight for environmental protection in several ways. First, environmental protection is sometimes exacerbated by policy failures, such as government subsidies to polluting and resource degrading industries. Agriculture, forestry, and fishing are primary examples. The WTO can help to correct these policy failures through international rules, particularly in connection with the WTO Agreement on Agriculture and the WTO Subsidies Agreement. In both, environmental subsidies have been addressed to a limited extent. In the future negotiating round, this should be a primary WTO objective.

The WTO also could aid environmental protection efforts by adopting a trade framework to facilitate environmental taxes, *i.e.*, taxes on the consumption of environmental resources. Such taxes may be anti-competitive for the country that adopts them if trading partners do not employ them. The WTO should examine its rules relating to border tax adjustments to remove any discrimination between product taxes on various inputs and components. Border tax adjustment should be allowed for taxes on resource inputs regardless of whether such inputs are consumed in the production process.

Finally, the WTO institutional model, with its associated agreements, could serve as a model for a new global architecture for the protection of the environment. Specifically, the UN Environment Programme, a weak body with a limited mandate, could be reformed along the lines of the WTO into a World Environmental Organization (WEO).

Fourth, it should be evident that the WTO cannot mandate environmental standards or adopt trade sanctions against environmentally deficient Members. This not only is beyond the scope of the WTO, trade barriers generally make for very poor environmental policy. They are ineffective to change behaviour in most cases and do not address root problems. Environmental problems are best addressed at their source. Trade, on the contrary, can help produce the resources and funding necessary to deal effectively with such problems.

## 3.2 Health

Trade restrictions to protect health are addressed by GATT Article XX(b) as well as the Sanitary and Phytosanitary Measures (SPS) Agreement discussed in Chapter 18. In judging the adequacy of this framework, it is noteworthy, first, that the *EC — Asbestos* decision specifically upholds a broad-based ban of a dangerous product in international trade. Second, although the *EC — Hormones* case ruled that a trade ban on hormone-fed beef was not in compliance with SPS Agreement norms, the Appellate Body made clear that a trade ban based upon scientific evidence after a scientific risk assessment would be upheld even if the standard applied was more stringent than international standards. Thus, health is protected under the international trading regime.

Despite this, it is evident that the WTO has further work to address health issues. First, the precautionary principle, present only to a limited extent in Article XX(b) and the SPS Agreement, should be incorporated into both norms so that under exigent circumstances, trade restrictions may be adopted to protect health even in the absence of scientific evidence. Second, the scope of an adequate risk assessment as well as the management and communication of risk should be more precisely defined. Third, the problem of labelling should be addressed so that WTO-consistent labelling may be used to inform consumers about such matters as the use of genetically modified foodstuffs. These three matters should be addressed through negotiation among WTO Members.

## 3.3 Workers' rights

Whether and to what extent workers' rights should be on the agenda of the WTO is a very controversial subject. Groups in favour of new WTO rules and the use of the WTO's dispute settlement process to upgrade labour standards argue that the trade community favours benefits for multinational corporations and investors while neglecting ordinary working people. They point out that, in many parts of the world, workers toil long hours for little pay under poor health and safety conditions. In many countries, fundamental rights of workers such as freedoms of association, to organize, to bargain with employers, and to resolve problems on the job are denied or not enforced. The WTO should, accordingly, ensure that social conditions improve as trade expands.[26]

The argument to the contrary[27] is that the WTO and the multinational trading system is a delicate structure that will collapse if burdened by the

[26] *See* John J. Sweeney [President of the AFL-CIO, The major association of unions in the United States], *Ignoring Ordinary Working People Won't Do*, INT'L HERALD TRIB., 15 December 1996.

[27] *See* Jose E. Alvarez, *How Not to Link: Institutional Conundrums of an Expanded Trade Regime*, 7 WIDENER L. SYMP. J. 1 (2001); Kristin Weldon, *Piercing the Silence or Lulling You to Sleep: The Sounds of Child Labor*, 7 WIDENER L. SYMP. J. 227 (2001).

responsibility for workers' rights around the world.[28] Furthermore, workers' wages, benefits, and working conditions vary from country to country; these differences are endemic and part of the theory of comparative advantage. GATT Article XX(e) allows import restrictions or products produced by forced labour, but this provision was added for economic reasons, not to protect workers. Additional rules on labour rights would not be acceptable to the majority of WTO Members.[29] Since the inception of the GATT in 1947, there have been many attempts to inject labour standards into trade negotiations at the GATT and the WTO; none of these efforts have been successful.[30] At the first WTO Ministerial Conference in Singapore in December 1996, the following five-point declaration was adopted:

- We renew our commitment to the observance of internationally recognized core labour standards.
- The International Labor Organization (ILO) is the competent body to set and deal with these standards, and we affirm our support for its work in promoting them.
- We believe that economic growth and development fostered by increased trade and further trade liberalization contribute to the promotion of these standards.
- We reject the use of labour standards for protectionist purposes and agree that the comparative advantage of countries, particularly low-wage developing countries, must in no way be put into question.
- In this regard, we note that the WTO and ILO Secretariats will continue their existing collaboration.[31]

Thus, the WTO has recognized the primacy of the International Labor Organization in developing and enforcing international rules with respect to workers' rights. The ILO has responded with a renewed effort to promote

[28] *U.N. Secretary General Says Environment, Labor Standards Should be Kept Out of the WTO*, 22 Int'l Trade Rep. Current Developments (BNA, July 21, 1999).

[29] *See* Paul Krugman, THE ACCIDENTAL THEORIST (AND OTHER STORIES FROM THE DISMAL SCIENCE) (1998).

[30] For a detailed summary, see Peter S. Watson, *The Framework for a New Trade Agenda*, 25 LAW & POL'Y INT'L BUS. 1237, 1525–57 (1994); Karen V. Champion, *Who Pays for Free Trade: The Dilemma of Free Trade and International Labor Standards, 22* N. C. J. INT'L L. & COM. REG. 181 (1996).

[31] WTO, Ministerial Conference, Singapore, 9–13 December 1996, *Singapore Ministerial Declaration*, WT/MIN(96)/DEC, 18 December 1996, para. 4.

international labour standards. In its 1998 Declaration,[32] the ILO defined four fundamental rights that are the subject of its conventions:

1. Freedom of association and the effective recognition of the right of collective bargaining;
2. The elimination of all forms of forced or compulsory labour;
3. The effective abolition of child labour; and
4. The elimination of discrimination in respect of employment and occupation.

The ILO has mounted new initiatives to inject these and other workers' rights into the new global economy.[33] Thus, the WTO will play only a cooperative role with respect to workers' rights. Labour standards will not be linked to trade sanctions at the WTO.[34]

Labour standards will continue to be linked with trade, however, in certain peripheral ways, such as through the generalized system of preferences,[35] regional agreements such as the North American Free Trade Agreement,[36] and voluntary codes of conduct.[37]

## 3.4 Human rights

The case for linking protection of human rights apart from workers' rights to the WTO rests on the idea that states that violate or turn a blind eye to the human rights infractions should not be allowed to participate in the international trading system. This view, in turn, rests on the premise that such exclusion will cause human rights violators to change their behaviour.

---

[32] ILO Declaration on Fundamental Principles and Rights at Work and its Follow-Up, 18 June 1998, reprinted in 37 I.L.M. 1233 (1998).

[33] *See* ILO, DECENT WORK (1999).

[34] For debate, see Note, *Linking Labor Standards and Trade Sanctions: An Analysis of Their Current Relationship*, 36 COLUM. J. TRANSNAT'L L. 659 (1998); Steve Charnovitz, *Trade, Employment and Labor Standards: The OECD Study and Recent Developments in the Trade and Labor Standards Debate*, 11 TEMPLE INT'L & COMP. L.J. 131 (1997); Raj Bhala, *Clarifying the Trade-Labor Link*, 37 COLUM. J. TRANSNAT'L L. 11 (1998).

[35] *E.g.*, the European Union has linked granting GSP treatment to labor standards. *EU Seeks More Labor, Environment Protection by Cutting GSP Tariffs*, INSIDE U.S. TRADE, 12 June, 1998, at 17.

[36] North America Agreement on Labor Cooperation, 13 September 1993, reprinted in 32 I.L.M. 1499 (1993).

[37] *See* Robert J. Liubicic, *Corporate Codes of Conduct and Product Labeling Schemes: The Limits and Possibilities of Promoting International Labor Rights Through Private Initiatives*, 30 LAW & POL'Y INT'L BUS. 111 (1998).

Thus, the case for linkage between trade and human rights depends on the power of the WTO to decree trade sanctions.

There are enormous problems with this reasoning. First, what human rights would the WTO seek to enforce? Arriving at an agreement on this would not be possible now. Second, there exist long established international and regional regimes for the promotion and enforcement of human rights, such as the UN Commission on Human Rights, the UN Committee on Human Rights, and the European Court of Human Rights.[38] Adding the WTO to these regimes would accomplish little and would pose the danger of conflicting interpretations and decisions. Third, although trade sanctions have emotional appeal to punish human rights violations, empirical studies have established that trade sanctions seldom accomplish their objectives and are not effective in accomplishing their objectives.[39] Fourth, if the WTO ever were to try to become a human rights enforcement agency, there is little chance its dispute settlement mechanism would survive; it soon would be engulfed in compliance problems, and the WTO itself would be under threat.

Nevertheless, the WTO has a role to play in promoting human rights. First, through its multilateral treaty framework that promotes principles of non-discrimination, the rule of law, economic liberalism, and peaceful dispute settlement, the WTO can be said to promote and protect human freedoms.[40] Second, Article XXI of the GATT permits WTO Members to participate in action involving trade sanctions decreed by the United Nations in cases of threats to peace and security. Moreover, WTO Members are permitted to use investment and trade as positive incentives to promote human rights in cases where infringement of WTO norms are not at stake.

## 3.5 The poor

Anti-globalists charge that liberalized trade benefits only the rich and transnational corporations at the expense of poor people and poor countries.[41] When this simplistic objection is analysed, it dissolves into two contradictory suppositions: (1) trade impoverishes the poor in importing

---

[38] *See generally* An Introduction to the International Protection of Human Rights (Raija Hanski and Markku Suksi eds., 2d ed. rev. 1999).

[39] *See* Gary Clyde Hufbauer et al., Economic Sanctions Reconsidered: History and Current Policy (1990).

[40] *See* Hoe Lim, *Trade and Human Rights: What's at Issue?*, 35 J. World Trade, No. 2, at 275 (2001).

[41] Mander and Goldsmith, above note 23.

(usually industrialized) countries by exporting jobs; and (2) workers in exporting (usually developing) countries suffer exploitation by multinational corporations. Obviously, there is something wrong with this picture. If jobs are exported causing unemployment and wage inequality in such countries, there must be corresponding gains by people in developing countries. Happily, the truth is more complex: trade is not, as the anti-globalists suppose, a zero-sum game. Rather, both sides in trade should win, in the sense that both should be better off than they would be without trade.

There are, however, kernels of truth in the anti-globalist charges that need to be addressed. First, while the WTO cannot take primary responsibility for improving the lot of the poor in rich countries, it remains true that trade and globalization does produce losers, in the sense that people in inefficient economic sectors may lose their jobs. In such cases, it is the primary responsibility of the state concerned to manage the situation; this can be done in a variety of ways, such as education, adjustment assistance, safeguards, or temporary trade restrictions. The role of the WTO is to allow reasonable safeguards while imposing discipline on such measures to avoid or minimize protectionism. The WTO Safeguards Agreement and other safeguard mechanisms represent the solution to this balancing act adopted by the 145 WTO Members.

When considering the charge that trade produces "pauperized" workers in rich countries, it is worthwhile to point out the nature and extent of the problem. While trade is responsible for some unemployment, it rarely, if ever, is the dominant factor. The unemployment effects of trade are local and limited to certain economic sectors. General unemployment results from broader macroeconomic conditions; trade often is the scapegoat.

Neither is trade the primary factor in growing wage inequality in industrialized countries. Empirical studies have established[42] that wage inequality between skilled and unskilled workers is due primarily to differences in education and access to technology, not trade. Moreover, economists point out that some wage inequality leads to the optimum conditions for job creation.[43] In addition, empirical studies establish that trade has little effect on wage stagnation in industrialized countries.[44] Wage stagnation is pri-

[42] Alan V. Deardorff, *Technology, Trade and Increasing Inequality*, 1 J. INT'L ECON. L. 353 (1998).

[43] *See Jobs and Wages Revisited*, ECONOMIST, 17 August 1996, at 62.

[44] Paul R. Krugman and Robert Z. Lawrence, *Trade, Jobs and Wages*, 274 SCIENTIFIC AMERICAN 44 (April, 1994); *Two Tales of Trade*, ECONOMIST, 19 July 1997, at 75.

marily due to domestic productivity considerations. Trade potentially brings prosperity both to rich and poor; thus, the economic effect of putative safeguard measures should be considered so that the cost of such measures does not exceed the temporary benefits.

A second charge is that the WTO does not do enough to benefit developing countries. This may be true, but it does not obscure the generally positive potential impact of trade on such countries. In this regard, the WTO should take steps to formally recognize the right to development as a fundamental human right. It should work with the UN units that have established that the right to development is best understood as a "right to a particular process of development" that should be implemented through "eliminating obstacles to development".[45] Once this is done, the WTO should strengthen its regime to benefit developing countries through (1) additional market access commitments; (2) additional special and differential treatment for developing countries in the WTO agreements; (3) new institutional help to implement the right to development; and (4) debt forgiveness.

## 3.6 Intellectual property

Developing countries should also be the focus of reforms relating to the WTO's intellectual property regime, the TRIPS Agreement. Three principal areas need to be addressed. First, mechanisms must be developed under the TRIPS Agreement to allow the production and importation of pharmaceuticals by developing countries to deal with health crises such as AIDS and malaria. Possible mechanisms include two-tier pricing (lower prices for developing countries), compulsory licensing, and parallel imports (allowing importation of the cheapest version of a product). In addition, an international fund should be constituted and approved by the WTO to allow the pricing of pharmaceuticals to be subsidized to benefit people in developing countries.

Second, the WTO should examine the issue of the impact of biotechnology patents on developing countries. This issue has several aspects: whether protection of plants breeders' rights and biotech rights has the potential to disrupt agriculture in developing countries; whether traditional knowledge and practices in developing countries receive adequate protection from uncompensated expropriation by transnational companies; and whether

[45] U.N. Doc. E/CN.4/1999/W6.18/26.18/2 Study on the Current State of Progress in the Implementation of the Right to Development, 14 and 10.

the intellectual property guarantees in the UN Convention on Biological Diversity receive adequate recognition in the TRIPS Agreement. These aspects relate to adequate compensation in return for access to genetic resources and the transfer of technology.

Third, the WTO should establish new mechanisms and incentives to encourage the transfer of technology to developing countries in a variety of fields consistent with the protection of intellectual property rights.

## 3.7 Transparency

The WTO must reform its culture from one of secrecy and opaqueness to openness and transparency. This transformation is already underway. Through its excellent web site, for example, the WTO makes documents, decisions, and even working papers available to the public. This process must continue; there should be a systematic and comprehensive review of WTO procedures to explore and promulgate transparency and public disclosure.

## 3.8 Governance

There is a debate about governance and the "democratic legitimacy" of the WTO. Some call for greater participation of non-governmental interests in the decision-making processes of the WTO.[46] Others advocate the creation of a Global Peoples' Assembly to influence globalization policy.[47] Another view is that broad principles of customary international law, such as human rights, environmental, and other norms are universal and superior to the treaty law of WTO agreements. Such norms should, therefore, supersede treaty language in particular cases.[48] Many challenge WTO decisions and authority on the basis that the WTO has an inherent "lack of democratic legitimacy".[49]

These criticisms of the democratic legitimacy of the WTO are wide of the mark because they demonstrate fundamental misunderstandings of the operation of international institutions. As a specialized international intergovernmental agency, the WTO cannot derive its constitutional legitimacy in the

[46] Steve Charnovitz, *Opening the WTO to Nongovernmental Interests*, 24 Fordham Int'l L.J. 173 (2000).

[47] Richard Falk and Andrew Strauss, *On the Creation of a Global Peoples Assembly: Legitimacy and the Power of Popular Sovereignty*, 36 Stan. J. Int'l L. 191 (2000).

[48] Robert Howse and Makau Mutua, Protecting Human Rights in a Global Economy: Challenges for the World Trade Organization 4 (2000).

[49] Markus Krajewski, *Democratic Legitimacy and Constitutional Perspectives of WTO Law*, 35 J. World Trade, No. 1, at 167, 168 (2001).

same way as nation-states. Rather, the WTO is the creation of nation-states and, therefore, its legitimacy is derivative in character. Norms established by the WTO are legitimized only by rigid adherence to the established procedures for the creation of international law.[50] The WTO itself has no power to create legal norms or policy. WTO adjudicating bodies and subsidiary councils cannot even render an official interpretation of existing WTO legal or policy norms; this is reserved to the WTO General Council and the Ministerial Conference.[51]

Thus, the "solutions" enumerated above would serve to detract, not add, to the legitimacy of the WTO. If the WTO were allowed to be influenced by a people's assembly or by vague overriding political norms, the WTO would be de-legitimized. Those who posit a "democratic deficit" in the WTO simply are uncomfortable with the established international order under which nation-states are the primary international participants. Their view cannot prevail in the absence of a far-reaching revolution in international law that is nowhere in sight.[51a]

Of course, the WTO can and should do more to further greater legitimacy. For example, with the consent of its Members, the WTO should promote greater openness and transparency, and allow qualified non-governmental organizations to participate in meetings as consultative organizations. Interest groups should also be encouraged to submit *amicus* briefs in dispute settlement proceedings.[52] In the last analysis, however, changing policy at the WTO will continue to depend on the will of its Members. NGOs and interest groups that desire changes in WTO policy must learn to work with and influence individual WTO Members. This is the key to policy change in the WTO. The WTO itself has no power of independent action.

## 4. The Doha negotiating agenda

The successful WTO Ministerial Conference held in Doha, Qatar in November 2001 effectively sets the direction of the organization for the

[50] *See generally* Thomas Franck, THE POWER OF LEGITIMACY AMONG NATIONS (1990).

[51] WTO Agreement Art. IX:2.

[51a] For a thoughtful review of how to correct the "democratic deficit" in the WTO, *see* Eric Stein, "International Integration and Democracy: No Love at First Sight", 95 A.J.I.L. 489 (2001).

[52] Andrea Kupfer Scheider, *Unfriendly Actions: The Amicus Brief Battle at the WTO*, 7 WIDENER L. SYMP. J. 887 (2001).

foreseeable future. In addition, the accession of China (and Taiwan) to WTO Membership is a precedent for the accession of other states, including Russia, and this sets the stage for the WTO to become as universal in membership as its sister organizations, the IMF and the World Bank.

The Work Programme concluded at Doha can be analysed in five parts: First, the largest category of negotiations concerns reform of existing agreements and rules to improve market access for trading goods and services. Second, developing country issues are extensive and pervasive. Third, globalization issues will be broached, notably competition policy, investment, and e-commerce. Fifth, dispute settlement issues must be agreed to address problems that have appeared.

The broadest category of agreed negotiations concerns issues to facilitate further market access for trade in goods and services. Continuing the trends of the Tokyo and Uruguay Rounds, these negotiations will concentrate on non-tariff trade barriers and will deal with reform of existing WTO agreements rather than break new ground. Market access negotiations will be broad-based, divided into three groups: agricultural products, non-agricultural products, and services.[53] In addition, the negotiating agenda concerns so-called "implementation issues," reform of existing WTO agreements on subsidies, dumping, customs matters, trade-related investment measures, intellectual property, and standards.[54]

Second, a host of trade and development issues will be considered, as the WTO is now seriously committed to reforms to ameliorate conditions in developing countries, which constitute the majority of WTO Members. Foremost is the commitment at Doha that the TRIPS Agreement must not prevent Members from taking measures to protect public health. This can mean not only the right of Members to grant compulsory licences for the manufacture of necessary pharmaceuticals, but also the right to trade such licensed products.[55] Developing countries also will obtain new concessions providing them with preferential conditions of access for their products in the markets of industrialized countries. In addition, new "special and differential" treatment provisions will be built into existing WTO agree-

[53] WTO, Ministerial Conference, Fourth Session, Doha, 9–14 November 2001, *Ministerial Declaration*, WT/MIN(01)/DEC/1, 20 November 2001, paras 13–16.

[54] Final Implementation Decision, Fourth WTO Ministerial Conference, Doha, 9–14 November 2001.

[55] WTO, Ministerial Conference, Fourth Session, Doha, 9–14 November 2001, *Declaration on the TRIPS Agreement and Public Health*, WTO/MIN(01)/DEC/2, 20 November 2001, paras 5–6.

ments, and perhaps a new SDT Framework Agreement will be concluded to grant developing countries concessions and flexibility in meeting WTO obligations.

Third, the WTO addressed the "globalization" issues of labour and the environment. Regarding labour, the Fourth Ministerial conference merely reiterated the First Ministerial Conference commitment at Singapore that Members should observe core labour standards but that ensuring this is the responsibility of the ILO.[56] Thus, there will be no negotiation concerning labour and no formal cooperation between the WTO and the ILO.

Regarding the environment, the WTO approved, for the first time, a negotiation agenda, which includes (1) the relationship of WTO rules to multilateral environmental agreements; (2) the elimination of tariff and non-tariff trade barriers to environmental goods and services; (3) criteria for granting observer status to environmental NGOs; and (4) reducing fisheries' subsidies. In addition, the WTO Trade and Environment Committee was instructed to bring additional items, such as intellectual property conflicts and labelling concerns, to the attention of WTO Members at the next Ministerial Conference to be held in 2003. This broad agenda enhances the likelihood of a new WTO agreement on the environment at the conclusion of the new trade round.

Fourth, the WTO will begin negotiations on controversial new issues, including competition policy and investment. Working Groups were established on both topics and the importance of international framework agreements on both was reaffirmed. Serious negotiations were put off, however, until after the WTO's Fifth Ministerial Conference in November 2003. Nevertheless, there is enhanced likelihood of WTO agreements on these two crucial economic topics. In addition, the WTO is continuing work on a new agreement involving trade-related aspects of electronic commerce.

Fifth, the WTO will have to address three different aspects of its highly successful dispute settlement system. First, myriad technical issues must be addressed to assure the smooth functioning of the system. These range from the "sequencing" problem, remand authority for the Appellate Body, and problems of conflicts of obligations to establishing a full-time Appellate Body. Second, issues relating to transparency and receiving *amicus* pleadings must be resolved. Third, the issue of the interface between the WTO dispute settlement system and the general system of international law and

56 *Singapore Ministerial Declaration*, above note 31, at para. 4.

dispute settlement should be clarified. Experience has established that the WTO legal system is not a self-contained regime but is part of the larger system of public international law.[57] Although the substantive jurisdiction of WTO panels is limited to the "covered agreements" of the WTO, the law applicable to any given dispute may include non-WTO rules of international law. The WTO has to develop principled ways of establishing its own jurisdiction, applicable law, and resolving conflicts between WTO law and general public international law.[58]

Summing up, the WTO in the twenty-first century will continue to play a vital role in the maintenance of international peace and prosperity. In short order, the WTO will become a universal economic organization, embracing virtually every country in the world. The scope of the WTO has expanded vastly as well; it will cover virtually every aspect of international trade and investment, exceeding the vision of its post-World War II founders. Yet, the WTO faces unprecedented new challenges: helping with other IGOs to manage the process of globalization with its attendant social dislocations, as well as helping to ameliorate poverty in the developing world and ending the north-south divide.

[57] Thomas J. Schoenbaum, *WTO Dispute Settlement: Praise and Suggestions for Reform*, 47 INT'L & COMP. L.Q. 647, 653 (1998).

[58] Joost Pauwelyn, *The Role of Public International Law in the WTO: How Far Can We Go?*, 95 AM. J. IN'TL L. 535 (2001); Gabrielle Marceau, *A Call for Coherence in International Law: Praises for the Prohibition Against "Clinical Isolation" in WTO Dispute Settlement*, 33 J. WORLD TRADE, No. 5, at 87, 110 (1999).

# INDEX